First published: 2013 ISBN: 978-0-9921829-6-0
2018 ISBN: 978-0-9921830-5-9

Published by Tracks4Africa (Pty) Ltd
270 Main Street, Paarl, 7646
SOUTH AFRICA
www.tracks4africa.com

Design Elsa Cade
Print production Les Martens (les@samedia-services.co.za)
SA Media Services (www.samedia-services.co.za)
Printer 1010 Printing, China

THE USE OF THE INFORMATION IN THIS BOOK IS SOLELY AT YOUR OWN RISK

Although every possible effort has been made to ensure that the information in this book is up to date and current at the time of going to print, Tracks4Africa (Pty) Ltd accepts no responsibility or liability for any loss, injury or inconvenience incurred by readers or travellers using this book.

GIVE US FEEDBACK

Tracks4Africa is, at its heart, a community-driven project; we collect, collate and process the travel experiences of a wide variety of travellers into various products. Your input, be it to this book, our website, our maps or our apps, is highly valued. Should you come across any errors in this book or on your travels discover worthy places not included, please let us know. Email us (newdata@tracks4africa.co.za) or visit our website (www.tracks4africa.com) to post your photographs, comments or corrections on existing listings. Similarly, if you're interested in contributing to our maps, go to Submit Data on our website.

Acknowledgements

The publication of the first self-drive guide was a bit of a gamble on the part of Tracks4Africa founders, Johann Groenewald and Wouter Brand. Book publishing was a whole new learning curve; and what's more, would there even be a market for the new product? Happily, the gamble turned out to be a solid bet as is evidenced by the new 2018 version you hold in your hands.

The formula hasn't changed, this is a guidebook by travellers for travellers. Much of the information here is gleaned from a community of overlanders, this ensures that the information in this book is relevant, up-to-date and born of actual on-the-ground experience.

What has changed is a great deal of the detail. Africa isn't a continent to sit still and Namibia is no exception to that adage. Uncountable hours have been spent checking and rechecking information.

We're very grateful to those in the Tracks4Africa community who share their GPS tracks, knowledge and experiences with us. And, in the case of this guide, particularly those who shared their images. All photographers are credited individually, in the caption to each image.

Besides our community, there's also a small, very busy team of people who are employed (both formally and informally) by Tracks4Africa. We must make mention of Karin Theron, editor of the first guide. Karin got the new book moving in the right direction before handing over to Neil Harrison. As project manager on the book Janine Reyneke had the unenviable task of keeping everything on track. Further thanks to Amy, Anet, Bessie, Elsa, Faith, Ian-Ray, Johann, Jurgen, Kate, Len and Lizette who all played vital parts in making this guide a reality.

Foreword

Growing up, I enjoyed regular access to the lush, tropical coastline of KwaZulu-Natal (South Africa) and this became the place where I wanted to spend my free time. If you had offered me a trip to Namibia back then I would have turned it down without a moment's hesitation. But then, in my late 30s, I had the opportunity to visit Namibia and a funny thing happened. I fell in love with a desert country.

The thing about Namibia is that it makes you feel small. And in a good way. The air is often so clear that distant objects seem near. At night, this feeling is amplified when you look up into the heavens and see a Milky Way startling in its colour, clarity and breadth. And should you should travel one of its remoter routes, you can easily drive for a day or more without seeing another soul.

Namibia has a great deal to offer, it's far more than a desert. And one of the best ways to enjoy this country, is by car - whether a normal sedan or a vehicle optimised for off-road travel.

This guide is aimed at people who intend to travel Namibia in their own vehicle. We'll show you what destinations and attractions are on offer and where to find them. You'll also be introduced to overland travel - the concept of self-contained vehicular travel. Much of the information in this book comes from a community of overlanders as well as a small committed team at Tracks4Africa.

So what makes this guide different to the first Namibia self-drive guide? Well, information really. Places change. Roads change. And we've added something new, our Atlas pages cover the whole country at a scale of 1:1 000 000. These pages include distance & travel times and should prove to be a great navigational aid.

We've also included two suggested routes, one which takes in most of what Namibia has to offer and another which will introduce you to both Botswana and Namibia in one long, glorious tour.

By buying this book you're on your way to joining this community of overlanders. Our fondest wish is that, in your hands, this guide becomes tattered and travel-worn, with scribbled notes in the margins and dog-eared pages tracking your progress across Namibia. And that it takes you to the places you've dreamed about, as well as those you've yet to imagine.

See you on the road!

Neil Harrison
EDITOR

contents

GENERAL INFORMATION

REGIONS & DESTINATIONS

HOW TO USE THIS GUIDE

IN ESSENCE, this guide is designed to help you to do two things, figure out where you want to go in Namibia, and once there, find places to stay. This makes it suitable for both trip planning and on-the-spot reference. There are sections dedicated to: Preparing for your trip; Deciding where to go (Regions, Destinations, Suggested Routes & Atlas); Route planning (Atlas); and, Finding places to stay (listings). You can also find out what facilities and services to expect at destinations and accommodation venues.

REGIONS, DESTINATIONS AND LISTINGS

To allow you to search more easily for specific places and areas, we've divided Namibia up into **15 regions**. It's important to note that while there are a few similarities, these DON'T match Namibia's official 14 regions. Our 15 regions represent a more colloquial or populist view of the country's different areas. This isn't an invention entirely of our own devising, just about all the regions we use are well known to, and well understood by, Namibian locals.

We've colour-coded our regions for quick reference. Look for the related colour strips when paging through this book.

Within these 15 regions we've identified **destinations.** These can take the form of a village, town, city or game reserve/ national park. So, you won't find all Namibia's towns and villages listed, we've purposefully left out those places which we feel will be of little interest or value to the overland traveller.

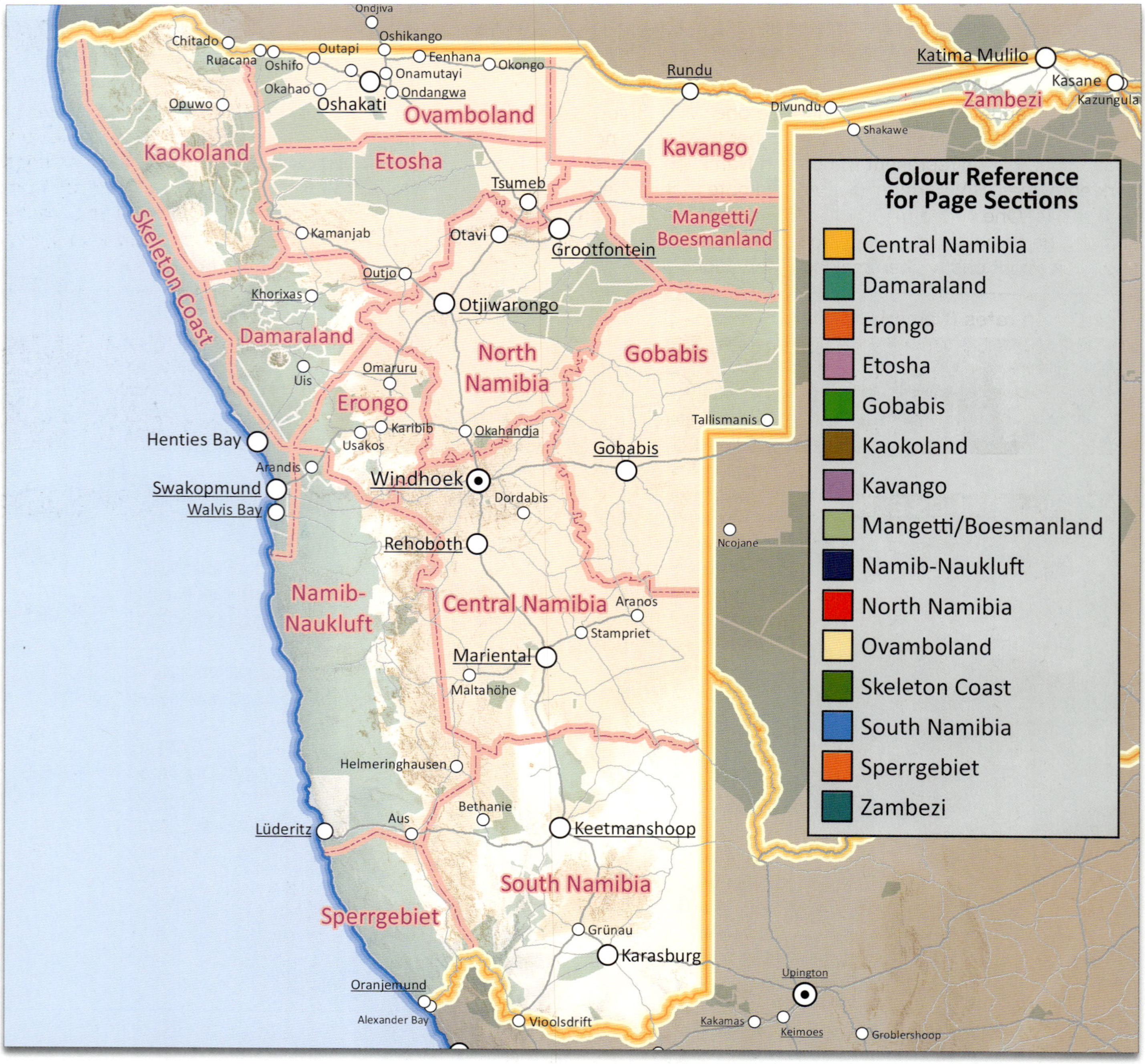

And lastly, within these regions, we've identified **accommodation listings.** Here, we've also attempted to concentrate on those we feel will be most relevant to the overland traveller. So you won't find every accommodation venue listed here and if you're looking for $1000-a-night full-board lodges, this is definitely the wrong guide for you! If we've been repeatedly unable to make contact with a venue, we've also left them out; community camps are the exception to this rule as they're often in remote areas and don't always have reliable communications.

Use the Contents pages at the beginning of the guide to look up regions and destinations. At the back of the guide you'll find an index with regions, destinations and listings arranged in alphabetical order.

LODGING VS. CAMPING

Our accommodation listings are divided into two groups: lodging and camping. These sport blue and green bands respectively. While these groupings would appear self-explanatory, there are a few points worth noting. Lodging is any form of accommodation where you don't have to camp so it includes hotels, lodges, B&Bs, guest-farms and even houseboats. It also includes tented camps which you'll often see referred to as permanent tents; this lodging subcategory describes accommodation in the form of existing erected tents; these belong to the venue and are typically furnished with beds and other furniture - some even have en-suite bathrooms. This is not the kind of tent that you quickly pack away after a night's rest!

Camping describes any venue where you're sleeping in your own structure, be it a ground or rooftop tent, caravan, camping trailer or motorhome. Such accommodation listings range from the most basic of bush camps with no facilities, to a campsite which offers powerpoints, shade structures, your own personal ablution facilities and access to a nearby restaurant and bar. There's camping and there's glamping!

LODGING RATES & CAMPING RATES

All accommodation listings include a rate indicator, the $ symbol, so you can easily tell whether you're looking at an affordable venue (**$**) or a very expensive one (**$$$**). If you see **$$$$**, well, lets just say that you should be rich in dollars or euros! Lodging rates are typically higher than camping rates so we've used two sets of rates to eliminate confusion. These price bands represent the cost in Namibian dollars per person per night. Where relevant, camping rates includes park entry fees (SADC rates). You should note that venues will differ in terms of what they include and what exclude from such costs. One venue might include a complimentary game drive in their price while another might charge you a hefty sum for the same service. It's impossible for us to reflect every possible price permutation so you should make your own enquiries about costs when making reservations.

Lodging rates (Namibian dollars)		Camping rates (Namibian dollars)	
$	0 - 500	$	0 - 150
$$	501 - 1 500	$$	151 - 250
$$$	1 501 - 5 000	$$$	251 - 500
$$$$	5 000 plus		

LODGING LISTINGS EXPLAINED

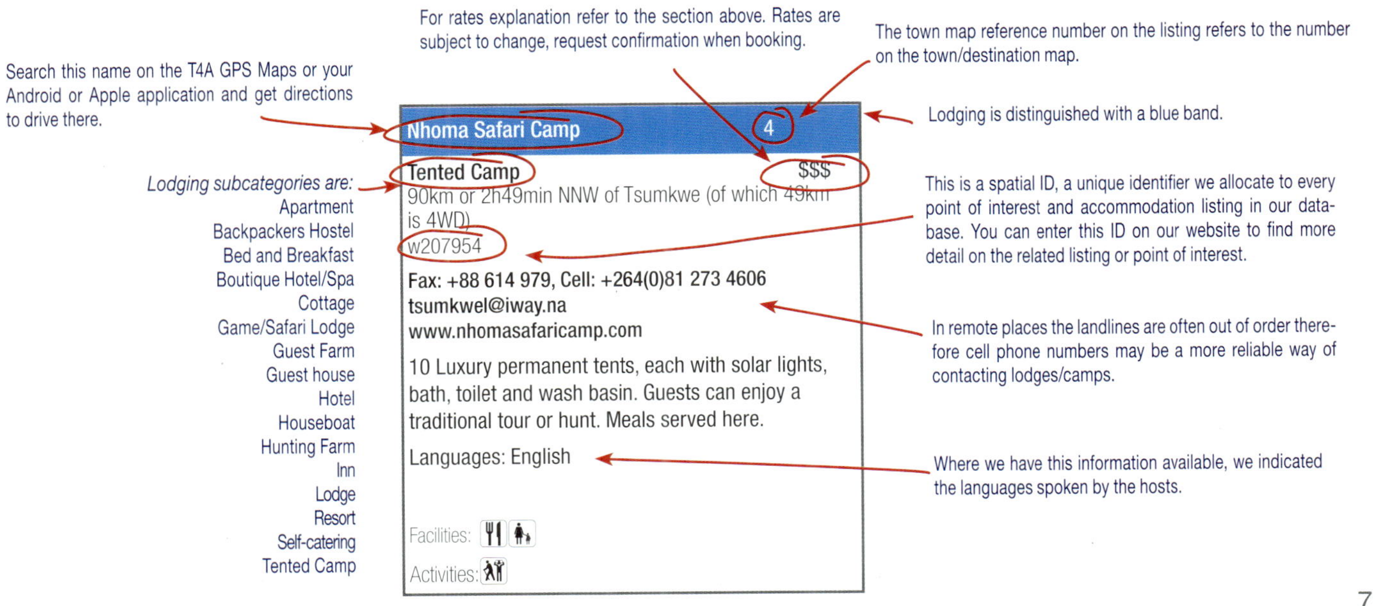

CAMPING LISTINGS EXPLAINED

The yellow paw indicates that this listing is a community camp or wildlife foundation. Tracks4Africa supports community efforts and conservation therefore we would in this way like to give extra free exposure to them.

Camping listings are distinguished with a green band.

Camping subcategories are:
Camping (ordinary camp)
4WD Trail Camp
Caravan Park
Community Camp
Farm Camp
Hiking Trail Camp
Holiday Resort
Lodge Camp
Park Camp
Tour Operator Camp
Transit Camp
Wilderness Camp

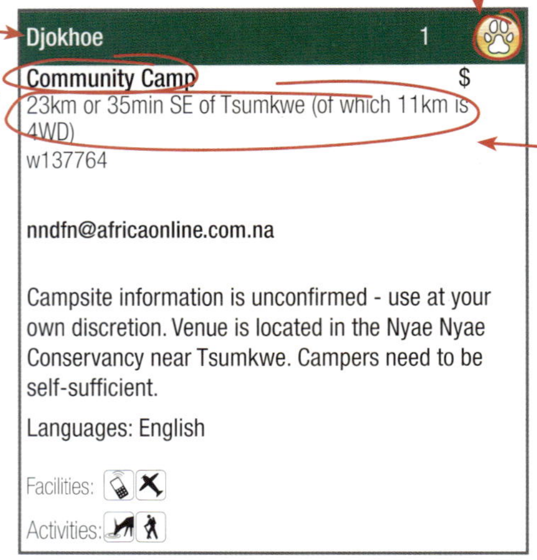

If accommodation is situated in a town or city, we provide the street address. For accommodation in the countryside, we provide the nearest town and the distance, time and direction from it. The distance and time is calculated using T4A GPS Maps and is a fair indication of how long it will take you to drive from the nearest town.

Where you see 4WD in the address line, it means that the lodge/camp is only reachable by off-road vehicle Where 4WD is not indicated, a sedan vehicle may in some cases be sufficient to gain access, but in some cases you may need a 4x2 to reach the lodge/camp. No self-drive access means that guests are not allowed to or are unable to drive to the lodge.

FACILITIES

Throughout this guide, you'll find the following icons used to describe facilities found in destinations (towns), lodging venues and camping venues. These are facilities that we have been able to verify at the time of writing.

Destination (town) facilities When looking at the maps on our destination pages, you won't necessary see the facilities indicated by the icons. If this is the case, you simply need to ask around to find out where they are.

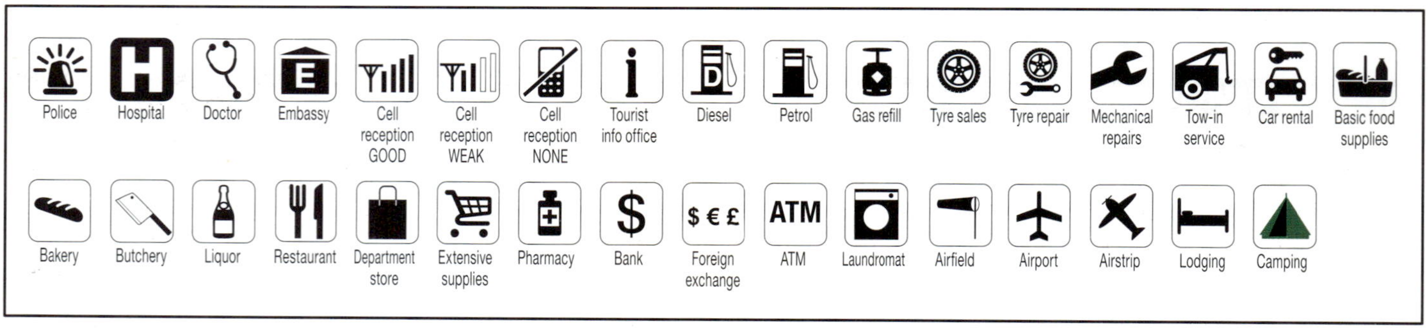

Lodging facilities Here, these icons indicate facilities found at the lodge venue. In the case of a landing strip, it might not be on the property but will be in the vicinity.

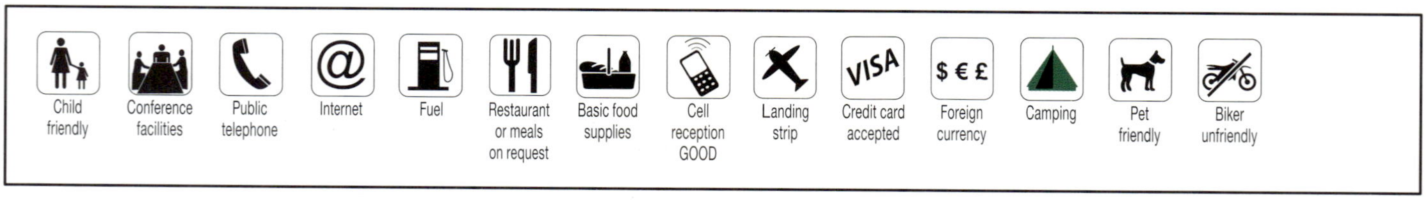

Camping facilities

Laundry · Kitchen area · Showers (hot) · Showers (cold) · Child friendly · Conference facilities · Shaded campsite · Public telephone · Internet · Power point · Fuel · Restaurant or meals on request · Basic food supplies · Cell reception GOOD · Landing strip · Credit card accepted · Foreign currency

Pet friendly · Wood is available · Ice is available · No drinking water · Biker unfriendly

LODGING AND CAMPING ACTIVITIES

These activities may be offered by the venue or a vendor nearby. Again, these are activities that we have been able to verify at the time of writing

Wildlife to view · Game drives · Guided walks · Hiking · Balloon trips · Swimming · Quad biking · Horse trails · Fishing

MORE INFORMATION

The descriptions in this book are highly summarised. To find out more information, we suggest you visit our other information platforms, like the T4A Africa Guide (included on the SD card for our GPS maps), our website, and our Apple and Android apps.

ATLAS PAGES

One of the things that makes this guide different to the previous guide is the inclusion of the atlas pages - these were drawn directly from our Traveller's Atlas Southern Africa. This means that, for the first time, this guide offers you a navigational function. That said, we would strongly recommend that you also use paper maps, like our Namibia Traveller's Map and a GPS loaded with the appropriate mapset – particularly if you plan on traversing remote areas within Namibia

378 - C3

On every destination listed, you'll find this icon. In this example, it tells you that you can find the destination on the Atlas map on page **378**. On this atlas map page, you can find the destination by using the coordinates **C3**.

WHY DON'T WE DISPLAY GPS COORDINATES

As a mapping company we have very accurate GPS coordinates of each place or accommodation listing shown in this book. So, why don't we publish these? Well, if you need a GPS coordinates, it means you're wanting to use a GPS device, and this being the case, we'd rather that you installed our GPS maps on your device. These maps include all the places mentioned in this book and more. This methodology prevents you entering such GPS coordinates incorrectly. In the remote wilderness, the consequences of such a mistake could be lethal.

SUGGESTED ROUTES

Another first for this guide is our Suggested Routes section. These routes have been compiled to give you a good introduction to the country and its neighbour, Botswana. Rather than see these routes as prescriptive, you should feel free to use them as it suits you. Cut out the parts that don't interest you and spend more days exploring the locations that do.

TIP

This symbol appears throughout the book and is used to highlight a noteworthy tip.

DISCLAIMER

Although Tracks4africa content is continuously updated, it is not possible to perfectly reflect the reality on the ground at all times. So while we strive to keep our information as up to date as possible, the high volume of listings in our database means that there's always the possibility of outdated information. For this reason, we ask you to treat the information you find here as a guide, and reconfirm important details with establishments directly. You can help us and other travellers, by submitting data corrections whenever you discover the need for such, by sending an email to newdata@tracks4africa.co.za.

SOUTHERN AFRICA OFFERS THE WORLD'S BEST SAFARI EXPERIENCE.
Make sure the vehicle does too.

COUNTRY INFORMATION

Brandberg, as seen from across the Ugab river. (photo: Heiner Dillmann)

NAMIBIA IS A BEAUTIFUL, UNSPOILT COUNTRY of memorable extremes. With a population of around 2.5 million citizens, it's sparsely populated (around three people per km^2) and its vast, open spaces make Namibia the ideal destination for first time visitors to Africa to discover the rich diversity of this continent.

Located in Southwest Africa (trivia tip: this was its previous name), Namibia is a gem for anyone itching to explore a wilderness. It has a great number of national parks, game reserves and conservation areas where a large variety of landscapes, vegetation and animals can be seen. But you don't have to restrict yourself to these protected areas in order to fully appreciate this country.

Namibia is also the ideal self-drive destination as it boasts a good infrastructure and friendly, welcoming locals. Essentially a desert land, this is a place of distant horizons and long, lonely roads where the urge to explore is difficult to resist. You'll enjoy an excellent road network, both tar and gravel. In remote areas, it's possible to drive for days without seeing another human being.

You'll discover places where the landscapes are almost surreal; you might well recognise scenes from some of your favourite movies! Happily, even with its vast, open spaces, there's a great deal to do and see, which makes it easy to keep your itinerary flexible and just enjoy your road trip!

Namibia offers a great range of accommodation, from basic campsites to well-equipped and comfortable camps, backpackers, tented camps, guest houses and lodges to the most luxurious of hotels. However, if you choose to venture into remote areas, you need to be a self-sufficient camper.

Windhoek is the nation's capital and the social, economic and cultural centre, it's a small modern city that's well worth a visit. You'll find it conveniently placed pretty much in the middle of the country.

GLOSSARY

Certain words in this guide are well known in Africa but may be unfamiliar to international visitors:

Boma: enclosure where people get together, commonly to eat.
Braai: barbeque (cooking meat over an open fire).
Long drop: a pit toilet.
Mokoro: a type of canoe made by hollowing out a tree trunk.
Rondavel: round house with a thatched roof.
Potjiekos: a stew cooked in a round, cast-iron pot (three-legged or flat bottomed) on an open fire, also referred to as a potjie in Afrikaans.
National Parks: generally owned and run by central government with the aim of natural conservation in perpetuity, and open to the public. Hunting is generally outlawed within such parks.
Game reserves: can be privately or government owned. If government owned they take second place to a national park but still allow public access. Occasional legal hunting takes place in these areas but it isn't widely publicised. Privately-owned game reserves don't offer public access and can be very exclusive and expensive, and for this reason often have far fewer visitors. Hunting is not uncommon here.
Conservancy: a legally registered, voluntary association of landowners and land users who band together to manage their natural resources in an ecologically sustainable manner. The group may be a group of private landowners, local communities, government, or any combination thereof. Benefits accrue to the members thereof. This is a fairly common way of involving and uplifting local communities who might otherwise be excluded from the benefits of tourism.
Transfrontier Parks / Peace Parks: national parks or game reserves located on national boundaries, thus requiring cooperation and collaboration between government conservation bodies in two countries. Managing the park as one entity requires that all human barriers are removed within the park so that animals can roam freely.
Transfrontier Conservation areas: as above, but will include areas of differing conservation status, from national parks to hunting concessions. While physical barriers remain in place here, the entire area is jointly managed for long term sustainability.
Co-Op or Agri-Mark: These stores cater for farmers. Almost a general dealer, they stock everything from ploughshares to pots, and some food items. They invariably also sell fuel. Their prices are reasonable and their range extensive. Always worth a visit.

CLIMATE

In winter (May - September), daytime temperatures in the interior range from 18 - 25° C. At night, freezing temperatures and ground frosts are common. In summer (October - April) the average interior daytime temperatures range from 20 - 34° C, but temperatures over 40° C are often recorded in the extreme north and south of the country. Along the coast the temperature varies less and seldom reaches higher than 25° C. Heavy fog is quite common, especially at night.

Namibia is a summer rainfall area at which time floods are common. The humidity is generally very low in most parts of Namibia, but in the extreme north it can be as high as 80% during summer.

In summer you should wear lightweight, light-coloured clothing, good sunglasses, a hat and suntan lotion with a high protection factor. During the winter months, or for visits to the coastal areas, you should pack warm clothing and enough bedding if you're camping.

In years gone by, Namibia used to have daylight savings time from the first Sunday of April to the first Sunday in September. Effective August 2017, this legislation was repealed and today the whole country operates on GMT+2 the whole year through.

BEST TIME TO VISIT

Most people feel that May to October is the best time to visit because it's cooler than summer. Most of the rain falls during February, March and April, and after this rainy season, the veld is green and beautiful.

If you do visit during the hot summer months, look for shade when you camp and don't walk around during the heat of the day. If possible, book accommodation at places with swimming pools. Even though it can be extremely hot, your body will quickly acclimatise to the temperature. Most people end up finding the heat tolerable and some actually prefer to visit during this time because there are fewer tourists.

During the rainy season in the national parks and game reserves, the animals become less dependent on the water holes and roam further afield, but the bird life remains fantastic and seeing game spread out over the plains is also a lovely sight. The bush is green and the vistas across the pans are spectacular, particularly when lightning storms approach. If the rains come early enough, you'll be able to see some of the flowering bulbs.

Always be very cautious of camping in dry riverbeds during the rainy season, these can unexpectedly flood due to rainfall kilometres away. Check the flow of these rivers on the T4A map and be on the lookout for rain clouds on

If this elephant could talk, he'd tell you that very dry riverbeds can quickly turn into raging torrents, like the one shown below. (photo: Heiner Dillmann)

Be very wary of crossing rivers. If you can't walk it, don't try and drive it. (photo: Frank Höppener)

the distant horizon. Also be aware that flash floods can damage roads, especially on D-routes which don't have bridges at river crossings.

If you plan to visit in June, July or August you're advised to book in advance, this is when many South Africans visit because it coincides with their school holidays. European visitors tend to prefer August. The Namibians themselves tend to flock to the coast during the December holidays, so bookings for this area in December/January are also advisable.

MONEY

Namibia's currency is the Namibian dollar (N$ or NAD), which is linked 1:1 to the South African rand (R or ZAR).

Credit cards are accepted in the cities and bigger towns. Just remember to let your bank know that you're travelling to Namibia and increase your credit limit for the duration of your stay if it's necessary. Major credit cards like Mastercard and Visa are accepted, but the latter enjoys better representation and acceptance. So it's advisable to carry both these credit cards in your travel party. You should be able to withdraw money from ATMs without any problems. In smaller towns you'll find that cash is king.

Officially, you can only pay for fuel, spares and repairs with cash, debit or credit cards (no garage or petrol cards), but some fuel stations may choose to only accept cash. Always ask what is accepted before you fill up, and if you're told that cards are accepted, confirm that the card machine is working! In rural areas, you can expect fuel stations to work on a cash basis. This doesn't mean you need to drive around carrying all your holiday funds in cash - there are ATMs in most towns. These are indicated in this guide to assist you with planning withdrawals.

Foreign currency and travellers cheques can be converted to Namibian dollars at any bank or Bureau de Change. Banking hours differ from bank to bank, branch to branch, and day to day, but for the most part you can expect banks to be open Mon – Fri, 09h00 - 15h30, and on Saturdays from 09h00 – 12h00.

Value Added Tax (VAT) is 15% on goods and services and is included in the price. Foreign tourists are exempt and can reclaim VAT on goods (not services) at their port of exit provided they have valid VAT receipts and present the goods.

(photo: Karin Theron)

LANGUAGE

The official language is English, but Afrikaans is more widely spoken; many European citizens also speak German. In total, 16 languages and dialects are spoken in Namibia.

PEOPLE

Namibia's earliest known inhabitants were the Khoisan (Khoikhoi and San tribes), the Nama and the Damara people. The Ovambo, Herero (of which the Himba is a sub-

Herero women (photo: Frank Höppener)

(above) Himba woman (photo: Frank Höppener)
(above right) Children of the Kavango region. (photo: Karin Theron)

tribe), Caprivian, Tswana, and Kavango people moved into the area later. Early Portuguese seafarers planted their crosses at what is today Cape Cross, just north of of Swakopmund, and Diaz Point near Lüderitz. Much later, an Afrikaner crossed the Orange River and mission stations were established in the hinterland by Europeans. The Afrikaans-speaking Basters are the descendants of Khoisan women and Dutch settlers who arrived in the mid-17th century.

For just over 100 years prior to to independence in 1990, the former South West Africa was first under German and then South African rule. Today, Namibia has a rich and diverse culture and the society is mostly westernised. However, if you travel the countryside, you will still see Herero women with impressive head gear, wearing colourful long dresses; and you'll see the Himba in their red leathery skins. There are even a few Bushman villages around where life is still lived the traditional way. You can recognise Nama people by the beautiful click sound in their language.

CONSERVATION

At present, almost half of Namibia is under some form of conservation management whether it be national parks, reserves, conservancies or private nature reserves. Local communities were given legislative power to create their own conservancies and to manage and benefit from the wildlife on communal land, allowing them to work with private companies to create their own tourism products. The first four communal conservancies were formed in 1998 and, to date, there are 82. We urge you to support community camps and wildlife foundations, as the proceeds go towards the preservation of the natural heritage of Namibia.

(below, main) Quiver tree (photo: Karin Theron). (insert top) Welwitschia, the living fossil. (photo: Frank Höppener). (insert middle & bottom) You won't always be lucky enough to spot a lion in Namibia whereas if you're bird watching you'll seldom return home without a sighting. (photos: Jurgen Blignaut)

FAUNA AND FLORA

Namibia has a high level of biodiversity and endemicity. Of the 217 mammal species found here, you will find unique desert-dwelling lion, rhino and elephant, and 26 other endemic species. Of the approximately 4 350 species and subspecies of vascular plant, 17% are endemic: most notable of which are the Quiver Tree and the living fossil plant, Welwitschia mirabilis. These last-mentioned plants live 1 000 years or more; some are said to be even 2 000 years old. More than 650 bird species have been recorded, of which 90 are endemic to southern Africa and 13 to Namibia.

RESPECTING THE ENVIRONMENT

What many visitors find enchanting about Africa is the freedom from overbearing rules and regulations. You'll arrive at a beautiful place or attraction and often you'll be free to walk around wherever you like and, seemingly, do whatever you like. We urge visitors to think carefully about the responsibility that goes with this freedom. Respect the places you visit, aim to leave them in the same state, or a better state than you found them. So, if you arrive at a remote campsite to find it a mess, tidy it up. To misquote Gandhi, be the change that you want to see in the world.

FOOD AND DRINK

Daytimes can be exceedingly hot in summer, winters slightly less so. For this reason you must always carry enough drinking water in case something goes wrong with your car and you're stranded while waiting for help. Work on two litres per person per day, for a few days.

Namibia's tap water quality is very good as it's sourced from deep wells, so you can drink it without having to add chemicals or boiling it. However, you should exercise caution if you think the water comes from a running river. As far as possible, don't use water from stagnant sources, and if you do, treat it first. A good rule of thumb is to boil any drinking water you're unsure about, or drink bottled water.

Using water purification tablets or a chlorine solution is a cheap and simple way to kill bugs in drinking water; wait 20 - 30 minutes for the tablets/solution to work before you drink the water. A better-tasting alternative is using one of the many water filtration devices available.

Every small village in Namibia has a shop where basic food can be purchased. If you require anything more exotic than the basics, you should stock up at supermarkets in bigger towns. Every destination in this book details the services available, this will assist you with your planning.

Namibia is renowned for good beer, the most popular being Tafel Lager and Windhoek.

ROAD CONDITIONS

Namibia has a very good road network. All national highways (B-routes) and national roads are paved (also referred to as surfaced or tarred roads). However, almost 90% of the country's roads are unpaved. These are referred to as unsurfaced, gravel or dirt roads. Namibia's gravel roads are world famous for their quality, as they are mostly of excellent standard and very well maintained.

Roads classified as C-routes, whether paved or unpaved, can usually be driven with any sedan vehicle, but a vehicle with high ground clearance is recommended. These roads have bridges over rivers and are regarded as all-weather roads.

D-routes may also be accessible to sedans but many are 4WD tracks; refer to T4A maps to check driving times and road types. These roads don't have bridges at river crossings so are more vulnerable to rain damage. Be aware that the salt roads near the coast are slippery all year round.

During the rainy season the roads can be very slippery and roads passing through river beds can be flooded. The smallest little stream can turn into a raging torrent. Never cross these streams unless you're absolutely sure how deep they are and how strongly they flow. Water levels drop just as quickly as they rise so you should rather wait a few hours or maybe a day if faced with a dangerous crossing.

Road signs are international and easy to understand. You should pay special attention to warnings of antelope, warthog and elephant, as these animals often graze along the road verges and can be unpredictable. Even though most roads are fenced, wild animals, donkeys, goats and cattle may still cross your path, even on the main tar roads in built-up areas. Always be on the lookout for animals beside the road. Kudu are often found on the roads at night, especially around Windhoek en route to the airport.

TOWING TIP: *You are advised NOT to travel Kaokoland or Damaraland with a trailer – not even the latest and most expensive off-road designs. These roads are not good for trailers and only a lucky few have managed to survive trips to these two regions.*

Road rules

- You must always carry a valid driver's licence issued in English. If your licence isn't issued in English, you have to get an international driver's licence.
- According to the Automobile Association of South Africa (AA) it is compulsory for any vehicle, caravan or trailer registered in South Africa to have a ZA sign displayed when it crosses any border. The ZA sign must be placed in a visible position on the rear of each vehicle, caravan and trailer and may not be within 150 mm of the rear number plate.
- Drive on the left side of the road.
- The speed limit is 60 km/h in urban areas and 120 on tarred roads outside urban areas. On gravel roads, it is 100 km/h. Speed limits are enforced via manned speed cameras, often positioned close to major towns. Vehicle rental companies impose a 80 km/h speed limit on gravel roads; should you have an accident, and should the vehicle be fitted with a tracking device, it'll be used to check whether you were exceeding this limit at the time.
- Driver and passengers must wear safety belts.

Van Zyl's Pass isn't for the inexperienced or poorly equipped. (photo: Heiner Dillmann)

(left) Most of Namibia's gravel roads are in top condition. (photo: Karin Theron)
(above) Always be on the lookout for cattle and wildlife on the roads. (photo: Karin Theron)
(above right) Driving difficult terrain requires patience, planning and a suitable vehicle. (photo: Frank Höppener)

- The use of a cell phone without a hands-free kit when driving is illegal.
- You must drive with your headlights on at all times.

Road advice

- Don't drive at night – if animals cross the road you won't see them until it's too late.
- Before you set off, check that your vehicle's tyre pressures are correct for the roads you plan to travel, as well as the load (luggage and passengers) you're carrying.
- Pack a reputable high-volume air compressor and pressure gauge so you can adjust your tyre pressure as needed.
- Carry two spare tyres, especially if you plan on travelling remote areas like Kaokoland.
- Carry a tyre repair kit and know how to use it.
- If you don't have 4WD experience, get training before venturing into remote areas.
- Vehicle fires are a real risk (due to electrical issues or long grass collecting near or on the exhaust) so carry a fire extinguisher.
- Any person injured in a road crash or a dependent of anyone killed in a road crash in Namibia can claim for assistance from the MVA Fund which derives its income from the fuel levy. Medical benefits, injury grants, funeral grants, loss of income and loss of support can be claimed by visiting the MVA Fund website (www.mvafund.com.na).

Driving tar roads

You wouldn't think there'd be any need to talk about this one, but there is. In Africa, you'll find tar roads and freeways that rival the world's best but you'll also come across tar roads in poor or very poor shape, often due to a lack of maintenance. This could mean that you're driving along what appears to be a great road when you suddenly have to swerve to avoid a pothole or other obstacle. There may have been a warning sign, or not. So, when you're travelling a tar road at speed, especially in rural areas, keep an eye on its overall condition, if you can see that it's not in the greatest shape then lower your speed and watch out for potholes and the like. This said, Namibia has very predictable tar roads which allow you to maintain a good average speed.

Driving gravel roads

If you deflate your tyres 20% below the pressure recommended for your vehicle/load/tyre combination, it will soften the ride and ensure better grip on gravel roads. Although the speed limit on gravel roads is 100 km/h, it's advisable to drive at 80 km/h, as these roads can be unpredictable and one can easily lose control. If you have no or little gravel driving experience you should never drive faster than 80 km/h.

If you overtake someone on a gravel road, drive to the far right and stay there until well clear of the vehicle you've passed. Your headlights should be on and you should be able to see far ahead. Pay attention to the direction the wind is blowing your dust, you don't want to blind the vehicle in front when you pass them.

When you encounter badly-corrugated roads, don't skirt around on the sides of the road. This makes the roads wider and wider, and causes what's known as vehicle track pollution. Be careful of the road edges; sometimes there is a very abrupt camber which can pull you off the road.

Driving thick sand

Lower your tyre pressure 40% below normal pressure. If this isn't enough, deflate further but note that this increases the chance of running the tyre off the wheel rim. Don't reduce radial tyres less than 0.8 bar and cross-ply tyres less than 1.2 bar. Note that the pressure depends on the load carried.

You need an off-road vehicle to drive in thick sand. Keep the vehicle in high-range and keep momentum. Drive as fast as possible but at a speed that's safe. If you cannot keep enough momentum, use first gear in low-range and if you get stuck, use your diff-lock as well before you bog down. Once you have bogged down, you will have to dig yourself out. Take your foot off the accelerator the moment the vehicle stops moving forward, otherwise you'll just dig yourself in.

If you need to stop in sand, don't use the brakes but rather roll to a halt. Applying brakes will cause a wall of sand to be built up in front of the wheel, which will make pulling away very difficult.

If possible, drive thick sand as early in the day as possible. As the day gets hotter the sand will get softer and your speed will be slower and your fuel consumption higher.

Driving rough terrain

There is no clear-cut tyre pressure for driving over sharp rocks and stones. Reducing tyre pressure can improve traction, but will expose the tyres to possible damage. On the other hand, increasing tyre pressure will protect the tyre but will compromise on traction. So it's best to keep to the pressure recommended by the manufacturer.

You need an off-road vehicle to drive rough terrain. Select first gear, low-range. It's always best to drive very slowly directly over sharp rocks instead of trying to avoid them, because damage happens when the sidewalls of your tyre, which are only a few millimetres thick, ride up against a knife-edged rock. The tread of a tyre is much thicker and is built to deal with these rocks.

Driving mud

Mud usually sits on top of a firm base so the trick is to let the tyres cut through the mud so they can get traction on the firm base below. Narrower tyres and high tyre pressure will normally be better than wide tyres which have been deflated.

You need an off-road vehicle to drive in mud. Select second gear, low-range. In most cases driving through mud requires momentum and a speed high enough to get you through the obstacle but not too fast to be unsafe.

Do not hold the steering wheel too tightly; feel the feedback from the tyres to the steering wheel and move with it rather than to fight it.

FUEL

Generally, fuel is reliably available in most towns and is of good quality. A very good rule is to fill up at each and every fuel station you pass, regardless how full your tank. The distances between towns can be large and occasionally towns run out of fuel or their pumps might be out of order.

This is especially true when the demand for fuel reaches a peak during the holiday season. Supply might be affected at smaller fuel stations, for this reason it's a good idea to always carry at least 40 litres of extra fuel.

Low sulphur diesel (50 ppm) is available all over Namibia, even at the smaller places. The only place you may not find it is at a container fuel stop, but here you can buy a few litres of normal diesel and mix it in (consult your owner's manual for advice on this subject).

The fuel price is regulated in Namibia. However, there might be marginal price differences from town to town; if fuel is sold in containers you will find these prices will be a bit higher. Check the Tracks4Africa website for the latest fuel price.

For an explanation on how to pay for fuel, spares and repairs turn to page 14.

CAMPING ETIQUETTE

The landscape, safety and weather all contribute to making Namibia a fantastic destination for people who love to camp.

The country offers a wide variety of camping options, all listed in this book. There are well-equipped campsites in and around every town, allowing you to camp in relative luxury with hot-shower ablutions and electricity. These are great if you need to clean up and check your equipment before heading for remoter destinations.

Many farms also offer camping facilities. These are closer to nature, but as you are on a working farm, the atmosphere may vary from tranquil to busy.

But Namibia's real camping gems are the bush camps in many of the nature reserves and/or conservancy areas. These may be very rustic with some having absolutely no facilities apart from a designated long drop. However, these camps offer the solitude that so many campers seek and they're well worth trying.

Namibia also has quite a few community camps. These are initiatives by the tourism industry of Namibia to assist local communities in running campsites in their areas. Some are brilliant and others not so much. But we ask that you support these community camps by staying there. You should offer constructive criticism which would enable these entrepreneurs to improve their offering.

If a campsite has a reception area, this is generally where you'll find a list of rules. Adhere to these at all times but also keep the following guidelines in mind.

Be quiet

People who prefer bush camping do so partly because they enjoy the solitude and sounds of the bush. They don't want to hear a drone buzzing about, or listen to loud music, kids' yelling or loud conversations. And they especially don't want to hear a generator! If you're travelling in a large group remember that you're prone to be noisier, so make a conscious effort to keep your noise down.

Don't disturb fellow campers' rest

Camp should be quiet by 22h00 and nobody should leave before sunrise. If you have to leave early, be considerate towards those still sleeping.

Honour bookings

Don't choose any campsite, unless you're told at reception that you may. Even remote camps often allocate campsites to specific bookings. You wouldn't like it if you found someone occupying the campsite you had booked well in advance and neither will you like it when the rightful occupier asks you to move from his camp.

Keep the donkey going

In campsites where a donkey boiler is used to heat up water for the ablutions, it is courteous to keep the fire going. You will benefit from other people's hot water as campers after you will benefit from yours.

The 'donkey boiler'. Keep the fire going! (photo: Frank Höppener)

(top) Endeavour to leave your campsite as clean or cleaner than how you found it. (photo: Karin Theron)

(above) The beautiful Granietkop Community campsite near Twyfelfontein. (photo: Björn Rehder)

Firewood is a scarce resource in many areas, so carry enough for your own needs. (photo: Frank Höppener)

BUSH CAMPING AND COMMUNITY CAMPS

For bush camping and some of the remote community camps we would like to suggest the following guidelines as the community camps are not always managed properly. Unless we campers do our bit to keep these scenic places in a serene condition, they will deteriorate.

Camp in designated areas

Disturb the environment as little as possible by camping

only in the designated area. Be on the lookout for animal trails leading to waterholes - don't camp on or near such paths. Never camp near a waterhole, animals going there to drink could be deterred by your presence; if it's a long trip to the next waterhole, your badly-located campsite could lead to the animal's demise. Lastly, don't camp in dry riverbeds in the rainy season - these are prone to flash floods.

Carry your own firewood

Don't collect firewood from the veld, this dead wood provides an ecosystem to a variety of organisms. Buy sufficient firewood or charcoal before you enter sensitive wilderness areas.

Do not feed wild animals

However much fun it seems to leave meat or bones out to attract wild animals for viewing around your camp, DON'T DO IT! They will learn to associate food with humans which will lead to them becoming a danger. You will not only put your own life at risk, but also the lives of future campers. Eventually, the park authorities will have to destroy habituated and now dangerous animals.

Fires

If there is a designated fire pit or place where previous campers made fire, stick to it otherwise the camp will be littered with leftover coals. Before you go to bed at night or leave your camp in the morning you must ensure that your fire is fully extinguished. Even a light breeze can cause smouldering coals to reignite, blow away and ignite the surrounding bush.

Waste management

Wilderness camps may be visited by officials only once a month. Under no circumstances should you leave your garbage behind even if bins are provided. Burn what rubbish you can in your campfire and take the remainder with you. Leave absolutely nothing behind and do not bury this type of waste, other than the ash from your fire.

The toilet

Use the toilet facilities provided, even if it is a long drop (pit toilet) which you might ordinarily avoid. Only enter a toilet when the door is open; otherwise knock, a closed door means the toilet is occupied. The breakdown of organic matter in these toilets is a natural process and shouldn't be interfered with by adding chemicals like antiseptics, disinfectant or anything else, to reduce bad odours.

If there are no facilities available, bury your waste; don't ever leave it or toilet paper uncovered! Ideally, paper should be burned rather than buried, but be very careful not to start a veld fire. It is quite difficult to burn wet toilet paper, so it's best to put it in a bag that you can either burn in your campfire or store with the rest of your garbage.

If you are big party, consider managing your toilet requirements as follows:

1. Dig a small ditch approximately 150mm wide (small spade width), 500mm deep and 2 - 3m long (depending on the number of people and duration of stay) at an appropriate place.
2. Agree amongst yourselves that this is the ONLY place that will be used for a toilet.

Fairy Circles in the Giribis Plains. (photo: Heiner Dillmann)

3. Start using it from one end. After each use, shovel closed the part you have just used. A toilet chair (toilet seat with legs) can also be used.
4. Cover the whole ditch with sand before your party leaves. Within a short time even the toilet paper will have decomposed.

FAIRY CIRCLES

When you travel Namibia, you might notice inexplicable bald patches in the landscape. These circles can be seen all over Namibia, but more often in western Kaokoland. They are 2 - 10m wide and on the edges of these circles grass grows rampantly while on the inside the circles are barren.

Tourists have often wondered if these were caused by radio activity, meteorites, UFOs or maybe even fairies. The indigenous San and Himba people believed that these circles may have been caused by dragons that stayed underground, evil spirits or gods. For the past 30 years scientist have also been researching this phenomenon.

In March 2012 a team of researchers from the University of Pretoria announced that, after intensive research, they believe that these so-called fairy circles are actually caused by earth gas bubbles which could possibly indicate oil reserves.

The research was led by Professor Gretel van Rooyen, a botanist from the University of Pretoria. She discounted the first scientific theory (that these circles were caused by radio activity) by testing the soil.

Another theory – that the soil is poisoned by the Damara Euphorbia *(Euphorbia damarana)*, also known as the Damaramelkbos plant – was discounted because they found that certain desert plants like annual rye grass *(Lolium multiflorum)* indeed flourishes under Damara Euphorbias.

A third theory - that Hodotermes mossambicus termites carry the plant material from the circles to their nests - was discounted by digging trenches of two metres deep inside and around the circles. No significant termite activity was found.

Professor Van Rooyen did two more experiments and realised that the soil inside the circles must be toxic and that the source of the toxins must be deep below the surface.

The university's Chemistry Department did various tests and found that the circles are caused by bubbles of gas underneath the earth that rise to the surface. The gas first moves through cracks and sink holes before it reach the sandy soil at the top.

Because of the homogeneous density of the soil, the gas that filters through small cracks, holes and the earth crust are distributed coniform. It breaks through the soil surface in an almost perfect circle. The earth gas takes the much needed oxygen from the soil and at the same time changes the chemistry of the soil.

However, in April 2013 prof. Norbert Jürgens, a German biologist from the University of Hamburg, claimed that sand termites *(Psammotermes allocerus)* are responsible for the fairy rings. According to his research they make the rings as part of their complicated water storage system. The termites kill the grass by eating the roots and that way the water stays in the ground for years.

According to him the reason why no one figured it out before is that the termites mostly move about at night and don't build big, noticeable nests.

However, Mr Walter Tschinkel, a biologist from the Florida State University, was not convinced by either theories because he himself could not find termites or anything toxic in the soil samples that he took.

At the same time a botanist from the University of Cape Town, Mr Michael Cramer, was researching his theory that the fairy circles are natural growth patterns caused by competition for scarce resources.

New Scientist reported in January 2017 that scientists from Princeton University found that two mechanisms acting simultaneously are responsible for the circles. Large-scale patterns are created by the termites that clear the vegetation in the area around their nests to establish water reservoirs while smaller patterns in the vegetation between the circles result from plants competing for water.

It does, however, seem like the last word was not yet spoken on fairy circles as Dr Stephan Getzin from the Helmholtz Center for Environmental Research in Leipzig, Germany, maintains that there are no termites in some areas where circles are found.

It is clear that these fairy circles will keep the romantics guessing and the scientists researching for quite some time!

(Sources: Beeld 7 March 2012, Republikein 3 April 2013 and New Scientist 18 January 2017)

DRONES

There are regulations governing the use of Remotely Piloted Aircraft. At the time of writing these were being revised and amended. If you plan to bring a drone into Namibia we would recommend you contact this country's Civil Aviation Authority (www.dca.com.na) for clarity on prevailing permissions and regulations. Drone use is strictly prohibited within game reserves and national parks.

USEFUL CONTACT NUMBERS

Police toll-free:	+264 (61) 10111
MedRescue:	+264 (61) 230 505/6/7
SOS International:	+264 (61) 289 0999
Ministry of Information & Communication Technology:	+264 (61) 283 9111

More than 50 countries have consular or embassy representation in Windhoek. For information, contact the ministry above.

GENERAL SAFETY PRECAUTIONS

(photo: Frank Höppener)

***AN ACCIDENT CAN RUIN A LONG-ANTICIPATED HOLIDAY** so it's worthwhile taking the time to consider some general safety precautions.*

RULE NUMBER ONE

Wherever you travel in Africa, the most important rule is to be as well informed as possible. Before your trip, read up about the areas you'll be visiting. There are various overland forums on the internet where you can ask experienced travellers just about anything you need to know.

Make sure that you have a good basic understanding of your vehicle and the equipment you'll be using. If you're planning a trip into remote areas, it's a good idea to do a bush mechanic course, or at the very least watch some online video clips on how to fix some basic mechanical problems, such as replacing a broken fanbelt or blocked fuel filter.

Ensure that more than one person is able to drive the vehicle, and is familiar with the basics, such as opening the bonnet, changing a wheel, checking oil and water, etc.

And should something should happen to you, does your travel partner or travelling companions know where you keep important information like emergency contact numbers?

BEWARE OF GROUP TRAVEL

Some people prefer to travel on their own and some prefer to travel in a group. Whatever your preference, always remember rule number one above and stay cautious.

It's often recommended that you don't travel alone to remote areas like Kaokoland. Group travel is, however, no guarantee for safety! If you prefer to travel in a group because you like the company or find it more convenient or economical, then do so. But never become complacent about safety because you're in a group. You must take personal responsibility for every aspect of your own safety.

Group travel can be just as dangerous as travelling solo because people in groups tend to do things they would never dream of doing alone. There's an overconfidence associated with travelling in a group. What's more, most vehicle damage occurs when people want to prove their driving skills or vehicle capability to the group.

Though there can be safety in numbers, be aware of the disadvantages of group travel too. (photo: Frank Höppener)

Whether you travel alone or in a group, avoid having to admit to yourself afterwards that a disaster happened because of your own stupidity or recklessness.

If you do travel in a group, give your vehicle's spare keys to another driver in your group, just in case you lose yours. But don't forget to collect them before you split up at the end of your journey!

CARRY WITH YOU

Carry your passport as well as copies of all your documents with you at all times. Don't leave these in your tent or wherever you're staying.

TRAVELLING REMOTE AREAS

When you travel remote areas like Kaokoland or Damaraland, carrying a satellite phone is advisable (see our special section on Communication on page 46). Satellite tracking devices are also a smart plan, these allow your friends and family to monitor your progress and location. Tracks4Africa has worked closely with one such provider, AfricanStuff. Find them at www.africanstuff.co.za

Apart from extra fuel, you must take extra water and dry food rations (and a few packets of rehydrate solution) so that you're able to survive five extra days in the bush should you become lost or stranded. It's possible to ration yourself to two litres of water per person per day, but remember to take that over and above your normal daily water ration. Under normal circumstances you could work on six litres of water per person per day for drinking, cooking and dishes. Ideally, you should always travel with at least 40 litres of water.

TIP: *In an emergency, stay with your vehicle. A search party will find a vehicle much more easily than it will find people walking around on foot, especially if it's an air search.*

PERSONAL SAFETY

Use common sense when you travel Namibia like you would when you travel anywhere else in the world. A universal truth is the greater the concentration of people, the higher the likelihood of crime, so you should be more cautious when you're in cities and big towns.

Crime is mostly limited to theft like pickpocketing, luggage theft and burglaries. You're an easy target if you leave your handbag or camera equipment in plain sight in an unattended vehicle. Leave the flashy jewellery at home and be careful of carrying your camera around your neck - rather carry it in a camera bag over your shoulder.

When you camp, you should rather stow your important personal belongings in the tent at night, especially if the campsite is in, or close to, a village or town. Loose camping gear should also be stowed away at night, because you never know whether a strong wind will come up during the night or hyenas carry it away. Should you experience a breakdown or accident and you cannot reach your planned destination, it's better not to pitch your tent right next to the road where everybody can see you.

INSURANCE

Make sure you have appropriate medical and vehicle insurance before you leave, and that your vehicle insurance includes vehicle recovery. You will find the numbers of tow-in services in this guide under the towns. Simply locate the town nearest your location.

(photo: Karin Theron)

Keep your insurance contact numbers with you. Remember that you cannot phone other countries' toll free numbers from Namibia, so make sure you're carrying the direct numbers.

It is advisable to contact your medical aid/insurance prior to your trip to obtain a document which states what you are covered for and what the claim procedure is when you're in a foreign country.

However, in case of a vehicle accident visitors can claim from the Namibian Motor Vehicle Accident Fund (MVA Fund) because a third party compensatory premium is included as a fuel levy when you purchase petrol/diesel. As a tourist you will automatically hold a visitor permit under the Immigration Control Act. A person involved in a motor vehicle accident is also entitled to medical treatment amounting up to N$1 500 000, an injury grant and funeral grant as well as loss of income and loss of support claims. Go to: www.mvafund.com.na for full details.

DRIVING THROUGH LONG, DRY GRASS

When driving through long, dry grass like that often found in Kaokoland and Damaraland, be aware of the danger of grass accumulating under your vehicle and catching fire. ALWAYS carry a fire extinguisher in your vehicle and stop at regular intervals to clear any grass around the

(photo: Frank Höppener)

(photo: Frank Höppener)

exhaust manifold. Never park your vehicle (or stop) on long, dry grass as it may catch fire. This risk is greater for petrol than it is for diesel vehicles because their exhaust temperatures are much higher, although turbo diesel engines also generate a lot of heat.

In places where the grass is long, stop every 20 km or so to check for grass collecting near or on the exhaust. The exhaust will be extremely hot, so always have a thick glove, similar to the ones used by welders, in the car.

***TIP:** Never install any additional electrical equipment to your vehicle without a proper fuse; not only is it better for the protection of the apparatus, but it also ensures your vehicle safety. Always verify the safety of any aftermarket work yourself by checking for any loose electric wiring underneath your vehicle. Sparks combined with a hot exhaust pipe and dry grass are a sure recipe for a fiery disaster!*

WILD ANIMALS

Most community camps in Namibia are unfenced so the wildlife can and will wander through. Always keep your eyes open for wild animals, especially at night. Remember that wild animals are just that, wild, and you're in their territory. It's never entirely safe to walk around in wildlife areas, even if it is allowed.

It's also not a good idea to swim or cool down in any of the rivers in northern Namibia as there are many hungry crocodiles in these parts. Also be careful of walking close to the water's edge; crocodiles are capable of lunging out the water and seizing their prey in milliseconds. Stay a minimum of 2m from the water's edge.

You should treat wild animals exhibiting any abnormally tame behaviour with suspicion because this docility could be a symptom of rabies. Children are most susceptible when they see these nice little 'doggies' approaching and they want to play with them. Reports were made of jackal, meerkat and even kudu approaching vehicles and people.

As previously mentioned, don't leave bones or other food out to attract animals to take photos. You will cause them to become tame and be shot when they inevitably become a threat to humans. Also, don't leave any refuse bags around your camp as the animals will tear them open.

Pack away all food to prevent wild animals, big or small, from tucking in when you go to bed. A little mouse burrowing into a plastic bag can cause great consternation in the middle of the night when you don't know where the noise is coming from. Hyenas are known for carrying off or chewing on anything lying around that's foreign to them. In areas where they're around, rather pack away everything at night and when leaving your camp.

In areas where there are elephant, you shouldn't keep fruit with you (especially citrus) as the elephants will do anything to get to it. Be vigilant of baboons and monkeys around your camp, for they are experts at stealing food. Always ask the local camp warden if they have any problems with monkeys or baboons.

Never ever sleep with your tent open where wild animals roam free – no matter how hot it is – as predators will drag you out of your tent and make a meal of you. As long as your tent is zipped up, you are safe. Predators like lion perceive a tent wall to be an impenetrable barrier - long may they labour under this misconception!

The desert elephants found in the riverbeds of Damaraland and Kaokoland have a comfort zone of about 500m. The dry riverbeds belong to them and they don't like to be disturbed, therefore you should drive slowly and be alert. An elephant encounter requires patience more than skill because these lords of the desert may take a long time to make way. People have been killed by elephant in Namibia's riverbeds so avoid driving there if you can.

In areas where hippos are found, be aware that at night they leave the water to graze. Never get between a hippo and the water, and do not pitch your tent on or near one of their pathways.

TAKING PHOTOGRAPHS

Respect people's privacy and ask for permission before photographing someone. Specific groups like the Himba and Herero are especially sensitive to tourists taking photographs of them. It is not uncommon to be expected to pay a fee for each photo you took of someone or his possessions.

In Africa you should avoid taking photographs of official buildings like airports or official residences. Roadblocks, guard posts, border posts and people in uniform are a definite no-no as well. You do not want to clash with anybody who is in a position of power.

(photo: Frank Höppener)

TRIP PLANNING GUIDE

(By Francois Visagie)

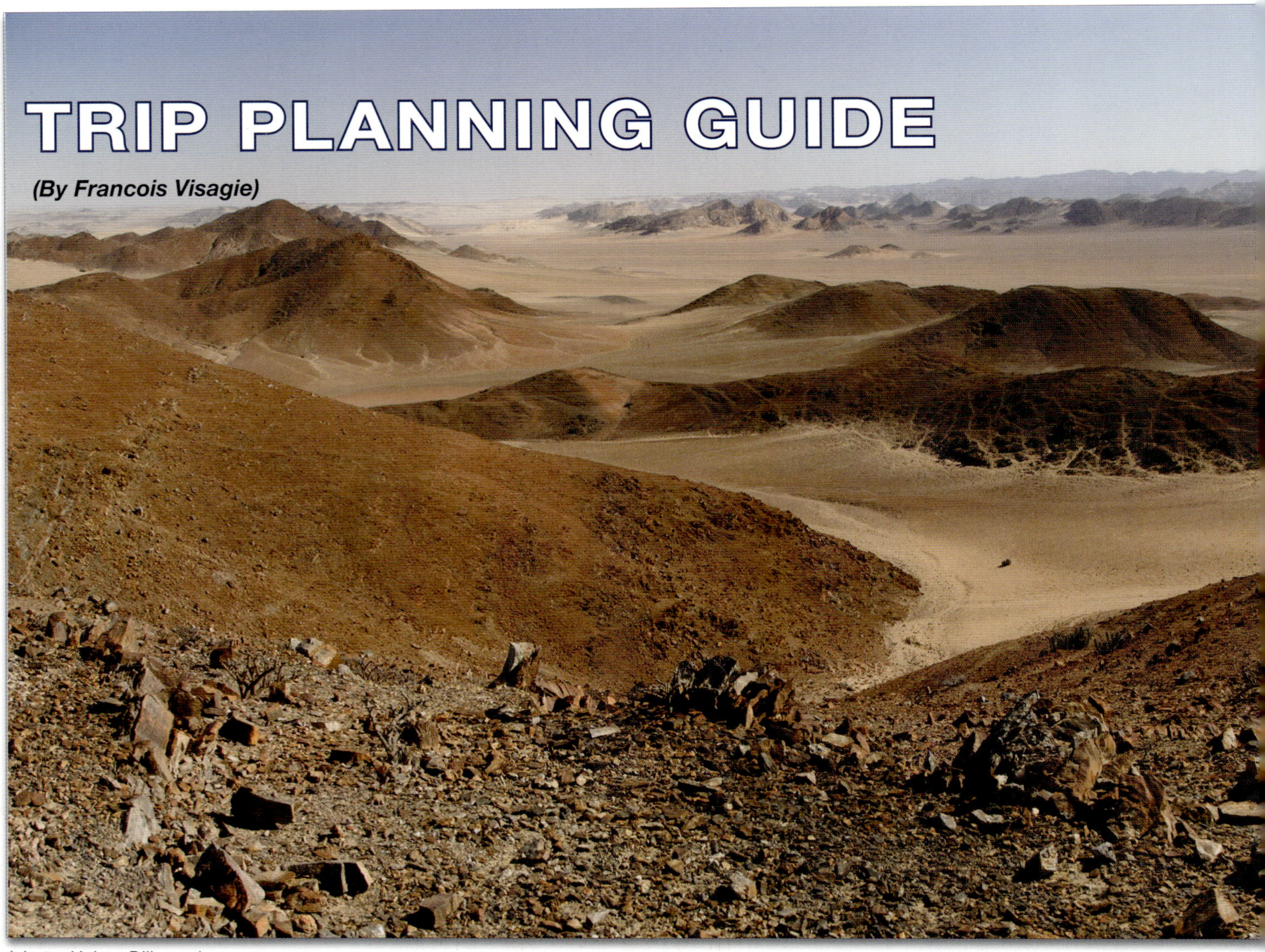

(photo: Heiner Dillmann)

***PEOPLE TRAVEL FOR DIFFERENT REASONS** but whatever your motivation, it's important that you do your homework before you set off. The more effort you put into your planning, the more you'll get out of your journey.*

THINGS TO CONSIDER

How flexible is your itinerary? Some people enjoy planning and travelling to a well-defined itinerary because they might not feel equipped to handle unforeseen circumstances, or they might not have enough leave time to accommodate delays. Others might find a fixed itinerary suffocating. Decide how structured or how flexible you want your itinerary to be.

Do you have enough time? Be realistic about the time you have for your trip. You might not be able to see and do everything you want because you simply don't have enough time. Be careful of trying to cram in too much; if you're driving every day from sunrise to sunset, you're not going to have a relaxing time of it. Less is more!

Do you want to travel in a group or on your own? If it's your first trip into Africa it would be wise to join a group of friends who are experienced overlanders, or a guided tour. Thereafter, if you want to go solo, you can begin with 'easy' routes and destinations. Travelling in a group can be very enjoyable and enlightening, but it can also put a big damper on your experience if they're not the kind of people you enjoy spending time with.

What are your personal capabilities? Be realistic about how much you enjoy camping, pitching a tent, cooking on a fire and off-road driving. Rather give yourself a gentle introduction to these sorts of activities.

What type of accommodation do you prefer? You might be a rough-and-tough bush camper or you might prefer to make camp in a venue with all the amenities. If you're not a camper, you can overnight in self-catering chalets or choose to splash out on luxury accommodation. Some people prefer a mix of everything. But remember, whether you're camping for one night or the whole trip, you'll need to carry the same amount of camping equipment. So, if your plans include very little camping, ask yourself whether it's worthwhile to camp at all.

The type of overnight accommodation you choose will influence your overnight choices; it'll also determine how much time you will need to settle in after arrival and how long it'll take you to get going again when you leave.

How safe are your destinations? Whether venturing into familiar or unfamiliar territory, the destinations may pose risks that your party members may not be aware of, or be accustomed to. You need to make sure your vehicle is suited to the kind of terrain you'll be driving (and every other vehicle in your group too). Remember, you may have to recover or repair vehicles.

Cultures differ and it will be worth your while to find out more about the people living in the areas that you want to visit. Find out about things like how to approach someone politely for advice and how to obtain permission to camp on communal land.

What bureaucratic challenges can you expect? If there are police/veterinary check points, or international border posts on the way, you should know what paperwork is need and what items are allowed and which are prohibited. Allow extra time in your itinerary for border crossings and checkpoints.

Do you have enough money? Assume that you'll consume at least the equivalent amount of food and refreshments you would at home, and allow extra money for fuel, levies, accommodation, park fees, shopping, activities etc. Draw up a rough budget for the trip to make sure you can afford it.

PLANNING

1. Make a rough list of attractions/destinations you want to visit and activities you want to take part in. This will form the basis of your trip plan.

2. Read up on your destinations. There are many excellent reference sources: most countries have official tourism websites and you'll find internet user forums dedicated to overland travel. These websites and forums are usually easy to find via search engines like Google, but you can also enquire on the Tracks4Africa forum (www.tracks4africa.co.za).

3. Update your destinations. Remove any you discover might be unsuitable and add any new or interesting ones you came across.

4. Now that you have an idea of where you'll be going, decide how many days of your holiday you want to be driving. You may want to consider building in a day or two spare for unforeseen delays/changes.

5. Determine how many hours you'll be able to travel per day, taking into account children in your party, people with special needs, lunch stops and the fact that it will take longer to drive scenic routes. If you camp, plan to be at your campsite well before nightfall. Avoid having to set up camp in the dark. Limit yourself to five hours of driving per day.

6. Mark your destinations on a map. You can use a paper map for this, or create waypoints in a mapping program like Garmin MapSource or BaseCamp. This could be useful later – see the section on Navigation. Viewing your route on Google Earth gives you a good indication of the terrain and population density of the areas you plan to travel.

7. Connect your destinations on the map to form the route you'll follow. Try to follow a logical sequence to prevent backtracks and unnecessary loops. Again, you could use a paper map or something like Garmin MapSource/ BaseCamp. The T4A paper maps indicate travel time between distances and MapSource/BaseCamp also calculates travel time.

8. When you start your detail planning, address issues like:
- Accommodation and the best time of the year to visit.
- Where to replenish fuel, water and food. And check that you can reach these points before supplies run low.
- Health and safety aspects. See our comprehensive section on health on page 54.
- Plan how much money you need and where you will exchange Namibian dollars or South African rands.
- Requirements for border crossings (see page 48).
- Current regulations governing the transportation of fresh produce and/or meat.
- Apply for guest licences for communications equipment like two-way radios.
- Apply for guest licences for drones.

FINAL TRIP PLANNING CHECKLIST

Money matters

- ☐ Draw up your budget.
- ☐ Collect adequate amounts of currency from your bank.
- ☐ Check you have both a Visa and Mastercard in your travel party.
- ☐ Notify your bank that you will be using these credit cards in Namibia.

Contact numbers to keep with you
(must be direct-dial numbers, not toll-free)

- ☐ To report lost or stolen bank cards.
- ☐ Medical aid plus the international SOS number for an emergency.
- ☐ Vehicle insurance in case of an accident.
- ☐ Vehicle mechanic or service centre closest to your route/destinations.
- ☐ A friend or family member at home who can assist with any emergency arrangements required.

Paperwork

- ☐ Passport, valid for six months after you are due to leave Namibia.
- ☐ Visa, if required.
- ☐ Border documents (see page 48 for more information about border post red tape).
- ☐ Medical and vehicle insurance details, and the claims procedure.
- ☐ Accommodation booking confirmations.
- ☐ Copies of your passport and all documents (kept separate from the originals).
- ☐ Digital copies of important documents, stored on a secure online server for remote access.

Medical

- ☐ Inoculations and prophylactics for malaria if you're going to the north of Namibia.
- ☐ Well-stocked first aid kit, check that medicines aren't expired.
- ☐ Yellow fever certificate - required if travelling from a country where yellow fever is endemic.

Technical gear

- ☐ The required Tracks4Africa maps, and your route, loaded onto your Garmin GPS. Or the Tracks4Africa Navigator app on your smartphone / tablet.
- ☐ If you're taking two-way radios, licences to use them in the areas you're visiting.
- ☐ If you are going into remote areas, rent or buy a satellite phone. Or hire a vehicle tracker so that your friends/family at home can follow your route.
- ☐ Camera and/or video camera, with extra batteries and your chargers. And enough data cards.
- ☐ Laptop with external storage to store and backup photos and videos.
- ☐ Adaptor for power points. Namibia uses the 15 A version of the BS 546 plug (also used in South Africa).
- ☐ Headlamp and/or torch with spare batteries.
- ☐ Binoculars
- ☐ Repair patches if you're using inflatable mattresses.

Vehicle

- ☐ Vehicle's services up to date. Trailer too, if you're taking one.
- ☐ If your overland vehicle has been in storage, make sure it was driven from time to time.
- ☐ Make sure your tyres (both vehicle and trailer) are in good condition and less than five years old.
- ☐ Check mechanicals like suspension and transmission components and steering linkages, or have them checked by a mechanic.
- ☐ Check tyre pressure, oil and coolant levels shortly before you leave.
- ☐ Make sure all fuel and water tanks and containers are filled before you leave.

Specific clothing

- ☐ Flip flops for showering. They protects your feet from bacteria and give you something to step onto when you get out of the shower.
- ☐ Buff for keeping your head and neck warm in winter and protecting it against mosquitoes in summer. Also handy if you're having a bad hair day.
- ☐ Long socks to keep you warm in winter and protect your legs from mosquitoes in summer.

- ☐ Wool cap and gloves if you're visiting in winter, Namibia can get quite cold at night.
- ☐ Hat and sunglasses (don't forget the sunblock).
- ☐ And don't forget the laundry bag!

Maps, books and print-outs

- ☐ Paper maps and your researched information (printed) on your planned route and destinations.
- ☐ Guide book. To provide lots of information on the region as well as practical advice to make travel easier.
- ☐ Books or apps on animals, birds, fauna and flora and / or trees of the region. Namibia is renowned for its natural capital so you'll enjoy the region much more if you can recognise the different lifeforms you encounter.
- ☐ Sunrise / sunset data. Check this against your destinations and plan your days around sunrise / sunset and moonrise / moonset. This info is online but Garmin's range of outdoor GPS devices have a 'Sun and Moon' feature which provides this info too. Plus, there are apps you can download which will provide the same.

And lastly, don't forget these two!

- ☐ Insect repellent.
- ☐ Spade and toilet paper.

Plan your route carefully - you don't want to end up driving terrain which is beyond your vehicle's capabilities.(photo: Heiner Dillmann)

NAVIGATION

(By Francois Visagie, Wouter Brand and Johann Groenewald)

(photo: Heiner Dillmann)

UNLIKE SO MANY ANIMAL SPECIES, remarkably few homo sapiens demonstrate a natural ability to navigate. To know where we are and to navigate from that point to another, usually requires some degree of intellectual effort.

Navigation is about constructing and maintaining a mental map of where we are in relation with our surroundings. The human mental map is, at best, only a relative map – in that it exists relative to known landmarks. Absolute directions (north, south, east and west) play little to no part in the human mental map. Often people will be able to point out the direction in which a landmark or place is found but won't have a clue where an absolute direction like North is found.

So, a good mental map must include absolute orientation – you must know (more or less) where North is. This is essential when travelling to new and unfamiliar places.

The ability to maintain and adjust a mental map to some degree, can be described as 'navigational skills'. To navigate, you first need to know where you are and thereafter, where you want to go to. Happily for us directionally-challenged humans, these days we can turn to maps for navigational assistance, both paper and GPS.

Some people prefer paper maps over electronic maps but there's really an argument for both when travelling Africa. A paper map allows you to more easily orientate yourself as to where you are in relation to the country you're travelling, while the electronic map allows you to zoom in and navigate to within a few meters of any given point. Where a paper map can give you accurate information within 50m, an electronic map can do it within 5m.

Even if you prefer not to rely on an electronic device, it may be a good idea to have one as a backup in case you need to find your location on the map or simply want to retrace your tracks.

Whether you use a paper map or an electronic map or both, invest in the best possible maps you can afford. Your maps must be accurate and be up-to-date on the areas you want to travel, this is especially vital if you're travelling remote areas.

Even if you have the best electronic device with the most accurate maps, you should also have auxiliary navigational aids such as paper maps and a compass. If you consult these from time to time this will ensure that your mental map stays in good shape in the event that your electronic devices stop working.

Whether using an electronic or a paper map, pay attention to your surroundings as you travel. Make a mental note when you take a turn, maybe even mark it on your map. If you find yourself testing a maze of tracks, you can also consider noting the odometer reading at each turn.

Your GPS should be set to voice-guided navigation. Not so that you can daydream the kilometres away but to allow you to devote your full attention to the road and your surroundings. When you pay attention to your changing surroundings, you'll be far better equipped to make navigational decisions. If you need to turn back, you will know which way to backtrack. If you need to take a detour, you'll know exactly where you are and what impact the detour will have on the route to your next stop.

But if you do get lost, don't panic. Although you might have missed an important turn, you're still a lot better off than someone who's been dropped blindfolded into the area. You will remember quite a bit about the terrain you travelled through, for how long, and so on. Use this information to locate yourself.

NAVIGATING WITH YOUR SMARTPHONE

Technological developments in recent years has led to an increasing number of people using their smartphones, tablets or iPads as navigation tools. Nowadays, the average smartphone comes equipped with a location service feature and one can further install a plethora of navigation applications - apps as they're known. Many people use their smartphones for city guidance so they're already familiar with this functionality.

Of course, some hardcore overlanders are more comfortable with their GPSs and will argue that their smartphones aren't up to the job. But while it's true that the average smartphone doesn't have all the features of a GPS, there's nothing to stop you from downloading and installing apps (often free or inexpensive) which replicate the features and functionality found on the average GPS.

ONLINE VS. OFFLINE APPS

Map or navigation apps can be divided into two categories: online and offline. Online apps require an internet connection to download map information as you travel, while offline apps store the maps on your device. In remote areas, or simply for the sake of reducing roaming charges, it's highly advisable that you use offline apps; these are also usually much faster. What's more, if there's no cellular reception - as is often the case in Namibia's remote regions - online apps won't work at all.

Google Maps and Apple Maps are two well-known examples of online apps. Some online apps do allow you to download and cache map data but with limited coverage of a temporary nature, so this isn't suited to overland trips. Many offline navigation apps are available, including such examples as Garmin's Navigation app, TomTom, Sygic, iGo, Here Maps and the Tracks4Africa Overland Navigator. These apps are downloaded when you first install them and are often large files which include various country maps. Once installed you don't require an internet connection anymore. However, some of these apps may require an internet connection for searches, so test them before you leave home.

(photo: Karin Theron)

The ***Tracks4Africa Overland Navigator*** app is available for Android and Apple devices. The ***Tracks4Africa Guide*** app (also available for both platforms) isn't a navigational app as such but it displays your GPS location on a digital paper map while you drive. This solves half your navigational problems and it comes with the same rich content you'll find in this guide book.

If you use your smartphone, tablet or iPad for overland navigation you must get a proper mount and a permanent power supply. Navigation apps keep your screen and GPS receiver on all the time, the combination of which consumes significant battery power.

NAVIGATION USING A GPS

Which GPS?

Before you can answer this question you have to consider what you will be using your GPS for. If you're considering a self-drive trip into remote areas you'll have a very different set of needs to someone who wants a GPS for activities like hiking, mountain biking or even just normal city navigation.

If you're a self-drive traveller who wants to explore Africa's remoter regions you'll want a Garmin GPS loaded with Tracks4Africa GPS maps. And to get the full potential from your navigation system you need a Garmin GPS which displays the maps in a particular way, otherwise you won't have all the information on the T4A maps at your disposal when you travel.

The Drive/Drive Assist models (once named Nuvi) in the Garmin range are largely intended for city navigation. They do a perfect job of getting you from point A to B, but they only display road labels and points of interest (POI) on the map screen at low zoom levels (50 – 80m). Such information is embedded in the T4A map and while you are able to search for it under 'Where to' > 'Points of interest (POI)', it isn't displayed at higher zoom levels when you look at the map under 'View map'.

(top) Garmin GPSMap 276Cx. (bottom) Garmin Montana

For this reason the Drive/Drive Assist range isn't ideal for travelling into remote areas. T4A road labels carry information such as 'off-road' or 'deep sand' which is critical to your decision making. The map also carries POIs which provide additional information, for example seasonal flood warnings or dangerous sections on a trail. You would want to see this type of information on the map as you drive or when you plan a route.

If you intend to record your route on your GPS, you need a GPS which can record and manage the tracks for the duration of your trip. GPS tracks can be used for your trip report and they're also very welcome at Tracks4Africa where we use them to update and improve our maps.

If you plan to venture into areas which aren't covered in detail by the maps you've have installed, then you might want to import tracks and waypoints to your GPS to use as a guide. This is another feature normally only associated with outdoors orientated GPS units.

You'll be using your GPS inside your vehicle so a high-sensitivity GPS receiver is required to ensure that your unit receives sufficient signal to make accurate location calculations. If your GPS struggles to pick up a signal inside the vehicle, or the signal isn't strong enough, consider fitting an external antenna.

On a motorbike you need a GPS with a screen which can be read in direct sunlight, and the unit has to be both water-resistant and dustproof.

There are two Garmin models which tick all of the above boxes, the Montana and the GPSMap 276Cx. They are rugged, have sufficiently large screens, display all map features and allow superior track management. But they're both expensive, so if you're just looking for routing instructions from A to B on known roads and tracks, then any of the entry-level Garmin Drive/Drive Assist devices will do the job at a fraction of the price. Bikers should consider the Garmin Zumo which is purpose-built with handy features for their type of usage.

Before you go

Don't leave map and GPS preparation until the last minute. Proper trip planning requires that you select and study the maps well in advance to make sure that the places you intend visiting are shown.

If you intend using a GPS for navigation on your trip, here are a few preparation tips:

1. Get to know your GPS and its peripherals before you go into unfamiliar territory. Test the features and maps, and consider a basic training course in how to use your GPS.
2. Make sure your GPS is running the manufacturer's latest firmware.
3. Ensure you have latest maps installed on your GPS and computer.
4. Make sure your GPS's route calculation method is on the right setting (normally, fastest time with no avoidances selected).
5. If you want to record tracks with your GPS bear in mind that older units won't have adequate memory to store the entire trip. The solution is to download your tracks to your laptop every day or two. Newer GPS devices will record tracks and archive your tracks. To access these archived tracks, look in the Garmin / GPX / Archive folder on your device's internal memory.
6. Transfer all the waypoints and tracks that you've come up with during trip planning to your GPS. Make sure you can find them under 'favourites' before you set off.
7. Get a sturdy GPS mounting bracket and place in a suitable position in your vehicle. You should be able to glance at the screen without looking away from the road for too long, and the unit shouldn't block important vehicle controls. Bear in mind that some units are prone to overheating if left in direct sunlight.
8. The GPS will probably have to draw power from the vehicle's battery; most commonly, via the cigarette lighter plug (take an extra fuse for this circuit). This is fine if your GPS has an internal battery but if it doesn't, you're going to experience power supply problems on corrugated roads and the like. In this instance, a permanently wired connection is a better bet.

TIP *It's not enough that you know how to operate your GPS, someone else in your party needs to have this skill too. This is in case something should happen to you, plus it'll allow you share this duty while you travel.*

How to use your GPS

When you set your destination, your GPS will display useful information like 'time to destination' and 'distance to destination' provided you have set up your map screen accordingly. These are handy measures to have, especially when the kids start asking the inevitable question! They're also useful for planning lunch stops.

Operating a GPS while driving is as dangerous as texting while driving. Don't do it. Rather pull over to the side of the road, or let one of your passengers operate the GPS.

Navigate to a destination

To navigate to a desired destination, follow these steps:

1. Ensure that the correct map, and only that map, is selected. Your GPS won't work properly if you have more than one map selected.
2. Know which route calculation method you have selected and know why you've selected it. The default should be 'Fastest time'. De-select 'All avoidances'.
3. Find the desired destination. Depending on how you did your trip planning, you'll look up intermediate destinations or waypoints from your 'Favourites'.
4. Then select 'Go' to start navigation on your Garmin device.
5. Review the calculated route to confirm that it's suitable. Pay attention to 'time to destination'. If this is very long in relation to the distance, it indicates that you're probably going to do some off-road driving. Use your common sense, don't be led astray by technology.
6. Follow the route instructions, paying careful attention to major turn-offs. Compare what you're seeing around you on the road with what your GPS is suggesting. For instance, does the road sign indicate the same distance as your GPS?

Direction of travel & map orientation

When you're stationary, your GPS won't show you which way you should be driving. It's only when you start moving that the GPS can pick up what direction you're travelling and orientate the map accordingly.

There are two ways to set up the map screen of your GPS when it comes to direction. You have north-up where the screen will always position the map with north aligned with the top of the screen, similar to a paper map view. Then there's track-up where the map will be rotated to always have the track you are supposed to be following pointing to the top of the screen. The choice is a matter of personal preference, but you may find track-up easier to use while navigating through towns.

TIP *On a long trip, it's entirely likely that you and your family will grow weary of the GPS guidance voice. You can still use the routing function with the voice guidance switched off. All it means is that you'll have to pay more attention to the screen in order to get routing instructions.*

ON THE ROAD

By now your trip planning is ancient history, and your electronic equipment has been checked and the appropriate apps and maps properly installed. You've also familiarised yourself with the operation of both hardware and software.

Depending on the app you've installed on your smartphone/iPad/tablet, this device can be a great source of information. Likewise, your GPS can serve as more than just a navigation device on the move. If, for instance, you're using the Tracks4Africa SD card, you'll also have access to the T4A Africa Travel Guide on your GPS. This is a rich source of information designed especially with the self-drive traveller in mind.

If you don't have your accommodation booked, you would want to start looking for a place to sleep, in the afternoon. You can find accommodation nearby if you have the Tracks4Africa Guide app installed on your phone or by browsing the contents of this book. You could also scroll down to the accommodation category on your GPS to find accommodation nearby.

Keep the direction of these places in mind as some may be behind you. Note that the distance indicated on your GPS is a straight-line distance and you first have to set your GPS to navigate to a particular place before it will calculate the proper distance and, more importantly, drive time. For each accommodation listing in this book we have indicated distance as well as travel time from the specified nearest town.

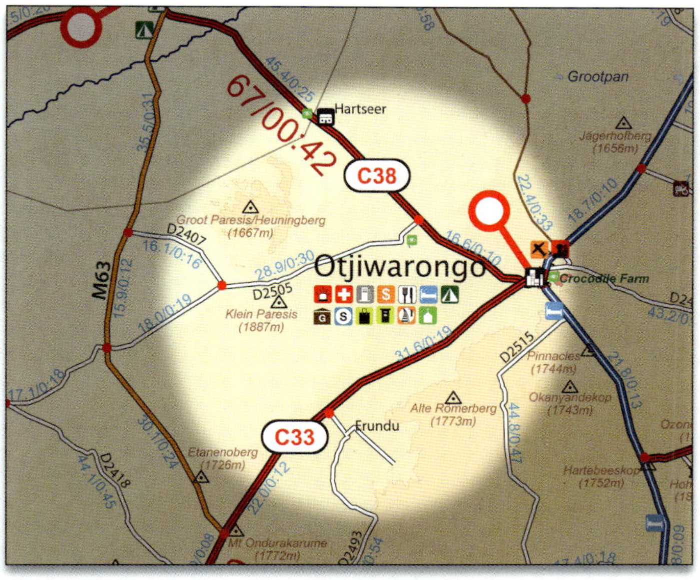

The T4A paper map is packed with useful detail.

NAVIGATION USING A PAPER MAP

Many people consider navigating with a paper map to be much more exciting and engaging than simply following the prompts from an electronic device. With a paper map you don't have a GPS signal to indicate your position on the map like you have on the digital map of your electronic device.

If you use a paper map, you need to be able to correctly orientate yourself on the map. If you're driving major routes it's easy to do by looking at road signs. However, when you're travelling remote areas where the landscape is unfamiliar and there are no road signs, it becomes much more difficult to plot your exact position on the map.

If you are going to rely solely on a paper map for navigation, you must study the map before you set off for the day. Look for prominent features which can help you to orientate yourself along the way, things like river crossings, major intersections, villages or mountain passes.

As you drive, plot your progress and mark the last position you're absolutely sure of, on the map. Also, keep an eye on the distance you've travelled and jot down odometer readings if necessary.

(above) Image what this landscape would look like if it were covered with multiple vehicle tracks! (photo: Frank Höppener).

(right) Better yet, follow the track shown on your T4A app or mapset. (photo: Karin Theron)

Pay careful attention to where north is and determine whether you're driving in the right direction. If you're using a Tracks4Africa paper map, you will find travel time as well as travel distance indicated. These are handy when planning your trip ahead.

If you get lost, stop and try your best to orientate yourself. You should be able to follow your tracks back by remembering prominent features you passed or by even following your own vehicle tracks. We trust that you have stayed on a designated track!

Get yourself to the last known position on the map and then start your route planning over again.

BE AN ECO-TRAVELLER

Vehicle tracks can cause irreparable damage to the environment. It can take hundreds of years for nature to repair the scars of vehicle track pollution. Such tracks are clearly visible from an aeroplane - they even show up on satellite images!

Namibia is an extremely popular self-drive destination; over the last decade, tourist traffic to places like Kaokoland and Damaraland has increased to the point where it's becoming a problem. These vast areas can't be fenced off or patrolled and it's this very 'freedom' which attracts so many visitors. We urge you to stay on designated roads and not to wild camp in these areas - it simply puts too much pressure on the environment.

Responsible travellers stick to existing tracks, but more importantly, they stick to the right tracks. Don't cause track pollution and unnecessary damage to fauna and flora.

There are numerous dead-end tracks leading into unspoilt areas. This is the result of indiscriminate leisure driving and people getting lost over many years. The problem is then made worse when travellers follow these erroneous tracks over and over again.

Navigating by means of a route or using a routable electronic map is an environmentally-friendly option, you can be sure you are taking the right track and therefore limiting track pollution.

Eco-travellers share information so that they can learn from each other's travel experiences. This is the only way we can protect and preserve this environment for future generations. If you love travelling Africa, share your tracks and experiences with fellow travellers on one of the many forums designed specifically for that purpose.

MAPS for Overlanders by Overlanders

Now in its 4th edition, the Tracks4Africa Namibia paper map is perhaps the largest paper map you'll ever buy. With its 1:1 000 000 scale (1cm = 10km), it's the perfect trip planning tool and navigational aid. Use it in conjunction with our T4A GPS Map of Namibia for a truly formidable solution.

What makes this map really unique is that its roads, tracks, places of interest, distance data and travel time estimates are all drawn from the collective travel experience of the Tracks4Africa community. Over the past 18 years, every single road or track shown on this map has been GPS recorded and verified.

What this means for you, is a map which reflects the reality of what you'll find on the ground. And a map that offers travel time information between towns for the entire road network, be it on tar, gravel or sand!

KEY FEATURES INCLUDE:

Printed on tearproof and water-resistant Polyart synthetic paper

Kaokoland shown in great detail, including all off-road tracks. Plus detailed maps for Swakopmund and Windhoek

Border Controls with opening and closing times

Place Name index

Find out more about our paper map at ***www.tracks4africa.co.za/maps/about/paper/***

TRACKS4AFRICA

VEHICLE PREPARATION

(By Francois Visagie, Johann Groenewald and Bessie Brand)

(photo: Frank Höppener)

WHEN YOU EMBARK ON AN OVERLAND TRIP, it's important to remember that your trip is vehicle dependent, so the selection and preparation of your vehicle is critical. Your vehicle must be safe, and it must be capable of traversing the kind of terrain you plan to travel. And, if you're planning to camp, it needs to be equipped accordingly.

VEHICLE DEFINITIONS

There's often debate around what type of vehicle is best suited for travelling in Africa. The truth is that it all depends on where you want to go, and what you want to do. You can see Africa from the tar but you'll see so much more if you venture off the tar, onto the dirt or gravel. And it's at this point that definitions begin to get very important - words can have different meanings in Africa! So, let's go through a few definitions relating to vehicles.

Sedan/hatchback: You could drive from Cape Town to Cairo in a 2WD sedan or hatchback, especially if you never left the tar. But it's also true that you can drive good gravel roads in such a sedan or hatchback. This type of vehicle wouldn't be our first choice, but if it's yours look for a model with good ground clearance and a full size spare wheel. During 2017 Julia Albu drove her 20 year old Toyota Conquest from Cape Town to Egypt. Julia herself was 80 years old at the time! So there really is no excuse! Go to www.myafricanconquest.com for more information on her incredible trip.

AWD: In this book we use the term AWD to describe a vehicle that has four driven wheels but no low-range gearing. Although this term can be used to describe some performance vehicles designed purely for tar roads, we use it to describe vehicles designed for a mixture of tar and gravel use. In Europe, such vehicles are sometimes referred to as 'gravel, grass and snow' machines. The BMW X3 is an example of such a vehicle. They typically offer a little more ground clearance than conventional sedans or hatchbacks and are entirely suitable for good gravel roads but we'd hesitate to use them on off-road routes.

SUV: We use this term to describe a vehicle that has raised clearance and 4WD, though no low-range gearing. They're suitable for gravel and off-road travel, but the lack of low-range gearing and off-road capable tyres doesn't make them a good choice for severe off-road routes or 4x4 trails.

Off-road vehicle: This is first prize for us. It describes a vehicle with raised clearance, 4WD, low-range and off-road tyres. It can be a pick-up (bakkie) or a station wagon type vehicle. In the right hands it can go almost anywhere.

Confusing terms: In Africa, if a vehicle looks like it can go off-road, people will often call it a 4x4 regardless of whether it actually has a 4WD drivetrain. Be aware of people's ignorance in this regard; for instance, if you ask a local whether a route or road is drivable they might look at your vehicle and make various incorrect assumptions about its capabilities.

When using Tracks4Africa maps and navigation guides, you'll find some routes and roads are marked '4WD', this means that an 'off-road vehicle' is required. We're also occasionally guilty of using the term 4x4 when we should refer to an 'off-road vehicle'.

CHOOSING A VEHICLE

Whichever vehicle you choose, it must large enough to accommodate you, your passengers, and your supplies and equipment.

It's entirely possible to tour Namibia in a sedan if you're comfortable driving such a vehicle on gravel roads. But although most roads in this country are good gravel roads, a vehicle with superior ground clearance and larger wheels is a more suitable fit than a sedan designed for tar road travel.

The comfort of bigger wheels on gravel roads makes a pick-up or an off-road vehicle the preferred choice of vehicle. The tyres fitted to off-road vehicles are also better suited to gravel roads. You can go far with a 2WD vehicle when conditions are dry, but in the rainy season it would be advisable to use an off-road vehicle.

If you're touring in a sedan you should stick to Namibia's B and C routes; don't travel any remote D routes unless you're absolutely certain that they're in good condition. It's best to speak to lodge/camp owners in the area you intend travelling to get the latest on road conditions.

An AWD or SUV is the first choice for touring the gravel roads and parks of Namibia. And if you're venturing into remote areas, an off-road vehicle is a necessity. You cannot travel Kaokoland, Damaraland, the Skeleton Coast and Khaudum Game Reserve without an off-road vehicle.

Adventure bike riders believe an off-road motorcycle is the best way to travel. A motorbike is economical and flexible because it gives you access to more roads than a 4-wheeled vehicle does. You can even take your bike over a river using two mokoros tied together if the ferry has broken down! Also, you don't need to plan for weeks and make lists of all the things that you need to take with, because you simply don't have space to take much gear. All this said, off-road travel in Africa on a motorcycle demands that you should be an experienced rider.

Although motorcycles aren't allowed in Namibia's national parks, the country remains an exciting destination for bikers as there are many great destinations where you'll be welcomed. Indeed, simply staying on public roads (gravel and tar) can add up to an unforgettable trip.

(photo: Peter Barber)

PREPARING YOUR MOTORBIKE

If you travel by bike, all you really need is money and your documents. Everything else is a luxury. The less weight you carry, the better your motorcycle will handle and the less chance there is of you falling off and damaging yourself and your bike.

To prepare for a biking expedition, you would prepare more or less like you would for a multi-day hiking trip. For inspiration look at what hikers use for camping, cooking and clothing; you need to drastically cut down on the weight of your equipment.

Extra fittings for overland biking

Fuel tank
You should seriously consider fitting a long-range fuel tank. You'll need a range of 400 km in order to cover most distances between fuel stops. If you need to carry extra fuel, a bladder system is better than extra fuel containers, because it can be easily stored when not in use.

Safety features
Fit handguards, and a bash plate to protect the sump.

Electronics
Fit a dual battery system with two external power outlets for your GPS and other electronic equipment. Most modern bikes have electronic starters; so it's best to protect the main battery from possible drainage.

Luggage carrier
The carrier system you choose should be dust- and waterproof, and packed as low as possible. Using dry bags is a better option than rigid boxes. If you fall, a rigid box can get damaged so badly that it becomes unusable. The best option is to strap waterproof dry bags to the carrier. Once your luggage is strapped on and secure, make sure that there are no loose straps which can foul the chain or wheels.

Tyres
In Namibia, you will inevitably ride a lot of gravel, so you should fit off-road tyres. If your itinerary consists of mostly

tar and good gravel roads, a dual-purpose tyre will be adequate. Get specialist advice on tubeless tyres.

Tools and spares
The basic equipment for every bike includes a toolset specific to your bike. A tyre repair kit includes spare tubes, tyre levers, tube patches, a valve spanner and, of course, an air pump.

Spares include an assortment of nuts and bolts, a spark plug, spare clutch and brake cables, epoxy glue and a chain breaker.

Camping equipment
For camping you will need a good lightweight, waterproof tent, a small but warm sleeping bag, a thin inflatable mattress and a groundsheet which can double as an emergency blanket. For cooking, you need a basic pot and pan set, a small gas stove and basic cutlery.

Personal items
You only have space for the bare minimum when it comes to toiletries. You should invest in good protective riding and rain gear. Take one set of riding gear and one set of clothes to wear in the evening.

Water and hydration backpack
You must always carry at least three litres of water and a hydration pack in your backpack. The best way to carry water is in a plastic bladder in your backpack.

PREPARING YOUR SEDAN, AWD OR SUV

If you are going to travel in a sedan, AWD, SUV or a 4x2 pick-up you'll probably stick to main roads and won't venture into rough or remote terrain. This may lead you to think you don't need to prepare for every eventuality. But in Namibia certain important preparations are still required.

Firstly, make sure you have a proper spare tyre and not one of the 'space saver' types fitted as standard to many vehicles these days. Check that all your tyres are in good condition and remember that the mileage tyres have travelled isn't necessarily an accurate prediction of their suitability to handle gravel roads. Tyres have a limited shelf life, about five to six years, irrespective of the distance they've travelled.

Make sure that your vehicle's service schedule is up to date before you leave. If you tow a trailer, make sure that its tyres are also in good condition, that you have a spare wheel and that the trailer has been serviced or inspected recently too.

Always carry at least 20ℓ of drinking water and some dry food rations for emergencies.

PREPARING YOUR OFF-ROAD VEHICLE FOR TRAVEL INTO REMOTE AREAS

If you plan on venturing into remote areas, vehicle prep becomes critically important. It's your responsibility to ensure that you and your fellow travellers can travel safely and that you'll be able to survive if you get into trouble.

Basics
You must be a self-sufficient and, preferably, an experienced camper. If you've never done an overland trip before, we recommend that you rent camping equipment and try it out close to home. It's the best way to figure out if you and your travel companions enjoy camping and it'll also help you decide what you do and don't need. Camping equipment is expensive and one is easily lured into buying a lot of unnecessary paraphernalia that will cost you a lot of money and use up an excessive amount of your vehicle's space and load capacities.

Many off-road vehicles are set up to allow quick access to the kitchen facilities! (photo: Karin Theron)

TIP: *Don't take anything you've never used before. And make sure you know how to use everything you take. In a crisis situation you don't want to discover that something doesn't work as it should, or that you don't know how to use it properly.*

When preparing your vehicle, the most important issue is to make sure that the manufacturer's services are up to date. And if your overland vehicle has been kept in storage, you must ensure it is used and serviced regularly.

Your tyres must be good quality items, in good condition, with lots of tread, and – preferably - no older than six years. Take at least one, but rather two, good spare tyres and a puncture repair kit. Invest in a good quality repair kit and make sure you know how to use it. Pack your tyre compressor and pressure gauge so that you can adjust tyre pressure as needed.

Thoroughly check your vehicle's mechanicals just before the trip. This is especially important if you haven't used your vehicle much since the previous service. This is a good time for the proverbial 'bumper-to-bumper' check that includes suspension and transmission components, steering linkages, healthy engine operation, etc. If you don't have the time or expertise, ask your favourite mechanic to do it.

If you have any aftermarket products or equipment fitted to your vehicle, make sure they are compliant with your vehicle's specifications. Pay particular attention to electrical equipment which could interfere with the vehicle's safety systems. Test drive your vehicle to make sure you're happy with any non-electrical and non-mechanical equipment fitted to your vehicle, like roof racks. Make sure everything is securely fitted.

Always pack cable ties, they're great for refastening things which rattle loose. Pack duct tape and a basic tool kit as well as a few basic spares like a fan belt and filters. Also

A tyre pressure gauge is an essential item.

Note the seed screen. (photos: Frank Höppener)

take spares for parts which are prone to failure on your particular vehicle. Take at least one spare of all the fuses on your vehicle, including the cigarette lighter plug that you use for your GPS, mobile phone, etc. Always have a fire extinguisher in your vehicle and make sure it's full and in working order.

Prepare your vehicle for any specific conditions you know you're likely to encounter. If you intend driving through long grass, take a seed screen to protect your radiator from being blocked. Select a net which is long enough to cover the radiator at the bottom as well, as most of the seeds are sucked up from below. Don't leave it on your vehicle all the time, it could increase your fuel consumption by almost 10%, especially if you have a turbo-diesel as these rely on cool intake air.

If you expect to encounter deep water crossings, take along a plastic or tarpaulin radiator cover and consider fitting a snorkel. A snorkel also helps to reduce the amount of dust sucked into your air filter.

Seek out knowledgeable advice to ensure you're on the right path without wasting your money. First prize is someone who's done a similar trip in a similar vehicle.

Beyond the basics

If you plan to explore seriously remote areas, you should be able to handle vehicle repairs yourself.

If the belts and hoses on your vehicle are more than a few years old, it's a good idea to pack replacement belts and hoses, they don't take up a lot of space. Pack them into a sealed plastic bag with a bit of silicon spray, and they'll last for many years. It's good practice to replace rubber components after a few years as they often become brittle.

Pack the following:

- Extra tyre valves and valve cores. When driving thick mud, valves are easily damaged, and once damaged, valves are often impossible to repair.
- Spare light bulbs for every light on the vehicle: headlights, running lights, indicators and brake lights.
- Spare fuel and oil filters.
- Air filters are easy to clean, so spares aren't normally necessary. But if there's a chance you might have to tackle a water crossing, take a spare. It's better to replace a wet air filter with a dry one, even if only temporarily.
- Oil for engine, gearbox and differential.
- If you have a long-range fuel tank with pump, get a

A snorkel allows your vehicle to breathe cleaner, cooler air when travelling dusty conditions. It's also useful for water crossings. (photo: Frank Höppener)

With a little mechanical insight and the right equipment, you should be able to tackle minor repairs and maintenance jobs yourself. (photo: Frank Höppener)

small spare pump with a hose you can put into the long-range tank and pump over to the main tank should the pump, electrics or switches fail.
- Spare wire, connectors, fuses, electrical tape and tools to work with them.
- Tow strap. If you're planning on driving muddy areas, you need one longer than 15 meters.
- Heavy-duty tow points. Standard tow points are typically not up to the job of being towed out of thick sand or mud.
- Bow shackles, rated to double the minimum specification required for your vehicle.
- Bottle jacks for changing tyres.
- Hi-lift jack. Make sure you know how to use it, it's a dangerous piece of equipment in novice hands.
- Jacking plates to prevent the jack from sinking into sand/mud. Improvise with existing gear.
- Jumper cables to charge a run-down battery.
- Construct a small wire tool (about 1m long) with a 'rake' on the end for cleaning out the grass from around the radiator and under the vehicle.
- If travelling in cold weather, take sufficient emergency gear to keep people warm, dry and visible.

Buying additional equipment

If you decide to fit accessories to your vehicle, remember to check your vehicle's warranty's terms and conditions. Don't forget that aftermarket products don't go through the same quality checks as your vehicle did so they're often the weakest link in your system.

Equipment can make one's life more comfortable and sometimes it can even save your life. But it comes at a price. The price for equipment is paid in extra weight, space taken up, adding to the bulk of your vehicle if fitted outside and, of course, the financial outlay.

Extra weight increases your vehicle's fuel consumption and stopping distance, and when carried on the roof-rack can make your vehicle significantly less stable. Extra weight can also take your vehicle or trailer (or combination thereof) closer to, or over, its legal weight limit.

Excess equipment could make your vehicle cramped, or could force you to leave behind other equipment you actually want to take with you.

Equipment mounted outside your vehicle – especially bulky equipment – increases its aerodynamic drag and therefore fuel consumption. This means more of your trip budget will go towards fuel, and less towards the activities you want to enjoy. With increased fuel consumption, you'll need to watch the distances between refuelling points more carefully than ever.

If you don't want to waste money on equipment, don't buy anything unless you're 100% sure you'll use it multiple times. Consider borrowing or renting equipment until you're sure of what you do and don't need. You will learn what works for you as you become more experienced.

Roof-racks

Advantages: Roof-racks make it possible to carry awkward, dirty or dangerous items outside the vehicle's cabin. People typically use them to transport items like camping equipment, firewood or gas cylinders.
Disadvantages: Items are more difficult to reach on a roof-rack and can increase your vehicle's fuel consumption.

Many types of roof-racks add significant wind noise when underway. The sturdier units may not be able to flex as much as your vehicle on very uneven terrain and thus could damage your vehicle's roof or its pillars, especially when mounted too rigidly. Items on the roof-rack, especially heavy things like a second spare wheel or toolbox, raise your vehicle's centre of gravity and reduce stability.
Suggestion: Any gap between the front of your roof-rack and the vehicle's roof can snag low-hanging branches. If this becomes a problem, consider fitting branch deflector cables.

Rooftop tents vs. ground tents

Rooftop tent advantages: A rooftop tent is the easiest way to sleep off the ground so it's helpful when your campsite is uneven, overgrown, water-logged or the soil is too soft to anchor a tent. Also, many people prefer to use rooftop tents in wilderness areas as this puts some distance between themselves and wild animals; however, this is a false sense of security. Rooftop tents are typically quicker to erect and break down than a ground tent. And fitted to the vehicle, rooftop tents can withstand wind speeds which might require additional strapping for ground tents.

Ground tent advantages: Ground tents can be left behind at your campsite when you go on a game drive whereas you'll have to close up your rooftop tent every time you drive your vehicle. Ground tents are cheaper than rooftop tents. What's more, a rooftop tent requires a roof-rack or luggage bars, so if you don't already have these, you'll have to add them to the cost of fitting a rooftop tent. Ground tents come in a greater variety of sizes for larger groups while most rooftop tents only cater for two people. Very few rooftop tents cater for up to four, and these tend to become heavy and bulky.

Keep heavy items off your roof rack.

Rooftop tents are a popular addition. (photos: Frank Höppener)

TIP *Most rooftop tents are fitted with canvas covers, these often get damaged by low-hanging branches, as would a ground tent packed on the roof-rack. Consider a hard-shell rooftop tent or a luggage carrier for your ground tent.*

Off-road trailers and off-road caravans

Advantages: These can be life-savers for larger families, they provide additional packing space and offer more flexibility. For instance, you can store your clothing, camping gear and groceries in the trailer or caravan, leaving only recovery gear and the picnic basket in your vehicle. You can even fit your rooftop tent (or an additional one) to some trailers. This way you can leave your whole camp behind when you go on day trips.
Disadvantages: When towing, your vehicle will be more unstable, especially in crosswinds. Before departing, make sure you're familiar and comfortable with your vehicle's handling when towing. A trailer or caravan increases the combined weight of your vehicle, which increases fuel consumption, makes overtaking and manoeuvering in tight off-road situations more difficult and increases braking distance. Make very sure that when laden, your trailer/caravan and vehicle combination complies with legislated weight limits. Individual and combined weight limits are determined by legislation pertaining to your vehicle's specifications, your trailer's or caravan's specifications as well as your driver's licence!
Suggestion: Ideally, you should buy a trailer or caravan with the same track width and tyres as your vehicle. This minimises off-road drag and gives you more swapping options in case of punctures.

Awnings

Advantages: Awnings provide shelter from sun and rain, but to do this they need to provide enough coverage as the sun doesn't always come from directly above. They make an exposed campsite pleasant – or at least bearable – and can also provide impromptu protection against rain and sun during roadside stops.
Disadvantages: Self-contained retractable awnings are easy to use but are limited in the cover they afford. Some of these awnings come with zip-on sides for rain protection but generally don't seem to withstand strong wind that well, even without the sides attached. Retractable swing-out awnings cover the rear and side of your vehicle and thus provide good shade, but they are more expensive. Fold-up, zip-away canvas awnings provide good shade and shelter but aren't quick and easy to erect.
Suggestion: Go for an awning which is easy to set up and stow away. If you fit one with a metal cover it won't get damaged by branches. If an awning protrudes from the front of the vehicle, branches can snag between the awning and roof-rack or the roof of the car so you should consider fitting branch deflector cables.

Camp showers

About 80% of Namibia's campsites have shower facilities so only pack a camp shower if you're sure you'll be camping at places which don't have such facilities. Experienced campers would argue that washing from a basin offers true quick-and-clean simplicity.

Advantages: Camp showers are the easiest way to wash long hair and offer an enjoyable way of cleaning up after a hot and sweaty day. Various types are available – the most basic ones consist of a suspended water container with shower head. Many types include a water pump; there are models that also provide warm water and some come with their own collapsible enclosures. You could also buy the bits and pieces separately and put together your own shower setup. Some of the basic suspended showers are made of black plastic so that you can warm your shower water by leaving the water bag in the sun.

Disadvantages: Showers can be cumbersome to set up, especially the more complex ones. These are less than ideal if you're breaking camp every day, but are great when staying over for a few days. Showers can waste precious drinking water if you're not careful.

Suggestion: If you're travelling daily and staying mostly at secluded or private campsites, you could make do without a shower enclosure. It's possible to heat your wash water in a fire bucket on the fire or by putting a water jerrycan close to the fire. Don't fill the can to the top and open the lid before you start heating the water so that the steam can escape. In hot weather you can get by without heating the water.

Inverters

Advantages: A 220 V inverter makes it unnecessary to take along a 12 V power supply for each of your electronic accessories – simply plug the 220 V adapters into the inverter.

Disadvantages: Being dependent on an inverter to power or charge your accessories introduces an additional potential point of failure. Quality and reliability vary widely, so pay some attention to back-up plans. The more powerful inverters also have significant 'stand-by' consumption – the power used when the inverter is on but not powering equipment.

Suggestion: Make sure your inverter is securely mounted, with enough ventilation to prevent heat build-up, and is protected against dust. The latter is especially important with inverters that have internal cooling fans.

Mobile fridges/freezers

Advantages: Mobile fridges/freezers make it possible to be self-sufficient for longer periods of time because they allow you to keep perishables for extended periods. Plus, they keep your drinks cool!

Disadvantages: They are generally fairly bulky. Construction materials have improved but many still tend to be quite heavy. However, the most common complaint in overlanding communities is that fridges/freezers drain battery power. With a mobile fridge/freezer your battery will need regular monitoring and when staying in one place for a couple of days, you'll probably need to run the engine for a few minutes every day.

Suggestion: If your fridge doesn't have a freezer compartment, create one on top by laying a newspaper sealed in plastic bag across the frozen goods. If you're catering for a larger group, instead of buying a large dual fridge/freezer or two separate units, you can save money by rotating ice packs between your freezer and cooler box. To minimise the power consumption of your mobile fridge/freezer, open it as little as possible and keep it well insulated. Also try to keep your vehicle as cool as possible by covering up windows against the sun, parking in the shade and opening vents and windows for ventilation. Ensure there's enough ventilation space around the fridge/freezer, especially around its ventilation outlet. Try to buy a dual 12 / 220 V freezer and use its 220 V inlet wherever you find a supply.

Dual battery systems

Advantages: With a dual battery system, your mobile freezer can run off its own dedicated battery. This way the vehicle's starter battery will not be drained. Any other 12 V accessory, like camp lights, inverters, electrical compressors, etc. can also be moved to the auxiliary battery.

Disadvantages: Although dual battery systems are quite simple in operation, they do add to the complexity of your vehicle's electrical system, and failures – although not common – are not unheard of. Conventional systems need to have the auxiliary battery close to the starter battery to prevent cable power loss. More advanced systems are available that provide the convenience of having the batteries further apart, but they cost more and cannot charge the auxiliary battery as quickly as conventional systems. What many people also don't realise is that battery capacity is like a bank loan. Even if you increase your battery capacity (loan), your sustainable power consumption (spending) is still limited by your alternator power (income). Most batteries will not fully recover their charge on a trip once drained; vehicle alternators simply weren't made to recondition batteries. Therefore, although dual battery systems protect your vehicle's starter battery, they aren't a blank cheque for unlimited power usage.

Suggestion: Look for a dual battery system which has at least a low-voltage alarm, and preferably also a so-called bridge function, with which you can connect your starter and auxiliary batteries together in emergencies. This is useful for winching or for when the starter battery is flat.

Solar panels

Advantages: If you carefully manage your power consumption, it's possible that with the right solar panel and enough sunshine, you can run your fridge/freezer almost indefinitely. With a good regulator working in tandem with the alternator, a solar panel can even help keep your aux-

This camping fridge/freezer has a 'jacket' for additional insulation and protection. (photo: Karin Theron)

iliary battery better charged than the alternator can on its own. As electricity sources independent of the vehicle, solar panels could also have some emergency use like charging a flat starter battery.
Disadvantages: Solar panels either take up space permanently (usually on the roof-rack), or need to be put in the sun and moved each time you pitch and break camp. Shade or overcast weather significantly reduces their output.
Suggestion: A good solar panel regulator integrates with your dual battery system in such a way that the solar panel operates in tandem with the vehicle's alternator, without requiring you to remember or do anything. When you decide on the size solar panel to buy, don't settle for one that provides your expected consumption requirements. You have to make provision for those less sunny days as well as the fact that you get on average maximum 10 hours of charging time on a sunny day. In addition to extra watts, make provision for extra amps on your solar regulator too because chances are good that your requirements will increase over time (due to more gadgets needing electrical power).

Portable generators

Carrying a portable generator is a bad idea. You will be very unpopular in a bush campsite if you start up a generator - most people go to remote areas to experience peace and quiet. And in lodges or towns, most campsites will have mains electricity. In fact, 53% of all campsites in Namibia have mains electricity.

Long-range fuel tanks

Advantages: Long-range fuel tanks allow your vehicle to carry more fuel and thus travel further before needing to refuel. Normally being fitted underneath the vehicle, long-range fuel tanks could actually improve a vehicle's centre of gravity, especially compared to jerrycans mounted on the roof-rack. Also, you don't need to carry extra fuel containers or pipes and funnels to get the fuel from the containers into your tank.
Disadvantages: Once fitted, long-range fuel tanks contribute to the permanent weight of your vehicle. They add a vulnerable area to your undercarriage and, depending on their shape, might even decrease its ground clearance. They add complexity and more potential points of failure to your vehicle's fuel system. Some chassis-mounted long-range fuel tanks may require a fuel pump to transfer fuel to the main tank. Failure of this fuel pump is a very real potential problem and it results in an out-of-fuel situation while there is still plenty of fuel in the reserve tank. Most frustrating!
Suggestion: Get a long-range tank of common construction that any competent welder could repair if need be during your trip. If a fuel transfer pump is used, purchase a spare one and make sure you know how to connect it. Have the tank fitted to your vehicle some time before leaving on your trip to ensure through normal daily use that there are no leaks or problems with the installation.

Though they require a little more effort, portable solar panels offer some clear advantages. (photo: Karin Theron)

Water tanks

Advantages: Water tanks allow you to leave behind the scores of bottles and little containers you would otherwise have had to carry for extended expeditions. They will make life a lot easier and enable you to carry more water for longer distances between replenishment stops. Like long-range fuel tanks, chassis-mounted water tanks are better for the vehicle's centre of gravity than containers mounted on the roof-rack or carried inside the vehicle.
Disadvantages: Once fitted, water tanks contribute to the permanent weight of your vehicle. They increase the vulnerable area underneath your vehicle and, depending on shape, might also decrease its ground clearance. You must always treat the water you fill your tank with, even if it comes from a clean natural source, otherwise it can go green and taste distinctly algal. A chlorine solution like Milton works well; remember to let the water stand for 30 minutes to permit the purifiers to take effect before you drink it.
Suggestion: Get a simple water tank that can be easily repaired if it starts leaking during a trip. Clean your tanks at the end of your trip by adding a strong chlorine solution to the remaining water and driving around with it for a day. Then let all the water out and keep the tank well ventilated, this will leave it clean and ready for your next trip.

You could also buy water in 5-litre containers in most major towns and, this way, keep your drinking water separate. However, we've found these containers have very thin sides so they don't stand up to the bumps and vibrations common to overland travel. Rather purchase a quality 10-litre fluids container. Once you've decanted your precious drinking water into this container, pack it securely in your vehicle.

Customised suspension

Advantages: Stiffer springs and/or shock absorbers may make your vehicle more stable when carrying a heavy load. Longer and/or softer springs may provide your vehicle with more articulation and traction on uneven terrain.
Disadvantages: Stiffer springs or shock absorbers can limit articulation and therefore traction on uneven terrain. Longer and/or softer springs may make your vehicle more unstable, especially at speed or on uneven terrain. Longer springs will also require you to fit longer shock absorbers.
Myth #1: 'A suspension upgrade increases your vehicle's ground clearance'. A suspension upgrade will only increase a vehicle's ground clearance marginally.
Myth #2: 'A suspension upgrade increases your vehicle's load-carrying capacity'. Your vehicle's load-carrying ca-

pacity is determined by its specification plate and the laws pertaining to this matter. Unless you're able to get the authorities to accept an amendment to your vehicle's capacities, a suspension upgrade won't legally increase your vehicle's load-carrying capacity.
Suggestion: From the advantages and disadvantages above you can see how these factors can work against one another. That's one problem. The other is that there doesn't seem to be many technical experts in the after-market suspension industry; people who are trained and skilled enough to calculate what a potential suspension change would do to your vehicle. Most dealers will just sell you a standard 'lift kit'. If you load and use your vehicle within the manufacturer's recommendations, your vehicle's standard suspension will normally be fine.

Differential locks

Advantages: Differential locks can provide extra traction on uneven terrain, thereby making it possible to get out of a tight spot without outside assistance.
Disadvantages: Differential locks add to the so-called unsprung weight of the modified axle. This can cause a form of instability – known as trammelling – on corrugated surfaces which can be very dangerous. They also add potential points of failure in your vehicle's drivetrain. Unless deactivated when turning, differential locks increase the vehicle's turning circle and can accelerate tyre and transmission wear as well as damage the road's surface. Under certain circumstances they can suddenly transfer all engine power to a single wheel. Unless the vehicle is driven with the limitations of differential locks in mind, this can cause a catastrophe in a situation where otherwise only wheel spin would have resulted.
Suggestion: Many modern four-wheel-drive vehicles are factory-fitted with some form of traction control. If you own such a vehicle, you may not need the additional cost and complexities of a differential lock, especially if you don't foresee driving really gruelling terrain on a regular basis.

Snorkels

Advantages: Snorkels raise your vehicle's air intake to roof height which means you'll draw cleaner, cooler air; this keeps the air filter cleaner for longer. A secondary benefit is that they allow you a greater wading depth because the engine is less likely to ingest water.
Disadvantages: Snorkels are fitted to the outside of the vehicle, usually to the side or along the front edge of the windscreen, and are therefore exposed to potential damage from low-hanging branches. Despite being fitted with intake grids, snorkels still collect leaves and twigs which find their way to the vehicle's air cleaner – this item still needs to be regularly inspected and cleaned.
Suggestion: To help reduce the amount of leaves and twigs collected, you can turn the snorkel's intake towards the back, although some people believe this reduces the snorkel's intake efficiency, especially at speed.

Sand/mud tracks

Advantages: These provide extra traction or better footing for recovering vehicles from ditches, sand or mud. Two types are available: a rigid type usually called sand tracks, and a roll-up type usually made from linked rubber segments and called mud tracks. Which one is the better, depends on how you think and work. For instance, both can be used to cross sharp ditches – sand tracks could be laid across a ditch, while rolled-up mud tracks would be used to fill the ditch.
Disadvantages: Both can get very dirty from work, especially in mud, so you would have to store them outside your vehicle.
Suggestion: If you have to store your muddy sand or mud tracks in your vehicle, cover them in empty firewood bags. If you don't have any, use black plastic bags (which you should always have with you in wilderness areas). Carefully consider which terrain you will drive before adding this extra weight to your vehicle.

Although winches are mostly used for recovery purposes, they also very useful for moving heavy trees off the road. (photo: Karin Theron)

Bash plate

Advantages: A bash plate will protect your engine's sump on very rocky roads and deeply-worn tracks where your vehicle will often bottom out.
Disadvantages: You will have to remove the bash plate every time you do an oil change.
Suggestion: Regularly inspect your bash plate to make sure the attachment bolts haven't come loose and fit lock nuts to the bolts.

Bull bar

Advantages: The main purpose of a bull bar is to protect the vulnerable front components of your vehicle like the radiator during a collision, but it's also used for winch fitment and recovery points to pull your vehicle out of sand or mud.
Disadvantages: A heavy-duty bull bar will add a lot of extra weight to the front of your vehicle and can thus possibly have a negative affect on steering and also make your front tyres wear faster. Bull bars effect aerodynamics and therefore fuel economy. It could also possibly interfere with the functioning of your vehicle's airbags and cause cracks in your chassis mounting.

Winch

Advantages: A winch can either pull you out of trouble or it can be used to clear the road of obstacles like fallen trees. A manual winch can be attached to any side of the vehicle, not just the front or the back. An electrical winch can move at least 1.5 times the gross vehicle mass (GVM) of the stricken vehicle and is much more convenient to use than a hand-operated item.
Disadvantages: A winch will add to the extra weight of your vehicle.
Suggestion: Instead of bolting your winch permanently to your bull bar, consider a detachable unit. A winch permanently fitted to the front of your vehicle is of little use if you need to be pulled backwards. Also, a detachable winch can be stored in a clean, dry place when you are back home.

TIP: *If you're shipping your vehicle from abroad, you can have it equipped in Namibia. There are a number of 4x4 fitment Centres in Namibia (Windhoek, Swakopmund and Walvis Bay). Shop around and find out who has the most experience.*

PACKING YOUR VEHICLE

Only pack the things you absolutely need. And understand the difference between 'need', 'want' and or 'might come in handy'. If you're still running out of space, you need to rethink your planning or your packing, otherwise the only solution is to buy a larger vehicle or a bigger trailer.

Pack the heaviest items as low as possible and between the vehicle's axles. This optimises your vehicle's stability and handling. Keep as little as possible on the roof; it is best not to have anything on the roof. If you have to pack on top, rather keep heavy items inside your vehicle and light stuff on the roof.

You may have to compromise in order to carry recovery equipment. This gear is typically heavy but you don't want to bury it at the bottom if there's a good likelihood you'll need it. See if you can pack it at the bottom in such a way that you can slide it in and out as required.

CAMPING CHECKLIST

Self-drive travellers have different overnight options. They can choose to stay in full board or self-catering accommodation, or to camp. Campers have the option of travelling with and staying in a mobile home or campervan, or camping the old-fashioned way. Well, not really the old-fashioned way, because nowadays there are so many new gadgets and gear available in the outdoor shops. You can decide which of these things you want to take along to add some convenience to your camping, but there are some basic things that you will need for shelter and preparing your food. Here are some must-haves:

Camping

- ☐ Tent with built-in ground sheet and mosquito net (if you're not using a rooftop tent)
- ☐ A gazebo with ground sheet is handy if you are using a rooftop tent
- ☐ Hammer and spade
- ☐ Stretcher or inflatable / foam mattress
- ☐ Sleeping bags, sheets and pillows
- ☐ Folding table and camp chairs
- ☐ 12 V DC LED lights (LED's advantage is that it draws low current from your vehicle battery)
- ☐ Clothes-line and pegs
- ☐ Wash-basin and toiletries
- ☐ Bag for carrying your towels, toiletries and clothes to the ablution block
- ☐ Cooler box or small refrigerator
- ☐ Water bottles filled with water from home (at least enough for the first day's drinking)
- ☐ Swiss Army knife or Leatherman
- ☐ Dustpan and brush
- ☐ Toilet paper
- ☐ Universal size plug
- ☐ Torch (a head lamp works the best)

Cooking

- ☐ Braai equipment: grid, triangle, tongs, gloves, matches and firelighters
- ☐ Gas cylinder and cooker head with spare rubber seals, key and nozzles
- ☐ Pots, frying pan and kettle
- ☐ Plates and salad/porridge bowls
- ☐ Coffee mugs and glasses
- ☐ Cutlery and can opener
- ☐ Chopping board, sharp knife and bread knife
- ☐ Egg lifter and little hand grater
- ☐ Paper towel, tin foil, refuse and jiffy bags (for leftovers)
- ☐ Washing-up bowl, dishcloths, scourers and detergents

Technical hardware

- ☐ 220 V extension lead
- ☐ Extender plug
- ☐ 220 V battery chargers (to charge deep-cycle batteries when mains power is available)
- ☐ Inverter
- ☐ Laptop with MapSource/BaseCamp, T4A maps and image software installed, to download tracks and photos
- ☐ External storage device to backup tracks and photos

COMMUNICATIONS

Namibia's Spitzkoppe and Pontoks mountains. (photo: Heiner Dillmann)

WHEN YOU TRAVEL, YOU NEED TO STAY IN CONTACT WITH the outside world. Some might argue that they travel in order to lose contact with the outside world! But even if this is the case, you still need to be able to make contact should circumstances demand it. And if you're travelling in a group, you need to stay in touch with your travel companions. These days, there are three main ways of staying in touch: by cellular phone, satellite phone or two-way radio.

CELL PHONE

The best way to communicate is via cell phone. Namibia's mobile networks are well developed with cell phone coverage just about everywhere, except for really remote areas in Kaokoland, the Skeleton Coast, Sperrgebiet and Namib-Naukluft.

International mobile phones can be used in Namibia without any problems but roaming costs are extremely high. Remember the international dialling code (+264) if you want to call local (Namibian) numbers from your cell phone network.

If you have a smart phone, remember to turn off data roaming when you leave your home country, otherwise you may end up paying for app and system updates at very expensive roaming rates. This way, you have all your contacts and should you need data connection for an emergency (like doing internet banking) it's available once you've turned the data connection back on.

But the cheapest way to use your smart phone is to visit an MTC service centre in any major town and ask their staff to advise you on the best data package. Such a package, together with an MTC SIM in your smart phone, will allow you to access the internet, email and WhatsApp at far more affordable local data rates. Then transfer your original SIM into an old cheap cell phone and use that just for voice calls and SMSs. It's worth noting that a conventional cell phone has much better battery life than a smart phone and this is another reason why many travellers prefer to use their old cell phones for basic voice and SMS communications when overlanding.

Data is very expensive while roaming so you should continue buying prepaid data packages for your local SIM card, or wait until you have access to a Wi-Fi connection before downloading data. Note that whilst you can buy airtime from even the tiniest remote little shop, data bundles aren't that readily available at smaller places so you may want to stock up on data bundles while you're in town.

There's 3G coverage in the main centres and good GPRS or EDGE along the main routes and in most towns or game park centres like Etosha. MTC offers 4G in the main centres like Windhoek, Keetmanshoop, Swakopmund, Walvis Bay, Henties Bay, Otjiwarongo, Tsumeb, Oshakati, Rundu and Katima Mulilo.

SATELLITE PHONE

You should seriously consider taking a satellite phone if you're travelling solo into remote areas. In the event of an accident or breakdown you could wait several days for another car to pass by. Satellite phones have wider coverage than cellular phones and might be the only way to call for help in these circumstances.

Under normal circumstances satellite phones work well, but there's no guarantee they'll work everywhere. If you have a mediocre satellite phone, reception can be adversely affected by cloud, tree cover and sitting in your car. So, it's worth your while to invest in the best satellite phone you can afford. Satellite phone airtime is far more expensive than cell phone airtime, but this is not normally a problem as you're generally only using your sat phone for emergencies. If you don't have a satellite phone, consider renting one. Note, many vehicle rental companies also rent satellite phones.

TWO-WAY RADIOS FOR GROUP TRAVEL

If you want to stay in contact with other vehicles in your group, two-way radios are the most effective method. Just remember that radio types and/or frequencies often require licences. Check whether yours requires a licence and if it does, find out where to apply for one.

VHF and UHF mobile (fixed) radios with external antennas offer the best range but these require commercial radio licences. Bear in mind that licences issued by the Independent Communications Authority of SA (ICASA) are only valid for South Africa, they have no standing in neighbouring countries.

29 MHz radios are also good for staying in contact with a group; these have a shorter range but can overcome obstacles like hills much better than VHF. They are very popular among 4WD travellers but you need a visitors' licence to use them. To apply for one, it's a good idea to work through a Namibian communications company.

If you're a radio ham (amateur radio), licensing is a lot easier. However, you will only be able to communicate with fellow radio hams, as you may only operate in your own frequency bands which don't overlap with commercial bands. Radio hams may not use their equipment to transmit on commercial bands, these require separate type approved radios and separate licences.

Licensed hand-held radios can be used for the above frequencies as well, but range will be severely limited unless they're connected to an external antenna. They have limited battery life so an external power source should be considered. These units are good enough for general convoy communication if the convoy is short. There isn't much of a price difference between these hand-held radios and the mobile (fixed) radios, but they have advantages like enabling you to stay in contact with the campsite when on walks in the surrounding area.

Licence-free hand-held radios can also be used and are much more affordable than the radios mentioned above. Licence-free radios cannot operate on the licensed frequencies and vice versa. Their range is a lot shorter and they are unsuitable for convoy work, unless the vehicles are close to one another, e.g. on slow trails. Range can be extended by connecting these radios to external antennas. There are many models available; not all have antenna connectors for external antennas which might be a consideration when purchasing a radio. These radios are ideal for around camp and hiking, if that is all you need. Many 4x4 and radio clubs will be happy to assist with detailed questions.

BORDER POSTS

The border post at Sendelingsdrift. (photo: Karen Theron)

NAMIBIA HAS A VERY MATURE IMMIGRATION AND CUSTOMS SYSTEM so passing through border posts is normally quite easy, given you have the correct documents. So make sure you have all the necessary official documents.

Some travellers have had unfortunate experiences with having to pay bribes at border posts elsewhere in Africa. Happily, Namibian border post officials tend to be efficient and not open to bribery. Service is not always delivered with a smile but if you take off your hat and sunglasses and adopt a cheerful manner, chances are good that you will receive a warmer reception.

You can travel Namibia for a maximum of 90 days per year, thereafter you have to apply at the Ministry of Home Affairs for an extended stay.

TIP: *Border officials often differ in how strictly they apply regulations; this means that nine times out of ten they might be happy to bend a rule or fast track a process but on the tenth time you might encounter an official who applies the rule to the letter. Be prepared for the tenth time!*

DOCUMENTS REQUIRED WHEN TRAVELLING BY VEHICLE

- A valid passport with at least six months remaining validity before expiry. Double check your passport is stamped with the correct date when entering the country.
- Original vehicle registration certificate (a certified copy is acceptable). Drivers whose vehicles are still financed by a bank will not have the original vehicle registration document and will have to use the vehicle licence papers (from which the renewal disc is cut out annually), or a copy of the vehicle registration certificate, which must be signed by a Commissioner of Oaths.
- If the car registration number on your registration papers is not the same as on the vehicle number plate (for instance if it was pre-owned) you must also present the registration paper from which your license disc was cut out.
- If you're not the registered owner of the vehicle (i.e. it's still being financed by the bank, you are renting a vehicle or you are driving a friend's vehicle), you must have a letter from the financial institution, company or friend giving you authorization to take the vehicle across the border. This letter must stipulate dates for which you are allowed to take

the vehicle out of the country and must also be signed by the owner and a Commissioner of Oaths.

- In the past Namibia required a Police Clearance Certificate but since 2015 the SA Police Service no longer issues vehicle Clearance Certificates for tourist cross border travel; only if the vehicle is being exported from the country or if you enter with a work permit.
- Drivers of vehicles arriving in Namibia from outside the Southern African Customs Union area (Botswana, Lesotho, South Africa, Swaziland and Namibia) must have a Carnet de Passage for the vehicle.
- Proof of vehicle insurance.
- A yellow fever certificate is strongly recommended. If you've been to an affected country, a yellow fever certificate is compulsory. Neighboring Angola has a history of yellow fever and the potential risk is high for this to spread to bordering countries like Namibia and Zambia.

TIP: *Keep your official documents together in a plastic envelope. Print your vehicle details (like VIN, engine and licence number as well as make) in large letter type and put that together with your registration paper, back to front in the envelope so that it is readable through the envelope. If you have a trailer, put its detail to be visible if you turn the envelope around. Whenever you are asked for your vehicle or trailer details, you just hold your handy envelope against the window for the official to read.*

BORDER CROSSING PROCEDURE

1. The driver and all passengers must present themselves to immigration to get their passports stamped. Always check that your passport has been stamped according to the correct dates of your stay and have it amended immediately if this isn't the case.
2. Each child and adult in your group will be required to fill in an Arrival/Departure form, so take a pen with you.
3. Once immigration is cleared, the driver must proceed to the Namibia Roads Agency counter. Have all the required vehicle documents ready. To enter Namibia with a foreign-registered vehicle you are required to pay a cross border charge of N$277 per vehicle and N$188 per trailer (at time of writing - 2018). ZAR also accepted. Cash payments only. Fees change every year.
4. Declare all valuables at customs. Have a list of all your cameras and electronic equipment with serial numbers and values ready; it will be much easier to complete the forms.
5. You can now proceed to the border gate. Have your gate pass (signed by both the customs and immigration departments) together with your passports ready for inspection. If your gate pass is not stamped, you will be sent back to the relevant counter for the additional stamp!

CUSTOMS

It is illegal to have any of the following goods in your possession:

- Narcotic, habit-forming drugs and related substances in any form.
- Firearms, ammunition and explosives.
- Indecent and obscene material such as pornographic books, magazines, films, videos, DVDs and software.

Namibia is a tourist-friendly country and allows visitors to take personal items like binoculars, cameras, clothing, jewellery, etc. into the country without having to pay customs duty. There are, however, restrictions on the duty-free quantities of the following consumables:

Cigarettes – 400
Cigars – 50
Tobacco – 250 g
Wine – 2 l
Spirits or other alcoholic beverages – 1 l
Perfume – 50 ml
Eau de Toilet – 250 ml

Other than your personal items, travellers can take new or used goods to the value of not more than the equivalent of 3 000 South African rand duty-free into Namibia. You are not allowed to take maize or firewood into Namibia.

TIP: *When you return to South Africa, if you have fuel in containers other than your fuel tank, these will attract an import duty so empty the containers into your vehicle before crossing the border.*

CROSSING INTO SOUTH AFRICA WITH CHILDREN

If you intend crossing into South Africa and you're travelling with children under 18, they must carry valid passports, unabridged birth certificates stating both parents' names, and affidavits from both parents (if either one or both aren't present). This rule applies whether the children require a visa or not, and applies again when they leave South Africa. There are a number of permutations of this rule relating to adoptive parents, guardians, children travelling alone etc. If one of these scenarios applies to you, look up the relevant requirements on the South African Department of Home Affairs website (www.dha.gov.za), 'CIVIC SERVICES' menu, 'Travelling with Children' item.

A SPECIAL NOTE ON MEAT, FRUIT AND VEGETABLES

The import regulations on meat, meat products, fruit and vegetables change frequently because they're based on disease outbreaks in the region. Unfortunately, at the time of writing there wasn't yet an official website with the latest such information so it's best to speak to people who've recently visited the country. You can also ask a trustworthy travel forum (www.tracks4africa.co.za/community, www.4x4community.co.za or www.overland.co.za) for an update, rather than relying on the personal experience of just one person.

From time to time there are outbreaks of foot-and-mouth disease in the region and during such times the import of all cloven hoof animals (including game) is banned. And this means you won't be allowed to take any raw meat or animal products like unpasteurised milk or cheese from the diseased country into Namibia. Veterinary staff at the border will ensure that such products are confiscated and destroyed.

Namibia has good quality meat at good prices, so you might as well buy your meat there. Any Spar, Pick n Pay or Shoprite has a good selection of fresh meat, as do many of the local butcheries. When there is an outbreak of foot-and-mouth disease, you are still allowed to take in fish and usually also chicken. However, when there is an outbreak of avian flu (bird flu) among e.g. ostriches, veterinary inspectors will also confiscate chicken or ostrich meat, and any other avian products such as eggs.

See more information about foot-and-mouth disease on page 52.

VISAS

Nationals from the countries listed below DON'T require visas to visit Namibia: Angola, Armenia, Australia, Austria, Azerbaijan, Belarus, Belgium, Botswana, Brazil, Canada, Cuba, Denmark, Finland, France, Germany, Hong Kong, Iceland, Ireland, Italy, Japan, Kazakhstan, Kenya, Kyrgyzstan, Lesotho, Liechtenstein, Luxembourg, Macau SAR, Malawi, Malaysia, Mauritius, Moldova, Mozambique, Netherlands, New Zealand, Norway, Portugal, Russia, Seychelles, Singapore, South Africa, Spain, Swaziland, Sweden, Switzerland, Tanzania, Turkmenistan, Ukraine, United Kingdom, United States of America, Uzbekistan, Zambia and Zimbabwe. (*Source: www.namibia.org.za*)

TIP: *Keep enough South African rand at hand because it will be accepted at all border posts. Namibia is a very popular destination for South Africans and during their June/July school holidays you may experience increased traffic and subsequent delays at the major border posts. In severe circumstances delays of a couple of hours have been reported. Rather plan to overnight close to the border post if you travel at the beginning or end of the holiday so that you can cross early in the morning when everybody is still fresh and friendly.*

NAMIBIA / SOUTH AFRICA BORDER

Klein Menasse/Rietfontein: 08h00 – 16h30
Tel: +264 (0)63 280 681.
Mata Mata: 07h00 – 16h30
Tel: +264 (0)63 683 297, +264(0)63 252 055.
If you want to enter Namibia at the Mata Mata border post, you have to spend two nights on the South African side of the Kgalagadi Transfrontier Park and show proof of such a reservation. If entering at Twee Rivieren you must spend two nights before exiting at Mata Mata.
Sendelingsdrift: 08h00 – 16h30
Tel: +264 (0)63 274 926, +27 (0)27 831 1506.
You need to pay R160 per vehicle and R60 per trailer/caravan to cross the river by pontoon (2018 fees).
Oranjemund/Alexander Bay: 06h00 – 22h00
Tel: +264 (0)63 232 756.
Noordoewer/Vioolsdrif: Open 24 hours
Tel: +264 (0)63 297 122.
Velloorsdrift/Onseepkans: 08h00 – 16h30
Tel: +264 (0)63 269 134.
Ariamsvlei/Nakop: Open 24 hours
Tel: +264 (0)63 280 057.
Klein Menasse/Rietfontein: 08h00 - 16h30
Tel: +264 (0)63 280 681.

NAMIBIA / BOTSWANA BORDER

Mohembo: 06h00 – 18h00
Tel: +267 (0)687 5505.
Ngoma Bridge: 07h00 – 18h00
Tel: +267 (0)620 0050.
Dobe: 07h30 – 16h30
Tel: +264 (0)67 243 328.
A very small border post - you have to open the gate between the two countries yourself! Very quiet, so no delays likely.
Trans Kalahari Border control (Buitepos/Mamuno): 07h00 – 24h00
Tel: +264 (0)62 560 404.
Impalila Island/Kasane: 07h30 – 16h30
There are no landlines on the island. The number on the Botswana side is +267 625 0252.
This border post crossing is for island lodge guests only. There's no vehicle access from Kasane so vehicles have to be left in the secure grounds of the immigration office. Guests are transported by small boat from there to the Namibian immigration, which is on Impalila Island. The trip takes about 15 minutes. At the end of their stay on Impalila Island, guests exit via Namibian immigration and are brought back by boat and re-enter Botswana at the office in Kasane. There is also an airstrip on Impalila Island for access by air.

NAMIBIA / ZAMBIA BORDER

Wenela/Sesheke (Katima Mulilo): 06h00 – 18h00
Tel: +264 (0)66 253 430, +264 (0)66 253 153.

NAMIBIA / ANGOLA BORDER

Katwitwi: 07h00 – 18h00
Tel: +264 (0)67 243 328 or Cell: +264 (0)81 142 2101.
Ruacana: 08h00 – 19h00
Tel: +264 (0)65 270 039.
Omahenene/Calueque: 08h00 – 19h00
Tel: +264 (0)65 259 504.
Oshikango/Santa Clara: 08h00 – 19h00
Tel: +264 (0)65 264 615.
This is a very busy border post with lots of trucks and pedestrians.

(photo: Frank Höppener)

Nkurenkuru: 07h00 – 19h00
Tel: +264 (0)66 255 356 or Cell: +264 (0)81 142 2101.
Rundu: 06h00 – 18h00 Tel: +264 (0)66 255 047.
This border crossing isn't suitable for overlanders, it's orientated towards local pedestrians, there's no road crossing.

INTERNATIONAL AIRPORTS

Most visitors enter Namibia at Hosea Kutako International Airport, located 45 km east of Windhoek. There are another 11 airports with immigration and customs facilities in Namibia: Windhoek Eros Airport, Keetmanshoop, Katima, Lüderitz, Mulilo (Mpacha Airport), Ondangwa, Oranjemund, Oshakati, Rundu, Grootfontein and Walvis Bay (Rooikop Airport).

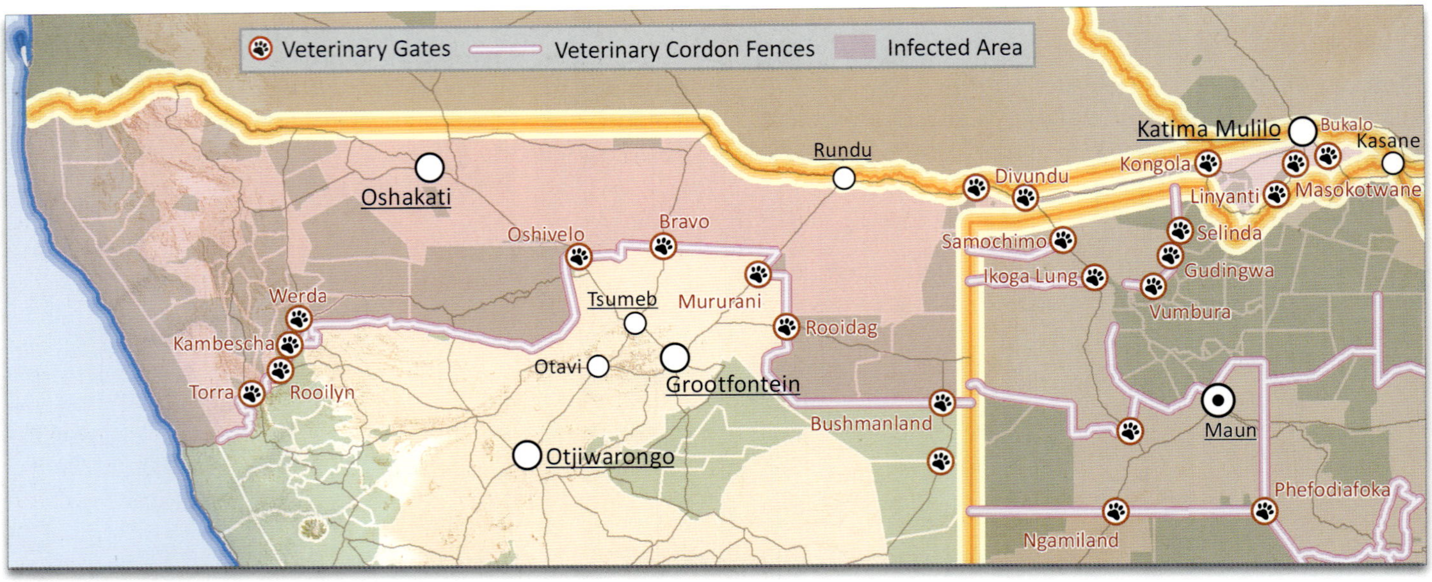

VETERINARY FENCES

IN SOUTHERN AFRICA FOOT-AND-MOUTH DISEASE IS CONTROLLED BY restricting the movement of animals by means of veterinary fences; and, by banning imports of raw meat and animal products like unpasteurised milk and cheese of cloven-hoofed animals. While import restrictions and veterinary fences are two forms of the same thing - animal disease control - the difference between them is that import restrictions apply to international border posts and veterinary fences apply to disease control within an affected country.

When state veterinarians put up veterinary fences in the 1960s their aim was to protect cattle against foot-and-mouth disease infections from buffalo. However, in the past 50 years, the number of diseases which potentially affect cattle and which now have to be considered as veterinary control problems has increased. The current veterinary fences are thus about more than just controlling foot-and-mouth disease.

WHAT IS FOOT-AND-MOUTH DISEASE?

Foot-and-mouth disease or hoof-and-mouth disease *(Aphtae epizooticae)* is an infectious and sometimes fatal viral disease that affects cloven-hoofed animals like African buffalo, antelope, impala, springbok, sheep, goats and domestic cattle. The virus is highly variable, which limits the effectiveness of vaccination.

The virus causes a high fever for two or three days, followed by blisters inside the mouth and on the feet that may rupture and cause lameness. Adult animals may suffer weight loss from which they do not recover for several months, as well as swelling in the testicles of mature males; in cows, milk production can decline significantly. Though most animals eventually recover from foot-and-mouth disease, the disease can lead to myocarditis (inflammation of the heart muscle) and death, especially in newborn animals. Some infected animals remain asymptomatic, but they nonetheless carry the virus and can transmit it to others.

Foot-and-mouth disease is a severe plague in animal farming, since it is highly infectious and can be spread by close contact with infected animals as well as over a long distance. Furthermore, it can be spread through contact with contaminated meat and animal products, farming equipment, vehicles, clothing and skin of animal handlers, animal feed, and by domestic and wild predators. Its containment demands considerable efforts in vaccination, strict monitoring, export bans on meat and other animal products, quarantine, and occasionally the elimination of millions of animals.

Hedgehogs and elephants may develop mild symptoms of foot-and-mouth disease, but are resistant to the disease and do not pass it on to other animals of the same species. Just as humans may spread the disease by carrying the virus on their clothes and bodies, animals that aren't susceptible to the disease may also aid in spreading it.

Humans can be infected with foot-and-mouth disease through contact with infected animals, but this is extremely rare. The disease is not to be confused with hand, foot and mouth disease (HFMD) which is usually caused by a Coxsackie virus and often seen in toddlers. Because foot-and-mouth disease rarely infects humans but spreads rapidly among animals, it is a much greater threat to the agriculture industry than to human health.

IMPORT RESTRICTIONS

The conditions for importing meat into Namibia vary according to the meat's origin. Imports of products for own consumption are the result of bilateral agreements and are subject to change depending on the prevailing animal health situation. Travellers are urged to check with the local Directorates of Veterinary Services for current regulations (www.mawf.gov.na/directorate-veterinary-services).

Some visitors don't take this prohibition seriously and try to hide their meat. However, you should be polite to your host country as something like foot-and-mouth disease can bring the whole meat industry of a region to its knees. The instant that foot-and-mouth disease is detected, all exports are suspended, and that includes exports to the EU which is a massive market for Namibia. Be a responsible visitor and respect your host country's regulations. Foot-and-mouth disease is not unique to Africa, but has been reported in countries like the USA, United Kingdom, Taiwan, China, Japan and Korea. (Source: Wikipedia)

VETERINARY FENCES

Veterinary cordon fences are physical fences demarcating control zones in accordance with the guidelines of the International Animal Health Authority. These fences are referred to as vet fences and they are indicated with red lines on T4A's GPS maps. The movement of raw meat and animal products, including unpasteurised milk, are allowed into but not out of an area classified as an infected zone.

Often visitors feel that their vacuum packed or deep frozen meat poses a minimal disease risk, but unfortunately the logistics of having every possible permutation of the rules in a form that can be understood by the vet fence guards, is quite impossible. Therefore you should rather not try to take raw meat in any form past a vet fence checkpoint.

In Namibia vet fence restrictions prevent you from moving meat from north to south and east to west, as foot-and-mouth disease occur in the northern parts of the country. Meat may be moved from the south to the north, and from the west to the east past the veterinary fences.

The vast majority of veterinary fences and the gates allowing access are static, therefore some checkpoints have been in operation at the same places for years. However, temporary veterinary gates are erected when it is possible to contain a foot-and-mouth disease outbreak within a smaller area, thus preventing it from spreading through the entire sector. The temporary gates operate similar to police road blocks; sometimes they are in operation, but more often not. It all depends on the veterinary health in the area at a specific point in time.

At some of these fences you may be asked to drive your vehicle through a dip filled with a disinfecting solution and you and your passengers will also have to exit the vehicle and walk on a mat impregnated with the solution to disinfect your shoes (the ones you are wearing plus extras) as the disease is also carried by the urine and faeces of infected animals.

Because of vet fences you may not:

- Take meat from Katima Mulilo to Rundu.
- Take meat from Rundu to Grootfontein.
- Take meat from Palmwag south into Damaraland.
- Take meat west past the vet fence between Tsumkwe and the main Rundu/Grootfontein road.
- Take meat from Etosha to the south. You can, however, take meat into Etosha coming from the south, but all the meat must be consumed before you return south.

If you need to travel in the 'right' direction past vet fences with meat, you should declare the meat and show your till slip indicating where you bought the meat. The official is then supposed to issue you with a permit. However, because of the human factor this system doesn't always work out well. If you are polite and courteous to the officials at these vet check points you will very seldom encounter any problems.

***TIP**: Have your shoes and cool boxes/fridges readily accessible as a nothing-to-hide attitude makes life so much easier. Keep all shoes in a box so that you won't need to unpack your luggage to find them at a control point. It also prevents the disinfectant from covering other gear.*

A typical veterinary control point. (photo: Karin Theron)

HEALTH & HYGIENE

(photo: Heiner Dillmann)

TRAVELLING IN AFRICA POSES HEALTH RISKS SO YOU SHOULD consult a medical practitioner at your local travel clinic to find out about the possible risks, and the inoculations and vaccinations required. This said, possibly the biggest risk to your health when travelling this continent, is driving!

Some health risks you can take precautions for and some you can't. Malaria is the most obvious health issue when you travel to Namibia. However, hepatitis A, cholera, typhoid and diarrhoea are also potential issues where water isn't 100% safe. You should also be aware of the risk of heat exhaustion or heat stroke.

Hepatitis B is transmitted like the AIDS virus which means that if you have to undergo dental or medical procedures while in Namibia you are at the same risk as anywhere in Africa.

What's more, the bush traveller may be exposed to tick-bite fever, rabies, bilharzia and other infections or parasitic diseases. And there are the risks of snake bites and scorpion stings which could be life-threatening.

BURNS

Second-degree burns are quite common when camping because you're making open fires and cooking over them. These burns are painful and usually accompanied by swelling and blisters. First- and second degree burns smaller than 7 cm in diameter or totalling less than 5% of your body's surface area are generally considered minor burns.

These types of burns usually heal quickly with minimal care. The only exceptions are burns in critical areas of the face, or burns around the circumference of a limb or finger - these require specialist care.

Prevention: The most important thing is to prevent burns – whether from an open fire or gas flame. Keep children and flammables (especially cooking oil) away from open flames. And don't start fires with petrol or diesel.

Treatment: The most important treatment is to immediately rapidly cool the area; heat below the surface can continue to cause tissue damage after the burn has occurred. Pouring cool water on the burn or holding it under a running tap is recommended.

Every camper should carry a few packets of Sterile Trauma Hydrogel Burn Dressings in their first aid kit. These are designed to cool and protect burns. The hydrogel has a long-term cooling and soothing effect and the dressing instantly shields and protects the wound against further contamination and infection. Fluid loss is kept to a minimum and the potential for shock is reduced.

Dressings should cover the whole of the burn area. The non-adhesive moist gel impedes bonding of the dressing to the wound and thereby facilitates easy removal of the dressing. You should take the dressing off within a day and apply antiseptic ointment to prevent infection.

If you have to clean the burn area/blisters, do so with a sterile saline solution. To make a sterile saline solution, mix 10 ml salt in a litre of water, boil the solution for a minute and let it cool down. Do not use an antiseptic liquid like Savlon or Dettol as it can cause chemical burns if not used in the correct dilution. Take a pain reliever if needed.

MALARIA

This is found north of Etosha, so northern Namibia is a high risk malaria area and you must take prophylaxis if you plan to visit there. In winter it's cooler and the risk is lower but there's still a lot of water around which acts as breeding grounds for mosquitoes.

Most doctors will advise you to keep toddlers under five out of malaria risk areas. You can take some precautions like spraying the children with mosquito repellents and keeping them inside mosquito nets in the afternoon and at night, but it's is a gamble and the stakes are high. Adults have almost 10 times more blood in their bodies so if they get infected, it takes far longer for the condition to get serious - not the case with youngsters.

Malanil and Malarone have paediatric versions for children of 11 kg and more, with the dosage determined by their weight; ask your travel clinic for more information. Malarone is extremely effective in preventing malaria and has few side effects, but can be expensive. You still need to take anti-biting precautions even if taking preventive drugs, as the drugs do not fully eliminate the risk.

Prevention: You can take measures to limit mosquito bites. Mosquitoes feed mainly between dusk and dawn. Female mosquitoes will take a blood meal just before laying their eggs, which is done at night. So it's important that repellents are used between dusk and dawn. Use a repellent which contains DEET or a natural repellent such as lemon and eucalyptus.

Clothing alone won't protect you from mosquito bites but it can help limit them when used with other preventative measures. Clothing which covers the body (long sleeves and long trousers tucked into socks) will lower the risk of being bitten. While mosquitoes can bite through many materials, canvas mosquito boots and thick denim jeans present them with a serious challenge.

Clothing impregnated with permethrin will also help repel mosquitoes. Such clothing, along with impregnated wrist and ankle bands, lower the risk of mosquito bites. If you're reluctant to impregnate everyday clothing, impregnated netting worn over your clothing will prevent contact between the chemicals and skin. Most travel clinics stock sprays for clothing and nets.
Research suggests that mosquitoes are attracted by sweat and dark colours; keeping clothes (especially socks) clean and wearing light colours or white clothing might also help prevent bites.

While air conditioning helps to keep mosquitoes away due to the lower temperature, it's important that it's left on all day and that the windows are kept closed. Carbon dioxide in the breath that you exhale will also attract mosquitoes so a sleeping in the breeze of a fan can help.

Using a mosquito net is a good idea. Ideally, the net should be impregnated with permethrin at least every six months or after every wash. If a bed net doesn't reach the floor it should be tucked in under the mattress.

Note, no precautionary measures are 100% effective.

Symptoms: Anyone experiencing flu-like symptoms shortly after returning from a malaria area must immediately consult a doctor and mention the visit to the malaria area. Make sure the clinic you attend can do a reliable malaria test: a blood slide with a microscope or one of the newer rapid diagnostic tests (RDT) dipstick tests on a drop of blood. The RDTs can be better than the microscope tests because they don't rely on the technician's expertise.

Other symptoms of malaria include body pain, diarrhoea and vomiting. The usual incubation period for malaria is 14 days, but it can take as little as a week or as long as two months to manifest itself.

HEPATITIS A

This is a viral infection of the liver which is generally transmitted via food and/or contaminated water.

Prevention: Although Namibia's water quality is good, it's safest to treat all drinking water or rely on bottled water (ensure these are sealed when purchased). Don't drink anything with ice, since you cannot determine the source of such. This infection can be prevented with two injections, six months apart, to give permanent immunity. Another option is a combination vaccine against hepatitis A and hepatitis B – a series of three injections.

Symptoms: Patients usually become jaundiced, nauseous, vomit and experience joint pain which may last up to 12 weeks.

HEPATITIS B

A viral infection of the liver which is contracted in the same way as the AIDS virus. You don't know beforehand if you might need to undergo dental or medical procedures while you travel.

Prevention: Three doses of vaccine, usually given one month apart, constitute the complete series of immunisation. You will only need a further booster in 25 years.

Symptoms: Most people remain healthy without any symptoms while they fight off the virus. Some will not even know they have been infected. However, until the virus has been cleared, they can remain infectious.

If there are any symptoms, these will develop an average of 60 - 90 days after exposure to the virus. Symptoms of include flu-like symptoms such as tiredness, general aches and pains, headaches and a high temperature. Further symptoms include a loss of appetite and weight loss, feeling sick, being sick, diarrhoea, pain in your upper right-hand side as well as yellowing of the skin and eyes. Symptoms usually pass in 1 - 3 months.

Hepatitis B is said to be chronic when you've been infected for longer than six months. The symptoms are usually much milder and tend to come and go. In many cases people with chronic hepatitis B infection will not experience any noticeable symptoms.

Symptoms of chronic hepatitis B may include feeling tired all the time, loss of appetite, feeling sick, abdominal pain, muscle and joint pains and itchy skin. This disease may eventually lead to liver cancer.

TRAVELLER'S DIARRHOEA

The reasoning 'What's good for the local people, cannot be bad', is only partially accurate. The local population may have developed resistance or tolerance to a number of harmful components in their food, such as parasites or other infectious agents.

Infections are the most important food-related hazards. They relate mainly to the contamination of food by parasites, but also bacteria or viruses present in human excreta. These can contaminate food through dirty hands or if the water used in food preparation has been soiled by sewage. Human excreta used as fertiliser can carry dangerous parasites or germs.

Improper hygiene of food and water leads to traveller's diarrhoea. Many of these infectious agents can be destroyed by heating, but some are found on the surface of foodstuffs such as fruit and vegetables which we don't cook. Meat and fish may contain parasites which undergo a biologic cycle ending in the animal. However, the intensive heat of frying, baking or stewing largely destroys these parasites.

Bacteria are responsible for 50 - 80% of cases of traveller's diarrhoea. E. coli will be the most likely cause.

Prevention: If you prepare your own food while you travel, you limit the risk of diarrhoea substantially. Good advice is to buy your food from a trusted supermarket rather than a street vendor or open-air market.

However, if you travel Africa you will miss out on the best and the freshest fruit and vegetables if you avoid local markets. The saying 'cook it, peel it or leave it!' carries considerable wisdom when you buy from the street markets. Otherwise a solution of 10 drops of unscented bleach per 1 ℓ water can be used to rinse all veggies and/or fruit that will be consumed raw. Treat non-bottled water with chlorine, iodine or silver-based purifiers, or boil it.

The human digestive system is home to more than 500 different types of bacteria. They help keep the intestines healthy and assist in digesting food. They are also believed to help the immune system. Taking probiotic supplements (so-called friendly bacteria) while you travel may help strengthen your immune system. Note that probiotics may be dangerous for people with weakened immune systems or serious illnesses.

Symptoms: Diarrhoea causes profuse watery stools which can lead to dehydration.

RABIES

No animal bite should be ignored! Since the disease is invariably fatal once symptoms appear, post-exposure treatment is based on the principle of inducing immunity before the virus gains access to the nervous system. Victims must get treatment without delay.

Prevention: Overland travellers should consider pre-exposure immunisation (three injections within one month) as there are many domestic dogs roaming around Namibia. Wild animals like bats, jackals, foxes, skunks, mongooses, meerkats and monkeys can also carry rabies. Be very suspicious if these animals behave in a tame manner.

No matter how tame an animal appears, it's not a pet! (photo: Karin Theron)

Symptoms: Rabies is a fatal disease contracted by virus-laden saliva after a bite from a rabid animal. The disease progresses to paresis or paralysis. Spasms of muscles on attempts to swallow will lead to a fear of water (hydrophobia). Delirium and convulsions follow. After two to ten days, death results (often due to respiratory paralysis).

CHOLERA

The mode of transmission is primarily through ingestion of water contaminated with faeces or vomit of infected people or, to a lesser extent, faeces of carriers. It is often associated with flooding, poor water supplies and/or poor sanitation.

Prevention: Cholera can be prevented by an oral vaccine dissolved in water. It's effective from six months to two years. You can avoid cholera by only drinking bottled water, especially in areas where you are not 100% sure of the water source.

Symptoms: Cholera is caused by bacteria and will usually cause profuse watery stools and vomiting. Rapid dehydration may follow which may lead to the patient's death within a few hours.

TYPHOID

This is a systemic bacterial disease, contracted when food or water contaminated with faeces or urine of an infected person or carrier is ingested.

Prevention: Inoculation with a typhoid injection is advised if you are travelling to remote areas where you are not 100% sure of the water source and are not able to take enough bottled water. The inoculation provides immunity for three years.

Symptoms: It may cause fever, headache and constipation (more common than diarrhoea). Intestinal haemorrhage or perforation may occur in untreated cases, which can lead to the death of the infected person.

YELLOW FEVER

A yellow fever certificate is strongly recommended as neighbouring Angola has a history of confirmed yellow fever cases so there's a risk that it can spread to bordering countries like Namibia and Zambia. If you've been to an affected country, a yellow fever certificate is compulsory.

Yellow fever is endemic in the tropics of Africa and America and is a much bigger problem in Africa than in America. It is a virus transmitted by a mosquito which flourishes in human habitations, especially under slum conditions. It is prevalent in the large urban informal settlements in tropical Africa.

Prevention: A single inoculation provides excellent immunity in over 95% of recipients, providing long-lasting immunity that will probably last a lifetime. International travel regulations, however, demand that boosters be administered every 10 years. The risk of infection can be minimised by taking general measures to prevent or reduce mosquito bites, as one would do for malaria.

***TIP:** Keep your inoculation certificate in your passport.*

Symptoms: The time between being infected with yellow fever and the start of symptoms is usually three to six days. This is known as the incubation period.

The symptoms of yellow fever usually appear in two stages. The initial symptoms (the acute first stage) can include a high temperature, headache, shivers, nausea and vomiting, aching muscles, backache and loss of appetite. Symptoms usually improve after three or four days.

After the initial symptoms of yellow fever, about 15% of people develop more severe symptoms. The symptoms of the toxic second phase can include a recurrent high temperature, abdominal pain, vomiting, a yellow tinge to the skin and whites of the eyes that is caused by liver damage, kidney failure, bleeding from the mouth, nose, eyes or stomach; you can also have blood in your vomit or stools.

Half of the people who have the second toxic phase of symptoms, die within 10 to 14 days. The other half recover with no major organ damage and are immune from the disease for life. Overall, this means that around seven or eight people out of every 100 who develop yellow fever, will die from it.

TICK-BITE FEVER

Tick-bite fever is a bacterial infection transmitted in the saliva of infected hard ticks (Ixodidae) when they bite humans. The arachnids which harbour the Rickettsial family of bacteria that cause tick-bite fever belong to either the Amblyomma, Dermacentor or Rhipicephalus family of ticks.

Since it's not possible to determine the infectious status of a tick, it's best to take preventative measures. It has been shown that ticks are infective at all stages of development (larva, nymph and adult) and there is hereditary transmission of the disease to succeeding generations through the tick eggs. This is believed to continue indefinitely.

Prevention: No vaccine is presently licensed for public use. This disease requires specific antibiotics for treatment. You should inspect yourself and your clothing for ticks at the end of each day, especially if you are camping in or walking through bush. Prompt removal of ticks can prevent some infections.

Symptoms: Tick-bite fever is characterised by a primary sore at the site of the bite (often having a blackish centre), swollen lymph nodes and, in most cases, intermittent fever lasting 10 to 14 days. The incubation period for this disease is about seven days. There is a sudden onset with significant malaise, deep muscle pain, severe headache and conjunctivitis. A rash, first appearing on the palms and soles on about the third day, rapidly spreads to most of the body. Bleeding underneath the skin is common. Blood tests may frequently show up negative in the early stages so an accurate diagnosis may be missed if tests are not repeated! The rash on the palms and soles is always a good clue.

BILHARZIA

This is a blood fluke infection with adult male and female worms living over a lifespan of many years in certain veins of the infected person. The infection is acquired from contact with water containing free-swimming larval forms which have developed inside snails.

Prevention: The only prevention is to avoid swimming in contaminated lakes and rivers. If you are not 100% sure that a lake or river is bilharzia-free, rather abstain from swimming. You should in any case be very cautious of crocodiles and hippos!

Symptoms: Severe liver complications and bladder cancer may result with chronic infections.

***TIP:** If you suspect that you might have been in contact with contaminated water, go for a bilharzia test at a pathologist when you return home.*

SCORPIONS

The majority of scorpions are harmless to us but their stings can be extremely painful requiring painkilling treatment.

However, Parabuthus Villosus, one of the deadliest scorpions in the world, can be found in the entire western region of Namibia. You should be very careful in the Namib Desert, Fish River Canyon, Epupa Falls, Brandberg, Spitzkoppe, Swakopmund and Walvis Bay. Some have even been found in the Windhoek area. Scorpions prefer rocky areas and mostly come out at night, apparently more so when the wind blows.

Prevention: Campers should always wear closed shoes after dusk. Outdoor lights attract insects and, in turn, the scorpions that feed on insects. Yellow outdoor lighting is less attractive to insects and is recommended in areas where scorpions are prevalent. And don't forget to shake out your shoes before you put them on in the mornings.

It is always a good idea to check for scorpion holes during daytime so that you know before nightfall if there might be any around. A scorpion hole is easy to recognise. The burrow entrances are usually situated in open ground and are smallish oval-shaped holes.

Symptoms: Moderate to more serious poisoning through scorpion stings causes malaise, sweating, heart palpitations, rise in blood pressure, salivation, nausea, vomiting and diarrhoea. Hyper acute (typically allergic) reactions include blurring of consciousness, unconsciousness, convulsions, fall in blood pressure, shock and even death.

Treatment: Pain at the site of a scorpion sting can sometimes be limited with an ice cube, but strong painkillers might be needed. In the case of more marked symptoms, treatment must be given as for snake bites, and the patient must receive medical treatment as quickly as possible.

TIP: *A compound in the exoskeleton of scorpions refracts ultraviolet (UV) light in the visible spectrum and causes them to fluoresce or glow. The fluorescence is thought to serve as an ultraviolet sensitivity mechanism, perhaps allowing the scorpion to avoid damaging light levels. Because the exoskeleton glows in UV light, it is very easy to find scorpions at night using a torch with UV LEDs. If you use a UV torch and walk around your campsite at night, you have an excellent chance of finding scorpions. Depending on the UV output of the torch you will be able to find scorpions from a distance of one to ten meters. The scorpions will have a greenish glow and will be easy to spot against the dark background of the ground. The scorpions do not seem to suffer any ill effect of the UV light and do not react to the UV light at all.*

Reference: www.wildlifephotography.nl)

SNAKES

Fatalities from snake bites are quite rare and the vast majority of snakes are not venomous. Less than 10% of bites ever require anti-venom. Most snakes will avoid humans and even if you're bitten by a venomous snake they rarely inject their full venom load. In Namibia the most deadly snakes are black mambas, puff adders, boomslang and Cape cobra. The Mozambique spitting cobra is found in the north of Namibia.

Prevention: Be on the lookout for snakes whenever you are in the bush. It's best to wear boots when you're out in the field and don't forget to shake them out in the morning before you put them on.

Symptoms: There are five types of snake venom, each associated with different species of snake, and each type of venom has a different effect on the victim's body.

Cobras and mambas have neurotoxic venom which attacks the central nervous system, affecting movement, breathing, swallowing, speech and sight.

The Black Mamba (Dendroaspis polylepis) is one of Africa's most feared venomous snakes.
(photo: Johan Marais www.africansnakebiteinstitute.com)

Boomslang have haematoxic venom which affects the blood, using up the clotting factors so it no longer coagulates. This leads to extensive blood loss into the tissues.

Puff adders have cytotoxic venom which attacks the body cells or tissues. The bite is extremely painful with much swelling and the victim experiences marked symptoms of shock.

The Mozambique spitting cobra has mixed neurotoxic and cytotoxic venom. It is considered one of the most dangerous snakes in Africa and it can spit its venom. Its bite can cause severe local tissue destruction (similar to that of the puff adder) while venom in the victim's eyes can cause impaired vision or blindness. *(Reference: http://goafrica.about.com)*

Treatment: Anybody bitten by a poisonous snake must get professional medical treatment as quickly as possible. Wash the bite with plain water and tightly bandage the limb. Note, this is not the same as a tourniquet, which should never be used.

Keep the victim as still as possible to slow the venom from entering the system. If you are spat on, rinse the affected area as soon as possible with clean water or milk.

Only if there's NO risk of the photographer getting bitten in the process, should a photo be taken of the snake for identification purposes. This will assist the doctor/hospital in treating the bite.

SLEEPING SICKNESS

African trypanosomiasis (generally known as sleeping sickness) is a parasitic disease transmitted by tsetse fly. Apparently, no new cases were reported in Namibia for decades, so it's not currently seen as a threat for visitors. There's no vaccine available.

HEAT EXHAUSTION OR HEAT STROKE

An adult should take in 4 - 6 litres of water or fluids (including what's in food) per day. But high temperatures can easily double this requirement. Loss of water and salt from the body causes heat exhaustion and ultimately heat stroke.

Prevention: Make sure you always have enough water with you and take special precaution when you travel into remote areas. You must remember to drink more on hot days, even if you don't feel thirsty, to prevent heat exhaustion.

Symptoms: Heat stroke occurs when the body can no longer sweat to cool itself while the body temperature rises. Heat stroke presents with a temperature of greater than 40.6° C in combination with vomiting, confusion and a fast pulse.

Treatment: People suffering from heat stroke must be cooled in the shade with water poured on them, after which they must slowly start drinking water.

MEDICAL INSURANCE

Ensure that your medical insurance provides you with good coverage for your overland trip; and if it doesn't, take out extra travel insurance. Make sure your insurance covers includes medical evacuation; Namibia has good private hospitals but because of its size, air evacuation could be required.

Evacuation doesn't include search and rescue so you should check that your insurance covers this too. International SOS Namibia operates a 24-hour medical assistance centre located in Windhoek, with bases in Windhoek, Swakopmund and Tsumeb. You can contact them on +264 61 289 0999.

FIRST AID KIT

You should always travel with a well-kitted first aid kit. Apart from special needs like chronic medication for adults and paediatric medicine, and a thermometer if you travel with children, there are a few basic things which should be in every first aid kit. If you already have a first aid kit for travelling, don't forget that medicines have limited life-spans. Check 'use by' dates and ask your pharmacist to check that the contents of your kit remain effective and safe to use. If you're travelling into remote areas, you're strongly advised to do a first aid course before departure.

Your first aid kit should contain the following at a minimum, you should add medicine according to your travel party's personal needs:

- 1 x Quicklot trauma pack
- 2 x Plastic SP Joints Stabilisers
- 2 x Dressings
- 3 x Bandages
- 2 x Gauze swabs
- 1 x Triangular bandages
- 2 x Conforming bandages
- 2 x Gauze
- 1 x Sterile dressing
- 1 x Sterile dressing pad
- 2 x Eye pads
- 1 x Sterile eye pad
- 1 x Eyebath
- 1 x Eye patch
- 2 x Big sterile trauma hydrogel burn dressing
- 1 x Small sterile trauma hydrogel burn dressing
- 1 x Roll clear Elastoplast
- 6 x Rehydrate packets
- 6 x Plasters
- Cotton wool
- Respirator mouthpiece
- Gloves, scissors, tweezers and safety-pins
- Antiseptic ointment (e.g. Bactroban)
- Antiseptic solution
- Anti-acid for heartburn and stomach acid
- Antihistamines
- Laxatives
- Imodium for mild diarrhoea
- A broad spectrum antibiotic
- Painkillers with aspirin or paracetamol and anti-inflammatories
- Skin-disinfecting agent or antiseptic wipes
- Water purification tablets

Having your own syringes, sterile needles and possibly scalpels, can help if you have to receive treatment at a place where you're unsure of the hygiene.

INDEMNITY

This information is NOT intended to be a complete list of all the risks encountered in Namibia. Consultation with a qualified doctor at a travel clinic is essential. Tracks4Africa is not responsible for any loss, infection, illness, injury or death resulting from the use of this information.

RENTING A FULLY-EQUIPPED 4X4

This rental camper features a double bed with twin reading lamps, 270° shade awning, kitchen, shower and much more. (photo: Avis Safari Rental)

IT'S POSSIBLE TO FLY TO NAMIBIA AND rent a 4WD vehicle which is fully equipped for camping. Many reputable and experienced companies offer this service and for many visitors this is a really good option. Namibia's rental companies compare to the best in the world!

But you should make your accommodation reservations before you book such a vehicle. Once your itinerary is settled, look for rental company recommendations on the internet. You'll often find personal recommendations on Africa forums like www.tracks4africa.co.za/community, www.namibia-forum.ch (German), www.4x4community.co.za or www.overland.co.za. If you can't find enough information, or if it's not up to date, you could start a new thread on one of these forums and ask for advice.

Another way of going about this is to search the internet for reviews on rental companies you've identified. Remember, not finding any reviews is not necessarily a negative sign. Most people tend to comment only about bad rentals or experiences. Also, don't let one bad review out of many good ones put you off a company.

When comparing rates, check the terms and conditions on insurance, applicable taxes and extra charges. The cheapest quote often works out not to be, because of hidden charges like VAT and credit card fees. Unlimited mileage seems to be the standard practice.

INSURANCE

Generally, vehicle insurance doesn't cover the loss of personal items. Check the insurance in your rental contract, and be aware of the following fine print:

- You can choose to pay zero excess, reduced excess or full excess in the event of loss of, or damage to, the vehicle This influences your daily rental rate.
- You might still be held responsible for damage to tyres, windscreen, glass, headlamps and paintwork.
- Most rental companies have conditions covering negligence and driving at night.
- Underbody- and clutch damage might not be covered by your insurance.
- Make sure your insurance covers tow-in.

Ask about backup vehicles in case of breakdown or recovery. You would not want to be stuck for several days waiting for a replacement vehicle or recovery.

EXTRA CHARGES

You might be charged extra for the following:

- Transfer to and from the airport.
- Vehicle cleaning upon return.
- Refuelling on return.
- Additional driver.
- Cross-border fees.
- An after-hour surcharge if you return the vehicle out side normal working hours or later than the agreed return date.
- An e-toll fee for vehicles departing from or returning to Johannesburg.
- A claims-handling fee, in case of an accident, irrespective of the liability cover you have chosen.
- Some companies charge a once-off contract or administration fee.
- A traffic fine admin fee if a fine was levied while you rented the vehicle.

GENERAL

When renting a 4WD through an international rental company, make sure you specify that you want an off-road vehicle. Some rental companies will advertise a 4x4 or similar vehicle and you might end up with something like an AWD or SUV which may not be suitable for off-road driving.

If you rent a vehicle with camping equipment, ask for the equipment list in advance. Not all vehicles are kitted out the same way. If you're travelling during winter, make sure enough warm bedding is included.

Namibia is predominantly an arid region and the majority of secondary routes travelled are gravel roads. As it's impossible to make vehicles dust-proof (and you cannot claim a refund for dust ingress) you should seriously consider taking a cover sheet to put between the tailgate and your gear. It will be messy every time you open the back door of the canopy and tailgate, but at least your gear will be protected from the dust.

For reasons of fuel economy, it's recommended to hire a diesel-powered off-road vehicle. Such a vehicle will thus give you a better range between refuels. A diesel engine also offers better low-end torque which is handy for driving in thick sand.

It's essential that you establish exactly what's included in your contract and what isn't before you rent a vehicle. Then, carefully check that you've got what you expected when you receive the vehicle. It is difficult when you've just arrived and you can't wait for the adventure to begin, but time spent checking the vehicle is time well spent.

Check that the vehicle has all the equipment you signed for and that it functions properly. Check for bad electrical connections if you rent a fridge/freezer.

It's important that the vehicle has good quality off-road tyres and that you have at least one, but preferably two, spare tyres of good quality if you intend travelling off-road. Your vehicle should be kitted with an electric compressor and pressure gauge so you can adjust tyre pressure as needed. When pumping high tyre pressures, make sure you do not overheat the compressor, give it short breaks to cool down. Check that there's a jack, wheel spanner and emergency triangles. And then check that the wheel spanner fits the wheel nuts. If a tyre repair kit isn't included, ask for one or buy one before departure to remote areas. Even if you don't know how to use it, someone passing by might be able to help.

Check the basic toolset which normally comes with the vehicle. Ask if they supply a spare fan belt and if not, what must be done if you have a breakage. Make sure that spare fuses are supplied and the vehicle is kitted with a fire extinguisher.

If you don't have any experience in off-road driving, you should only rent through a company that offers you 4WD driving instructions.

Vehicle maintenance is critical to the successful operation of a 4x4 hire company. The lack of proper preventative maintenance is primary source of problems with rental vehicles. A company should schedule a few days at least between hires. If you discover that the maintenance work has not been done, ask for another vehicle.

Many routes involve long distances and/or a considerable number of days of game driving. Long range tanks are advisable over carrying too many jerrycans on a roof-rack. Besides the danger aspect, it raises the centre of gravity and with a rooftop tent you will exceed the recommended rooftop mass.

Most companies that rent vehicles also rent satellite phones and GPSs. If you rent a GPS, check that the latest version of T4A is loaded. Some companies also provide assistance with route planning, camp bookings and cross border documentation at an extra fee.

When you collect the vehicle, check for any damage on the paint and bumpers, and for windscreen cracks as well as pitting. Note any damage on the form you have to sign and take photographs of the damage to cover yourself further. Ask the rental company about their policy on fair wear and tear and the type of damage for which they charge clients. Find out what their dispute policy is.

Finally, make sure you have a list of emergency contact numbers for the company you're renting from. If you intend crossing a border with the vehicle, make sure you have a letter of authorization from the vehicle rental company and a certified copy of the vehicle's registration papers.

Don't travel too far on the first day as you'll probably be tired or suffering from jetlag. Also, if you find anything wrong during the first day/night shakedown it'll be quicker to put right if you don't have a long trek back to the rental company to sort it out.

SPICE UP YOUR JOURNEY

A balloon trip over the desert has to be one of the most memorable ways to experience the sheer grandeur of this part of the world. (photo: www.balloon-safaris.com)

EXPERIENCED OVERLANDERS WILL TELL YOU it's a good idea to give yourself the occasional break from the routine of driving and camping. A good way to do this is to seek out unique experiences. Indeed, temporarily swopping your vehicle for an aeroplane, boat, hot air balloon, mountain bike, donkey, mokoro, horse or even just a pair of hiking boots, will introduce you to facets of Namibia that many visitors miss out on altogether.

When doing your trip planning look out for these sorts of activities and try to work a few into your itinerary; also, be open to activities that you come across while on the road. You may want to search the internet for reviews on the operators that you've identified but remember that the absence of reviews isn't necessarily a negative sign; people often comment more about bad services or experiences than they do about good ones. You should also make use of the 'bush telegraph', chat to other travellers you meet on the road or in the campsites, ask for recommendations.

There are a number of tour operators who'll take you into the desert on day trips. (photo: Frank Höppener)

Another way to enrich your trip is to make an effort to step outside the tourist circle - it's something that comes naturally to some travellers but requires conscious effort for others. What we mean by this is that you try to engage with Namibia as though

you were a resident rather than someone just passing through. This could mean that instead treating yourself with a meal out at a fancy lodge, you find out where the locals eat and visit there. If you hear of an everyday event, like a church fete or a soccer match, make an effort to attend and engage with the people around you.

When you ask locals for recommendations in this regard, you might find that they instinctively provide you with tourist options and you might have to be quite clear that you're looking for something 'ordinary'! Namibians are friendly people and natural engagements with them in everyday venues and settings can lead to great encounters and lasting memories.

(top left) The Orange River offers a number of different canoe trip options. (photo: Frank Höppener)
(left) A guided quad trip into the desert on the Skeleton Coast is a great way to let off some steam.
(above) Sea kayaking will give you a different perspective of the coastline. (photo: www.emkayak.iway.na)
(below) Horseback safaris in the Kambaku Game Reserve just north of the Waterberg. (photo: www.kambaku.com)

Namibia/Angola
Namibia/Botswana
Epupa Falls 11
Chitado
Ondjiva
Outapi
Oshikango
Eenhana
Ruacana
Oshifo
Onamutayi
Okongo
Okahao
Ondangwa
Oshakati
Rundu
Opuwo
10
Namutoni
15
Olifantsrus
12
14
Ongongo Hot Spring
Okaukeujo
13
Halali
Tsumeb
Grootfontein
Kamanjab
Otavi
Outjo
Palmwag
Khorixas
Otjiwarongo
Twyfelfontein 9
16 Waterberg Plateau NP
Organ Pipes & Burnt Mountain
Brandberg 8
Uis
Omaruru
Cape Cross Seal Colony
Spitzkoppe 7
Karibib
Henties Bay
Usakos
Okahandja
Arandis
17
Swakopmund
6
Moon Landscape
Windhoek
1
Gobabis
5
Walvis Bay
Dordabis
Ncojane
Rehoboth
Aranos
Stampriet
Mariental
Sossusvlei
4
Maltahöhe
Helmeringhausen
1 - 17 See days referenced in text
Bethanie
Keetmanshoop
Garub Pan
Lüderitz
Aus
3
Fish River Canyon
2
Grünau
Karasburg
Aussenkehr
DURATION
Windhoek to Windhoek:
17 days / 4 400 km
If driving from Cape Town, add:
4 days / 3 200 km (return)
If driving from Johannesburg, add:
4 days / 2 900 km (return)

(photo: Karin Theron)

Namibia Grand Tour

The Namibia Grand Tour is a round trip from the south of the country to north, taking in all the major parks and attractions. While you can drive this route in a 2WD vehicle, on some of the gravel roads generous ground clearance and big wheels will be an advantage. Also, some of the final sections to camps may well require 4WD but we've indicated this on each listing so you can select your accommodation accordingly.

The Namibia Grand Tour covers Fish River Canyon, Lüderitz , Sossusvlei, Namib Naukluft Park, Swakopmund, Brandberg, Twyfelfontein, Epupa Falls, Etosha National Park, Waterberg Plateau National park and Windhoek. Of course, you could also do the Tour in the reverse order.

While this tour is designed as a circular route, starting and ending in Windhoek, you can also access it from your nearest borderpost. If coming from South Africa, you would probably want to begin at Fish River Canyon or Waterberg depending on where you've entered the country - Gauteng visitors may want to extend the tour into the Zambezi (old Caprivi) region and return home via Botswana.

DETAILED ITINERARY

If you fly in to Windhoek we suggest you take the day to sort out your hire vehicle and do your shopping - so the next day when you begin your journey, you'll be well rested and ready. If you don't feel like overnighting in Windhoek, you could drive for an hour towards Rehoboth and camp (or rent a chalet) at Lake Oanob Resort just outside Rehoboth. If you've decided to do the tour in the reverse order, Okahandja could be your overnight stop outside Windhoek.

Day 1: WINDHOEK TO FISH RIVER CANYON (AI-AIS OR HOBAS)

(700 km - 7 hrs 15 min)

A long drive but mostly on good national road. Don't set off too late as the last hour or two will be on gravel. As you pass Hobas towards Ai-Ais, driving through the Gondwana Canyon Park, you'll find yourself in an area which offers great possibilities for landscape photos.

Day 2: FISH RIVER CANYON

We'd actually suggest you stay two nights here. This will give you the opportunity to experience both a sunrise and a sunset at the canyon lookout points, these are spectacular photo opportunities. It's worth noting that the view from the lookout will be in a westerly direction. The camp at Ai-Ais is much larger than the one at Hobas and it allows you the use of the hot water swimming pool as well as day hiking access to the canyon. You can also climb the nearby peaks, just ask the staff for directions. The newly-renovated camp at Hobas is about 10 km from the canyon lookout points so don't expect to be near the canyon. You are not allowed to hike down into the canyon from the Hobas lookout points unless you're setting off on the 5-day Fish River Canyon hiking trail (with the necessary permit). This trail starts here and ends at Ai-Ais. Booking for this trail is essential and you need to be fit, well prepared and self-sufficient. The drive from Ai-Ais to the canyon lookout via Hobas will take you about 1hr 15min so allow enough time and check gate closing times.

Day 3: FISH RIVER CANYON TO LÜDERITZ
(460 km - 5 hrs 10 min)

Today you drive to Lüderitz. Your GPS will tell you that the quickest route from Ai-Ais is north via Seeheim, and it would be correct in doing so. However, we suggest you incur ten minutes more on the road and drive south from Ai-Ais, following the winding Orange River as it flows west towards the Atlantic, until you turn north via Rosh Pinah. The gravel road along the river is prone to flooding after heavy rains so make the necessary enquiries if there has been rain in the region.

The water from the Orange makes grape cultivation possible on a large scale at Aussenkehr, you may want to take a little detour to see this unlikely sight. En route, a lunch stop at Aus will be a welcome break before you visit the feral horses of the Namib at Garub Pan just outside Aus. Once you're in Lüderitz be sure to visit Kolmanskop ghost town, a deserted, old German diamond mining town.

Optional detour: A number of tour operators in the Aussenkehr/ Noordoewer area offer adventure canoe holidays on the Orange River. These fully-catered trips are typically four days long and include all the necessary gear.

Note: *In Namibia, the Orange River is also occasionally referred to as the iGariep River.*

Day 4: LÜDERITZ TO SOSSUSVLEI
(490 km - 5 hrs)

Sossusvlei is a highlight for most first-time visitors to Namibia, here you can experience and climb the country's famous red dunes. Today calls for an early departure from Lüderitz, aiming for an early lunch in Helmeringhausen or simply a stop to sample their famous apple strudel pie - it's delicious!

The duration of your stay at Sossusvlei will depend on the number of activities you have planned; if you're a keen landscape photographer you may want to stay longer to take advantage of different light conditions (stay inside the main gate to take advantage of an early start to the dunes). The best visiting times are late afternoons and early mornings, as midday temperatures can be scorching.

Day 5 & 6: SOSSUSVLEI TO SWAKOPMUND
(380 km - 4 hrs)

The road from Sossusvlei to Swakopmund carries a lot of tourist traffic and is almost always heavily corrugated, so take it easy. Also note that you are driving through the Namib-Naukluft Nature Reserve, if you want to drive into the smaller tracks you require a permit. Swakopmund has much to offer on the activity front but if you simply want to eat out and wander through the curio shops you'll also be very happy. If neither of those make your heart beat faster, consider a day drive to the Moon Landscape (permit required) or Cape Cross seal colony. During the winter months, we suggest you opt for self-catering accommodation rather than camping as the weather could be miserable at times, this will also give you the chance to catch up on your washing!

Optional detour: Naukluft Mountain Zebra Park is about 115km or 1hr 40min from Sossusvlei on the D854 near Buellsport. Apart from being a beautiful drive, this gives you the chance to leave Sossusvlei later in the day or simply to spend some time wandering around the rest camp, exploring the mountain. The drive from here to Swakopmund is about 4 hrs.

Day 7: SWAKOPMUND TO SPITZKOPPE
(155 km - 1 hr 40 min)

Spitzkoppe offers a truly unique camping experience, the sites are located in the midst of huge granite koppies. It's a short drive from Swakopmund but if you arrive in the early afternoon, this'll give you lots of time to set up your camp and explore the area on foot. This place will have most people reaching for their cameras, you'll get the most beautiful shots in the late afternoon or early morning.

Day 8: SPITZKOPPE TO BRANDBERG
(130 km - 2 hrs)

This short drive via Uis to White Lady Lodge will allow you plenty of time to explore. Take a walk up to the White Lady painting after which the lodge was named. If you have an off-road vehicle you could take a drive down the Ugab river just be sure to ask the lodge staff about water levels. Fill your fuel tank at Uis.

Optional detour: Brandberg itself is a majestic place and if you are seeking more solitude you may want to skip White Lady Lodge and drive to the Ugab Rhino Camp on the western side of the mountain, on the Ugab River. The drive is beautiful and there are many opportunities to take small tracks towards the mountain. To reach Ugab Camp itself you may not need an off-road vehicle but one is recommended, especially if you intend exploring around the main tracks. The area is remote and you need to be self-sufficient with water and food. It's 200 km from Spitzkoppe to Ugab Camp and will take 3 hrs travel.

Warning: Should you want to drive from here to Twyfelfontein, your GPS will probably direct you via the river and over some bad 4WD tracks since this is the fastest way to get to Twyfelfontein. Avoid this routing by inserting Uis as your first destination. We don't recommend you drive down the river or over these 4WD tracks unless you are an experienced off-road driver and know how to recover your vehicle and have plenty of provisions with you. This is a very remote and potentially dangerous area. The 240 km from Ugab Rhino Camp to Twyfelfontein via Uis will take you about 3hrs 30min.

Day 9: BRANDBERG TO TWYFELFONTEIN
(135 km - 2 hrs)

From White Lady Lodge the GPS may direct you via some sand tracks northwest of the campsite, avoid these and drive back to the main road on gravel. The river tracks are shorter but you run the risk of getting properly stuck even in an off-road vehicle.

It's a short drive to Twyfelfontein and there are many camping options but beware that some require an off-road vehicle to reach. Nothing too serious but it may result in some bruised egos!

Visit the Twyfelfontein or /Ui-//aes world heritage site to see ancient rock engravings. It's best in the afternoon when it's not too hot but allow more than an hour for the guided tour. Wear comfortable walking shoes and take a hat.

(photo: Richard Randall)

You may also want to visit other sites like Burnt Mountain and the Organ Pipes but for these a good imagination is required. We would rather suggest a drive past the Burnt Mountain site into the Valley of Desolation, stop 15min in and experience the dead silence. The tracks are rocky but not difficult to drive and if you encounter an obstacle that you feel uncomfortable with, simply turn back. Take a GPS with you and make sure you have water, there are not many vehicles in this area and if you get stuck you might have to wait for a while. Not one to tackle in the heat of the day.

Day 10: TWYFELFONTEIN TO SESFONTEIN (OR OPUWO)

(215 km - 2 hrs 45 min or 340 km - 4 hrs 20 min to Opuwo)

Depending on how much you want to explore the Sesfontein and Palmwag areas, you may want to stay over somewhere between Palmwag and Sesfontein or push through to Opuwo to stock up on supplies. There are several community campsites in the Palmwag to Sesfontein area, some are great, others are definitely not. A visit to the Palmwag concession is worth a visit, various game viewing activities are on offer. You may also want to visit Ongongo Hot Spring where they now have a luxury campsite in place of the old, rundown community campsite.

Day 11: SESFONTEIN OR OPUWO TO EPUPA FALLS

(326 km - 4 hrs 20 min or 180 km - 2 hrs 30 min from Opuwo

If you decided to drive from Sesfontein area you may want to leave early and allow some time to stock up on supplies in Opuwo. The town caters for travellers and there are lots of specialties on offer. Consider buying wood here as the area around Epupa Falls is being stripped of all wood. Also, fill up with fuel in Opuwo as this is the last fuelstop before you reach Epupa Falls and you have to come back the same way.

Epupa Falls is a true oasis after the long dusty drive north. This is the land of the Himba people and you may see them on the road. Respect their privacy by first asking if you may take a photo and expect to have to pay for this privilege.

Day 12: EPUPA FALLS TO ETOSHA (OLIFANTSRUS)

(440 km - 5 hrs 45 min)

We suggest that you enter Etosha from the western side via the Galton gate and camp at Olifantsrus the first night.

On your way via Opuwo, be sure to buy enough provisions for the next couple of days and fill up your fuel tank again. There are shops and fuel inside the park but it's better to come prepared.

Day 13 to 15: ETOSHA NATIONAL PARK

(270 km +)

Take the next three days to leisurely tour from the west to the east of the park. There are several rest camps in the park, most of which have magnificent water holes. We suggest you spend your early mornings and late afternoons at these waterholes and wait for the animals to walk past. On the roads between the camps there are plenty of waterholes spread out along the route which animals will visit.

We suggest that, after Olifantsrus, you camp at Okaukeujo, Halali and Namutoni, one night each. If you feel like staying in one place for a while, rather drive to Halali and spend two nights there.

Etosha offers a wonderful game viewing experience. Although it's a popular park with many visitors the waterholes and variety of game makes up for it. The waterholes are a dream come true for wildlife photographers. In the bigger camps, you can lounge by the pool or spend hours on end at the waterhole. You do not have to drive great distances per day to see game as they frequent these waterholes.

Day 16: ETOSHA TO WATERBERG PLATEAU NATIONAL PARK

(315 km - 3 hrs 30 min from Namutoni)

The drive from Namutoni is mostly on good tar roads and you pass through three towns before you reach Waterberg Plateau National Park. You can again stock up after Etosha at any of these towns. The park itself is really small in relation to where you've come from but as its name suggests it's a mountainous area and has a completely different feel. Do a day hike from the rest camp and get 'high' on the scenery!

Day 17: WATERBERG PLATEAU NATIONAL PARK TO WINDHOEK

(300 km - 3 hrs 15 min)

The drive back to Windhoek is along good tar roads and you could choose to make a leisurely start to the day and still arrive in the afternoon. At Okahandja there's a big craft market where you can buy some momentos of your Grand Tour.

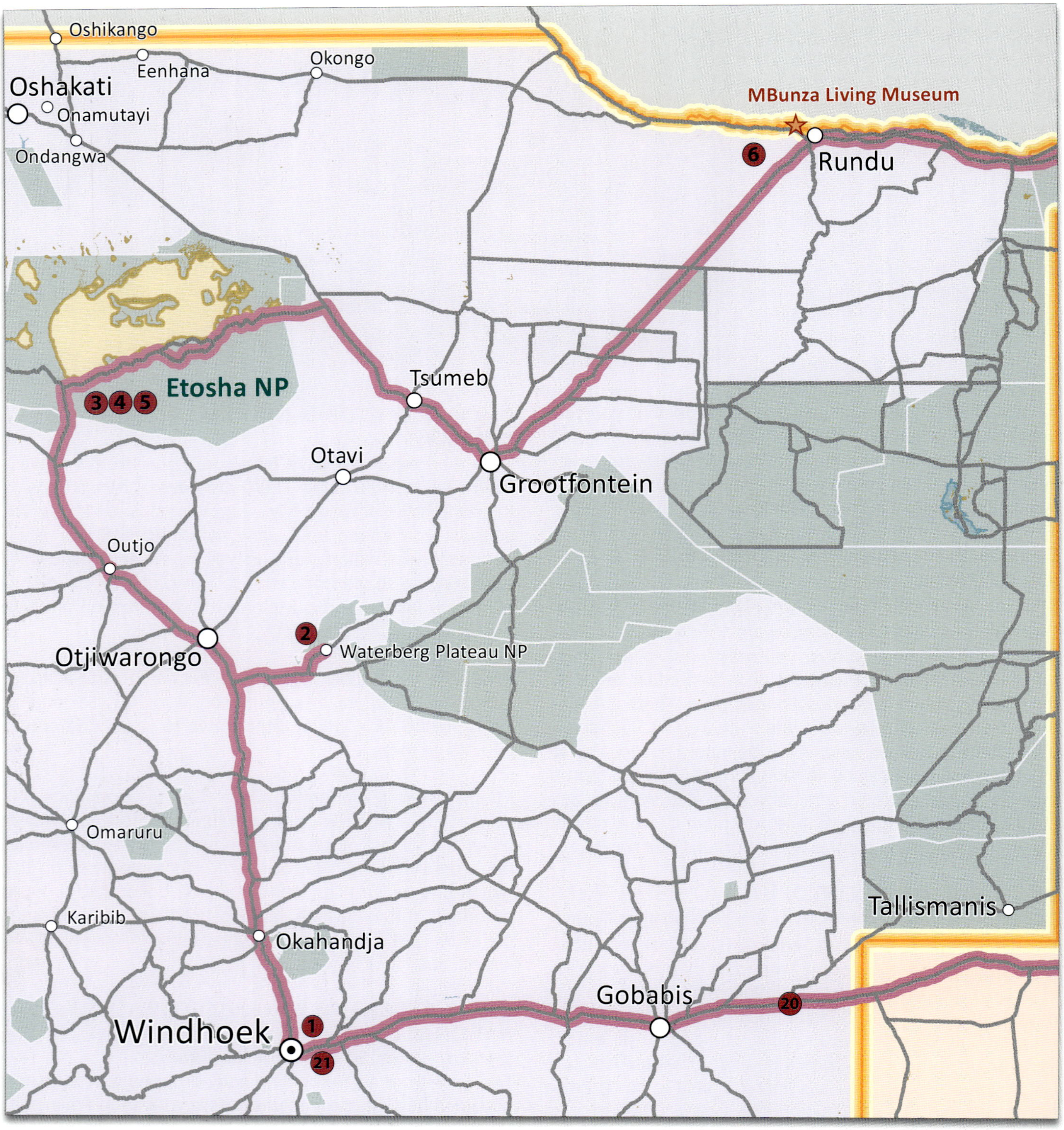

Namibia & Botswana Grand Tour

(With thanks to namibia-forum.ch)

THE NAMIBIA & BOTSWANA Grand Tour aims to introduce you to the top attractions of two countries. Of course, you won't see everything that Namibia and Botswana have to offer but it's a great start, a good way to get to know the lay of the land. This route visits some National Parks where an off-road vehicle is required. If you are driving a 2WD vehicle, you should make the following changes. On Day 12, take a trip to Chobe National Park with one of the game lodges, in their vehicle. On Day 13, drive south to Elephants Sands on the A33. From here you can go on various off-road day trips in the lodges' vehicles. On Day 14, drive south to Nata and then west on the A3 to Planet Baobab, a lodge which offers various trips and activities. From here, you'll drive through to Maun where you can pick up the rest of the original route, Day 19 onwards.

DURATION
Windhoek to Windhoek:
21 days 4 410 km
If driving from and returning to Cape Town, add:
4 days and 3 200 km to your itinerary.
If driving from and returning to Johannesburg, start in Maun and add:
4 days and 2 300 km to your itinerary.

This tour has also been designed as a clockwise circular route starting and ending in Windhoek. But there's nothing to stop you from driving it in a counter clockwise direction, or beginning and ending the tour in Maun, Botswana.

Day 1: ARRIVE IN WINDHOEK
(50 km – 45 min)

It is important to stay the first night in Windhoek. Whether you've flown in, or driven to Windhoek, the chances are good that you'll be tired. On your arrival there's still quite a lot to do. Pick up your rental vehicle if you're getting one and take the time to get acquainted with it. Stock up on provisions and fill up your tanks. If you've still got time, take in a city tour and then end off the day with dinner at the famous Joe's Beerhouse.

Day 2: WATERBERG PLATEAU NATIONAL PARK

(290 km, 3 hrs)

You'll pitch camp for the first time in Namibia beneath the Waterberg's red sandstone cliffs. Once you've got your gear sorted out, take the chance to stretch your legs on one of the nine trails found around the base of the plateau.

The Waterberg Plateau. (photo: Frank Höppener)

Day 3: ETOSHA NP

(280 km, 3 hrs; game drive 100 km, 3 hrs)

Regardless of where you choose to base yourself at this park, you're in for a treat. Etosha is one of Namibia's most popular game parks, a place where you can expect to see small and large animal species. Six camps in the park offer camping and lodging, and you can explore the park on a good gravel road.

Day 4: ETOSHA NP

(70 km, 2 hrs; game drive 100 km, 3 hrs)

Spend some time bird watching. There are 46 raptors to be found here, including the Egyptian vulture. If you're visiting after heavy rains, you'll see the pan covered by a shallow layer of water. In particularly rainy years, the pan becomes a breeding ground for flamingos which arrive in their thousands.

(photo: Hannes Thirion)

Day 5: ETOSHA NP

(70 km, 2 hrs; game drive: 100 km, 3 hrs)

Even though you've got your own vehicle, consider signing up for a guided game drive. This will give you the benefit of a knowledgeable guide who's sure to point out things you'd miss on your own. Also consider a night game drive where you'll get to see animals not often seen in the daylight hours. Okaukuejo camp is famous for its floodlit waterholes, a great way to spend your last evening at Etosha.

The old water mill at Andara Mission Station on the banks of the Kavango River. (photo: Karin Theron)

Day 6: KAVANGO RIVER

(430 km – 4 hrs 30 min)

Head northeast for the Kavango River in Kavango Region, and find a place to stay on the riverbanks. In Botswana, this same river is called the Okavango. A visit to the Mbunza Living Museum, some 15 km from Rundu, is well worth your time, here you can learn about the region's fascinating cultures.

Day 7: DIVUNDU

(200 km – 2 hrs; game drive 100 km – 3 hrs)

Heading due east now, your next stop is the small village of Divundu, just into the Caprivi strip. Nearby, you'll find Popa Falls (more rapids than waterfalls) which are most impressive in the dry season. Or, you could choose to explore the Mahango Game Reserve.

Day 8: BUFFALO CORE AREA

(150 km - 6 hrs) 4WD required

Take a day trip to the Buffalo Core Area. Here you can sign up for a boat trip or spend some time relaxing at the river, watching the game. See if you can find the old South African army base. The tracks in this area are best traversed in an off-road vehicle with an experienced person at the wheel. Note: hunting is permitted in this area.

Day 9: KONGOLA

(200 km – 2 hrs; game drive 100 km – 3hrs)

You're continuing east along the Caprivi corridor to the town of Kongola. Visit the Horse Shoe, an oxbow lake on the Kwando river, or the Mafwe Living Museum. Places to stay include Nambwa, Mavunje, Namushasha or Mazambala. Be prepared for stretches of very deep sand, lowering your tyre pressures is a must.

Day 10: KASANE
(230 km – 2 hrs 30 min)
It's time to cross over into Botswana where you'll be spending three nights in the Kasane area. Allow an hour for the border crossing. A three-hour boat cruise in the Chobe National Park is a visit to elephant central and one of the best ways to get close to the game.

Day 11: VICTORIA FALLS
(Full day)
Take a day trip to Victoria Falls in nearby Zimbabwe. The border post is more easily negotiated if you leave your vehicle behind and take a taxi or shuttle – the drivers typically know how to organise formalities. Otherwise, allow anything from one to three hours for the border post. Once at the falls, take your time, the walk to the various viewpoints is well worth it. If you have the funds, a helicopter flip over the falls will give you a memorable perspective.

Day 12: CHOBE WATERFRONT
(Game Drive: 150 km – 6 hrs) 4WD required
Back to Chobe, but this time on land. Drive the famous 'Chobe Waterfront' to see who's come down to the water to drink.

Day 13: SAVUTI
(170 km – 3 hrs; game drive 50 km – 2 hrs) 4WD required
Drive to Savuti, stay at the Savuti Camp. This is a place to spot lions and leopards, both of whom exhibit behaviours unique to this area. The camp is unfenced so care should be taken when walking to the ablutions at night. This is a very popular venue, you'll need to book up to a year in advance.

Day 14: SAVUTI GAME DRIVE
(150 km – 6 hrs) 4WD required
The rainy season here lasts from November to April. And if you're here during the first couple of months, you'll be able to witness thousands of zebra moving south to the Mababe Depression grasslands. In the dry season make your way towards the artificial waterholes – predators gather here so you could have some exciting sightings.

Day 15: KHWAI
(110 km – 3 hrs; game drive 50 km – 2 hrs) 4WD required
Make your way south to the Khwai region. Stay at the community campsite here (advance bookings required) or in the Moremi Game Reserve. You're on the easternmost tip of the Okavango Delta, one of Africa's most celebrated game reserves.

DAY 16: KHWAI
The choice is yours, make this a lazy day in the camp, catch up on your reading and watch animals pass by. Or you could organise a bushwalk via the Khwai Development Trust, this is one of the few places you can explore the Delta on foot. Whatever you decide, ending the day with a two hour sunset cruise will finish your day in memorable fashion.

Day 17: MOREMI GAME RESERVE
(50 km – 2 hrs; game drive 100 km – 3 hrs) 4WD required
Stay at a camp in the Moremi Game reserve e.g. Xakanaxa or Third Bridge Campsites. Take a game drive in the reserve.

If you're visiting during the rainy season expect a great deal of water and mud. You will get stuck! (photo: Mietsie Visser)

Day 18: MOREMI GAME DRIVE / BOAT TRIP
(game drive 150 km – 6 hrs; boat trip) 4WD required
No trip to Moremi is complete without a mokoro trip. These hollowed-out tree trunks (or modern replicas) are poled by experienced local guides who'll take you deep into the Delta's papyrus-fringed channels. This is a side of the Delta you'll never forget so splash out! Bookings are recommended.

A deep water crossing in Moremi Game Reserve. (photo: Lizette Swart)

Day 19: MAUN
(160 km – 3 hrs 30 min)
Drive to Maun. Once settled in, take an hour's flight over the Okavango Delta. An aerial view of the waters you've just visited will round off your perspective of this amazing place. If you still have time in hand, Maun has much to offer. From basket-weaving classes, to museums, restaurants and bars. You're back in civilisation – African style!

Day 20: NAMIBIA
(500 km – 5 hrs)
Drive back to Namibia, overnighting along the road. Stay at Zelda Game & Guestfarm, East Gate rest camp or Kalahari Bush Breaks, not far past the border crossing. Allow one hour for border crossing.

Day 21: WINDHOEK
(300 km – 3 hrs)
Drive back to Windhoek, spend one last night or dash to the airport to start the journey home.

BOESMANLAND

The Dorsland Grootboom baobab just south of Khaudum NP. (photo: Karin Theron)

BOESMANLAND IS A HISTORIC REGION in north-eastern Namibia that's home to the largest remaining group of San people (aka Bushman) who still live on their ancestral land (Nyae Nyae Conservancy). As you might have guessed, the region's name means 'land of the bushman'.

The Bushman occupied the southern African continent long before black and white settlers invaded their territories. They lived in the Kalahari for some 20 000 years as hunter-gatherers and survived by hunting, and gathering edible plants. The Bushman at the Nyae Nyae Conservancy still follow a very traditional lifestyle since they've only had contact with western influences since 1950.

Boesmanland is a vast, sparsely-populated area and although not as lush as the more northern parts of Namibia, there's an abundance of game, flora and bird species. The terrain ranges from pans and stony plains, to dune fields and open woodland.

Mangetti National Park, situated 110 km south of Rundu, is home to a thriving collection of wildlife, including large mammal species like elephant, eland, rhino, blue wildebeest, zebra, giraffe, sable antelope as well as predators like leopard, hyena and the endangered wild dog. One of Namibia's latest parks, Mangetti was fenced off in the early 70s as a game camp with the aim to generate an income for local communities through game farming, trophy hunting and live game sales. It was proclaimed a National Park in 2008 and officially opened in 2014. The park has 4x4 tracks with deep sand so you'll need an off-road vehicle if you want to explore it. Park infrastructure - like overnight facilities - is under development.

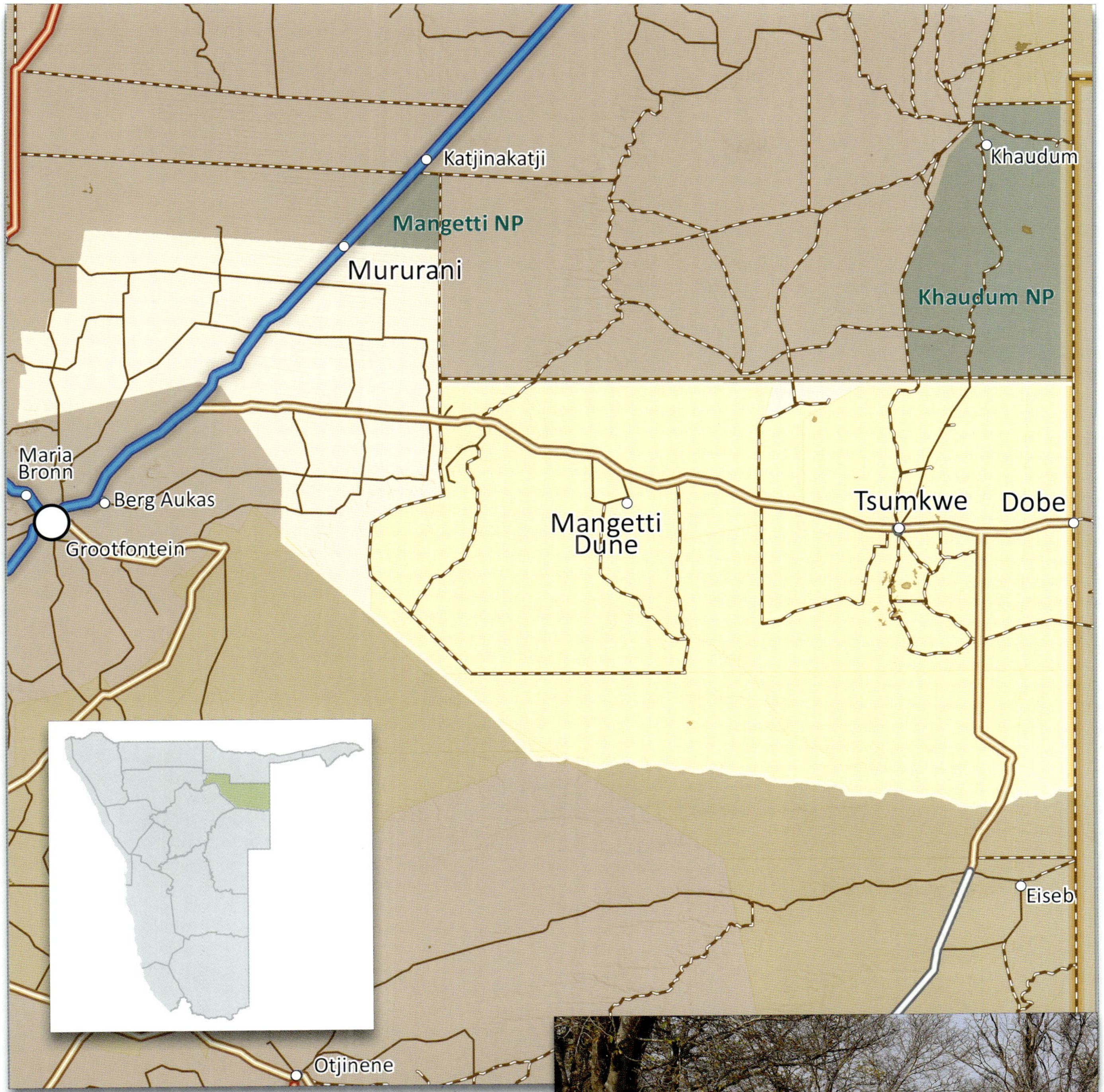

Mangetti National Park (photo: Frank Höppener)

MAJOR ATTRACTIONS

- Craft market at Tsumkwe which sells Bushman arts and crafts.
- At the 'Living Museum of Ju/'Hoansi-San' you can see first-hand how Bushman hunt with bow and poisoned arrows, dig out springhares and porcupines, and catch guinea fowl and other game birds for food.
- The Dorsland Grootboom is an ancient baobab tree which is still growing despite having fallen over and losing some of its branches. When you see it from afar, it's difficult to believe that this is a single tree.

More details about the attractions are available on our website (www.tracks4africa.co.za) or our Guide App. Our GPS Map can navigate you to each of these attractions.

Tsumkwe

(photo: Karin Theron)

THE SMALL TOWN OF TSUMKWE was the capital of the former Bushmanland District which now forms part of the Otjozondjupa region. Before Namibian independence from South Africa, the town was home to the 36th Battalion of the South African Defence Force. These days the town is a lot smaller but you'll still find an airstrip, a few houses, some shops and a fuel station.

Traveller Description

Tsumkwe is situated in the Nyae Nyae Conservancy, it's the last town you'll drive through before entering Khaudum National Park from the south, or entering Botswana through the Dobe border post to the east. It's also significant to travellers as the place to visit Bushman (San) villages. Visitors should stop at the G!hunku Craft Centre which both exhibits and sells, arts and crafts made by the local San; items like ostrich egg jewellery, glass beads and hunting bows.

Travel Info

The Ju/'Hoansi-San people live in small family groups throughout the conservancy, on land left to them by their forefathers. Visitors can arrange to visit these settlements accompanied by a local guide; enquire at the Nyae Nyae Conservancy Office in town or at one of the lodges in the area. Visitors must bear in mind that the San people's lifestyle has become largely westernised, so their traditional culture can best be observed at The Living Museum of the Ju/'Hoansi-San, 150km west of Tsumkwe. Tsumkwe Lodge has comfortable bungalows, a small pub and restaurant, a camping area, and offers the guided San walks referred to previously.

TRAVEL TIP! The C44 between Tsumkwe and the intersection with the B8 is a good gravel road accessible to sedan vehicles. But note that all other roads are either deep sand (or mud in the Jan - Mar rainy season) and should only be driven in an off-road vehicle, preferably with an experienced off-road driver. Although the Dobe border post can be reached in a sedan with reasonable ground clearance (depending on seasonal rains), travellers wishing to enter Botswana will need an off-road vehicle on that side. There's a veterinary fence on the C44 at Rooidag, 145km west of Tsumkwe, which limits the transport of raw meat and unpasteurised milk from east to west, but not from west to east. However, this could change in the event of a foot-and-mouth outbreak. The General Dealer is well stocked with food, liquor, fresh bread, frozen meat and hardware. But they don't have fresh meat, vegetables or fruit.

Town Info: Hospital: +264(0)67 248 170 Police: +264(0)67 300 600 Tow-in: +264(0)81 269 9832

Djokhoe 1

Community Camp $
23km or 35min SE of Tsumkwe (of which 11km is 4WD)
w137764

nndfn@africaonline.com.na

Campsite information is unconfirmed - use at your own discretion. Venue is located in the Nyae Nyae Conservancy near Tsumkwe. Campers need to be self-sufficient.

Languages: English

Facilities:

Activities:

Elephant Song (Little Hunter's Ju/'Hoansi-San) 2

Community Camp $
25km or 27min NNE of Tsumkwe (of which 1km is 4WD)
w274152

Cell: +264(0)81 803 8136
contact@lcfn.info
www.lcfn.info

Two campsites, each with a dry toilet, bucket shower and braai facilities. Water and wood available. Book at reception at Living Museum of the Ju-Hoansi-San.

Languages: English

Facilities:

Activities:

Ju/'Hoansi-San Campsite Grashoek 3

Community Camp $
150km or 1h58min WNW of Tsumkwe
w279434

contact@lcfn.info
www.lcfn.info

Located at the Living Museum of the Ju/'Hoansi-San. Three shaded campsites, each with a dry toilet, bucket shower and braai area. Wood and water available.

Languages: English

Facilities:

Activities:

Nhoma Safari Camp 4

Tented Camp $$$
90km or 2h49min NNW of Tsumkwe (of which 49km is 4WD)
w207954

Fax: +88 614 979, Cell: +264(0)81 273 4606
tsumkwel@iway.na
www.nhomasafaricamp.com

10 Luxury permanent tents, each with solar lights, bath, toilet and wash basin. Guests can enjoy a traditional tour or hunt. Meals served here.

Languages: English

Facilities:

Activities:

Nhoma Safari Camp 5

Camping $$
90km or 2h49min NNW of Tsumkwe (of which 49km is 4WD)
w360368

Fax: +88 614 979, Cell: +264(0)81 273 4606
tsumkwel@iway.na
www.nhomasafaricamp.com

Campsite with ablutions. Benefits the //nhoq'ma community. Free firewood. Traditional tours or hunts available.

Languages: English

Facilities:

Activities:

Omatako Valley Rest Camp 6

Community Camp $
132km or 1h37min WNW of Tsumkwe
w219547

cb@indigosafaris.com
www.omatakovalley.com

Spacious, shady campsites on sand, each with braai area, table, tap and sink. Ablutions have flush toilets, sinks and showers. Water carried from well.

Languages: English

Facilities:

Activities:

Tucsin Tsumkwe Lodge 7

Lodge $$
2km or 4min SW of Tsumkwe (of which 1km is 4WD)
w137910

Tel: +264(0)67 240 901 , Fax: +264(0)67 240 902
reservations.tsumkwe@travel-weaver.com
www.tsumkwe-lodge.com

En-suite accommodation. Venue offers guided walks with Bushman and visits to Bushman Village.

Languages: English, Afrikaans

Facilities:

Activities:

Tucsin Tsumkwe Lodge 8

Lodge Camp $
2km or 4min SW of Tsumkwe (of which 1km is 4WD)
w239952

Tel: +264(0)67 240 901 , Fax: +264(0)67 240 902
reservations.tsumkwe@travel-weaver.com
www.tsumkwe-lodge.com

Five campsites, each with their own braai facilities and power points. Communal ablution blocks.

Languages: English, Afrikaans

Facilities:

Activities:

"Not all those who wander are lost."

JRR Tolkien
The Fellowship of the Ring

CENTRAL NAMIBIA

(photo: Guy Harwood)

THIS REGION IS HOME TO Namibia's capital, Windhoek; a large, modern city which boasts a mix of modern and old colonial architecture. Many of the tourist attractions in the town's centre hark back to the German presence in Namibia in the 1900s. This is a lush, hilly and clean city, and its inhabitants are warm and friendly. You can easily spend two to three days here as there is lots to see and do.

Windhoek has lots to offer visitors so you'll find everything you need, even long-term storage facilities for your vehicle. Many overseas visitors who regularly visit Namibia, store their vehicles on one of the surrounding farms. These 'vehicle hotels' offer good security, are spotlessly clean and have workshops. They'll even start and run your vehicle regularly.

Because of its high altitude, Windhoek can get extremely cold at night, especially in winter. The landscape around Windhoek consists mainly of dense acacia growth, and swaying grass which appears white in the late afternoon sun.

The Central Namibia plateau is enclosed by two deserts, the Namib to the west and the Kalahari to the east.

You'll find the Genocide Statue in front of the Alte Feste fort and next to the Independence Memorial Museum, in Windhoek. (photo: Karin Theron)

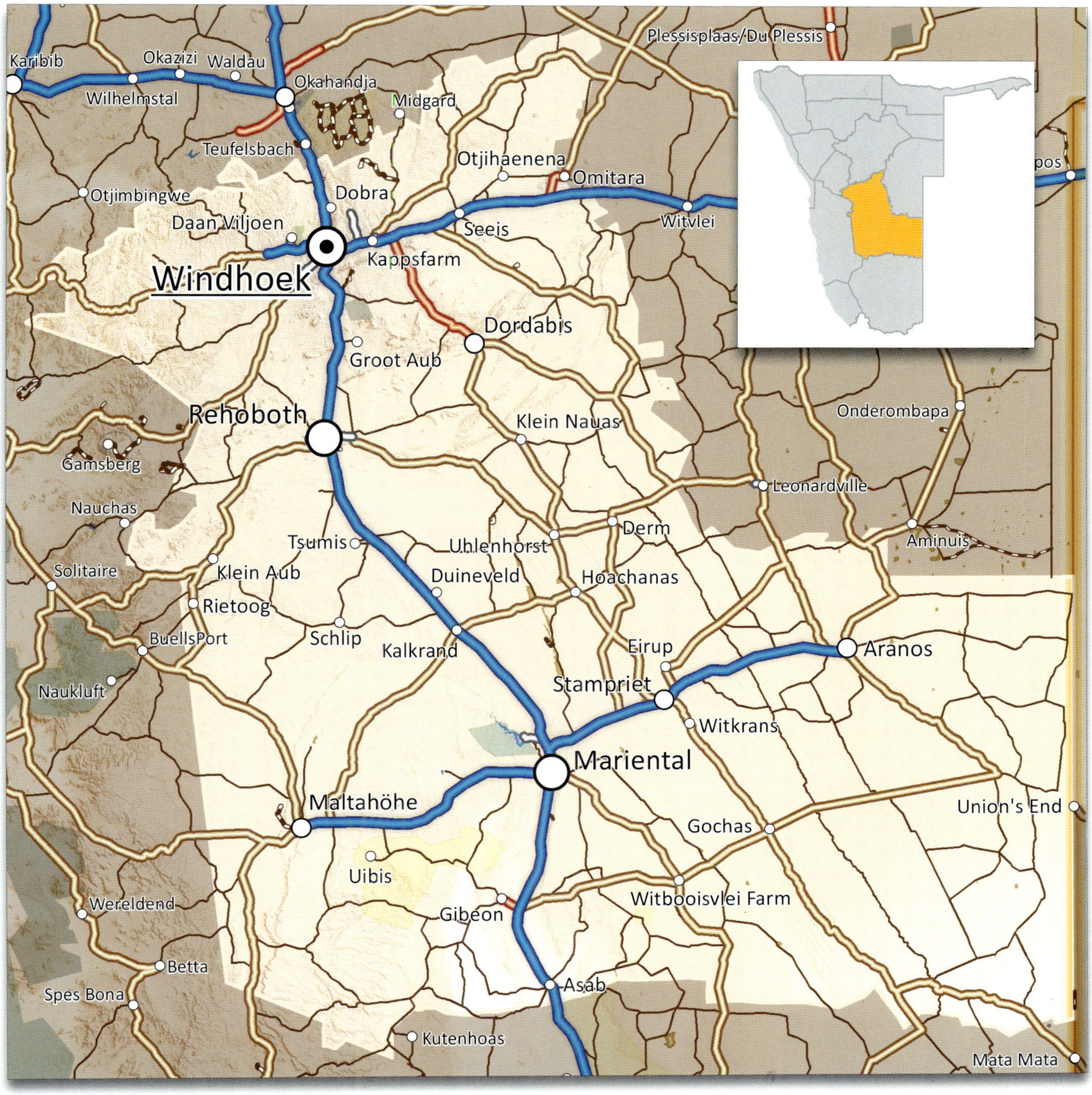

MAJOR ATTRACTIONS

- Windhoek attractions include Christuskirche (Christ Church), Alte Feste Museum (old German Fort), Namibia Crafts Market, State House, Genocide Memorial, Independence Museum and Gibeon Meteorites Display.
- Attractions on the city's outskirts include German War Graves and Heroes' Acre. The Daan Viljoen Game Reserve offers hiking and mountain biking trails.
- Hardap is Namibia's largest dam; the Hardap Resort is a popular stop-over for self-drive travellers.
- Arnhem Cave, which is said to be inhabited by six different bat species.
- Bitterwasser Pan is about 3 km wide and used as a glider port during the summer months.

More details about the attractions are available on our website (www.tracks4africa.co.za) or our Guide App. Our GPS Map can navigate you to each of these attractions.

Aranos

(photo: Johann Groenewald)

LOCATED IN A SEA OF RIPPLED RED Kalahari sand dunes, the small town of Aranos is surrounded by nature reserves and commercial livestock farms. The Natural Namibia Meat Producer's (NNMP) abattoir in town is an approved export facility for lamb, mutton and beef to South Africa and the EU. Livestock roams freely between the dunes, giving the meat a uniquely natural flavour and taste.

Traveller Description

The dry Nossob River Basin, originating in the Anas Mountains near Windhoek, passes south of the town before entering the Kgalagadi Game Reserve in South Africa. Wildlife flourishes in the area and ostrich, springbok and gemsbok (oryx) are regularly seen.

Aranos offers all basic facilities as well as an information centre. Note that the fuel station closes at 16:30.

Travel Info

The border post at Union's End is closed - travellers from Aranos who wish to visit the Kgalagadi Transfrontier Park will have to travel south to the Mata Mata border post to enter South Africa. Note that the border post opening and closing times (07:00 and 15:30) differ from the park gate times, and visitors making use of the Mata Mata border post have to stay two nights in the Kgalagadi Transfrontier Park before exiting at Twee Rivieren.

Useful numbers:

Aranos Village Council (tourist information):	+264(0)63 272 051
Agrimark:	+264(0)63 272 375/470
Spar Food Store:	+264(0)63 272 016
Strauss Butchery:	+264(0)63 272 251

TRAVEL TIP! This town is easily reached via the tarred C20 from Mariental.

Town Info:
Hospital: +264(0)63 276 900, Police: +264(0)63 272 002, Doctor: +264(0)63 272 085, Tow-in: +264(0)63 272 644

Aranos Hotel 1

Hotel $
125 Nossob St, Aranos
w138425

Tel: +264(0)63 272 031, Cell: +264(0)81 220 0780,
Fax: +264(0)63 272 300
aranoshotel@iway.na

This venue hosts up to 22 people in eight en-suite rooms (air-conditioning, TV, coffee/tea facilities) and three rooms which share an ablution facility.

Languages: English, Afrikaans

Facilities:

Activities:

Blue Bull Lodge 2

Self-catering $
On the C20 Rd, Aranos
w361729

Tel: +264(0)63 272 450, Cell: +264(0)81 262 8620
bloubu@iway.na
www.bluebull-aranos.com

Four self-catering units, each sleeping 2 - 6 people. Each unit has a fully-equipped kitchenette, bathroom with shower and a braai area.

Languages: English

Facilities:

Activities:

Ley-Lia Guest House 3

Self-catering $
6 Sarel Theron St, Aranos
w360818

Cell: +27(0)81 376 3549
leyliaguesthouse@gmail.com

Self-catering rooms with TV, kitchenette and kettle. Breakfast and braai packs can be arranged.

Languages: English, Afrikaans

Facilities:

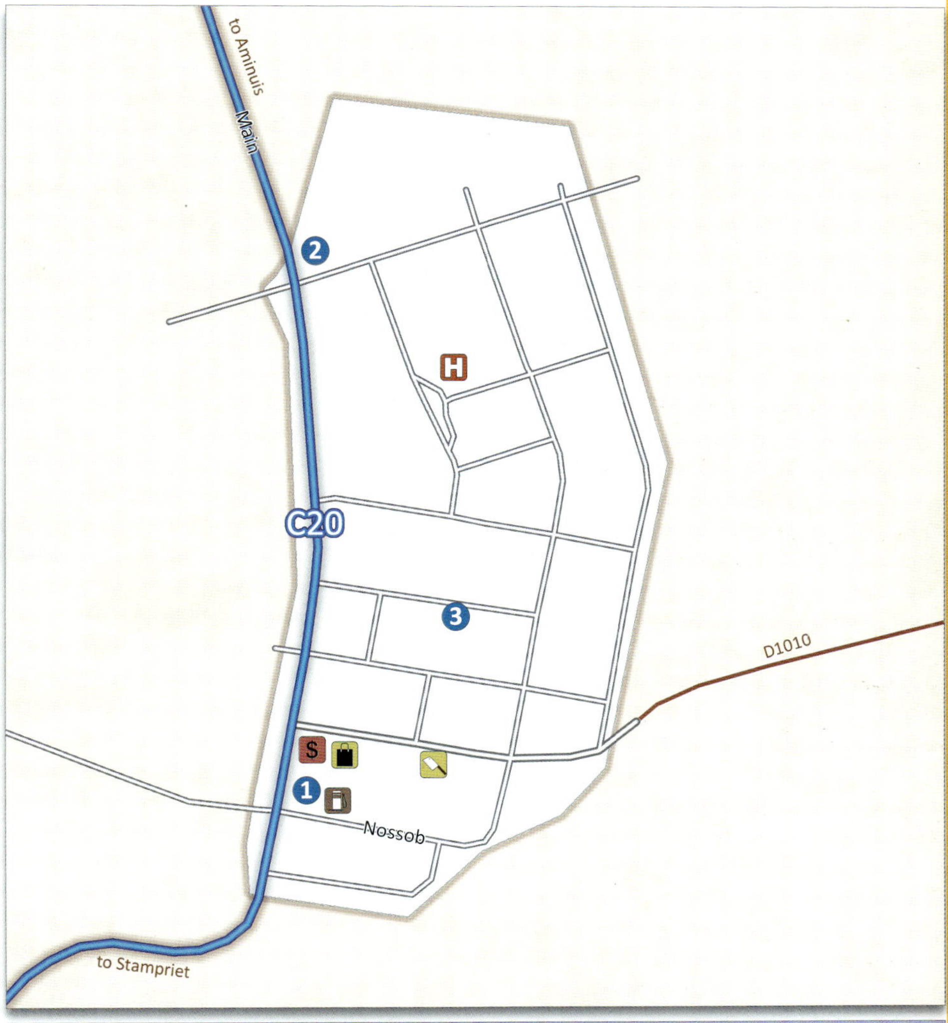

(photo: Frank Höppener)

Dordabis

(photo: Ian-Ray Nel)

THE HISTORICAL VILLAGE OF DORDABIS was established in the early 20s by August Stauch who purchased the Dordabis, Ibenstein and Protea farms to develop as a trade centre. Stauch had originally established a diamond claim at Kolmanskop outside Lüderitz in 1908. His daughter Marianne, and her husband Nicolai Krafft, started Karakul sheep farming and opened the first carpet weavery in Namibia on the farm Ibenstein.

Dordabis mostly serves the farming community which is focused on hunting or livestock farming.

Traveller Description

The Arnhem Cave, 67km north-west of Dordabis, is at 4.5km in length, Namibia's largest and longest cave. It was discovered in 1930 and is inhabited by six different bat species, including the giant leaf-nosed bat which is the largest insect-eating bat in the world. Guided tours offered by the nearby lodge last up to three hours.

Travel Info

There is a police station and a state clinic in town (open 08:00 - 17:00), as well as a fuel station and small shops. Mechanical and tyre repairs can be done by local mechanic, Eddy Krems. Ask for him at the fuel station or contact him on the number below.

Useful numbers:
Clinic: +264(0)62 513 516
Dordabis store: +264(0)62 573 500
Mechanical repairs (Eddy Krems): +264(0)81 129 7490

TRAVEL TIP! Dordabis is 90km from Windhoek and easily reached by sedan vehicle on a tarred road. The general dealer sells bread and frozen meat, but availability of produce cannot be guaranteed. Rather stock up in larger towns or call ahead to check on availability.

Town Info:

Police: +264(0)62 573 514

Tow-in: +264(0)81 129 7490

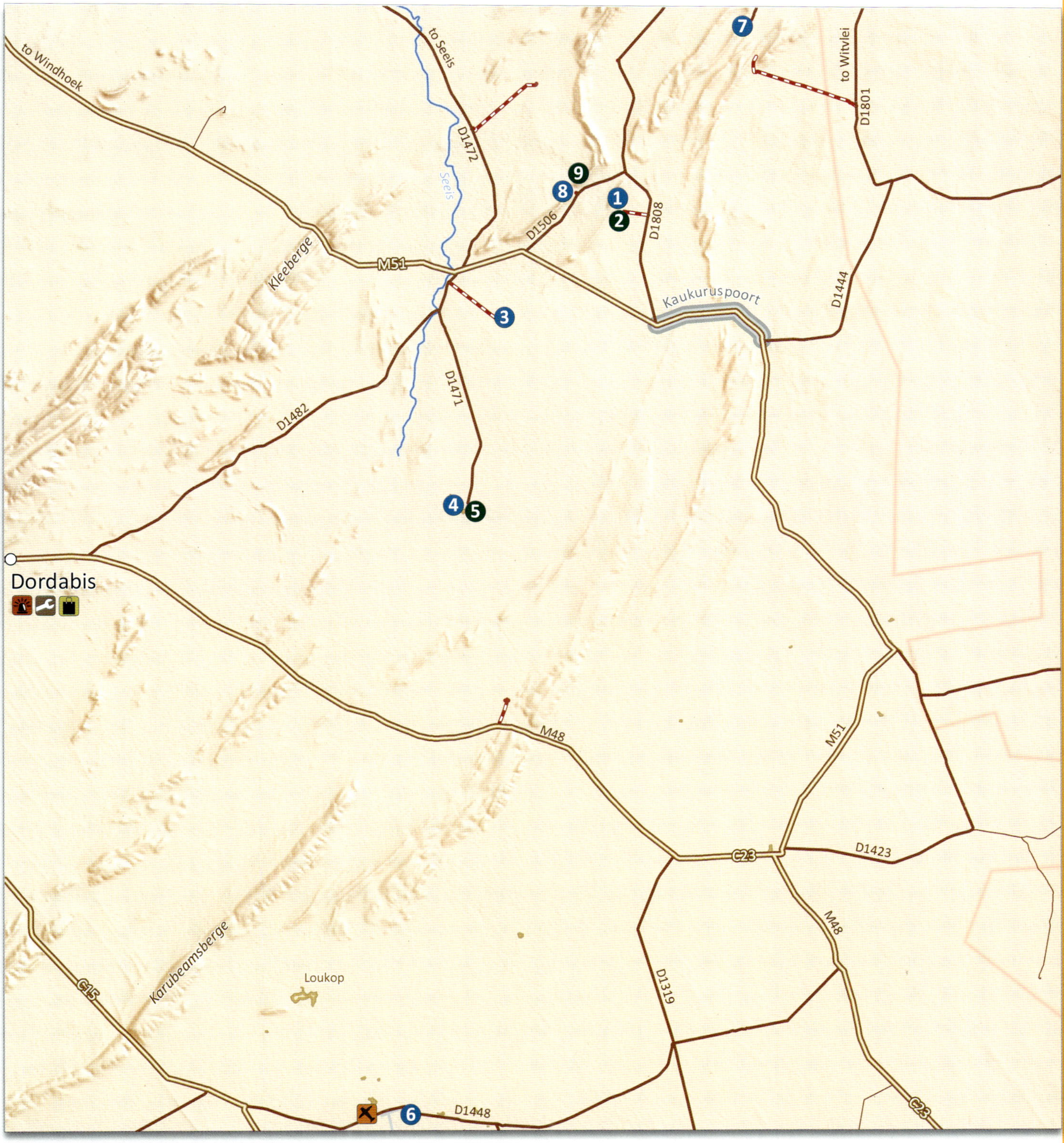

Dordabis

Arhem Cave & Lodge 1

Lodge $
64km or 1h6min ENE of Dordabis
w138445

Tel: +264(0)62 581 885, Cell: +264(0)81 259 6434,
Fax: +264(0)62 581 885
arnhem@afol.com.na

The lodge provides accommodation in thatched chalets with en-suite bathrooms. A thatched lapa houses the dining area, swimming pool and bar. Cave tours offered.

Languages: English, Afrikaans

Facilities: FC

Activities:

Arnhem Cave & Lodge 2

Lodge Camp $
64km or 1h6min ENE of Dordabis
w227573

Tel: +264(0)62 581 885, Cell: +264(0)81 259 6434,
Fax: +264(0)62 581 885
arnhem@afol.com.na

Campsites with ablution facilities and braai areas. Guests can visit the Arnhem Caves, the longest caves in Namibia.

Languages: English, Afrikaans

Facilities: FC

Activities:

Eningu Clayhouse Lodge 3

Lodge $$
48km or 55min ENE of Dordabis
w138455

Tel: +264(0)64 464 144, Fax: +264(0)64 464 155
info@eningulodge.com
www.eningulodge.com

Nine private, individually-styled guest rooms. The venue offers a rooftop sundeck, lounge, indoor and outdoor dining areas, archery range, wine cellar and souvenier shop.

Languages: English, German

Facilities: VISA @

Activities:

Farm Heimat 4

Guest Farm $$
56km or 1h1min E of Dordabis
w189027

Tel: +264(0)62 581 650, Cell: +264(0)81 247 1004,
Fax: +264(0)88 620 042
info@farm-heimat.com, www.farm-heimat.com

Comfortable, luxurious rooms with en-suite bathrooms. There's also a bungalow with fully-equipped kitchen (includes cutlery, crockery, fridge and stove).

Languages: English, German, Afrikaans

Facilities: VISA FC @

Activities:

Farm Heimat 5

Farm Camp $
56km or 1h1min E of Dordabis
w360401

Tel: +264(0)62 581 650, Cell: +264(0)81 247 1004,
Fax: +264(0)88 620 042
info@farm-heimat.com, www.farm-heimat.com

Camping (with ablution facilities) is available on this working farm.

Languages: English, German, Afrikaans

Facilities: VISA FC @

Activities:

Kiripotib Guest Farm 6

Lodge $$
65km or 45min SE of Dordabis
w254409

Tel: +264(0)62 581 419, Fax: +264(0)62 581 429
reservations@kiripotib.com
www.kiripotib.com

Chalets, guest rooms and tents. The rooms are en-suite. There's a thatched lapa with bar and fireplace. This venue is closed for the month of February.

Languages: English, German, Afrikaans

Facilities: VISA @

Activities:

Okambara Elephant Lodge 7

Lodge $$
95km or 1h35min NE of Dordabis
w207916

Tel: +264(0)64 405 157, Cell: +264(0)81 467 6448,
Fax: +264(0)88 625 692
info@okambara.de, www.okambara.de

Situated on a large game ranch, this lodge offers comfortable accommodation in the main house or in big chalets that have separate bathrooms. Self-drive access by prior arrangement only.

Languages: English, German, Afrikaans

Facilities: FC

Activities:

Scheidthof Guest Farm And Foto Safaris 8

Guest Farm $$
55km or 53min ENE of Dordabis
w138421

Tel: +264(0)62 581 884, Cell: +264(0)81 249 6333,
Fax: +264(0)62 581 884
grahl@iway.na

Accommodation in single or double en-suite rooms, as well as double rooms sharing a bathroom. Guests have total privacy and a choice of different boarding options.

Languages: English, German, Afrikaans

Facilities: FC @

Activities:

Scheidthof Guest Farm And Foto Safaris 9

Farm Camp $
55km or 53min ENE of Dordabis
w254376

Tel: +264(0)62 581 884, Cell: +264(0)81 249 6333,
Fax: +264(0)62 581 884
grahl@iway.na

As well as camping facilities, this venue offers photographic safaris throughout Namibia. During the rainy season the roads are very slippery and only accessible with an off-road vehicle.

Languages: English, German, Afrikaans

Facilities: FC @

Activities:

(photo: Ian-Ray Nel)

(photo: Stephen Cunliffe)

Gochas

(photo: Johann Groenewald)

GOCHAS IS ONE OF THE SMALLEST TOWNS in Namibia, and has been the main settlement of the !Kharakhoen Nama people since 1889. They named the village Gochas, Nama for "the place of many !Go bushes", after the many candle-pod trees (*Acacia hebeclada*) that grow in the area.

Gochas is situated in the Aoab River Valley, an area where frequent skirmishes took place between the German Schutztruppe and Nama people during the War of Resistance from 1904 to 1907. Several war graves of German Schutztruppe can be seen in the cemetery in town, and a few monuments along the C15 commemorate battles which took place along the Aoab Riverbed.

Fruit and vegetables are cultivated in the area surrounding the nearby village of Stampriet, these are irrigated from artesian water wells supplied from the catchment area south-west of Windhoek.

Traveller Description

Gochas has a few small shops, a fuel station and an airstrip, but the beauty of the surrounding red Kalahari dunes with their feathery golden tufts of bushman-grass, makes this a popular stopover for travellers using the Mata Mata border post. A number of activities are available in the area, including hiking, dune boarding, bird watching, game viewing and desert safaris.

Travel Info

The OK Grocer is very well stocked and gas bottles can be refilled here or at the Agri Co-Op. The farms under irrigation along the Aoab Riverbed make for a very scenic drive from Gochas to Mata Mata. The Kalahari Farmstall, 15km before reaching the border post, offers fresh produce, curios, good coffee and mouth-watering lunches (pre-order from the number below).

Useful numbers:

Clinic +264(0)63 250 020, OK Grocer +264(0)63 250 003, Mata Mata Border Post (07:00 to 15.30): +264(0)63 252 055 Kalahari Farmstall: +264(0)63 252 017, Alternative tow-in numbers: +264(0)62 500 132 / +264(0)62 504 250

TRAVEL TIP! You can buy fresh fruit and vegetables and some of the best Kalahari meat in Gochas but there is no guarantee that they will always have fuel. Diesel (incl. 50ppm) is available from the Agri Mark during business hours. The Mata Mata border post opening and closing time (07:00 and 15:30) does not coincide with the entry gate into the Kgalagadi and travellers making use of this border post have to stay a compulsory two nights in the Kgalagadi Transfrontier Park before exiting the park at Twee Rivieren.

Town Info: Police: +264(0)63 250 001 Tow-in: +264(0)81 129 7490

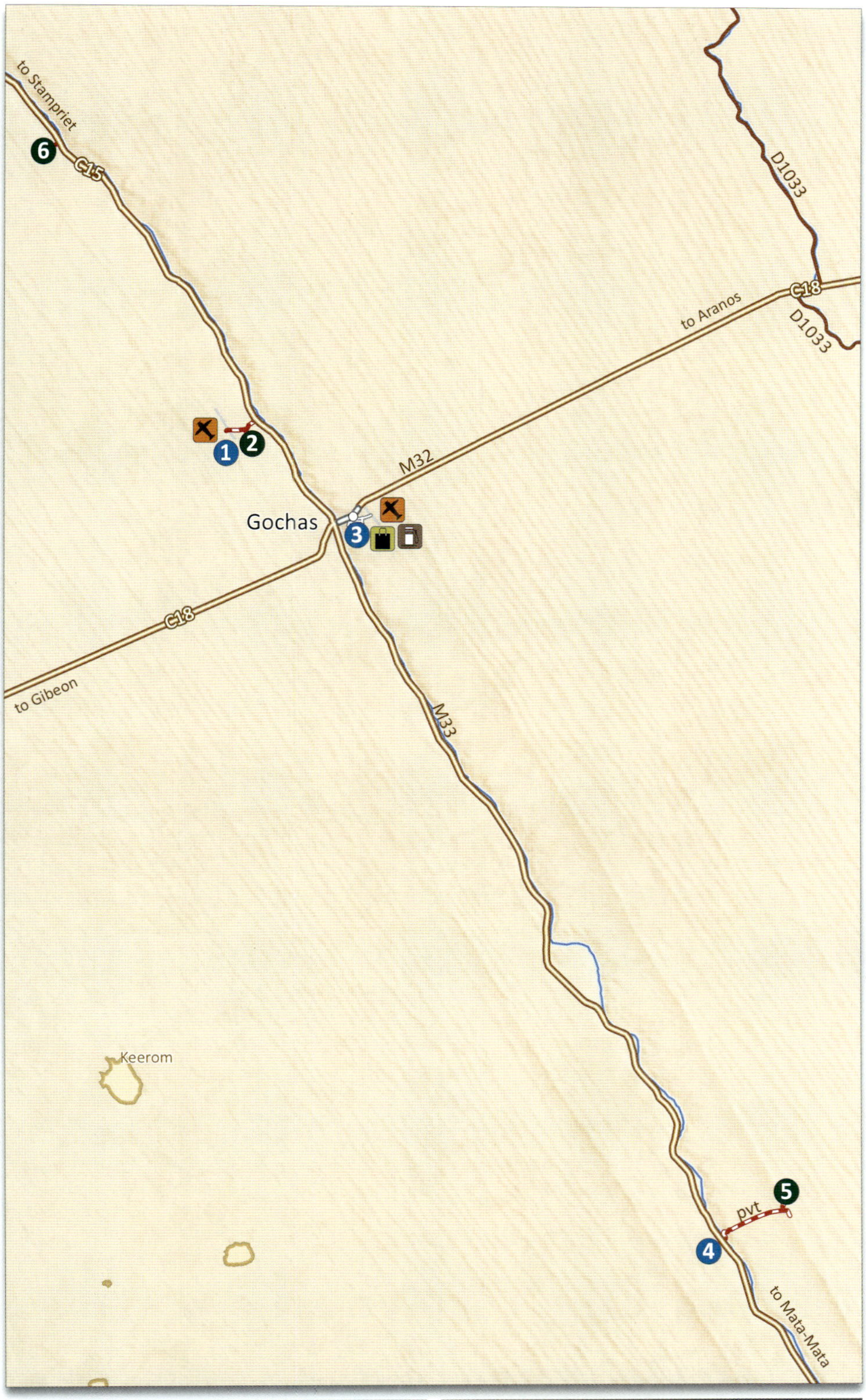

Auob Lodge 1

Lodge $
6km or 5min NW of Gochas
w138325

Tel: +264(0)61 374 750, Fax: +264(0)61 256 598
auob@ncl.com.na

Situated on the banks of Auob river, this venue offers double en-suite rooms with air-conditioning, TV, mosquito nets, coffee/tea facilities and internet access.

Languages: English, German, Afrikaans

Facilities:
Activities:

Auob Lodge 2

Lodge Camp $
6km or 5min NW of Gochas
w232884

Tel: +264(0)61 374 750, Fax: +264(0)61 256 598
auob@ncl.com.na

The lodge offers camping facilities; campers are welcome to use lodge facilities and join activities offered at the lodge.

Languages: English, German, Afrikaans

Facilities:
Activities:

Kamelruhe Guest House 3

Guest House $
In Gochas
w142885

Tel: +264(0)63 250 224, Cell: +264(0)81 321 7480
kamelruhe@gmail.com
www.kamelruheguesthousenamibia.com

Double rooms with en-suite bathrooms and air-conditioning. There's Wi-Fi and DStv in the lounge. They offer hearty, Namibia-style dinners, breakfasts and lunches.

Languages: English, Afrikaans

Facilities:
Activities:

Red Dune Camp 4

Guest Farm $
35km or 26min SSE of Gochas
w232783

Tel: +264(0)63 250 164, Cell: +264(0)81 421 0927
reddunecamp@iway.na
www.reddunecamp.com

Two air-conditioned rooms (breakfast or self-catering). A permanent tent with two single beds, flush toilet, wash basin & hot water bush shower. Dinner can be booked in advance.

Languages: English

Facilities:
Activities:

Red Dune Camp 5

Farm Camp $
39km or 35min SSE of Gochas
w138055

Tel: +264(0)63 250 164, Cell: +264(0)81 421 0927, Fax: +264(0)88 617 718
reddunecamp@iway.na,
www.reddunecamp.com

Four campsites with flush toilet, hot shower and a braai area. Campsites can be reserved for one group if booked.

Languages: English

Facilities:
Activities:

Wildmoor Nature Camp 6

Farm Camp $
21km or 16min NW of Gochas
w232539

Tel: +264(0)61 306 423, Cell: +264(0)81 127 6282
nfjunius@gmail.com

A choice of campsites (with ablutions) under huge trees, or rustic campsites against the cliffs (only accessible by off-road vehicle).

Languages: English, German, Afrikaans

Facilities:
Activities:

Kalkrand

(photo: Johann Groenewald)

KALKRAND IS SO SMALL it can hardly be called a town but its general dealer, fuel station, school, police station and public clinic comfortably sustains the local farming community. The town is situated on the B1 national road between Mariental and Windhoek; the pans to its east are a big tourist attraction and various upmarket lodges can be found in amongst the red Kalahari dunes. Activities offered nearby include game drives, guided dune hikes, and mountain biking.

Traveller Description

The area around Kalkrand is renowned for its pans, of which Bitterwasser is the most famous. Situated 62km east of Kalkrand, it offers excellent thermal conditions for gliders and thus many gliding records are broken during the annual gliding season (Oct - Feb). A palm tree is planted for every record that falls and these line the avenue leading to the airfield.

Travel Info

Fresh meat, takeaways and basic necessities are available at the general dealer, but fuel supplies aren't guaranteed. There is a small government clinic in town.

Useful numbers: Clinic: +264(0)63 264 072 Kalkrand Fuel Station: +264(0)63 264 114

TRAVEL TIP! At the turnoff to Duineveld, 20km north of Kalkrand, there are a few roadside stalls where one can buy springbok rugs.

Town Info: Police: +264(0)63 264 015 Tow-in: +264(0)81 129 7490

Bitterwasser Lodge & Flying Centre 1

Lodge $$
61km or 59min ENE of Kalkrand
w138029

Tel: +264(0)63 265 300, Cell: +264(0)81 128 8657, Fax: +264(0)63 265 355
info@bitterwasser.com,
www.bitterwasser.com

Situated on the edge of the Bitterwasser Pan, you'll find accommodation in 13 rondavels, 22 en-suite bungalows and a country house. Bookings required.

Languages: English, German, Afrikaans

Facilities:

Activities:

Camelthorn Kalahari Lodge 2

Lodge $$
66km or 1h3min E of Kalkrand
w305237

Tel: +264(0)61 237 294, Fax: +264(0)61 237 295
intu-afrika@exclusive.com.na
www.intu-afrika.com

12 rooms featuring large showers, air-conditioning and a tea/coffee facilities. Venue offers restaurant, lounge, pool and bar.

Languages: English, German

Facilities:

Activities:

Intu Afrika Kalahari Reserve & Lodges 3

Game/Safari Lodge $$$
71km or 1h1min N of Mariental
w138423

Tel: +264(0)61 237 294, Fax: +264(0)61 237 295
intu-afrika@exclusive.com.na
www.intu-afrika.com

The Intu Africa Kalahari Private Game Reserve has three lodges: Suricate Tented Lodge, Zebra Kalahari Lodge and Camelthorn Kalahari Lodge. Venues offer bushman walks in the desert.

Languages: English, German

Facilities:

Activities:

Jansen Kalahari Guest Farm 4

Guest Farm $
43km or 45min ENE of Kalkrand
w361658

Tel: +264(0)63 265 323, Cell: +264(0)81 372 5147
jansen.louise01@gmail.com

Two self catering units. Enjoy magnificent view of sand dunes amongst the camelthorn trees.

Languages: English, Afrikaans

Facilities: FC @

Activities:

Jansen Kalahari Guest Farm 5

Farm Camp $
43km or 45min ENE of Kalkrand
w361659

Tel: +264(0)63 265 323, Cell: +264(0)81 372 5147
jansen.louise01@gmail.com

Five campsites enjoy hot showers, electricity and shade.

Languages: English, Afrikaans

Facilities: FC @

Activities:

Kalahari Auob Camp 6

Tented Camp $
65km or 1h8min NE of Kalkrand
w360446

Tel: +264(0)63 265 304, Cell: +264(0)81 480 7264
kalahariauob@gmail.com
www.kalahariauob.com

En-suite rooms at the farmstead or luxury tents on the banks of the dry Auob river.

Languages: English

Facilities: FC @

Activities:

Kalahari Red Dunes Lodge 7

Lodge $$$
10km or 8min ESE of Kalkrand
w228740

Tel: +264(0)61 240 020, Cell: +264(0)81 407 9127,
Fax: +264(0)63 264 029
reservations@reddduneslodge.com,
www.redduneslodge.com

12 Chalets with thatched roofs and canvas / stone walls. The main house has a restaurant, bar and pool. All the buildings are connected by boardwalks.

Languages: English, German, Afrikaans

Facilities: VISA @

Activities:

Teufelskrallen Tented Lodge 8

Tented Camp $$
737m or 1min N of Kalkrand
w255843

Tel: +264(0)61 240 020, Cell: +264(0)81 325 3023,
reservations@teufelskrallenlodge.com
www.teufelskrallenlodge.com

Six luxury tents on platforms overlooking the Kalahari landscape. Each with bathroom and fridge. Reception, restaurant and swimming pool are located 3km away at the Altes Farmhaus.

Languages: English, German, Afrikaans

Facilities: VISA FC @

Activities:

Zebra Kalahari Lodge 9

Lodge $$$
67km or 1h4min E of Kalkrand
w279378

Tel: +264(0)61 237 294 , Fax: +264(0)61 237 295
intu-afrika@exclusive.com.na
www.intu-afrika.com

8 Twin bedrooms connected to the main lodge building. Each room is air-conditioned and has an en-suite bathroom.

Languages: English, German

Facilities: VISA @

Activities:

Maltahöhe

(photo: Johann Groenewald)

MALTAHÖHE WAS ESTABLISHED IN 1899 as an outpost for the German Schutztruppe. The Maltahöhe Hotel, founded in 1907, is the oldest country hotel in Namibia and part of the original building is still in use. In the 1900s the bar was a popular watering hole for Hans Heinrich Von Wolf, master of Duwisib Castle; it still serves the same purpose for thirsty locals and travellers today.

These days the town is a business centre for sheep and cattle farmers, and serves as a tourist gateway for popular destinations such as Sossusvlei, Solitaire, Sesriem and Duwisib Castle.

Leliepan (Lily pan), 41km north of Maltahöhe, is usually bone-dry but after good rains this salt pan fills with water; a few days later the entire 800 hectare surface of the pan becomes covered with Amaryllis lilies (Crinum paludosum). This beautiful display of white and pink flowers only lasts for a week and usually takes place around February.

Traveller Description

Maltahöhe offers most facilities and services that travellers may need and is a popular overnight destination for travellers en-route to Sossusvlei, Sesriem and the Namib-Naukluft National Park. The Duwisib Castle is worth a visit too. The cemetery at the farm Nomtsas, 60km west of Maltahöhe, contains the graves of German pioneers and is a national monument. The site is situated on a private farm and thus, permission must be obtained before visiting the graves.

Travel Info

The Woermann Brock supermarket is well-stocked with fresh produce and meat; gas refills are available at Agra or Maraun's Garage.

Useful numbers: Clinic: +264(0)63 293 025   Agra: +264(0)63 293 029

TRAVEL TIP! If you are interested in seeing the Amaryllis lilies bloom on Leliepan, phone the Maltahöhe Hotel on +264(0)63 293 013 to find out when they're likely to be flowering.

Town Info: Police: +264(0)63 293 005   Tow-in: +264(0)81 298 1259

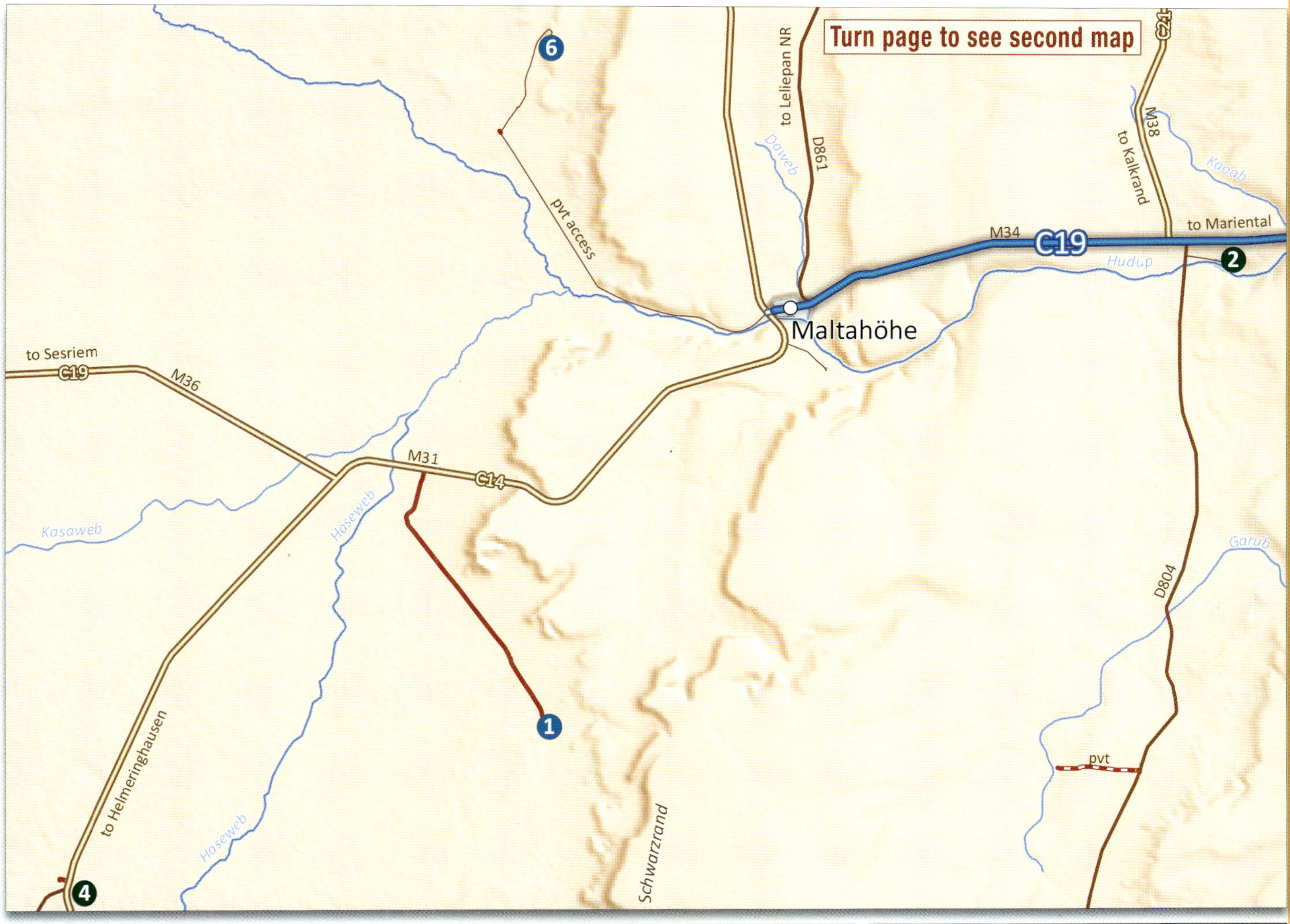

Gaste Farm Burgsdorf	**1**
Guest Farm	$$

27km or 41min SSW of Maltahöhe
w217089

Tel: +264(0)63 293 200, Cell: +264(0)81 128 6772,
Fax: +264(0)63 683 140
bookings@burgsdorf.org,
www.burgsdorf.org

Nine en-suite rooms with bath and toilet. Other facilities include swimming pool, restaurant, open-air grill and bar.

Languages: English, German, Afrikaans

Facilities:

Activities:

Hudup Campsite	**2**
Lodge Camp	$

15km or 11min E of Maltahöhe
w140248

Tel: +264(0)63 293 512, Cell: +264(0)81 226 9518,
Fax: +264(0)88 617 811
ottohunt@mweb.com.na

Located the banks of the Hudup River, these spacious campsites have clean ablutions. Activities include excellent bird viewing, hiking trails, 4x4 trails and more.

Languages: English, German, Afrikaans

Facilities:

Activities:

Hudup Guest House	**3**
Guest House	$

198 Johan Albrecht Street, Maltahöhe, Namibia
w142444

Cell: +264(0)81 323 0410
steyn.venter@outlook.com

Six en-suite rooms of which three are family rooms. One room is disabled-friendly. Under new management since June 2017.

Languages: English, Afrikaans, Italian, German

Facilities:

Lisbon Road House & Camping	**4**
Camping	$

37km or 24min SW of Maltahöhe
w267832

Tel: +264(0)63 293 107, Cell: +264(0)81 129 3201
judith@iway.na

Campsites with showers, toilets and braai facilities. An en-route stop that sells food and farm-fresh products.

Languages: English

Facilities:

Maltahöhe Hotel	**5**
Hotel	$

Johan Albrecht st, Maltahöhe
w140246

Tel: +264(0)67 240 901
maltahohe@travel-weaver.com
www.maltahoehe-hotel.com

Cosy country hotel that offers en-suite double rooms or family rooms with shared bathroom facilities. There's also an 18-bed backpackers dormitory.

Languages: English, German, Afrikaans

Facilities:

Activities:

Namseb Lodge	**6**
Game/Safari Lodge	$

18km or 26min NW of Maltahöhe
w140286

Tel: +264(0)63 293 166, Cell: +264(0)81 325 4790
reservation@namseb.com
www.namseb.com

Double rooms as well as self-catering chalets within a private game reserve on top of the Namseb Plateau.

Languages: English, German, Afrikaans

Facilities:

Activities:

Maltahöhe

Oa Hera Namib Campsite 7

Camping $
8 Main St, Maltahöhe
w207486

Tel: +264(0)63 293 028, Cell: +264(0)81 215 2595, Fax: +264(0)88 635 417
oaheraa@iway.na

Each campsite has a bathroom (cold showers), stone tables and chairs and a private braai. There's also a restaurant, curio shop and secure parking.

Languages: English

Facilities:

Pappot Accommodation 8

Bed and Breakfast $
116 Main St, Maltahöhe
w360456

Tel: +264(0)63 293 397, Cell: +264(0)81 271 9414
pappot@iway.na

Accommodation in rooms, includes breakfast. Nearby you'll find a supermarket, arts and crafts, coffee shop, local wines, ice and soft drinks.

Languages: English, Afrikaans, German

Facilities:

Pappot Campsites 9

Caravan Park $
116 Main St, Maltahöhe
w142598

Tel: +264(0)63 293 397, Cell: +264(0)81 271 9414
pappot@iway.na

Campsites with shade nets, braai areas and clean ablutions. Two rooms available too. Pappot is a well-known coffee shop and supermarket in the main road of Maltahöhe.

Languages: English, Afrikaans, German

Facilities:

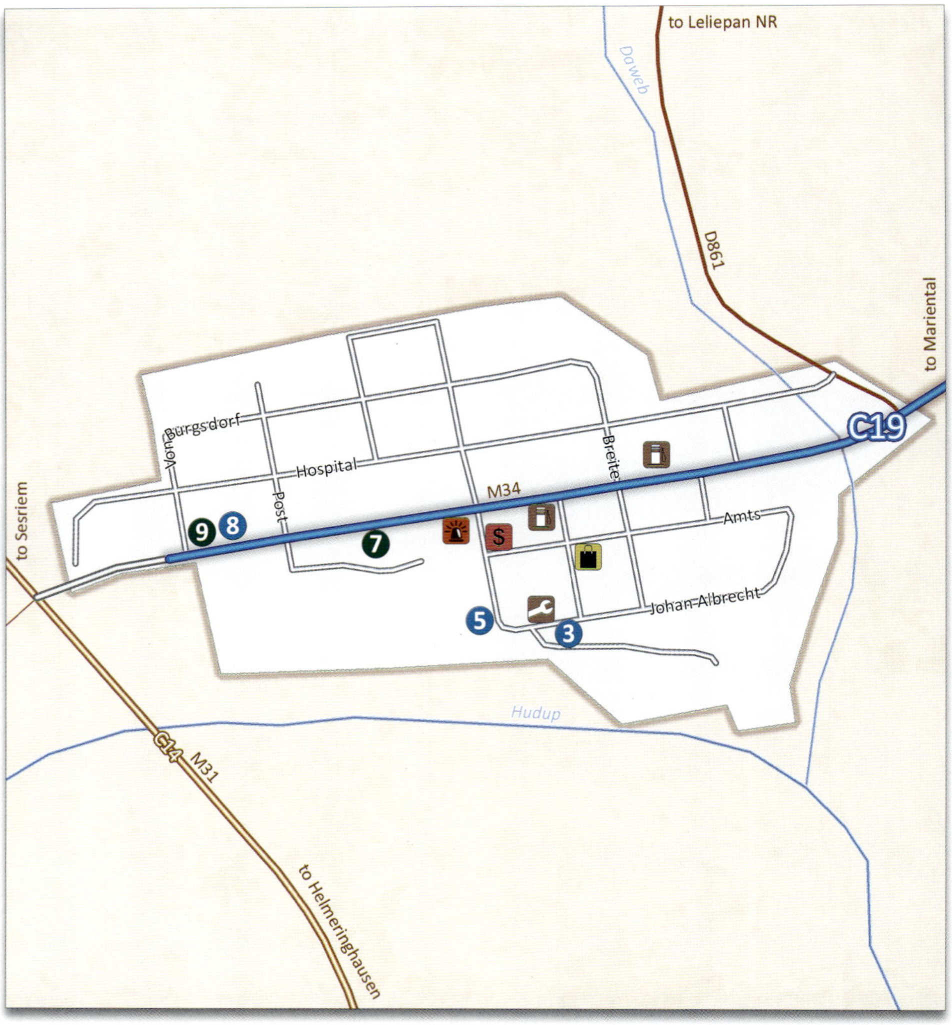

"The real voyage of discovery consists not in seeking new landscapes, but in having new eyes."

Marcel Proust

right: Amaryllis in flower at Leliepan just north of Maltahöhe. (photo: Heiner Dillmann)

opposite page: A thunderstorm brews below the Tsaris Pass, west of Maltahöhe. (photo: Heiner Dillmann)

N 43988 W

Mariental

(photo: Ian-Ray Nel)

MARIENTAL WAS FOUNDED IN 1912 as a railway stop between Windhoek and Keetmanshoop. It's one of the main towns of south-central Namibia and serves as a business centre for the surrounding commercial cattle farms. For travellers passing through on the B1 highway it offers good facilities and services.

The Hardap Game Reserve 45km west of Mariental is home to several bird and large mammal species. It encloses Namibia's largest dam, the Hardap Dam, which is situated on the Fish River. With a surface area of 25km², the dam is a popular angling destination and home to a successful freshwater fish institute.

Hendrik Witbooi, the Nama leader during the War of Resistance (1904-1907) against German rule, had his home in Gibeon, a small village 65km south of Mariental. The town is better known for the discovery of large pieces of the 15+ ton Gibeon meteorite. These pieces are on display in the Post Street Mall in Windhoek.

Traveller Description

The town offers all the facilities and services a traveller may need before heading off into the surrounding Namib and Kalahari deserts. The local Spar is well stocked with supplies and has its own bakery and Tops liquor store next door. Gas can be refilled at Von Watzdorf Hardware or Agra.

Travel Info

The nearby Hardap Game Reserve is a very popular destination amongst locals and tourists alike. Activities like game drives, bird watching, guided walks and boat trips are available. Camping as well as self-catering accommodation is offered.

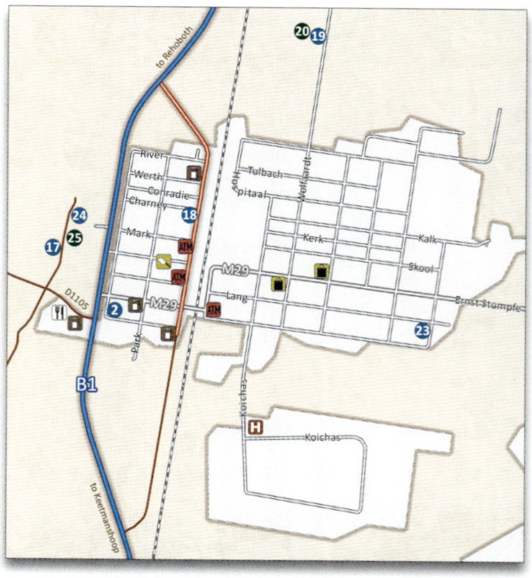

TRAVEL TIP! Hardap Dam is home to the largest breeding colony of pelicans in Namibia, a species listed as vulnerable in Southern Africa.

Town Info:

Hospital: +264(0)63 245 250
Doctor: +264(0)63 242 007

Police: +264(0)63 345 000
Tow-in: +264(0)81 250 1774

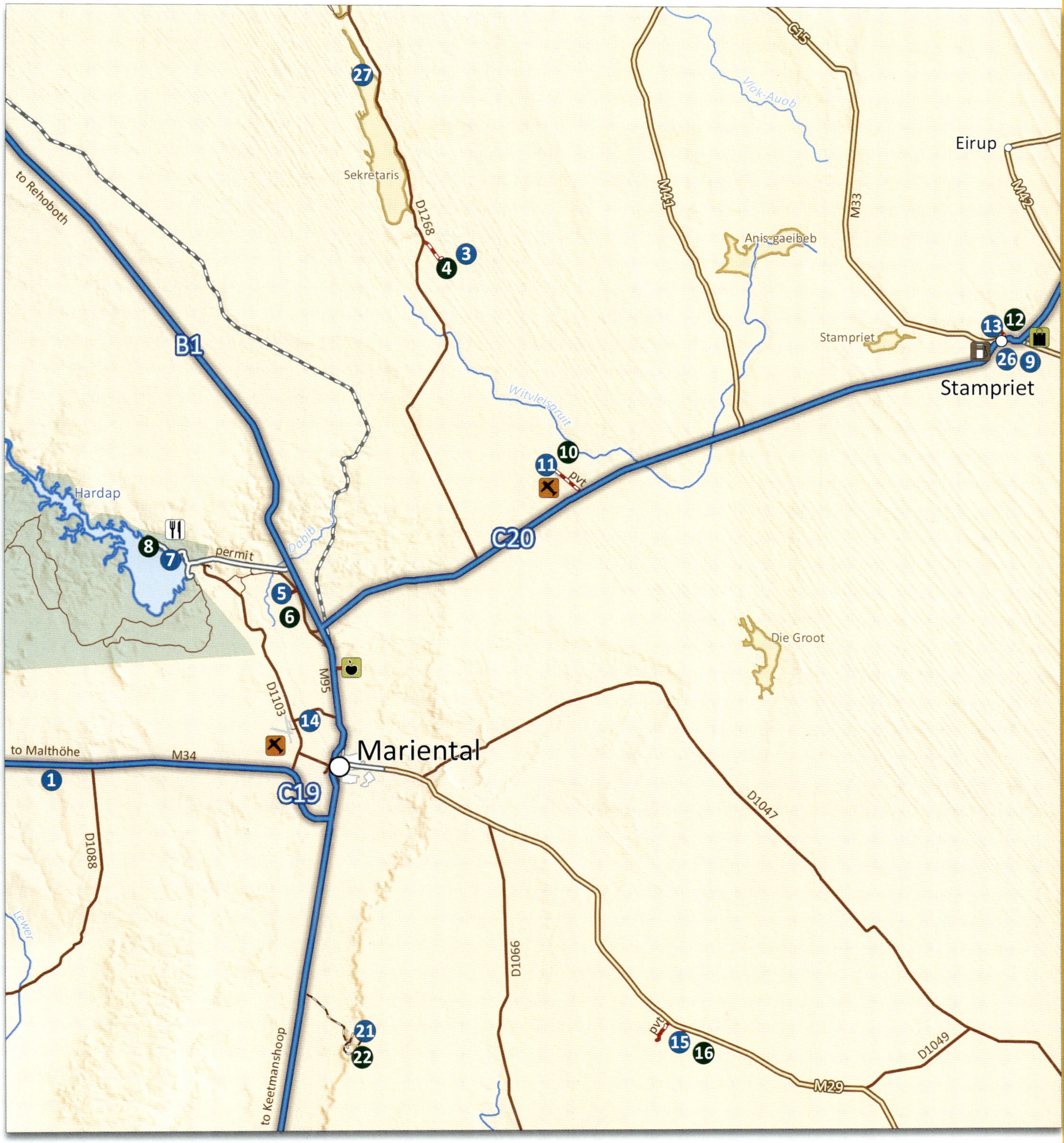

Africa Safari Lodge — 1

Lodge — $$
18km or 15min W of Mariental
w272017

Tel: +264(0)63 243 411
bookings@africasafarilodge.com.na
www.africasafarilodge.com.na

20 Chalets with views of the plains. Each chalet has a bathroom, tea/coffee facilities, satellite TV and air-conditioner.

Languages: English

Facilities:

Activities:

Anandi Guesthouse — 2

Guest House — $
15 River St, Mariental
w142515

Tel: +264(0)63 242 220, Cell: +264(0)81 241 1822, Fax: +264(0)63 242 223
anandi@iway.na,
www.anandiguesthouse.com

Luxury, air-conditioned, en-suite bedrooms, all with separate garden entrance, DStv, tea tray and fridge. Most with spa bath and shower. Secure parking.

Languages: English, Afrikaans

Facilities:

Activities:

Bagatelle Kalahari Game Ranch — 3

Game/Safari Lodge — $$$
51km or 48min NNE of Mariental
w142843

Tel: +264(0)63 240 982, Fax: +264(0)63 241 252
bagatelle@resdest.com
www.bagatelle-kalahari-gameranch.com

Three different styles of luxurious chalets, all with en-suite bathrooms. Airport transfers available.

Languages: English, German, Afrikaans

Facilities:

Activities:

Mariental

Bagatelle Kalahari Game Ranch — 4

Farm Camp — $$
52km or 49min NNE of Mariental
w228038

Tel: +264(0)63 240 982, Fax: +264(0)63 241 252
bagatelle@resdest.com
www.bagatelle-kalahari-gameranch.com

Five campsites, each with its own ablution facilities. The venue is located on the edge of the southern Kalahari Desert.

Languages: English, German, Afrikaans

Facilities:
Activities:

Bastion Farmyard B&B — 5

Bed and Breakfast — $
15km or 35min NNW of Mariental
w193051

Tel: +264(0)63 240 827, Cell: +264(0)81 274 5574, Fax: +264(0)88 630 431
bastion@iway.na,
www.bastionfarmyard.com

Accommodates 16 people in five spacious rooms, all with private entrances, air-conditioning, ceiling fans, heaters, coffee/tea facilities, fridges etc. Free Wi-Fi.

Languages: English, Afrikaans

Facilities:
Activities:

Bastion Farmyard B&B — 6

Farm Camp — $
15km or 35min NNW of Mariental
w254366

Tel: +264(0)63 240 827, Cell: +264(0)81 274 5574, Fax: +264(0)88 630 431
bastion@iway.na,
www.bastionfarmyard.com

Four paved, shady, spacious campsites can accommodate six people each. Each site has its own ablution and kitchen area, lights, braai facility and power point.

Languages: English, Afrikaans

Facilities:
Activities:

Hardap Resort — 7

Resort — $$
23km or 32min NW of Mariental
w137434

Tel: +264(0)61 285 7200, Cell: +264(0)81 218 1613, Fax: +264(0)63 247 770
reservations@nwr.com.na,
www.nwr.com.na

Accommodation in VIP, family and bush chalets. There's a restaurant overlooking the dam (popular for angling and watersports) Venue is motorbike-friendly.

Languages: English

Facilities:
Activities:

Hardap Resort — 8

Holiday Resort Camp — $
25km or 35min NW of Mariental
w140790

Tel: +264(0)61 427 200, Cell: +264(0)81 218 1613, Fax: +264(0)63 247 770
reservations@nwr.com.na,
www.nwr.com.na

This venue encompasses Namibia's largest dam and offers camping. Popular spot for anglers.

Languages: English

Facilities:
Activities:

Indigo Self-Catering — 9

Self-catering — $
62km or 39min ENE of Mariental
w361748

Tel: +264(0)63 260 032, Cell: +264(0)81 294 7337
w.m.snyman@gmail.com
www.indigoselfcatering.com

Luxurious double and single rooms with air-conditioning and fully-equipped kitchenettes.

Languages: English

Facilities:
Activities:

Kalahari Anib Campsite — 10

Lodge Camp — $$
35km or 27min NE of Mariental
w221354

Tel: +264(0)61 427 200 , Cell: +264(0)81 129 2424, Fax: +264(0)61 251 863
info@gondwana-collection.com,
store.gondwana-collection.com

Private, well-spaced campsites, each with its own ablution facilities, power points and braai area. Reservations advisable.

Languages: English

Facilities:
Activities:

Kalahari Anib Lodge — 11

Lodge — $$
34km or 26min NE of Mariental
w138443

Tel: +264(0)61 427 200 , Cell: +264(0)81 129 2424, Fax: +264(0)61 251 863
info@gondwana-collection.com,
store.gondwana-collection.com

Venue caters for groups as well as individual travellers. A choice of rooms with private verandas leading onto a courtyard, or chalets. There's a bar. Reservations mandatory.

Languages: English

Facilities:
Activities:

Kalahari Farm Campsite — 12

Camping — $$
63km or 40min ENE of Mariental
w360392

Tel: +264(0)61 427 200, Cell: +264(0)81 129 2424, Fax: +264(0)61 251 863
info@gondwana-collection.com,
store.gondwana-collection.com

Private campsites located in a grove of palm trees. Reservations advisable.

Languages: English

Facilities:
Activities:

Kalahari Farmhouse — 13

Guest Farm — $$
63km or 40min ENE of Mariental
w219520

Tel: +264(0)61 427 200 , Cell: +264(0)81 129 2424, Fax: +264(0)61 251 863
info@gondwana-collection.com,
store.gondwana-collection.com

Accommodation in comfortable bungalows. The restaurant serves delicious fresh farm produce. There are many activities on the farm for guests to enjoy. Reservations mandatory.

Languages: English

Facilities:
Activities:

Koha Guest House — 14

Guest House — $
6km or 8min NW of Mariental
w141430

Tel: +264(0)63 242 915, Cell: +264(0)81 124 6613, Fax: +264(0)63 240 836
bookings@kohaguesthouse.com,
www.kohaguesthouse.com

Six luxury, en-suite rooms. Satellite television is available in the lounge. Campsites have electricity and hot showers.

Languages: English, German, Spanish, Afrikaans

Facilities:
Activities:

Lapa Lange Game Lodge — 15

Lodge — $$$
34km or 26min SE of Mariental
w207988

Tel: +264(0)63 241 801, Cell: +264(0)81 129 1085, Fax: +264(0)63 240 384
lapalange@iway.na,
www.lapalange.com

Located on the Kalk Plateau, this lodge offers 18 luxury double rooms and permanent tents. Guests can enjoy warm Namibian hospitality, good food and trips into the Kalahari Desert.

Languages: English, Afrikaans

Facilities:
Activities:

Lapa Lange Game Lodge 16

Lodge Camp $$
34km or 26min SE of Mariental
w247250

Tel: +264(0)63 241 801, Cell: +264(0)81 129 1085,
Fax: +264(0)63 240 384
lapalange@iway.na,
www.lapalange.com

Six campsites on grassed stands. Campers can enjoy lodge activities like trips into the Kalahari Desert, photographic tours and sundowner drives.

Languages: English, Afrikaans

Facilities:

Activities:

La Vida Inn B&B and Camping 17

Inn $
West of B1, 1km or 1min WNW of Mariental
w142534

Tel: +264(0)63 242 121, Cell: +264(0)81 122 9148,
Fax: +264(0)63 241 600
lavidainnbb@gmail.com

Accommodation in comfortable, spacious, en-suite rooms; all equipped with free Wi-Fi, air-conditioning, satellite TV and more. Secure parking.

Languages: English

Facilities:

Activities:

Mariental Hotel 18

Hotel $
c/o Hendrik Witbooi Ave & Charney Rd, Mariental
w140262

Tel: +264(0)63 242 466, Fax: +264(0)63 242 493
mrlhotel@iafrica.com.na
www.marientalhotel.com

Comfortable, air-conditioned, en-suite rooms, all with DStv and coffee/tea facilities. And there's a ladies bar, lapa, braai facilities and secure parking.

Languages: English, Afrikaans

Facilities:

Activities:

Mariental Restcamp 19

Self-catering $
1km or 3min N of Mariental
w362062

Fax: +264(0)63 241 549, Cell: +264(0)81 034 0310
mrc@iway.na

Overnight boma for tour groups, plus self-catering rooms. There's also a small shop and 24-hour security. Reservations mandatory.

Languages: English, Afrikaans

Facilities:

Activities:

Mariental Restcamp 20

Camping $
1km or 3min N of Mariental
w362061

Fax: +264(0)63 241 549, Cell: +264(0)81 034 0310
mrc@iway.na

10 Private campsites, each with bathroom and braai. Plus, 10 campsites with braais. There's also a small shop and 24-hour security.

Languages: English, Afrikaans

Facilities:

Activities:

Oppikopi Resort 21

Self-catering $
22km or 26min S of Mariental (of which 6km is 4WD)
w188890

Tel: +264(0)63 240 682, Cell: +264(0)81 424 2491
oppikopi@yahoo.com

Two-room chalets available. As well as one chalet which sleeps four (double bed and two singles). Bathrooms and kitchens are seperate from the chalets.

Languages: English, Afrikaans

Facilities: FC

Activities:

Oppikopi Resort 22

Camping $
22km or 26min S of Mariental (of which 6km is 4WD)
w188945

Tel: +264(0)63 240 682, Cell: +264(0)81 424 2491
oppikopi@yahoo.com

All campsites have water, electricity, lighting and braai area. Off-road vehicle required for access.

Languages: English, Afrikaans

Facilities: FC

Activities:

Rest Nest Accommodation 23

Self-catering $
334 Lang St, Mariental
w267830

Tel: +264(0)63 242 219, Cell: +264(0)81 148 6211,
Fax: +264(0)88 644 244
hardpmrl@iway.na,
www.restnestaccommodation.com.na

Accommodation includes budget, standard and self-catering rooms. All of which have air-conditioning and free Wi-Fi. Secure, off-street parking available.

Languages: English, Afrikaans

Facilities:

Activities:

River Chalets 24

Self-catering $$
Main Road, Mariental
w142533

Tel: +264(0)63 240 515, Cell: +264(0)81 128 2601,
Fax: +264(0)63 242 601
garbers@iway.na,
www.riverchalets.com

Luxury, air-conditioned chalets with DStv, private braai facilities and shaded parking. Breakfast, and packs available on request. Security on duty 12 hours per day.

Languages: English, Afrikaans

Facilities:

Activities:

River Chalets 25

Camping $
B1 Main Road, Mariental
w360398

Tel: +264(0)63 240 515, Cell: +264(0)81 128 2601,
Fax: +264(0)63 242 601
garbers@iway.na,
www.riverchalets.com

Private campsites, each with their own electricity, braai and ablution facilities.

Languages: English, Afrikaans

Facilities:

Activities:

Stampriet Historical Guesthouse 26

Guest House $$
62km or 39min ENE of Mariental
w232540

Tel: +264(0)63 260 013, Cell: +264(0)81 244 7448,
Fax: +264(0)63 260 215
stampriet@iway.na,
www.stamprietguesthouse.com

En-suite rooms decorated in an antique fashion. Each room is equipped with air-conditioner, Wi-Fi and patio. Ideal stopover on your way to the Kalahari Desert.

Languages: English, Afrikaans

Facilities:

Activities:

Suricate Tented Lodge 27

Tented Camp $$$
67km or 54min N of Mariental
w305244

Tel: +264(0)61 237 294 , Fax: +264(0)61 237 295
intu-afrika@exclusive.com.na
www.intu-afrika.com

12 permanent tents, each with open-air, en-suite bathroom, deck, mini bar, safe and mosquito net. A honeymoon tented suite is also available.

Languages: English, Dutch

Facilities:

Activities:

Rehoboth

(photo: Ian-Ray Nel)

IN 1845 A GERMAN MISSION was established among the resident Nama (Khoikhoi) in the place known today as the town of Rehoboth. However, the mission was closed after coming under frequent attack from the Nama. In 1868 Hermanus van Wyk, of mixed race or 'Baster' family, left the Cape Colony to escape discrimination and harassment. In 1870 Van Wyk's clan discovered the fertile area around Rehoboth, which at that time had largely been abandoned by the Nama people who'd came under attack of the Oorlam Afrikaners. In the late 18th century Oorlam Afrikaners, a sub-tribe of the Nama people, migrated out of the Cape Colony and were assimilated into Damaraland.

In 1885 Captain Hermanus van Wyk, who was the leader of the Rehoboth people, negotiated with the German Empire for protection against the local tribes. In return he supported the German Empire during the War of Resistance (1904-1907), the Herero and Nama uprising against German colonial rule. During the WW1 they refused to take up their weapons against South Africa, with the result that they gained several privileges above the Herero and Nama during the subsequent South African occupation of South West Africa (now Namibia).

Today the town is inhabited by the Baster community, the racially mixed descendents of Hermanus Van Wyk and the local Khoikhoi people. Their language is still Afrikaans and they are a highly respected minority community with strong political influences.

Traveller Description

Rehoboth is located 95km south of Windhoek on a plateau covered in dense Acacia woodland and sporting several hot springs. These are the first lush green surroundings the traveller sees when travelling up from the south.

The history of the Rehoboth Basters is recorded in the museum in town. It details their cultural heritage as well as the archaeological and geological finds in the area. The Lutheran Paulus Church was inaugurated in 1908 and is a well-known landmark in Rehoboth. There is a large Acacia forest within the municipal boundaries of Rehoboth, with some camel thorn trees estimated to be more than 2 000 years old. The Rehoboth Spa has an outside thermal pool as well as an indoor one but the facilities aren't on par with other hot Namibian springs, such as Gross Barmen or Ai-Ais.

Five kilometres west of the town is Lake Oanob, the town's main water supply since 1990. It's enclosed in a private nature reserve, Oanob Lake Resort where you'll find several species of antelope and numerous birds. This popular resort offers a variety of aquatic sports, picnic facilities and overnight accommodation (camping or chalets). It also caters for conferences; a traveller in search of peace and quiet may be disappointed by the number of delegates sharing the facilities.

Travel Info

There are several good shops in town, as well as a bakery and liquor store. Gas can be refilled at Afrox. The town also boasts a big shopping centre conveniently located right next to the highway.

Useful numbers:

Rehoboth Museum: +264(0)62 522 954

TRAVEL TIP! The Rehoboth museum is open Mondays to Fridays from 09:00 to 16:30 (closed for lunch between 12:30 and 14:00). It's best to call and confirm that they're open before taking the drive to Rehoboth to visit the museum. The Lutheran Paulus Church is also well worth a visit.

(photo: Ian-Ray Nel)

Town Info:

Hospital:	+264(0)62 522 006
Police:	+264(0)62 523 223
Doctor:	+264(0)62 522 006
Tow-in:	+264(0)81 292 8833

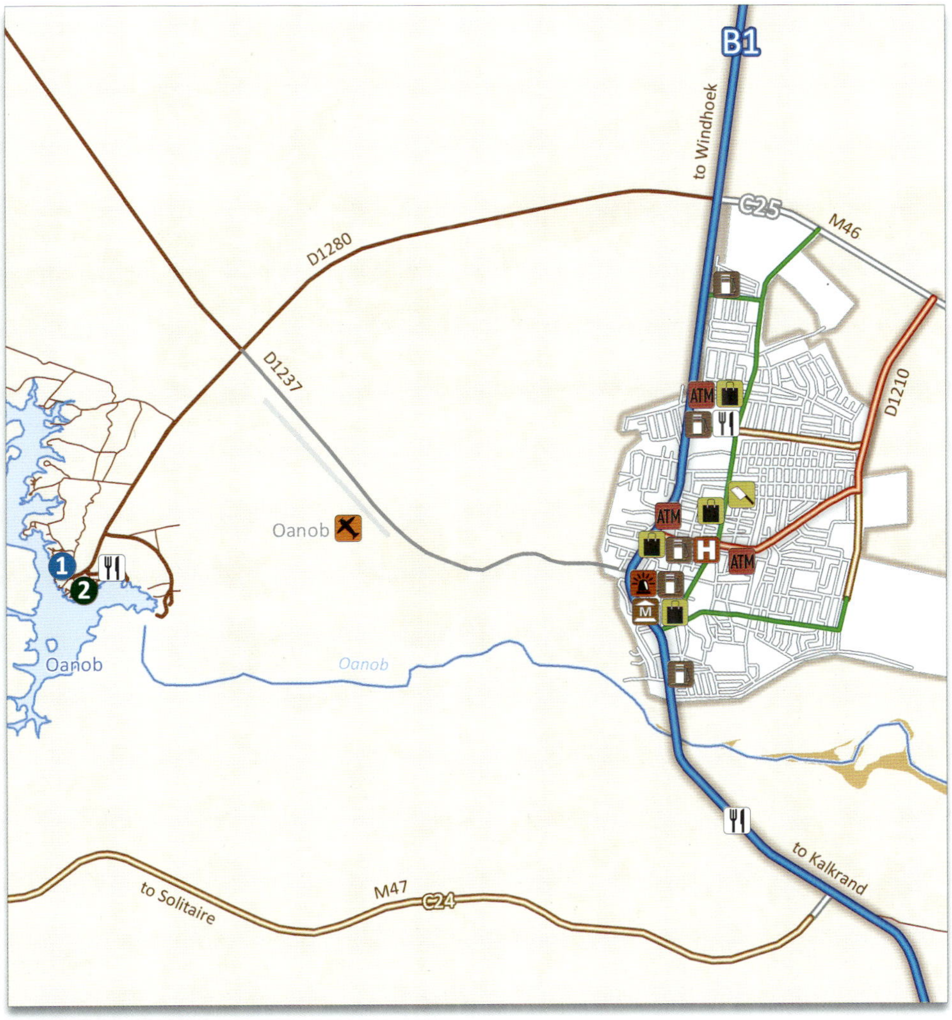

Lake Oanob Resort 1

Resort $$
8km or 12min W of Rehoboth
w138807

Tel: +264(0)62 522 370, Cell: +264(0)81 124 0874, Fax: +264(0)62 524 112
reservations@oanob.com.na,
www.oanob.com.na

Luxury accommodation in self-catering 2- and 3-bedroom chalets as well as in single, double or family size en-suite rooms. This resort is popular for its wide variety of water sports.

Languages: English

Facilities:

Activities:

Lake Oanob Resort 2

Holiday Resort Camp $
8km or 12min W of Rehoboth
w189186

Tel: +264(0)62 522 370, Cell: +264(0)81 124 0874, Fax: +264(0)62 524 112
reservations@oanob.com.na,
www.oanob.com.na

Campsites are situated on the waterfront and have individual braai areas; they share neat ablution facilities. This resort has a lot to offer in terms of water sport activities.

Languages: English

Facilities:

Activities:

Windhoek

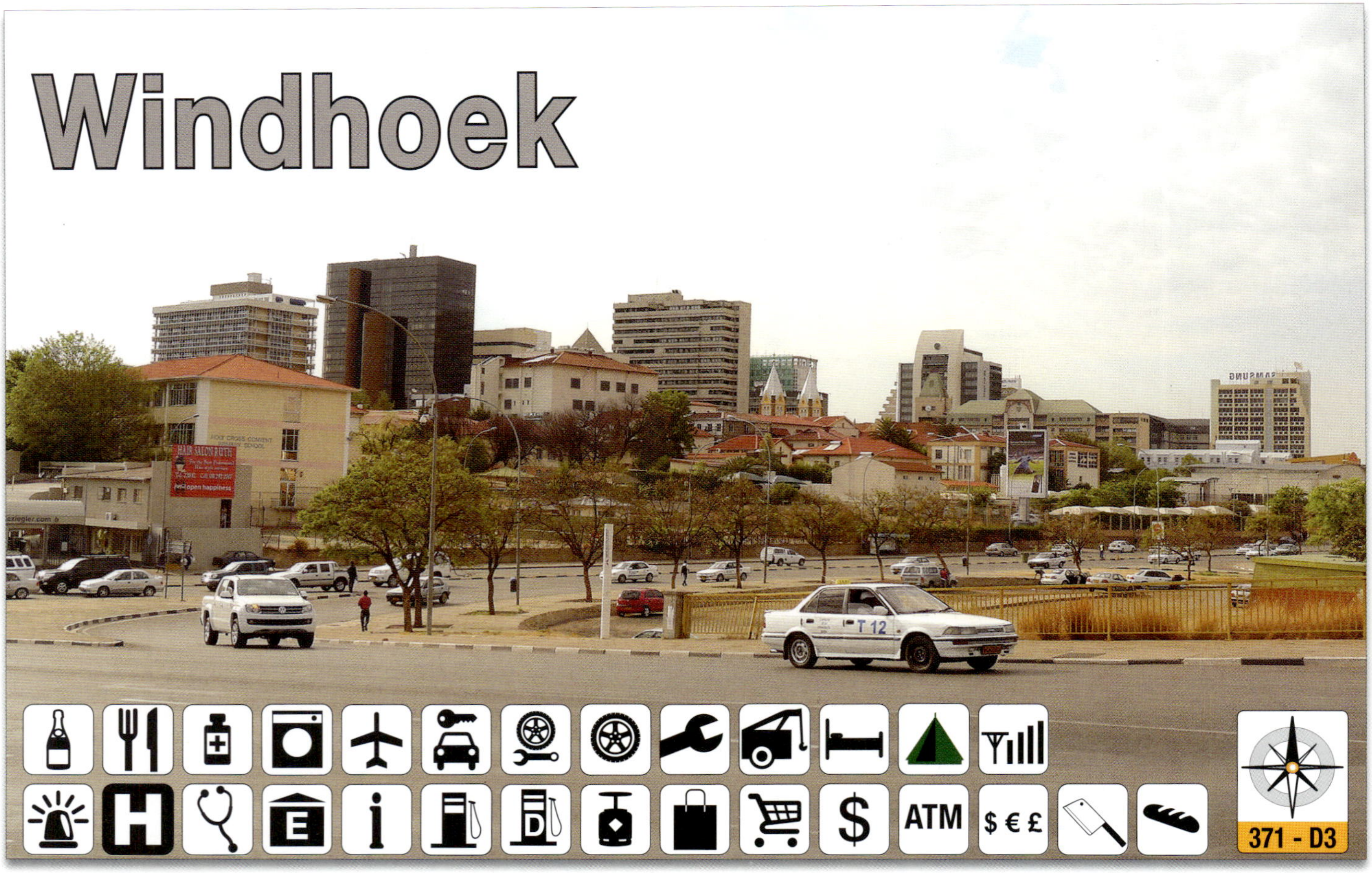

(photo: Frank Höppener)

WITH A POPULATION OF MORE THAN 325 000 PEOPLE, the capital is the country's largest city and its social, economic and cultural centre. Its origins date back to 1849 when the Oorlam Captain, Jan Jonker Afrikaner, settled at the site of the strongest spring in the area. It's unclear where the name Windhoek originates from, but one theory is that Afrikaner called it Windhoek (Afrikaans for windy corner) as the area experiences windy days for more than 70% of the year. The Namas called it "/Ai-//Gams" (Fire Water) and the Herero named it "Otjomuise" (Place of Steam), after the vapour escaping from the hot springs in the area.

Captain Afrikaner built a stone church which was also used as a school but the settlement was destroyed during the war between the Nama and Herero. In 1884 South West Africa was declared a German protectorate and on 18 October 1890 Major Curt Von Francois laid the foundation stone for a fort in Windhoek, from where the Schutztruppe could maintain order. The strong springs in the area provided water for drinking and irrigation, and Windhoek formed a buffer between the warring Herero and Ovambo.

After the War of Resistance ended in 1907 development accelerated as people migrated from the countryside to the city and soon there was also a large influx of European settlers from Germany and South Africa. The German influence can still be seen today.

Traveller Description

Windhoek is a beautiful, friendly, modern city that's well worth a couple of days of your time. The historical city centre is easily explored on foot and there are other attractions worthy of a visit.

- The Independence Museum was erected in 2014 and showcases Namibia's history of anti-colonial resistance and the national liberation struggle.
- Christuskirche near the Independence Museum is the oldest Evangelical Lutheran church in Namibia. This beautiful church was built in the Gothic revival style with Art Nouveau elements.
- Alte Feste is the original fort built by Curt von Francois and is the oldest building in Windhoek. A statue of a soldier on a horse, Reiterdenkmal, which commemorated the German people who died during the Namibian War of Resistance, was removed from its position in front of the fort in 2013 and replaced with a Genocide Memorial. A statue of Sam Nujoma, founding President of the Namibia nation, was erected on the same hill overlooking the city.
- Tintenpalast ('Ink Palace') houses the parliament and gets its name from the high amount of ink used by the members of parliament, this building was completed in 1913.

- The Parliament Gardens are one of the most beautiful gardens in Namibia and the perfect place for a relaxing stroll or a picnic.
- The National Botanical Garden displays Namibia's plants in a 12-hectare nature reserve. Note, it's closed on weekends and public holidays.
- Heroes' Acre is Namibia's official war memorial. Built on one of the hills just south of Windhoek, it was designed to foster a spirit of patriotism and nationalism.
- The Gibeon Meteorites Display showcases 30 pieces of a large meteorite weighing more than 15 tons, said to be over 600 million years old.
- The Namibia Craft Centre is situated inside the old breweries complex on Tal Street and houses Namibian arts and crafts, bookshops, a restaurant and coffee shop. It is the city's tourist hub.

Travel Info

Windhoek meets all a traveller's requirements. There are modern, well-stocked grocery stores, specialist shops selling camping and travel gear, banks for foreign exchange, and much more.

The hospital number quoted is for the private Roman Catholic hospital. The contact number for the Medi-Clinic hospital in Windhoek is +264(0)61 433 1000.

TRAVEL TIP! You are not allowed to take photographs of government buildings in Namibia, even if there are no signs to this effect. Opening hours of museums may be restricted to office hours so it's best to confirm these before planning your day.

Town Info:

Hospital:+264(0)61 433 1000
Tow-in: +264(0)61 222 067
Police: +264(0)61 209 4111
Tourism: +264(0)61 290 6000
Doctor: +264(0)61 222 749
Embassy: +264(0)61 205 7111

African Kwela Guest House 1

Guest House $
18 Palm St, Suiderhof, Windhoek
w208764

Tel: +264(0)61 227 029, Cell: +264(0)81 122 8108,
Fax: +264(0)61 227 032
kwela@internet.com.na,
www.africankwela.com

Clean, comfortable single, double or family en-suite rooms. Last mentioned can accommodate three adults.

Languages: English, German

Facilities: FC @

Activities:

African Nest Accommodation 2

Lodge $
c/o Caprivi St & Nelson Mandela Ave, Eros, Windhoek
w252783

Tel: +264(0)61 306 192, Cell: +264(0)81 777 9100
africannest10@gmail.com

Clean, non-smoking, en-suite rooms. Each with TV, fridge and free Wi-Fi. Some rooms have air-conditioning, others have fans. Very close to the famous restaurant, Joe's Beerhouse.

Languages: English

Facilities: @

Activities:

Airport Hunting And Guest Farm 3

Guest Farm $$
51km or 43min ENE of Windhoek
w206683

Tel: +264(0)62 540 475, Cell: +264(0)81 128 8288,
Fax: +264(0)62 540 475
info@airportfarm-namibia.com,
www.airportfarm-namibia.com

Spacious double rooms with own bathrooms and porch. There's also a lounge, dining room and lapa.

Languages: English, German, Afrikaans

Facilities: FC

Activities:

Airport Hunting And Guest Farm 4

Farm Camp $
51km or 43min ENE of Windhoek
w255814

Tel: +264(0)62 540 475, Cell: +264(0)81 128 8288,
Fax: +264(0)62 540 475
info@airportfarm-namibia.com,
www.airportfarm-namibia.com

Spacious campsites with a hot water 'donkey'. This venue also offer secure storage for camping equipment and vehicles.

Languages: English, German, Afrikaans

Facilities: FC

Activities:

Airport Lodge 5

Lodge $$
22km or 19min E of Windhoek
w141622

Tel: +264(0)61 231 491, Cell: +264(0)81 122 6101,
reservations@airportlodgenamibia.com
www.airportlodgenamibia.com

Full-board or self-catering thatched chalets, with en-suite bathrooms, mini-bars, coffee/tea facilities, satellite TV, private wooden decks and braai areas.

Languages: English, German, Afrikaans, Otjiherero

Facilities: VISA @

Activities:

Aloe Travel Lodge 6

Lodge $
8-12 Wika Drive, Olympia, Windhoek
w208755

Tel: +264(0)61 251 306, Cell: +264(0)81 127 2339,
Fax: +264(0)61 272 110
aloe@iway.na,
www.aloetravellodge.com

Single, double or family rooms, and self-catering chalets. All situated on a 9hectare area in the southern part of Windhoek. Quiet but close to the city.

Languages: English

Facilities: VISA

Activities:

Windhoek

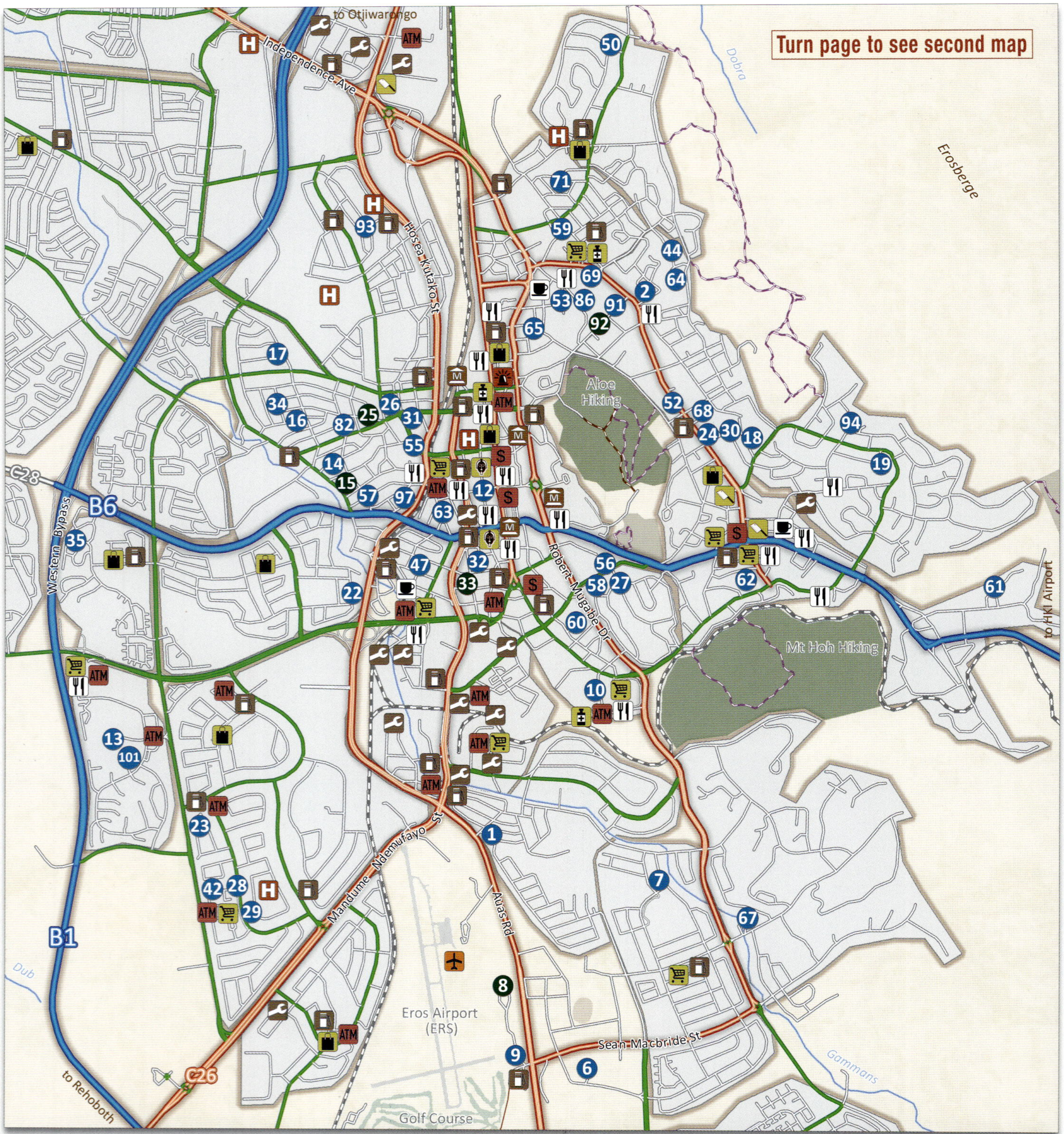

AnJo Villa Guesthouse 7

Guest House $
16 Mose Tjitendero St, Olympia, Windhoek
w208760

Tel: +264(0)61 252 027, Cell: +264(0)81 122 7022, Fax: +264(0)61 255 006
anjo@mtcmobile.com.na, www.anjogroup.com

This venue offers a full breakfast, as well as access to dining & entertainment areas, lounge, pool and secure undercover parking.

Languages: English

Facilities:
Activities:

Arebbusch Rest Camp 8

Lodge Camp $
c/o B1 & Sean Mcbride St, Windhoek South
w138376

Tel: +264(0)61 252 255, Fax: +264(0)61 251 670
reservations@arebbusch.com
www.arebbusch.com

Caravan and camping sites available - communal ablution facilities. Popular stopover for overlanders. Restaurant and bar on site.

Languages: English, Afrikaans

Facilities:
Activities:

Arebbusch Travel Lodge 9

Lodge $$
c/o B1 and Sean Mcbride St, Olympia, Windhoek South
w138100

Tel: +264(0)61 252 255, Fax: +264(0)61 251 670
reservations@arebbusch.com
www.arebbusch.com

Standard rooms with en-suite bathrooms. Self-catering en-suite chalets with kitchenette and braai stands. Or budget rooms with communal ablution facilities.

Languages: English, Afrikaans

Facilities:
Activities:

Auas City Hotel 10

Hotel $$
Centaurus St, Maerua Park, Windhoek Central,
w198516

Tel: +264(0)61 239 805, Fax: +264(0)61 239 826
info@auascityhotel.com
www.auascityhotel.com

Comfortable, affordable rooms with air-conditioning, coffee/tea facilities and Wi-Fi. Conveniently-located venue.

Languages: English, Afrikaans

Facilities: VISA FC @

Activities:

Auas Safari Lodge 11

Lodge $$$
48km or 45min SE of Windhoek
w139465

Tel: +264(0)61 228 104, Cell: +264(0)81 317 1207, Fax: +264(0)88 625 903
auassafarilodge@journeynamibia.com, www.auas-safarilodge.com

14 Comfortable, double, en-suite bedrooms. Ideal for smaller groups and families. Panoramic views.

Languages: English, Afrikaans

Facilities: VISA FC @

Activities:

Avani Windhoek Hotel & Casino 12

Hotel $$$
129 Independence Ave, Gustav Voigts Centre, Windhoek Central
w138957

Tel: +264(0)61 280 0000, Fax: +264(0)61 222 260
windhoek@avanihotels.com
www.minorhotels.com

173 Rooms on 14 floors. All rooms have en-suite bathrooms and air-conditioning. This venue was formerly the Kalahari Sands Hotel.

Languages: English, German, Afrikaans

Facilities: VISA @

Activities:

A-Z Boutique Guesthouse 13

Bed and Breakfast $
17 Range St, Pionierspark Ext 1, Windhoek
w208771

Tel: +264(0)61 244 445, Cell: +264(0)81 879 7789
reservations@a-zguesthouse.com
www.a-zguesthouse.com

Venue is reserved for Angolan residents. Offers single and double en-suite rooms with satellite TV.

Languages: Portuguese, English, Afrikaans

Facilities: VISA @

Activities:

Backpacker Unite 14

Backpackers Hostel $
5 Grieg St, Windhoek West
w208805

Tel: +264(0)61 259 485, Cell: +264(0)81 129 8093, Fax: +264(0)61 259 812
magicbus@iafrica.com.na

Dorms and rooms sleep up to 22 people. Bed and breakfast option available. Venue has kitchen, TV, sauna, pool table and secure off-street parking.

Languages: English, Afrikaans

Facilities: @

Activities:

Backpacker Unite 15

Camping $
5 Grieg St, Windhoek West, Windhoek
w360469

Tel: +264(0)61 259 485, Cell: +264(0)81 129 8093, Fax: +264(0)61 259 812
magicbus@iafrica.com.na

Campsites with ablution facilities.

Languages: English, Afrikaans

Facilities: @

Activities:

Banting Self-catering Accommodation Cc 16

Apartment $
16 Banting St, Windhoek West, Windhoek
w313090

Tel: +264(0)61 234 207, Cell: +264(0)81 128 5830, Fax: +264(0)61 308 941
bsca@iway.na, www.bsca.com.na

Fully-equipped, air-conditioned, self-catering units. Each with terrace and TV. The private bathrooms have a bath or shower.

Languages: English

Facilities: @

Activities:

Baumgartner Holiday Apartments 17

Apartment $
21 Hahnemann St, Windhoek West
w208809

Tel: +264(0)61 224 852, Cell: +264(0)81 127 9158, Fax: +264(0)61 224 852
bbfritz@iway.na

Six rooms with en-suite bathrooms. Each room has air-conditioning, coffee/tea facilities, wall safe, fridge and satellite TV. Secure parking is available.

Languages: English, Afrikaans

Facilities:

Activities:

Bella-Mia Holiday Apartments 18

Apartment $$
14B Lotz St, Klein Windhoek, Windhoek
w208926

Tel: +264(0)61 226 888, Cell: +264(0)81 124 8926, Fax: +264(0)88 648 116
bellamia@afol.com.na

Two types of comfortable luxury apartments on offer. Each with en-suite bathroom, lounge, work table, satellite TV, fully-equipped kitchen and own garden.

Languages: English, German, Afrikaans

Facilities: FC @

Activities:

Belvedere Boutique Hotel 19

Hotel $$
76 Dr Kwame Nkrumah Ave, Ludwigsdorf, Windhoek
w142577

Tel: +264(0)61 258 867, Cell: +264(0)81 128 4241, Fax: +264(0)61 258 867
belvedere@afol.com.na,
www.belvedere-boutiquehotel.com

Comfortable, air-conditioned rooms and a beautiful garden. All rooms have satellite TV. Most rooms have showers. Only luxury rooms have full en-suite bathroom.

Languages: English

Facilities: VISA @

Activities:

Big 5 Mini Lodge 20

Tented Camp $
14km or 22min N of Windhoek
w177694

Cell: +264(0)81 122 0020
futuretecnam@gmail.com

Luxury permanent tents and self-catering. Great views from the lodge. Close to Windhoek.

Languages: English, Afrikaans

Facilities: FC

Activities:

Big 5 Mini Lodge 21

Lodge Camp $
14km or 22min N of Windhoek
w222194

Cell: +264(0)81 122 0020
futuretecnam@gmail.com

Camping in a beautiful setting. Tranquil surrounds and great scenery.

Languages: English, Afrikaans

Facilities: FC

Activities:

CENTRAL NAMIBIA • Windhoek

Windhoek

Butterfly B&B — 22

Bed and Breakfast — $
58 Papageien Rd, Hochland Park, Windhoek
w310764

Tel: +264(0)81 129 4065
butterflybnb58@gmail.com

Each room has a bathroom, satellite TV, patio and kitchenette. There are also braai facilities. Shuttle service available, at additional cost.

Languages: English, German, Afrikaans

Facilities:
Activities:

Caotinha Guest Cottage — 23

Guest House — $$
45 Schlettwein St, Pionierspark, Windhoek
w314287

Cell: +264(0)81 446 5625
caotinhaguest@hotmail.com
www.caotinha-guest-cottage-na.book.direct

Rooms have air-conditioning and a TV with satellite channels. There's also a terrace and snack bar.

Languages: Portuguese, French, Spanish, English

Facilities:
Activities:

Capbon Guesthouse — 24

Guest House — $$
10 Friedrich-Giese St, Klein Windhoek
w314641

Cell: +264(0)81 127 1013
capbon@iway.na

10 Comfortable, double en-suite rooms with fully-equipped kitchenette. A few minutes drive from the city centre.

Languages: English, German, Afrikaans

Facilities:
Activities:

Cardboardbox Backpackers — 25

Camping — $
15 Johann Albrecht St, Windhoek West
w255819

Tel: +264(0)61 228 994, Cell: +264(0)81 233 1833,
Fax: +264(0)61 245 595
info@cardboardbox.com.na,
www.cardboardbox.com.na

The backpackers has campsites available with modern bathrooms. Campers may use the backpackers' facilities.

Languages: English

Facilities: FC
Activities:

Cardboardbox BackPackers — 26

Backpackers Hostel — $
15 Johann Albrecht St, Windhoek West
w139603

Tel: +264(0)61 228 994, Cell: +264(0)81 233 1833,
Fax: +264(0)61 245 595
info@cardboardbox.com.na,
www.cardboardbox.com.na

Singles, twins, doubles, triples or dorm rooms. Restaurant, kitchen, bar and pool on site. Oldest and biggest backpackers hostel in Windhoek.

Languages: English

Facilities: FC
Activities:

Casa Africana Hotel Pension — 27

Hotel — $
21 Heinitzburg St, Luxury Hill, Windhoek
w360386

Fax: +264(0)61 306 634, Cell: +264(0)61 306 633
info@casa-africana.com
www.casa-africana.com

Various self-catering options. Includes complimentary breakfasts. Light lunch and dinner available on request.

Languages: English

Facilities:
Activities:

Casa Blanca Boutique Hotel — 28

Hotel — $$
52 Fritsche St, Pionierspark, Windhoek
w177692

Tel: +264(0)61 249 623, Fax: +264(0)61 249 622
casablanca@afol.com.na

Comfortable, luxurious, en-suite rooms. All with air-conditioning, mini-bar, free internet, safe, DStv and telephone.

Languages: English, German, Afrikaans

Facilities:
Activities:

Casa Onganga Bed & Breakfast — 29

Bed and Breakfast — $
63 Fritsche St, Pionierspark, Windhoek
w141419

Tel: +264(0)61 242 622, Cell: +264(0)81 275 6954,
Fax: +264(0)88 625 141
rosigi@mweb.com.na

En-suite rooms with linen, cutlery and crockery. Gym facilities across the street in the Baines Shopping Centre.

Languages: English, German, Afrikaans

Facilities:
Activities:

Casa Piccolo Apartments — 30

Apartment — $$
6 Barella St, Klein Windhoek
w208927

Tel: +264(0)61 221 155, Fax: +264(0)61 221 187
casapiccolo@iafrica.com.na
www.casa-piccolo.com

Comfortable single and double en-suite rooms which have air-conditioning, satellite TV, coffee/tea facilities and mini bar. Secure parking area.

Languages: German, English, Afrikaans

Facilities:
Activities:

Cela Hotel Pension — 31

Hotel — $
82 Dr. Frans Indongo St, Windhoek West
w139112

Tel: +264(0)61 223 322, Cell: +264(0)81 200 3000,
Fax: +264(0)61 226 246
info@hotelcela.com

En-suite rooms are air-conditioned and have satellite TV, mini bar and internet. There's a 24-hour reception service and secure parking.

Languages: English

Facilities:
Activities:

Chameleon Backpackers Lodge — 32

Backpackers Hostel — $
5-7 Voigt St, Windhoek Central
w139640

Tel: +264(0)61 244 347, Cell: +264(0)81 128 4624,
Fax: +264(0)88 639 275
chameleonbackpackers@iway.na,
www.chameleonbackpackers.com

18 single, double, triple or luxury rooms, most en-suite but some with shared bathroom facilities. All rooms have either a ceiling fan, standing fan or air-conditioning.

Languages: English

Facilities: FC
Activities:

Chameleon Backpackers Lodge — 33

Lodge Camp — $
5-7 Voigt St, Windhoek Central
w208772

Tel: +264(0)61 244 347, Cell: +264(0)81 128 4624,
Fax: +264(0)61 220 885
chameleonbackpackers@iway.na,
www.chameleonbackpackers.com

Very small camp, just three campsites operated on a first come first served basis, no bookings. Venue is centrally situated in the city, close to all amenities.

Languages: English

Facilities:
Activities:

Daniel's Guest House — 34

Self-catering $
17 Galen St, Windhoek West
w208806

Tel: +264(0)61 236 644, Cell: +264(0)81 298 2903, Fax: +264(0)61 236 644
request@danielsguesthouse.com, www.danielsguesthouse.com

Self-catering units with fully-equipped kitchens. Each has two to five beds and air-conditioning. There's braai area at the pool and secure parking.

Languages: English

Facilities: @

Activities:

Discovery Guest House — 35

Guest House $$
Tauben St, erf 1506, Hochland Park, Windhoek
w359276

Fax: +264(0)88 621 375, Cell: +264(0)81 141 2230
bookings@discoveryguesthouse.com
www.discoveryguesthouse.com

En-suite rooms with kitchenette, satellite TV and a bathroom (bath and shower). There are braai facilities, a bar and a shared lounge.

Languages: English

Facilities: VISA @

Activities:

Düsternbrook Safari Guest Farm — 36

Guest Farm $$
59km or 55min S of Okahandja
w138454

Tel: +264(0)61 232 572, Cell: +264(0)81 864 3000, Fax: +264(0)61 257 112
info@duesternbrook.net, www.duesternbrook.net

Comfortable double rooms with en-suite bathrooms (solar-heated showers). Chalets are self-catering.

Languages: English, German, French, Afrikaans

Facilities: VISA FC @

Activities:

Düsternbrook Safari Guest Farm — 37

Camping $$$
59km or 55min S of Okahandja
w255825

Tel: +264(0)61 232 572, Cell: +264(0)81 864 3000, Fax: +264(0)61 257 112
info@duesternbrook.net, www.duesternbrook.net

Two camping areas: Bush camp and Pioneer camp. The first is fenced with plug points while Pioneer campsite has 'bush' shower and toilets.

Languages: English, German, French, Afrikaans

Facilities: VISA FC @

Activities:

Eagle Rock Guest Farm & Business Lodge — 38

Guest Farm $$
38km or 33min W of Windhoek
w313545

Tel: +264(0)61 257 187, Cell: +264(0)81 622 0162
aw@buchaw.de
www.eaglerock.de

Spacious two-bed bungalows with large bathrooms, Wheelchair- and children-friendly. Free Wi-Fi and pool.

Languages: German, English

Facilities: VISA @

Activities:

Eden Chalets Self Catering — 39

Self-catering $
20km or 17min E of Windhoek
w247239

Tel: +264(0)61 234 836, Cell: +264(0)81 170 7575, Fax: +264(0)61 234 877
reservations@edenchalets.com, www.edenchalets.com

Air-conditioned, self-catering chalets with lapa, braai and pool. Game and parrot viewing included. Game drives available.

Languages: English

Facilities: VISA @

Activities:

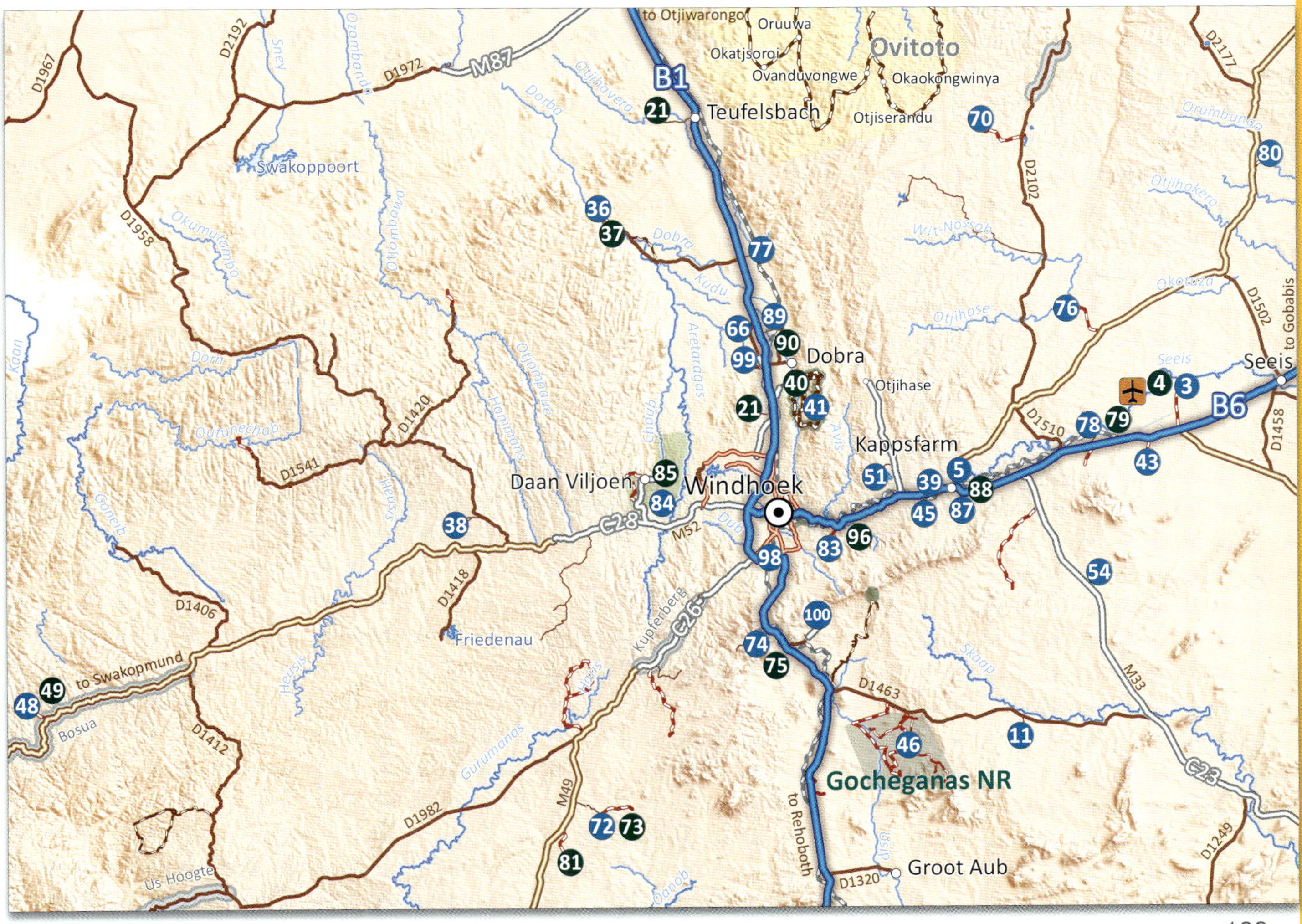

Windhoek

Elisenheim Campsites — 40

Farm Camp — $
17km or 27min N of Windhoek (of which 1km is 4WD)
w143010

Tel: +264(0)61 264 429, Cell: +264(0)81 124 4373,
Fax: +264(0)61 264 429
elisenheimgf@afol.com.na

Five campsites on a lawn, each with its own tap and braai pit. Electricity available on request. Clean ablution facilities. Closed 15 Dec to 15 Jan.

Languages: English

Facilities:
Activities:

Elisenheim Guest Farm — 41

Guest Farm — $$
17km or 26min N of Windhoek
w138806

Tel: +264(0)61 264 429, Cell: +264(0)81 124 4373,
Fax: +264(0)61 264 429
elisenheimgf@afol.com.na

Comfortable, fully-furnished, en-suite rooms with braai facilities. Includes cutlery, crockery, gas stove, outside bathroom (hot shower), flush toilet and basin.

Languages: English, German

Facilities:
Activities:

Etambi Guesthouse — 42

Guest House — $$
6 Gous St, Pionierspark, Windhoek
w139469

Tel: +264(0)61 241 763, Cell: +264(0)81 285 2969,
Fax: +264(0)61 242 916
etambi@mweb.com.na,
www.etambi.com

11 Comfortable rooms with en-suite bathrooms (shower, bath and toilet). As well as air-conditioning, satellite TV, safe and mini bar.

Languages: English

Facilities:
Activities:

Etango Ranch Guest Farm — 43

Guest Farm — $$
45km or 34min E of Windhoek
w254411

Tel: +264(0)62 540 451, Cell: +264(0)81 256 9017,
Fax: +264(0)88 643 168
etango@resdest.com,
www.etangoranch.com

Bungalows with two spacious, air-conditioned, en-suite twin/double rooms. Six en-suite rondavels, or two en-suite double rooms. All meals must be booked.

Languages: English

Facilities:
Activities:

Felsenblick Accommodation Self Catering — 44

Self-catering — $$
8 Gutsche St, Klein Windhoek, Windhoek
w177699

Tel: +264(0)61 232 739, Cell: +264(0)81 129 9562,
Fax: +264(0)61 250 318
monica@namibiastay.com,
www.namibiastay.com

Comfortable rooms, each with satellite TV, coffee/tea facilities, stove, mini bar, under-floor heating and wall safe. Secure parking available.

Languages: English, German, Afrikaans

Facilities:
Activities:

Finkes Sicht Guest House — 45

Guest House — $
18km or 13min E of Windhoek
w316170

Tel: +264(0)61 225 025, Cell: +264(0)81 423 9335
utefinke@iway.na
finkessicht.wordpress.com

Comfortable accommodation, all rooms have electric heaters and en-suite bathrooms (hot showers).

Languages: German, English, Afrikaans

Facilities:
Activities:

Gocheganas Private NR & Wellness Village — 46

Lodge — $$$
38km or 40min SSE of Windhoek
w139832

Tel: +264(0)61 224 909, Cell: +264(0)81 122 4833,
Fax: +264(0)61 224 924
reservations@gocheganas.com,
www.gocheganas.com

Sixteen secluded, luxury chalets with private verandas and en-suite bathrooms. One Crown suite with kitchenette and living room. Massages and other body treatments offered.

Languages: English, German

Facilities:
Activities:

Guesthouse Tamboti — 47

Guest House — $
9 Kerby St, Windhoek Central
w208773

Tel: +264(0)61 235 515, Fax: +264(0)61 259 855
tamboti@afol.com.na
www.tamboti-namibia.com

Single, double and family en-suite rooms. With air-conditioning, satellite TV, telephone, fridge, laundry services, internet access and secure parking.

Languages: English, German

Facilities:
Activities:

Harmonie C28 Self-Catering — 48

Self-catering — $
93km or 1h23min WSW of Windhoek
w360841

Tel: +264(0)61 681 065, Cell: +264(0)81 127 2709
harmonie@iway.na

Self-catering accommodation that sleeps two people, with a sleeper couch for a child or third person. Equipped with cutlery, fridge, small stove and braai facilities. No internet.

Languages: English, Afrikaans

Facilities: FC
Activities:

Harmonie Farm — 49

Farm Camp — $
93km or 1h23min WSW of Windhoek
w239938

Tel: +264(0)61 681 065 , Cell: +264(0)81 127 2709
harmonie@iway.na

Campsite with beautiful scenery in the Khomas Hochland Mountains. On 4x4 routes, game like Kudu, Klipspringer and Oryx can be seen, as well as 80 bird species.

Languages: English, Afrikaans

Facilities: FC
Activities:

Haus Sonneneck — 50

Guest House — $$
1 Robyn St, Erospark, Windhoek
w177702

Tel: +264(0)61 225 020, Fax: +264(0)61 225 020
haussonneneck@afol.com.na
www.haussonneneck.com

Luxurious, air-conditioned, en-suite rooms with modern furnishings and a mini bar, satellite TV and safe.

Languages: English, German, Afrikaans

Facilities: FC
Activities:

Heja Game Lodge — 51

Lodge — $
22km or 24min ENE of Windhoek
w138435

Tel: +264(0)61 257 151, Fax: +264(0)61 257 148
info@hejalodge.com
www.hejalodge.com

Standard or luxury rooms, and fully-equipped bungalows. All rooms have air-conditioning, mini safe, satellite TV and free Wi-Fi.

Languages: English, German

Facilities:
Activities:

Hillside Executive Accommodation 52

Self-catering $$
93 Nelson Mandela St, Klein Windhoek,
w267897

Tel: +264(0)61 248 300, Cell: +264(0)81 748 2558,
Fax: +264(0)61 248 301
admin@hillsidewindhoek.com,
www.hillsidewindhoek.com

Upmarket, self-catering venue with services like laundry, Wi-Fi etc. Restaurants are within walking distance and shopping complexes are in a 2km radius.

Languages: English, Afrikaans

Facilities: VISA FC @

Activities:

Hilltop Guest House 53

Guest House $$
12 Lessing St, Klein Windhoek, Windhoek
w208799

Cell: +264(0)81 245 2750
info@hilltop.com.na
www.hilltop.com.na

Seven elegant, air-conditioned, en-suite rooms (three luxury and four standard). All rooms have DStv and Wi-Fi. Families can be accommodated.

Languages: English, Afrikaans

Facilities: VISA FC @

Activities:

Hohewarte Guest Farm 54

Guest Farm $$
44km or 42min ESE of Windhoek
w139468

Cell: +264(0)81 426 1893
info@hohewarte.com
www.hohewarte.com

Comfortable double en-suite rooms equipped with all modern amenities. Secure parking area. There are many activities to be enjoyed on the farm.

Languages: English, German, Afrikaans

Facilities: VISA

Activities:

Hotel Fürstenhof 55

Hotel $$
4 Frans Indongo St, Windhoek West, Windhoek
w140935

Tel: +264(0)61 237 380, Fax: +264(0)61 237 855
furstenhof@proteahotels.com.na

Air-conditioned, en-suite rooms with all the modern amenities. The bar offers an exclusive selection of SA wines. Car rentals available on site.

Languages: English

Facilities: VISA @

Activities:

Hotel Heinitzburg 56

Boutique Hotel/Spa $$$
22 Heinitzburg St, Luxury Hill, Windhoek
w140460

Tel: +264(0)61 249 597, Fax: +264(0)61 249 598
heinitzburg@heinitzburg.com
www.heinitzburg.com

Sixteen rooms, gourmet restaurant, wine cellar and pool. All just five minutes' drive from the city.

Languages: English, German

Facilities: VISA FC @

Activities:

Hotel Pension Alexander 57

Boutique Hotel/Spa $
10 Beethoven St, Windhoek West, Windhoek
w208758

Tel: +264(0)61 240 775, Cell: +264(0)81 149 0009,
Fax: +264(0)61 271 892
pensionalex@iway.na

Simple and affordable single, double and family rooms. All rooms have tiled floors, satellite TV and fans. Secure parking available.

Languages: English

Facilities: VISA FC @

Activities:

Hotel Pension Christoph 58

Bed and Breakfast $$
33 Heinitzburg St, Windhoek
w208776

Tel: +264(0)61 240 777, Cell: +264(0)81 237 7644,
Fax: +264(0)61 248 560
christoph@afol.com.na

10 En-suite double rooms, with secure parking.

Languages: English, German, Afrikaans

Facilities: VISA

Activities:

Hotel Pension Eros 59

Hotel $
21 Omuramba Road, Erospark, Windhoek
w138739

Tel: +264(0)61 227 020, Fax: +264(0)61 242 919
eros@iway.na

21 En-suite bedrooms with air-conditioning, satellite TV and well-stocked mini bar. There's also a braai lapa and a pool. Secure parking available.

Languages: English, Afrikaans

Facilities: VISA FC @

Activities:

Hotel Pension Moni 60

Hotel $
7 Rieks van der Walt St, Windhoek Central, Windhoek
w206819

Tel: +264(0)61 228 350, Cell: +264(0)81 127 0112,
Fax: +264(0)61 227 124
reswhk@monihotel.com,
www.monihotel.com

All the rooms have DStv, telephones and Wi-Fi. There's a tranquil garden with good bird watching, and a fully-licensed bar.

Languages: English, German

Facilities: VISA FC @

Activities:

Hotel Pension Onganga 61

Hotel $
11 Schuckmann St, Avis, Windhoek
w139474

Tel: +264(0)61 241 701, Cell: +264(0)81 127 3494,
Fax: +264(0)61 241 676
ongangahotel@gmail.com

Ten well-appointed, spacious, air-conditioned rooms. Venue also has bar, restaurant, pool and great views of the Auas mountain range.

Languages: English, German

Facilities: VISA FC @

Activities:

Hotel Pension Palmquell 62

Hotel $$
60 Jan Jonker Rd, Klein Windhoek
w208784

Tel: +264(0)61 234 374, Fax: +264(0)61 234 483
hotel.palmquell@iafrica.com.na
www.palmquell.com

16 Comfortable, air-conditioned, en-suite rooms. Each with satellite TV, telephone, coffee/tea facilities, heater, safe and a mini bar. Secure parking area.

Languages: English

Facilities: VISA @

Activities:

Hotel Pension Steiner 63

Hotel $$
11 Wecke St, Windhoek Central
w208808

Tel: +264(0)61 414 400 , Fax: +264(0)61 224 234
hotelpensionsteinernamibia@gmail.com

16 rooms, four are family-friendly. All are en-suite and have mini bars and satellite TV. Buffet breakfast and light lunches served. Secure parking

Languages: English, German, Afrikaans

Facilities: VISA

Activities:

Windhoek

Hotel Thule 64

Hotel $$$
1 Gorges St, Eros, Windhoek
w138956

Tel: +264(0)61 371 950, Fax: +264(0)61 371 967
reservations@hotelthule.com
www.hotelthule.com

Has the feeling of a remote country estate but only five minutes from city centre.

Languages: English

Facilities:

Activities:

Hotel Uhland 65

Hotel $
147 Dr Kenneth David Kaunda St, Windhoek Central
w177704

Tel: +264(0)61 389 700, Cell: +264(0)81 856 3423,
Fax: +264(0)61 389 713
info@hoteluhland.com,
www.hoteluhland.com

En-suite rooms with telephone, mini bar, coffee / tea facilities, TV and ceiling fans. Superior rooms have air-conditioning and heating.

Languages: English, German, French, Afrikaans

Facilities: FC

Activities:

Immanuel Wilderness Lodge 66

Lodge $$
23km or 30min N of Windhoek
w139036

Tel: +264(0)61 260 901, Cell: +264(0)81 324 8198,
Fax: +264(0)61 260 903
office@immanuel-lodge.de,
www.immanuel-lodge.de

Comfortable rooms with en-suite bathrooms. Thatched roofs and ceiling fans provide a comfortable climate inside the huts at all times of the year.

Languages: English, German

Facilities:

Activities:

Jordani B&B 67

Bed and Breakfast $$
55 Hamutenya Wanahepo Ndadi St, Olympia, Windhoek
w224555

Tel: +264(0)61 220 141, Cell: +264(0)81 124 0090,
Fax: +264(0)63 238 007
Jordani@iway.na,
www.jordanibb.com

Five comfortable en-suite rooms with air-conditioning, free Wi-Fi and satellite TV.

Languages: English

Facilities: FC

Activities:

Klein Windhoek Guest House 68

Bed and Breakfast $$
2 Hofmeyer St, Klein Windhoek, Windhoek
w141590

Tel: +264(0)61 239 401, Cell: +264(0)81 366 8216,
Fax: +264(0)61 234 952
kwgh@iway.na,
www.kleinwindhoekguesthouse.com

Self-catering flats and guest rooms. Latter are inclusive of breakfast, air-conditioning, satellite TV and free Wi-Fi.

Languages: English, German, Afrikaans

Facilities:

Activities:

Kubata City Hotel 69

Lodge $$
151 Nelson Mandela Ave, Windhoek Central, Windhoek
w139471

Tel: +264(0)61 224 608, Cell: +264(0)81 240 3713,
Fax: +264(0)61 224 610
kubata@iway.na,
www.kubata.com.na

20 Thatched standard, single, double, en-suite (3) and VIP (10) rooms.

Languages: English, Portuguese, Afrikaans, Dutch

Facilities:

Activities:

Leopard Lodge 70

Lodge $$
73km or 1h19min NNE of Windhoek
w209680

Fax: +264(0)62 540 444, Cell: +264(0)81 128 0202
bookings@leopardlodge.com
www.leopardlodge.com

Fully-equipped single and double rooms, serviced daily. Laundry services available. Neat and comfortable lodge.

Languages: English

Facilities:

Activities:

Londiningi Guest House 71

Guest House $
11 Winterberg St, Eros, Windhoek
w141526

Tel: +264(0)61 242 378, Cell: +264(0)81 128 1017,
Fax: +264(0)61 226 201
londiningi@mweb.com.na,
www.londiningi.com

10 En-suite rooms in a venue conveniently close to the city centre. Secure parking.

Languages: English, Afrikaans, French

Facilities:

Activities:

Melrose Game Farm 72

Guest Farm $$
47km or 42min SSW of Windhoek
w139534

Tel: +264(0)61 234 298, Cell: +264(0)81 219 3221
melrose@mweb.com.na

Accommodation in the main house - nine double rooms, all en-suite, with a private terrace.

Languages: English, Afrikaans

Facilities: FC

Activities:

Melrose Game Farm 73

Farm Camp $
47km or 42min SSW of Windhoek
w222189

Tel: +264(0)61 234 298, Cell: +264(0)81 219 3221
melrose@mweb.com.na

Campsites with clean ablution facilities, electricity and braai areas. Campers are welcome to partake in all the activities offered on the farm.

Languages: English, Afrikaans

Facilities: FC

Activities:

Monteiro 74

Self-catering $$
17km or 16min S of Windhoek
w261553

Cell: +264(0)81 129 1172
monteiro@iway.na
www.monteironamibia.com

Chalets and permanent tents. Spacious, en-suite guest rooms (bath/shower or just shower). Three bedroom house also available.

Languages: English, Afrikaans

Facilities:

Activities:

Monteiro 75

Lodge Camp $
17km or 16min S of Windhoek
w141727

Cell: +264(0)81 129 1172
monteiro@iway.na
www.monteironamibia.com

Shaded or bush campsites. Each campsite has lights, water, power points and braai facilities. There's a communal bush kitchen and ablution facilities. Meals on request.

Languages: English, Afrikaans

Facilities:

Activities:

N/a'an ku Sê Lodge And Wildlife Sanctuary 76

Lodge $$$
53km or 51min NE of Windhoek
w143260

Tel: +264(0)61 307 338, Cell: +264(0)81 461 8655, Fax: +264(0)61 307 337
lodge@naankuse.com,
www.naankuselodge.com

Six luxurious, individual chalets and 10 beautiful holiday homes. The lodge is crafted from logs and glass and a beautiful dining area with great views.

Languages: English, Afrikaans

Facilities:

Activities:

Okapuka Ranch 77

Game/Safari Lodge $$
33km or 36min N of Windhoek
w138440

Tel: +264(0)61 234 607, Cell: +264(0)81 128 7310, Fax: +264(0)61 234 690
okapuka@iafrica.com.na,
www.okapuka-ranch.com

Comfortable, en-suite rooms with air-conditioning, coffee/tea facilities, bar fridge and satellite TV.

Languages: English

Facilities:

Activities:

Ondekaremba Africa Farm 78

Guest Farm $$
40km or 33min ENE of Windhoek
w139464

Tel: +264(0)62 540 424, Fax: +264(0)88 635 249
info@ondekaremba.com
www.ondekaremba.com

Single, double and triple en-suite rooms. Each room has a mini bar and private terrace.

Languages: English

Facilities:

Activities:

Ondekaremba Africa Farm 79

Farm Camp $$
41km or 35min ENE of Windhoek
w143296

Tel: +264(0)62 540 424, Fax: +264(0)88 635 249
info@ondekaremba.com
www.ondekaremba.com

Campsites have clean ablution facilities and electricity.

Languages: English

Facilities:

Activities:

Onjala Lodge 80

Lodge $$$
76km or 1h14min NE of Windhoek
w207900

Tel: +264(0)61 259 325, Cell: +264(0)81 122 7171, Fax: +264(0)61 247 755
res@onjala.com,
www.onjala.com

11 Rooms, four bungalows and four Panorama Suites. The venue is situated in a private nature reserve.

Languages: English

Facilities:

Activities:

Prospect Guest Farm 81

Farm Camp $
50km or 44min SSW of Windhoek
w207862

Tel: +264(0)61 234 441
prospect19@iway.na

Camping area on a lawn with ample shade provided by big trees, and ablution blocks. Campers need to be self-sufficient.

Languages: English, German, Afrikaans

Facilities:

Activities:

Rivendell Guest House 82

Bed and Breakfast $$
40 Beethoven St, Windhoek West
w137860

Tel: +264(0)61 250 006, Fax: +264(0)88 650 3354
rivendell@infotour-africa.com
www.rivendell-namibia.com

Furnished, en-suite, double rooms. Some with shared bathrooms. Flat with kitchen and lounge. Located in leafy suburb within walking distance of city centre.

Languages: English

Facilities:

Activities:

River Crossing Lodge 83

Lodge $$
9km or 15min ESE of Windhoek
w228210

Tel: +264(0)61 246 788, Cell: +264(0)81 127 7161, Fax: +264(0)61 243 079
reservations@rivercrossing.com.na,
www.rivercrossing.com.na

Located on a game reserve. The main building offers a dining room, bar, lounge with fireplace, and curio corner. There's also a lap pool and elevated wooden sun deck.

Languages: English

Facilities:

Activities:

Sun Karros Lifestyle Safaris At Daan Viljoen 84

Game/Safari Lodge $$$
22km or 20min WNW of Windhoek
w138385

Cell: +264(0)83 323 2393
reservations@sunkarros.com
www.sunkarros.com

19 Luxurious chalets. Each chalet fully equipped with air-conditioned rooms, satellite TVs and private braai.

Languages: English

Facilities:

Activities:

Sun Karros Lifestyle Safaris At Daan Viljoen Camp 85

Park Camp $$$
22km or 20min WNW of Windhoek
w189024

Cell: +264(0)83 323 2393
reservations@sunkarros.com
www.sunkarros.com

Each campsite has a braai, wash-up area, electric lights and power points. There are three ablution blocks (showers & toilets). Some campsites have their own ablution facilities.

Languages: English

Facilities:

Activities:

The Olive Exclusive Boutique Hotel 86

Hotel $$$
22 Promenaden Rd, Klein Windhoek, Windhoek
w279640

Tel: +264(0)61 383 890, Fax: +264(0)61 383 885
info@theolive-namibia.com
www.theolive-namibia.com

Junior and premier suites. All rooms are air-conditioned and en-suite, with DStv and coffee/tea facilities. There's an on-site restaurant and bar.

Languages: English, German, Afrikaans

Facilities:

Activities:

Trans Kalahari Inn 87

Lodge $
23km or 20min E of Windhoek
w138897

Tel: +264(0)61 222 877, Fax: +264(0)61 226 100
tki@iway.na
www.transkalahari-inn.com

En-suite bungalows with mini bar and beautiful views. Great restaurant with cosy bar. Long term parking available.

Languages: English, German, Dutch, Afrikaans

Facilities:

Activities:

Windhoek

Trans Kalahari Inn — 88

Lodge Camp — $
23km or 20min E of Windhoek
w198390

Tel: +264(0)61 222 877, Fax: +264(0)61 226 100
tki@iway.na
www.transkalahari-inn.com

Situated next to the lodge with great views of Aus Mountains. Campers are welcome to enjoy a drink or dinner at lodge restaurant. Long-term parking for private vehicles.

Languages: English, German, Dutch, Afrikaans

Facilities:
Activities:

Umti Lodge — 89

Lodge — $
22km or 26min N of Windhoek
w255876

Tel: +264(0)61 303 977, Cell: +264(0)81 568 2006, Fax: +264(0)61 304 977
umti@iway.na,
www.umtinam.com

10 Standard rooms and four family bungalows. There's also a bar and pool.

Languages: English

Facilities:
Activities:

Umti Lodge — 90

Lodge Camp — $
22km or 26min N of Windhoek
w255875

Tel: +264(0)61 303 977, Cell: +264(0)81 568 2006, Fax: +264(0)61 304 977
umti@iway.na,
www.umtinam.com

Basic campgrounds with clean ablution facilities. Campers may use the lodge's entertainment area and bar.

Languages: English

Facilities:
Activities:

UrbanCamp.net — 91

Tented Camp — $
2 Schanzen Rd, Klein Windhoek
w361045

Tel: +264(0)61 244 251, Cell: ?+264(0)81 162 0761, Fax: +264(0)61 370 797
booking@urbancamp.net,
www.urbancamp.net

Two tented camps: Garden Tent or Explorers Delight. Enjoy big shade trees, Wi-Fi, en-suite bathrooms and pool.

Languages: English, German

Facilities:
Activities:

UrbanCamp.net — 92

Camping — $$
2 Schanzen Road, Klein Windhoek
w254377

Tel: +264(0)61 244 251, Cell: ?+264(0)81 162 0761, Fax: +264(0)61 370 797
booking@urbancamp.net,
www.urbancamp.net

Campsites with individual ablution facilities. Venue is centrally located within walking distance of shops, banks and Joe's Beerhouse.

Languages: English, German

Facilities:
Activities:

Vee's Self Catering Accommodation — 93

Self-catering — $
7311 Elephant St, Rhino Park, Windhoek
w208801

Tel: +264(0)61 221 598, Cell: +264(0)81 129 5773, Fax: +264(0)61 221 598
vikki@africaonline.com.na

En-suite single, double or family rooms. All with fans and TV (with DVD player). There's an outdoor patio with braai and fully-equipped kitchen.

Languages: English

Facilities:
Activities:

Villa Moringa Guest House — 94

Guest House — $$
111A Joseph Mukwayu Ithana St (old Gloudina St), Ludwigsdorf
w139867

Tel: +264(0)61 224 472, Cell: +264(0)81 124 0617, Fax: +264(0)61 231 957
info@villa-moringa.com,
www.villa-moringa.com

Modern, luxurious en-suite rooms. Venue is 10 minutes from Windhoek CBD and offer airport transfers.

Languages: English, German, French, Portuguese, Spanish

Facilities:
Activities:

Vineyard Country B&B — 95

Bed and Breakfast — $
7km or 9min ESE of Windhoek
w279624

Tel: +264(0)61 224 144, Cell: +264(0)81 124 3620
info@vineyard.com.na
www.vineyard.com.na

Eight en-suite bedrooms leading onto gardens, with custom-made furniture.

Languages: English, German, Afrikaans

Facilities:
Activities:

Vineyard Country B&B — 96

Camping — $$
7km or 9min ESE of Windhoek
w279625

Tel: +264(0)61 224 144, Cell: +264(0)81 124 3620
info@vineyard.com.na
www.vineyard.com.na

Campsites have private luxury bathrooms (solar-heated shower, wash basin and toilet).

Languages: English, German, Afrikaans

Facilities:
Activities:

Vondelhof Guest House — 97

Guest House — $$
2 Puccini St, Windhoek West, Windhoek
w177706

Tel: +264(0)61 248 320, Fax: +264(0)88 614 352
reservations@vondelhof.com
www.vondelhof.com

En-suite rooms, each with ceiling fans, mini bar, TV, safe, mosquito nets and coffee/tea facilities. Breakfasts and light lunches are available.

Languages: English, Afrikaans, Dutch, German

Facilities:
Activities:

Windhoek Country Club Resort — 98

Resort — $$
7km or 9min S of Windhoek
w139024

Tel: +264(0)61 205 5911, Fax: +264(0)61 205 2797
windhoek@legacyhotels.com
www.legacyhotels.co.za

A resort within the city. Offers businessmen, conference delegates or families luxury accommodation in a tranquil setting.

Languages: English

Facilities:
Activities:

Windhoek Game Camp — 99

Self-catering — $$
20km or 28min N of Windhoek
w254450

Fax: +264(0)88 627 918, Cell: +264(0)81 272 1594
info@windhoekgamecamp.com
www.windhoekgamecamp.com

Eight luxury, self-catering permanent tents, all with en-suite facilities. Each tent has a fully-equipped kitchen and wooden deck.

Languages: English, Afrikaans

Facilities:
Activities:

Windhoek Mountain Lodge	100
Lodge	$$

22km or 20min SSE of Windhoek
w200955

Tel: +264(0)61 257 053, Cell: +264(0)81 466 6801, reservations@windhoek-mountain-lodge.de
www.gravel-travel.com

Nine comfortable rooms. Breakfast and dinner included. Bar on site. Sundowner trips and motorcycle tours offered.

Languages: English

Facilities:

Activities:

Winnie Guest House	101
Guest House	$

9 Range St, Erf 1490, Pionierspark Ext 1, Windhoek
w255874

Tel: +264(0)61 418 200, Cell: +264(0)81 825 9354, Fax: +264(0)61 418 233
reservations@winnieguesthouse.com,
www.winnieguesthouse.com

20 Spacious, en-suite rooms with air-conditioning and Wi-Fi. There's also a bar and pool. Centrally located.

Languages: Portuguese, English

Facilities:

Activities:

The D1958 is favourite for cyclists in the Windhoek area. (photo: Frank Höppener)

(photo: Frank Höppener)

DAMARALAND

(photo: Frank Höppener)

THIS IS A SEMI-DESERT AREA EAST OF the Skeleton Coast and south of Kaokoland that offers a great deal in terms of natural beauty and interesting attractions. Travellers can enjoy striking rock formations, geological and cultural sites, as well as some of Namibia's most famous landmarks, including Mount Brandberg and Twyfelfontein.

Taking in the sunset on the western face of Mount Brandberg is an unforgettable experience. This Massif is also well-known for the 'White Lady' bushman painting and wonderful wilderness hiking opportunities.

The mountains in the Twyfelfontein area are extraordinary. The Mowani Mountains are also called the Red Mountains because of their flame colour. Himba and Herero women in traditional garb sell stones and crafts on the road between Twyfelfontein and Uis.

One cannot go to Damaraland without exploring the Messum Crater where one of the oldest plant species (Welwitschia mirabilis) flourishes. If you travel by off-road vehicle you should spend a day enjoying the Doros Crater and the interesting landscape just north of it.

If you camp close to the Huab or Aba-Huab Rivers, chances are good that you will encounter desert elephant or black rhino. The desert elephants are not as used to humans as the elephants in Etosha and they don't like being disturbed. They have a comfort zone of at least 500m. As the dry riverbeds belong to them, you are advised to rather stay out of there. An elephant encounter requires patience more than skill, because these lords of the desert may take a long time to make way – and sometimes they don't! Be very cautious, elephants have killed people in Namibia's riverbeds.

Be careful when driving in Damaraland in the rainy season. Because of seasonal flooding, the roads can be very submerged. Many vehicles had to be rescued from rivers like the Aba-Huab, so always enquire about road conditions during the rainy season. Because of the possibility of flash floods you should not camp in the dry riverbeds during the rainy season.

Please stay on existing tracks or roads when driving on the pebble desert plains in Damaraland. New roads are the worst example of 'vehicle track pollution' as a new track will be visible for up to 600 years before the desert winds can wipe it out.

Damaraland is mainly communal land divided into conservancies. The conservancies are managed by the local communities who own the land rights and are responsible for the wild game. Money spent at community camps stays in the communities, being used for education, medical treatment, and other improvements.

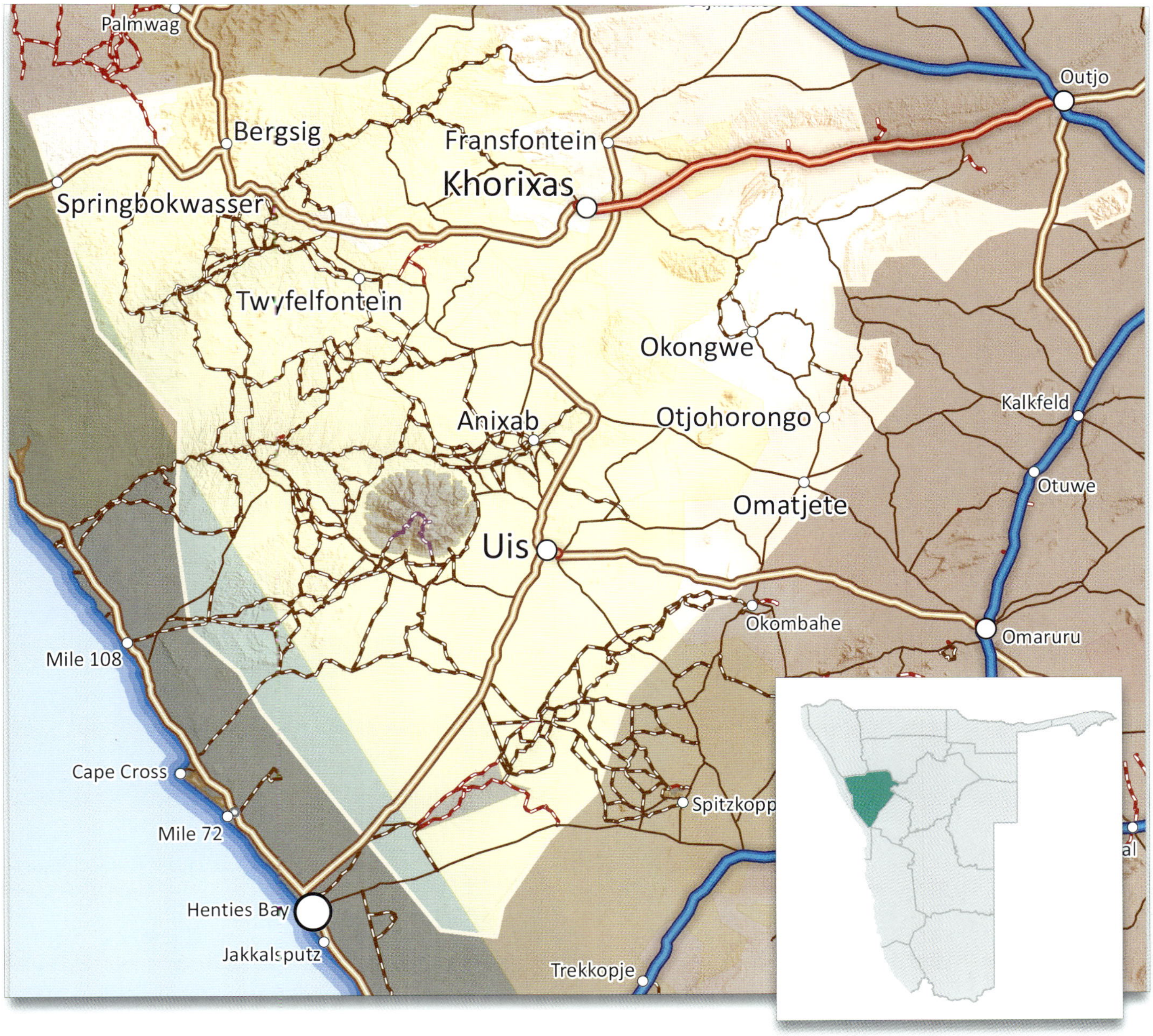

Unfortunately some visitors see the area as a 4x4 playground where anything goes. As this attitude can cause resentment, we urge you to respect the people and what is, in effect, their backyard. When you drive past a village, keep your speed down so as not to cover them in your dust and always give them a polite wave. Remember to dispose of your own litter in a proper way and respect the local people and their cultures.

If you want to enjoy the off-road driving opportunities that this vast and remote region has to offer, do one of the popular eco-trails like the Upper-Huab Trail or the Ruspoort Trail.

MAJOR ATTRACTIONS

- Doros Crater
- Messum Crater
- The Living museum of the Damara is a cultural village open to visitors.
- The fascinating White Lady Bushman painting was discovered on Mount Brandberg in 1918.
- Desolation Valley is a harsh and remote valley along the Huab River with remarkable rock formations.
- With at least 2 500 individual open-air rock engravings, Twyfelfontein is one of the largest and most important concentrations of rock art in Africa. Twyfelfontein was proclaimed as Namibia's first World Heritage Site in 2007.
- Close to Twyfelfontein you can visit the Organ Pipes, Burnt Mountain (not the same as Brandberg) and the Petrified Forest.
- The 35m high pillar of rock called Vingerklip/Rock Finger is situated between Outjo and Khorixas.

More details about the attractions are available on our website (www.tracks4africa.co.za) or our Guide App. Our GPS Map can navigate you to each of these attractions.

Khorixas

(photo: Ian-Ray Nel)

ORIGINALLY NAMED 'NUWE DORP', the town was established in 1936 as a trading post for the region's farming community. It was later renamed Khorixas after the water bush, Salvadora persica ('Gorigas' or 'Khoris' in Khoekhoegowab, the Damara language), which are found in Damaraland. This shrub grows approximately 3m tall and has succulent leaves sought after by the desert elephant which roam the Kunene region. The Damara use the plant to make a potent beer.

Khorixas used to be the capital of Damaraland, but after Namibia's independence Damaraland was incorporated into the Kunene region, with Opuwo as the administrative capital.

The town is home to the Damara people who keep small livestock like goats and sheep; unfortunately, unemployment is high.

Traveller Description

There are several good lodges, game farms and camping facilities in the surrounding area, from where one can explore attractions like Vingerklip (Rock Finger), the Petrified Forest, Organ Pipes, Burnt Mountain and the world heritage site at Twyfelfontein. Khorixas itself is not a touristy town but you will be able to stock-up and find basic facilities.

Travel Info

Travellers should be very cautious crossing the dry riverbeds of the ephemeral Unib and Ugab Rivers during the rainy season as flash floods can occur. You'll encounter many dry riverbed crossings while exploring the tourist attractions in the area so it's best to deflate your tyres a bit before you set out for the day.

Phone the hospital if you need to see a doctor. Private doctors only come in from Otjiwarongo on certain days.

TRAVEL TIP! If you enjoy hiking, you must experience the Brandberg hiking trail and visit the famous 'White Lady' San painting.

Town Info:

Hospital: +264(0)67 335 100 Police: +264(0)67 331 003 Doctor: +264(0)67 335 100

Bambatsi Guest Farm — 1

Guest Farm — $$

62km or 45min ENE of Khorixas

w138134

Fax: +264(0)88 615 627, Cell: +264(0)81 245 8803

info@bambatsi.com

www.bambatsi.com

Comfortable bungalows with en-suite bathrooms. View wildlife from the main veranda or enjoy a drink at the bar.

Languages: English, German, Afrikaans

Facilities: VISA FC

Activities:

Bambatsi Guest Farm — 2

Farm Camp — $

62km or 43min ENE of Khorixas

w232622

Fax: +264(0)88 615 627, Cell: +264(0)81 245 8803

bambatsi@iway.na

www.bambatsi.com

Two camps here. Biro Camp only accommodates one group while Camp Gik can accommodate two groups.

Languages: English, German, Afrikaans

Facilities: VISA FC

Activities:

Damara Mopane Lodge — 3

Lodge — $$

26km or 18min ENE of Khorixas

w255824

Tel: +264(0)61 427 200, Fax: +264(0)67 687 186

info@gondwana-collection.com

www.gondwana-collection.com

Accommodation in air-conditioned double rooms. Meals prepared with ingredients sourced from their own vegetable garden. Reservations mandatory.

Languages: English

Facilities: VISA @

Activities:

Huab Lodge — 4

Lodge — $$$

86km or 1h24min NNW of Khorixas

w139462

Tel: +264(0)67 312 070, Cell: +264(0)81 242 7375,

Fax: +264(0)88 637 655

info@huab.com,

www.huab.com

Eight spacious bungalows accommodating a maximum of 16 guests. The venue is strategically situated in Damaraland en-route to Etosha.

Languages: English, German, Dutch, Afrikaans

Facilities: VISA FC @

Activities:

iGowati Lodge — 5

Lodge — $

King Justus Garoeb Ave, Khorixas

w137501

Tel: +264(0)67 331 592, Cell: +264(0)81 450 8790,

Fax: +264(0)67 331 594

igowati@mweb.com.na,

www.igowatilodge.com

30 comfortable, en-suite rooms. Each with fans, television and coffee/tea facilities. Guest can enjoy traditional dances and learn about the Damara culture.

Languages: English, Afrikaans

Facilities: VISA

Activities:

iGowati Lodge — 6

Lodge Camp — $$

King Justus Garoeb Avenue, Khorixas

w255833

Tel: +264(0)67 331 592, Fax: +264(0)67 331 594

igowati@mweb.com.na

www.igowatilodge.com

Grassed, shaded campsites have shared ablutions and wash-up area. One private site with its own facilities is available. Campers may use lodge facilities.

Languages: English, Afrikaans

Facilities: VISA

Activities:

Khorixas

Khorixas Rest Camp — 7

Lodge Camp — $
3km or 4min NW of Khorixas
w138532

Tel: +264(0)61 285 7200, Fax: +264(0)61 224 900
reservations@nwr.com.na
www.nwr.com.na

Campsites, caravan sites and bungalow accommodation. There's also a restaurant and curio shop.

Languages: English

Facilities:
Activities:

Khorixas Rest Camp Chalets — 8

Resort — $$
3km or 4min NW of Khorixas
w313104

Tel: +264(0)61 285 7200, Fax: +264(0)61 224 900
reservations@nwr.com.na
www.nwr.com.na

Ideally located between Etosha, the Kunene region and the Skeleton Coast, this venue offers family and bush chalets, and single rooms. There's also a pool, restaurant and curio shop.

Languages: English

Facilities:
Activities:

Ugab Terrace Lodge — 9

Lodge — $$
66km or 48min E of Khorixas
w207675

Tel: +264(0)64 461 677, Cell: +264(0)81 140 0179,
Fax: +264(0)88 636 170
info@ugabterracelodge.com,
www.ugabterracelodge.com

16 En-suite bungalows, each with private veranda. Facilities include a bar. The lodge is situated on a plateau and enjoys panoramic views.

Languages: English, German, Afrikaans

Facilities:
Activities:

Ugab Terrace Lodge — 10

Lodge Camp — $
66km or 48min E of Khorixas
w255846

Tel: +264(0)64 461 677, Cell: +264(0)81 140 0179,
Fax: +264(0)88 636 170
info@ugabterracelodge.com,
www.ugabterracelodge.com

Five campsites where you can park your RV or caravan or set up tent. The campsites are located at the foot of the hill overlooking the Ugab Terrace and Valley.

Languages: English, German, Afrikaans

Facilities:
Activities:

Vingerklip Lodge — 11

Lodge — $$$
64km or 1h11min E of Khorixas
w138041

Tel: +264(0)61 255 344, Fax: +264(0)88 623 642
vingerkl@mweb.com.na
www.vingerklip.com.na

Double and family rooms, as well as a suite. There are two swimming pools and a jacuzzi. The restaurant is situated on top of the plateau. Activities include sundowner drives and cultural trips.

Languages: English

Facilities:
Activities:

"When you travel, remember that a foreign country is not designed to make you comfortable. It is designed to make its own people comfortable."

Clifton Fadiman

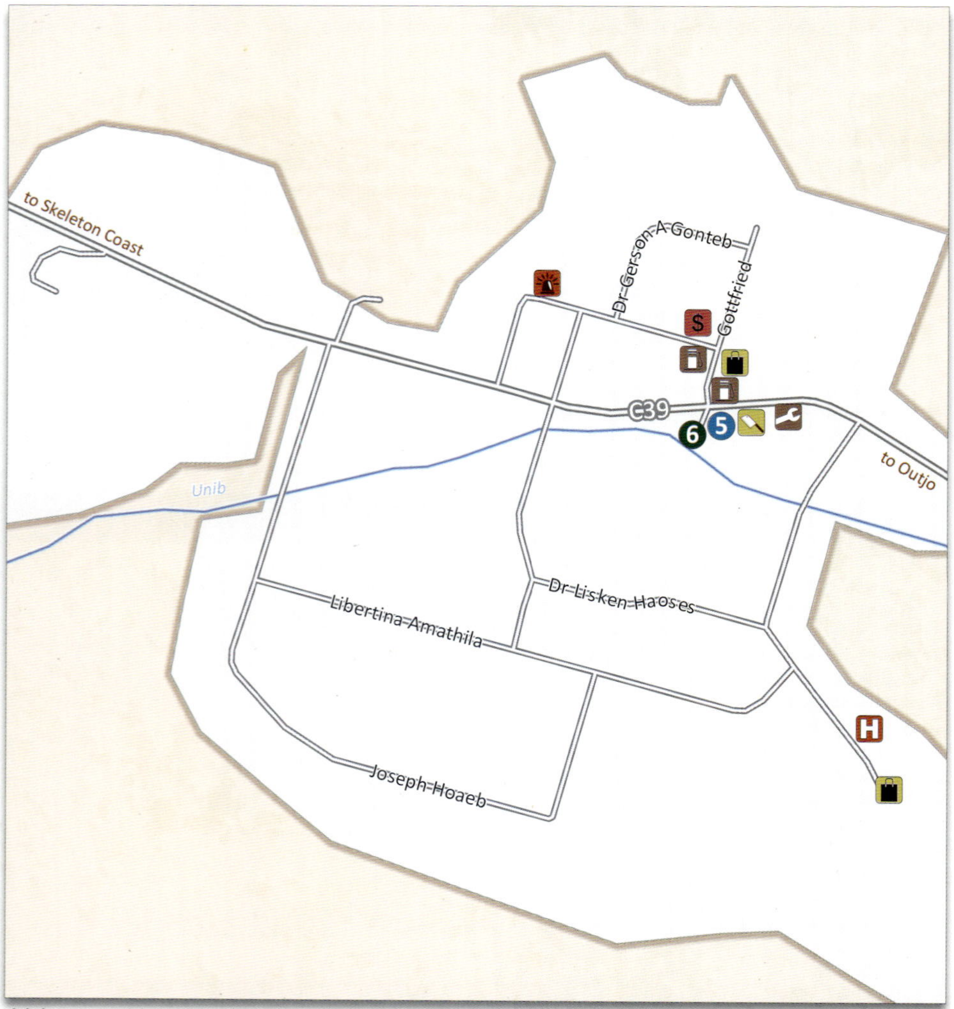

right: Located halfway between Khorixas and Outjo, Vingerklip ('Finger rock') is one of Namibia's most famous rock formations.
(photo: Heiner Dillmann)

Twyfelfontein

An example of the rock engravings at Twyfelfontein. (photo: Frank Höppener)

ORIGINALLY KNOWN AS !UI-!!AIS (Damara for the jumping waterhole), the first European farmer in the region, David Levin, named this spot Twyfelfontein (doubtful fountain); he was unsure whether the fountain would supply enough water for his livestock. In 1971 the area was given back to the Damara farmers as communal land for their exclusive use.

The first reports of the rock engravings at Twyfelfontein were made in 1921 by the topographer, Reinhard Maack, who also reported the White Lady painting in the Brandberg. Thorough investigation of the site was only done in 1950, when more than 2 000 rock engravings, as well as a few rock paintings, were identified. This is one of the largest concentrations of rock petroglyphs in Africa and was declared a national monument in 1952; later, in 2007, it became Namibia's first World Heritage Site.

Traveller Description

Twyfelfontein is one of Namibia's most popular tourist destinations, with more than 40 000 people visiting this open-air gallery annually. The visitor's centre was designed to blend in with the red sandstone environment and is constructed from natural material which is completely removable and reusable. All visitors must be accompanied by a guide and have the option of following one of two routes, lasting between 45 and 90 minutes.

The Dancing Kudu route includes a detour to the original spring and features an unusual engraving of a female kudu with several geometric shapes. The return route passes the Zwei Schneider shelter where the only remaining rock paintings can be seen.

The Lion Man route is longer and rougher but has been upgraded with walking aids. This route with its steel bridges and stairs isn't recommended for people with restricted mobility. From viewing platforms visitors enjoy excellent views of the major engravings. The route includes the 'Lion Man', in which elements of a human and a lion are combined, indicating that this is an engraving of a 'shaman', a man who has transformed into a lion. The return route passes the ruins of the Levin farm house.

Other attractions nearby include the Living Museum of the Damara (a cultural village), the Organ Pipes (a rock formation resembling the pipes of a large church organ), and the blackish rock of the Burnt Mountain (not to be confused with Brandberg, 65km south of Twyfelfontein).

Travel Info

There are no shops in the Twyfelfontein area, but limited fuel and a mechanical workshop is available at the Twyfelfontein Country Lodge.

There are many dry riverbed crossings in the area so be aware of possible flash floods during the rainy season, and be prepared for deep sand driving during the dry season.

Useful numbers:

Twyfelfontein Country Lodge:	+264(0)67 697 021
Alternative tow-in numbers:	+264(0)62 500 132 / +264(0)62 504 250

TRAVEL TIP! The late afternoon sun provides excellent light for photographing the engravings but this is also a common time for tour buses to arrive, so be sure to arrive early! Please refrain from touching or wetting the rock as this causes deterioration of the paintings and etchings.

Keep an eye open for the Namibian desert elephants which frequent the Aba-Huab riverbed.

Town Info: Tow-in: +264(0)81 129 7490

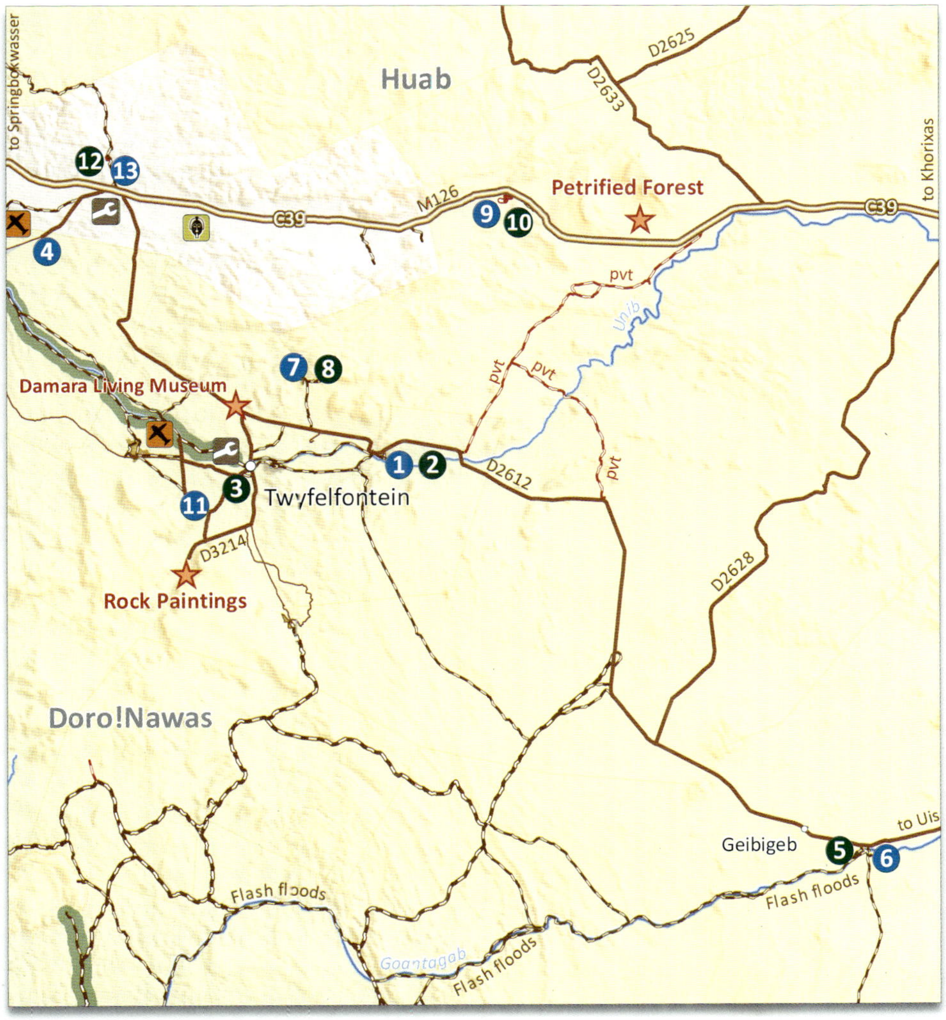

Aabadi Mountain Camp 1

Tented Camp $$
8km or 12min E of Twyfelfontein (of which 7km is 4WD)
w206679

Tel: +264(0)61 265 446 , Cell: +264(0)81 230 3797
aabadi@face2facenamibia.com
www.aabadimountaincamp.com

You'll find with fifteen permanent tents with private open-air bathrooms on the Aba Huab riverbed. The restaurant offers both European and African dishes.

Languages: English, Afrikaans

Facilities: FC

Activities:

Aabadi Mountain Camp 2

Lodge Camp $
8km or 13min E of Twyfelfontein (of which 7km is 4WD)
w208208

Tel: +264(0)61 265 446 , Cell: +264(0)81 230 3797
aabadi@face2facenamibia.com
www.aabadimountaincamp.com

The camp is located on the Aba Huab riverbed and features open-air ablution facilities with running water and flush toilets.

Languages: English, Afrikaans

Facilities: FC

Activities:

Aba-Huab Community Camp 3

Community Camp $
5km or 07h00min SE of Twyfelfontein
w137967

No detailed information available as we were unable to make contact. But the venue was visited by Tracks4-Africa travellers at the time of writing and found to be operational.

Languages: English, Afrikaans

Facilities:

Activities:

Twyfelfontein

Doro Nawas Camp 4

Lodge $$$
23km or 25min NW of Twyfelfontein
w139900

Tel: +264(0)61 274 500, Fax: +264(0)61 239 455
enquiry@wilderness.co.za
www.wilderness-safaris.com

16 Chalets with private verandas, en-suite bathrooms and outdoor showers. The main building offers a dining room, meal terrace, bar, curio shop and art gallery.

Languages: English

Facilities:

Activities:

Madisa Camp 5

Lodge Camp $
43km or 1h12min ESE of Twyfelfontein (of which 28km is 4WD)
w360870

Cell: +264(0)81 698 2908
bookings@madisacamp.com
www.madisacamp.com

Nine private, spacious campsites, each with their own ablutions, braai areas and lights; all on the riverbed. There are also five large overland campsites that have communal ablutions.

Languages: English

Facilities: FC

Activities:

Madisa Camp Safari Tents 6

Tented Camp $
43km or 1h15min ESE of Twyfelfontein (of which 29km is 4WD)
w255892

Cell: +264(0)81 698 2908
bookings@madisacamp.com
www.madisacamp.com

Luxury, private permanent tents, each with its own en-suite rock bathroom with beautiful views. Bring your own drinking water. Located next to the Gauntegab River

Languages: English

Facilities: FC

Activities:

Mowani Mountain Camp 7

Lodge $$$
8km or 15min NNE of Twyfelfontein (of which 6km is 4WD)
w138652

Tel: +264(0)61 232 009, Fax: +264(0)61 222 574
mowani@visionsofafrica.com.na
www.mowani.com

Twelve luxurious, thatched rooms with en-suite bathrooms, dressing rooms and spectacular viewing decks. Also three suites, with a rock pool and a drinks spot on the boulders.

Languages: English

Facilities:

Activities:

Mowani Mountain Camp Campsites 8

Camping $
7km or 14min NE of Twyfelfontein (of which 6km is 4WD)
w138680

Tel: +264(0)61 232 008, Fax: +264(0)61 222 574
mowani@visionsofafrica.com.na
www.mowani.com

Basic camping at three campsites where there's a pit toilet. Campers should be self-sufficient. Campers do not have access to lodge facilities.

Languages: English

Facilities:

Activities:

Tsubes Restcamp 9

Tented Camp $
37km or 37min NE of Twyfelfontein
w361509

Cell: +264(0)81 127 9829
fransa@iway.na

Four permanent tents, each with bedding and their own ablution facilities. Each tent has two beds, two camping chairs and a table.

Languages: English

Facilities:

Activities:

Tsubes Restcamp 10

Camping $
37km or 36min NE of Twyfelfontein
w360948

Cell: +264(0)81 127 9829
fransa@iway.na

Situated between Khorixas and Twyfelfontein on the C39 road, these shaded campsites have braai areas and ablution facilities.

Languages: English

Facilities:

Activities:

Twyfelfontein Country Lodge 11

Lodge $$$
5km or 9min SW of Twyfelfontein
w138566

Tel: +264(0)61 374 750, Fax: +264(0)61 256 598
twyfelfontein@ncl.com.na
www.twyfelfonteinlodge.com

En-suite double rooms and an executive bungalow. All developed to impact minimally on the environment. Responsible bikers welcome.

Languages: English, German, Afrikaans

Facilities:

Activities:

Xaragu Camp 12

Camping $$
20km or 23min NNW of Twyfelfontein (of which 3km is 4WD)
w315260

Cell: +264(0)81 124 5612
info@xaragu-damaraland.com
www.xaragu-damaraland.com

12 Campsites with communal ablution facility.

Languages: English

Facilities:

Activities:

Xaragu Tented Camp 13

Tented Camp $
20km or 22min NNW of Twyfelfontein (of which 2km is 4WD)
w138808

Cell: +264(0)81 124 5612
info@xaragu-damaraland.com
www.xaragu-damaraland.com

12 Permanent en-suite tents, either single, double or triple (families only). The tented camp rate per person per night includes dinner and bed & breakfast.

Languages: English

Facilities:

Activities:

(above) The Twyfelfontein Country Lodge. (photo: Peter Barber)
Below (photo: Frank Höppener)

Uis

(photo: Basil Calitz)

HUGE WHITE MOUNDS of processed tin ore to the east of Uis make this tiny town hard to miss, they also tell the story of its success and decline. Tin was discovered here in 1911, with large scale mining starting in 1958 when Iscor installed an extraction plant. The plant was enlarged in 1966 and the town of Uis was established for the mine's employees. The plant was enlarged again in 1980, producing 140 tons of ore per hour and operating 24/7; this made it the largest hard-rock tin mine in the world. When the tin market crashed in October 1985, recovering the ore became uneconomical and the plant was closed in 1990, leaving the residents unemployed.

In 1994 a small mining project was introduced with support from the Swedish Raw Materials Group, and a small plant was installed that produces 2 - 3kg of tin ore per hour. In April 2017, Bushveld Minerals, a company with interests in South Africa and Madagascar, agreed to terms to purchase the mine; and once finalised, this project will create new opportunities for the residents of this small town.

Traveller Description

Uis is situated at the foot of the Brandberg Mountain, home to the White Lady rock painting which is believed to be over 20 000 years old. It's this rock art site which brings travellers to Uis, residents also make a living from the passing traffic into Damaraland.

The Brandberg Massif is Namibia's highest mountain; its highest point, the Königstein, towers some 2 759m above sea level. The name means 'burning mountain' and refers to the mountain's appearance at sunset. The Brandberg hiking trail is a strenuous three day guided trail to the Königstein Peak. Guides must be booked beforehand through the Brandberg Mountain Guides.

The area around Uis is rich in minerals and rare rocks are often found on the ground rather than on top of a mountain or underground. Locals collect these rocks and sell them to the passing tourist trade.

To the south of Uis, just outside the town boundary, are 16 graves which tell a tragic story. A group of travellers was making their way to the coast when they reached the main road to Swakopmund, where Uis is now located. Stopping for the night they collected dead branches of the Damara milk bush (Euphorbia damarana) to cook their evening meal, not knowing that the bush is toxic. Their food absorbed the toxic smoke and they went to sleep never to wake again. They were buried where they died, and their graves are still visible today.

Travel Info

There's a variety of accommodation in Uis, as well as a small supermarket, fuel station and restaurant. If you're travelling from the west coast via Uis and the Brandberg towards Twyfelfontein and Etosha, Uis is the last fuel stop until Khorixas. Fuel may be available at Twyfelfontein Country Lodge, but isn't guaranteed, so be sure to fill up at Uis.

The tow-in service is located in Okahandja. Alternative numbers include +264(0)62 500 132 / +264(0)62 504 250.

Useful numbers:

Info Centre for Brandberg Mountain Guides: +264(0)64 504 162
Uis Clinic: +264(0)64 504 011

TRAVEL TIP! The well-stocked Brandberg Supermarket sells fresh meat and bread.

Town Info:

Police: +264(0)64 504 007
Tow-in: +264(0)81 129 7490

Turn page to see second map

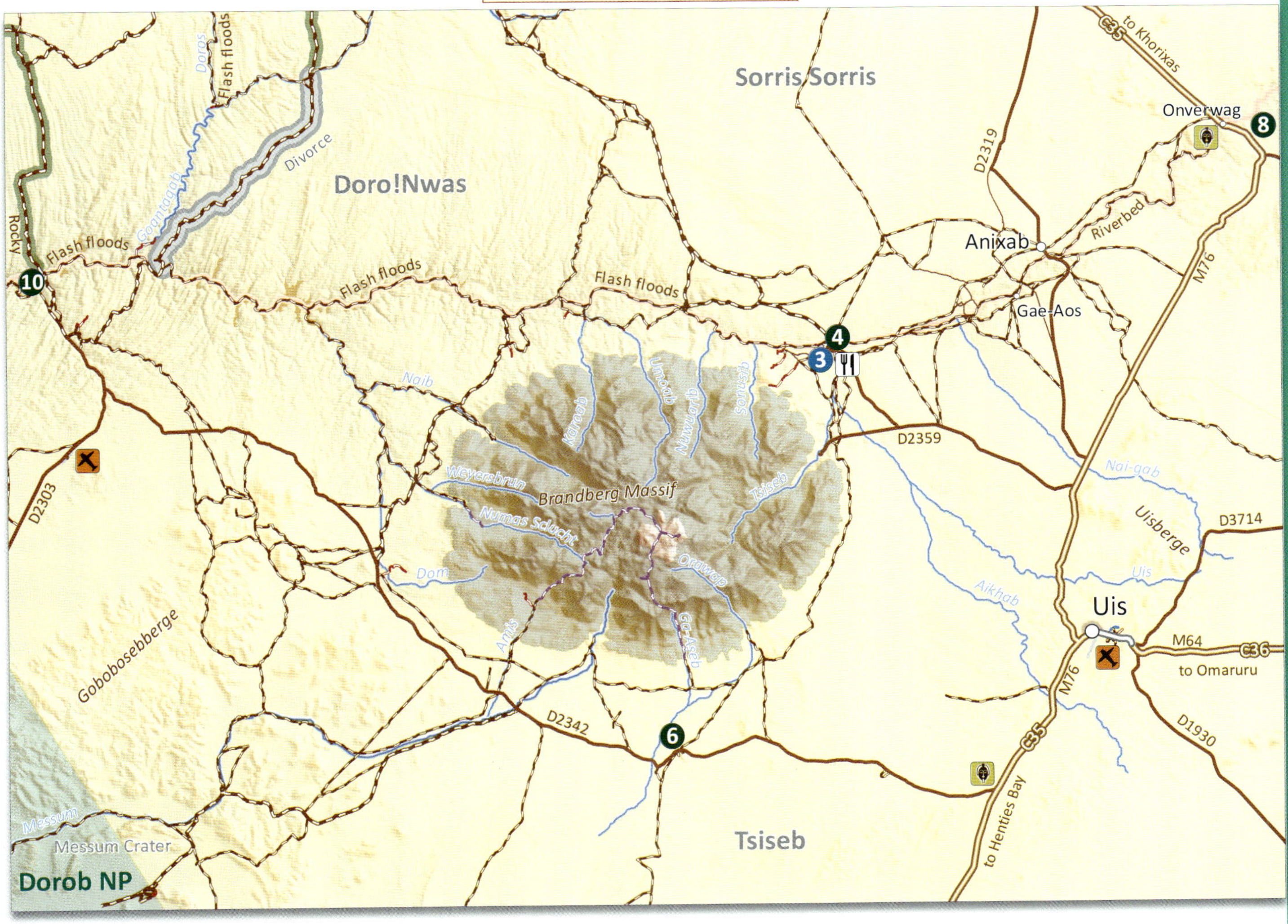

Uis

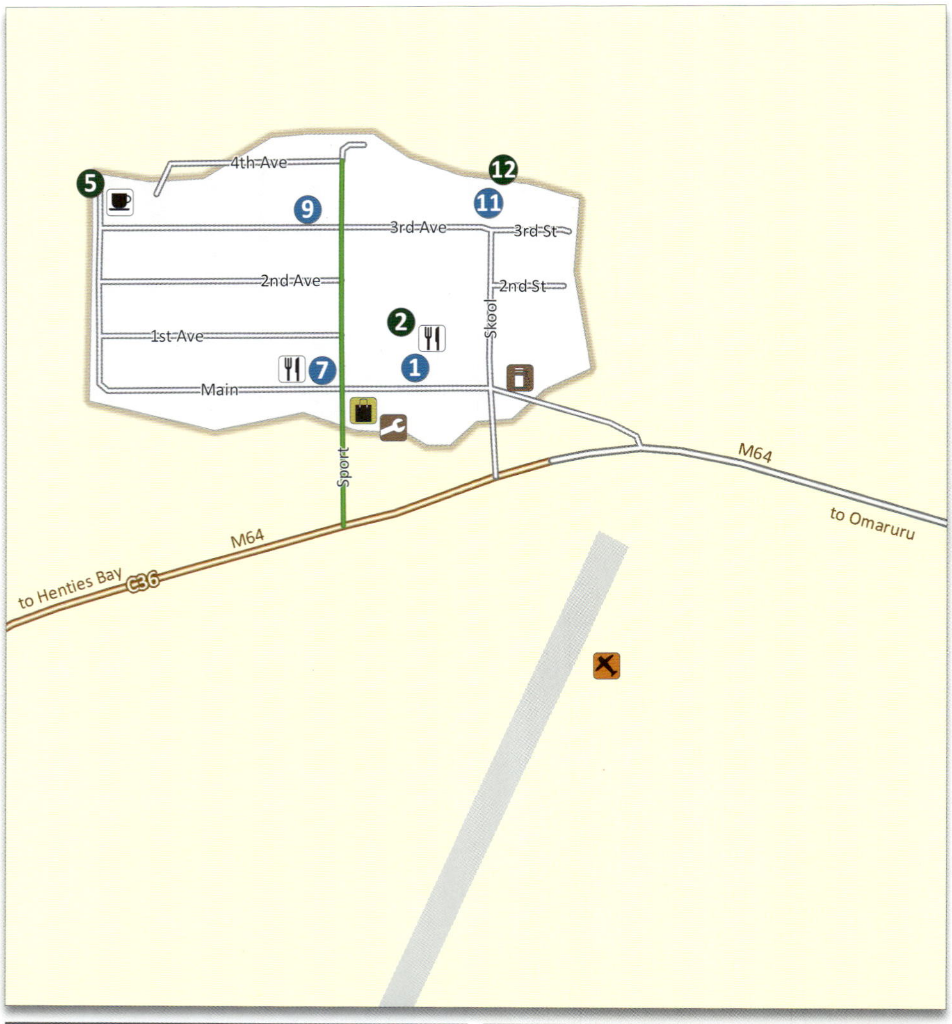

Brandberg Rest Camp 1

Self-catering $
3 Uis St, Uis
w140345

Tel: +264(0)64 504 038, Cell: +264(0)81 128 3775, Fax: +264(0)64 504 037
brandberg@africaonline.com.na,
www.brandbergrestcamp.com

Affordable accommodation in en-suite, self-catering rooms. There are also campsites, a pool, restaurant, bar and internet facilities.

Languages: English, German, Afrikaans

Facilities:
Activities:

Brandberg Rest Camp 2

Lodge Camp $
3 Uis St, Uis
w208193

Tel: +264(0)64 504 038, Cell: +264(0)81 128 3775, Fax: +264(0)64 504 037
brandberg@africaonline.com.na,
www.brandbergrestcamp.com

Campsites have power points, braai facilities and communal ablutions. Campers may use lodge swimming pool. Bikers welcome. Bookings can be made online.

Languages: English, German, Afrikaans

Facilities:
Activities:

Brandberg White Lady Lodge 3

Lodge $$
38km or 37min NW of Uis
w138473

Tel: +264(0)64 684 004, Cell: +264(0)81 791 3117, Fax: +264(0)64 684 006
ugab@iway.na,
www.brandbergwllodge.com

Eight chalets, fifteen en-suite rooms and six rustic permanent tents. Facilities include a dining room (dinner bookings required), bar, lounge and two pools.

Languages: English, Afrikaans

Facilities:
Activities:

Brandberg White Lady Lodge 4

Lodge Camp $
38km or 37min NW of Uis (of which 1km is 4WD)
w139235

Tel: +264(0)64 684 004, Cell: +264(0)81 791 3117, Fax: +264(0)64 684 006
ugab@iway.na,
www.brandbergwllodge.com

Campsites have a water point and braai area, but no electrical points. The lodge offers a dining room, bar, lounge and two pools.

Languages: English, Afrikaans

Facilities:
Activities:

Daureb Isib Campsite 5

Camping $
c/o Golf course Rd & Third Ave, Erf 672, Uis
w360951

Tel: +264(0)64 504 106, Cell: +264(0)81 127 0170, Fax: +264(0)64 504 138
dairebisib@gmail.com,
www.daurebisib.com

Five private and secure campsites, each with its own shower, toilet, kitchenette and braai area. Shaded parking is available (high enough for roof-top tents).

Languages: English

Facilities:
Activities:

Elephant Rock Community Camp 6

Community Camp $
40km or 34min WSW of Uis
w317221

Cell: +264(0)81 333 0387

Located a few meters away from the Brandberg Elephant Rock formation, these campsites have a toilet, shower and water points within a short walk. Cold drinks on sale at reception.

Languages: English

Facilities:

Montis-Usti Guest House 7

Guest House $$
c/o Main Road & Sport St, Erf 83, Uis
w142800

Tel: +264(0)64 504 219, Cell: +264(0)81 257 1307, Fax: +264(0)64 504 219
montis-restaurant@iway.na

Self-catering rooms with fully-equipped kitchenettes. Montis-Usti also offers a restaurant.

Languages: English

Facilities:
Activities:

Ozohere Campsite 8

Camping $$
45km or 39min NNE of Uis
w315169

Cell: +264(0)81 370 8298
ozoherelodge@gmail.com
www.ozoherelodge.com

Located on the banks of the Ugab River, this venue features basic, shaded campsites in and around huge boulders. Well placed to sleep over while traveling from the coast to Etosha.

Languages: English

Facilities:
Activities:

Petras Guesthouse 9

Guest House $
12 3rd Street, Uis
w255878

Cell: +264(0)81 129 9565
hot.air.ballooning.namibia@gmail.com
www.petras-gaestehaus.com

Spacious en-suite rooms overlooking the garden with pool. Private parking available.

Languages: English

Facilities:

Activities:

Rhino Ugab Camp - Ugab Save The Rhino Trust Camp 10

Community Camp $
107km or 1h56min WNW of Uis (of which 6km is 4WD)
w139148

www.savetherhinotrust.org

Basic campsites but good & clean. Showers (buckets filled by water heated via a 'donkey') and pit toilets. Camping is free, on first-come-first-served basis. Donations welcome.

Languages: English, Afrikaans

Facilities:

Activities:

Uis White Lady Guest House 11

Bed and Breakfast $$
1 & 2 Third Avenue, Uis
w139052

Tel: +264(0)64 504 102, Cell: +264(0)81 128 0860,
Fax: +264(0)64 504 102
whitelady@iway.na,
www.uiswhiteladyguesthouse.com

13 En-suite rooms with air-conditioning. Birdwatchers will enjoy all the birds visiting the waterhole. Bookings essential.

Languages: English, German, Afrikaans

Facilities:

Activities:

Uis White Lady Guest House 12

Camping $
1 & 2 Third Avenue, Uis
w142801

Tel: +264(0)64 504 102, Cell: +264(0)81 128 0860,
Fax: +264(0)64 504 102
whitelady@iway.na,
www.uiswhiteladyguesthouse.com

Clean, well-kept camp with ablution block and braai areas. 35km from the Brandberg.

Languages: English, German, Afrikaans

Facilities:

Activities:

Travel is fatal to prejudice, bigotry, and narrow-mindedness, and many of our people need it sorely on these accounts. Broad, wholesome, charitable views of men and things cannot be acquired by vegetating in one little corner of the earth all one's lifetime."

Mark Twain,
The Innocents Abroad

Desolation Valley (photo: Heiner Dillmann)

ERONGO

Sunrise and sunset are the best times to haul out your camera. (photo: Mietsie Visser)
(below, middle) The road to Spitzkoppe. (photo: Frank Höppener)

THIS REGION GETS ITS NAME from the Erongo Mountains where beautiful gemstones are found - these are often sold, informally, along the roads.

Spitzkoppe (meaning sharp hill) is one of Namibia's most recognisable landmarks and most famous mountain, it's also an outstanding camping spot. Although it's not the highest mountain in Namibia, it is popular for rock climbing. Even though it looks like it has a sharp peak when viewed from afar, Spitzkoppe actually consists of a series of rounded granite boulders.

Erongo is a farming area with lots of game farms that offer accommodation. The B2 highway between Windhoek and Swakopmund traverses this region and offers easy access to its attractions.

Omaruru is a charming and tourist-friendly town where you can visit one of Namibia's few wineries, Kristall Kellerei. Though small in size, the town is well worth a visit if you're interested in arts and culture.

On the Erindi Private Game Reserve visitors can enjoy wildlife from the smallest insects to the largest land mammals, as well as a multitude of rare and endangered species.

(right) The granite boulders of the Spitzkoppe have secrets, like this rock pool. (photo: Heiner Dillmann)

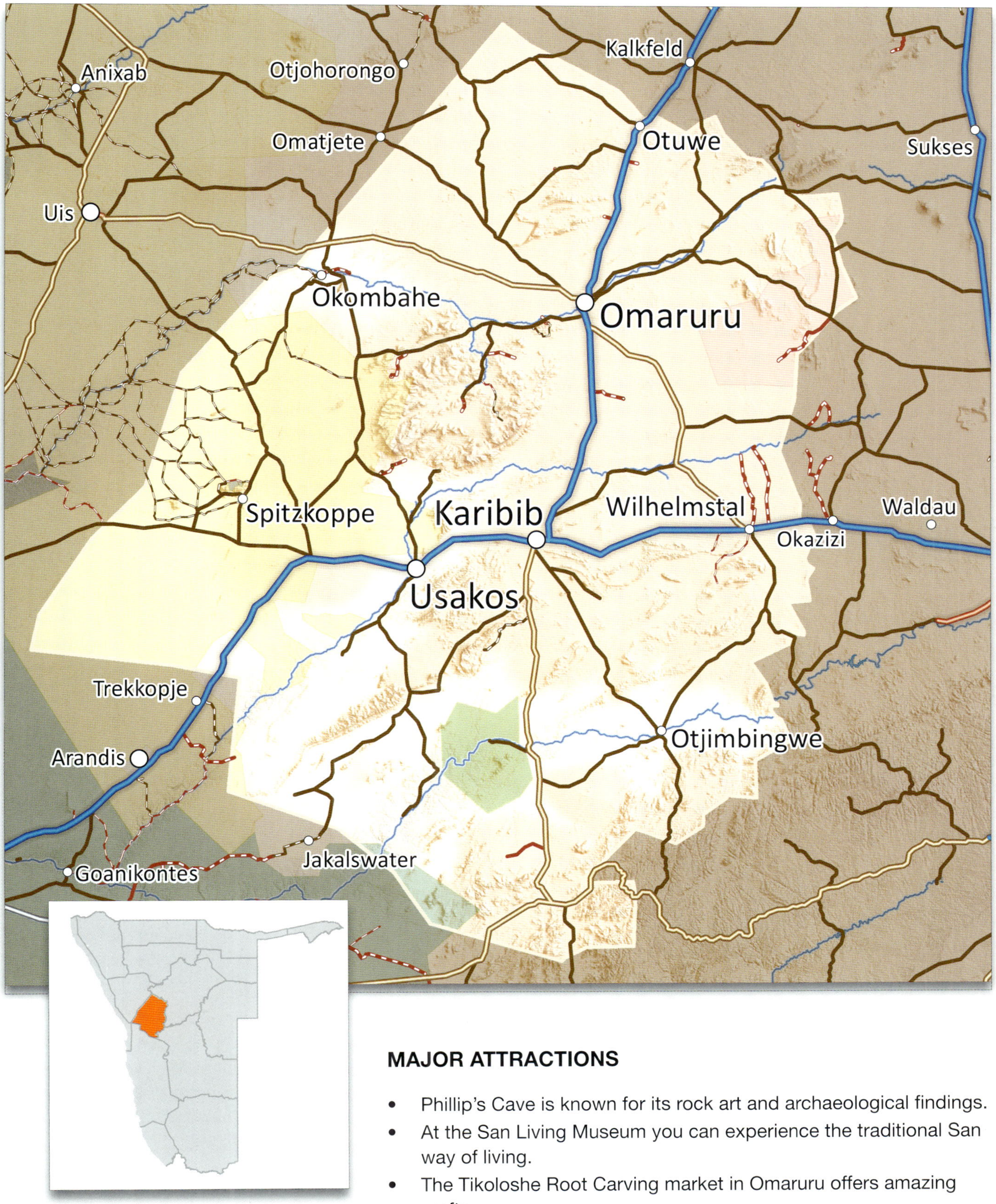

MAJOR ATTRACTIONS

- Phillip's Cave is known for its rock art and archaeological findings.
- At the San Living Museum you can experience the traditional San way of living.
- The Tikoloshe Root Carving market in Omaruru offers amazing crafts.
- You can either camp at Spitzkoppe Nature Reserve or enjoy a day visit to these extraordinary rock formations and Bushman Paradise cave with rock paintings.
- The rock paintings in Ekuta Cave are believed to have been made between 4 400 BC and 100 AD.
- The Erongo Singing rocks make metallic melodious sounds when beaten with a rock.
- Kristall Kellerei is one of Namibia's few wineries and a lovely spot to enjoy lunch in the garden.

More details about the attractions are available on our website (www.tracks4africa.co.za) or our Guide App. Our GPS Map can navigate you to each of these attractions.

Karibib

(photo: Janine Reyneke)

THE TOWN OF KARIBIB HAS A RICH HISTORY. Expecting business opportunities to arise from the railway construction between Swakopmund and Windhoek, Eduard Hälbich, a merchant from Otjimbingwe, bought a nearby waterhole called Otjandjomboimwe as well as 20 000 hectares of surrounding land from Herero headman Zacharias Zeraua. The deal was finalised on 7 January 1895 and two years later Hälbich opened a branch at what would later become known as Karibib.

Karibib grew rapidly when the railway construction reached the newly founded town. 1 June 1900 marks the day of the official foundation of Karibib when the first train arrived from Swakopmund. The railway station was built, a medical practice, storage facilities, a prison as well as living quarters for the railway workers. But when the railway workers moved on towards Windhoek in 1902, business quietened down.

However, in 1904 the place experienced a revival as a railway hub for ferrying troops during the Herero Revolt. On 8 December 1907 a reserve for the Herero was proclaimed in the vicinity of Otjimbingwe, whilst the remaining Herero land was confiscated and offered to the resident farmers in the district, a process which lasted until 1909, by which time Karibib district already numbered 837 white settlers, traders and farmers. Over the following few years the farming community grew strongly; later, high quality marble and gold were found and mined in the area.

Traveller Description

The beautiful Erongo Mountains dominate the Karibib skyline. There are a number of tourist attractions in the vicinity, like Spitzkoppe, Philipp's Cave (known for its rock art and archaeological findings) and the Erongo Singing Rocks. The town itself is not really a touristy town, but rather a stop for refreshments, replenishing stocks and refuelling. The Old Station Building is a national monument and places worth visiting include Hälbich House, Christ Church and the Henckert Tourist Centre in the main street.

Travel Info

Between the Agra Retail and OK Bazaars shops travellers will be able to replenish stocks and refill gas bottles.

Useful numbers:
Town clinic: + 264(0)64 550 073

TRAVEL TIP! At the Henckert Tourist Centre beautiful karakul rugs and wall hangings are woven. They also sell an excellent selection of curios and Namibian jewellery.

Town Info:
Police: +264(0)64 550 008 Doctor: +264(0)64 550 050 Tow-in: +264(0)81 129 7490
Tourism: +264(0)65 404 827

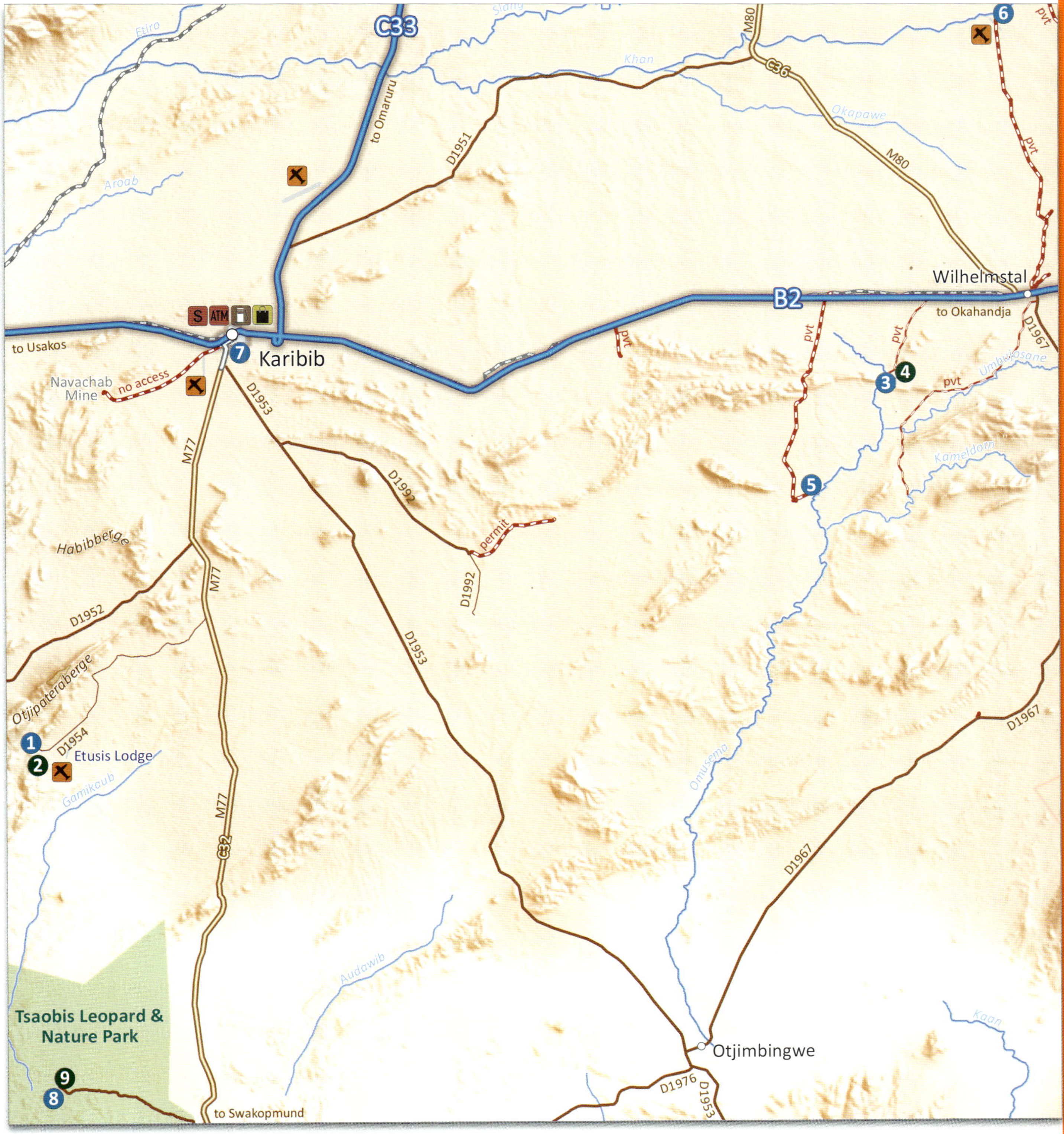

Karibib

Etusis Lodge — 1

Lodge $$
35km or 41min SSW of Karibib
w142653

etusis@resdest.com
www.etusis.de

Choose between comfortable bungalows or luxury permanent tents. Venue is located in savannah and mountainous bushveld. 4WD recommended in the rainy season.

Languages: English, German, Afrikaans

Facilities:
Activities:

Etusis Lodge — 2

Lodge Camp $
35km or 41min SSW of Karibib
w361804

Tel: +264(0)64 550 826
etusis@resdest.com
www.etusis.de

The five shaded campsites are 20km from the lodge, each has its own braai but shares ablution facilities. Lodge facilities not available to campers. You must be self-sufficient.

Languages: English, German, Afrikaans

Facilities:
Activities:

Kaliombo Safari Lodge — 3

Lodge $$
51km or 46min E of Karibib (of which 7km is 4WD)
w142660

Tel: +264(0)64 404 561, Cell: +264(0)81 129 4561,
Fax: +264(0)64 404 923
sunrisetours@iafrica.com.na,
www.sunrisetours.com.na

5 Permanent tents, each with en-suite bathroom and a private patio with spectacular views.

Languages: English

Facilities:
Activities:

Kaliombo Safari Lodge — 4

Lodge Camp $
51km or 46min E of Karibib (of which 7km is 4WD)
w142661

Tel: +264(0)64 404 561, Cell: +264(0)81 129 4561,
Fax: +264(0)64 404 923
sunrisetours@iafrica.com.na,
www.sunrisetours.com.na

The camp is situated on a dry riverbed and has one campsite for a maximum of 10 people. There's no power.

Languages: English

Facilities:
Activities:

Kansimba Game Lodge — 5

Game/Safari Lodge $$$
54km or 50min ESE of Karibib
w224556

Tel: +264(0)62 503 966, Cell: +27(0)81 687 5782,
Fax: +264(0)62 503 967
kansimba@iafrica.com.na,
www.kansimba.com

Each room has a balcony leading onto the garden while the luxury suites have balconies overlooking the river and waterhole. Bookings required.

Languages: English, German, Afrikaans

Facilities:
Activities:

Khan River Lodge — 6

Lodge $$
70km or 1h4min ENE of Karibib
w138464

Tel: +264(0)62 503 883, Cell: +264(0)81 386 7077,
Fax: +264(0)62 682 333
info@khanriverlodge.com,
www.khanriverlodge.com

Offers accommodation in comfortable rustic chalets with en-suite bathrooms. Self-catering units also available.

Languages: English, Afrikaans

Facilities:
Activities:

Klippenberg Guest House — 7

Guest House $$
1km or 2min SSE of Karibib
w206849

Tel: +264(0)64 550 693, Cell: +264(0)81 124 8730,
Fax: +264(0)64 550 693
kcc@iway.na

10 Standard and five economic rooms. This venue has tennis courts, a small golf course and is located close to Klippenberg Mountain.

Languages: English

Facilities:
Activities:

Tsaobis Nature Park Restcamp — 8

Self-catering $
64km or 1h4min SSW of Karibib
w138679

Tel: +264(0)64 684 060, Cell: +264(0)81 319 8333
booking@tsaobisnaturepark.com
www.tsaobisnaturepark.com

Accommodation in eight bungalows/chalets. The ideal setting for geological trips and one-day excursions. Activities include sundowner drives and 4x4 trails.

Languages: English, German, Afrikaans

Facilities:
Activities:

Tsaobis Nature Park Rest Camp — 9

Camping $
64km or 1h5min SSW of Karibib
w141116

Tel: +264(0)64 684 060, Cell: +264(0)81 319 8333
booking@tsaobisnaturepark.com
www.tsaobisnaturepark.com

Spacious camp with shady trees and an open-air shower. Situated within the Tsaobis Nature Park.

Languages: English, German, Afrikaans

Facilities:
Activities:

> *"So shut up, live, travel, adventure, bless and don't be sorry"*
>
> *Jack Kerouac*

Approaching the Spitzkoppe and Pontok Mountains. (photo: Heiner Dillmann)

(photo: Frank Höppener)

Omaruru

(photo: Ian-Ray Nel)

THE NAME OMARURU MEANS 'BITTER MILK' in the local Otjiherero language - their cattle used to browse on a local bush which turned their milk bitter.

Omaruru was established in 1863 by Wilhelm Zeraua, the first chief of the White Flag clan of the OvaHerero people. In 1871 Anders Ohlsson and Axel Eriksson established a brewery at Omaruru; Eriksson also established a trading post, which flourished thanks to long distance trading between southern Angola and the Cape Colony.

The town also grew thanks to a mission built in 1872 by Gottlieb Viehe; this was attacked in 1904 during the Herero Revolt and is today a museum. Franke Tower was later erected to commemorate the relief of the local garrison by Hauptmann Victor Franke's troops, the garrison was besieged by Herero tribesmen who'd risen up against the German colonial presence. Interestingly, descendants of Lothar von Trotha and the Von Trotha family travelled to Omaruru in October 2007 by invitation of the royal Herero chiefs and publicly apologised for Von Trotha's role in the Herero genocide.

Von Trotha was governor of German South West Africa and Commander-in-Chief of its colonial forces, in which role he suppressed a native rebellion during the Herero Wars. He was widely condemned for his brutality in the Herero Wars, particularly for his role in the genocide that led to the near-extermination of the Herero.

Traveller Description

Omaruru is a quaint and tourist-friendly town, there's lots of accommodation here as well as on surrounding guest farms. The town is situated on the Omaruru River which is usually dry; despite this Omaruru appears quite lush and green due to an abundant groundwater supply. In fact, the town receives all its water from boreholes along the Omaruru River. This town is both the commercial centre for the surrounding cattle and game farms, and an excellent springboard for touring the nearby Erongo Mountains. It's an interesting place with some artistic inhabitants making chocolates, cheese and wine as well as various forms of art and carvings. The main road boasts a couple of excellent coffee shops and restaurants - this welcoming town offers all the services that a traveller may need.

Travel Info

Omaruru is known for its annual festival when the Hereros commemorate their past chiefs. Nearby attractions include dinosaur footprints on a farm north-east of town, Paula's Cave with rock art south-west of town as well as the popular Erindi Private Game Reserve east of Omaruru. Historical points of interest in town include the Rhenish Mission House which has been transformed into the town museum, and Franke Tower. Travellers can restock their pantries and refill gas bottles at both the Spar and Agra.

TRAVEL TIP! Visit the Tikoloshe Africa Centre at the town's entrance, it sells sculptures carved from hardwood tree roots. At Kristall Kellerei, one of four wine producers in Namibia, visitors can taste and buy brandy, a variety of wines and schnapps. The Sand Dragon Restaurant and art centre is located in a historic building on the main street and has a shaded garden. Unlimited Home Industries produces a range of handmade chocolates using local ingredients such as dates, rosella, kumquat, oranges, choc-mint and honey.

Town Info:

Hospital: +264(0)64 572 900
Police: +264(0)64 570 340 / +264(0)64 570 010
Doctor: +264(0)64 570 033
Tow-in: +264(0)85 571 7034 / +264(0)64 571 109

Turn page to see second map

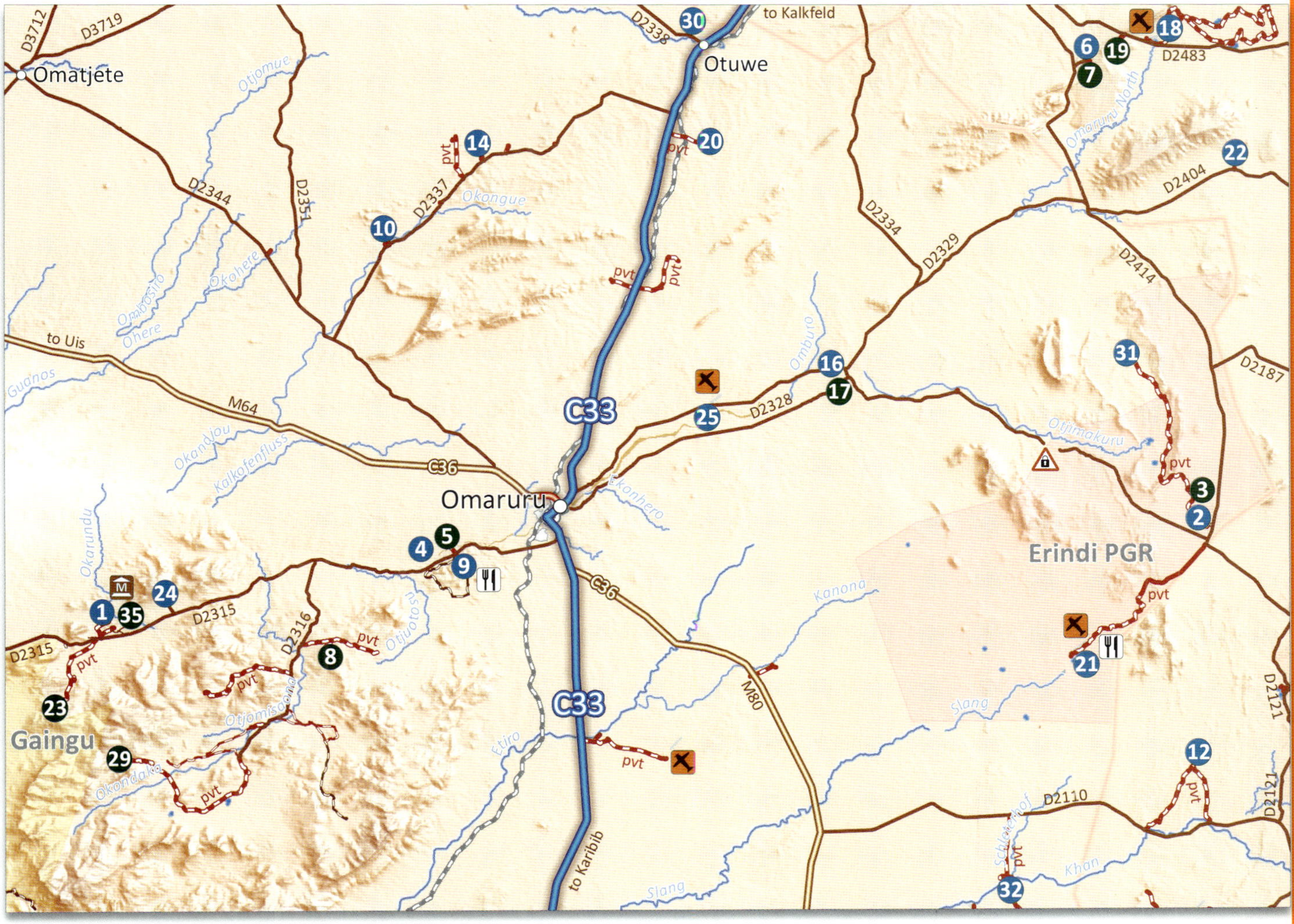

"I can speak to my soul only when the two of us are off exploring deserts or cities or mountains or roads."

Paulo Coelho

Omaruru

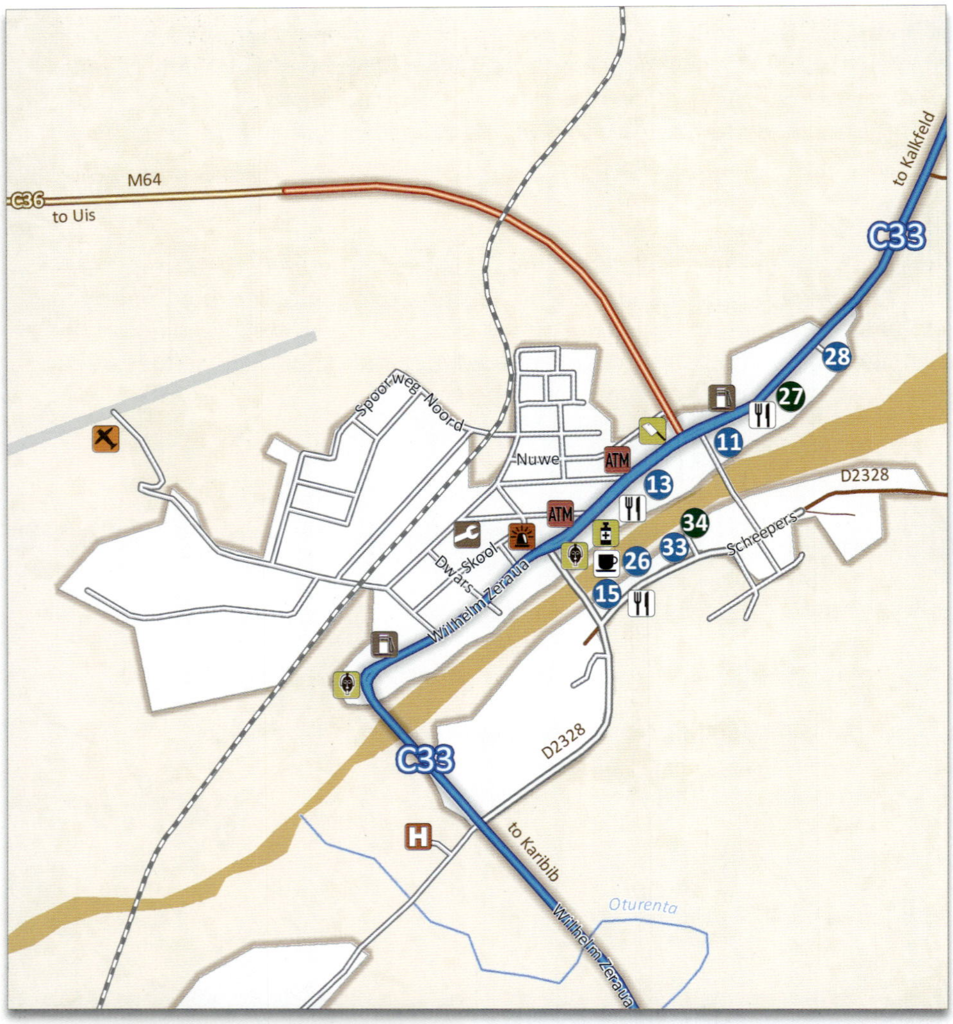

Ai Aiba Rock Painting Lodge 1

Lodge $$
49km or 1h14min WSW of Omaruru
w140281

Tel: +264(0)61 239 199, Fax: +264(0)64 570 557
info@aiaiba-namibia.com
www.aiaiba.com

Double bungalows with private patios. Facilities include a bar. Activities include walking safaris, sun downer drives, tours to historic rock art and Etemba picnic tour.

Languages: English

Facilities:

Activities:

Camp Elephant (Erindi Private GR) 2

Self-catering $$
67km or 1h4min E of Omaruru
w262380

Fax: +264(0)64 570 801, Cell: +264(0)83 330 1111
reservations1@erindi.com
www.erindi.com

Fifteen luxury chalets. All with air-conditioning, satellite TV, and braai area on outside patio. Maximum six people per chalet. Shaded parking.

Languages: English

Facilities:

Activities:

Camp Elephant (Erindi Private GR) 3

Park Camp $$$
67km or 1h3min E of Omaruru
w261525

Fax: +264(0)64 570 801, Cell: +264(0)83 330 1111
reservations1@erindi.com
www.erindi.com

30 Luxury campsites, each with its own private bathroom, braai area, table seating, private lawn, wash area and shaded parking. Maximum six people per site.

Languages: English

Facilities:

Activities:

Camp Mara 4

Self-catering $$
14km or 22min WSW of Omaruru
w262361

Tel: +264(0)64 571 190, Cell: +264(0)81 128 1203, Fax: +264(0)64 571 190
campmara@iway.na,
www.campmara.com

Two self-catering units, with two extra double rooms. Plus one cottage. Venue is 13km from Omaruru on the edge of the Erongo Mountains.

Languages: English, German, Afrikaans

Facilities:

Activities:

Camp Mara 5

Camping $$
14km or 22min WSW of Omaruru
w262360

Tel: +264(0)64 571 190, Cell: +264(0)81 128 1203, Fax: +264(0)64 571 190
campmara@iway.na,
www.campmara.com

Campsites suitable for tents and caravans on the banks of the Omaruru River. With toilets, showers and braais. On the edge of the Erongo Mountains.

Languages: English, German, Afrikaans

Facilities:

Activities:

Dinosaur's Tracks Guestfarm Namibia 6

Guest Farm $
30km or 27min SE of Kalkfeld
w137683

Tel: +264(0)67 290 153, Cell: +264(0)81 462 2983
dinotracks@afol.com.na
www.dinosaurstracks.com

Three comfortable three-bed rooms, each room with en-suite bathroom and its own terrace with beautiful view of mountain scenery.

Languages: English, German

Facilities:

Activities:

Dinosaur's Tracks Guestfarm Namibia 7

Farm Camp $
30km or 27min SE of Kalkfeld
w222195

Tel: +264(0)67 290 153, Cell: +264(0)81 462 2983
dinotracks@afol.com.na
www.dinosaurstracks-guestfarm.com

Five shady campsites right at the fossilized dinosaur tracks (a National Monument).

Languages: English, German

Facilities:

Activities:

Erongo Plateau Camp 8

Farm Camp $
38km or 51min WSW of Omaruru
w138812

Tel: +264(0)61 221 567, Cell: +264(0)81 277 1668, Fax: +264(0)88 642 716
erongo@iway.na,
www.erongo.iway.na

Campground is small and secluded, the campsites are all private. No credit card facilities here, bring cash.

Languages: English, Afrikaans

Facilities:

Activities:

Erongo Wilderness Lodge 9

Lodge $$$
14km or 21min WSW of Omaruru
w138814

Tel: +264(0)61 239 199, Cell: +264(0)81 128 0951,
info@erongowilderness-namibia.com
www.erongowilderness-namibia.com

Ten luxury, tented bungalows, built on stilts and shaded by thatched roofs, located amongst granite boulders. Visit local rock art and enjoy excellent birding.

Languages: English

Facilities:
Activities:

Etendero Guest Farm 10

Guest Farm $$
37km or 52min NNW of Omaruru
w142105

Tel: +264(0)64 570 927, Fax: +264(0)64 571 082
etendero@iway.na
www.etendero.de

20 comfortable, en-suite rooms. Farm-style meals prepared from fresh farm produce.

Languages: English, German

Facilities:
Activities:

Evening Shade Self Catering And Main Street Café 11

Bed and Breakfast $$
116 Wilhelm Zeraua Rd (Main Str), Omaruru
w315077

Tel: +264(0)64 570 303, Cell: +264(0)81 124 6184
info@evening-shade.com
www.evening-shade.com

Three double/single and two family rooms, sleeping 17 in all. Full kitchens are available for self-catering or breakfast as part of the room rate.

Languages: English, German, Afrikaans

Facilities:
Activities:

Haasenhof Guest Farm 12

Guest Farm $$
80km or 1h4min ESE of Omaruru
w138525

Tel: +264(0)62 503 827, Cell: +264(0)81 275 2177,
Fax: +264(0)88 651 7643
haase@iway.na,
www.haasenhof.com

Comfortable single or double rooms with private bathrooms. A lovely garden surrounds the pool.

Languages: German, English, Afrikaans

Facilities:
Activities:

Hotel Central 13

Hotel $
Wilhelm Zeraua st, Omaruru
w140440

Tel: +264(0)64 570 030, Fax: +264(0)88 655 9806
centralhotel@iway.na
www.centralhotelomaruru.com

Eight double and five single rooms, in comfortable bungalows; each with own veranda and bathroom.

Languages: English, Afrikaans

Facilities:
Activities:

Immenhof Guest Farm 14

Guest Farm $$
49km or 1h25min NNW of Omaruru
w139470

Tel: +264(0)61 234 342, Cell: +264(0)81 629 3270,
Fax: +264(0)88 627 420
eden@africaonline.com.na,
www.immenhofnamibia.com

Nine spacious, en-suite rooms, each individually decorated. Bookings required.

Languages: English, Afrikaans

Facilities:
Activities:

Kashana Lodge 15

Lodge $$
Dr. I Scheepers Drive, Omaruru
w262340

Tel: +264(0)64 571 434, Fax: +264(0)64 571 107
info@kashana-namibia.com
www.kashana-namibia.com

Comfortable accommodation in standard or luxury chalets, with double or king-size beds. Well-furnished family rooms can accommodate up to four people.

Languages: English, Afrikaans, German

Facilities:
Activities:

Klein Eden Guest Farm 16

Guest Farm $$
29km or 24min ENE of Omaruru
w207972

Tel: +264(0)64 570 620, Fax: +264(0)64 570 630
kleinedengasteplaas@iway.na
www.kleinedenguestfarm.com

Eight self-catering units with air-conditioning, fans, bathroom (shower) and fully-equipped, open-plan kitchen. There are indoor braai areas as well as a boma.

Languages: English

Facilities:
Activities:

Klein Eden Guest Farm 17

Farm Camp $$
30km or 27min ENE of Omaruru
w358688

Tel: +264(0)64 570 620, Fax: +264(0)64 570 630
kleinedengasteplaas@iway.na
www.kleinedenguestfarm.com

Camping with hot water, power points, indoor and boma braais.

Languages: English

Facilities:
Activities:

Mount Etjo Safari Lodge 18

Lodge $$$
105km or 1h19min SSW of Otjiwarongo
w138437

Tel: +264(0)67 290 173, Cell: +264(0)81 799 7643,
Fax: +264(0)67 290 172
mount.etjo@iway.na,
www.mount-etjo.com

Standard or luxury en-suite rooms, with jacuzzis.

Languages: English, German, French, Afrikaans

Facilities:
Activities:

Mount Etjo Safari Lodge 19

Lodge Camp $$
95km or 1h26min NE of Omaruru
w243167

Tel: +264(0)67 290 173, Cell: +264(0)81 799 7643,
Fax: +264(0)67 290 172
mount.etjo@iway.na,
www.mount-etjo.com

The camp has private showers and toilets, and each campsite has its own braai area with wood provided. Campers are welcome to eat at the lodge and join activities there.

Languages: English, German, French, Afrikaans

Facilities:
Activities:

Okosongoro Guest Farm 20

Guest Farm $$$
40km or 26min NNE of Omaruru
w142793

Tel: +264(0)67 290 161, Fax: +264(0)67 290 170
clausen@okosongoro.com.na
www.okosongoro.com.na

Farm-style accommodation in en-suite guest rooms, for hunters and non-hunters. Laundry facilities available. Guests enjoy delicious farm-cooked meals.

Languages: English

Facilities:
Activities:

Omaruru

Old Traders Lodge (Erindi Private GR) 21

Game/Safari Lodge $$$
82km or 01h46min ESE of Omaruru
w140557

Tel: +264(0)64 570 802, Cell: +264(0)83 330 1114, Fax: +264(0)64 570 801
reservations@erindi.com,
www.oldtraderslodge.com

Situated within Erindi Private Game Reserve, the lodge offers luxury, family and standard suites, each equipped with TV, fridge and air-conditioner.

Languages: English

Facilities:

Activities:

Omaha Guest Farm & Estate 22

Self-catering $$
72km or 1h4min ENE of Omaruru
w143305

Tel: +264(0)67 306 556, Cell: +264(0)81 124 7687, Fax: +264(0)88 645 472
omaha@mweb.com.na,
www.namibia-farm-accommodation.com

Five double and one family room. Rates are for self-catering. Omaha is situated at the base of Mount Etjo.

Languages: English

Facilities:

Activities:

Omandumba Guest Farm Three Elephant Campsite 23

Lodge Camp $
56km or 1h21min WSW of Omaruru
w274113

Tel: +264(0)64 571 086, Cell: +264(0)81 245 3713
omandumba@iway.na
www.omandumba.de

The camp is located at the base of a rock wall, under shady trees. It's completely wild besides a flush toilet and 'donkey' shower.

Languages: English

Facilities:

Activities:

Omandumba Self Catering Farmhouse 24

Guest Farm $$
41km or 48min WSW of Omaruru
w274110

Tel: +264(0)64 571 086, Cell: +264(0)81 217 0879
omandumba@iway.na
www.omandumba.de

Accommodation includes a farm house and self-catering options. Located on the north-western slopes of the Erongo Mountains.

Languages: English

Facilities:

Activities:

Omaruru Game Lodge 25

Lodge $$$
17km or 16min ENE of Omaruru
w137647

Tel: +264(0)64 570 044, Fax: +264(0)64 570 134
omlodge@iafrica.com.na
www.omaruru-game-lodge.com

En-suite bungalows with thatched roofs and natural stone walls. Self-catering bungalows also available, each with kitchen and braai facility.

Languages: English, Afrikaans

Facilities:

Activities:

Omaruru Guest House 26

Guest House $
Dr Scheepers Drive, Omaruru
w138366

Tel: +264(0)64 570 035, Fax: +264(0)88 621 005
hello@omaruru-guesthouse.com
www.omaruru-guesthouse.com

18 Double and one single room. Located under big shady trees on the banks of the Omaruru River. Meals are served on the veranda.

Languages: English

Facilities:

Activities:

Omaruru Rest Camp 27

Camping $
Wilhelm Zeraua Rd, Omaruru
w274144

Tel: +264(0)64 570 516, Fax: +264(0)64 571 017
omarururestcamp@iway.na

Campsites with clean individual ablutions, ideal for campers or caravaners. Family-friendly, self-catering units also available.

Languages: English, Afrikaans

Facilities:

Activities:

Omaruru Rest Camp Guest House 28

Guest House $$
Wilhelm Zeraua Road, Omaruru
w142391

Tel: +264(0)64 570 516, Fax: +264(0)64 571 017
omarururestcamp@iway.na

24 Self-catering, air-conditioned rooms with internet access. There's also a restaurant and sports bar. Great spot for bird lovers.

Languages: English, Afrikaans

Facilities:

Activities:

Omukutu Nature Farm and Black Rock Campsite 29

Camping $$
66km or 1h32min WSW of Omaruru (of which 2km is 4WD)
w360754

Cell: +264(0)81 128 3234
pangolin@iafrica.com.na

Pristine location with only one farm road in and out. Wildlife meander past the campsite on their way to a small dam.

Languages: English

Facilities:

Activities:

Ondombo Hunting & Guestfarm 30

Guest Farm $$
47km or 29min NNE of Omaruru
w142645

Tel: +264(0)67 290 009, Cell: +264(0)81 302 2896, Fax: +264(0)88 615 158
kfriedensdorf@iway.na,
www.namibia-jagdfarm.com

Comfortable accommodation in double rooms. There's a braai area, beautiful garden and secure parking.

Languages: English

Facilities:

Activities:

Otjikoko Game Ranch 31

Guest Farm $$$
88km or 1h36min ENE of Omaruru
w233713

Tel: +264(0)64 570 500, Cell: +264(0)81 235 1755, Fax: +264(0)88 653 0707
haag@otjikoko.com,
www.otjikoko.com

Four en-suite rooms in the main farmhouse. Venue is a hunting and guest farm with a variety of game. 4WD needed during rainy season. Bookings essential.

Languages: German

Facilities:

Activities:

Ozongwindi Lodge 32

Lodge $$$
80km or 1h9min WNW of Okahandja
w262335

Tel: +264(0)62 503 981, Cell: +264(0)81 129 7602, Fax: +264(0)62 500 832
info@ozongwindi.com,
www.ozongwindi.com

10 Free-standing bungalows, each with its own deck. Plus an old-style renovated farmhouse with four double rooms. All bathrooms en-suite. No camping facilities.

Languages: English, German, Afrikaans

Facilities:

Activities:

River-Guesthouse 33

Guest House $
Dr I Scheepers Drive, Omaruru
w141178

Tel: +264(0)64 570 274, Cell: +264(0)81 269 5949, Fax: +264(0)64 570 274
riveromaruru@gmail.com

Rooms with all modern amenities. Plus a pool, beautiful garden, lapa and sundowner deck.

Languages: English, German, Afrikaans

Facilities: FC

Activities:

River-Guesthouse 34

Lodge Camp $
Dr I Scheepers Drive, Omaruru
w261557

Tel: +264(0)64 570 274, Cell: +264(0)81 269 5949, Fax: +264(0)64 570 274
riveromaruru@gmail.com, www.river-guesthouse.com

Six campsites with ablution facilities for men and women. Power points at an extra charge, and braai facilities.

Languages: English, German, Afrikaans

Facilities: FC

Activities:

San Living Museum 35

Camping $
46km or 55min WSW of Omaruru
w274112

Tel: +264(0)64 571 086, Cell: +27(0)81 245 3713
omandumba@iway.na
www.omandumba.de

This small camp is located close to the living museum. There are reed showers and toilets, and braai stands at each site. But no power.

Languages: English

Facilities:

Activities:

(photo: Ian-Ray Nel)

Usakos

(photo: Janine Reyneke)

HERERO CHIEF SAMUEL MAHARERO sold some land to Europeans in the early 1900s, they in turn resold it to the Otavi Mining and Railway Company (OMEG). OMEG operated an industrial railway line from Swakopmund to Tsumeb and thus established a railway station and a repair shop at the settlement which became known as Usakos. Mining operations slowed down in the 60s, but Usakos remained important as a drive-through from the Namibian interior to the coast.

Traveller Description

Surrounded by mountains, Usakos is picturesque with uninterrupted views of the horizon. It's quite an important tourist town in the Erongo area as there are many attractions in the vicinity. It is the closest town to Spitzkoppe, one of Namibia's most recognisable landmarks, and worth a refreshment stop. Although the facilities at the Spitzkoppe Community Camp are basic, it is so amazing that you simply have to spend two nights.

You will find a variety of accommodation in and around Usakos, you can visit the nearby Philipp's Cave (known for its rock art and archaeological findings) and the Erongo Singing Rocks. Historic buildings in Usakos are the Roman Catholic church (erected in 1905) and the old hotel. Also worth seeing is the steam locomotive, Class NG No.40, in front of the old station building.

Travel Info

There's a doctor in Karibib 35km away. His contact number is +264(0)64 550 050.

TRAVEL TIP! If you're on your way to Swakopmund, stop at the Namib Oasis Farmstall on your way out. They serve a great breakfast and lunch and sell homemade preserves and good biltong. The Uiba-Oas Crystal Market at the D1918 / B2 junction is also worth a visit.

Town Info:

Hospital:	+264(0)64 530 067
Police:	+264(0)64 530 003
Tow-in:	+264(0)81 311 8318

Ameib Gästehaus — 1

Guest House $$
27km or 28min N of Usakos
w137362

Cell: +264(0)81 857 4639
ameib@erongosafaris.com
www.ameib.com

Accommodation in farm-style guest rooms, thatched bungalows and cabins. Ameib is part of the Erongo Mountain Rhino Sanctuary Trust. Reservations mandatory.

Languages: English, German, Afrikaans

Facilities:
Activities:

Ameib Gästehaus — 2

Lodge Camp $
27km or 29min N of Usakos
w140627

Cell: +264(0)81 857 4639
ameib@erongosafaris.com
www.ameib.com

Ten campsites with concrete bases and braai areas. Electricity available in the ablution block. Reservations mandatory.

Languages: English, German, Afrikaans

Facilities:
Activities:

Bahnhof Hotel Usakos — 3

Hotel $
22 Theo Ben Gurirab St, Usakos
w141549

Fax: +264(0)64 530 765, Cell: +264(0)81 124 9008
bahnhof@iway.na

Comfortable single and double rooms with en-suite bathrooms, air-conditioning, satellite TV, Wi-Fi, pool, restaurant, beer garden and secure, undercover parking.

Languages: English, Afrikaans

Facilities:
Activities:

Hohenstein Lodge — 4

Game/Safari Lodge $$$
27km or 24min NNW of Usakos
w142109

Tel: +264(0)64 530 900, Fax: +264(0)64 530 931
info@hohensteinlodge.com
www.hohensteinlodge.com

14 Spacious rooms with en-suite shower/toilet and safe. All the bungalows as well as the restaurant at Hohenstein have great views.

Languages: German, English

Facilities:
Activities:

Spitzkoppe — 5

Camping $
54km or 43min WNW of Usakos
w138624

Tel: +264(0)64 464 144, Cell: +264(0)81 850 2566
reservations@logufa.com
www.spitzkoppe.com

31 Campsites, a few of which are for overlanders only. Maximum of 8 people allowed per site. There are dry toilets at the campsites and hot showers at reception.

Languages: English, Afrikaans

Facilities:
Activities:

Spitzkoppen Lodge — 6

Self-catering $$$
54km or 43min WNW of Usakos
w261558

Tel: +264(0)64 464 144, Cell: +264(0)81 850 2566
reservations@logufa.com
www.spitzkoppenlodge.com

15 spacious, tastefully-furnished chalets, each with private bathroom and outside viewing deck.

Languages: English, Afrikaans

Facilities:
Activities:

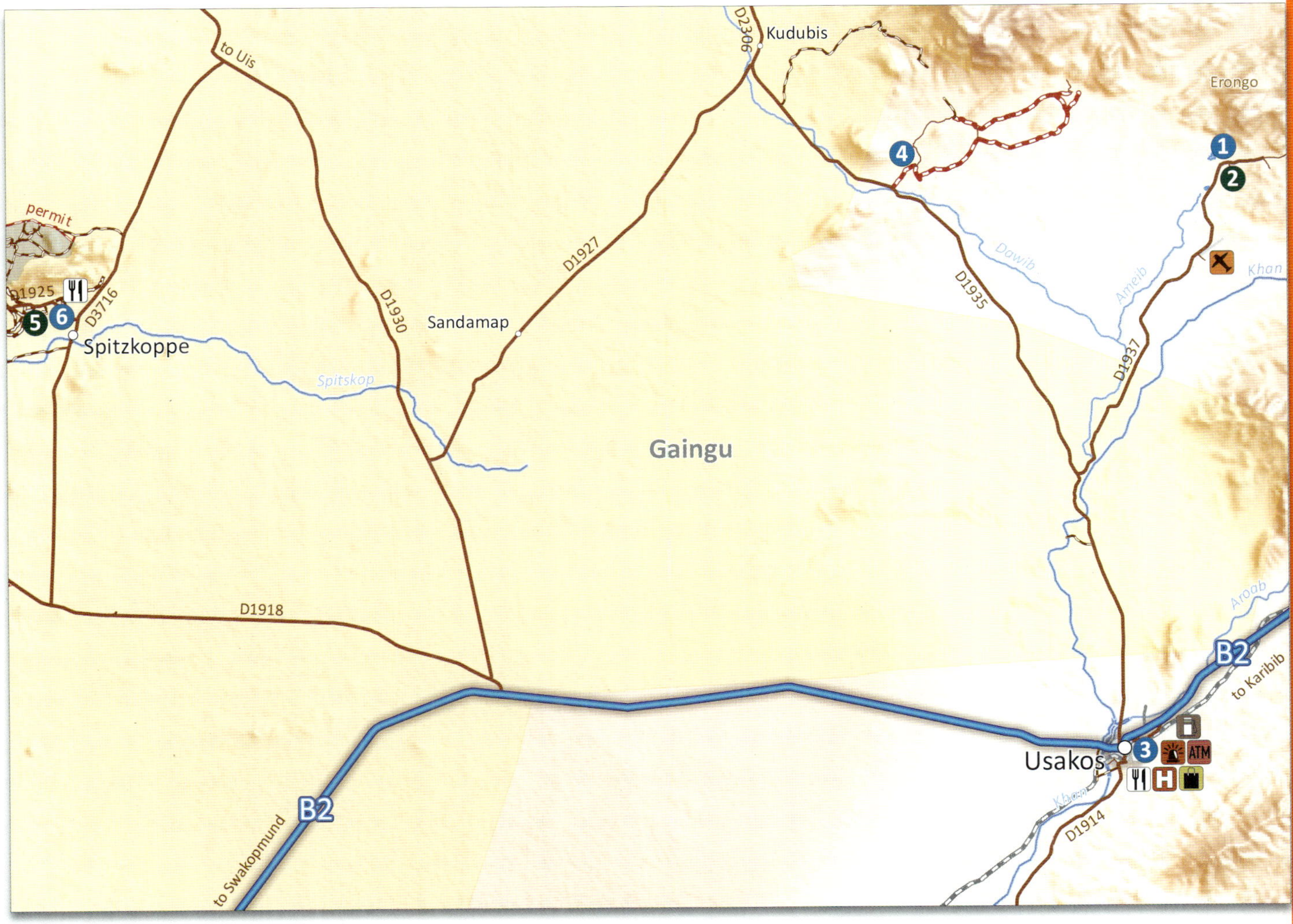

(above) An implausibility of wildebeest drift across a far plain. (photo: Frank Höppener)
(bottom) Okaukuejo waterhole (photo: Mietsie Visser)

ETOSHA IS ONE OF NAMIBIA'S finest national parks and offers spectacular game viewing. The park has 86 springs, fountains and waterholes (some natural and some fed by boreholes), where the game tends to concentrate in the dry season. Visitors can expect to see a host of small and large animal species, including elephant, lion, giraffe, rhino and a variety of antelope, including the elusive Damara Dik-Dik, Namibia's smallest antelope.

Thousands of years ago Etosha Pan would have been a lake fed by the Kunene River but today the pan only holds water after heavy rains. During this time, for a short while, it plays host to flamingos, pelicans and wading birds. The rainy season generally offers excellent birding opportunities with some 340 species present, about a third of which are migratory.

Part of the reason Etosha is so popular is because it offers good facilities and is accessible by sedan. The park has a few points from which to enter or exit but the main ones are: Galton Gate in the southwest, Anderson Gate in the south, Von Lindequist Gate in the east and King Nehale Gate in the northeast. The park is serviced by a good gravel road and it has six camps which offer excellent camping and/or lodging facilities. Olifantsrus is the newest camp in the park, offering just camping. Each camp is unique and has different vegetation which attracts different animals.

When it was proclaimed in 1907, the park was one of the largest reserves in the world, but it has since shrunk in size to an area consisting mainly of Etosha Pan which is 130 km long and 50 km wide. The western section of the park was restricted for many years but now visitors are allowed to use Galton Gate and stay over at Dolomite luxury camp.

There also are reserves just outside Etosha which offer their own game drives and beautiful scenery; for instance, Onguma Private Game Reserve to the east near Namutoni Gate and Ongawa Private Game Reserve to the south near Anderson Gate.

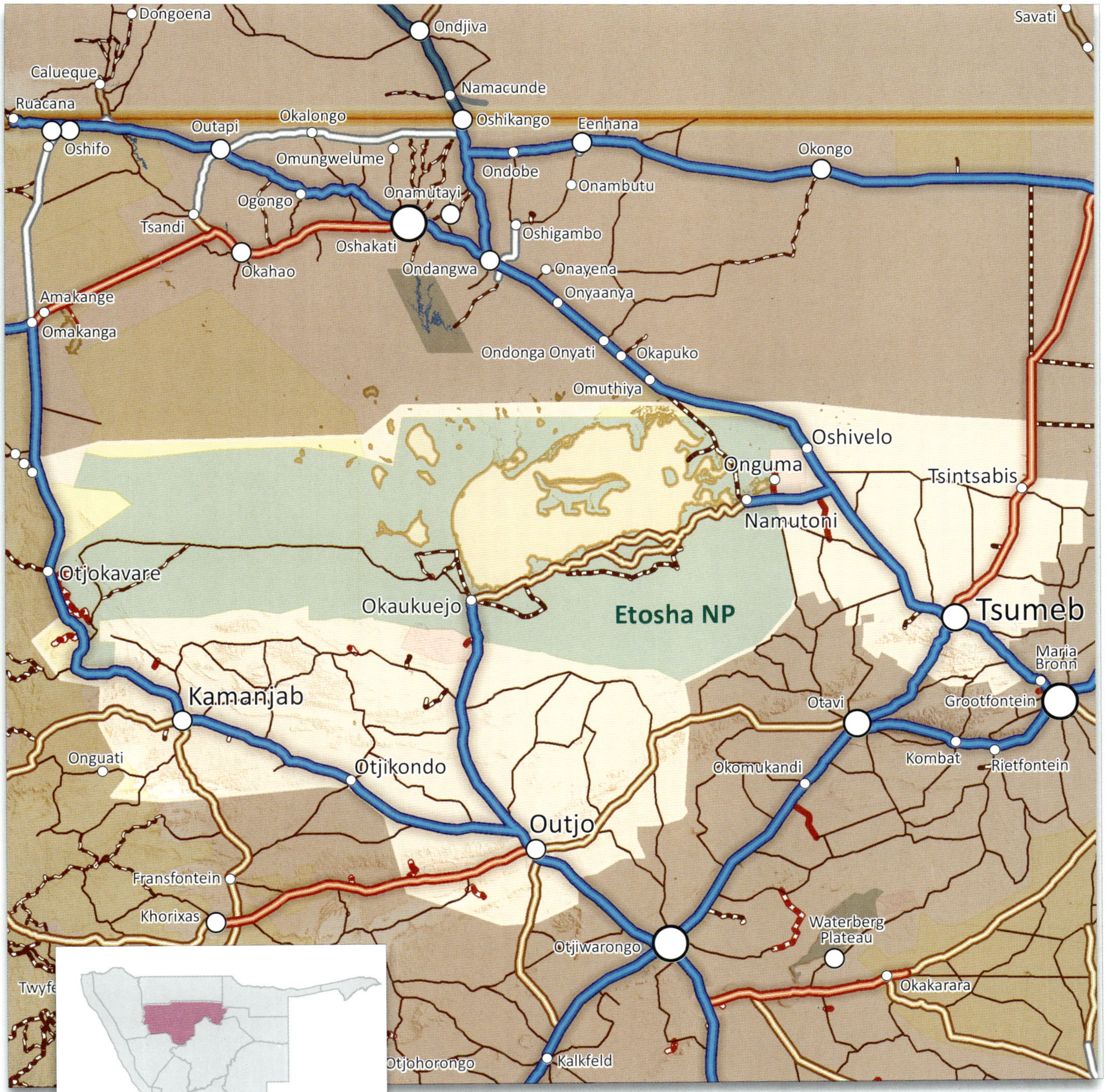

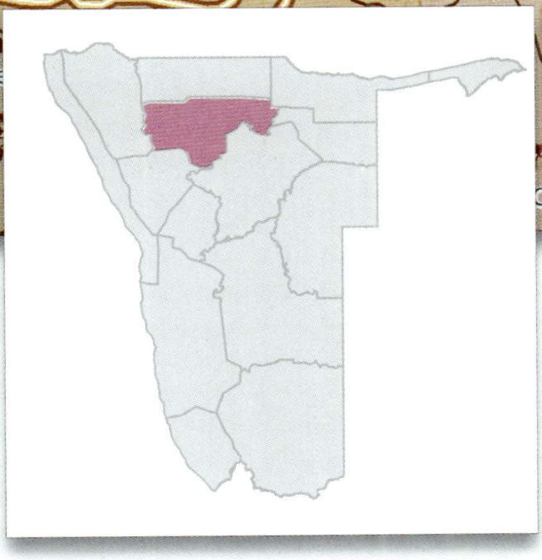

MAJOR ATTRACTIONS

- Etosha National Park
- Onguma and Ongawa Private Game Reserves
- Phantom Forest is a dense stand of *Moringa ovalifolia* trees, also known as Phantom or Ghost trees
- Lake Guinas and Lake Otjikoto are natural sinkholes formed by collapsing caves.
- Tsumeb Craft Market sells traditional arts and crafts from northern Namibia.
- The Open-air Museum of Cultural Villages in Tsumeb gives visitors an insight into the lives of various Namibian tribes.
- Museums at Outjo and Tsumeb display some of the history of the area.
- The Kamanjab rock engravings site is the second largest such site in Namibia.

More details about the attractions are available on our website (www.tracks4africa.co.za) or our Guide App. Our GPS Map can navigate you to each of these attractions.

Etosha National Park

(photo: Frank Höppener)

EXPLORERS CHARLES JOHN ANDERSSON AND FRANCIS GALTON were the first Europeans to record the existence of the Etosha Pan on 29 May 1851. They were travelling with Ovambo copper ore traders when they left Omutjamatunda (now known as Namutoni) to travel north. The name Etosha means Great White Place. In 1885, entrepreneur William Worthington Jordan bought a huge tract of land from Ovambo chief Kambonde. The land spanned nearly 170 kilometres from Okaukuejo in the west to Fischer's Pan in the east. Jordan gave 2 500 hectares of this land at no charge to Dorsland Trekkers who were on their way back from Angola. However, they had to abandon their newly-acquired farms just a year later, after clashes with a subtribe of the Ovambo people.

At the same time German troops occupied Okaukuejo, Namutoni and Sesfontein in order to kill migrating wildlife, this in an attempt to stop the spread of rinderpest to their cattle. A fort was built by the German cavalry in 1889 at the site of the Namutoni spring. On 28 January 1904, 500 men under Nehale Mpingana, chief of the Ovambo subtribe that drove the Dorsland Trekkers out, attacked the German Schutztruppe at Fort Namutoni and completely destroyed it, driving out the colonial forces and plundering their horses and cattle. The fort was rebuilt and troops stationed there once again when the area was declared a game reserve in 1907, Lieutenant Adolf Fischer of Fort Namutoni became the first game warden.

Etosha National Park is Namibia's most famous and popular national park. The park has an abundance of game and about 340 bird species have been counted. Game viewing is easy as most animals come to drink at one of the few watering holes. It's only after heavy rains that the Etosha Pan fills up and becomes a water source for wading birds and other animals. This is also the time when the bulbs flower.

Traveller Description

Galton Gate and the associated West Etosha route is now open to self-drive tourists. Self-drive visitors can also use Namutoni Gate in the east, Anderson Gate in the south or King Nehale Gate north of Namutoni. The park is serviced by a good gravel road which can be negotiated in a normal sedan vehicle. However, you are advised to use an SUV or pick-up vehicle during the rainy season. The main camps (Okaukuejo, Namutoni and Halali) offer a good variety of accommodation while Onkoshi and Dolomite are exclusive camps.

Travel Info

All three main camps (Okaukuejo, Namutoni and Halali) have fuel stations, restaurants and shops with basic food supplies. Okaukuejo has laundry facilities and a basic clinic. Namutoni Camp has the best shade but most people regard the waterhole at Okaukuejo as the park's star attraction, especially at night when elephant, rhino and lion come down to drink.

TRAVEL TIP! You're allowed to take raw meat from cloven-hooved animals and unpasteurised milk into Etosha if you travel from the south. However, veterinary fence restrictions don't allow you to take it out past the same control point, unless the meat is cooked.

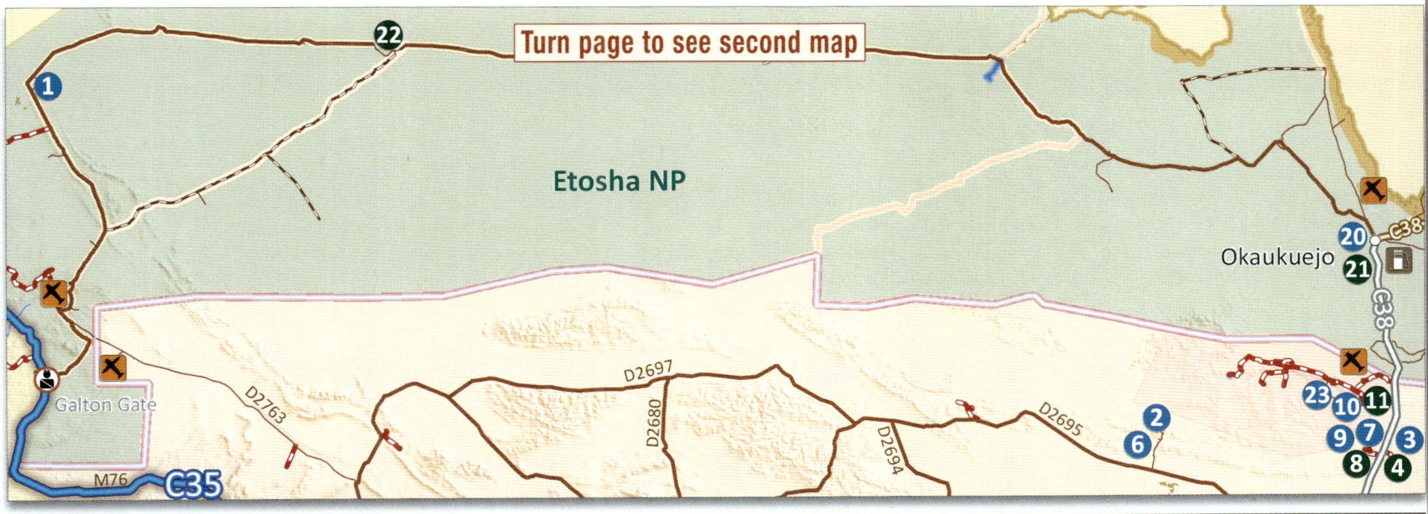

Dolomite Camp 1

Bed and Breakfast $$$
110km or 1h42min NNW of Kamanjab
w254368

Tel: +264(0)61 285 7200, Fax: +264(0)61 224 900
reservations@nwr.com.na
www.nwr.com.na

Luxury accommodation in en-suite chalets on elevated wooden decks, with dinner, bed and breakfast. Reservations mandatory.

Languages: English

Facilities:
Activities:

Eagle Tented Lodge & Spa 2

Tented Camp $$$
58km or 38min SW of Anderson Gate
w140279

Tel: +264(0)61 375 300, Cell: +264(0)81 293 3522, Fax: +264(0)61 375 333
res@nuvella.com.na,
www.epacha-lodge.com

Eight standard and eight luxury permanent tents, all en-suite and with private, raised balconies with splash pools. Lodge built from natural rock with thatch roof.

Languages: English

Facilities:
Activities:

Eldorado Guest House 3

Bed and Breakfast $$
10km or 8min S of Anderson Gate
w227570

Tel: +264(0)67 333 421, Cell: +264(0)81 302 2290
hanel@iway.na
www.etosha-camping.com

Owner-run venue offers full-board accommodation and great hospitality. Located on the doorstep of Etosha National Park.

Languages: English, Afrikaans

Facilities:
Activities:

Eldorado Guest House 4

Lodge Camp $
10km or 7min S of Anderson Gate
w227907

Tel: +264(0)67 333 421, Cell: +264(0)81 302 2290
hanel@iway.na
www.etosha-camping.com

Grassed camping area. You can also buy meat here. Ideal location for day trips into Etosha.

Languages: English, Afrikaans

Facilities:
Activities:

Emanya@Etosha 5

Game/Safari Lodge $$$
33km or 27min E of Namutoni Gate
w239883

Tel: +264(0)61 222 954, Fax: +264(0)61 260 458
bookings@emanya.com
www.emanya.com

20 Luxury, air-conditioned, en-suite rooms with laundry service on request. African cuisine with grill & buffet, and bar. Wildlife viewing at waterhole.

Languages: English, Afrikaans

Facilities:
Activities:

Epacha Game Lodge 6

Lodge $$$
57km or 36min NW of Anderson Gate
w140280

Tel: +264(0)61 375 300, Fax: +264(0)61 375 333
epacha@nuvella.com.na
www.epacha-lodge.com

Luxury, en-suite chalets with private balconies. As well as twin and double rooms and a presidential suite. Facilities include a spa with a sauna and jacuzzi.

Languages: English

Facilities:
Activities:

Etosha National Park

Etosha Safari Camp 7

Self-catering $$
9km or 6min S of Anderson Gate
w254370

Tel: +264(0)61 427 200, Cell: +264(0)81 129 2424, Fax: +264(0)67 333 455
info@gondwana-collection.com, store.gondwana-collection.com

50 Fully-equipped, twin-bed chalets. Great birding opportunities. Reservations mandatory.

Languages: English

Facilities:

Activities:

Etosha Safari Camp 8

Camping $
9km or 8min SSW of Anderson Gate
w138856

Tel: +264(0)61 427 200, Cell: +264(0)81 129 2424, Fax: +264(0)67 333 455
info@gondwana-collection.com, store.gondwana-collection.com

Fully-equipped campsites. Popular activities include bird watching and hiking. Reservations advisable. 4WD recommended during rainy season.

Languages: English

Facilities:

Activities:

Etosha Safari Lodge 9

Lodge $$
11km or 10min SSW of Anderson Gate
w219518

Tel: +264(0)61 427 200, Cell: +264(0)81 129 2424, Fax: +264(0)61 251 863
info@gondwana-collection.com, store.gondwana-collection.com

Comfortable, fully-serviced bungalows, each with own veranda. Facilities include a bar. Reservations mandatory.

Languages: English

Facilities:

Activities:

Etosha Village 10

Lodge $$
4km or 4min SSW of Anderson Gate
w184841

Tel: +27(0)21 930 4564, Fax: +27(0)21 914 9930
reservations@etosha-village.com
www.etosha-village.com

45 Luxury suites, each with an air-conditioned bedroom (and en-suite bathroom) and a patio.

Languages: English, Afrikaans

Facilities:

Activities:

Etosha Village Campsite 11

Lodge Camp $
4km or 4min SSW of Anderson Gate
w360960

Tel: +27(0)21 930 4564, Fax: +27(0)21 914 9930
reservations@etosha-village.com
www.etosha-village.com

Two spacious group sites and four individual sites. Partially shaded. All with running water, lights and well-kept ablutions.

Languages: English, Afrikaans

Facilities:

Activities:

Halali Camp 12

Lodge $$
69km or 1h24min WSW of Namutoni Gate
w139150

Tel: +264(0)61 285 7200, Fax: +264(0)61 224 900
reservations@nwr.com.na
www.nwr.com.na

Double rooms and luxury chalets. Some chalets are equipped with kitchens, braai facilities and even jacuzzis. The venue has lots of amenities, including a bar. Reservations advisable.

Languages: English

Facilities:

Activities:

Halali Rest Camp 13

Park Camp $$
70km or 1h25min WSW of Namutoni Gate
w232876

Tel: +264(0)61 285 7200, Fax: +264(0)61 224 900
reservations@nwr.com.na
www.nwr.com.na

Plenty of campsites, all equipped with electricity, water and braai area. Park fees payable at the gate on arrival. Reservations advisable.

Languages: English

Facilities:

Activities:

Mokuti Etosha Lodge 14

Lodge $$$
13km or 14min E of Namutoni Gate
w137384

Tel: +264(0)61 431 8000, Fax: +264(0)88 652 3230
mokuti.res@ol.na
www.mokutietoshalodge.com

106 Rooms and suites, two restaurants and two bars. Recreational facilities include a gym, tennis courts and a spa. Private and scheduled game drives available.

Languages: English

Facilities:

Activities:

Mushara Bush Camp 15

Tented Camp $$
21km or 20min E of Namutoni Gate
w209635

Tel: +264(0)61 241 880, Fax: +264(0)67 229 107
reservations@mushara-lodge.com
www.musharabushcamp.com

Accommodation for 32 guests and eight children in permanent tents. Meals served on the veranda at the main house.

Languages: English

Facilities:

Activities:

Mushara Lodge 16

Lodge $$$
20km or 20min E of Namutoni Gate
w143027

Tel: +264(0)61 241 880, Fax: +264(0)67 229 107
reservations@mushara-lodge.com
www.mushara-lodge.com

Ten thatched chalets, one triple room and one family house. As well as two exclusive villas.

Languages: English

Facilities:

Activities:

Mushara Outpost 17

Tented Camp $$
23km or 22min E of Namutoni Gate
w216444

Tel: +264(0)61 241 880, Fax: +264(0)67 229 107
reservations@mushara-lodge.com
www.musharaoutpost.com

Permanent tents on raised wooden decks. All have air-conditioning, open-plan bathrooms, mini-bars, safes, mosquito nets and hair dryers. No children under 12.

Languages: English

Facilities:
Activities:

Namutoni Camp 18

Park Camp $$
12km or 15min E of Namutoni Gate
w232875

Tel: +264(0)61 285 7200, Fax: +264(0)61 224 900
reservations@nwr.com.na
www.nwr.com.na

Maximum of eight people per campsite. At the centre of this venue a beautiful old German Fort overlooks the flood-lit King Nehale waterhole. Reservations advisable.

Languages: English

Facilities:
Activities:

Namutoni Resort 19

Lodge $$
12km or 12min W of Namutoni Gate
w139151

Tel: +264(0)61 285 7200, Fax: +264(0)61 224 900
reservations@nwr.com.na
www.nwr.com.na

Comfortable, en-suite double rooms which are interconnected via elevated wooden walkways. Spacious bush chalets also available. Park fees payable at the gate. Reservations advisable.

Languages: English

Facilities:
Activities:

Okaukuejo Camp 20

Self-catering $$$
18km or 18min N of Anderson Gate
w137913

Tel: +264(0)61 285 7200, Fax: +264(0)61 224 900
reservations@nwr.com.na
www.nwr.com.na

Fully-catered chalets or rooms. As well as self-catering family chalets with kitchens and braai areas. Reservations advisable.

Languages: English

Facilities:
Activities:

Okaukuejo Rest Camp 21

Park Camp $$
18km or 18min N of Anderson Gate
w232877

Tel: +264(0)61 285 7200, Fax: +264(0)61 224 900
reservations@nwr.com.na
www.nwr.com.na

37 Campsites with basic facilities. Campsites must be booked through NWR who will allocate a campsite upon your arrival. Reservations advisable.

Languages: English

Facilities:
Activities:

Olifantsrus 22

Camping $$$
90km or 1h40min NE of Galton Gate
w279491

Tel: +264(0)61 285 7200
reservations@nwr.com.na
www.nwr.com.na

10 Campsites with power points. Maximum of eight people per site. No chalets available. Reservations advisable.

Languages: English

Facilities:
Activities:

Ongava Lodge (Ongava GR) 23

Lodge $$$$
9km or 13min W of Anderson Gate
w137368

Tel: +264(0)83 330 3920, Cell: +264(0)81 155 8979
reservations@ongava.com
www.ongava.com

Ongava Game Lodge overlooks a watering point and the plains beyond. Located along the southern boundary of Etosha. Reservations mandatory.

Languages: English, Afrikaans

Facilities:
Activities:

Onguma Bush Camp Bungalows (Onguma GR) 24

Lodge $$$
20km or 25min NE of Namutoni Gate
w143233

Tel: +264(0)61 237 055, Fax: +264(0)61 235 677
reservations@onguma.com
www.onguma.com

Venue offers three twin-bed thatched bungalows, three twin-bed rooms, two four-bed family units and a honeymoon suite.

Languages: English

Facilities:
Activities:

Onguma Bush Camp (Onguma GR) 25

Lodge Camp $$
20km or 25min NE of Namutoni Gate
w143310

Tel: +264(0)61 237 055, Fax: +264(0)61 235 677
reservations@onguma.com
www.onguma.com

Six campsites, each with own ablutions, kitchen and braai. Firewood available. Breakfast, lunch or dinner can be ordered.

Languages: English

Facilities:
Activities:

Onguma Etosha Aoba Lodge (Onguma GR) 26

Lodge $$$
24km or 30min ENE of Namutoni Gate
w137419

Tel: +264(0)61 237 055, Fax: +264(0)61 235 677
reservations@onguma.com
www.etosha-aoba-lodge.com

Luxury, thatched cottages with verandas. The main thatched building houses the dining area, bar and library, and overlooks the plunge pool.

Languages: English, German, Afrikaans, Owambo, Damara, San

Facilities:
Activities:

Onguma Tamboti Luxury (Onguma GR) 27

Camping $$
15km or 18min ENE of Namutoni Gate
w277773

Tel: +264(0)61 237 055, Cell: +264(0)81 671 9659, Fax: +264(0)61 235 677
reservations@etosha-aoba-lodge.com,
www.onguma.com

15 private, spacious campsites in amongst trees, each with its own ablution facilities.

Languages: English

Facilities:
Activities:

Onguma Tented Camp (Onguma GR) 28

Tented Camp $$$
23km or 31min NE of Namutoni Gate
w143317

Tel: +264(0)61 237 055, Cell: +264(0)81 129 7180, Fax: +264(0)61 235 677
reservations@onguma.com,
www.onguma.com

Seven permanent tents with en-suite facilities, all located around a waterhole in the Onguma Private Game Reserve. No children under 12.

Languages: English

Facilities:
Activities:

Etosha National Park

Onguma Tree Top Camp (Onguma GR) 29

Lodge $$$
25km or 34min NE of Namutoni Gate (2km is 4WD)
w279636

Tel: +264(0)61 237 055, Cell: +264(0)81 129 7180, Fax: +264(0)61 235 677
reservations@onguma.com, www.onguma.com

Four tree houses, each with outside showers, all overlooking the waterhole. The entertainment area consists of a deck overlooking the waterhole.

Languages: English

Facilities:

Activities:

Onkoshi Camp 30

Lodge $$$
No self-drive access allowed
w209689

Tel: +264(0)61 285 7200, Fax: +264(0)61 224 900
reservations@nwr.com.na
www.nwr.com.na

Chalets with indoor & outdoor showers, plus a honeymoon suite. Onkoshi Camp is accessed from Namutoni via a Namibia Wildlife resort vehicle and guide. Reservations mandatory.

Languages: English

Facilities:

Activities:

Sachsenheim Guest Farm 31

Guest Farm $$
39km or 32min E of Namutoni Gate
w139684

Tel: +264(0)67 230 011, Cell: +27(0)81 215 0100
sachse@iway.na

Comfortable double, single or family units.

Languages: English, German, Afrikaans

Facilities:

Activities:

Sachsenheim Guest Farm 32

Farm Camp $
39km or 32min E of Namutoni Gate
w360958

Tel: +264(0)67 230 011, Cell: +27(0)81 215 0100
sachse@iway.na

Private, communal or bush camp campsites for overlanders, trucks, caravans and motorhomes. Clean, spacious, electrified ablutions blocks.

Languages: English, German, Afrikaans

Facilities:

Activities:

Banded mongoose live in large packs and are frequently seen in Etosha. (photo: Mietsie Visser)

(photo: Frank Höppener)

top and above: (photo: Frank Höppener)

Kamanjab

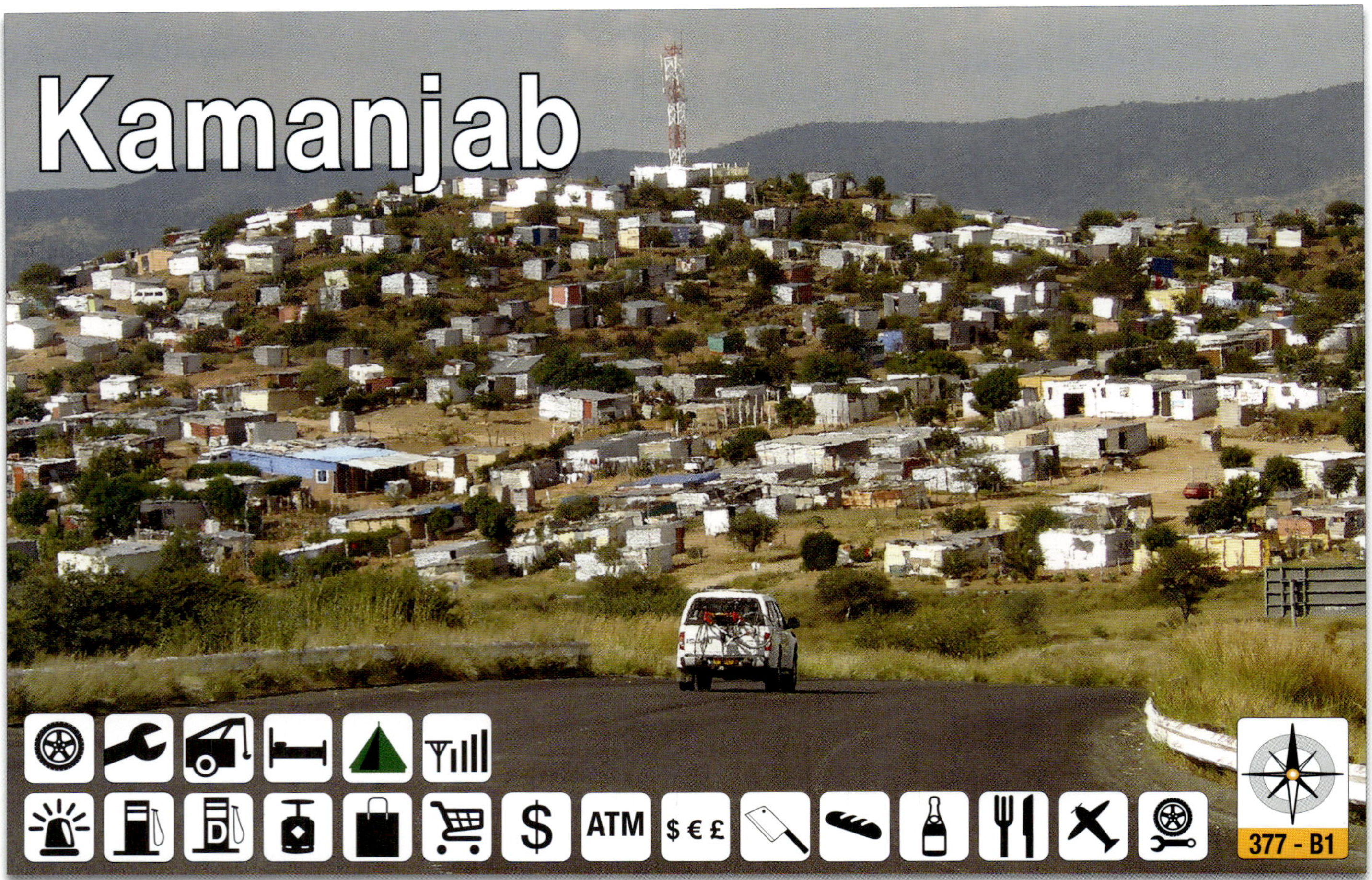

(photo: Frank Höppener)

KAMANJAB IS AN IMPORTANT TOWN in the Etosha region and offers the traveller essential facilities. It's centrally situated for those en-route to Kaokoland, whether they come from Etosha, Windhoek, Swakopmund or from the northern parts of Namibia. While the town itself is fairly plain, the surrounding area is very scenic and has a lot to offer. The C40 gravel road, from which Kamanjab is accessed, leads directly to the Grootberg Pass and Palmwag, while the nearest entry into Etosha National Park, Galton Gate, is only 70km away on tar.

Traveller Description

If heading north, Kamanjab is a good place to draw money and fill up with fuel and provisions, it's the last place you can do so before reaching Opuwo or Ruacana. The general dealer is well-stocked with everything from a needle to a bottle of wine and there's a wide range of accommodation in the area. Attractions include the rock engravings at Peet Alberts Koppie, the Otjikandero Himba Orphan Village and the Otjitotongwe Cheetah Park.

To reach the rock engravings at Peet Alberts Koppie requires a short hike up the koppie but it's worth the effort. You'll find over 1 500 Bushmen engravings, mainly of animals; the view over Kamanjab and surrounding landscape is also worth the price of admission.

At the Otjikandero Himba Orphan Village visitors can witness the Himba way of life, while at Otjitotongwe Cheetah Park you are allowed to touch tame cheetah.

Travel Info

Contact the town clinic at +264(0)67 330 031 if you require medical services. An extra landline number for the tow-in service is +264(0)67 330 104.

TRAVEL TIP! You need a key for the gate to the rock engravings on Peet Alberts Koppie; get it from your accommodation hosts. An off-road trip into the dry riverbeds will lead you to some exquisite scenery. Okaukuejo can easily be reached within a day via Galton Gate.

Town Info:

Police: +264(0)67 330 004 Tow-in: +264(0)81 283 2420

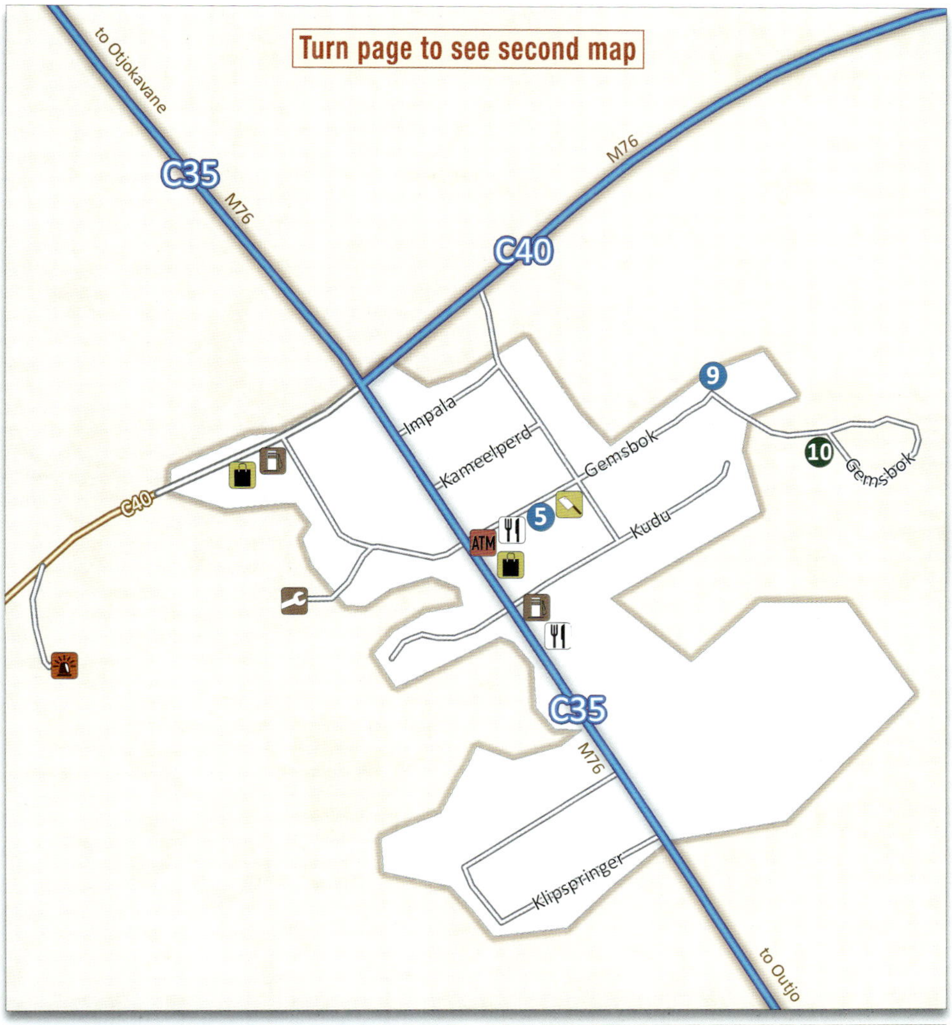

Hobatere Lodge 1

Lodge $$
83km or 1h21min WNW of Kamanjab
w137695

Tel: +264(0)61 228 104
reservations@journeysnamibia.com
www.hobatere-lodge.com

Six twin rooms, six double rooms (on request, these can accommodate a third person) and two single rooms. Each room has a shower, toilet and washbasin.

Languages: English

Facilities:
Activities:

Kamanjab Rest Camp 2

Park Camp $
4km or 5min WSW of Kamanjab
w139453

Tel: +264(0)67 330 247, Cell: +264(0)81 323 8370,
Fax: +264(0)88 633 178
kamanjabrestcamp@iway.na,
www.kamanjab-camp-namibia.com

Owner-run venue with eight well-kept campsites with various amenities. Located in natural surroundings on the C40 not far from Kamanjab.

Languages: English, German, Afrikaans

Facilities:
Activities:

Kaoko Bush Lodge 3

Tented Camp $$
10km or 12min N of Kamanjab
w243166

Fax: +264(0)88 655 9079 , Cell: +264(0)81 342 0788
alpecbushcamp1@gmail.com
www.kaoko-bush-lodge.com

Self-catering chalets situated in a game park.

Languages: English, Afrikaans, German

Facilities:
Activities:

Kaoko Bush Lodge 4

Park Camp $
10km or 12min N of Kamanjab
w243165

Fax: +264(0)88 655 9079 , Cell: +264(0)81 342 0788
alpecbushcamp1@gmail.com
www.kaoko-bush-lodge.com

Four spacious, shaded campsites, large enough for caravans/bush trailers. Each with its own ablutions (hot shower, toilet and electric plug), and nearby tap. Max four people per site.

Languages: English, Afrikaans, German

Facilities:
Activities:

Oase Guest House 5

Guest House $
30 Gemsbok St, Kamanjab
w139193

Tel: +264(0)67 330 055
reservations@exclusive.com.na
www.oasegh.com

18 Double rooms with en-suite bathrooms. The guests can enjoy Himba cultural visits and nature walks to see rock engravings.

Languages: English, Afrikaans

Facilities:
Activities:

Onjowewe Bush Camp 6

Tented Camp $$
21km or 14min ESE of Kamanjab
w359862

Fax: +264(0)88 621 665, Cell: +27(0)79 583 1165
namibiajjtours@gmail.com
www.namibiajjtours.com

Three large permanent tents sitting between Mopane trees. The venue has hot water but no electricity - paraffin lamps/candles are provided.

Languages: English, German, Afrikaans

Facilities:
Activities:

Onjowewe Camping - Duncan's Campsite 7

Camping $
21km or 14min ESE of Kamanjab
w232271

Fax: +264(0)88 621 665, Cell: +27(0)79 583 1165
namibiajjtours@gmail.com
www.namibiajjtours.com

Four campsites with hot showers, braai facilities and clean ablutions.

Languages: English, German, Afrikaans

Facilities:
Activities:

Onjowewe House In The Rocks 8

Lodge $$
21km or 15min ESE of Kamanjab
w232269

Fax: +264(0)88 621 665, Cell: +27(0)79 583 1165
namibiajjtours@gmail.com
www.namibiajjtours.com

Open-plan house with two double en-suite rooms and one double room with outside bathroom. As well as two large permanent tents, each with two twin beds and an outside shower & toilet.

Languages: English, German, Afrikaans

Facilities:
Activities:

Kamanjab

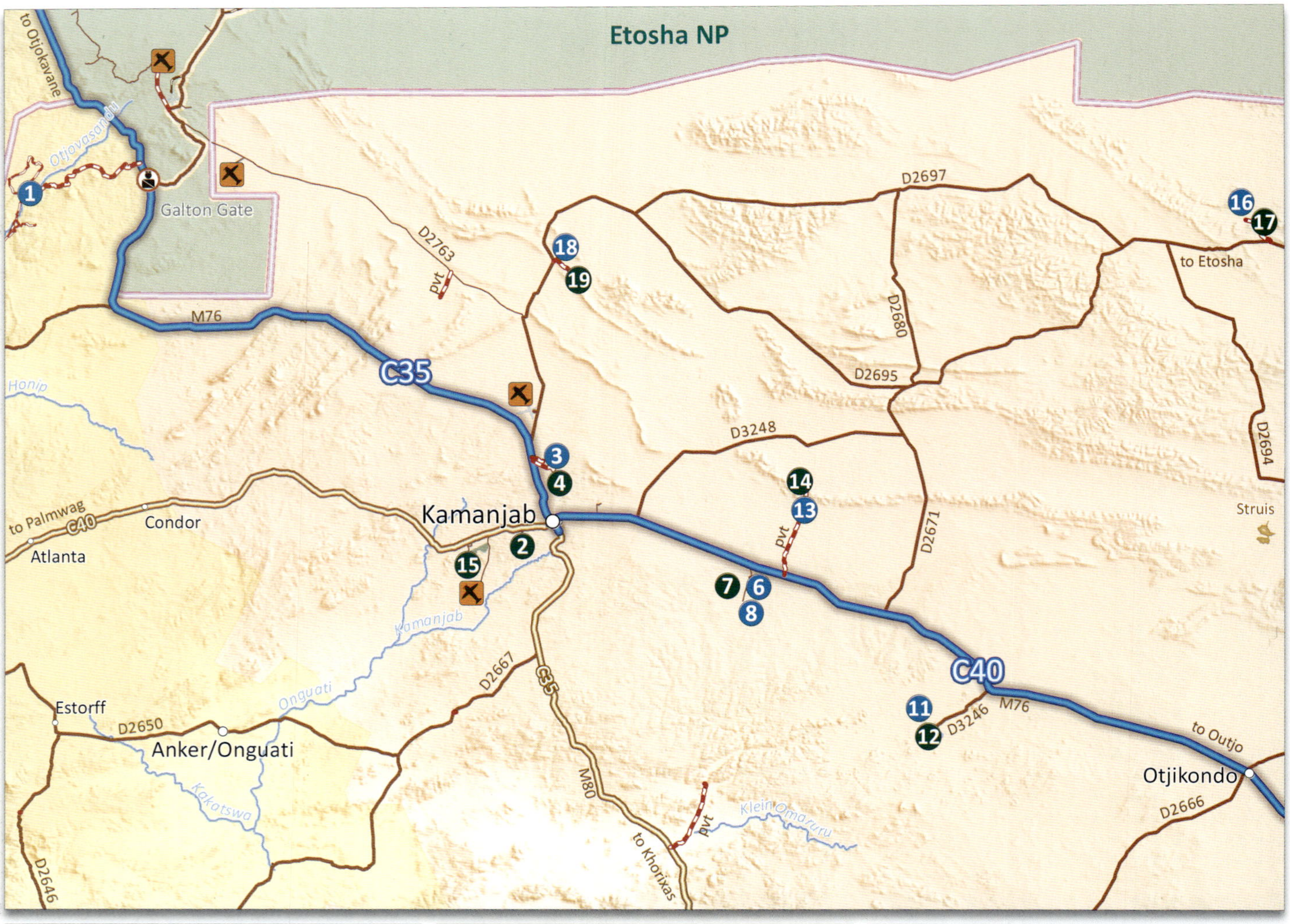

Oppi-Koppi Restcamp 9

Lodge $$
300m from Kamanjab centre
w255837

Tel: +264(0)67 330 040, Fax: +264(0)67 330 184
info@oppi-koppi-kamanjab.com
www.oppi-koppi-kamanjab.com

Chalets and bungalows with either single or double rooms.

Languages: English, Afrikaans, Dutch, German

Facilities:
Activities:

Oppi-Koppi Restcamp 10

Lodge Camp $
In town of Kamanjab
w138474

Tel: +264(0)67 330 040, Fax: +264(0)67 330 184
info@oppi-koppi-kamanjab.com
www.oppi-koppi-kamanjab.com

Comfortable campsites with clean ablution blocks, 24-hour electricity and hot water.

Languages: English, Afrikaans, Dutch, German

Facilities:
Activities:

Otjitambi Guest Farm 11

Guest Farm $$
54km or 41min ESE of Kamanjab
w137699

Tel: +264(0)67 312 138, Cell: +264(0)81 201 4233,
Fax: +264(0)67 687 141
jcsotjitambi@iway.na,
www.otjitambi.iway.na

Comfortable, elegant rooms with en-suite bathrooms. Bookings essential.

Languages: English, German, Afrikaans

Facilities:
Activities:

Otjitambi Guest Farm 12

Farm Camp $
54km or 41min ESE of Kamanjab
w361046

Tel: +264(0)67 312 138, Cell: +264(0)81 201 4233,
Fax: +264(0)67 687 141
jcsotjitambi@iway.na,
www.otjitambi.iway.na

Four campsites with water, ablution block (hot showers) and fire wood. No electricity.

Languages: English, German, Afrikaans

Facilities:
Activities:

Otjitotongwe Cheetah Guest Farm 13

Guest Farm $$
31km or 26min E of Kamanjab
w137684

Tel: +264(0)67 330 201
cheetahs@iway.na
www.cheetahparknamibia.com

Six thatched chalets and two conventional chalets, all with en-suite facilities. This venue is home to a non-profit organisation which promotes cheetah conservation.

Languages: English, German

Facilities:
Activities:

Otjitotongwe Cheetah Guest Farm 14

Lodge Camp $$$
33km or 30min E of Kamanjab
w192195

Tel: +264(0)67 330 201
cheetahs@iway.na
www.cheetahparknamibia.com

Pleasant campsite with plenty of shade, grassed sites and clean ablution blocks. There's a bush bar with a pool table. Cheetah feeding every day.

Languages: English, German

Facilities:
Activities:

Porcupine Camp	15
Camping	$

10km or 10min WSW of Kamanjab
w140061

Fax: +264(0)67 330 274, Cell: +264(0)81 270 3587
restcamp@iway.na
www.porcupine-camp.com

Eight campsites with two ablution blocks. Hot showers via a donkey system. No electricity.

Languages: English, German, Afrikaans

Facilities:

Activities:

Tandala Ridge B&B	16
Bed and Breakfast	$$

90km or 1h17min ENE of Kamanjab
w228031

Cell: +264(0)81 124 5202
kori@iway.na
www.tandalaridge.com

Two en-suite, thatched chalets overlooking a waterhole. Both chalets are private and quiet.

Languages: English

Facilities:

Activities

Tandala Ridge B&B	17
Lodge Camp	$

90km or 1h17min ENE of Kamanjab
w227956

Cell: +264(0)81 124 5202
kori@iway.na
www.tandalaridge.com

Three campsites under shady Mopane trees. Ablution blocks with hot showers, flush toilets and sink. Firewood provided.

Languages: English

Facilities:

Activities:

Toko Lodge	18
Lodge	$$

29km or 27min N of Kamanjab
w141091

Tel: +264(0)61 234 342, Cell: +264(0)81 629 3270,
Fax: +264(0)67 687 094
toko@jandpgroup.biz,
www.tokolodgesafaris.com

14 Large, comfortable en-suite rooms with private verandas.

Languages: English, German

Facilities:

Activities:

Toko Lodge	19
Lodge Camp	$

31km or 33min N of Kamanjab
w141092

Tel: +264(0)61 234 342, Cell: +264(0)81 629 3270,
Fax: +264(0)67 687 094
toko@jandpgroup.biz,
www.tokolodgesafaris.com

Three campsites with good ablutions, situated a little way from the lodge. Firewood is supplied and lodge dinners can be booked.

Languages: English, German

Facilities:

Activities:

A rare Black Rhino seen at Etosha. (photo: Mietsie Visser)

Outjo

(photo: Ian-Ray Nel)

OUTJO CAN BE FOUND tucked away among some small hills and is best known for being a cattle farming centre and the gateway to Etosha National Park. The town was founded by Germans under the command of Colonel Theodor von Leutwein in 1897 as a small military base; it was used primarily as a base from which to explore the northern reaches of German South West Africa.

Places of interest in the town include the Naulila Monument, commemorating the 1914 massacre of German soldiers and officials by the Portuguese near Fort Naulila on the Kunene River in Angola. It also commemorates soldiers killed when attempting to avenge the earlier losses. The Windmill Tower, east of Outjo, was constructed in 1900 to provide fresh water for German soldiers, their horses and the hospital.

Traveller Description

Outjo is the primary gateway to the Etosha National Park (Anderson Gate is only about 100km north of the town) as well as the last stop before Damaraland and the Kaokoveld. This is the ideal town to stock up on food and fuel supplies, get your tyres checked or repaired, draw some money and even see the doctor if you need one. Outjo offers a variety of camping and lodging accommodation to suit your needs and pocket.

The local museum (Franke Haus Museum) details the campaign of Major Viktor Franke in Ovamboland. The Bäckerei Outjo offers tasty German cakes, strudel bread and coffee and shouldn't be missed. Apart from Etosha, nearby attractions include the Ugab Terraces and 'Vingerklip' south-west of Outjo en-route to Khorixas.

TRAVEL TIP! Gamkarab is a working cattle farm north-east of Outjo which offers camping facilities to nature lovers keen on exploring the Gamkarab Cave. This cave was originally used as a water source by the Bushman and local wildlife. Visitors can explore the cave which leads 60 meters down to the water point. The cave system fans out underwater and researchers are still exploring its myriad tunnels. Explorers need to bring their own headlights and wear old clothes and comfortable shoes.

Town Info:
Hospital: +264(0)67 313 250, Police: +264(0)67 313 005, Doctor: +264(0)67 313 020, Tourism: +264(0)67 313 072

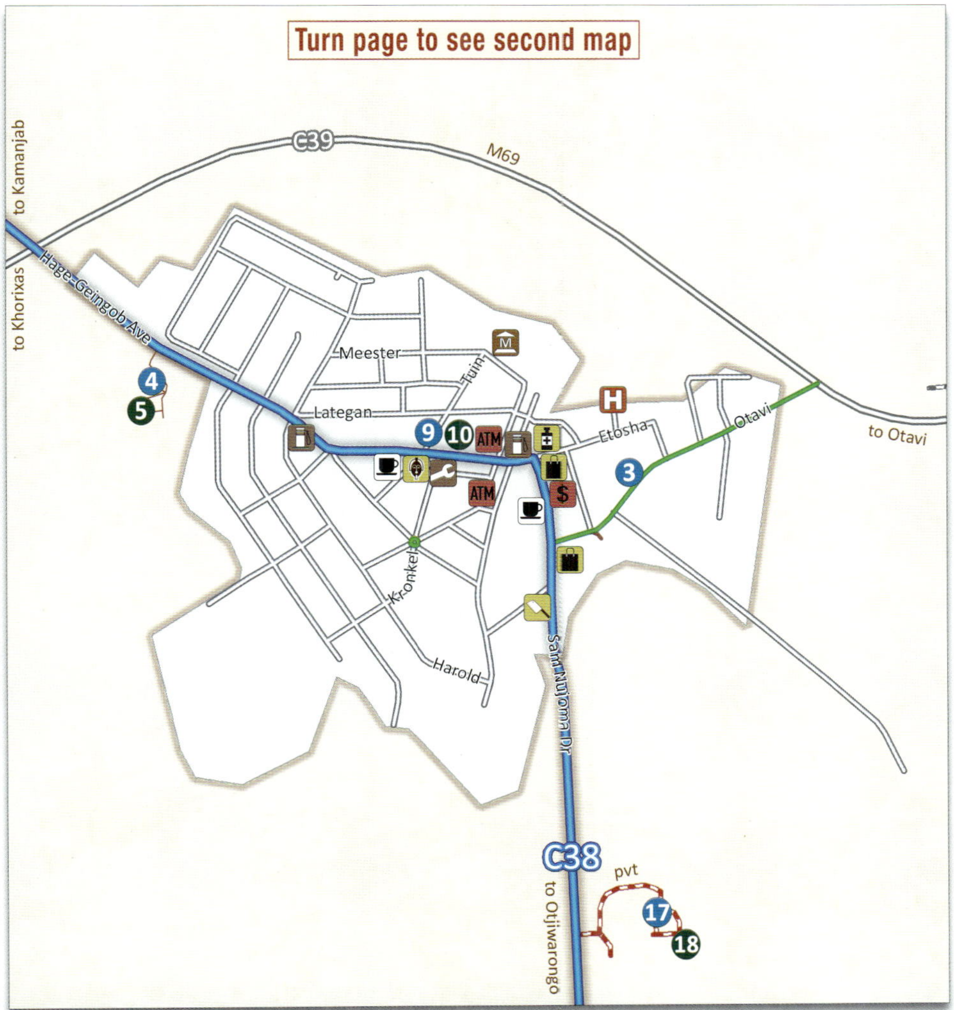

Buschberg Guest Farm 1

Guest Farm $$
80km or 52min NW of Outjo
w140306

Cell: +264(0)81 279 5667
info@buschberg.com
www.buschberg.com

Comfortable accommodation with en-suite bathrooms. Guests can enjoy hiking, drives on the farm, bird watching or visits to nearby Etosha.

Languages: English, Afrikaans

Facilities:
Activities:

Buschberg Guest Farm 2

Farm Camp $
80km or 52min NW of Outjo
w255818

Cell: +264(0)81 279 5667
info@buschberg.com
www.buschberg.com

Camping facilities with clean ablutions. Located close to the Etosha's gate.

Languages: English, Afrikaans

Facilities:
Activities:

Etosha Garden Hotel 3

Hotel $
6 Otavi St, Outjo
w142087

Tel: +264(0)61 259 372, Fax: +264(0)61 226 286
etoshahotel@iway.na
www.etosha-garden-hotel.com

20 Affordable en-suite rooms. There's a pool in a tropical garden. Safe parking is available.

Languages: English

Facilities:
Activities:

Etotongwe Lodge 4

Lodge $$
1km or 2min WNW of Outjo
w209632

Tel: +264(0)67 313 001, Fax: +264(0)88 619 441
comms@etotongwelodge.com
www.etotongwelodge.com

Comfortable overnight accommodation in 21 en-suite rooms. Each room has air-conditioning and mosquito nets. Venue operates on a bed and breakfast basis. Rooms are disability friendly.

Languages: English, German, Afrikaans

Facilities:
Activities:

Etotongwe Lodge 5

Lodge Camp $
1km or 2min W of Outjo
w227579

Tel: +264(0)67 313 001, Fax: +264(0)88 619 441
comms@etotongwelodge.com
www.etotongwelodge.com

Grassed campsites, each with its own electricity point and tap. Ample, clean ablution facilities and a lapa with central braai area.

Languages: English, German, Afrikaans

Facilities:
Activities:

Outjo

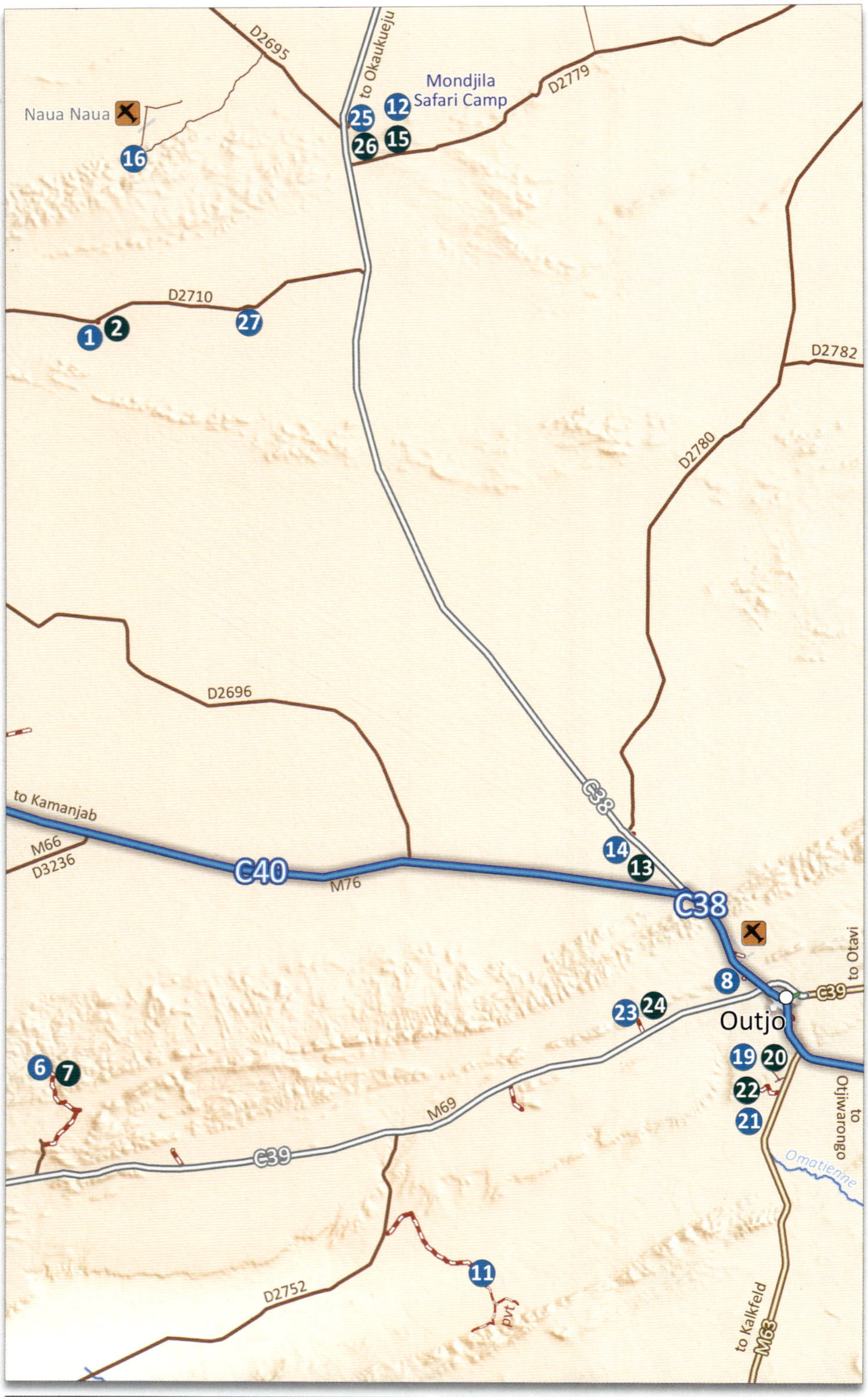

Gelukspoort Guest Farm — 6

Guest Farm — $$
63km or 52min W of Outjo
w137915

Tel: +264(0)67 312 025, Cell: +264(0)81 285 2972,
Fax: +264(0)67 312 025
info@gelukspoort.com,
www.gelukspoort.com

Double and luxury rooms with balconies. As well as thatched chalets with balconies overlooking a waterhole. Rates include dinner, bed and breakfast.

Languages: English, Afrikaans

Facilities: FC

Activities:

Gelukspoort Guest Farm — 7

Farm Camp — $
63km or 52min W of Outjo
w255830

Tel: +264(0)67 312 025, Cell: +264(0)81 285 2972,
Fax: +264(0)67 312 025
info@gelukspoort.com,
www.gelukspoort.com

Three campsites under big shady trees. Each equipped with showers, toilets, braai facilities and a wash-up area.

Languages: English, Afrikaans, German

Facilities: FC

Activities:

Ijaba Lodge at Buschfeld Park — 8

Lodge — $$
4km or 5min WNW of Outjo
w137964

Tel: +264(0)67 313 665
ijabalodge@gmail.com
www.ijaba-lodge.com

A range of accommodation options in bungalows plus two permanent tents and a grassed camping area. 45 minutes from Etosha's Okaukeujo gate.

Languages: English, German, Afrikaans

Facilities: VISA @

Activities:

Kai-Oms Backpackers Lodge — 9

Backpackers Hostel — $$
Cnr. Harold and Meester Strs, Outjo
w243162

Tel: +264(0)67 313 597, Cell: +264(0)81 375 0152,
Fax: +264(0)67 313 598
vzyl.deon@yahoo.com

Accommodation in dormitories and self-catering rooms. Meals available on request.

Languages: English, German, Afrikaans

Facilities: FC

Activities:

Kai-Oms Backpackers Lodge — 10

Lodge Camp — $
Meester Laan 2, Outjo
w267891

Tel: +264(0)67 313 597, Cell: +264(0)81 357 0152,
Fax: +264(0)67 313 598
vzyl.deon@yahoo.com

Campsites with braai facilities and a communal kitchenette.

Languages: English, German, Afrikaans

Facilities: FC

Activities:

Kudu Game Ranch — 11

Game/Safari Lodge — $
45km or 42min SW of Outjo
w221737

Cell: +264(0)81 127 2571
lukas@afrikajag.com

Five thatch roof bungalows set up for hunters. Lapa with inside dining room & bar. Separate kitchen.

Languages: English

Facilities: VISA

Activities:

Mondjila Safari Camp

Mondjila Safari Camp 12

Tented Camp. $$ 72km or 43min NNW of Outjo. w361809

Tel: +264(0)61 237 294, Fax: +264(0)61 237 295, reservations@exclusive.com.na

11 Luxury en-suite permanent tents. Each equipped with twin beds and a standing fan.

Language: English

Facilities: Activities:

Mamselle Nature Camp 13

Camping $
15km or 13min NW of Outjo
w189060

Fax: +264(0)67 303 998, Cell: +264(0)81 218 3904
mamsellenaturecamp@yahoo.com

Two shaded campsites, each with its own ablution block (flush toilet and hot shower).

Languages: English, Afrikaans

Facilities:
Activities:

Mamselle Nature Camp Luxury House 14

Self-catering $
15km or 13min NW of Outjo
w255835

Fax: +264(0)67 303 998, Cell: +264(0)81 218 3904
mamsellenaturecamp@yahoo.com

Luxury house that sleeps four. Bedding and cutlery provided. There's also a bungalow that sleeps two.

Languages: English, Afrikaans

Facilities:
Activities:

Mondjila Safari Camp 15

Lodge Camp $
72km or 43min NNW of Outjo
w361808

Tel: +264(0)61 237 294, Fax: +264(0)61 237 295
reservations@exclusive.com.na

Five campsites, each with its own power point, light and braai area. Clean, communal ablutions available.

Languages: English

Facilities:
Activities:

Okutala Etosha Lodge 16

Lodge $$$
90km or 1h6min NW of Outjo
w138459

Tel: +264(0)67 333 461, Cell: +264(0)81 126 4324
bookings@okutala.com
www.okutala.com

21 Luxury units, each unit boasting a seating area and veranda with a view. The lodge has a lapa & deck overlooking a waterhole.

Languages: English, German

Facilities:
Activities:

Ombinda Country Lodge 17

Lodge $
2km or 3min SSE of Outjo
w138783

Tel: +264(0)67 313 181, Cell: +264(0)81 129 9680,
Fax: +264(0)67 313 478
ombindagerald@iway.na,
www.ombindalodge.com

Thatched bungalows with en-suite bathrooms. There are also self-catering units.

Languages: English, Afrikaans

Facilities:
Activities:

Ombinda Country Lodge 18

Lodge Camp $
2km or 3min SSE of Outjo
w206730

Tel: +264(0)67 313 181, Cell: +264(0)81 129 9680,
Fax: +264(0)67 313 478
ombindagerald@iway.na,
www.ombindalodge.com

Grassed, well-equipped campsites with spotless ablution blocks. Campsites located close to the lodge where there's a bar and conference facilities.

Languages: English, Afrikaans

Facilities:
Activities:

Outjo

Oppiklippe — 19

Self-catering — $
8km or 9min SSW of Outjo
w207973

Tel: +264(0)67 313 836, Cell: +264(0)81 280 2010
gogabi11@gmail.com
www.etosha-namibia.com

Fully-equipped thatched house and an overnight cabin. Guests can go for walks on the 'Outjo terraces' and enjoy the local wildlife.

Languages: English, Afrikaans

Facilities:
Activities:

Oppiklippe — 20

Camping — $
8km or 9min SSW of Outjo
w361020

Tel: +264(0)67 313 836, Cell: +264(0)81 280 2010
gogabi11@gmail.com
www.etosha-namibia.com

Family-friendly venue in beautiful surroundings offers nine shaded campsites.

Languages: English, Afrikaans

Facilities:
Activities:

Sâsa Safari Camp — 21

Self-catering — $$
10km or 12min SSW of Outjo
w274147

Fax: +264(0)88 641 499, Cell: +264(0)81 129 0658
bookings@sasasafaricamp.com
www.sasasafaricamp.com

10 Twin-bed chalets with a large communal kitchen. Venue is built with natural rock stone from the area.

Languages: English, Afrikaans

Facilities:
Activities:

Sâsa Safari Camp — 22

Camping — $
10km or 12min SSW of Outjo
w137846

Fax: +264(0)88 641 499, Cell: +264(0)81 129 0658
bookings@sasasafaricamp.com
www.sasasafaricamp.com

Each campsite has its own braai area, table and chairs.

Languages: English, Afrikaans

Facilities:
Activities:

Sophienhof Lodge — 23

Lodge — $$
11km or 10min W of Outjo
w217010

Tel: +264(0)67 312 999, Cell: +264(0)81 353 5135,
Fax: +264(0)67 313 955
bertie@sophienhof-lodge.com,
www.sophienhof-lodge.com

Bungalows with en-suite bathrooms. Plus, a farmhouse and VIP house with en-suite, air-conditioned rooms. All units have a dining area and/or terrace.

Languages: English

Facilities:
Activities:

Sophienhof Lodge — 24

Lodge Camp — $$
11km or 10min W of Outjo
w222196

Tel: +264(0)67 313 999, Cell: +264(0)81 353 5135,
Fax: +264(0)67 313 955
bertie@sophienhof-lodge.com,
www.sophienhof-lodge.com

Two separate camping venues with electricity, water, showers and toilets. The campsites are shaded and suitable for caravans or trailers.

Languages: English

Facilities:
Activities:

Toshari Lodge — 25

Lodge — $$
71km or 46min NNW of Outjo
w140957

Tel: +264(0)67 333 440, Cell: +264(0)81 382 2655,
Fax: +264(0)67 333 444
toshari@iway.na, www.toshari.com

Standard, family and luxury rooms, all equipped with mosquito nets and air-conditioning.

Languages: English, German

Facilities:
Activities:

Toshari Lodge — 26

Lodge Camp — $
71km or 45min NNW of Outjo
w261560

Tel: +264(0)67 333 440, Cell: +264(0)81 382 2655,
Fax: +264(0)67 333 444
toshari@iway.na, www.toshari.com

Each campsite has its own ablution facility, 220v power point and a braai.

Languages: English, German

Facilities:
Activities:

Vreugde Guest Farm — 27

Guest Farm — $$
69km or 45min NW of Outjo
w209691

Fax: +264(0)88 636 664, Cell: +264(0)81 418 4865
info@vreugdeguestfarm.com
www.vreugdeguestfarm.com

Double, twin and family rooms with en-suite bathrooms. Large, shady garden and a lapa. Enjoy tours of this working cattle and sheep farm.

Languages: English, German, Afrikaans, French

Facilities:
Activities:

Okaukuejo waterhole in Etosha, north of Outjo. (photo: Frank Höppener)

The German Evangelical Lutheran Church in Outjo. (photo: Ian-Ray Nel)

(photo: Ian-Ray Nel)

Tsumeb

(photo: Ian-Ray Nel)

THE TOWN'S RECENT HISTORY BEGINS IN 1905 when a huge mineralized ore pipe was discovered at Tsumeb. The same pipe was mined in prehistoric times but those ancient workers barely scratched its surface. Most of the ore was removed in the 20th century by cut-and-fill methods; copper, lead, zinc and germanium were extracted. Since its founding, Tsumeb has been primarily a mining town. The mine was originally owned by OMEG (Otavi Mining and Railway Company) and later by TCL (Tsumeb Corporation Limited) before its closure a few years ago when the ore ran out and the main shafts became flooded by ground water. The mine has since been reopened by a group of local entrepreneurs (Ongopolo Mining) since a fair amount of oxidized ore remains to be recovered in the upper levels of the mine. The town also boasts a metal smelter, currently owned by Namibia Custom Smelters.

Traveller Description

Tsumeb is the gateway to the north and the closest town to Etosha National Park. It's a welcoming town with colourful Jacaranda, Flamboyant and Bougainvillea trees lining its streets. Tsumeb offers all the services and facilities that a traveller might need as well as plenty of interesting attractions. Visitors will find the Tsumeb Museum fascinating while the Tsumeb Cultural Village and Arts and Crafts Centre is perfect for those with a taste for local culture and art. The annual Copper Festival, organised by the Tsumeb Municipality during the second half of the year, is a well-known event on the local calendar. For visitors with an interest in gemstones and minerals, there are a number of historic German mines to visit, like Alt Bobos and !Uris west of town. About 20km northwest of town you'll find two natural sinkholes, Lake Otjikoto and Guinas, both are popular scuba diving sites. The exact depths of these lakes are unknown, but they're at least 80m. The water in Guinas is completely clear and is the habitat for a unique and critically-endangered species of fish, Tilapia guinasana - also known as the Nguni fish or African Koi. Otjikoto has poor visibility but is of particular interest as the retreating German forces dumped a lot of their weaponry and supplies into the lake in 1914. Some of it has been recovered for display in museums.

Travel Info

There's a Spar, Shoprite and Pick 'n Pay in town, as well as fuel stations, repair shops and restaurants.

Travel North Namibia Guesthouse offers a range of convenient traveller services and you can contact them on +264(0)67 220 728 or cell +264(0)81 220 1222 or +264(0)81 299 4214

To find out about the Copper Festival, which is normally held around October, contact the chairman of the organising committee, Julius Gaeseb, at the Municipality on +264(0)67 221 056 / 7

TRAVEL TIP! Watch out for cattle on the B1 road between Tsumeb and Ondangwa. There's a vet control point at Oshivelo, just north of Tsumeb; you're allowed to take raw meat from cloven-hoofed animals north, but not south past this point.

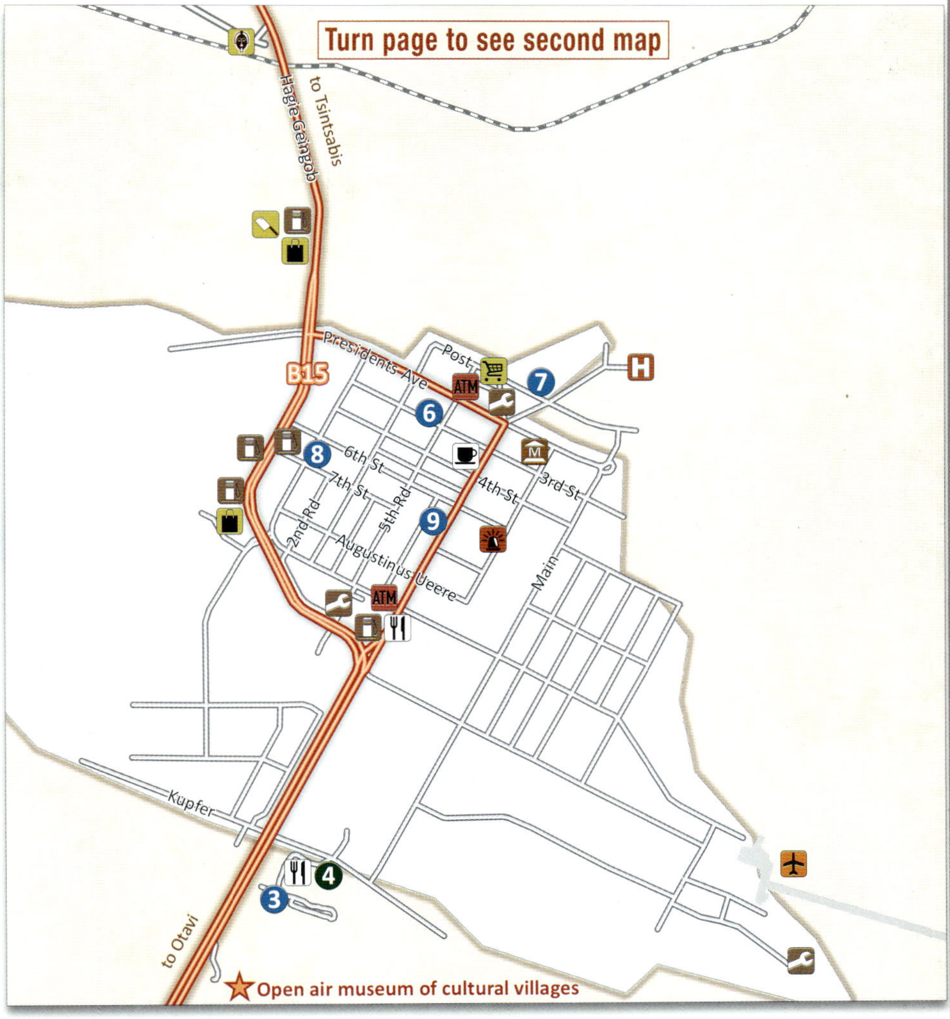

Town Info:

Hospital:	+264(0)67 221 002
Police:	+264(0)67 223 5017
Doctor:	+264(0)67 222 400
Tow-in:	+264(0)67 222 412/3

Ghaub Guest Farm 1

Guest Farm $$
54km or 42min S of Tsumeb
w140590

Tel: +264(0)67 240 188, Fax: +264(0)67 240 554
ghaub@iway.na
www.ghaub.com

Spacious, en-suite twin rooms with private verandas, overlooking lawns. There's also a dining area, cosy bar and lounge.

Languages: English, German, Afrikaans

Facilities:
Activities:

Ghaub Guest Farm 2

Farm Camp $$
54km or 42min S of Tsumeb
w270499

Tel: +264(0)67 240 188, Fax: +264(0)67 240 554
ghaub@iway.na
www.ghaub.com

Three grassed, shaded campsites, each with its own shower and toilet. Other facilities include kitchen area, braai and electricity; plus, access to pool and Wi-Fi at the lodge.

Languages: English, German, Afrikaans

Facilities:
Activities:

Kupferquelle Resort 3

Self-catering $$
Kupfer St, Tsumeb
w255834

Tel: +264(0)67 220 139, Fax: +264(0)67 220 149
booking@kupferquelle.com
www.kupferquelle.com

15 Luxury and 25 standard chalets. Offered on a half and full board basis.

Languages: English

Facilities:
Activities:

Kupferquelle Resort 4

Holiday Resort Camp $
Kupfer St, Tsumeb
w142343

Tel: +264(0)67 220 139, Fax: +264(0)67 220 149
booking@kupferquelle.com
www.kupferquelle.com

25 Fully-equipped campsites set in tranquil, oasis-like landscape.

Languages: English

Facilities:
Activities:

La Rochelle Guest Farm 5

Guest Farm $$$
44km or 40min NNE of Tsumeb
w139332

Tel: +264(0)67 221 326, Cell: +264(0)81 855 5788, Fax: +264(0)67 220 761
contact@larochellelodge.com, www.larochellelodge.com

Thatched-roofs bungalows with air-conditioned rooms, separate toilet & shower, mini-bar, telephone and private patio.

Languages: English

Facilities:
Activities:

Makalani Hotel 6

Hotel $
Ndilimani Cultural Troupe St, Tsumeb
w142363

Tel: +264(0)67 221 051, Fax: +264(0)67 221 575
mail@makalanihotel.com
www.makalanihotel.com

Situated in the town centre, this venue offers 28 rooms with en-suite bathrooms. There's also an a la carte restaurant, bar and gambling house.

Languages: English

Facilities:
Activities:

> *"...there ain't no journey what don't change you some."*
>
> *David Mitchell,* Cloud Atlas

Tsumeb

Minen Hotel 7

Hotel $$
7 Omeg Allee St, Tsumeb
w142350

Tel: +264(0)67 221 072, Fax: +264(0)67 221 750
minen@mweb.com.na
www.minen-hotel.com

Comfortable en-suite rooms and good German cuisine. There's also a veranda, pool and ladies bar. Free airport transfers available.

Languages: English, German, Afrikaans, Oshiwambo, Herero

Facilities:
Activities:

The Copper Guesthouse 8

Bed and Breakfast $
c/o Linekela Kalenga & 7th St, Tsumeb
w254416

Tel: +264(0)67 220 310, Fax: +264(0)67 222 110
info@copperguesthouse.com.na
www.copperguesthouse.com.na

17 En-suite single, double, executive and family rooms. A fully-equipped kitchen is available for guests' use.

Languages: English

Facilities:
Activities:

Travel North Guesthouse 9

Guest House $$
Omeg Allee st, Tsumeb
w142344

Tel: +264(0)67 220 728, Cell: +264(0)81 299 4214,
info@travelnorthguesthouse.com
www.travelnorthguesthouse.com

Single and double rooms with air-conditioning, TV, coffee/tea facilities, mini-fridge and shower/toilet.

Languages: English, German, Afrikaans, Oshiwambo, Damara

Facilities:
Activities:

Treesleeper Camp 10

Community Camp $
64km or 43min NNE of Tsumeb
w142643

Cell: +264(0)81 698 3374
treesleeper.booking@gmail.com
treesleeper.wordpress.com

Six private campsites. Five with wooden decks, picnic tables and fireplaces. Three with their own ablution blocks (hot showers).

Languages: English

Facilities:
Activities:

!Uris Safari Lodge 11

Lodge $$
27km or 29min W of Tsumeb
w142642

Tel: +264(0)67 221 818, Fax: +264(0)67 220 242
marketing@uris-safari-lodge-namibia.com
www.uris-safari-lodge-namibia.com

14 Rooms in seven semi-detached chalets, all equipped with all modern amenities. Disabled access.

Languages: English, German, Afrikaans

Facilities:
Activities:

!Uris Safari Lodge 12

Lodge Camp $$
27km or 29min W of Tsumeb
w227572

Tel: +264(0)67 221 818, Fax: +264(0)67 220 242
marketing@uris-safari-lodge-namibia.com
www.uris-safari-lodge-namibia.com

Two campsites, each with its own ablutions (hot shower), outside basin, extra tap and built-in table.

Languages: English, German, Afrikaans

Facilities:
Activities:

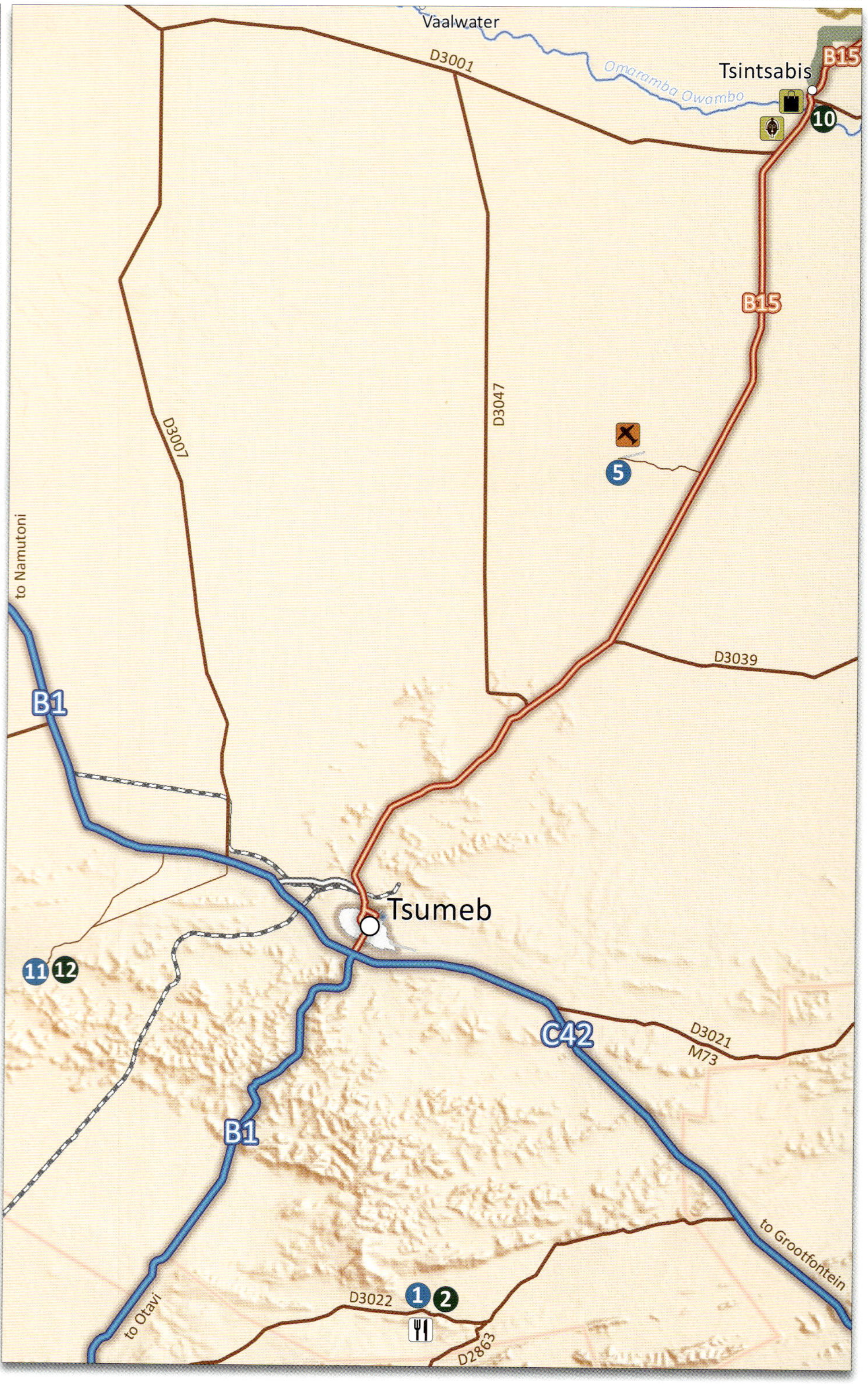

top: Lake Otjikoto, to the north of Tsumeb. (photo: Heiner Dillmann)

The St. Barbara Roman Catholic Church is named after the patron saint of miners and was erected in 1913; it's also one of Tsumeb's oldest buildings and its first church. (photo: Ian-Ray Nel)

GOBABIS

An example of traditional Herero dress. (photo: Karin Theron)

THOUGH MAINLY A CATTLE-FARMING REGION, the area also offers lots of hunting opportunities. This is the 'Little Texas' of Namibia and the statue of a large Brahman bull in the middle Gobabis town confirms that this is indeed serious cattle farming country.

The area around Gobabis is beautiful with long, soft grass and big acacia trees. Here and there, the red sand dunes of the Kalahari Desert are visible.

You will find a lot of game along the roads, especially between Gobabis and Hochfeld, therefore you should rather not drive after dark. Be on the lookout for jackal, warthog, kudu, oryx, red hartebeest, steenbok, springbok and aardvark.

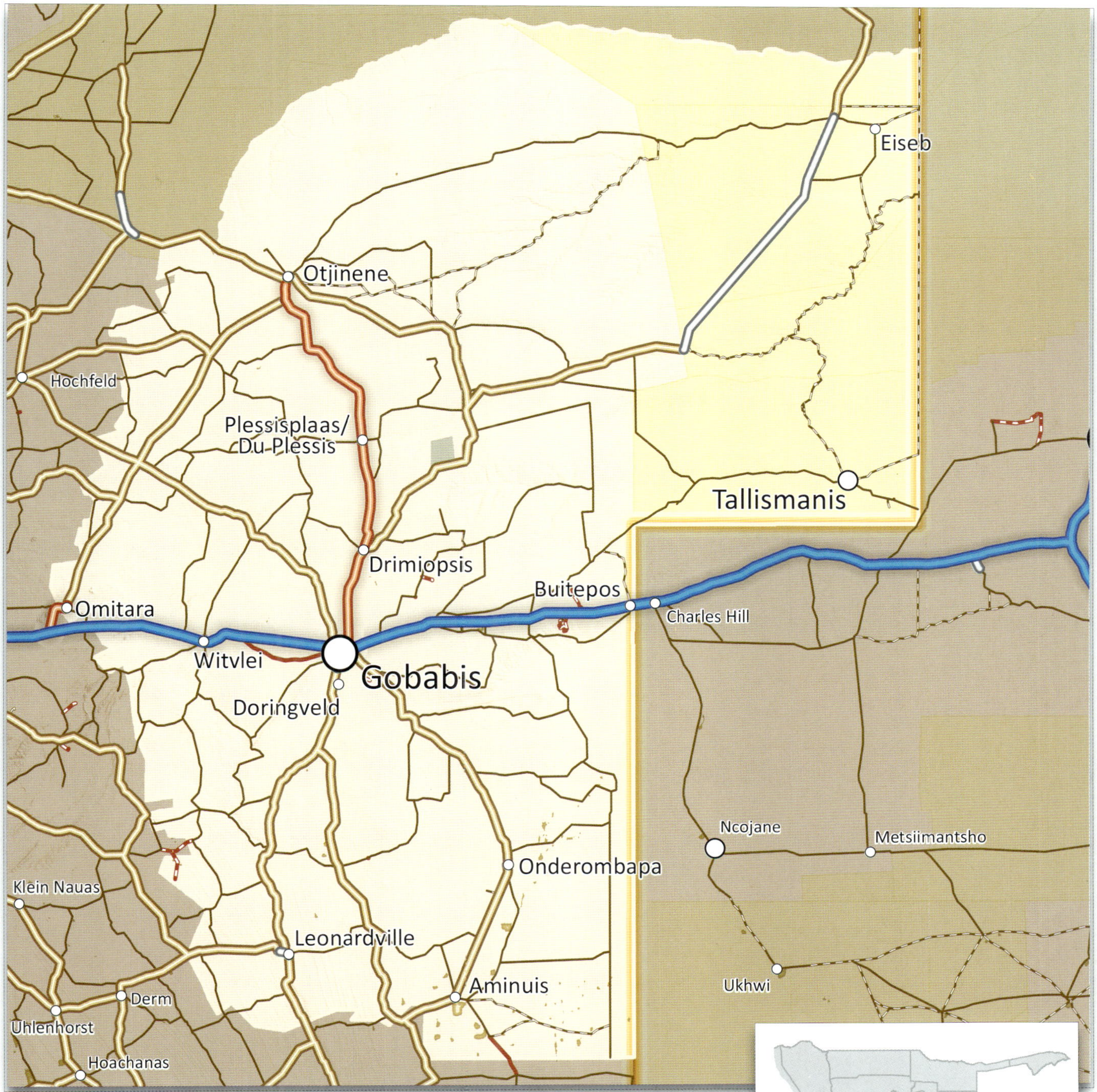

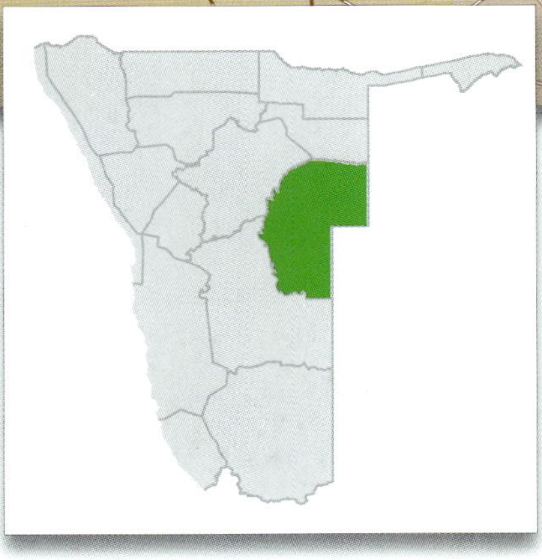

Gobabis is not a touristy area itself, but it is the closest town to the Buitepos border post and a convenient stopover on the Trans-Kalahari Highway which links Namibia, Botswana and South Africa. So it offers a lot in terms of accommodation and stock-replenishment.

Gobabis is home to the Herero people. And, although this is a modern town, many Herero women still wear their traditional clothing. Always ask before you take a photo of these women with their colourful dresses and beautiful head gear.

MAJOR ATTRACTIONS

- The Gobabis Museum displays a variety of agricultural implements and historical artefacts.
- Harnas Wildlife Foundation is an animal sanctuary which welcomes visitors.

More details about the attractions are available on our website (www.tracks4africa.co.za) or our Guide App. Our GPS Map can navigate you to each of these attractions.

Buitepos

(photo: Johann Groenewald)

THE FARM SANDFONTEIN, 110km east of Gobabis, served as a resting place for the Dorsland Trekkers on their return from Angola in the 20s. Some decided to settle here and an outpost was established to maintain law and order in the region. The farm's name changed to Buitepos, meaning outpost. With the establishment of the Buitepos/ Mamuno Border Post it became a thoroughfare to Ghanzi, Botswana. In the beginning there was only a two-spoor track on the Botswana side so there wasn't much traffic but the completion of the Trans-Kalahari Highway in 1999 heralded a new border post, fuel station and shop. The village of Charles Hill in Botswana, 7km from the Mamuno border post, has grown rapidly and boasts a fuel station, store, ATM and Bureau de Change.

Traveller Description

The Trans-Kalahari Highway offers the most direct route between Johannesburg (South Africa) and Windhoek (Namibia) via the Buitepos/Mamuno Border Post (1 100km from Johannesburg, and 320km from Windhoek). On the Botswana side, there are three rock art paintings in the vicinity of Mamuno. There are also engravings behind the Customs and Immigration staff houses, although very faint.

Travel Info

East Gate rest camp in Buitepos is located on the original Sandfontein Farm, and offers lodging and camping, as well as a restaurant, fuel station and a shop selling basic supplies, fresh produce and wine & malt.

There's also comfortable lodging and camping options on surrounding game farms, many of which offer hunting safaris. Some lodges offer cultural activities with the Kalahari San including bush walks, village visits and cultural dancing displays.

The tow-in service number is for Polka 24-hour service in Namibia who can assist anywhere in that country (they're based in Okahandja). Alternative numbers are +264(0)62 500 132 / +264(0)62 504 250. The police number is for the Buitepos Police Station in Namibia.

Useful numbers:

Mamuno Border Post (Botswana): +267 659 2013 (07:00 to 00:00), Buitepos Border Post (Namibia): +264(0)62 56 0404 (07:00 to 00:00), East Gate Rest Camp: +264(0)62 560 405

TRAVEL TIP! When the sun sets, the ground cools down quicker than tarred roads, like the Trans-Kalahari Highway. Domestic animals like cattle and donkeys move onto the tar to enjoy the lasting heat. Plus, the open space of the road offers predators no place to hide. If you drive at night you run a high risk of colliding with such domestic animals - they're often not seen until it's too late.

Town Info: Police: +264(0)62 560 400 Tow-in: +264(0)81 129 7490

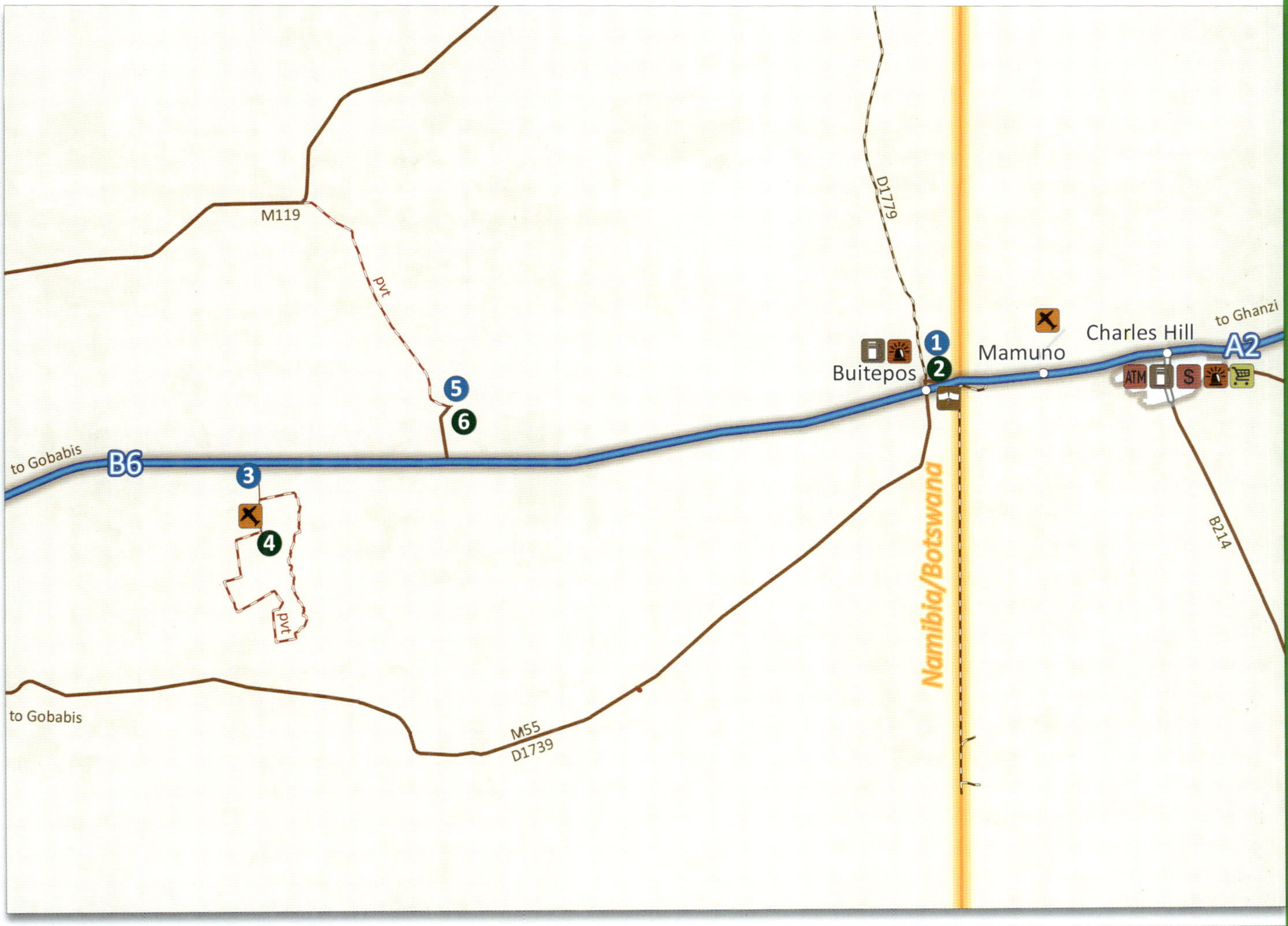

East Gate Rest Camp — 1

Self-catering — $
Buitepos border post
w254369

Tel: +264(0)62 560 405, Cell: +264(0)81 129 0686,
Fax: +264(0)62 560 406
bookings.eastgate@iway.na,
www.eastgate-namibia.com

Bungalows sleep up to four adults, with fully-equipped kitchen and private bath facilities. Plus a cabin for two, with ablution facilities.

Languages: English, Afrikaans

Facilities:
Activities:

East Gate Rest Camp — 2

Lodge Camp — $
Buitepos border post
w137323

Tel: +264(0)62 560 405, Cell: +264(0)81 129 0686,
Fax: +264(0)62 560 406
bookings.eastgate@iway.na,
www.eastgate-namibia.com

Venue is mainly for stopovers. Separate ablution facilities. Fuel station on premises.

Languages: English, Afrikaans

Facilities:
Activities:

Kalahari Bush Breaks — 3

Lodge — $$
28km or 20min WSW of Buitepos
w139608

Tel: +264(0)64 464 144, Cell: +264(0)81 244 4844,
Fax: +264(0)64 464 155
reservations@logufa.com,
www.kalaharibushbreaks.com

En-suite bedrooms as well as en-suite chalets. Thatched lapa with bar overlooks shaded garden and lit waterhole.

Languages: English, German, Afrikaans

Facilities:
Activities:

Kalahari Bush Breaks — 4

Lodge Camp — $
25km or 16min W of Buitepos
w137977

Tel: +264(0)64 464 144, Cell: +264(0)81 244 4844,
Fax: +264(0)64 464 155
reservations@logufa.com,
www.kalaharibushbreaks.com

Luxury campsites with power points, and eco campsites. Ablution facilities are open-air and the water is heated via a 'donkey'.

Languages: English, German, Afrikaans

Facilities:
Activities:

Zelda Game Guest Farm — 5

Guest Farm — $$
20km or 14min W of Buitepos
w138424

Tel: +264(0)62 560 427, Fax: +264(0)62 560 431
bookings@zeldaguestfarm.com
www.zeldaguestfarm.com

En-suite twin and family rooms. Choose between B&B and more inclusive option.

Languages: English, Afrikaans

Facilities:
Activities:

Zelda Game Guest Farm — 6

Farm Camp — $
20km or 14min W of Buitepos
w361021

Tel: +264(0)62 560 427, Fax: +264(0)62 560 431
bookings@zeldaguestfarm.com
www.zeldaguestfarm.com

Ten shaded campsites on lawn, each with access to hot water and electricity. Clean ablutions (four showers and toilets).

Languages: English, Afrikaans

Facilities:
Activities:

Gobabis

(photo: Johann Groenewald)

LIKE MANY NAMIBIAN TOWNS, Gobabis developed around a mission station; in this instance one established in 1856 by the Rhenish Missionary Society. But this spot was also once a base camp for ivory hunters and a trading post for elephant tusks. In the latter half of the 1800s and the early 1900s several conflicts flared up between the Mbanderu and the Khauas Khoikhoi, as well as between the settlers and the indigenous people. Herero and Nama people fought wars against one another, as well as with settlers from the Cape Colony who occupied the land. Perhaps for that reason the spot became known as Gobabis which means 'The place where people quarrelled'. Gobabis district was proclaimed by the German authorities in February 1894 and in June of the following year Gobabis was occupied by a German garrison.

These days Gobabis is an important link on the Trans-Kalahari Corridor between South Africa, Botswana and Namibia. It is about 110km from the Buitepos/Mamuno border post and serves as an important node between the mines of landlocked Botswana and the Namibian port of Walvis Bay. This route is also used for transporting consumer goods imported from Gauteng, South Africa into Namibia.

Traveller Description

Gobabis is a large town and considered as the capital of eastern Namibia. The settlement borders the Kalahari Desert, and is traditionally the land of the Herero people. It is the ideal stopover as it offers all services and facilities that a traveller might need. The greater Gobabis area is cattle farming country with a number of hunting lodges too. Gobabis is so proud of its cattle farming that a statue of a large bull with the inscription 'Cattle Country' greets visitors to the town.

Of special interest is the Gobabis Museum on the outskirts of the town, where a variety of old agricultural implements are displayed as well as a collection of historic artefacts that depicts the history of the people in the region. While the German military fort, which was built in 1896/7, has long since disappeared, one of the few buildings dating back to that era is the field hospital, or Lazarette, which has been declared a national monument.

A large amount of wildlife can be seen on surrounding farms and many travellers find a visit to the Harnas Wildlife Sanctuary, some 100km north-east of Gobabis, to be worthwhile.

Travel Info

Tow-in services are performed by Kuhn Panel beaters, their number is +264(0)62 562 438. The internet café is at Rosy Hair Salon. The number given is for the private hospital, which is better than the state hospital. There is a Spar in town and gas bottles can be refilled at Agra.

TRAVEL TIP! Be on the lookout for the Herero ladies with their beautiful, traditional dresses and headgear. Travellers who are interested in cultural tours, can contact Uakii Wilderness Survival, a community-based tour agent which offers cultural guided tours of the Kalahari Bushmen, Ovaherero and Batswana people. You can contact them on +264(0)62 562 324 or +264(0)81 252 1270.

Town Info:

Hospital: +264(0)62 563 980 Police: +264(0)62 566 100 Doctor: +264(0)62 562 084
Tow-in: +264(0)81 243 2169 / +264(0)81 122 0597 Tourism: +264(0)62 562 324 / +264(0)81 252 1270

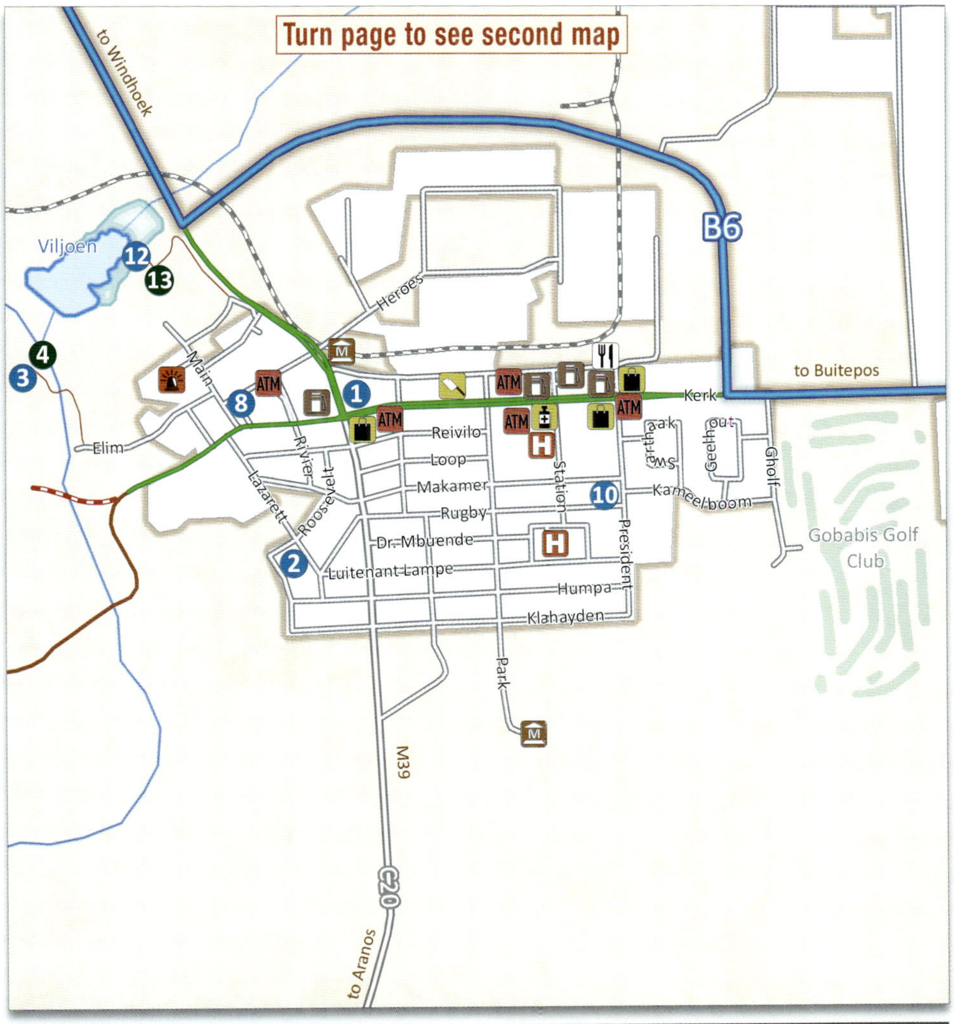

Erni's Bistro B&B — 1

Bed and Breakfast — $
29 Quito Cuanavale St, Gobabis
w138801

Tel: +264(0)62 565 222, Fax: +264(0)62 565 221
ernisbistro@iway.na

Good, clean accommodation in basic rooms behind the restaurant. With TV, fridge and bathroom. Bookings essential.

Languages: English, Afrikaans

Facilities:

Activities:

Gobabis Guest House — 2

Guest House — $
8 Lazarette St, Gobabis
w138803

Tel: +264(0)62 563 189, Cell: +264(0)81 292 5086, Fax: +264(0)62 564 125
gghnam@mtcmobile.com.na,
www.gobabisguesthouse.com

Six en-suite, double rooms with air-conditioning and fridges. There's also a fully-equipped self-catering family unit.

Languages: English

Facilities:

Activities:

Goba Lodge — 3

Lodge — $$
2km or 5min W of Gobabis
w138798

Tel: +264(0)62 564 499, Fax: +264(0)62 564 466
goba@iway.na
www.goba.iway.na

Single, double and family chalets.

Languages: English

Facilities:

Activities:

Goba Lodge & Rest Camp — 4

Lodge Camp — $
2km or 5min W of Gobabis
w208034

Tel: +264(0)62 564 499, Fax: +264(0)62 564 466
goba@mweb.com.na
www.goba.iway.na

Camping area on grass with clean ablution blocks and braai facilities. Recreational facilities include tennis courts.

Languages: English

Facilities:

Activities:

Good Hope Country House — 5

Guest House — $$
54km or 55min NE of Gobabis
w208161

Fax: +264(0)62 563 700
goodhope@sanworld.com.na

Comfortable, air-conditioned double rooms.

Languages: English

Facilities:

Activities:

Gobabis

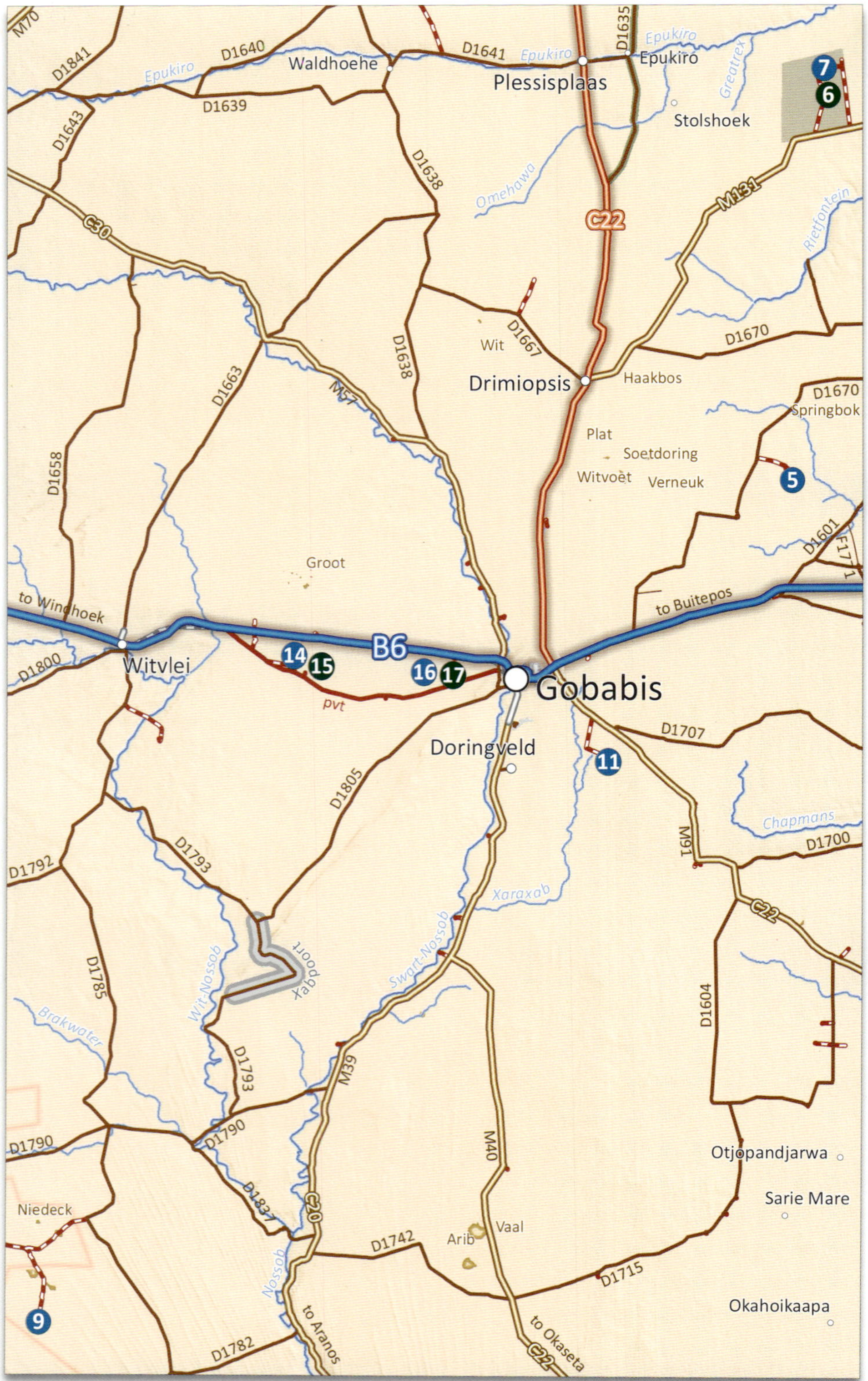

Harnas Wildlife 6

Camping $$$
107km or 1h29min NNE of Gobabis
w139361

Tel: +264(0)62 568 828, Cell: +264(0)81 140 3322,
Fax: +264(0)62 568 842
bookings@harnas.org,
www.harnas.org

The campsites have fully-equipped kitchens and clean ablutions. Campers can enjoy morning and evening animal feeding.

Languages: English, Afrikaans

Facilities:

Activities:

Harnas Wildlife Foundation & Guest Farm 7

Guest Farm $$$
107km or 1h28min NNE of Gobabis
w138434

Tel: +264(0)62 568 828, Cell: +264(0)81 140 3322,
Fax: +264(0)62 568 842
bookings@harnas.org,
www.harnas.org

Rustic, en-suite, air-conditioned chalets of various sizes.

Languages: English, Afrikaans

Facilities:

Activities:

Kalahari Gateway & Conference Centre 8

Hotel $
In Gobabis
w141960

Tel: +264(0)62 564 878, Fax: +264(0)62 564 878
kalaharicc@iway.na

Comfortable holiday accommodation in en-suite rooms. Facilities include a tea garden, beer garden and sports bar.

Languages: Afrikaans

Facilities:

Activities:

Kuzikus Wildlife Reserve 9

Game/Safari Lodge $$
129km or 2h18min SW of Gobabis
w142647

Tel: +264(0)61 253 076, Cell: +264(0)81 475 7957,
Fax: +264(0)61 255 508
outdoor-adventure@mweb.com.na,
www.kuzikus-namibia.de

Comfortable, luxurious, en-suite rooms equipped with all modern amenities. Reservations mandatory.

Languages: English, German, French

Facilities:

Activities:

Onze Rust Guest House 10

Guest House $
95 Rugby St, Gobabis
w208035

Tel: +264(0)62 562 214, Cell: +264(0)81 128 4668,
Fax: +264(0)62 565 060
onzerust@iafrica.com.na

Single and double rooms with air-conditioning, TV and fridge. They also have a braai area and inside parking.

Languages: English

Facilities:

Activities:

SanDüne Game Lodge 11

Lodge $$
20km or 23min SE of Gobabis
w177663

Tel: +264(0)62 563 559, Cell: +264(0)81 328 6763,
Fax: +264(0)62 563 557
info@sandune.com.na,
www.kwathabeng.co.za

Safari-style, en-suite rooms with electric lights. Accommodation is also available at the main guest-house, bush villa and tents.

Languages: English, German, Afrikaans

Facilities:

Activities:

Transkalahari End Resort / Die Dam — 12

Self-catering — $
1km or 2min NW of Gobabis
w255845

Tel: +264(0)62 565 656, Cell: +264(0)81 470 2311,
Fax: +264(0)62 565 656
gobabisdam@mweb.com.na

Self-catering chalets with braai facilities.

Languages: English, Afrikaans

Facilities:

Activities:

Transkalahari End Resort / Die Dam Campsites — 13

Holiday Resort Camp — $
1km or 2min NW of Gobabis
w138799

Tel: +264(0)62 565 656, Cell: +264(0)81 470 2311,
Fax: +264(0)62 565 656
gobabisdam@mweb.com.na

Situated at the Viljoen Dam, this resort offers a caravan park and campsites with individual electricity points and braai facilities.

Languages: English, Afrikaans

Facilities:

Activities:

West Nest Lodge — 14

Lodge — $$$
43km or 39min W of Gobabis
w255870

Tel: +264(0)62 570 343, Cell: +264(0)81 124 5295,
Fax: +264(0)62 570 363
info@westnestlodge.com,
www.westnestlodge.com

Luxury chalets, cozy thatched rooms, comfortable tented chalets and private campsites.

Languages: English, Afrikaans

Facilities:

Activities:

West Nest Lodge — 15

Lodge Camp — $$
43km or 39min W of Gobabis
w267578

Tel: +264(0)62 570 343, Cell: +264(0)81 124 5295,
Fax: +264(0)62 570 363
info@westnestlodge.com,
www.westnestlodge.com

Four private campsites. Facilities consists of a lapa, restaurant, bar, conference facility, gym, kitchen, boma and chapel.

Languages: English, Afrikaans

Facilities:

Activities:

Xain Quaz Rest Camp — 16

Lodge — $
10km or 8min WNW of Gobabis
w261562

Tel: +264(0)62 562 688, Cell: +264(0)81 218 9800,
Fax: +264(0)62 562 824
xainquaz@iway.na

Thatched chalets, cottages and bungalows on full-board or self-catering. Large bar and pool.

Languages: English, Afrikaans

Facilities:

Activities:

Xain Quaz Rest Camp — 17

Lodge Camp — $
10km or 8min WNW of Gobabis
w138315

Tel: +264(0)62 562 688, Cell: +264(0)81 218 9800,
Fax: +264(0)62 562 824
xainquaz@iway.na

Well spaced campsites with communal ablution facility. Set on the grounds of a leisure resort complete with a large bar and pool.

Languages: English, Afrikaans

Facilities:

Activities:

(photo: Johann Groenwald)

KAOKOLAND

A Himba kraal deep in the Marienfluss. (photo: Mietsie Visser)

IT'S ONE OF THE LAST remaining wilderness areas in Africa, so it's not surprising that Kaokoland attracts hardcore travellers and explorers. Make no mistake, you must be self-sufficient and an experienced off-road traveller if you're going to venture into this remote region in the extreme north-western corner of Namibia.

Do your preparations and you'll experience a harsh but nevertheless beautiful and rewarding journey. You definitely need an off-road vehicle to tour Kaokoland and you'd be wise not to take a trailer. Seriously consider taking a satellite phone if you travel Kaokoland on your own.

The routes here are dusty sand or gravel roads, often no more than simple tracks; they can easily become flooded depending on the season or a nearby rainstorm. If you're an off-road driving enthusiast or a very skilled adventure bike rider, you might want to tackle the notorious Van Zyl's Pass.

The Kaokoland landscape ranges from sweeping plains, to rugged mountains and dry riverbeds seamed with lush riparian bush. It deserves your respect, so be an eco-traveller and don't create track pollution; stay on the beaten tracks or roads and don't disturb any plants, especially the Welwitschia (no matter what size or age).

As in Damaraland, you have to be aware of desert elephant, especially in the dry riverbeds. The desert elephants are not used to humans and they don't like being disturbed. They have a comfort zone of at least 500m and are best observed from afar. As the dry riverbeds belong to them, you are advised to rather stay out of there. Chances are good that you might also encounter rhino, lion and leopard.

(photo: Frank Höppener)

(photo: Heiner Dillmann)

Kaokoland is mainly communal land that is divided into conservancies. The conservancies are managed by the local communities, who own the land rights and are responsible for the wild game. Money spent at community camps stays in the communities. Remember to take your own litter with you when you leave, as the communities here live in a very natural way and don't have facilities for disposing your rubbish.

The area is sparsely inhabited by nomadic Himba who are cattle herders and live in simple round huts. Respect them and their culture. They have a number of sacred places spread throughout Kaokoland and you need to ensure that you do not camp on or near them. These sacred places are indicated on Tracks4Africa's GPS maps with roads marked 'no access'.

When you drive past a village, keep your speed down so as not to cover the residents in your dust and give them a polite wave. Beware of large herds of cattle if you camp near Himba villages. The cattle have adapted to feeding as far as 35 km away from water and only return to drink every second or third day. The return to water normally happens at nightfall or later. Over the last 5 km the smell of water excites them, often causing a stampede. And you don't want to be camped in their way!

Kaokoland has a lot to offer in terms of natural beauty. The life-giving Kunene River has many waterfalls and rapids of which the most spectacular are the Ruacana Falls and Epupa Falls. The Marienfluss Conservancy is a wide and long valley covered in soft wavering grass for most of the year, set between high, stark mountain ranges. You can

(below) Epupa Falls (photo: Frank Höppener)
(bottom left) Himba woman and child. Ask for permission before taking photographs of these people. A fee is often required. (photo: Mietsie Visser)
(bottom right) The statuesque secretary bird. (photo: Jurgen Blignaut)

Hartmann's Valley rock formations. (photo: Frank Höppener)

enter the Marienfluss in the south via the nerve-wracking Van Zyl's Pass, or the track passing Rooidrom.

Rooidrom is a red, 45 gallon Caltex drum that was put there many years ago by Bantu Affairs Commissioner Ben van Zyl as a way of storing petrol for when he would pass there again and need it. Its purpose, however, changed to that of being a road marker (it is at a split in the road) and this is how it got its name. Rooidrom became a well-known landmark in Kaokoland and fellow travellers regularly paint it. It later became a memorial for one Jan Joubert, a pioneer in marking the 4x4 trails of Namibia; he was murdered north of Gobabis while on a trip into Hereroland.

Recently the mysterious Lone Men have become an attraction. The Lone Men are nearly life-size rock sculptures, masterfully created from rock prevailing in the area. They blend in perfectly with their surroundings and take on different poses. Each sculpture bears a disc with a number and a message. At the time of going to press a sculpture numbered 27 has been seen. The name of the artist and the exact location of the sculptures haven't been made public and travellers seem to be in agreement that their GPS co-ordinates should remain a secret so that the Lone Men can remain mysterious. The sculptures have been spotted along the road on the routes between Puros in the south, Van Zyl's Pass in the east, Otjinhungwa in the north and the Skeleton Coast Park in the west.

MAJOR ATTRACTIONS

- Epupa Falls
- Sesfontein Fort, a German fort from World War One
- Ongongo Hot Spring near Sesfontein
- Rooidrom
- Van Zyl's Pass
- Marienfluss
- Ruacana Falls
- Fairy circles
- Lone men rock sculptures

More details about the attractions are available on our website (www.tracks4africa.co.za) or our Guide App. Our GPS Map can navigate you to each of these attractions, apart from all the fairy circles and Lone men.

Epupa Falls

Epupa Falls, as seen from the air. (photo: Heiner Dillmann)

ON THE OTHER SIDE of the Kunene river in Angola, Epupa Falls are known as the Monte Negro Falls. The river is half a kilometre wide at this point and features a series of waterfalls ranging from 1.5m to 37m in height. Epupa is a Herero word meaning foam, named after the foam created by the falling water. These unique falls form a habitat for a few endemic fish and other aquatic species.

Traveller Description

It's recommended that you travel from Opuwo to the falls with an off-road vehicle. Even though the falls are difficult to reach it's still a major tourist attraction in Namibia. What makes it so special is the unspoilt environment, an area covered with fig trees, Baobabs and Makalani palms. The falls are framed by walls of coloured rock.

There are two possible routes from Epupa Falls to Ruacana Falls. The inland route via Okangwati is about 160km along good dirt roads and takes a morning. The off-road route next to the river is very scenic but takes one to two days, depending on the water level. Avoid this one if you're towing and/or driving alone. During the rainy season (December to March) the route can be a technical challenge.

Travel Info

Polka 24hr tow-in is based in Okahandja and services this area +264(0)81 129 7490. Alternative tow-in numbers: +264(0)62 500 132 or +264(0)62 504 250.

TRAVEL TIP! Contact local tour guide, Joao Murotua, on +264(0)81 276 6019 if you wish to visit a Himba village or do hiking trails. He has a vast knowledge on crocodiles, trees and birds found here. Some 240 bird species have been recorded in the Kunene region, including specials like the bare-cheeked babbler, rufous-tailed palm-thrush and scarlet chested sunbird.

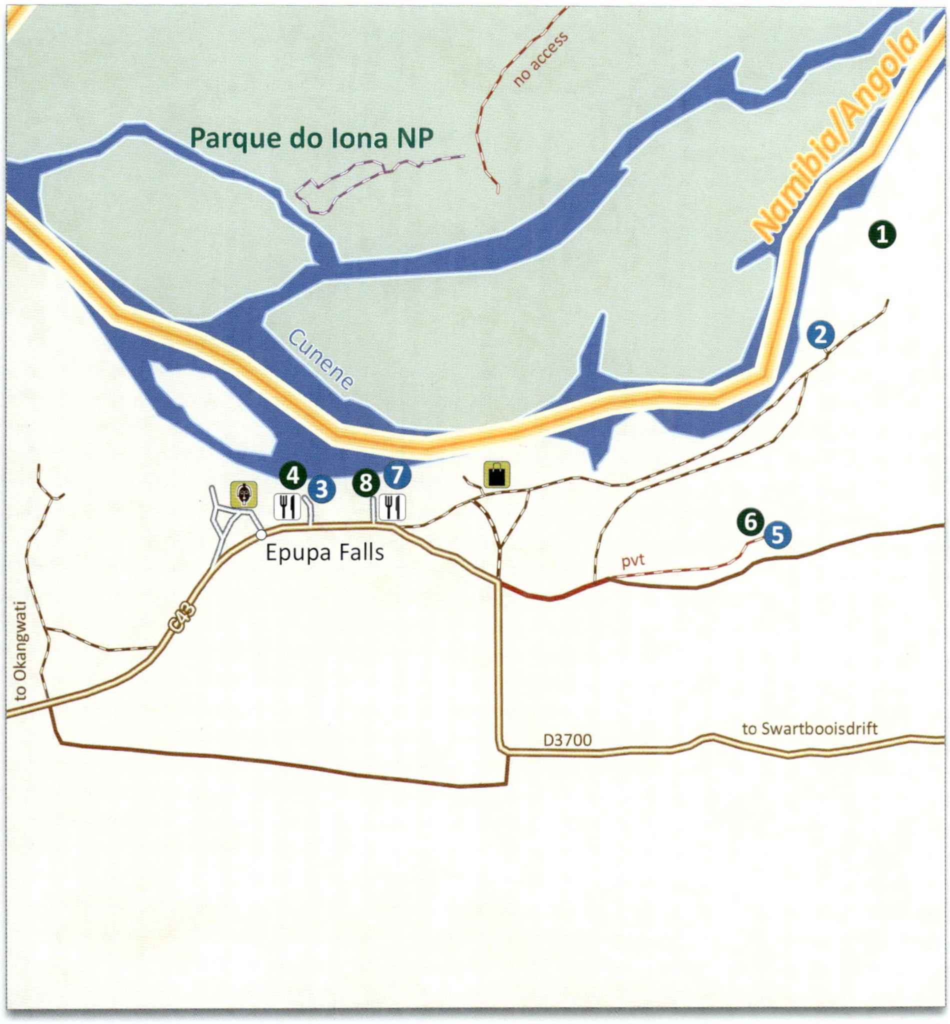

Epupa Camp — 1

Lodge Camp — $$
1km or 3min ENE of Epupa Falls
w255826

Tel: +264(0)61 232 740, Cell: +264(0)81 366 4003,
Fax: +264(0)61 249 876
reservations@epupa.com.na,
www.epupa.com.na

Each campsite has a river view and private ablution facilities (hot shower, flush toilets and two hand basins). As well as a braai area and a sink for dishes.

Languages: English, Afrikaans

Facilities:

Activities:

Epupa Camp Tented Camp — 2

Tented Camp — $$
1km or 3min ENE of Epupa Falls
w141499

Tel: +264(0)61 232 740, Cell: +264(0)81 366 4003,
Fax: +264(0)61 249 876
reservations@epupa.com.na,
www.epupa.com.na

Nine en-suite permanent tents with private balconies. The lodge has a dining room and lounge overlooking the Kunene River.

Languages: English, Afrikaans

Facilities:

Activities:

Epupa Falls Lodge — 3

Lodge — $$$
Directly at Epupa falls
w255827

Tel: +264(0)65 695 108, Cell: +264(0)81 149 2840,
Fax: +27(0)88 617 368
bookings@epupafallslodge.com,
www.epupafallslodge.com

Five chalets with a beautiful deck overlooking the falls. Each chalet has two single beds which can be pushed together to make a double.

Languages: English, German, Afrikaans

Facilities:

Activities:

Epupa Falls Lodge — 4

Lodge Camp — $
Epupa Falls, Kaokoland, Namibia
w142431

Tel: +264(0)65 695 108, Cell: +264(0)81 149 2840,
Fax: +27(0)88 617 368
bookings@epupafallslodge.com,
www.epupafalls.com

Seven campsites of which five are river-facing. Each campsite has its own braai and washing area, but shares ablution facilities.

Languages: English, German, Afrikaans

Facilities:

Activities:

Kapika Waterfall Lodge — 5

Lodge — $$$
1km or 2min E of Epupa Falls (4WD)
w216437

Tel: +264(0)65 685 111, Cell: +264(0)81 470 9312,
Fax: +264(0)65 685 110
pam.morgan111@gmail.com,
www.kapikafalls.com

Ten chalets with solar electricity and mosquito nets. Set on a terrace overlooking the Kunene River.

Languages: English, German

Facilities:

Activities:

Kapika Waterfall Lodge — 6

Camping — $$
1km or 2min E of Epupa Falls (4WD)
w361034

Tel: +264(0)65 685 111, Cell: +264(0)81 470 9312,
Fax: +264(0)65 685 110
kapika.epupa@gmail.com

Ten basic campsites with no electricity, situated on a hill above the Epupa settlement.

Languages: English, German

Facilities:

Activities:

Omarunga Lodge — 7

Lodge — $$$
In Epupa Falls town
w227910

Cell: +264(0)81 620 6887
bookings@damaraland-namibia.com
www.omarungalodge.com

13 En-suite, thatched chalets. And one family chalet which sleeps up to five. Guests can relax at the bar and stroll over to view Epupa Falls.

Languages: English

Facilities:

Activities:

Omarunga Lodge — 8

Lodge Camp — $
In Epupa Falls town
w137649

Cell: +264(0)81 620 6887
bookings@damaraland-namibia.com
www.omarungalodge.com

Nine campsites, each with its own braai pit and water tap. Clean ablution blocks. Campers are welcome to use the lodge restaurant and bar.

Languages: English

Facilities:

Activities:

Opuwo

(photo: Ian-Ray Nel)

OPUWO WAS ORIGINALLY CALLED Otjihinamaparero by the Himba, and some still refer to it by that name. The name Opuwo originated when the commissioner of Ondangwa, Hugo Hahn, came in search of land to build an office. Upon arrival he asked local headmen to give him some land where he could build an office. When the headmen wanted to give him more than the small plot he needed, Hahn said “Opuwo” which means ‘enough for me’. Opuwo is the capital of the Ovahimba people and the Kunene Region.

Traveller Description

Opuwo is the biggest town in the area and an important base from which to explore Kaokoland. The C43 road from Palmwag north to Opuwo as well as the C41 from Ruacana south to Opuwo are gravel roads in relatively good condition and can generally be traversed in a sedan car. During the dry season it is possible to drive north from Opuwo towards Epupa on the C43 in a sedan vehicle. However, the rest of the roads around Opuwo are little more than tracks and generally require an off-road vehicle. During the rainy season the entire road system in the region becomes challenging even if you’re driving an off-road vehicle.

The town is not a tourist destination in itself but Opuwo is the last place to get fuel, food supplies and services before you enter the remote Kaokoland.

Travellers heading north to Okangwati can visit the Living Museum of the Ovahimba which is situated just off the C43. Apart from providing an insight into the Himba culture, visitors can also enjoy a guided tour to a cave with Bushman rock paintings and a giant Baobab with an interesting history. Camping is also offered.

Travel Info

Most campsites in town are quite noisy so the best place to camp is at the Opuwo Country Hotel. The Kaoko Information Centre in town offers a nice taste of the Himba lifestyle. They can also arrange tours to Puros to search for desert elephant. Their contact number is +264(0)81 691 7378.

Useful Numbers:

Alternative tow-Ins: +264(0)62 500 132 or +264(0)62 504 250

TRAVEL TIP! You should not attempt Van Zyl's Pass towing a trailer and you should only ever descend it, i.e. travel the pass in an east to west direction. If you want to travel the Marienfluss with a trailer, rather take the road via Etanga and Rooidrom. From Opuwo to Etanga it's a good gravel road and from Etanga you are generally on a reasonably good two-spoor track up to Marble Community Camp (a good stopover). Even though there is a difficult section between the camp and Rooidrom, it should not be a problem for off-road trailers.

Town Info:

Hospital: +264(0)65 272 800, Police: +264(0)65 273 148, Doctor: +264(0)81 421 2743, Tow-in: +264(0)81 310 0787

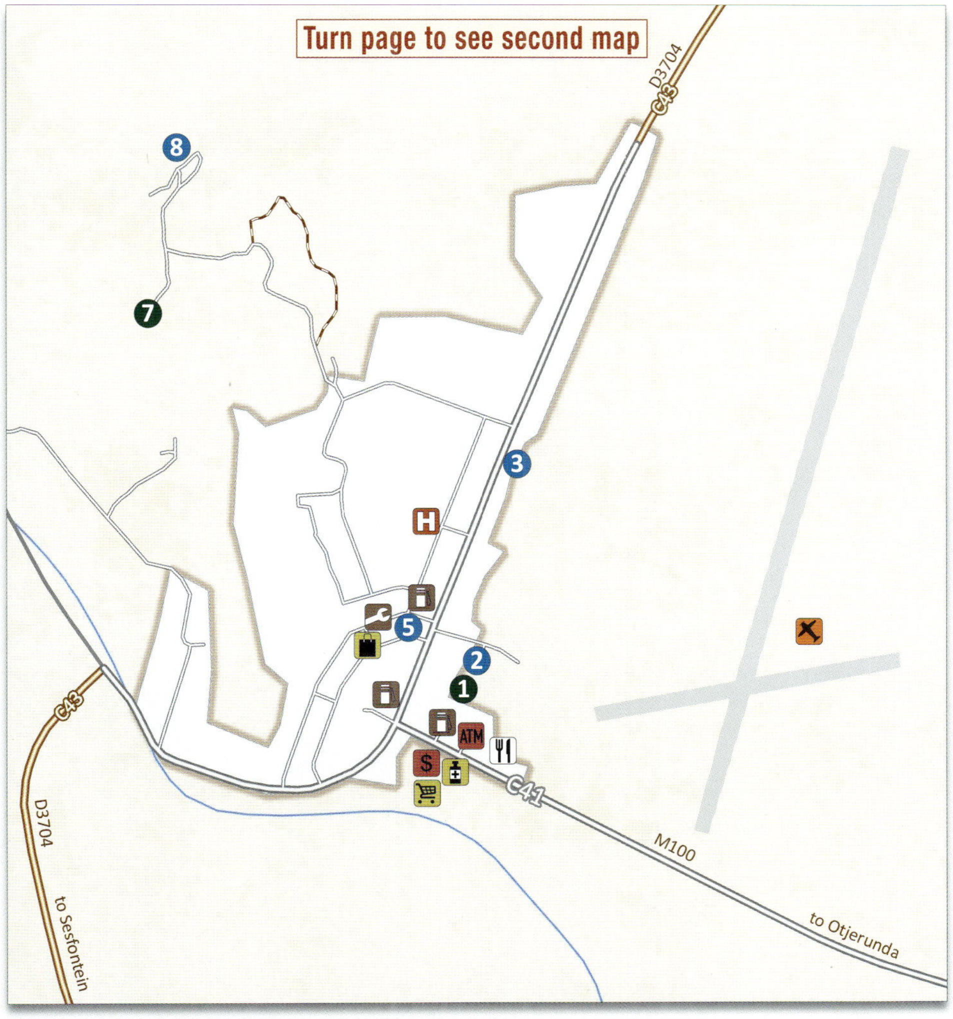

Aameny Rest Camp 1

Camping $
In Opuwo
w139183

Tel: +264(0)65 273 572, Cell: +264(0)81 260 2089, Fax: +264(0)65 273 230
aamenylodge@yahoo.com

Spacious campsites located in a beautiful garden. With communal ablution blocks. Facilities include a braai area and secure parking.

Languages: English

Facilities:
Activities:

Aameny Rest Camp Bungalows 2

Bed and Breakfast $
In town of Opuwo
w361059

Tel: +264(0)65 273 572, Cell: +264(0)81 260 2089, Fax: +264(0)65 273 230
aamenylodge@yahoo.com

Comfortable rondavels situated in a beautiful garden.

Languages: English

Facilities:
Activities:

Opuwo

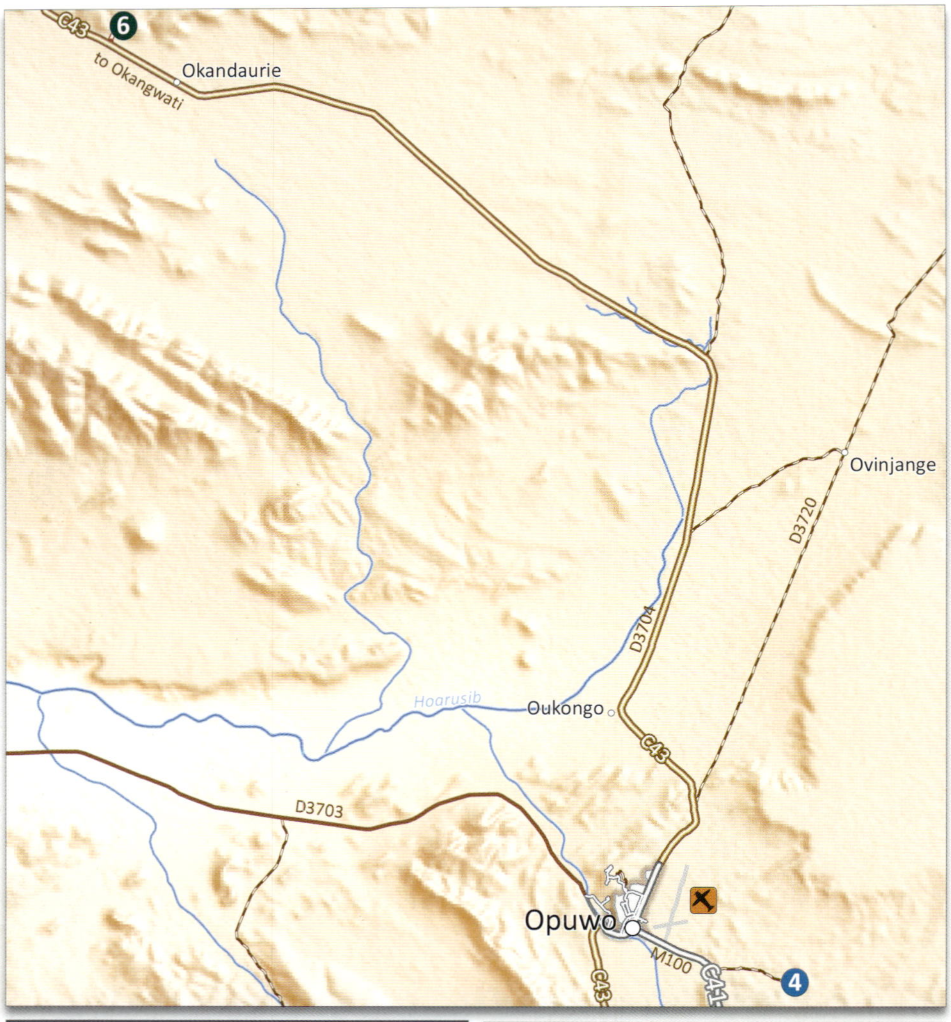

ABBA Guest House 3

Guest House $
Mbumbijazo Muharukua Avenue, Opuwo
w219538

Tel: +264(0)65 273 155, Cell: +264(0)81 234 6810,
Fax: +264(0)88 614 177
abba@iway.na,
www.abbaguesthouse.com

Four budget, six standard and five luxury rooms, all with en-suite bathrooms. Breakfast is an optional extra.

Languages: English, German, Afrikaans, Otjiherero, Oshiwambo

Facilities:

Activities:

Mopane Lodge 4

Tented Camp $
5km or 7min ESE of Opuwo (of which 3km is 4WD)
w189421

Fax: +264(0)61 401 593, Cell: +264(0)81 127 2660
mopanelodge01@gmail.com

15 En-suite, luxury, permanent tents located in a Mopane grove. Breakfast and dinner served in the lapa.

Languages: English

Facilities:

Activities:

Okahane Guest House 5

Guest House $$
Marthi Athisaari st, Opuwo
w138158

Tel: +264(0)65 273 031, Cell: +264(0)81 295 9024,
Fax: +264(0)65 273 025
ohakane@gmail.com

13 Air-conditioned rooms with en-suite bathrooms. Breakfast and 3-course dinners served at the lapa. Excursions to Himba Villages and Epupa Falls are available.

Languages: English, German, Afrikaans

Facilities:

Activities:

Omungunda Campsite (Living Museum) 6

Community Camp $
43km or 3h10min NNW of Opuwo
w227985

Cell: +264(0)81 838 2556
tjipuruaj@yahoo.com
www.lcfn.info

Spacious campsites with shade trees, hot water and flush toilets. No electricity or firewood. All campsites have braai facilities. Museum tours on the Himba culture.

Languages: English, Afrikaans, Herero, Ovambo

Facilities:

Opuwo Country Hotel 7

Lodge Camp $$
3km or 8min NNW of Opuwo
w140994

Tel: +264(0)64 418 661, Fax: +264(0)64 405 596
reservations@opuwolodge.com
www.opuwolodge.com

12 Campsites on the hotel grounds. Clean ablution blocks with hot water; plus, braai facilities, wash basins and power points.

Languages: English, German, Afrikaans

Facilities:

Activities:

Opuwo Country Lodge 8

Lodge $$
3km or 8min NNW of Opuwo
w140988

Tel: +264(0)64 418 661, Fax: +264(0)64 405 596
reservations@opuwolodge.com
www.opuwolodge.com

28 Luxury and 12 standard rooms, all en-suite. The venue is situated on a hilltop with spectacular views of the valleys and mountains.

Languages: English, German, Afrikaans

Facilities:

Activities:

(photo: Ian-Ray Nel)

above: (photo: Ian-Ray Nel)

below: (photo: Frank Höppener)

Otjinhungwa (Marienfluss Conservancy)

(photo: Donald Roberts)

OTJINHUNGWA IS LOCATED in the Marienfluss Conservancy near the Angolan border. There is a school, a few huts and a little shop selling basic supplies. The Marienfluss is surrounded by mountains, most of which are regarded as sacred by the Himba people. Respect their culture and do not camp there. Travellers love the wide open spaces of the Marienfluss and the challenge of driving the nearby Van Zyl's Pass.

Traveller Description

The road to Otjinhungwa is very sandy and only accessible with an off-road vehicle. From the east you can reach the Marienfluss and Otjinhungwa either via Van Zyl's Pass or via Etanga. You should not attempt Van Zyl's Pass with a trailer! If you want to travel through the Marienfluss with a trailer, rather take the road via Etanga and Rooidrom. From Opuwo to Etanga is a good gravel road and from Etanga you are generally on a reasonably good two-spoor track up to Marble Community Camp, which is a good stopover. Even though there is a difficult section between the camp and Rooidrom, it should not be a problem for off-road trailers.

Remember, you can only traverse Van Zyl's Pass from the east to the west (going down) and not going up. You should budget two days for both routes as driving is slow; rather stop over at one of the community campsites.

Travel Info

There's no cellphone reception in northwest Kaokoland (except for Puros, Epupa and Opuwo) so travellers are advised to carry a satellite phone for emergencies. Also, carry enough water. Even if you aren't travelling during the hottest time of the year, temperatures can still be very high and shade is sparse. If your car breaks down you can easily wait several days before another vehicle drives by.

Polka 24 hour tow-in service is based in Okahandja and services this area. Alternative tow-in numbers:
+264(0)62 500 132 or +264(0)62 504 250

TRAVEL TIP! When the wind blows in the Marienfluss, everything gets covered in sand and dust. Pack netting which can serve as a wind break. Be on the lookout for fairy circles and enjoy the prolific birdlife!

Town Info: Tow-in: +264(0)81 129 7490

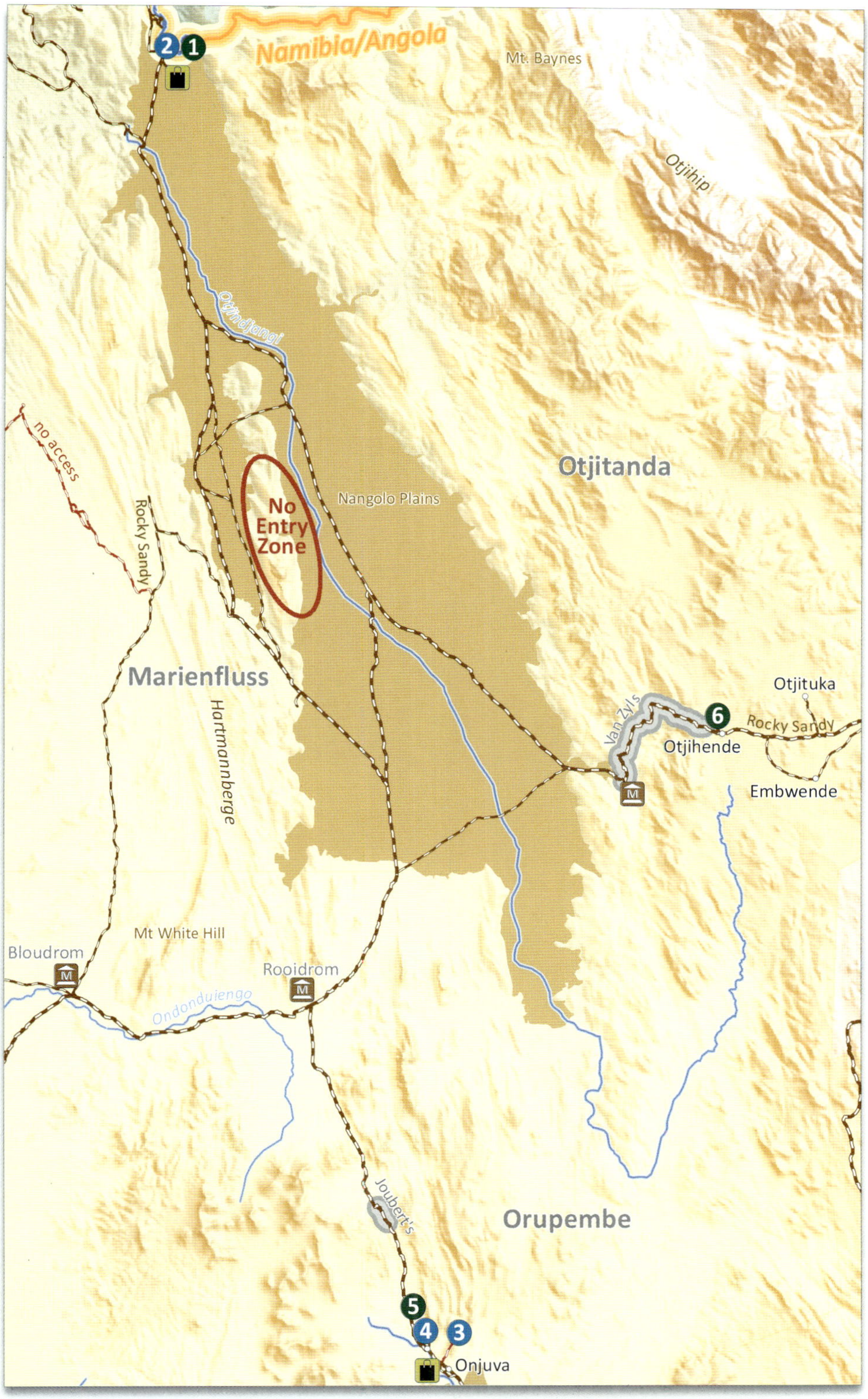

Camp Syncro 1

Camping $
1km or 1min NE of Otjinhungwa (Marienfluss Conservancy) (Off-road vehicle required)
w137591

christinger@campsyncro.com
www.campsyncro.com

Four campsites on the edge of the Kunene river, each with fireplace. Shared ablution blocks - hot showers and flush toilets.

Languages: English, German, French, Swiss

Facilities:

Activities:

Camp Syncro Bungalows 2

Self-catering $$
1km or 1min NE of Otjinhungwa (Marienfluss Conservancy) (Off-road vehicle required)
w359855
christinger@campsyncro.com
www.campsyncro.com

Two basic but spacious self-catering bungalows. Each with double bed and en-suite (hot shower). There's also an outside fireplace.

Languages: English, German, French, Swiss

Facilities:

Activities:

Etambura Camp 3

Tented Camp $$
25km or 41min NNE of Orupembe (Off-road vehicle required)
w254451
Tel: +264(0)64 40 6136, Cell: +264(0)81 149 7611,
Fax: +264(0)64 40 6135
info@kcs-namibia.com.na, www.kcs-namibia.com.na

Five canvas & thatch en-suite chalets (twin-bed) with private decks and 360° views. Bookings essential.

Languages: English

Facilities:

Activities:

House on The Hill 4

Self-catering $
26km or 41min N of Orupembe (of which 26km is (Off-road vehicle required)
w222156

Cell: +264(0)81 124 6826
houseonthehill.nott@gmail.com
www.houseonthehillnam.com

Three cottages. Unit 1 with two bedrooms (two beds in each) and a shared bathroom. Units 2 and 3, both with two beds, own bathroom and kitchen.

Languages: English

Facilities:

Marble Campsite 5

Community Camp $
26km or 41min N of Orupembe (Off-road vehicle required)
w184829

Secluded campsites with braai areas, communal showers (unreliable hot water) and toilets. No electricity. No bookings accepted.

Languages: English

Facilities:

Activities:

Van Zyl's Pass Community 6

Community Camp $
73km or 3h1min WSW of Okangwati/Okanguati (Off-road vehicle required)
w201097

One campsite with 'donkey' shower and toilet. Pay on the morning of departure, at reception desk, ask for official receipt. Use this venue at your own discretion.

Languages: English

Facilities:

Palmwag

(photo: Frank Höppener)

THE PALMWAG CONSERVANCY COVERS an area of 400 000 hectares. Wildlife includes Hartman's Mountain Zebra, giraffe, oryx, springbok and kudu. The predator population is the largest outside of the Etosha National Park, with lion, cheetah and leopard; as well as brown and spotted hyena. Birdlife is prolific and diverse with most of Namibia's endemic species present. There is also a healthy population of desert-adapted rhino (managed by the Save the Rhino Trust) and elephant.

Damaraland sand frogs (Tomopterna damarensis) inhabit the Uniab Riverbed near Palmwag. They have reddish-brown upperparts with dark patches, and white undersides. They have stout bodies and rounded snouts and their calls are a series of high-pitched tut-tut notes, repeated at around seven per second. These frogs are only found in Namibia and Southern Angola.

Traveller Description

Palmwag is one of Kaokoland's major attractions. Accommodation options vary from lodging and camping to staying at tented camps. Visitors can enjoy guided walks and game drives to observe the diverse range of free-roaming game. You can enjoy lion, elephant or rhino tracking with a qualified and experienced guide. Always wear proper hiking boots and neutral coloured clothing (not white, yellow or red) when you go for a guided walk. These animals have a keen sense of smell so do not spray perfume or deodorant on your body before your excursion.

Travel Info

If you are particularly interested in the rhino or elephant populations of this area, you can experience these desert dwelling animals in their natural environment at the Desert Rhino Camp.

Palmwag is a good place to refuel as supplies can be very unreliable further north. Take enough cash as debit/credit cards may not be accepted.

Polka 24 hour tow-in service is based in Okahandja and services this area.
Alternative tow-in numbers: +264(0)62 500 132 or +264(0)62 504 250

TRAVEL TIP! Due to the vet fence at Palmwag you can take raw meat or animal products like unpasteurised milk into Palmwag when you come from the south, but you are not allowed to take it back south or past Palmwag if you come from the north.

Town Info: Tow-in: +264(0)81 129 7490

Aub Combretum Camp — 1

Camping $
29km or 1h22min WNW of Palmwag (of which 26km is 4WD)
w204858

Tel: +264(0)67 333 214, Cell: +264(0)81 124 2468
bookings@damaraland-namibia.com

This venue is located in the Palmwag concession area. There no facilities. You need to take your own water, firewood and all other supplies.

Languages: English

Facilities:

Activities:

Blackridge Campsites — 2

Wilderness Camp $
113km or 4h41min WNW of Palmwag (of which 111km is 4WD)
w204852

Tel: +264(0)67 333 214, Cell: +264(0)81 124 2468
bookings@damaraland-namibia.com

This camp has no facilities. Permit required - obtain from Palmwag Lodge or any entrance gate to the concession.

Languages: English

Activities:

Crowther's Campsite — 3

Wilderness Camp $
74km or 3h11min W of Palmwag (of which 71km is 4WD)
w204854

Tel: +264(0)67 333 214, Cell: +264(0)81 124 2468
bookings@damaraland-namibia.com

This camp has no facilities. Permit required - obtain from Palmwag Lodge or any entrance gate to the concession.

Languages: English

Activities:

Etendeka Mountain Camp — 4

Tented Camp $$$
18km or 55min N of Palmwag (Off-road vehicle required)
w189423

Tel: +264(0)61 239 199, Cell: +264(0)81 124 6479, Fax: +264(0)61 234 971
info@etendeka-namibia.com, www.etendeka-namibia.com

Permanent tents with clean ablution blocks. Available on a full board basis. No children under 8. Bookings mandatory.

Languages: English

Facilities: FC

Activities:

"I have found out that there ain't no surer way to find out whether you like people or hate them than to travel with them."

Mark Twain, Tom Sawyer Abroad

Palmwag

Grootberg Lodge 5

Lodge $$$
27km or 32min E of Palmwag
w139133

Tel: +264(0)61 228 104, Fax: +264(0)88 625 903
reservations@grootberg.com
www.grootberg.com

Comfortable, thatched chalets with en-suite bathrooms and fully-furnished rooms.

Languages: English

Facilities:
Activities:

Hein's Campsite 6

Wilderness Camp $
22km or 1h0min WNW of Palmwag (of which 20km is 4WD)
w204857

Tel: +264(0)67 333 214, Cell: +264(0)81 124 2468
bookings@damaraland-namibia.com

This camp is located in the Palmwag concession area. No facilities. Permit required - obtain from Palmwag Lodge.

Languages: English

Facilities:
Activities:

Hoada 7

Camping $$
52km or 48min ENE of Palmwag
w140773

Tel: +264(0)61 228 104, Fax: +264(0)88 625 903
reservations@grootberg.com
www.grootberg.com

Seven campsites, each with their own ablution facilities (shower & toilet), braai and kitchen. One overland site. Please report to reception on arrival.

Languages: English, Afrikaans

Facilities:
Activities:

Palmwater Camp 11

Camping $
8km or 9min SE of Palmwag (of which 1km is 4WD)
w140010

Reportedly, no facilities or water. At the time of writing we were unable to make contact with this venue. Use at your own discretion.

Languages: English

Facilities:
Activities:

Theun's Campsite 12

Wilderness Camp $
102km or 3h NW of Palmwag (of which 84km is 4WD)
w204853

Tel: +264(0)67 333 214, Cell: +264(0)81 124 2468
bookings@damaraland-namibia.com

This camp is located in the Palmwag concession area. No facilities. Permit required - obtain from Palmwag Lodge.

Languages: English

Xai Ais 13

Wilderness Camp $
54km or 2h26min WNW of Palmwag (of which 52km is 4WD)
w204855

Tel: +264(0)67 333 214, Cell: +264(0)81 124 2468
bookings@damaraland-namibia.com

Wilderness campsite, only a tree for shade. Waterhole nearby. Guest only pay the concession fee.

Languages: English

Activities:

Mbakodja River Campsite — 8

Camping — $

54km or 1h0min NNW of Palmwag (of which 8km is 4WD)

w139643

Five campsites, each with tap and braai area. No electricity. 'Donkey' shower doesn't work properly, warmish water only. There may be a fee for camping. Use at your own discretion.

Languages: English

Facilities:

Palmwag Lodge — 9

Lodge — $$$

At Palmwag

w139346

Tel: +264(0)64 403 096, Cell: +264(0)81 620 6887, Fax: +264(0)64 402 097
bookings@damaraland-namibia.com, www.palmwaglodge.com

12 Thatched bungalows with en-suite bathrooms. 12 Luxury en-suite tents. Entry by permit only - obtain at reception.

Languages: English

Facilities: VISA FC

Activities:

Palmwag Lodge — 10

Lodge Camp — $$

At Palmwag

w139665

Tel: +264(0)64 403 096, Cell: +264(0)81 620 6887, Fax: +264(0)64 402 097
bookings@damaraland-namibia.com, www.palmwaglodge.com

Eight campsites with braai areas and communal ablution facilities. Campers may use the lodge facilities like the bar.

Languages: English

Facilities: VISA FC

Activities:

(photo: Frank Höppener)

Puros

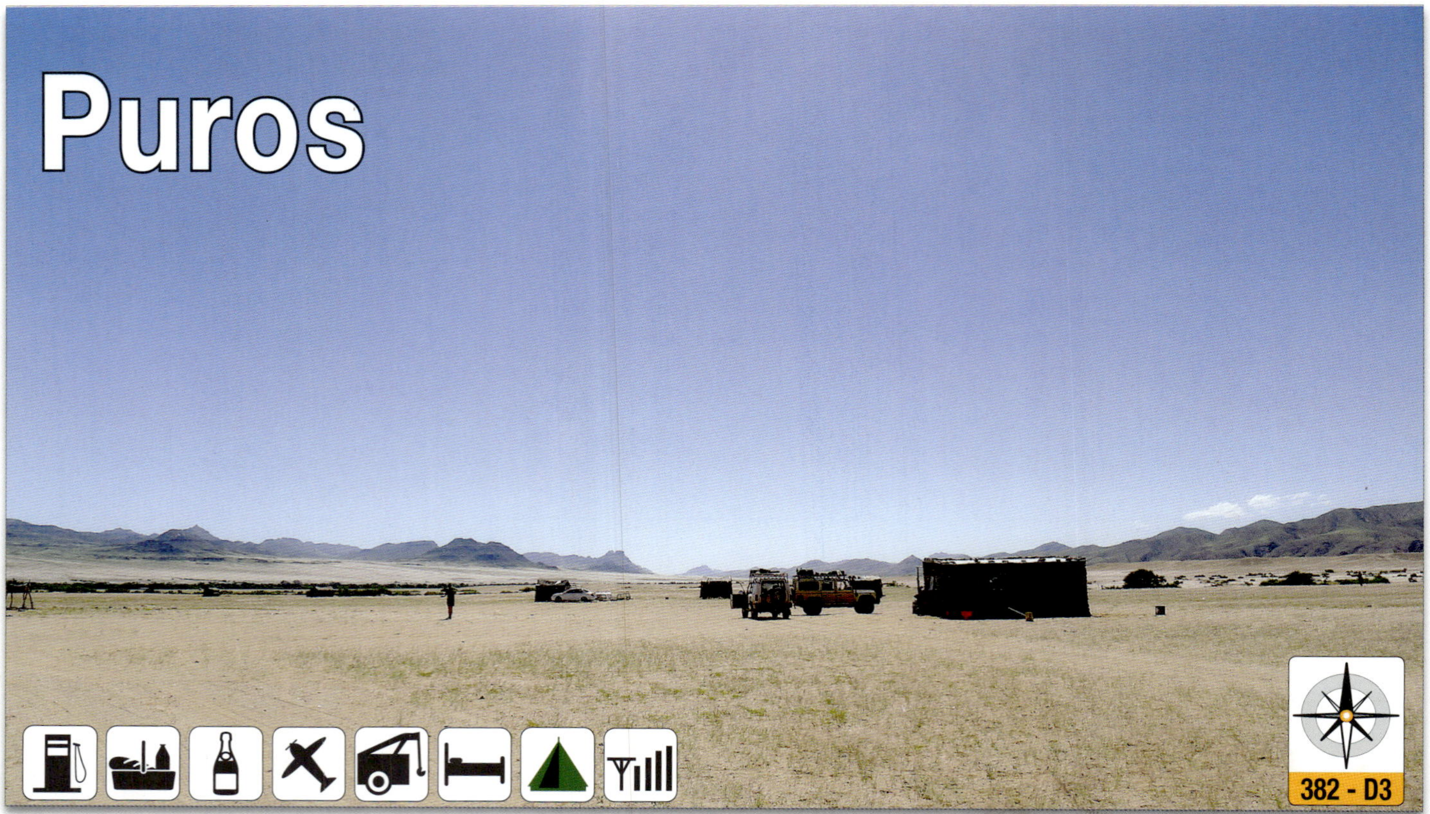

(photo: Frank Höppener)

BEFORE COLONIAL TIMES, KAOKOLAND was mostly inhabited by the Ovambo, Nama and Herero people. In the second half of the 19th century, a group of Herero crossed the Kunene River, migrating north to what is now Angola, joining with the Bushman in Southern Angola. The modern day Himba people, which is the most represented ethnic group in Kaokoland, originated from this Angolan Herero group. In 1884, Kaokoland became part of German South West Africa and Namibian Herero changed much of their habits and costumes as a consequence of German rule. However, the Himba retained much of their traditional, nomadic and pastoral habits.

Traveller Description

Although Puros doesn't offer much as a town, the area is very popular amongst overlanders as it offers a taste of the real beauty and remoteness of Kaokoland. Puros can be reached with a sedan vehicle with high clearance but you will need an off-road vehicle if you want to explore the dry riverbeds.

The Puros elephants are one of only two desert-dwelling elephant populations in the world that live in dry riverbeds. The Hoarusib riverbed is not only frequented by desert-adapted elephant but also giraffe, rhino, kudu, zebra, ostrich and smaller animals like jackal and the desert chameleon.

Travel Info

The shop is very basic, but does sell cold beer! Fuel is only available in containers, at a higher price.

Useful Numbers:

Alternative tow-in numbers: +264(0)62 500 132 or +264(0)62 504 250.

TRAVEL TIP! Get a local guide to take you on a day trip down the dry Hoarusib riverbed. You will see breathtaking landscapes and vistas down to the Skeleton Coast. You will also cross mountain ranges and many wet and dry riverbeds. You will marvel at the variety of animals and birds to be seen, and learn about the plants and people of the region when you visit a Himba village.

Town Info: Tow-in: +264(0)81 129 7490

Puros Bush Lodge 1

Self-catering $
5km or 10min N of Puros (Off-road vehicle required)
w193080

Cell: +264(0)81 455 8180

This community-owned lodge offers basic, self-catering accommodation. Bed linen and towels provided. Campsites with clean ablutions (hot showers). No bookings required outside of season.

Languages: English

Activities:

Puros Ngatutanga Camp 2

Community Camp $
5km or 10min N of Puros (Off-road vehicle required)
w137726

Cell: +264(0)81 455 8180

Six campsites, each with tap and braai pit. Ablutions with flush toilets and hot water via 'donkey' system. Trips to local villages can be arranged. Reservations advisable.

Languages: English

Facilities:

Activities:

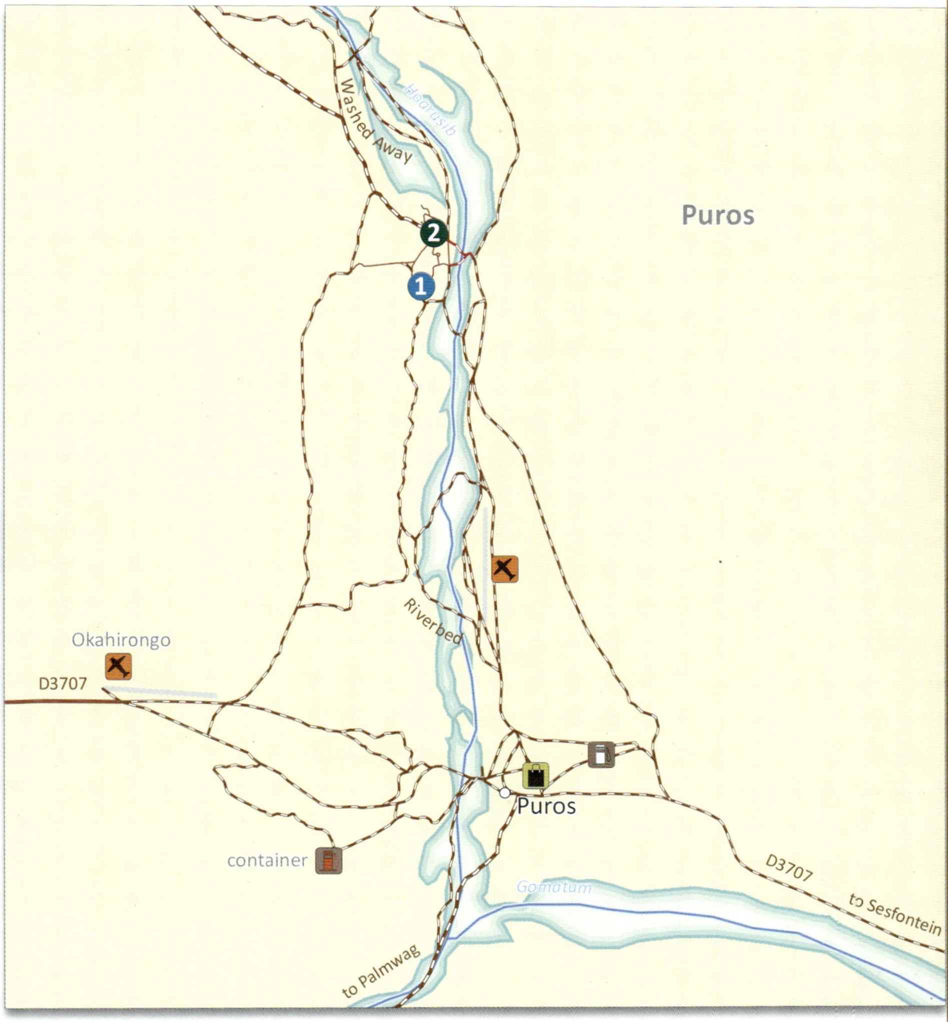

(photo: Karin Theron)

Ruacana

(photo: Ian-Ray Nel)

RUACANA IS LOCATED ON THE KUNENE RIVER, the border between Angola and Namibia. The town was developed around an underground hydroelectric plant which was linked to the nearby dam. This was bombed by a Cuban airstrike in 1988 during the Angolan Civil War. The plant was partially repaired and today it is used by Nampower which operates three turbines. Etunda is a community project located near Ruacana which produces maize, wheat, watermelons, bananas and other produce. Half of the 600 hectares is commercially-irrigated farmland and the rest is allocated to small-scale farmers.

Traveller Description

Ruacana is a small, peaceful settlement offering basic facilities. The Kunene Mini Market at the only fuel station has an ATM and excellent food supplies. They stock frozen meat, fresh bread, liquor and ice. The town is known for the Ruacana Falls which are located nearby and a must-see after good rains. Tours to the Hydro Electric Power Plant run by Nampower can be arranged.

Travel Info

Ruacana border post is open 08:00 - 19:00 and the number is +264(0)65 270 290. You should have N$295 (2018 fee) cash available to pay the cross border charge. You can either pay in South African rand or Namibian dollars.

Useful telephone numbers:

Clinic: +264(0)65 270 054
Alternative tow-in numbers: +264(0)62 500 132 or +264(0)62 504 250

TRAVEL TIP! Accommodation is available in town, or you can camp at nearby Hippo Pools, a nice Himba community camp on the Kunene River.

Town Info:

Police: +264(0)65 270 089
Tow-in: +264(0)81 129 7490

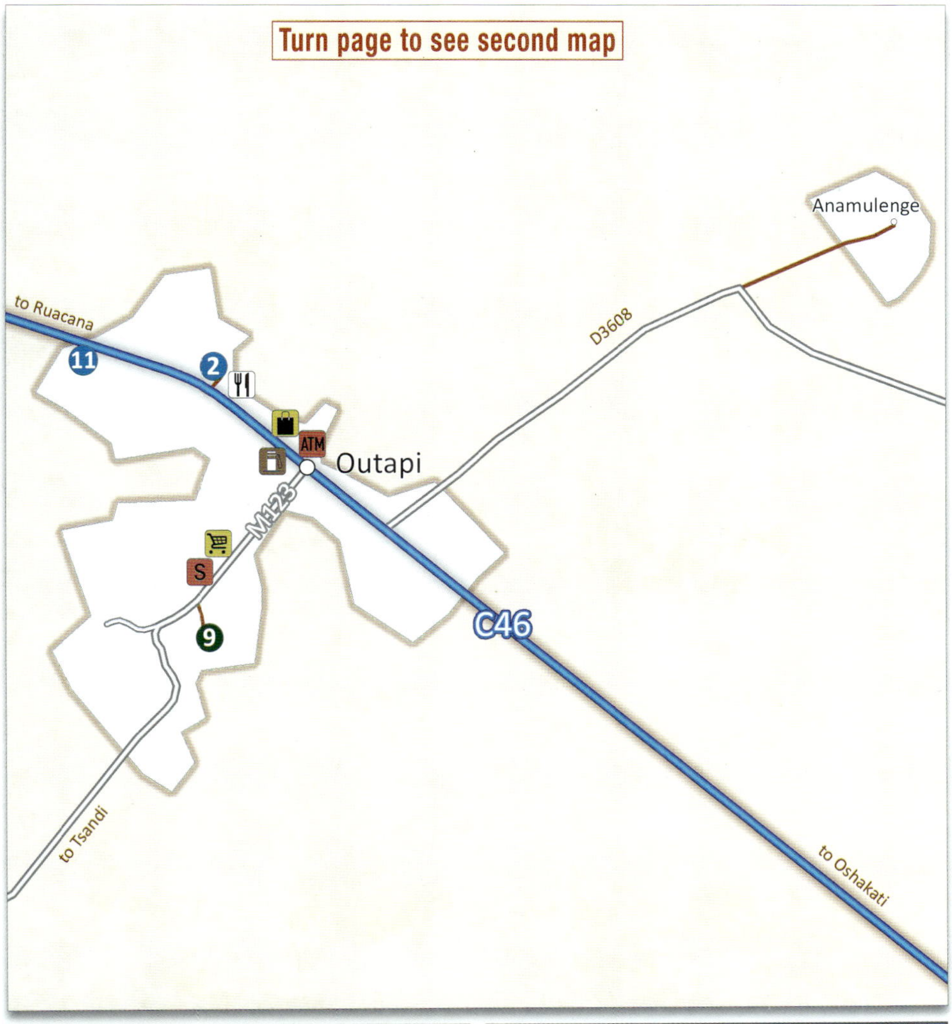

Hippo Pools Community Camp — 1

Community Camp $
21km or 21min WNW of Ruacana
w138588

Cell: +264(0)81 260 8840

10 Campsites under Mopane trees, each with braai facilities. Very neat ablutions. Venue is run by the local Himba people.

Languages: English

Facilities:

Activities:

Keelu Guesthouse — 2

Lodge $
Main Road, Outapi
w241423

Tel: +264(0)65 251 313, Cell: +264(0)81 335 0116,
Fax: +264(0)65 251 313
keeluguesthouse1@gmail.com,
www.outapiminilodge.iway.na

Single and double rooms with bathrooms, air-conditioning and TVs. Includes breakfast. Located alongside Oshakati / Ruacana road.

Languages: English

Facilities:

Kunene Islands — 3

Lodge Camp $
31km or 34min W of Ruacana
w189043

Fax: +264(0)88 650 9918, Cell: +264(0)81 129 3931
unicorn@iway.na

Located close to Angolan border and Kunene River in an unspoilt area. Communal ablution blocks.

Languages: English

Facilities:

Activities:

Kunene River Lodge — 4

Lodge $$
71km or 3h9min W of Ruacana (of which 10km is 4WD)
w137410

Tel: +264(0)61 228 104
reservations@journeysnamibia.com
www.kuneneriverlodge.com

Air-conditioned rooms and rustic en-suite chalets. 4WD required during rainy season.

Languages: English, German, Afrikaans

Facilities:

Activities:

Kunene River Lodge — 5

Lodge Camp $$
71km or 3h9min W of Ruacana (of which 10km is 4WD)
w141076

Tel: +264(0)61 228 104
reservations@journeysnamibia.com
www.kuneneriverlodge.com

12 Well-equipped campsites under canopy of mature trees overlooking the Kunene River. Campers can enjoy lodge facilities and activities.

Languages: English, German, Afrikaans

Facilities:

Activities:

Mavinga — 6

Camping $$
34km or 42min W of Ruacana (of which 3km is 4WD)
w193072

Cell: +264(0)81 128 6890

Located next to the Kunene River near Ruacana. The campsite is basic but perfect for overnight stay in an outdoor area.

Languages: English

Facilities:

Activities:

Mavinga Lodge — 7

Lodge $$
34km or 44min W of Ruacana (of which 3km is 4WD)
w361603

Tel: +264(0)81 128 6890

Located along the Kunene River near Ruacana, this lodge offers spacious, comfortable single and double rooms.

Languages: English

Facilities:

Activities:

Okapupa Camp — 8

Camping $
55km or 2h41min W of Ruacana (of which 10km is 4WD)
w137648

Tel: +264(0)65 273 570, Cell: +264(0)81 124 3212
okapupacamp@yahoo.com

Located on the banks of the Kunene River, this venue offers clean ablution facilities and a large thatched bar and dining area.

Languages: English, Afrikaans

Facilities:

Activities:

Ruacana

Ombalantu Baobab Tree Heritage Centre and Campsite	9
Camping	$

In Outapi
w316412

Tel: +264(0)65 251 005, Cell: +264(0)81 438 4705,
Fax: +264(0)65 251 005

Four campsites with clean ablutions, each with braai area. Wash-up facilities also available.

Languages: English

Facilities:

Omunjandi Restcamp	10
Camping	$

30km or 31min W of Ruacana (of which 1km is 4WD)
w138328

Cell: +264(0)81 358 5865
omunjandi@gmail.com
www.omunjandirestcamp.com

Large, shady campsites with pool and ablution facilities. There's also a stone hut. Amenities are very rustic.

Languages: English, Afrikaans

Facilities:

Activities:

Outapi Town Hotel	11
Hotel	$

Main Road, Outapi
w255888

Tel: +264(0)65 251 029, Fax: +264(0)65 251 032
outapith@iway.na
www.outapith.iway.na

Air-conditioned, en-suite rooms, each with TV, telephone and fridge. Located seven minutes from the famous Ombalantu Baobab Tree.

Languages: English

Facilities: VISA

Activities:

Ruacana Eha Lodge	12
Lodge	$$

1km or 2min W of Ruacana
w139116

Tel: +264(0)65 271 500, Cell: +264(0)81 124 7758,
Fax: +264(0)65 270 095
info@ruacanaehalodge.com.na,
www.ruacanaehalodge.com.na

21 Double en-suite rooms with private verandas, a family suite and six huts with braai areas.

Languages: English

Facilities: VISA @

Activities:

Ruacana Eha Lodge	13
Lodge Camp	$

1km or 2min W of Ruacana
w141154

Tel: +264(0)65 271 500, Cell: +264(0)81 124 7758,
Fax: +264(0)65 270 095
info@ruacanaehalodge.com.na,
www.ruacanaehalodge.com.na

15 Campsites with their own braai areas and a communal ablution block.

Languages: English

Facilities: VISA @

Activities:

Ruacana Guest House	14
Guest House	$

Dr. Sam Nujoma Drive, Ruacana
w315008

Cell: +264(0)81 243 4030
ruacanaguesthouse@gmail.com

Self-catering units, each with own, satellite TV, Wi-Fi, queen-size beds, bathroom, fully-equipped kitchen, braai and air-conditioning.

Languages: English, Portuguese, Afrikaans

Facilities: FC @

When the river levels are low, the Ruacana Falls can be rather uninspiring. (photo: Ian-Ray Nel)

Opposite page, bottom (photos: Sebastian Dürrschmidt LCFN www.lcfn.info)

Sesfontein

(photo: Ian-Ray Nel)

SESFONTEIN'S NAME IS DERIVED FROM THE SIX FOUNTAINS located in the vicinity. A well-known landmark is the old German fort, Fort Sesfontein, which has graves from the First World War. The fort's many palm trees were planted by the German police officers who were stationed here to combat weapon smuggling as well as elephant and rhino poaching. Today the fort is a historical monument which has been rebuilt and equipped to accommodate tourists.

Traveller Description

The area around Sesfontein and Puros is very popular because of the fountains, hot springs and beautiful landscape. There are many off-road riverbed trails which are often frequented by desert elephants. Lion still roam the area along with other game. Spoil yourself with a swim in the Ongongo Hot Spring, 27km east of Sesfontein. After a few days' hard travelling the lukewarm water which cascades over a waterfall into a crystal-clear pool will invigorate you. Although it's possible to reach the spring with a sedan vehicle with high clearance, a 4x4 is recommended as the 6km off-road track from Warmquelle is rough and very rocky in parts, sandy in others, and at one point you have to cross a dry riverbed.

Travel Info

Fort Sesfontein Lodge offers guided off-road day trips as well as local guides for those who prefer to use their own vehicles. If you want to traverse Robbies Pass to Kaoko Otavi to visit the Dorsland Trekker remains, you should budget 5 to 6 hours travel time as the drive is difficult with extremely slow rock-crawling.

Useful numbers:

Clinic: +264(0)65 275 511
Alternative tow-in numbers: +264(0)62 500 132
+264(0)62 504 250

TRAVEL TIP! The dry riverbeds can become very wet and muddy during the rainy season and extremely dusty during the dry season. As you get into the dry Hoanib Riverbed from Sesfontein, make sure all your windows are closed against the penetrating powder dust. On the popular Hoarusib Riverbed trail, you should stay on the main tracks because there are some spots with deep soft mud. On both tracks you can expect very deep sand, so you must lower your tyre pressures. Visiting here in a single vehicle is very risky unless you are an experienced off-road driver with good recovery gear.

Town Info:
Police: +264(0)65 275 515
Tow-in: +264(0)81 129 7490

Sesfontein

Cameltop Community Camp 1

Community Camp $
3km or 4min WSW of Sesfontein
w139085

Five large, shaded campsites with hot water, flush toilets and braai facilities. Drinkable water. Use at your own discretion, this information could not be confirmed at time of writing.

Languages: English

Facilities:

Camp Aussicht 2

Lodge Camp $
65km or 1h5min NNE of Sesfontein (of which 7km is 4WD)
w139836

Tel: +264(0)61 234 342, Cell: +27(0)81 629 3270, Fax: +264(0)61 233 872
eden@africaonline.com.na

Five campsites with clean ablutions. Wood is supplied. High-clearance vehicle required to reach camp.

Languages: English, German, Afrikaans

Facilities:

Activities:

Elephant Song Campsite (Hoanib River) 3

Wilderness Camp $
24km or 47min WSW of Sesfontein (of which 16km is 4WD)
w193088

This campsite is beautifully located, but deserted with no facilities. It has been visited by the Tracks4Africa community of travellers. You need to be self-sufficient.

Languages: English

Activities:

Fort Sesfontein Lodge 4

Lodge $$
In Sesfontein
w137605

Tel: +264(0)65 685 034, Fax: +264(0)65 685 033
fsesfontein@gmail.com
www.fort-sesfontein.com

This restored German fort offers double, en-suite rooms. Electricity via generator. 4WD recommended during the rainy season.

Languages: English

Facilities: VISA

Activities:

Khowarib Community Rest Camp 5

Community Camp $
35km or 27min ESE of Sesfontein (of which 2km is 4WD)
w141946

Cell: +264(0)81 407 9539

Camp with braai and ablution facilities. We suggest you just show up, the community will help you.

Languages: English

Facilities:

Activities:

Khowarib Lodge 6

Tented Camp $$$
34km or 26min ESE of Sesfontein (of which 2km is 4WD)
w138139

Tel: +264(0)64 402 779, Cell: +264(0)81 219 3291, Fax: +264(0)88 641 314
reservations@khowarib.com, www.khowarib.com

En-suite twin & double canvas chalets, or 3-bed family chalets. All chalets have mains electricity, coffee/tea facilities, a veranda and an open-air bathroom.

Languages: English

Facilities: VISA FC

Activities:

Khowarib Lodge 7

Lodge Camp $
34km or 27min ESE of Sesfontein (of which 2km is 4WD)
w227908

Tel: +264(0)64 402 779, Cell: +264(0)81 219 3291, Fax: +264(0)88 641 314
reservations@khowarib.com, www.khowarib.com

Eight campsites, each with light, tap, wash-up area, shade port and braai pit. Campers have full access to lodge facilities. Bookings required.

Languages: English

Facilities: VISA FC

Activities:

Ongongo Waterfall Campsite 8

Community Camp $$$
27km or 30min E of Sesfontein (of which 6km is 4WD)
w139343

Cell: +264(0)61 23 9643
ongongo@naturefriendsafaris.com
www.ongongo.com

Luxury campsites with private ablutions. No electrical points but there are 12 V solar-powered lights. Ongongo means 'magical' in Herero.

Languages: English, Afrikaans, Ovaherero

Facilities:

Activities:

Sesfontein Guesthouse 9

Guest House $$
In Sesfontein
w361570

Tel: +264(0)61 239 643, Cell: +264(0)81 473 2926
ongongo@naturefriendsafaris.com
www.sesfontein-guesthouse.com

Six rooms each with one double and one single bed. No en-suite bathrooms; four communal shower & toilet units. Restaurant serves lunch and dinner.

Languages: English

Facilities: VISA

Activities:

Zebra Community Camp 10

Community Camp $
D3707, 1km or 2min WSW of Sesfontein
w139086

Cell: +264(0)81 614 1410

Basic campsites with hot shower ('donkey' system), and bucket-flush toilets. No running water - it's available in containers.

Languages: English

Facilities:

(photo: Heiner Dillmann)

Ongongo Hot Springs, east of Sesfontein, as seen from under the waterfall. (photo: Heiner Dillmann)

(photo: Ian-Ray Nel)

KAVANGO

Top and bottom (photos: Heiner Dillmann)

THE KAVANGO RIVER FORMS THE NORTHERN BORDER of Namibia and the Kavango region. Most of the attractions of this region are located along the river, like Popa Falls near Divundu. After good rains these falls, which are in fact rapids rather than falls, are quite spectacular.

The B8 highway which runs from Grootfontein to Rundu (the capital of this region), is the main artery linking the heart of Namibia with the old Caprivi strip which stretches out like an arm over Botswana. The B8 also runs through the Bwabwata National Park which straddles both the Kavango and Zambezi regions. Formed in 2007, the park is managed by government in conjunction with the local community; it's made up of three core conservation areas as well as 'multiple use areas' where people farm with livestock and grain in the small villages. The park's office and main entrance is located near Kongola in the Zambezi (Caprivi) region; tourists can visit three 'core areas' dedicated to conservation: Mahango and Buffalo in this region and Kwando in the Zambezi region.

With over 600 bird species, this park is a real paradise for bird watchers. There's also plenty of game to be seen - herds of elephant migrate freely through the region, crossing between Botswana and Angola. Unguided walking is permitted but be aware that hunting concessions were given to the local community and hunting takes place, especially in the Buffalo and Kwando Core Areas.

The Mahango Game Reserve with its magnificent baobab trees borders the Bwabwata National Park. These ancient trees look like they were planted the wrong way around, especially when they shed their leaves in the dry season.

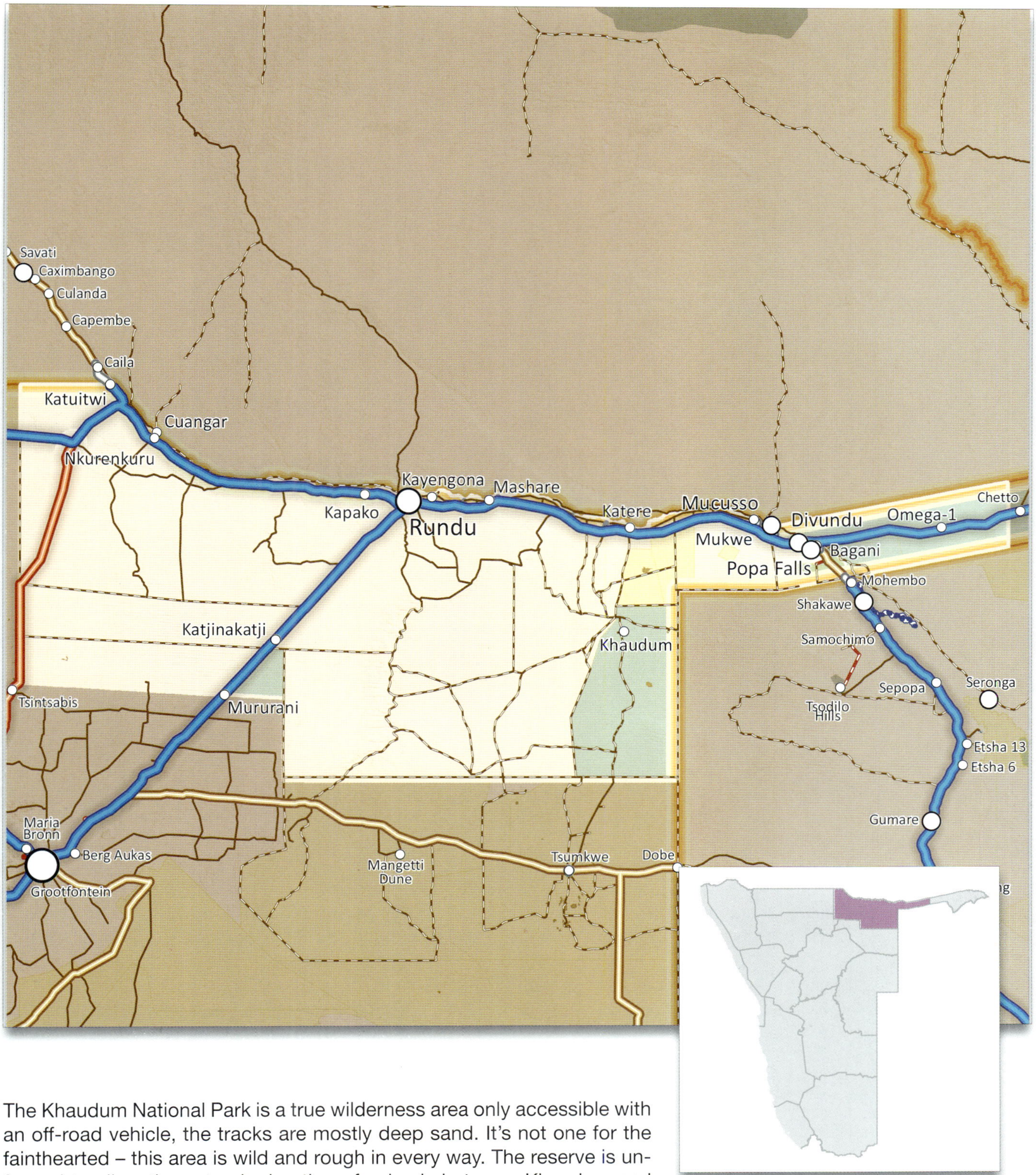

The Khaudum National Park is a true wilderness area only accessible with an off-road vehicle, the tracks are mostly deep sand. It's not one for the fainthearted – this area is wild and rough in every way. The reserve is unfenced to allow the natural migration of animals between Khaudum and Botswana. It is home to herds of elephant, a variety of antelope, giraffe, hyena, leopard, lions and the African wild dog. For a real African experience there are two basic rest camps, also unfenced. Visitors should take malaria precautions when visiting this region.

MAJOR ATTRACTIONS

- Khaudum National Park
- Mahango Core Area
- Popa Falls
- The Andara Mission Station church is open to visitors.

More details about the attractions are available on our website (www.tracks4africa.co.za) or our Guide App. Our GPS Map can navigate you to each of these attractions.

Divundu

(photo: Johann Groenewald)

DIVUNDU IS A SMALL VILLAGE on the south-eastern bank of the Kavango River and is home to the Mbukushu kings. It's situated on the B8 highway, the main artery linking the Kavango region to the Caprivi Strip (recently renamed as the Zambezi region).

In 1913, Alexander Ndara, chief of the Hambukushu tribe, accepted and welcomed some Catholic missionaries. The Catholic church and hospital at the Andara Mission Station 15km west of Divundu are still functional and the original water mill is a reminder of the days when the station's fertile farmland was irrigated with river water.

The Okavango River is the fourth-longest river system in southern Africa, running south-eastward for 1 600km. It rises in Angola, where it is known as the Cubango River. Further south it forms part of the border between Angola and Namibia (where it's known as the Kavango river), and then flows into Botswana, draining into the Okavango Delta. Before entering Botswana, the river drops four meters, across its full 1.2km width, in a series of rapids known as Popa Falls. These are visible when the river runs low during the dry season, and is the main attraction near Divundu.

Traveller Description

There is a large variety of accommodation options in the Divundu area. The town itself isn't pretty but travellers can stock up at the two general dealers before venturing into the Zambezi region. Birding, fishing, game viewing and boat cruises are some of the most popular activities offered here.

The riverine habitat is a bird watcher's paradise and to date some 430 species, nearly 70% of Namibia's total number of species, have been recorded. The Kavango River with its 71 fish species is a very popular angling spot and the nearby Mahango Core Area offers a diversity of wildlife in typical riverine and swampland habitat.

Travel Info

The Mahango Core Area is well worth a visit. The River loop can be accessed in a sedan and will take one to two hours whereas the western loop requires an off-road vehicle and will take at least two hours to complete.

A few of the local lodges offer boat cruises to Popa Falls. From the Popa Falls Rest Camp, upgraded in 2013, you can walk to the rapids and have refreshments at the restaurant that overlooks them. Some lodges offer guided tours to nearby villages.

Tow-in numbers: +264(0)62 500 132 or +264(0)62 504 250

The nearest hospital is at Andara, 15km west of Divundu.

TRAVEL TIP! The road between Rundu and Katima Mulilo has cell phone reception most of the way. Because of veterinary fence restrictions you cannot take raw meat from Katima Mulilo to Rundu. There is a vet fence control point just east of Divundu where your vehicle will be checked and sprayed.

Town Info:
Police: +264(0)66 259 432

Turn page to see second map

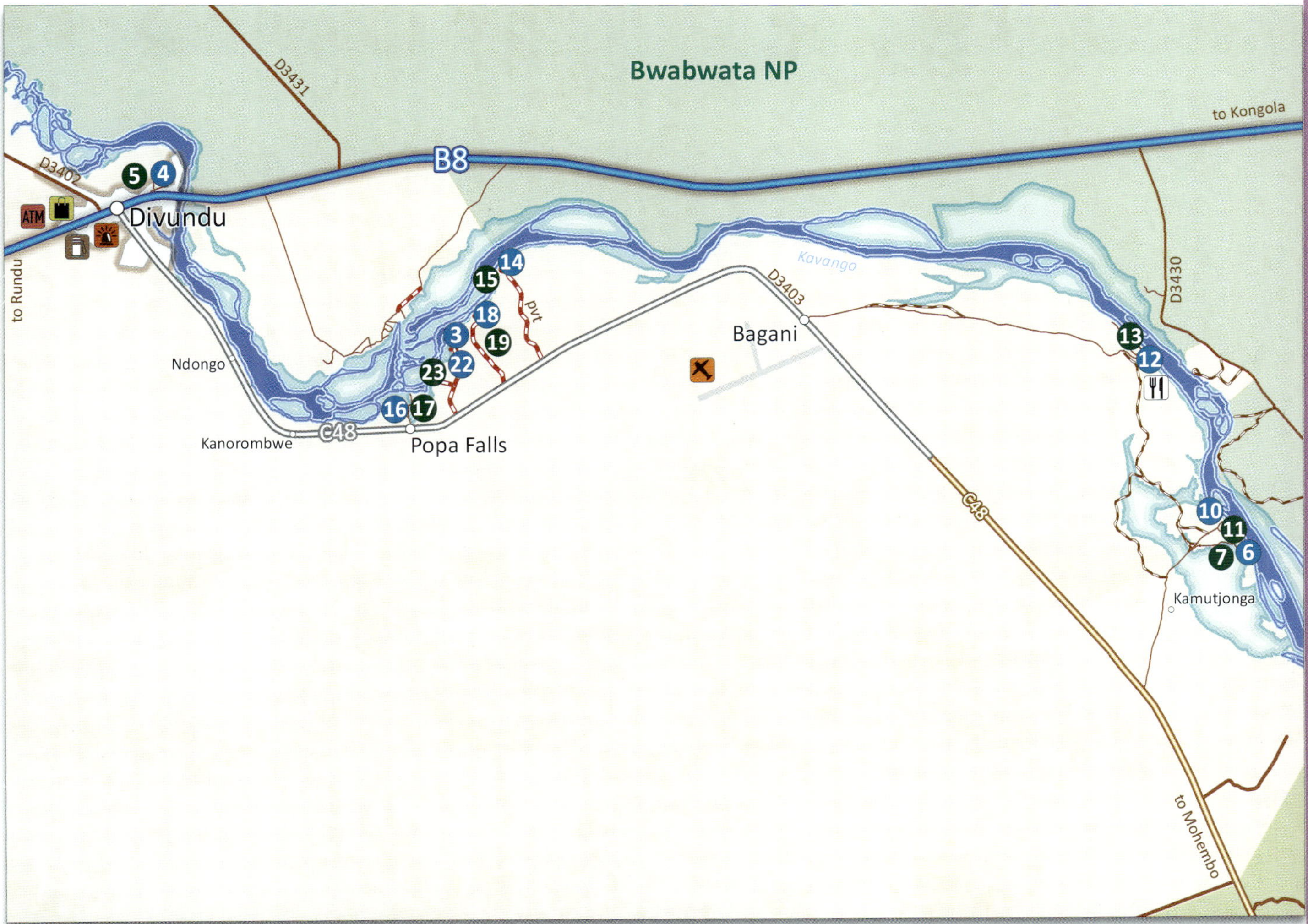

Camp Ndurukoro 1

Camping $
53km or 50min WNW of Divundu
w305987

Cell: +264(0)81 124 1051
campndurukoro@icloud.com

Shaded campsites, each with own braai and tap. Neat and clean ablutions. Tents available.

Languages: English

Facilities:
Activities:

Camp Ndurukoro & Chalets 2

Self-catering $
53km or 50min WNW of Divundu
w305986

Cell: +264(0)81 124 1051
campndurukoro@icloud.com

Two self-catering wooden chalets on stilts, with bathrooms (warm showers & flush toilets).

Languages: English

Facilities:
Activities:

Divava Okavango Lodge & Spa 3

Lodge $$$
7km or 7min ESE of Divundu
w138183

Tel: +264(0)66 259 005, Cell: +264(0)81 819 1779,
Fax: +264(0)88 654 7537
reservation@resdest.com, www.divava.com

20 Luxurious chalets with bar, restaurant, pool and deck overlooking the Kavango River.

Languages: English

Facilities:
Activities:

Divundu

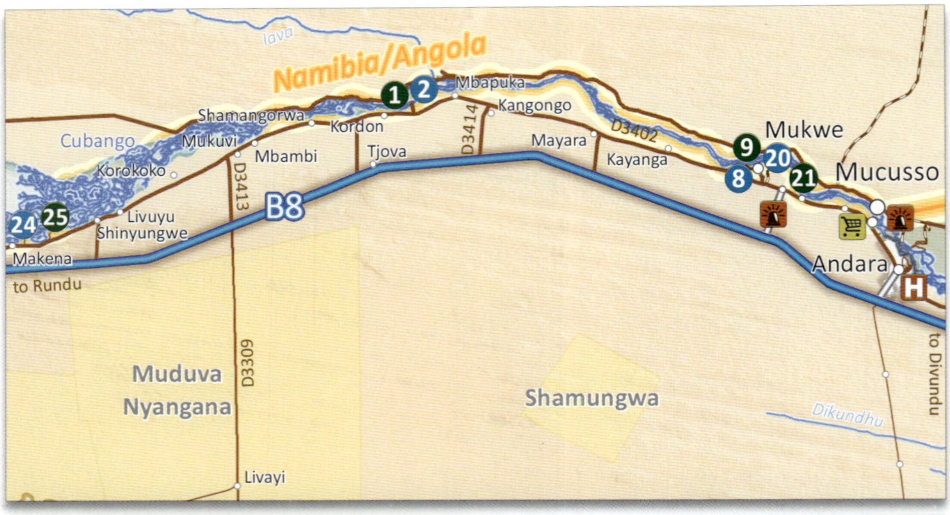

Divundu Guest House — 4

Guest House — $$
On B8 highway, near bridge over Kavango River
w224554

Tel: +264(0)66 259 031, Cell: +264(0)81 127 8565,
Fax: +264(0)88 613 754
divundu@afol.com.na

Six bungalows, and 30 backpacker rooms with shared facilities.

Languages: English, Afrikaans

Facilities:

Activities:

Divundu Guest House — 5

Camping — $
On B8 highway, near bridge over Kavango River
w255823

Tel: +264(0)66 259 031, Cell: +264(0)81 127 8565,
Fax: +264(0)88 613 754
Divundu@afol.com.na

The campsite is situated on the Kavango river, with running water, toilets, and shower ablutions with hot water.

Languages: English, Afrikaans

Facilities:

Activities:

Mahangu Safari Lodge — 6

Lodge — $$
19km or 31min ESE of Divundu (of which 4km is 4WD)
w137844

Tel: +264(0)66 259 037, Cell: +264(0)81 127 1347,
Fax: +264(0)66 259 115
mahangulodge@iway.na,
www.mahangu.com.na

Ten thatched, en-suite bungalows and six luxury permanent tents, also en-suite. Bookings required.

Languages: English, German, Afrikaans

Facilities:

Activities:

Mahangu Safari Lodge — 7

Lodge Camp — $$
19km or 32min ESE of Divundu (of which 4km is 4WD)
w192958

Tel: +264(0)66 259 037, Cell: +264(0)81 127 1347,
Fax: +264(0)66 259 115
mahangulodge@iway.na,
www.mahangu.com.na

Campsites close to the river. Campers may use the lodge facilities like the restaurant and bar.

Languages: English, German, Afrikaans

Facilities:

Activities:

Mobola Lodge — 8

Self-catering — $$
29km or 33min WNW of Divundu (of which 2km is 4WD)
w255812

Cell: +264(0)81 230 3281
mobolalodge@gmail.com
www.mobola-lodge.com

Four bungalows: two units for 4 - 6 persons, and two double-bed units. Kitchen and braai facilities. Breakfast on request. On the Kavango river.

Languages: German

Facilities:

Activities:

Mobola Lodge — 9

Lodge Camp — $
29km or 33min WNW of Divundu (of which 2km is 4WD)
w255811

Cell: +264(0)81 230 3281
mobolalodge@gmail.com
www.mobola-lodge.com

Six campsites, each with own braai, power and water. Shared ablution block. Located next to the Kavango river.

Languages: German

Facilities:

Activities:

Ndhovu Safari Lodge — 10

Tented Camp — $$$
18km or 31min ESE of Divundu (of which 4km is 4WD)
w141576

Tel: +264(0)61 224 712, Fax: +264(0)66 259 153
ndhovu@resdest.com
www.ndhovu.com

Fully-equipped, en-suite permanent tents with all the modern amenities. Activities include bird watching, sundowner cruises and tours to local villages.

Languages: English

Facilities:

Activities:

Ndhovu Safari Lodge — 11

Lodge Camp — $$
19km or 31min ESE of Divundu (of which 4km is 4WD)
w221710

Tel: +264(0)61 250 725, Fax: +264(0)88 642 978
ndhovu@resdest.com
www.ndhovu.com

One exclusive campsite located next to the river under shady trees. Can accommodate up to 15. Reservations mandatory.

Languages: English

Facilities:

Activities:

Ngepi Camp — 12

Lodge — $$
15km or 23min E of Divundu
w139367

Tel: +264(0)66 259 903, Cell: +264(0)81 202 8200,
Fax: +264(0)66 259 906
bookings@ngepicamp.com,
www.ngepicamp.com

En-suite tree houses as well as en-suite family bush huts. Environmentally-friendly camp run on solar power.

Languages: English

Facilities:

Activities:

Ngepi Camp — 13

Lodge Camp — $
15km or 23min E of Divundu
w138399

Tel: +264(0)66 259 903, Cell: +264(0)81 202 8200,
Fax: +264(0)66 259 906
bookings@ngepi.com,
www.ngepicamp.com

Private, grassed campsites on an island. Separate overlander sites. Their ablutions and bush pub are famous.

Languages: English

Facilities:

Activities:

Nunda Safaris & Lodge — 14

Lodge — $$
9km or 8min E of Divundu
w192363

Tel: +264(0)66 259 093, Cell: +264(0)81 310 1730, Fax: +264(0)66 259 094
bookings@nundaonline.com, www.nundaonline.com

Seven large, tastefully-furnished, twin bed, en-suite permanent tents on wooden decks. And eight large, thatched, twin bed, en-suite bungalows.

Languages: English, German, Afrikaans

Facilities: VISA FC @
Activities:

Nunda Safaris & Lodge — 15

Lodge Camp — $
9km or 9min E of Divundu
w222186

Tel: +264(0)66 259 093, Cell: +264(0)81 310 1730, Fax: +264(0)66 259 094
bookings@nundaonline.com, www.nundaonline.com

Grassy camp on the riverbank. Each campsite has a braai, seating, tap, light and power point. Communal ablutions. Drinking water is available.

Languages: English, German, Afrikaans

Facilities: VISA FC @
Activities:

Popa Falls Resort — 16

Self-catering — $$$
5km or 6min SE of Divundu
w274145

Tel: +264(0)61 285 7200, Fax: +264(0)66 259 108
reservations@nwr.com.na
www.nwr.com.na

10 River cabins, each containing four beds. Plus a store selling basic essentials.

Languages: English

Facilities: VISA
Activities:

Popa Falls Resort — 17

Park Camp — $$
5km or 6min SE of Divundu
w138292

Tel: +264(0)61 285 7200, Fax: +264(0)66 259 108
reservations@nwr.com.na
www.nwr.com.na

15 Campsites on the banks of the Kavango River. Venue has a beautiful reception area, restaurant and bar (right at the falls).

Languages: English

Facilities: VISA
Activities:

Rainbow River Lodge — 18

Lodge — $$
8km or 9min ESE of Divundu
w139337

Tel: +264(0)66 259 067, Cell: +264(0)81 210 6678
info@rainbowriverlodgenamibia.com
www.rainbowriverlodgenamibia.com

20 Semi-luxury chalets with mosquito nets, and furniture handmade from local wood.

Languages: English, German, Afrikaans

Facilities: FC @
Activities:

Rainbow River Lodge — 19

Lodge Camp — $
8km or 9min ESE of Divundu
w361575

Tel: +264(0)66 259 067 , Cell: +264(0)81 210 6678
info@rainbowriverlodgenamibia.com

Campsites for big groups and small. Each with its own braai, power point and light. Four ablution blocks.

Languages: English, German, Afrikaans

Facilities: FC @
Activities:

RiverDance Lodge — 20

Lodge — $$
28km or 34min WNW of Divundu (of which 3km is 4WD)
w254372

Tel: ?+264(0)66 258 401, Cell: ?+264(0)81 366 9775, Fax: +264(0)88 614 995
reservations@riverdance.com.na, www.riverdance.com.na

RiverDance Lodge is located on the banks of the Kavango River and offers luxurious accommodation with river views. Owner managed.

Languages: English, German, Afrikaans

Facilities: VISA @
Activities:

RiverDance Lodge — 21

Lodge Camp — $
28km or 34min WNW of Divundu (of which 3km is 4WD)
w254373

Tel: +264(0)66 258 401, Cell: +264(0)81 366 9775, Fax: +264(0)88 614 995
reservations@riverdance.com.na, www.riverdance.com.na

Exclusive campsites with individual bathrooms, on the river. Campers are welcome to join activities offered at the lodge.

Languages: English, German, Afrikaans

Facilities: VISA @
Activities:

Shametu River Lodge — 22

Lodge — $$
7km or 9min ESE of Divundu
w255842

Tel: +264(0)66 259 035, Cell: +264(0)81 653 1901
shameturiverlodge@iway.na
www.shameturiverlodge.com

12 En-suite chalets: ten double units, one wheelchair-friendly and one family chalet.

Languages: English, Afrikaans

Facilities: FC
Activities:

Shametu River Lodge — 23

Lodge Camp — $$
7km or 7min ESE of Divundu
w255822

Tel: +264(0)66 259 035, Cell: +264(0)81 653 1901
shameturiverlodge@iway.na
www.shameturiverlodge.com

Eight private campsites and four campsites for large groups. Each campsite has its own kitchenette and ablutions. Fresh vegetables for sale.

Languages: English, Afrikaans

Facilities: VISA FC
Activities:

Shamvura Camp — 24

Tented Camp — $$
82km or 1h42min W of Divundu
w141017

Tel: +264(0)66 264 007, Cell: +264(0)81 241 7473, Fax: +264(0)66 258 297
shamvura@iway.na, www.choosytravellers.co.za

Tented camp ideal for fishing and birding. Children under 12 require supervision - there's a resident otter and an unfenced pool.

Languages: English

Facilities: FC @
Activities:

Shamvura Camp — 25

Camping — $
82km or 1h42min W of Divundu
w361558

Tel: +264(0)66 264 007, Cell: +264(0)81 241 7473, Fax: +264(0)66 258 297
shamvura@iway.na

Six campsites on the banks of the Kavango River. Ideal for self-catering guests but meals also available on request.

Languages: English

Facilities: FC @
Activities:

Khaudum National Park

The roads in this national park often feature thick sand. (photo: Karin Theron)

KHAUDUM NATIONAL PARK BORDERS BOTSWANA and is unfenced to allow animals to follow their natural migration routes from the Okavango Delta and Kavango River. The park is famous for its large herds of elephant, but giraffe, African wild dog and predators like lion, leopard, spotted hyena and jackal also occur. A wide variety of antelope and some 320 bird species have been recorded. In addition, Khaudum is the only park in Namibia which protects the Northern Kalahari Sandveld biome with its forest savannah and woodland.

For millennia, the land in and around what is now the Khaudum National Park has been home to clans of hunter/gatherers. With the disruption of traditional social systems, these groups now inhabit a cultural hinterland in conservancies and villages around the park which blend ancient and modern. Hunting within park boundaries is prohibited but conservation-driven community development is promoted. The absence of fences allows free movement of wildlife into locally-owned land, enhancing tourism potential and providing much needed income to communities.

Khaudum was proclaimed a Nature Reserve in 1989 but was given National Park status in 2007. The park can be described as Namibia's 'forgotten wilderness' as it attracts few visitors, is large and extremely wild with a very rudimentary tourist infrastructure.

Traveller Description

Long grass can sometimes make it difficult to spot animals. Deep sand and hidden tree roots will slow you down and you also need to take care of branches pushed onto the tracks by elephants. The park has two camps: Khaudum in the north and Sikereti in the south. Both are very basic so you need to be self-sufficient. Travelling the eastern route from Khaudum to Sikereti can be problematic during the rainy season but it's worthwhile as it passes many waterholes. If in doubt, phone the park officials on +264(0)61 284 2111 to inquire about road conditions. The drive can take up to a day, depending on your stops.

Travel Info

You need an off-road vehicle to visit Khaudum and for your own safety it's recommended that you travel in a party of at least two vehicles. You should not attempt to tow a trailer in the park. No fuel is available in the park so you need to carry extra - remember that the park's deep sand tracks will drastically increase your vehicle's fuel consumption.

The nearest towns for food supplies and fuel are Tsumkwe, Rundu, Divundu and Grootfontein. The nearest clinic to the northern part of the park is 37km north of Khaudum Camp on the Katere-Khaudum road; in the south you'll find one at Tsumkwe.

TRAVEL TIP! Allow yourself enough time when you head south out of Khaudum NP. You will want to stop at the Dorsland Grootboom, an ancient Baobab tree (find it on your T4A GPS map) and the Living Museum of the Ju/'Hoansi-San, which you will pass on your way to Tsumkwe.

If you head west for Grootfontein or Rundu from Tsumkwe, you will pass through a veterinary control point before you reach the B8 highway. You are not allowed to take raw meat past this point.

(photo: Stephen Cunliffe)

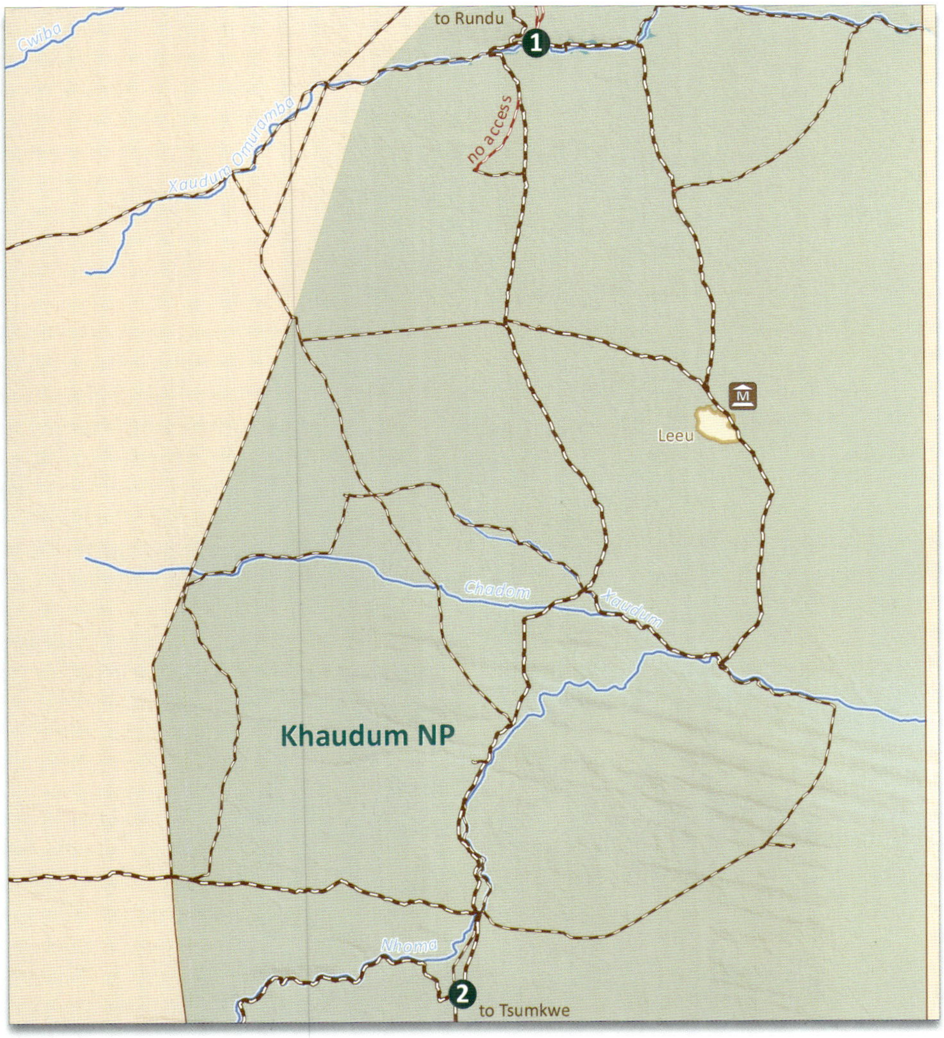

Khaudum Camp 1

Park Camp $$$
164km or 4h14min ESE of Rundu (of which 54km is 4WD)
w137713

Tel: +264(0)61 227 519, Fax: +264(0)61 229 936
reservations@khaudumcamping.com

Six campsites uncer Camelthorn trees, overlooking the Omuramba. Each site has a braai area, private ablutions and seating. Reservations mandatory.

Languages: English

Facilities:

Activities:

Sikereti Camp 2

Park Camp $
60km or 1h18min NNE of Tsumkwe (of which 8km is 4WD)
w137753

Tel: +264(0)67 244 017, Fax: +264(0)61 229 936

Basic campsites, no electricity. Communal ablution facility. Reservations mandatory.

Languages: English

Facilities:

Activities:

Rundu

(photo: Johann Groenewald)

RUNDU LIES ON THE BORDER WITH ANGOLA; this fast-growing town is the capital of the Kavango region as well as its administrative centre and main economic hub. While not a particularly scenic spot, its location on the Kavango River allows for some beautiful waterfront views.

The B10, which runs west from Rundu to Oshikango/Ondangwa, is a wide single-lane, dual-traffic highway, as is the B8, which runs east to Katima Mulilo and south to Grootfontein. Due to its location, Rundu has always been a gathering point for local men seeking work; from here they would be bussed to farms and mines in central Namibia. This exodus of young locals from the Kavango region to urban centres continues to this day. The military base opposite the airport was built in 1972 while South West Africa was under South African occupation, these days it's used by the Namibian Defence Force.

Traveller Description

Rundu's location, and the good accommodation offered in and around town, makes it the ideal stopover, especially when heading for Etosha National Park, Bwabwata National Park, the Zambezi region (Caprivi Strip) or Botswana. The town has several big retail outlets like Shoprite, Pick 'n Pay, Spar, Pep, OK Foods and Woermann Brock, so stocking up is a pleasure.

Rundu is home to many woodcarvers and you'll find a woodcarvers' market near the big open market. Several local restaurants serve traditional food, including mahangu, ground nuts, stewed meats, and fish from the Kavango river.

Rundu is a bustling town and you should anticipate an element of petty crime - be vigilant of opportunists who target vehicle contents. If you do have any problems or feel particularly uncomfortable you can contact the Tourism Task Force (Police Inspector Eben Muyambo +264(0)81 247 1018) directly.

Travel Info

A visit to the Mbunza Living Museum 14km west of Rundu is worthwhile. Here visitors can experience everything about the everyday life of the Mbunza, the local Kavango people. Activities to be observed include fishing, land cultivation, traditional cuisine and fire making as well as specialised techniques like basket and mat weaving, blacksmithing, pottery and the making of drums.

The Rundu border crossing isn't suitable for overlanders as there's only a motorboat crossing for pedestrians to Calai, Angola. Rundu is serviced by Namibia Air who offers flights to Windhoek.

Rundu has no less than seven doctors and the Rundu Medical Centre is an impressive private facility offering most medical services under one roof. Their contact number is +264(0)66 267 233. Bon's Coffee Shop on the 1st floor of the Rundu Medical Center is recommendable.

Other Useful Numbers:
Kavango Mechanical Services: +264(0)81 129 1252

TRAVEL TIP! You can't take raw meat or unpasteurised milk from Rundu to Grootfontein because of the vet fence at Mururani. While Rundu is known for its beautiful wood carvings, curios made of wood are not allowed past the Mururani control point, unless you have a permit from the Department of Forestry in Rundu.

Town Info:
Hospital: +264(0)66 265 500. Police: +264(0)66 266 300. Doctor: +264(0)66 255 803

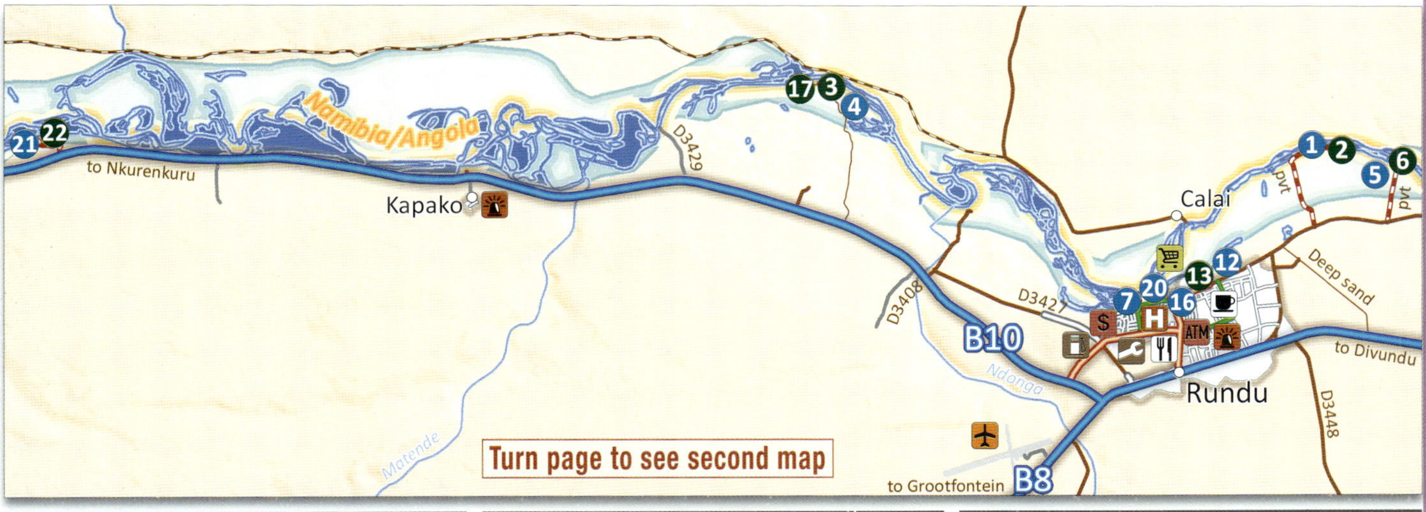

Camp Hogo — 1

Tented Camp — $
9km or 13min NE of Rundu
w226870

Cell: ??+264(0)81 251 0002
camphogokavango@gmail.com

Luxury permanent tents on stilts on the banks of the Kavango River. As well as budget tents, serviced campsites, bar and restaurant.

Languages: English, Afrikaans

Facilities:
Activities:

Camp Hogo — 2

Camping — $
9km or 13min NE of Rundu
w316034

Cell: +264(0)81 251 0002
camphogokavango@gmail.com

Six serviced campsites on the banks of the Kavango River.

Languages: English, Afrikaans

Facilities:
Activities:

Hakusembe Campsite — 3

Camping — $$
17km or 22min WNW of Rundu
w361129

Tel: +264(0)61 427 200, Cell: +264(0)81 129 2424, Fax: +264(0)61 251 863
info@gondwana-collection.com,
store.gondwana-collection.com

Each campsite has its own bathroom facilities, and can host eight people. There's also a shop. Reservations advisable.

Languages: English, Afrikaans

Facilities:
Activities:

Hakusembe River Lodge — 4

Lodge — $$$
17km or 22min WNW of Rundu
w139394

Tel: +264(0)61 427 200, Cell: +264(0)81 129 2424, Fax: +264(0)61 251 863
info@gondwana-collection.com,
store.gondwana-collection.com

Eight comfortable, en-suite chalets and a honeymoon suite. Reservations mandatory.

Languages: English, Afrikaans

Facilities:
Activities:

Kaisosi River Lodge — 5

Lodge — $$
9km or 11min ENE of Rundu
w137796

Tel: +264(0)66 267 125, Cell: ?+264(0)81 249 5090
kaisosi@iway.na
www.kaisosiriverlodge.com

Sixteen spacious rooms (eight twin, four triple, four family) overlooking the Kavango river. Plus a la carte restaurant and river cruises.

Languages: English

Facilities:
Activities:

Kaisosi River Lodge — 6

Lodge Camp — $
9km or 12min ENE of Rundu
w267913

Tel: +264(0)66 267 125, Cell: ?+264(0)81 249 5090
kaisosi@iway.na
www.kaisosiriverlodge.com

16 Shaded, grassed campsites - each with private shower (warm water) & toilet, electricity and braai area.

Languages: English

Facilities:
Activities:

Rundu

Kavango River Lodge	7
Lodge	$$

1A Fish Eagle St, Rundu
w138804

Tel: +264(0)66 255 244, Cell: +264(0)81 127 4695, Fax: +264(0)66 255 013
kavangolodge@gmail.com

All rooms have air-conditioning and TV. Breakfast and dinner served. Views over the Kavango River.

Languages: English, Afrikaans

Facilities:

Activities:

Mukuku Rest Camp	8
Self-catering	$$

59km or 59min E of Rundu (of which 10km is 4WD)
w361750

Cell: +264(0)85 574 1520
mukuku11@gmail.com

Three self-catering units. All with kitchen (with fridge), seating area, balcony and/or patio. Bed linen available.

Languages: English

Facilities:

Activities:

Mukuku Rest Camp	9
Lodge Camp	$

59km or 59min E of Rundu (of which 10km is 4WD)
w361754

Cell: +264(0)85 574 1520
mukuku11@gmail.com

Grassed and shaded camp with clean ablutions - hot showers and flush toilet.

Languages: English

Facilities:

Activities:

Muramba River Lodge	10
Lodge	$

81km or 49min E of Rundu
w361752

Cell: +264(0)81 779 0255
mparekerandolph@gmail.com

Single or double rooms, on the banks of the Kavango River.

Languages: English

Facilities:

Activities:

Muramba River Lodge	11
Lodge Camp	$

81km or 49min E of Rundu
w361760

Cell: +264(0)81 779 0255
mparekerandolph@gmail.com

Basic campsites on grass. Facilities include ablution blocks with flushing toilets.

Languages: English

Facilities:

Activities:

Ngandu Safari Lodge	12
Lodge	$$

Usivi Road, Rundu
w137335

Tel: +264(0)66 256 723, Fax: +264(0)66 265 999
ngandu@iafrica.com.na

41 Chalets with great views of the Kavango River.

Languages: English

Facilities: VISA FC

Activities:

Ngandu Safari Lodge	13
Lodge Camp	$

Usivi Road, Rundu
w232328

Tel: +264(0)66 256 723, Fax: +264(0)66 265 999
ngandu@iafrica.com.na

Campsites near the lodge, facilities include bar and braai area.

Languages: English

Facilities: VISA FC

Activities:

n'Kwazi Lodge	14
Lodge	$$

17km or 23min ENE of Rundu
w137842

Fax: +264(0)66 255 452, Cell: +264(0)81 242 4897
reservations@nkwazilodge.com
www.nkwazilodge.com

14 Comfortable, thatched, en-suite chalets with mosquito nets, gas and paraffin lamps and private verandah.

Languages: English

Facilities: VISA

Activities:

n'Kwazi Lodge	15
Lodge Camp	$

17km or 21min ENE of Rundu
w138753

Fax: +264(0)66 255 462, Cell: +264(0)81 242 4897
reservations@nkwazilodge.com
www.nkwazilodge.com

16 Grassed, shaded campsites, each with electricity and their own ablution facilities.

Languages: English

Facilities: VISA

Activities:

Omashare Hotel 16

Hotel $$
1223 Maria Mwengere Road, Rundu
w139473

Tel: +264(0)66 266 600, Fax: +264(0)66 256 111
bookings@omasharehotel.com
www.omasharehotel.com

20 Air-conditioned, luxury rooms located in town centre. Great views of Kavango River and Angola beyond.

Languages: English

Facilities:

Activities:

Samsitu Riverside Camp 17

Camping $
17km or 23min WNW of Rundu
w140499

Tel: +264(0)66 257 023, Cell: +264(0)81 129 3290, Fax: +264(0)66 256 091
kavpharm@iafrica.com.na

Grassed campsites on the banks of the Kavango River, each with braai area, tap and light. Clean ablutions with plenty of hot water.

Languages: English

Facilities:

Activities:

Shankara Rest Camp 18

Self-catering $
83km or 1h11min E of Rundu
w361136

Tel: +264(0)66 258 616, Cell: +264(0)81 240 2933
shankararestcamp81@gmail.com

Self-catering single, double or family chalets, all with fully-equipped kitchenettes. Access to a communal TV.

Languages: English

Facilities:

Activities:

Shankara Rest Camp 19

Camping $
83km or 1h11min E of Rundu
w261513

Tel: +264(0)66 258 616, Cell: +264(0)81 240 2933
shankararestcamp81@gmail.com

Shaded campsites. Ablution blocks with hot showers.

Languages: English

Facilities:

Activities:

Tambuti River Lodge 20

Lodge $
Tambuti Lodge, Beach Rd, Rundu
w138805

Tel: +264(0)66 255 711, Cell: +264(0)81 483 4113, Fax: +264(0)66 255 131
tambuti@iway.na, www.tambuti.com.na

Spacious bungalows overlooking the floodplains, just above the Kavango River.

Languages: English

Facilities:

Activities:

Taranga Safari Lodge 21

Lodge $$$
37km or 32min W of Rundu
w254417

Tel: +264(0)66 257 236 , Cell: +264(0)81 169 2186, Fax: +264(0)88 633 554
info@taranganamibia.com, www.taranganamibia.com

Four open-fronted, luxury, riverbank chalets, on the banks of the Kavango River.

Languages: English, Afrikaans

Facilities:

Activities:

Taranga Safari Lodge 22

Lodge Camp $
37km or 32min W of Rundu
w261559

Tel: +264(0)66 257 236 , Cell: +264(0)81 169 2186, Fax: +264(0)88 633 554
info@taranganamibia.com, www.taranganamibia.com

Eight private, grassed campsites and ablution block. Each campsite has a fireplace with grid, and tap.

Languages: English, Afrikaans

Facilities:

Activities:

(photo: Karin Theron)

NAMIB-NAUKLUFT

Rainbow in the Namib-Naukluft National Park, west of the Kuiseb Pass. (photo: Heiner Dillmann)

STRETCHING FROM THE SWAKOP RIVER in the north to the Aus/Lüderitz road (B4) in the south, the Namib-Naukluft region is comprised mostly of the Namib-Naukluft National Park. It's the fourth largest park in Africa and includes sections of the still restricted Diamond Area.

A huge part of the region consists of conservation areas. Besides the Namib-Naukluft National Park, you'll also find the Naukluft Mountain Zebra Park as well as the Gamsberg and Namibrand Nature Reserves.

The word Namib means 'open space' and this is a strong theme in this breathtakingly-beautiful landscape. The Namib Desert, with its towering orange-red sand dunes, is one of the world's oldest deserts. The colour of the sand developed over millions of years as iron in the sand oxidised, like rusting metal.

The Namib Desert was the first natural site in Namibia to be inscribed on the World Heritage List, an honour bestowed in 2013. According to UNESCO the Namib is composed of two dune systems, an ancient semi-consolidated one overlain by a younger active one. The desert dunes are formed after soil and sand material is transported thousands of kilometres from the hinterland, by river into the ocean; then, these materials are washed ashore and distributed by the wind. The dunes themselves are formed when an obstacle (for example, a bush or some rough soil) breaks the force of the wind, and causes sand to be deposited. The Namib features gravel plains, coastal flats, rocky hills, inselbergs within the sand sea, a coastal lagoon and ephemeral rivers. Fog is the primary source of water, accounting for a

(opposite bottom) Elephant Rock can be seen on the 3-hour Rock Sculpture Trail in the Namib-Naukluft National Park. (photo: Heiner Dillmann)

(right) Sossusvlei, an aerial perspective. (photo: Heiner Dillmann)

Even on an overcast day, Sossusvlei dunes offer unique photographic opportunities. (photo: Mietsie Visser).

(above and right) The buildings of Lüderitz and Kolmanskop respectively. (photos: Mietsie Visser)

unique environment in which endemic invertebrates, reptiles and mammals adapt to an everchanging variety of microhabitats and ecological niches.

Lüderitz, in the south, is the main town of the region and is a tourist hub. It's a beautiful, historical town from where most guided 4WD desert trails and extreme hiking trails begin. Close to Lüderitz is Kolmanskop, a ghost town with a rich diamond mining history. This is a fascinating open-air museum and popular tourist stop.

As you travel east from Lüderitz towards Aus, you'll come across one of the few populations of desert-dwelling feral horses in the world. There's a special lookout point at Garub Pan where you can view these beautiful wild horses of the Namib.

The biggest tourist attraction within this region is without doubt Sossusvlei. Although the name is used to describe the area, it in fact only refers to the dry salt pan stretched out amongst the undulating red sand dunes. The Sossusvlei dunes are regarded as some of the highest in the world.

The gates to Sossusvlei open at sunrise and close at sunset. There is a 4x2 parking area just before the vlei; beyond this area a 4x4 vehicle is a necessity. Guests can either walk from there to the pan (about 10km return, through deep sand) or make use of the 4x4 shuttle service to and from the sites. It's best to visit Sossusvlei early in the morning when the red colour of the sand is strong and bright and the light and shadows offer breathtaking views. Otherwise, visit in the late afternoon when the sun isn't baking down.

MAJOR ATTRACTIONS

- Namib-Naukluft National Park with the iconic dunes at Sossusvlei and nearby Deadvlei, which are of photographic significance.
- Namibrand is one of the largest private nature reserves in Southern Africa and boasts breathtaking Namib Desert landscapes and a variety of wildlife.
- The Naukluft Mountain Zebra Park is a hiking paradise.
- The Gamsberg Mountain within the Gamsberg Nature Reserve resembles the famous Table Mountain in Cape Town and is 2 346m high. The Reserve is ideal for activities like star gazing, hiking and bird watching.
- The 1 200m high Flying Fox Cable Slide northeast of Swakopmund provides a huge adrenaline rush.
- The Solitaire bakery has become famous for its excellent apple strudel and confectionary.
- Natural attractions include a Quiver Tree Forest near Keetmanshoop and endemic Welwitschia, also known as living fossil plants since they live 1 000 years or more.
- The Flintstone Caves offers interesting rock formations and a braai area.
- Kolmanskop once was an important diamond mining town, but is now a fascinating ghost town.
- The Sesriem Canyon is a fissure in the sandstone carved 30m deep in places by the Tsauchab River.
- Commonwealth War Graves near Gibeon.
- German geologists Henno Martin and Hermann Korn hid in a shelter for eight months to avoid South African internment during World War II.
- Seeing the Namib Desert from a hot air balloon is quite spectacular.
- The Duwisib Castle was built by German Baron von Wolf for his bride in 1909 and today it gives an insight of the colonial times.
- The Moon Landscape is extraordinarily dry and barren, yet with interesting colours and undulations.
- Attractions in or near Lüderitz include the memorial to Adolf Lüderitz, after whom the town was named; the Bartolomeo Diaz cross, errected when he landed there in December 1487 and (only accessible at low tide); Haus Goerke, the 1910 mine manager's residence (tours offered daily); the Lüderitz Museum which covers the town's history and the diamond mining industry; and, Felsenkirche (Church on the rock), a national monument built in 1911.
- Neuras is one of only a few wineries in Namibia and it is open to the public.
- The feral horses at Garub Pan are one of the main attractions of the region.
- HESS is an international telescope with high optical sensitivity.

More details about the attractions are available on our website (www.tracks4africa.co.za) or our Guide App. Our GPS Map can navigate you to each of these attractions.

(left) (photo: Heiner Dillmann)

(bottom) Diaz Point. At the time of writing this walkway was out of service, restricting access to low tide. (photo: Frank Höppener)

NAMIB-NAUKLUFT

Aus

(photo: Janine Reyneke)

AUS IS A TRANQUIL DESERT TOWN some 125km east of Lüderitz on the B4 which runs between Lüderitz and Keetmanshoop. The railway service used to run between the two towns but the train from Keetmanshoop now terminates at Aus. The village was formerly the site of a prisoner-of-war camp established by the South African army in 1915 to house German Schutztruppe captured during the First World War. The inmates initially lived in tents but later built brick houses. The number of prisoners reached 1 500 but by May 1919 the last inmates left and the camp closed. A plaque marks the site today and some of the houses have been reconstructed.

There is a Commonwealth gravesite just north of Aus. What makes this cemetery unusual is that both German and Allied forces rest here together, most were killed by the Spanish flu in 1918.

Traveller Description

Aus is the ideal stopover if you're on your way to Lüderitz from Keetmanshoop. It's a small town but it has all the basic necessities travellers might need, as well as good accommodation. Here you can soak up the peace and quiet of the Namib Desert and the magnificence of the Aus Mountains. The climate is usually hot and arid but snow has been recorded in winter. The biggest attraction is without a doubt the feral horses which can be sighted at the nearby Garub Pan. The Prisoner of War Camp and Commonwealth War Graves are also worth a visit.

Travel Info

There's a clinic in town if you need medical services. You can contact them at +264(0)63 258 008. You can buy basic medication at the shop.

TRAVEL TIP! Popular activities include mountain biking and hiking in the Aus Mountains. Short hikes from Klein Aus Vista Lodge include the Sunset Trail (4km, 1h45) and Schutztruppe Trail (9km, 3h).

Town Info:

Police: +264(0)63 258 005
Tow-in: +264(0)81 298 1495

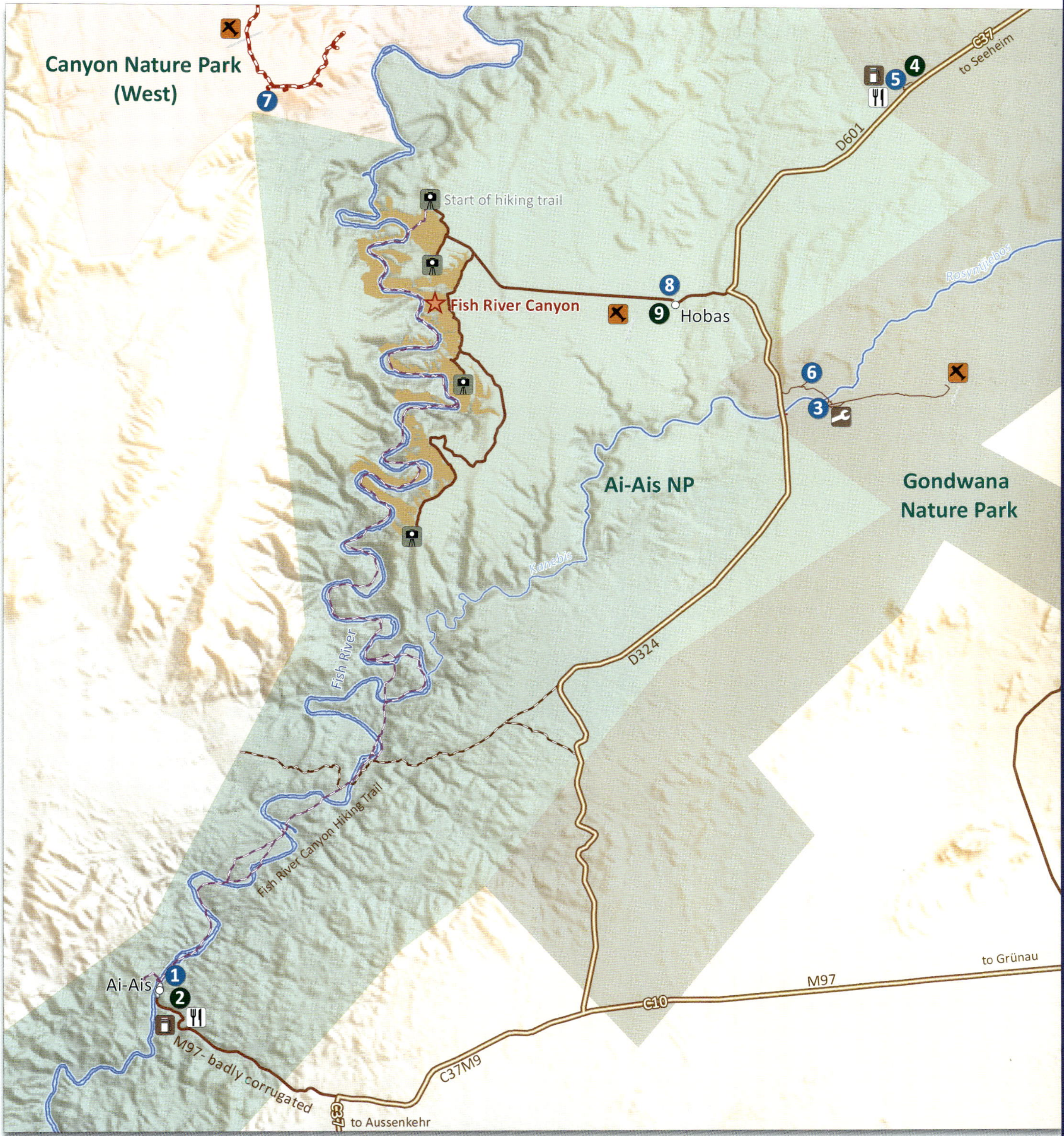

Aus Haven & Rest Camp — 1

Self-catering — $$
St Theresia, Aus
w140300

Tel: +264(0)63 258 029, Cell: +264(0)81 298 1495, Fax: +264(0)88 612 614
namibaus@afol.com.na,
www.ausnamibia.co

Three self-catering, double and single rooms. Two single bed & breakfast rooms. All rooms en-suite with TV, air-conditioning, Wi-Fi and secure parking. Braai facilities available.

Languages: English, Afrikaans

Facilities:

Activities:

Aus Haven & Rest Camp — 2

Camping — $
St Theresia, Aus
w255815

Tel: +264(0)63 258 029, Cell: +264(0)81 298 1495, Fax: +264(0)88 612 614
namibaus@afol.com.na,
www.ausnamibia.co

Six campsites with electricity. Secure parking.

Languages: English, Afrikaans

Facilities:

Activities:

Bahnhof Hotel Aus — 3

Hotel — $$
20 Lüderitz St, Aus
w142179

Tel: +264(0)67 240 901, Cell: +264(0)81 232 9483, Fax: +264(0)63 258 092
reservations.bahnhof@travel-weaver.com,
www.hotel-aus.com

26 Double rooms as well as a 4-bed family room, all en-suite. There's also a wheelchair-friendly room.

Languages: English, Afrikaans, German

Facilities:

Activities:

Aus

Klein-Aus Vista Campsite 4

Camping $
5km or 8min WNW of Aus
w142204

Tel: +264(0)63 258 116, Fax: +264(0)88 623 302
reservations@klein-aus-vista.com
www.klein-aus-vista.com

Spotless camping area with clean ablution blocks (flush toilets & hot showers). Enjoy hiking and sunset drives. Reservations advisable.

Languages: English, Afrikaans

Facilities:

Activities:

Klein-Aus Vista: Desert Horse Inn 5

Lodge $$
3km or 4min NW of Aus
w137552

Tel: +264(0)63 258 116, Fax: +264(0)88 623 302
reservations@klein-aus-vista.com
www.klein-aus-vista.com

Twin rooms, 3-bed and 4-bed units. All en-suite with verandas.

Languages: English, Afrikaans

Facilities:

Activities:

Klein Aus Vista - Eagle's Nest Chalets 6

Self-catering $$$
10km or 19min WSW of Aus
w274160

Tel: +264(0)63 258 116, Fax: +264(0)88 623 302
reservations@klein-aus-vista.com
www.klein-aus-vista.com

Seven natural-rock chalets nestled against the mountain slope. Each chalets sits between massive granite boulders. Reservations mandatory.

Languages: English, Afrikaans

Facilities:

Activities:

Klein-Aus Vista Geisterschlucht Cabin 7

Self-catering $
26km or 2h7min WSW of Aus
w228051

Tel: +264(0)63 258 116, Fax: +264(0)88 623 302
reservations@klein-aus-vista.com
www.klein-aus-vista.com

Two rooms, each sleeps 4 people. Full ablutions, cooking facilities and braai place. Reservations mandatory.

Languages: English

Facilities:

Activities:

Orange House Self-Catering 8

Self-catering $$
20 Lüderitz St, Aus
w361709

Tel: +264(0)67 240 901, Cell: +264(0)81 232 9483,
reservations.bahnhof@travel-weaver.com
www.bahnhof-hotel-aus.com

Located on a hill overlooking the town, this self-catering house has two double rooms. Both en-suite (shower & toilet) with mosquito nets, fan, built-in cupboards. Satellite TV and braai included.

Languages: English, Afrikaans, German

Facilities:

Activities:

Tirool Guest Farm 9

Farm Camp $
48km or 37min NE of Aus
w267870

Cell: +264(0)81 217 6932
mail@tirool.com
www.tirool.com

Spacious, private campsites. Ablution facilities with hot showers. Each campsite has its own braai and washing-up basin.

Languages: English

Facilities:

Activities:

The road from Aus to Helmeringhausen. (photo: Frank Höppener)

Tirool Guest Farm Chalets	10
Self-catering 48km or 37min NE of Aus w270495	$$

Cell: +264(0)81 217 6932
mail@tirool.com
www.tirool.com

Fully-equipped chalets with braai area, lounge and bathroom. Warm water via 'donkey' system and solar power for lights.

Languages: English, Afrikaans

Facilities:

Activities:

right (photo: Mietsie Visser)
below (photo: Neil Harrison)

Betta

(photo: Ian-Ray Nel)

BETTA IS A FARM situated at a strategic point where the road from Duwisib Castle joins the C27 from Helmeringhausen/Sesriem. The farmer has put up a 24-hour fuel stop, kiosk and a restcamp which offers accommodation in rooms as well as camping facilities.

Traveller Description

Betta Rest Camp is a popular stopover for travellers on their way to Sossusvlei. Make sure you have enough time available to visit the Duwisib Castle, 20km north of Betta.

Travel Info

You can pre-book meals at the rest camp or braai for yourself. Their shop is well stocked with food for campers, including meat and cold beer.

Useful Numbers:
Tow-in: +264(0)81 129 7490 Alternative tow-in numbers: +264(0)62 500 132 or +264(0)62 504 250

Betta Rest Camp 1

Self-catering $
In Betta
w232883

Tel: +264(0)67 240 901, Cell: +264(0)81 122 2626,
Fax: +264(0)88 631 720
reservations.betta@travel-weaver.com,
www.bettacamp.net

Self-catering bungalows, and tents with clean ablution blocks and braai facilities.

Languages: English, Afrikaans

Facilities:
Activities:

Betta Rest Camp 2

Camping $
In Betta
w139178

Tel: +264(0)67 240 901, Cell: +264(0)81 122 2626,
Fax: +264(0)88 631 720
reservations.betta@travel-weaver.com,
www.bettacamp.net

Shaded camp with clean ablutions and braai facilities. Kiosk sells everything from food to car lubricants. Right next to garage.

Languages: English, Afrikaans

Facilities:
Activities:

Duwisib Guest Farm 3

Guest Farm $$
21km or 16min NE of Betta
w140370

Tel: +264(0)63 293 344, Cell: +264(0)81 354 3619,
Fax: +264(0)88 632 619
duwisib@iway.na,
www.farmduwisib.com

Self-catering units for 2 - 8 people, as well as castle-view double rooms on a dinner, bed & breakfast basis.

Languages: English, German, Afrikaans

Facilities:
Activities:

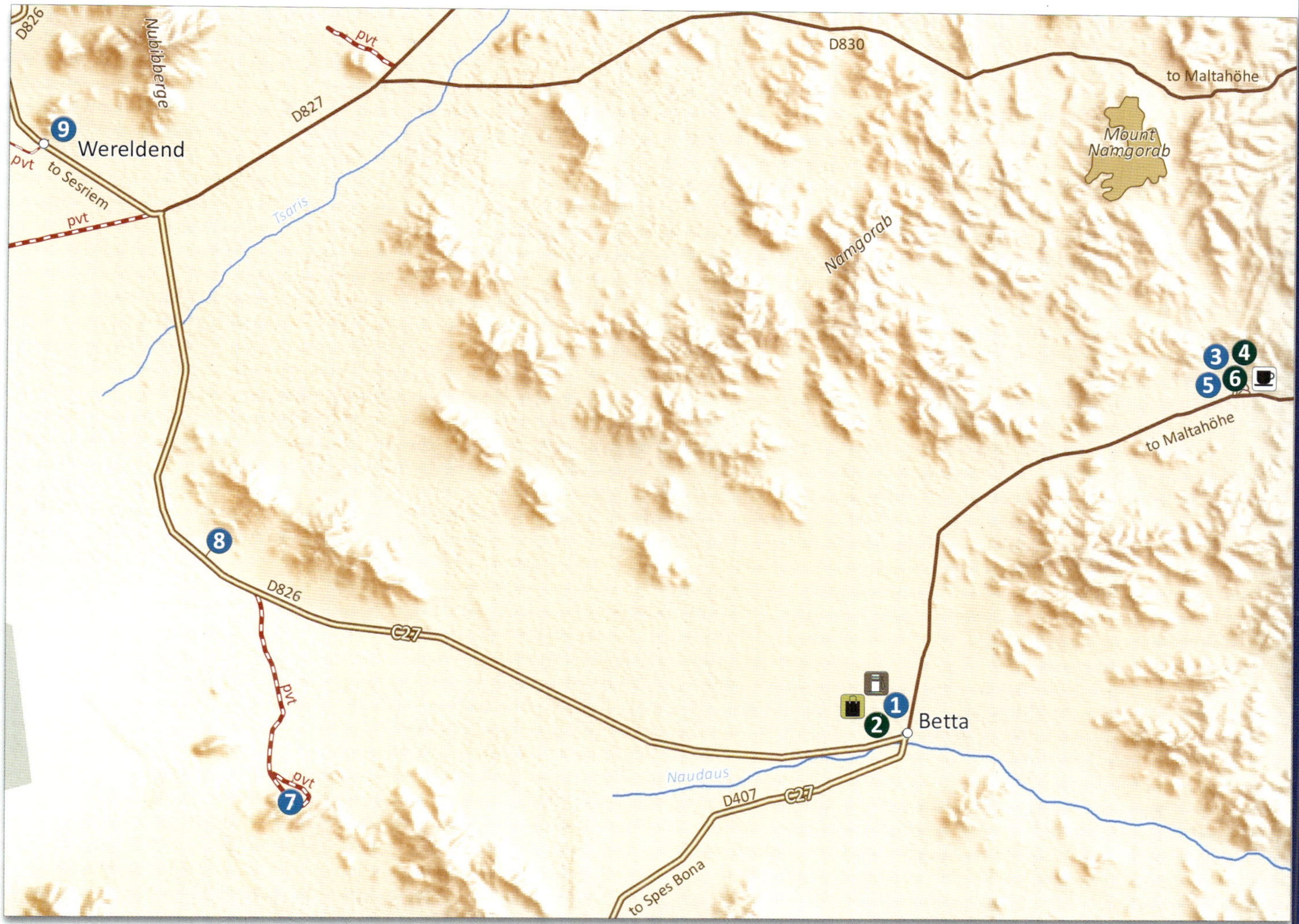

Duwisib Guest Farm — 4

Farm Camp — $
21km or 14min NE of Betta
w142175

Tel: +264(0)63 293 344, Cell: +264(0)81 354 3619,
Fax: +264(0)88 632 619
duwisib@iway.na,
www.farmduwisib.com

Shaded campsites, each with seating, braai area and tap. Central ablution facilities with electric light. Great views. No power points.

Languages: English, German, Afrikaans

Facilities:
Activities:

Duwisib Rest Camp — 5

Bed and Breakfast — $$
21km or 15min NE of Betta
w361048

Tel: +264(0)61 285 7200, Cell: +264(0)81 291 5280,
Fax: +264(0)61 224 900
reservations@nwr.com.na,
www.nwr.com.na

Five rooms. Motorbike-friendly venue run by Namibia Wildlife Resorts. Near Duwisib Castle.

Languages: English

Facilities:
Activities:

Duwisib Rest Camp — 6

Camping — $$
21km or 15min NE of Betta
W142163

Tel: +264(0)61 285 7200, Cell: +264(0)81 291 5280,
Fax: +264(0)61 224 900
reservations@nwr.com.na,
www.nwr.com.na

10 Campsites, with picnic spot and kiosk. Run by Namibia Wildlife Resorts and located near Duwisib Castle.

Languages: English

Facilities:
Activities:

Greenfire Desert Lodge — 7

Game/Safari Lodge — $$$
33km or 33min W of Betta
w224553

Tel: +27(0)11 888 1160, Fax: +27(0)11 888 1020
drifters@drifters.co.za
www.drifters.co.za

12-Bed lodge offers a comfortable stay and excellent game-viewing opportunities. Venue is situated on a 20 000 hectare game farm.

Languages: English

Facilities:
Activities:

Tolous Lodge — 8

Lodge — $$
27km or 22min WNW of Betta
w137793

Tel: +264(0)61 234 342, Cell: +264(0)81 629 3270,
Fax: +264(0)61 233 872
eden@mweb.com.na

15 Twin bungalows, each with private patio, open-air bathroom and bedrooms. Solar powered. Plus restaurant and ladies bar.

Languages: English, Afrikaans

Facilities:
Activities:

Wereldend Rest Camp — 9

Self-catering — $
46km or 36min NW of Betta
w361518

Cell: +264(0)81 291 0676
wereldend@gmail.com

Chalet with four beds, shower, toilet, solar lights, basin, gas geyser, kitchenette and built-in braai. No electricity.

Languages: English

Facilities:

Gamsberg

The Gamsberg Pass. (photo: Frank Höppener)

THE FLAT-TOPPED GAMSBERG MOUNTAIN is part of the Great Escarpment which separates the Khomas Highland to the east from the low-lying Namib Desert to the west. The mountain within the Gamsberg Nature Reserve resembles the famous Table Mountain in Cape Town and is 2 346m high.

The Gamsberg area is a stargazing mecca with clear skies and little-to-no light pollution. There are some great hiking trails in the reserve which offer awesome views of beautiful, unspoilt scenery.

The Gamsberg Pass is traversed by the C26, a gravel road. This pass is one of Namibia's most popular, it's also the highest and longest. Its elevation and the fact that you overlook the Kuiseb River in the valley below makes it one of the most scenic 4x4 routes you can travel in Namibia. Because of its beautiful scenery, Gamsberg is sometimes called the Garden Route of Namibia.

Traveller Description

Good accommodation is available on guest farms in the area but there no other facilities. This is a very popular tourist destination because of the natural beauty of the area. Historical sites in the area include the Henno Martin shelters where Henno and Hermann Korn hid in 1941 to avoid internment during WW2. The adventure of these two German geologists is told in Henno Martin's novel 'The Sheltering Desert'. Another historical point of interest is an old Schutztruppe well. These attractions can be found on the T4A GPS map.

Travel Info

Be aware that rain can cause roads in the area to become decidedly hazardous thanks to fast-flowing creek crossings and slippery mud.

Apart from the excitement of Gamsberg Pass and Spreetshoogte Pass, there are various 4WD trails on farms in the area. Register at the Isabis farmhouse for trails varying in length from 16 to 40km (3 hours to 2 days) on Isabis and neighbouring Hornkranz farm. You can also rent mountain bikes to explore the farms. Hiking and climbing along Leopard Gorge, a spectacular 120m deep canyon of the Gaub River, is another breathtaking experience.

TRAVEL TIP! Visit the Hess Gama Ray Telescope or the Rooisand Observatory if you're into stargazing. However, since the telescopes need to be protected from the dust generated by vehicles, access to the Hess site is restricted. You need to arrange your visit in advance and be accompanied by an authorized guide.

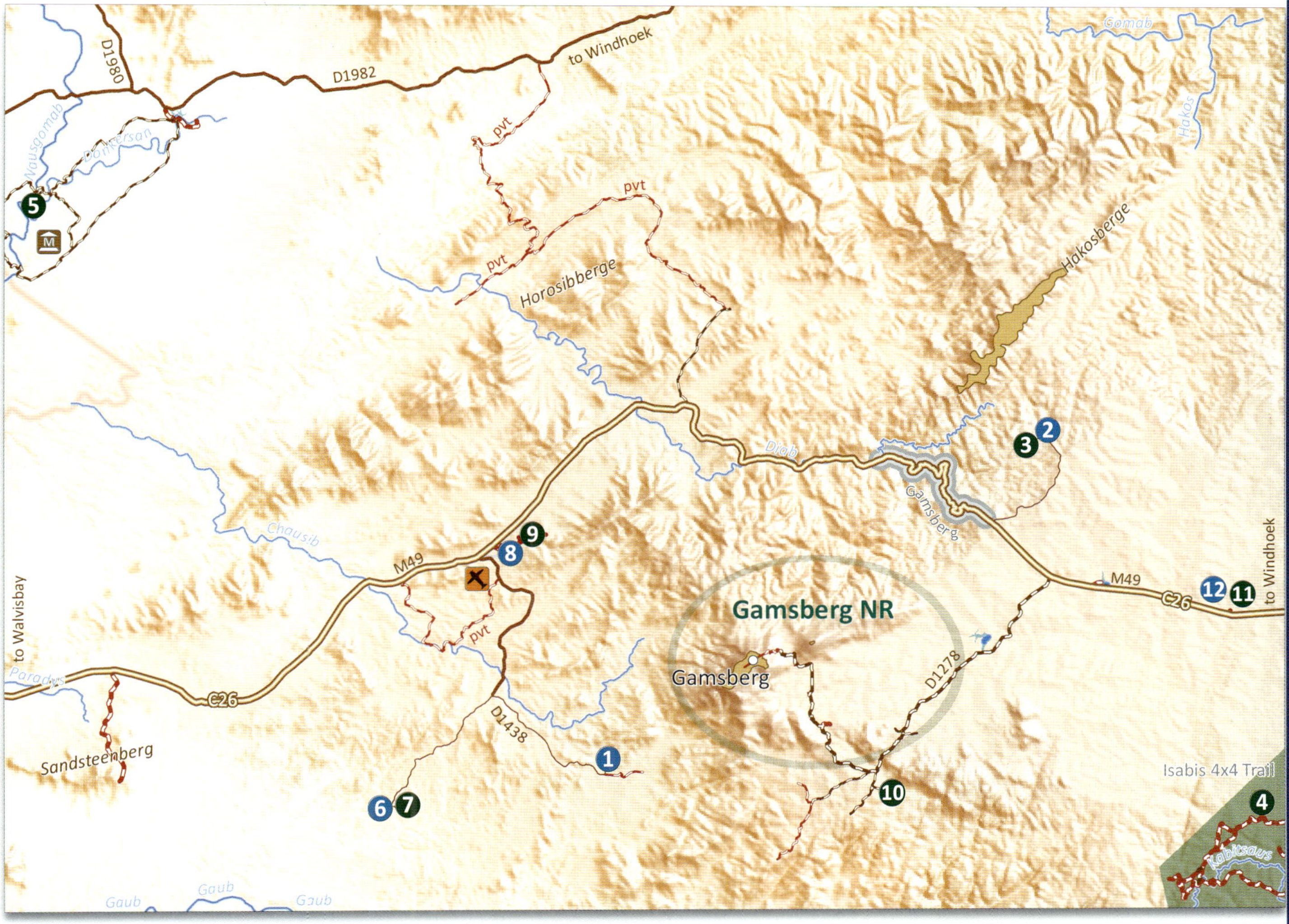

Corona Guest Farm 1

Guest Farm $$
120km or 1h46min NNE of Solitaire
w139546

Tel: +264(0)61 681 045, Fax: +264(0)61 681 046
corona@resdest.com

Three suites and six standard rooms, all en-suite with double and single beds, and air-conditioning. Four luxury permanent tents, also en-suite.

Languages: English, German, Afrikaans

Facilities: VISA @

Activities:

Hakos Guest Farm 2

Guest Farm $$
141km or 2h3min NNE of Solitaire
w141604

Tel: +264(0)62 572 111, Cell: +264(0)81 277 4535, Fax: +264(0)62 572 111
hakos@mweb.com.na,
www.hakos-astrofarm.com

Half and full-board accommodation in 14 guestrooms, each with shower and bathroom. Plus indoor braai facilities and indoor pool.

Languages: English, German, Afrikaans

Facilities: VISA FC @

Activities:

Hakos Guest Farm 3

Farm Camp $
141km or 2h4min NNE of Solitaire
w141634

Tel: +264(0)62 572 111, Fax: +264(0)62 572 111
hakos@mweb.com.na
www.hakos-astrofarm.com

Four shaded and wind-sheltered campsites, with braais. Two hot showers and two toilets. Great views.

Languages: English

Facilities: VISA @

Activities:

Klipdam Camp (Isabis 4WD trail) 4

4WD Trail Camp $
106km or 02h12min NE of Solitaire (of which 7km is 4WD)
w140435

Tel: +264(0)62 572 133, Cell: +264(0)81 124 5588, Fax: +264(0)62 572 133
info@isabis4x4.com,
www.isabis4x4.com

Klipdam Camp is situated on the Isabis 4x4 Trail and offers basic facilities. The camp can accommodate up to 50 people and has a flush toilet and running water.

Languages: English, German, Afrikaans

Facilities: FC

Activities:

Niedersachsen Guest Farm 5

Farm Camp $
188km or 3h7min N of Solitaire (of which 27km is 4WD)
w204847

Tel: +264(0)62 572 200, Cell: +264(0)81 244 5958, Fax: +264(0)62 572 201
sachsen@iway.na,
www.farmniedersachsen.com

Two campsites, one close to the farmhouse and the other 11 km away (only accessible with 4WD).

Languages: English, German, Afrikaans

Facilities:

Activities:

Rooiklip Guest Farm 6

Guest Farm $$
120km or 1h50min N of Solitaire
w142153

Tel: +264(0)61 681 031, Cell: +264(0)81 128 7844, Fax: +264(0)61 681 032
rooiklip@iway.na,
www.rooiklip.iway.na

Two guest houses with six comfortable standard rooms. Plus, self-catering Camp Flintstone, fully-equipped with a big lapa and kitchen.

Languages: English, German, Afrikaans

Facilities: @

Activities:

Gamsberg

Rooiklip Guest Farm 7

Farm Camp $$
121km or 1h54min N of Solitaire
w207594

Tel: +264(0)61 681 031, Cell: +264(0)81 128 7844,
Fax: +264(0)61 681 032
rooiklip@iway.na, www.rooiklip.iway.na

Cave campsites with showers, rock bathrooms and wash basins. The venue is only accessible with off-road vehicles.

Languages: English, German, Afrikaans

Facilities:

Activities:

Rooisand Desert Ranch 8

Guest Farm $$
103km or 1h24min N of Solitaire
w137724

Fax: +264(0)88 625 004, Cell: +264(0)81 127 7629
lifestyle@rooisand.com
www.rooisand.com

Four single and five double en-suite rooms, as well as a private, self-catering house on top of the mountain.

Languages: English, German, French, Afrikaans

Facilities: VISA

Activities:

Rooisand Desert Ranch 9

Farm Camp $$
105km or 1h27min N of Solitaire
w198388

Fax: +264(0)88 625 004, Cell: +264(0)81 127 7629
lifestyle@rooisand.com
www.rooisand.com

Five campsites on level, sandy ground. Each site has a tap, power point, clean ablutions and a braai area. Wood is available for purchase.

Languages: English, German, French, Afrikaans

Facilities: VISA

Activities:

Waterval Camp (Camp Weener) 10

Camping $
146km or 2h35min NNE of Solitaire (of which 16km is 4WD)
w198289

Cell: +264(0)81 289 5257
zunicabonsmaras@gmail.com

Two campsites - Panorama and Waterval. Both with ablution facilities (cold showers and toilet).

Languages: English, Afrikaans

Facilities:

Activities:

Weissenfels Guest Farm 11

Farm Camp $
121km or 1h45min NE of Solitaire
w361580

Tel: +264(0)62 572 112, Cell: +264(0)81 124 1818,
Fax: +264(0)62 572 102
rowins@iafrica.com.na, www.weissenfelsnamibia.com

Campsites with clean ablution blocks. Guests can camp at the dam too.

Languages: English

Facilities: VISA FC

Activities:

Weissenfels Guest Farm & Vortex Wellness Centre 12

Guest Farm $$
121km or 1h45min NE of Solitaire
w142644

Tel: +264(0)62 572 112, Cell: +264(0)81 124 1818,
Fax: +264(0)62 572 102
rowins@iafrica.com.na, www.weissenfelsnamibia.com

Comfortable, budget rooms as well as luxury, en-suite, air-conditioned rooms. Breakfast and dinner included.

Languages: English

Facilities: VISA FC

Activities:

Camping at Rooiklip Guest Farm near Gamsberg. (photo: Frank Höppener)

Helmeringhausen

(photo: Johann Groenewald)

HELMERINGHAUSEN WAS ORIGINALLY founded as a farm by a member of the Schutztruppe, the colonial armed force of Imperial Germany. Today it's still a privately-owned farm from which two plots were sold to the garage and the general dealer. Apart from these two businesses and the public roads, everything is owned by Farm Helmeringhausen.

Traveller Description

Helmeringhausen is located 500km south of Windhoek and 200km northeast of Lüderitz on the crossing of the C13 and C14 national roads. It's a popular stopover for tourists heading north for Sossusvlei and beyond. The farm owners established the Helmeringhausen Hotel which offers rooms as well as camping facilities. They also have self-catering accommodation across the road. Although their menu is limited in size, the hotel offers excellent meals and high tea. There's a variety of camping and lodging options on offer on farms in the area. The Tirasberg area southwest of Helmeringhausen is particularly beautiful - these mountains turn deep carmine red in the late afternoon.

Travel Info

The Helmeringhausen Farming Association established an Agricultural Museum next to the Helmeringhausen Hotel. This open-air museum displays all sorts of old farming implements as well as an antique fire engine. Activities include guided drives on Farm Helmeringhausen.

The nearest police station and hospital is at Aus, 110km southwest of Helmeringhausen.

Tow-in service is provided by Polka, based in Okahandja. Alternative tow-in numbers are +264(0)62 500 132 or +264(0)62 504 250.

TRAVEL TIP! You simply have to stop for tea and apple crumble at the Helmeringhausen Hotel but you may prefer to stay over on one of the other farms where you can enjoy the solitude and beauty of the Tirasberg Mountains.

Town Info:

Tow-in: +264(0)81 129 7490

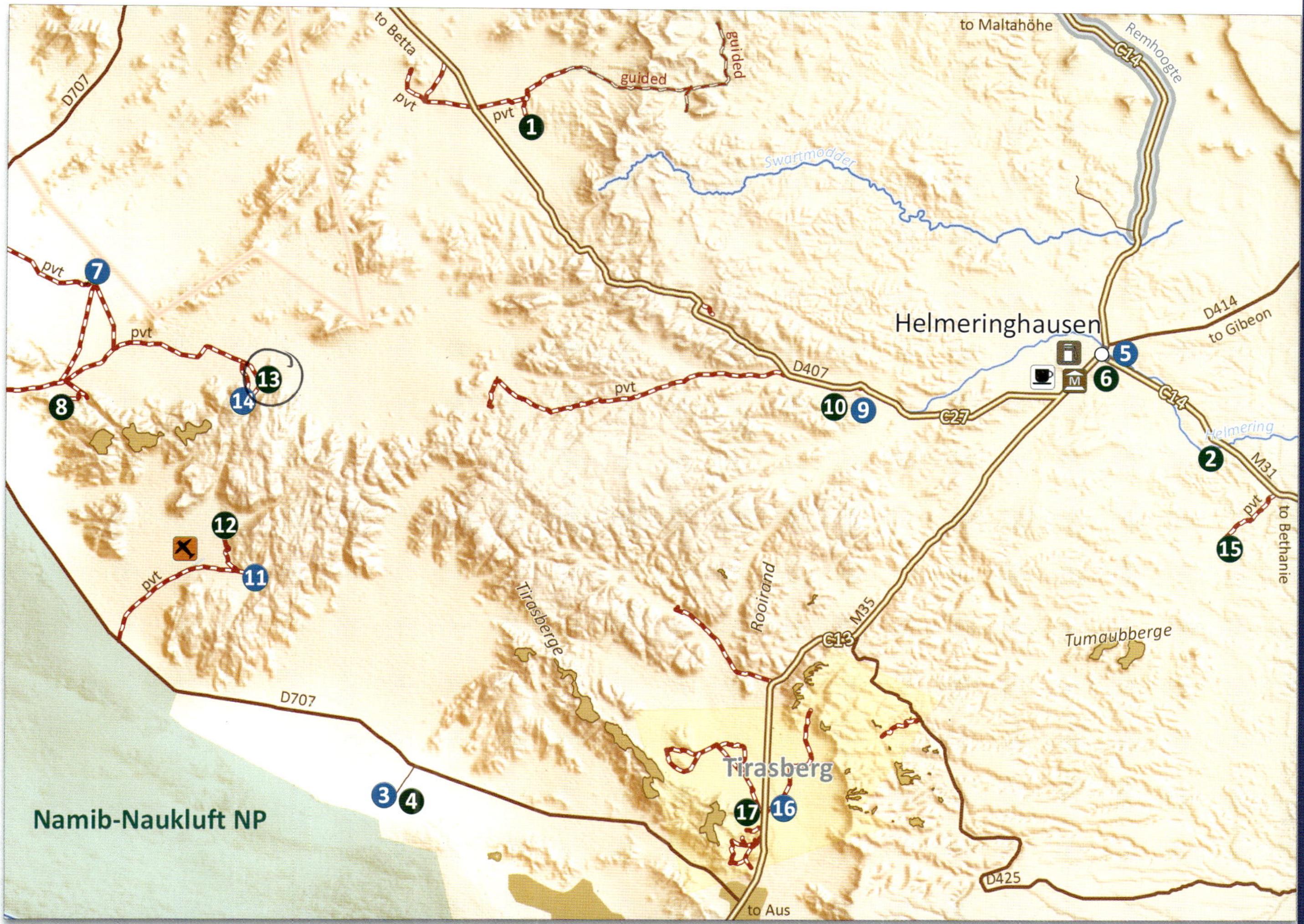

Aubures Camp — 1

Farm Camp — $
60km or 1h2min WNW of Helmeringhausen
w140974

Tel: +264(0)63 683 314
amiller@iway.na

Six campsites, with fireplace and drinking water. Ablutions with hot water and flush toilets. There's also a scullery area.

Languages: English, German, Afrikaans

Facilities:
Activities:

Goais — 2

Camping — $
16km or 11min SE of Helmeringhausen
w310760

Cell: +264(0)81 255 1535
goaisnr13@gmail.com

Three campsites which can accommodate up to 12 people. Ablutions include flush toilet and hot shower.

Languages: English

Facilities:
Activities:

Gunsbewys Guest Farm — 3

Guest Farm — $
77km or 1h7min WSW of Helmeringhausen
w206806

Tel: +264(0)63 683 053
grabnergertrud@gmail.com
www.tirasberge.de

Two en-suite rooms with a kitchen in the original farm house. This also houses the Tiras Conservancy Info Centre. Plus a self-catering house.

Languages: English, German

Facilities:
Activities:

Gunsbewys Guest Farm — 4

Camping — $$
77km or 1h7min WSW of Helmeringhausen
w261546

Tel: +264(0)63 683 053
grabnergertrud@gmail.com
www.tirasberge.de

Two campsites with clean ablution blocks - toilet and hot showers. Solar energy for cooking, lighting and heating water.

Languages: English, German

Facilities:
Activities:

Helmeringhausen Hotel — 5

Hotel — $$
In Helmeringhausen
w138042

Tel: +264(0)63 283 307, Cell: +264(0)81 603 2171, Fax: +264(0)63 283 308
helmering@iway.na, www.helmeringhausennamibia.com

22 Comfortable, en-suite rooms in peaceful setting. Beautiful beer garden.

Languages: English, German, Afrikaans

Facilities:
Activities:

Helmeringhausen Hotel — 6

Lodge Camp — $$
In Helmeringhausen
w209726

Tel: +264(0)63 283 307, Cell: +264(0)81 603 2171, Fax: +264(0)63 283 308
helmering@iway.na, www.helmeringhausennamibia.com

Shaded campsites, each with their own braai. Neat ablutions. Campers may not use the hotel pool. Reservations mandatory.

Languages: English, German, Afrikaans

Facilities:
Activities:

Helmeringhausen

Kanaan Guest Farm — 7

Guest Farm — $$$
131km or 1h59min W of Helmeringhausen
w143050

Tel: +264(0)63 683 119, Fax: +264(0)88 628 762
kanaan@naankuse.com
www.kanaannamibia.com

Four en-suite, double rooms with a modern architectural style. There's a lapa, braai area, and sitting room with cosy fireplace.

Languages: English, Afrikaans

Facilities:

Activities:

Kanaan Mountain Camp 707 — 8

Farm Camp — $$
126km or 1h51min W of Helmeringhausen
w193053

Tel: +264(0)63 683 119, Cell: +264(0)81 251 1373, Fax: +264(0)88 628 762
kanaan@naankuse.com, www.kanaannamibia.com

Unfenced venue. Neat ablutions but water is only available at the farmhouse, 14km away. Bottled drinking water is available. Bookings essential.

Languages: English, Afrikaans

Facilities:

Activities:

Lovedale Farm Holidays — 9

Self-catering — $
19km or 17min W of Helmeringhausen
w189028

Fax: +264(0)88 624 627, Cell: +264(0)81 281 9074
stay@lovedale-namibia.com
www.lovedale-namibia.com

Two self-catering units, one is wheelchair-friendly. Venue features Aloe Trail, a one hour walk with nice viewpoints.

Languages: English, Afrikaans

Facilities: VISA FC @

Activities:

Lovedale Farm Holidays — 10

Farm Camp — $
19km or 17min W of Helmeringhausen
w222190

Fax: +264(0)88 624 627, Cell: +264(0)81 281 9074
stay@lovedale-namibia.com
www.lovedale-namibia.com

Luxury camping facilities. The Aloe Trail on the farm is about one hour's walk with nice viewpoints for game and bird watching.

Languages: English, Afrikaans

Facilities: VISA FC

Activities:

NamTib Desert Lodge — 11

Lodge — $$
108km or 1h37min WSW of Helmeringhausen
w188973

Tel: +264(0)63 683 055, Fax: +264(0)88 633 459
stay@namtib.net
www.namtib.net

Five bungalows, one family chalet and two single rooms. Venue is a privately-owned reserve in the Tiras Mountains.

Languages: English

Facilities: FC

Activities:

NamTib Desert Lodge - Little Hunter's Rest — 12

Camping — $
109km or 1h38min WSW of Helmeringhausen
w207457

Tel: +264(0)63 683 055, Fax: +264(0)88 633 459
stay@namtib.net
www.namtib.net

Five campsites under large Camel Thorn trees. Each site has braai facilities.

Languages: English

Facilities:

Activities:

(photo: Frank Höppener)

4/4/19.

Ranch Koiimasis Camping 13

Farm Camp $$
138km or 2h6min W of Helmeringhausen
w141712

Tel: +264(0)63 683 052, Cell: +264(0)81 262 8545
info.koiimasis@gmail.com
www.namibia-farm-lodge.com

Comfortable campsites, all with their own braai areas & clean drinking water. Bookings required.

Languages: German, English, Afrikaans and Croatian

Facilities:

Activities:

Ranch Koiimasis Fest In Fels Farm Lodge 14

Guest Farm $$
139km or 2h8min W of Helmeringhausen
w138853

Tel: +264(0)63 683 247, Cell: +264(0)81 262 8545
fifkoiimasis@gmail.com
www.namibia-farm-lodge.com

Accommodation on a Dinner-Bed-and-Breakfast, or self-catering basis. Bookings required.

Languages: German, English, Afrikaans and Croatian

Facilities:

Activities:

Sterreprag 15

Farm Camp $
23km or 29min SE of Helmeringhausen
w216357

Cell: +264(0)81 128 7101
andrecoetzee@mtcmobile.com.na

Camping under a huge Camel Thorn tree. Open-air ablutions with flush toilet, hot shower and wash-up basin. Venue is a working sheep and goat farm.

Languages: English, Afrikaans

Facilities:

Tiras Guest Farm 16

Guest Farm $
44km or 33min SW of Helmeringhausen
w140241

Tel: +264(0)63 683 048
kidogo@mweb.com.na
www.tirasberge.de

Two double, en-suite rooms, and two-bed chalet. Both on a self-catering basis, no meals served.

Languages: English, German

Facilities:

Activities:

Tiras Guest Farm 17

Farm Camp $$
43km or 33min SW of Helmeringhausen
w139644

Tel: +264(0)63 683 048
kidogo@mweb.com.na
www.tirasberge.de

Campsites on a former livestock breeding farm. Mountain climbing is one of the activities available here.

Languages: English, German

Facilities:

Activities:

"I am not the same having seen the moon shine on the other side of the world."

Mary Anne Radmacher

(photo: Frank Höppener)

Lüderitz

(photo: Frank Höppener)

WHAT IS TODAY KNOWN AS LÜDERITZ was founded in 1487 by Bartolomeu Diaz as Angra Pequena (Portuguese for Small Bay). During the early 19th century it became a trading post and in 1883 Adolf Lüderitz from Germany purchased Angra Pequena from the local Nama chief. When he did not return from an expedition to the Orange River in 1886 Angra Pequena's name was changed to Lüderitzbucht in his honour.

Initially, Lüderitz was a trading post, whale and seal hunting station, fishing village and guano-harvesting town but it enjoyed a temporary surge of prosperity when diamonds were discovered in 1909 in the nearby Kolmanskop. In those days the railway line ran between Keetmanshoop and Lüderitz and the harbour town flourished.

In 1905 German authorities established a concentration camp on Shark Island. The camp operated for two years during the Herero Wars and almost 3 000 Hereros and Namas died here as a result of the tragic conditions of forced labour. Their labour was used for expansion of the town, railway and port and they also worked on the farms of white settlers. A movement to change the town's name back to !Nami#Nûs, its name prior to 1884, has been going on for some time. The appeal of this harbour town lies in the fact that little has changed since the early 20th century. Although this coastline might be inhospitable to people, it is important for coastal seabird breeding.

Traveller Description

Lüderitz is a charming town with beautiful colonial architecture and a touristy waterfront. Apart from a few museums that are worth visiting, Felsenkirche (Church of the Rock) is a well-known attraction. Historical sites worth seeing are the stone cross erected by Bartolomeu Diaz at Diaz Point, and the lighthouse. Activities include wind- and kite-surfing during the windy months and boat cruises for an opportunity to see whales, seals, dolphins and penguins as well as other marine life and sea birds. Visitors should note that the wooden walkway to Diaz Cross has been damaged and is no longer in use, but that the cross can still be reached via the path at low tide. One of the town's biggest attractions is a visit to the nearby Kolmanskop ghost diamond town. Guided tours into the Namib Desert and to Pomona and Bogenfels ghost diamond towns in the Sperrgebiet, are also available.

Travel Info

The only way to enter the Sperrgebiet National Park is when travelling with a Ministry of Environment and Tourism concessionaire. Tours with the concessionaires begin in Lüderitz. Travellers will find everything they need in this town, the local Spar sells good quality meat.

TRAVEL TIP! If you are lucky enough to get a wind-free day at Shark Island, stay for longer as this is the most beautiful campsite right on the sea. Visit the Adolf Lüderitz Memorial that was erected at Shark Island in 1953.

Town Info:

Hospital: +264(0)63 202 446
Police: +264(0)63 202 255
Doctor: +264(0)63 202 515
Tow-in: +264(0)63 203 669

Alte Loge — 1

Guest House — $
Mabel Street, Lüderitz
w267836

Cell: +264(0)81 636 7485
alte.loge@gmail.com
www.historisches-ferienhaus-namibia.de

En-suite rooms with breakfast.

Languages: English, German, Afrikaans

Facilities:

Hansa Haus Guest House — 2

Guest House — $
85 Mabel St, Lüderitz, Namibia
w142509

Tel: +264(0)63 203 699 , Cell: +264(0)81 128 4336, Fax: +264(0)63 204 031
hansahaus@iway.na

Venue accommodates ten people. Two rooms with double beds and three rooms with two single beds. The balcony has a sea view and braai.

Languages: English, Afrikaans

Facilities:

Haus Sandrose — 3

Self-catering — $
15 Bismarck St, Lüderitz
w219546

Tel: +264(0)63 202 630, Fax: +264(0)63 202 365
haussandrose@iway.na
www.haussandrose.com

Self-catering units in a beautiful, sheltered garden in town centre. Rooms are fully-equipped and linen / towels are high quality.

Languages: English, German, Afrikaans

Facilities:

Activities:

Lüderitz

Island Cottage 4

Cottage $
Shark Island, Lüderitz
w193054

Tel: +264(0)63 203 626, Cell: +264(0)81 292 2984,
Fax: +264(0)63 204 113
retha.c@mweb.com.na

Comfortable, en-suite rooms with double beds, fully-equipped kitchenettes, private patios, braai areas and satellite TV.

Languages: English, Afrikaans

Facilities: VISA FC @

Activities:

Kairos Cottage B&B 5

Bed and Breakfast $
Kreplin Street, Shark Island, Lüderitz
w277711

Tel: +264(0)63 203 080, Cell: +264(0)81 650 5598
christo.b@iway.na
www.kairoscottage.com

Five en-suite rooms, each with its own shower and great sea views.

Languages: English

Facilities: VISA

Kratzplatz B&B 6

Bed and Breakfast $
5 Nachtigal St, Lüderitz
w140980

Tel: +264(0)63 202 458, Cell: +264(0)81 129 2458,
Fax: +264(0)63 202 458
kratzmr@iway.na,
www.kratzplatz.info

Comfortable single, double and family en-suite rooms in converted old church.

Languages: English, German, Afrikaans

Facilities: VISA

Activities:

Lüderitz Backpackers Lodge 7

Backpackers Hostel $
2 Ring Street, Lüderitz
w142507

Tel: +264(0)63 202 000, Cell: +264(0)81 261 2174,
luderitzbackpackers@hotmail.com
www.luderitzbackpackers.weebly.com

Self-catering accommodation in dormitories, double and family rooms. There's a fully-equipped kitchen, braai facilities and laundry services.

Languages: English, Afrikaans

Facilities:

Lüderitz Nest Hotel 8

Hotel $$
820 Dias St, Oostend, Lüderitz
w140304

Tel: +264(0)63 204 000, Fax: +264(0)63 204 001
reservations@nesthotel.com
www.nesthotel.com

Luxurious beachfront accommodation for holiday-makers and businessmen.

Languages: English

Facilities: VISA FC @

Activities:

Obelix Guest House 9

Guest House $$
Between Bay and Bismarck Road, Lüderitz
w138862

Tel: +264(0)63 203 456, Cell: +264(0)81 227 7735,
Fax: +264(0)63 203 457
kalahari@iway.na

11 Double and five family rooms. Includes lapa, restaurant, bar and braai facilities.

Languages: English, Afrikaans, German

Facilities: VISA @

Activities:

(photo: Karin Theron)

Sea-View Zum Sperrgebiet 10

Hotel $$
Woermann St, Lüderitz
w142511

Tel: +264(0)63 203 411, Cell: +264(0)81 1 282 264, Fax: +264(0)63 203 414
res.sperrgebiet@united.com.na,
www.unitedafricagroup.com.na

Comfortable, en-suite rooms, each equipped with TV and coffee/tea facilities. The hotel also offers laundry and airport transfer services.

Languages: English

Facilities:

Activities:

Shark Island Rest Camp 11

Camping $$
Shark Island, Lüderitz
w137935

Tel: +264(0)61 285 7200, Fax: +264(0)61 256 320
reservations@nwr.com.na
www.nwr.com.na

Each campsite has its own electricity point and built-in braai. One large ablution facility and additional smaller ones between the campsites.

Languages: English

Facilities:

Activities:

Shark Island Rest Camp Lighthouse 12

Self-catering $
Shark Island, Lüderitz
w279628

Tel: +264(0)61 285 7200, Fax: +264(0)61 256 320
reservations@nwr.com.na
www.nwr.com.na

Lighthouse accommodation! Two rooms (two beds in each) and two bathrooms. Fully-equipped with sitting room and TV.

Languages: English

Facilities:

Activities:

Zum Anker Accommodation 13

Self-catering $$
299 Bulow St, Lüderitz
w277708

Cell: +264(0)81 129 4390
randd@iway.na
www.zumanker-luderitz.com

Four self-catering units, ranging from one-bedroom flats to a four-bedroom home. Each apartment has its own lounge, kitchen and bathroom.

Languages: English, German, Afrikaans

Facilities:

Zur Waterkant B&B 14

Bed and Breakfast $
Bremer St, Lüderitz
w139168

Tel: +264(0)63 203 145, Fax: +264(0)63 203 145
Zur-Waterkant@Raubkatzen.de
www.raubkatzen.de

Double rooms with bathrooms. Or self-catering family rooms with small kitchenette.

Languages: German, English

Facilities:

"The traveler sees what he sees. The tourist sees what he has come to see."

GK Chesterton

(photo: Frank Höppener)

Namib-Naukluft National Park

(photo: Mietsie Visser)

THE NAMIB-NAUKLUFT NATIONAL PARK is said to be the the fourth largest park in the world, it includes sections of the still restricted Diamond Area. The park offers breathtaking landscapes and natural wonders like Sossusvlei, Tinkas Flats, Kuiseb Canyon, Sesriem Canyon, Moon Landscape and the Koichab Depression. The park is bordered by the Sperrgebiet National Park in the south and the Dorob National Park to the north. Apart from a small area around Lüderitz, the coast from Oranjemund almost up to Walvis Bay is included in the park.

The Namib Desert, with its towering orange-red sand dunes, is one of the world's oldest deserts. The burnt orange colour of the sand developed over millions of years as iron in the sand oxidised, like rusting metal. The biggest attraction within the park is Sossusvlei which boasts some of the highest dunes in the world.

Wildlife in the park includes gemsbok, Hartmann's zebra, black rhino, giraffe, springbok, brown hyena, leopard and baboon. The 348 bird species recorded include lappet-faced vulture, Ludwig's bustard, Rüppell's korhaan, dune lark, Herero chat and African black oystercatcher.

Evidence of Stone Age life in the Kuiseb River dates back 200 000 years. Archaeological finds indicate that the area was used by semi-nomadic communities when rain provided enough grazing for animals. The Topnaar people still live along the Kuiseb River inside the park.

Traveller Description

The word Namib means 'open space' and that is largely what epitomises this extraordinary conservation area. The southern and coastal sections of the park are closed to self-drive travellers and can only be accessed by tour operators. If you want to explore the desert, there are many guided coastal and desert trails starting from Lüderitz. Shipwrecks found along the coast include the Otavi at Spencer Bay, the Eduard Bohlen at Conception and the Eagle at Sandwich Harbour. Sossusvlei, in the centre of the park, is easily accessed from Sesriem. Most of the national park campsites are located in the northern section. The Welwitschia Plains 4WD Trail is a nice loop off the C28 which affords beautiful views of the surreal Moon Landscape.

Travel Info

Apart from the rest camp at Sesriem, all the campsites within the park are very basic so visitors need to be self-sufficient campers. You need an off-road vehicle to traverse remote areas like Tinkas Flats but you can reach the Sossusvlei parking area with a sedan vehicle, from there 4WD shuttles will take you to the dunes.

TRAVEL TIP! You don't need a permit to traverse the park via the C28 and C14 roads to Swakopmund and Walvis Bay, but you're not allowed to venture off these roads. Permits for the park can be obtained in Windhoek, Swakopmund or at the park's office at Sesriem. See page 234 on Sesriem for more information about visiting Sossusvlei.

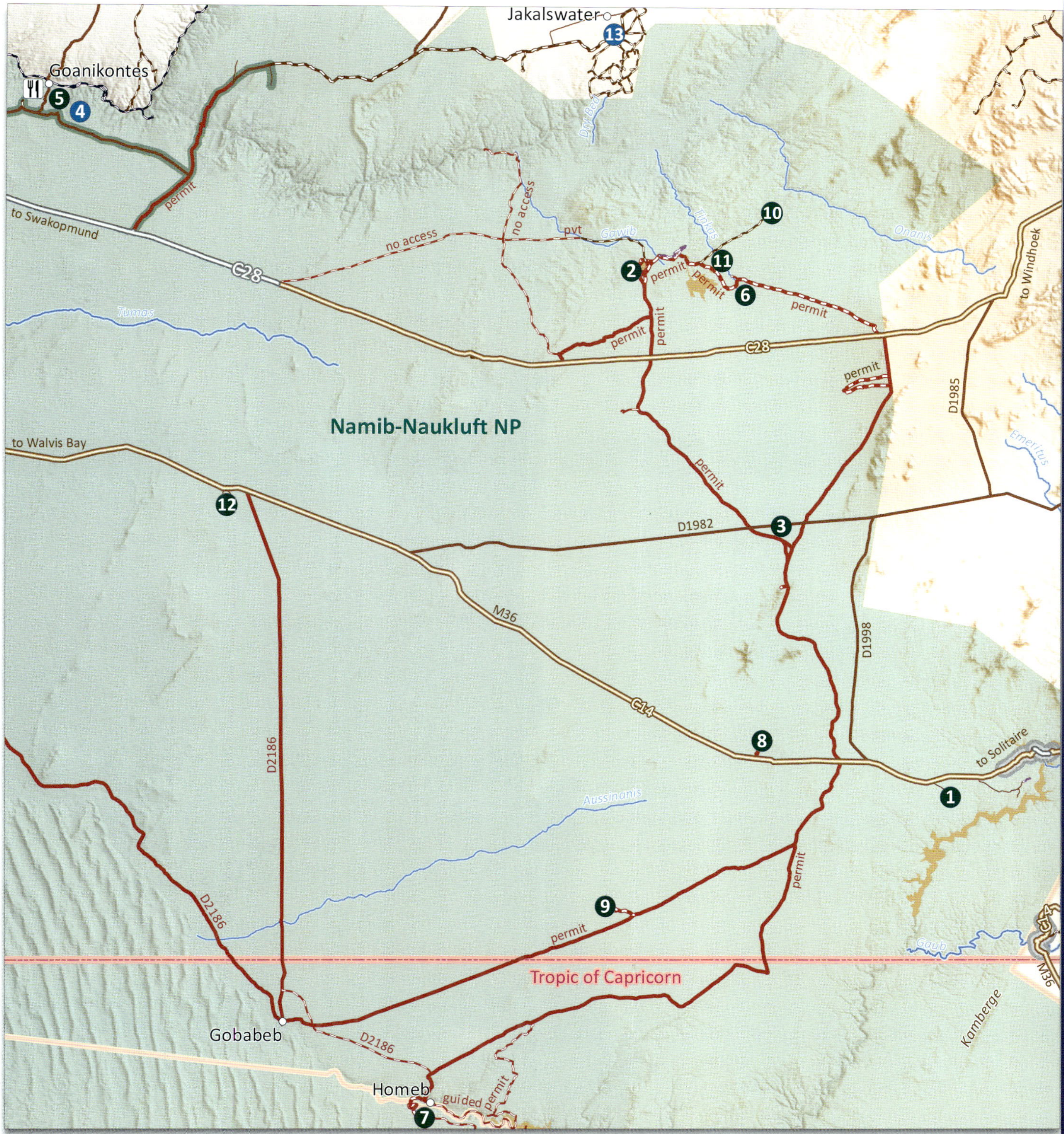

Namib-Naukluft National Park

Aruvlei Campsite — 1

Park Camp — $
131km or 1h43min ESE of Walvis Bay
w137895

Tel: +264(0)64 404 576

Basic campsites, campers need to be self-sufficient. Obtain permits from the Ministry of Environment & Tourism offices in Swakopmund or Sesriem. No bookings.

Languages: English

Facilities:

Activities:

Blutkuppe/Bloedkoppie Campsite — 2

Park Camp — $
137km or 1h49min E of Walvis Bay (of which 2km is 4WD)
w141618

Tel: +264(0)64 404 576

Campsites not marked, you have to choose where you want to camp. Permit required from Ministry of Environment & Tourism in Swakopmund or Sesriem. No bookings.

Languages: English

Facilities:

Activities:

Ganab Campsite — 3

Park Camp — $
107km or 1h22min E of Walvis Bay
w141617

Tel: +264(0)64 404 576

No facilities other than braais, campers need to be self-sufficient. Get permits from the Ministry of Environment & Tourism in Swakopmund or Sesriem. No bookings.

Languages: English

Facilities:

Activities:

Goanikontes Oasis Rest Camp — 4

Self-catering — $
40km or 53min E of Swakopmund
w247251

Tel: +264(0)64 405 976
info@goanikontes-oasis.com

Family units, 2-sleeper bungalows or two luxurious, double-storey, A-frame bungalows built into the natural boulders of the valley. Reservations mandatory.

Languages: English, German, Afrikaans

Facilities:

Activities:

Goanikontes Oasis Rest Camp — 5

Camping — $$
40km or 53min E of Swakopmund
w137960

Tel: +264(0)64 405 976
info@goanikontes-oasis.com

11 Campsites, each with their own braai area and electricity. Ablutions - toilets and showers. Campers can dine at the lodge restaurant. Reservations mandatory.

Languages: English, German, Afrikaans

Facilities:

Activities:

Groot Tinkas Campsite — 6

Park Camp — $
148km or 2h23min E of Walvis Bay (of which 17km is 4WD)
w137703

Tel: +264(0)64 404 576

Located among small hills, close to dam. Campers must be self-sufficient. Obtain permits from the Ministry of Environment & Tourism in Swakopmund or Sesriem. No bookings.

Languages: English

Facilities:

Activities:

Homeb Camp — 7

Park Camp — $
116km or 1h50min SE of Walvis Bay (of which 13km is 4WD)
w137566

Tel: +264(0)64 404 576

Basic campsites. Campers must be self-sufficient. Obtain permits from Ministry of Environment & Tourism in Swakopmund or Sesriem. No bookings.

Languages: English

Facilities:

Activities:

Kries Se Rus — 8

Park Camp — $
112km or 1h26min ESE of Walvis Bay
w175340

Tel: +264(0)64 404 576

Basic campsites with no facilities. Obtain permits from Ministry of Environment & Tourism in Swakopmund or Sesriem. No bookings.

Languages: English

Facilities:

Activities:

Mirabib Campsite — 9

Park Camp — $
134km or 2h9min ESE of Walvis Bay
w138109

Tel: +264(0)64 404 576

Basic campsites with no facilities. Obtain permit from Ministry of Environment & Tourism in Swakopmund or Sesriem. No bookings.

Languages: English

Facilities:

Activities:

Rock Arch Camp — 10

Park Camp — $
121km or 2h18min E of Swakopmund (of which 25km is 4WD)
w207590

Tel: +264(0)64 404 576

Two campsites with no facilities. Guests can camp in a cave. Obtain permits from Ministry of Environment & Tourism offices in Swakopmund or Sesriem. No bookings.

Languages: English

Facilities:

Activities:

Tinkas Campsite — 11

Park Camp — $
113km or 1h59min E of Swakopmund (of which 17km is 4WD)
w140164

Tel: +264(0)64 404 576

Basic campsites, you must be self-sufficient. Obtain permits from Ministry of Environment & Tourism in Swakopmund or Sesriem. No bookings.

Languages: English

Facilities:

Activities:

Vogelfederberg Campsite — 12

Park Camp — $
52km or 37min ESE of Walvis Bay
w137893

Tel: +264(0)64 404 576

Campsite with basic facilities, you must be self-sufficient. Obtain permits from Ministry of Environment & Tourism in Swakopmund or Sesriem. No bookings.

Languages: English

Facilities:

Activities:

Wüstenquell Lodge	13
Guest Farm	$$

106km or 02h20min E of Swakopmund
w139138

Tel: +264(0)61 234 342, Cell: +264(0)81 140 5987, Fax: +264(0)88 648 879
info@wustenquell.com, www.wustenquell.com

One rondavel, two mountain chalets and the 'Zebra Outpost', a self-catering house for four people.

Languages: English

Facilities:

Activities:

Namib Naukluft Railway (photo: Mietsie Visser)

Tsondab Vlei (photo: Heiner Dillmann)

NamibRand Nature Reserve

(photo: Mietsie Visser)

COVERING AN AREA OF 215 000 HECTARES, NamibRand Nature Reserve is one of the largest private nature reserves in southern Africa. It was established in 1984 by J A Brückner, a Windhoek businessman, who integrated 15 former sheep farms into one single conservation unit to help conserve the ecology and wildlife of the southwestern Namib Desert. To date, seventeen former livestock farms have been rehabilitated into a single continuous natural habitat.

The predominant large mammals in the reserve are oryx and springbok. Other large mammals include kudu, Hartman's and Burchell's zebra, giraffe, klipspringer, steenbok, hartebeest and baboon. Predators include leopard, spotted and brown hyena, black-backed jackal, aardwolf, bat-eared fox, Cape fox, African wildcat, caracal and genet. To date more than 150 bird species have been identified.

Traveller Description

This upmarket nature reserve isn't cheap but seeing as the number of guest beds here is restricted to one per 1 000 hectares, exclusivity is guaranteed. Presently, there are five concessionaires conducting tourism operations in the reserve. The reserve can be explored by 4WD or on foot, as well as from the air by hot air balloon or with scenic flights. Other activities offered in the reserve include dune boarding and horse riding.

Travel Info

Internet is only available at reception and only for urgent matters. There is a curio shop, wine cellar and bar. Tourism information is available at the Sossusvlei Lodge Adventure Centre near Sesriem.

TRAVEL TIP! The reserve offers spectacular photographic opportunities for people who want to photograph the red sand dunes of the Namib Desert. As it's one of the least light-polluted areas in the world, it also offers amazing star-gazing opportunities. Another special feature of the reserve is the numerous magical fairy circles which dot the grass plains.

NamibRand Family Hideout 1

Self-catering $$
58km or 55min NW of Betta (of which 5km is 4WD)w139655

Tel: +264(0)61 226 803, Cell: +264(0)81 127 2957,
Fax: +264(0)88 619 115
ambruck@afol.com.na,
www.nrfhideout.com

Farmhouse accommodates up to 10. Has gas fridge, freezer, stove and braai facilities. Solar power. Bedding available on request. Reservations mandatory.

Languages: English, German, Afrikaans

Facilities:

Activities:

NamibRand Family Hideout 2

Park Camp $$$
59km or 57min NW of Betta (of which 6km is 4WD) w224552

Tel: +264(0)61 226 803, Cell: +264(0)81 127 2957,
Fax: +264(0)88 619 115
ambruck@afol.com.na,
www.nrfhideout.com

Two campsites (both very private), under camel thorn trees. Each takes eight people and two vehicles max. Private ablution block (hot shower & flush toilet). Reservations mandatory.

Languages: English, German, Afrikaans

Facilities:

Activities:

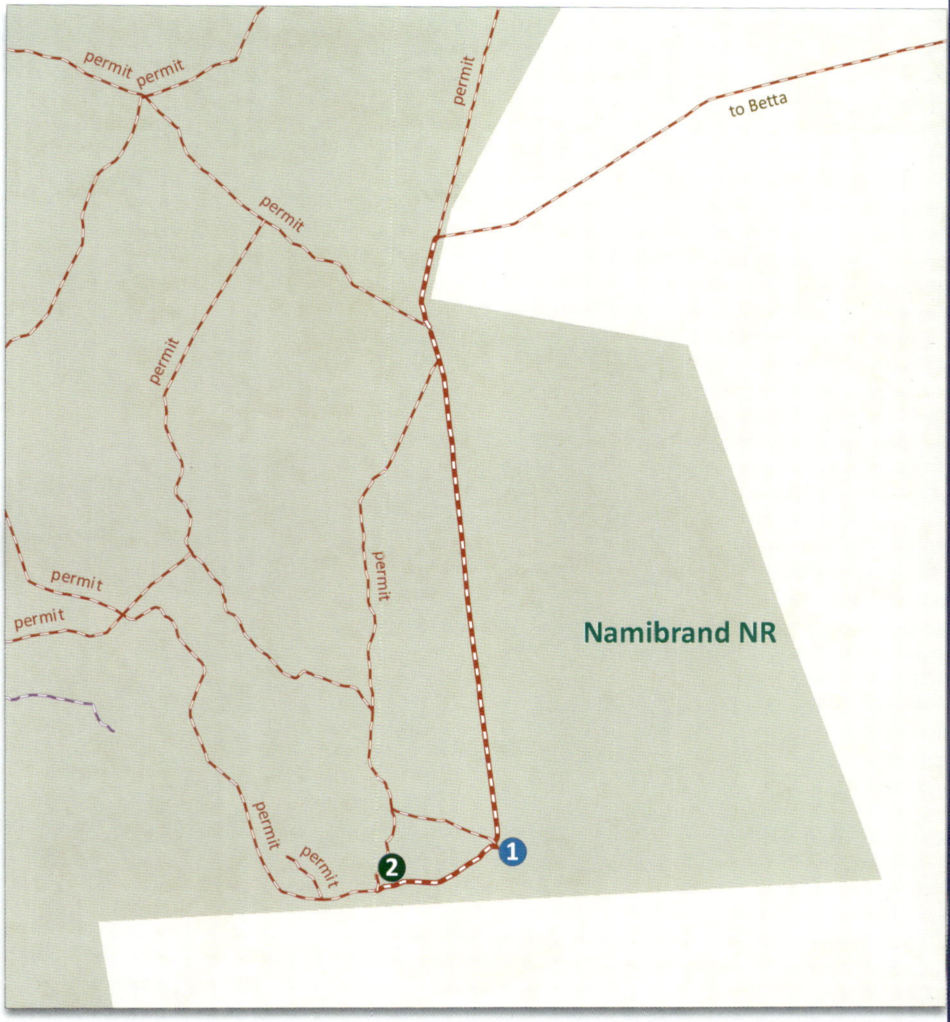

(photo: Heiner Dillmann)

Sesriem

(photo: Ian-Ray Nel)

SESRIEM IS A SMALL SETTLEMENT in the Namib Desert, renowned for the Sesriem Canyon, Sossusvlei and Deadvlei. The name Sesriem ('six belts' in Afrikaans) was given to the settlement by settlers returning from the Dorsland Trek. They tied together six straps made of Oryx hide to lower buckets into the canyon to get water. The canyon, a narrow gorge about a kilometre in length and 30 to 40 metres deep, was formed by erosion over many centuries.

Sossusvlei is possibly Namibia's most spectacular and best-known attraction. Surrounded by some of the highest dunes in the world (reaching almost 400m), Sossusvlei is a large, white, salt and clay pan. Sossusvlei literally translates to 'dead-end marsh', it's the place where dunes come together to prevent the Tsauchab River from flowing any further. However, due to the dry conditions in the Namib Desert the river seldom flows this far and the pan remains bone-dry most years. Only during an exceptionally good rainy season will the Tsauchab River fill the pan to create a truly spectacular sight.

Deadvlei is an area very close to Sossusvlei where, ages ago, the Tsauchab River used to settle in a small pan. Bushes and trees used to grow in the pan until a sand dune blocked the flow of the river and diverted the water into Sossusvlei. The bushes and trees in Deadvlei died but due to the exceptional dry desert conditions the tree stumps have petrified and remain to this day. Visitors are requested not to climb on these ancient trees.

Traveller Description

Sesriem is the main access point to the Namib-Naukluft National Park - get permits from the Nature Conservation offices in Sesriem. The settlement has a filling station with a shop where you can get basics like food and water. Apart from the park's restcamp, there are many upmarket lodges and campsites in the vicinity.

Travel Info

The gate to Sossusvlei opens at sunrise and closes at sunset. There is a 4x2 parking area just before the vlei; beyond this area an off-road vehicle is a necessity. Guests can either walk to the pan (about 5km one way), or make use of the 4x4 shuttle service to and from the sites. It is best to visit Sossusvlei early in the morning when the red colour of the sand is brightest and the light and shadows offer breathtaking scenery. Otherwise, visit in the late afternoon when the sun isn't baking down relentlessly on the desert sands. The nearby Deadvlei is of great photographic significance with the skeletons of Acacia trees dotting a dry white pan. Another natural phenomena near Sesriem is Elim, a petrified dune.

Sossusvlei Lodge can assist with mechanical repairs, and tyre repairs can be done at the Engen fuel stop. Oasis Coffee Shop next to the garage sells basic foods, fresh bread and takeaways; the shop inside the Sesriem Rest Camp sells curios as well as basic food supplies.

Tow-in services is provided by Polka 24 hour service, based in Okahandja. Alternative tow-in numbers include +264(0)62 500 132 or +264(0)62 504 250.

TRAVEL TIP! If you're a keen photographer you might prefer to stay at Sesriem Rest Camp inside the park. This will allow you more time in the early morning and late afternoon to take photographs of the Sossusvlei dunes before and after the park gates open and close.

Town Info:
Tow-in: +264(0)81 129 7490

A Little Sossus Lodge 1

Lodge $$
39km or 32min SE of Sesriem
w139503

Tel: +264(0)64 464 144, Cell: +264(0)81 127 9920, Fax: +264(0)64 464 155
reservations@logufa.com,
www.littlesossus.com

20 Chalets, all en-suite. The lodge is 35km from the entrance gate to Sossusvlei.

Languages: English

Facilities: VISA FC

Activities:

A Little Sossus Lodge 2

Lodge Camp $
39km or 32min SE of Sesriem
w227576

Tel: +264(0)64 464 144, Cell: +264(0)81 127 9920, Fax: +264(0)64 464 155
reservations@logufa.com,
www.littlesossus.com

Each campsite has its own en-suite bathroom with hot water.

Languages: English

Facilities: VISA FC

Activities:

Desert Camp 3

Self-catering $$
5km or 6min E of Sesriem
w142888

Tel: +27(0)21 930 4564, Fax: ?+27(0)21 914 9930
reservations@desertcamp.com
www.desertcamp.com

20 Luxury, eco-friendly, self-catering, en-suite units under canvas with adobe-style walls. With verandas to enjoy the views.

Languages: English

Facilities: VISA FC @

Activities:

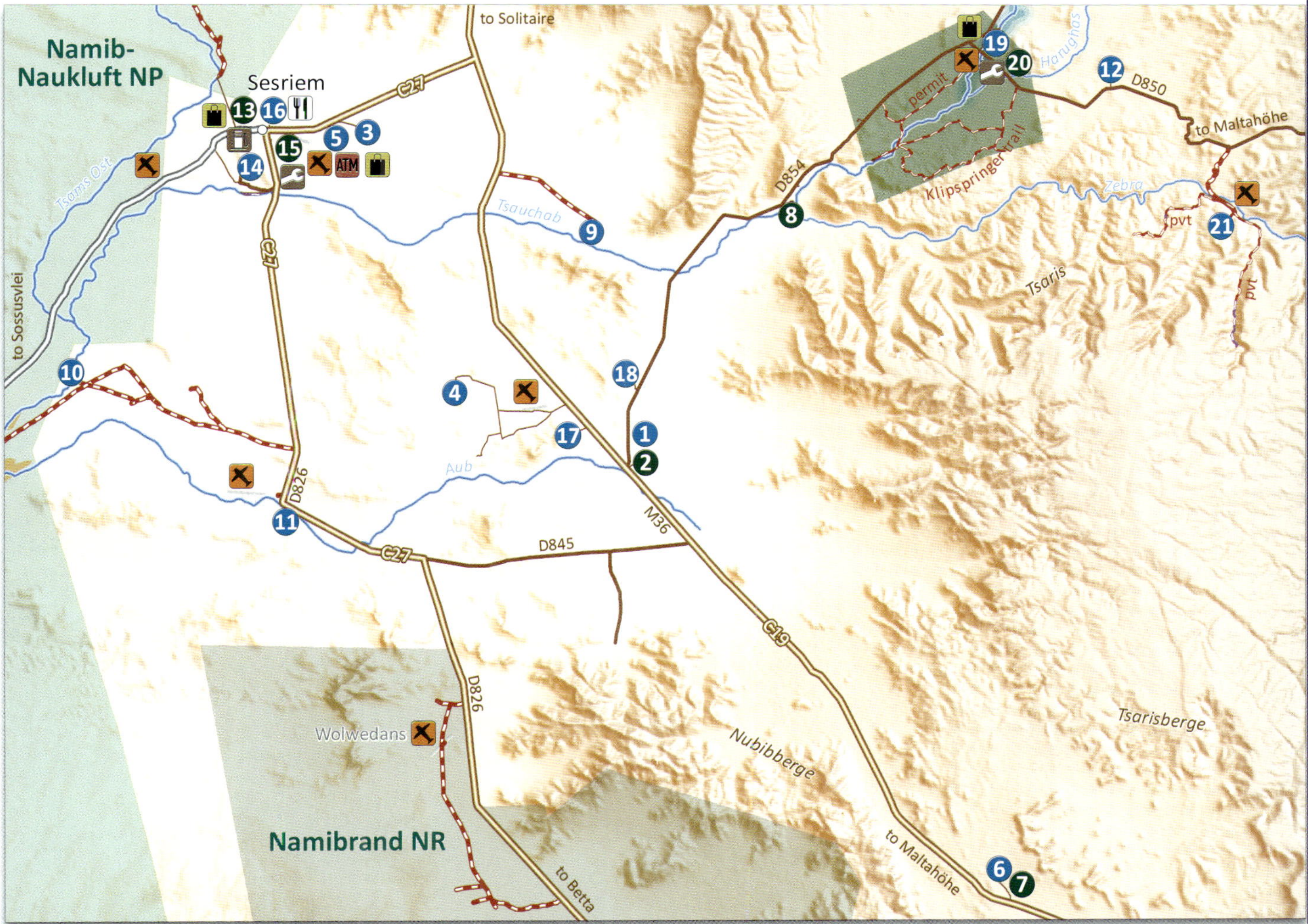

Sesriem

Desert Homestead Outpost 4

Tented Camp $$$
42km or 40min SE of Sesriem
w140192

Tel: +264(0)61 240 020, Cell: +264(0)81 578 4700,
reservations@homestead.com.na
www.deserthomesteadoutpost.com

Enjoy panoramic views from the 12 thatch, canvas & stone abodes or the main house. There's also a restaurant, lounge and pool.

Languages: English

Facilities:

Activities:

Desert Quiver Camp 5

Self-catering $$
5km before the Gate to Sesriem and Sossusvlei - Namib Naukluft Park
w360961

Tel: +27(0)21 930 4564, Fax: +27(0)21 914 9930
reservations@desertquivercamp.com
www.desertquivercamp.com

24 Self-catering, en-suite units with spacious bedrooms and patio with braai. Fresh food can be ordered daily.

Languages: English, Afrikaans

Facilities:

Activities:

Hammerstein Lodge 6

Lodge $$
72km or 55min SE of Sesriem
w140283

Tel: +264(0)63 693 111, Cell: +264(0)81 146 3221,
Fax: +264(0)63 693 112
hammerst@hammerstein.com.na,
www.hammerstein.com.na

51 Standard hotel rooms and five self-catering units. Bookings essential.

Languages: English, Afrikaans

Facilities:

Activities:

Hammerstein Lodge 7

Lodge Camp $
72km or 55min SE of Sesriem
w138035

Tel: +264(0)63 693 111, Cell: +264(0)81 146 3221,
Fax: +264(0)63 693 112
hammerst@hammerstein.com.na,
www.hammerstein.com.na

Each campsite has its own ablutions and braai area. The lodge has a bar. Bookings essential.

Languages: English, Afrikaans

Facilities: FC

Activities:

Hauchabfontein Camping Area 8

Farm Camp $
57km or 51min E of Sesriem
w206812

Tel: +264(0)63 293 433, Cell: +264(0)81 233 4436,
Fax: +264(0)63 293 433
edithh@iway.na,
www.hauchabfontein.com

Shaded campsites with hot showers and braai areas. Venue is located between Sossusvlei and the Naukluft, along the Tsauchab River.

Languages: English

Facilities:

Activities:

Hoodia Desert Lodge 9

Lodge $$$
26km or 37min ESE of Sesriem
w219519

Tel: +264(0)61 237 294, Cell: +264(0)81 306 6931,
Fax: +264(0)61 237 295
hoodia@exclusive.com.na,
www.hoodiadesertlodge.com

12 Comfortable air-conditioned, en-suite rooms. Plus, tented bungalows with shaded porches and open-air bathrooms.

Languages: English

Facilities:

Activities:

Kulala Desert Lodge 10

Lodge $$$
31km or 38min SW of Sesriem
w138448

Tel: +264(0)61 274 500, Fax: +264(0)61 239 455
enquiry@wilderness.co.za
www.wilderness-safaris.com

14 Beautifully-furnished, thatched, en-suite chalets with rooftop verandas.

Languages: English

Facilities:

Activities:

Le Mirage Desert Lodge & Spa 11

Lodge $$$
23km or 19min S of Sesriem
w139486

Tel: +264(0)63 683 019, Cell: +264(0)81 355 7749,
Fax: +264(0)88 654 7536
lemirage@resdest.com,
www.mirage-lodge.com

27 Luxury, en-suite rooms; each with air-conditioning, safe, mini-bar and coffee/tea facilities.

Languages: English

Facilities: FC

Activities:

N/aan ku sê Charity Lodge & Wildlife Sanctuary 12

Guest Farm $$$
81km or 1h17min E of Sesriem
w139530

Tel: +264(0)63 293 417, Cell: +264(0)81 859 4608
neuras@naankuse.com
www.naankuselodge.com

Six en-suite chalets, all rooms have large twin beds and their own private verandas overlooking the bushveld.

Languages: English, Italian, Afrikaans

Facilities:

Activities:

Sesriem Rest Camp 13

Park Camp $$
At Sesriem
w138658

Tel: +264(0)61 285 7200, Fax: +264(0)61 224 900
reservations@nwr.com.na
www.nwr.com.na

24 Campsites, each with own braai area, tap and power point. Communal ablution facilities.

Languages: English

Facilities:

Activities:

Sossus Dune Lodge 14

Lodge $$$
6km or 8min SSW of Sesriem
w204883

Tel: +264(0)61 285 7200, Fax: +264(0)61 224 900
reservations@nwr.com.na
www.nwr.com.na

25 Thatched chalets on raised wooden platforms, each with a private veranda.

Languages: English

Facilities:

Activities

Sossus Oasis 15

Transit Camp $$
1km or 1min SE of Sesriem
w228698

Tel: +27(0)21 930 4564, Fax: +27(0)21 914 9930
reservations@sossus-oasis.com
www.sossus-oasis.com

Campsites, each with its own ablutions, power point, braai, paved veranda and wash-up facility.

Languages: English

Facilities: FC

Activities:

Sossusvlei Lodge 16

Lodge $$
At Sesriem
w137830

Tel: +27(0)21 930 4564, Fax: +27(0)21 914 9930
reservations@sossusvleilodge.com
www.sossusvleilodge.com

Spacious, air-conditioned, en-suite, twin-bed room with patio.

Languages: English

Facilities:
Activities:

The Desert Homestead / Horse Trails 17

Bed and Breakfast $$
36km or 30min SE of Sesriem
w139282

Tel: +264(0)61 240 020, Fax: +264(0)63 293 301
desert.homestead281@gmail.com
www.deserthomesteadlodge.com

Individual two-bed chalets with en-suite toilet/shower.

Languages: English

Facilities:
Activities:

The Elegant Desert Lodge 18

Lodge $$
43km or 37min SE of Sesriem
w140858

Tel: +264(0)63 693 253, Cell: +264(0)81 302 8255
info@the-elegant-collection.com
www.elegant-desert-lodge.com

29 Tastefully-furnished, modern, stylish rooms with en-suite bathrooms. Enjoy the atmosphere of a true Namibian guest lodge.

Languages: English, Afrikaans

Facilities:
Activities:

Tsauchab River Camp 19

Self-catering $$
72km or 1h7min E of Sesriem
w141990

Tel: +264(0)64 464 144, Fax: +264(0)88 613 906
reservations@logufa.com
www.tsauchab.com

Six private, exclusive chalets situated on the banks of the Tsauchab River.

Languages: English

Facilities:
Activities:

Tsauchab River Camp 20

Lodge Camp $
72km or 1h7min E of Sesriem
w138094

Tel: +264(0)64 464 144, Cell: +27(0)81 232 6721,
Fax: +264(0)88 613 906
reservations@logufa.com,
www.tsauchab.com

12 Private campsites on the banks of the Tsauchab River.

Languages: English

Facilities:
Activities:

Zebra River Lodge 21

Lodge $$
94km or 1h34min E of Sesriem
w139529

Tel: +264(0)63 693 265, Fax: +264(0)63 693 266
eden@africaonline.com.na
www.zebra-river-lodge.com

13 Double or triple, en-suite rooms. Five rock chalets. Honeymoon suite. And seven standard family rooms.

Languages: English

Facilities:
Activities:

Sesriem Canyon (photo: Karin Theron)

Solitaire

(photo: Peter Barber)

IN 1948 WILLEM VAN COLLER bought 33 000 hectares of land to farm with Karakul. His wife named the farm Solitaire as the word has two possible meanings: a single set diamond or loneliness. Both are equally fit to describe this one-of-a-kind place. Van Coller later built the small shop and petrol pump as well as a small chapel. He sold the farm in 1968 and today it's a popular stopover for tourists travelling to and from the Namib-Naukluft National Park.

Traveller Description

Solitaire is situated at the junction of the C14 (Walvis Bay - Bethanie) and the C24 (Rehoboth - Sossusvlei), both are major tourist routes through the Namib-Naukluft National Park. It offers a welcome stop to dusty, weary travellers and has become famous for the apple crumble served at the bakery. Café Van der Lee serves excellent Italian coffee and on a hot day the ice cold drinks go down well.

Solitaire is surrounded by nice campsites and lodging options. This small outpost has a bakery, restaurant, general dealer with ATM, fuel station and the Solitaire Lodge.

Travel Info

If you're on your way to Solitaire on the C14 from Walvis Bay, please take care at the Guab Pass. There are a lot of accidents in this area as people tend to speed because they've become used to driving in the desert where they can see for miles. The road surface of the narrow pass is normally good but drivers tend to cut corners. This is dangerous as people sometimes stop in the road to take photographs.

TRAVEL TIP! The roads in the area often get washed away in heavy rains. Fill up your tank as this will be the last fuel station in many miles.

Town Info:
Tow-in: +264(0)81 129 7490

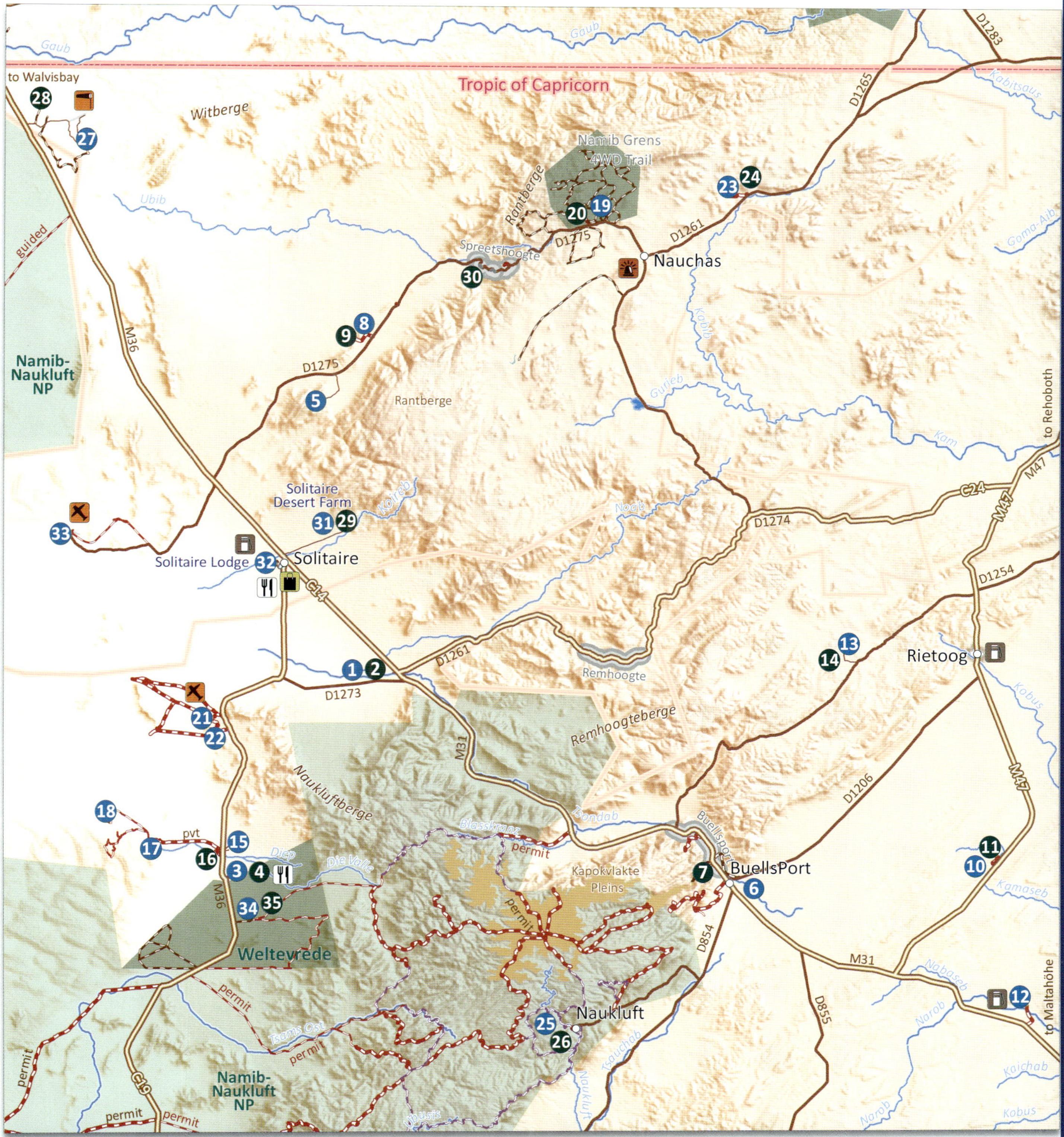

Ababis Guest Farm	1

Game/Safari Lodge $$
14km or 10min SE of Solitaire
w138439

Tel: +264(0)63 293 362, Cell: +264(0)81 782 8965,
Fax: +264(0)63 293 364
info2@ababis-gaestefarm.de,
www.ababis-gaestefarm.de

Four standard twin/ triple rooms with en-suite bathrooms, two comfort rooms with air-conditioning and a self-catering house.

Languages: English, German

Facilities: VISA @

Activities:

Ababis Guest Farm	2

Farm Camp $$
14km or 10min SE of Solitaire
w227575

Tel: +264(0)63 293 362, Cell: +264(0)81 782 8965,
Fax: +264(0)63 293 364
info2@ababis-gaestefarm.de,
www.ababis-gaestefarm.de

Four shady campsites, each with own braai. Hot water ablutions with separate kitchen sink. No electricity. Campers can dine at the guest house.

Languages: English, German

Facilities: VISA @

Activities:

Agama River Camp	3

Lodge $$
32km or 24min S of Solitaire
w143273

Tel: +264(0)61 250 725 , Cell: +264(0)81 242 7375,
Fax: +264(0)88 637 655
agama@resdest.com,
www.agamarivercamp.com

Ten chalets furnished to fit your needs.

Languages: English

Facilities: VISA FC @

Activities:

Solitaire

Agama River Camp — 4

Camping — $$
32km or 25min S of Solitaire
w143271

Tel: +264(0)63 683 245, Cell: +264(0)81 127 0177, Fax: +264(0)63 683 245
agama@resdest.com,
www.agamarivercamp.com

Eight private, shaded campsites with hot water. Each campsite has its own washing-up facility, braai and light.

Languages: English

Facilities:
Activities:

Barchan Dune Retreat — 5

Guest Farm — $$
28km or 23min NNE of Solitaire
w140472

Tel: +264(0)62 682 031, Cell: +264(0)81 231 6204
barchan@iway.na
www.barchandunes.com

Six en-suite rooms built into a dune. Delightful meals served in the dining room.

Languages: English, German, Afrikaans

Facilities:
Activities:

BuellsPort Guest Farm — 6

Guest Farm — $$
53km or 39min SE of Solitaire
w138451

Tel: +264(0)63 293 371, Fax: +264(0)88 625 749
info@buellsport.com
www.buellsport.com

Comfortable accommodation in newly-refurbished luxury and standard rooms. Venue is a working cattle and horse stud farm.

Languages: English, German, Afrikaans

Facilities:
Activities:

BuellsPort Guest Farm Campsites — 7

Farm Camp — $$
51km or 38min SE of Solitaire
w139531

Tel: +264(0)63 693 371, Fax: +264(0)88 625 749
info@buellsport.com
www.buellsport.com

Exclusive campsite for one group, or a shared campsite where more than one group can stay at a time. Hot water via wood oven. Report to guest farm reception on arrival.

Languages: English, German, Afrikaans

Facilities:
Activities:

Camp Gecko — 8

Tented Camp — $$
30km or 23min NNE of Solitaire
w138462

Fax: +264(0)62 572 017, Cell: +264(0)81 270 9064
geckonam@iway.na
www.campgecko.net

Bush tents, double-storey bush hideaways with en-suite bathrooms, and self-catering huts.

Languages: English, German, French, Italian, Spanish etc.

Facilities:
Activities:

Camp Gecko — 9

Camping — $
31km or 27min NNE of Solitaire
w232785

Fax: +264(0)62 572 017, Cell: +264(0)81 270 9064
geckonam@iway.na
www.campgecko.net

Four campsites with natural shade, and two private campsites with private ablution blocks and braai area.

Languages: English, German, French, Italian, Spanish etc.

Facilities:
Activities:

Capricorn Rest Camp — 10

Guest House — $$
83km or 1h1min ESE of Solitaire
w261542

Fax: +264(0)88 641 407, Cell: +264(0)81 364 2931
capricorn@iway.na
www.capricorn-naukluft.weebly.com

Four bungalows equipped with twin beds, warm shower & toilet, terrace, braai and electrical lights. Parking nearby.

Languages: English, German

Facilities:
Activities:

Capricorn Rest Camp — 11

Camping — $
83km or 1h2min ESE of Solitaire
w254426

Fax: +264(0)88 641 407, Cell: +264(0)81 364 2931
capricorn@iway.na
www.capricorn-naukluft.weebly.com

Four campsites with shadow netting, braais and benches/tables. Communal toilet and shower. Ideal stopover spot.

Languages: English, German

Facilities:
Activities:

Gamis Farm — 12

Guest Farm — $$
84km or 1h7min ESE of Solitaire
w198563

Cell: +264(0)81 128 4959
gamisfarm@mtcmobile.com.na
www.gamisfarm.com

Two double rooms with one shared bathroom. Also, self-catering units with dining room, kitchen, two verandas, and outside toilet.

Languages: English, German, Afrikaans

Facilities:
Activities:

Garies Rest Camp — 13

Guest House — $$
71km or 1h11min E of Solitaire
w139429

Cell: +264(0)81 409 2829
garies@iway.na

Seven rooms accommodating up to 14 adults. Located on the C24 between Windhoek & Sossusvlei, this venue is a great stopover.

Languages: English, Afrikaans, Dutch

Facilities:
Activities:

Garies Rest Camp — 14

Camping — $
71km or 1h11min E of Solitaire
w361586

Cell: +264(0)81 409 2829
garies@iway.na

Three private campsites which can accommodate up to 10 people. Shared ablutions.

Languages: English, Afrikaans, Dutch

Facilities:
Activities:

Moon Mountain Lodge — 15

Tented Camp — $$$
29km or 21min SSW of Solitaire
w232430

Tel: +264(0)67 240 901 , Cell: +264(0)81 122 2626
reservations@travel-weaver.com
www.moonmountain.biz

17 units, each with a private plunge pool. Rooms offer great views of adjacent mountain ranges and desert landscape.

Languages: English, Afrikaans

Facilities:
Activities:

Namib Desert Campsite 16

Lodge Camp $$
54km or 42min NNE of Sesriem
w222192

Tel: +264(0)61 427 200 , Cell: +264(0)81 129 2424, Fax: +264(0)61 251 863
info@gondwana-collection.com, store.gondwana-collection.com

Small campsites with little shade. Good ablutions with hot showers. Campers welcome to use lodge facilities, including Wi-Fi. Reservations advisable.

Languages: English, Afrikaans

Facilities:

Activities:

Namib Desert Lodge 17

Lodge $$
59km or 52min NNE of Sesriem
w138126

Tel: +264(0)61 427 200 , Cell: +264(0)81 129 2424, Fax: +264(0)61 251 863
info@gondwana-collection.com, store.gondwana-collection.com

Comfortable, en-suite rooms with private verandas. Venue is spread out along the foot of fossilized Namib dunes. Reservations mandatory.

Languages: English, Afrikaans

Facilities:

Activities:

Namib Dune Star Camp 18

Lodge $$$
42km or 1h17min SW of Solitaire (of which 25km is 4WD)
w361032

Tel: +264(0)61 427 200, Fax: +264(0)61 251 863
info@gondwana-collection.com
store.gondwana-collection.com

This venue has nine cabins, fairly widely spaced. Each cabin has a large, en-suite bedroom and a spacious deck. Reservations mandatory.

Languages: English

Facilities:

Activities:

Namibgrens Guest Farm 19

Guest Farm $$
54km or 52min NE of Solitaire
w138879

Tel: +264(0)61 304 051, Cell: +264(0)81 148 5020, Fax: +264(0)61 304 053
enquiry@namibgrens.com, www.namibgrens.com

The Old Guest House offers 11 en-suite rooms; there are also luxury villas and a thatched house. Venue is a fully-operational cattle and sheep farm. Reservations mandatory.

Languages: English

Facilities:

Activities:

Namibgrens Guest Farm 20

Farm Camp $$
56km or 55min NE of Solitaire (of which 1km is 4WD)
w142538

Tel: +264(0)61 304 051, Cell: +264(0)81 148 5020, Fax: +264(0)61 304 053
enquiry@namibgrens.com, www.namibgrens.com

12 Private campsites, each accommodating 2 - 30. All sites have their own private, open-air ablutions. Wood is available.

Languages: English

Facilities:

Activities:

Namib Naukluft Lodge 21

Lodge $$
18km or 13min SSW of Solitaire
w137527

Tel: +264(0)61 372 106, Fax: +264(0)61 215 356
trixim@afex.com.na
www.namib-naukluft-lodge.com

Comfortable, en-suite rooms with private patios. Enjoy a meal on the veranda or at the boma near the pool.

Languages: English, German

Facilities:

Activities:

Namib Naukluft Lodge - Soft Adventure Camp 22

Lodge $$
19km or 16min SSW of Solitaire
w233696

Tel: +264(0)61 372 106, Fax: +264(0)61 215 356
nnlreservations@afex.com.na
www.namib-naukluft-lodge.com

15 Private, en-suite chalets. There are dining and kitchen facilities, and an entertainment area.

Languages: English, German, Afrikaans

Facilities:

Activities:

Nauams Rest Camp 23

Guest Farm $
70km or 1h6min NE of Solitaire
w361571

Tel: +264(0)61 307 251, Cell: +264(0)81 469 7219
info@nauamsrestcamp.com
www.nauamsrestcamp.com

Three en-suite rooms in the main house, with cooling fan and safe. Meals on request.

Languages: English, Afrikaans

Facilities:

Activities:

Nauams Rest Camp 24

Farm Camp $
70km or 1h6min NE of Solitaire
w219503

Tel: +264(0)61 307 251, Cell: +264(0)81 469 7219
info@nauamsrestcamp.com
www.nauamsrestcamp.com

Each campsite is equipped with its own braai area, toilet & basin, and kitchenette area with clean running water.

Languages: English, Afrikaans

Facilities:

Activities:

Naukluft Camp 25

Bed and Breakfast $$
75km or 1h2min SSE of Solitaire
w274151

Tel: +264(0)61 285 7200, Cell: +264(0)81 144 3478
reservations@nwr.com.na
www.nwr.com.na

Six single/double bush chalets. The venue is located southeast of Solitaire in the Naukluft mountains.

Languages: English

Facilities:

Activities:

Naukluft Camp 26

Camping $$
75km or 1h3min SSE of Solitaire
w137887

Tel: +264(0)61 285 7200, Cell: +264(0)81 144 3478
reservations@nwr.com.na
www.nwr.com.na

21 Campsites with braai facilities. Communal ablutions with showers, flush toilets and wash basins.

Languages: English

Facilities:

Activities:

Rostock Ritz Desert Lodge 27

Lodge $$$
51km or 43min NNW of Solitaire
w137818

Tel: +264(0)64 694 000, Cell: +264(0)81 258 5722, Fax: +264(0)88 616 556
rostock@iway.na, www.rostock-ritz-desert-lodge.com

14 Standard rooms, three luxury suites and two wheel-chair-friendly rooms. All with ceiling fan, toilet, shower and private balcony.

Languages: English, German, Afrikaans

Facilities:

Activities:

Solitaire

Rostock Ritz Desert Lodge 28

Lodge Camp $
47km or 38min NNW of Solitaire (of which 2km is 4WD)
w137473

Tel: +264(0)64 694 000, Cell: +264(0)81 258 5722,
Fax: +264(0)88 616 556
rostock@iway.na,
www.rostock-ritz-desert-lodge.com

Four campsites with solar lights, braai facilities and taps. Ablutions include showers and four flush toilets. There's a big lapa with fireplace.

Languages: English, German, Afrikaans

Facilities: VISA FC

Activities:

Solitaire Desert Farm 29

Farm Camp $
7km or 8min ENE of Solitaire
w140695

Tel: +264(0)67 240 901, Cell: +264(0)81 232 9483,
Fax: +264(0)67 240 902
camping@solitairenamibia.com,
www.solitairenamibia.com

Solitaire Guest Farm has three campsites with braai areas and ablution facilities. It's best to call ahead to make sure they have campsites available.

Languages: English

Facilities: VISA @

Activities:

Spreetshoogte 30

Farm Camp $
42km or 35min NE of Solitaire (of which 1km is 4WD)
w139894

Fax: +264(0)88 651 7719, Cell: +264(0)81 268 8259
namibpersiestoet@africaonline.com.na

Spacious campsites, each with its own toilet, shower, solar lights and braai.

Languages: English, Afrikaans

Facilities:

Activities:

Solitaire Desert Farm 31

Lodge $$$
7km or 8min ENE of Solitaire
w140702

Tel Direct: +264(0)62 572 024
sdf-reservations@solitairenamibia.com
Book Online: www.solitairenamibia.com

Solitaire Desert Farm offers en-suite rooms equipped with all the modern amenities, on a B&B basis. Includes air-conditioning, Wi-Fi, private decks, pool, open thatch bar and restaurant, marked hiking trails and a 45 000 acre private conservation area. Courtesy shuttle from airstrip for fly-ins. Reserve online or call ahead for camping availability.

Languages: English, German, Afrikaans, Portuguese, French

Facilities: VISA @ Activities:

Solitaire Lodge 32

Lodge $$$
In Solitaire w232882

Tel Direct: +264(0)63 293 621
reservations@solitairenamibia.com
Book Online: www.solitairenamibia.com

B&B accommodation offered in spacious en-suite rooms, with air-conditioning, coffee/tea service, outdoor seating areas, courtyard pool and garden, There's also Wi-Fi, a bakery, bar and restaurant, and an air strip. Venue offers marked hiking trails and activies within a 45 000 acre private conservation area.

Languages: English, German, Afrikaans, Portuguese, French

Facilities: VISA FC @

Activities:

Tsondab Valley Scenic Reserve 33

Bed and Breakfast $$$
27km or 36min W of Solitaire
w206439

Tel: +264(0)63 293 383 , Cell: +264(0)81 128 3266,
Fax: +264(0)88 636 266
info@tsondab.com,
www.tsondab.com

Five en-suite bungalows with great views of the dunes. Tsondab Valley is a private nature reserve bordering the Namib Naukluft National Park.

Languages: English

Facilities:

Activities:

Weltevrede Guest Farm 34

Guest Farm $$
37km or 28min S of Solitaire (of which 2km is 4WD)
w138023

Tel: +264(0)63 293 208, Cell: +264(0)81 685 3433,
Fax: +264(0)63 293 209
info@weltevredeguestfarm.com,
www.weltevredeguestfarm.com

12 En-suite bungalows with private verandas, and three family rooms with en-suite bathrooms.

Languages: English, Afrikaans

Facilities: VISA @

Activities:

Weltevrede Guest Farm 35

Farm Camp $
37km or 28min S of Solitaire (of which 2km is 4WD)
w270500

Tel: +264(0)63 293 208, Cell: +264(0)81 685 3433,
Fax: +264(0)63 293 209
info@weltevredeguestfarm.com,
www.weltevredeguestfarm.com

Four campsites, each with its own toilet, shower and basin.

Languages: English, Afrikaans

Facilities: VISA @

Activities:

(photo: Frank Höppener)

(photo: Frank Höppener)

NORTH NAMIBIA

Near the Waterberg. (photo: Heiner Dillmann)

IN THE AREA NORTH OF WINDHOEK you'll come across a few major settlements like Okahandja, Otjiwarongo, Otavi and Grootfontein. The landscape is covered in grey grass and speckled with acacia trees, shrubs and termite mounds that point skywards meters high. There are many hunting and cattle farms in this area so you should be very aware of wild animals along the roads and avoid travelling at night.

The most notable attraction of this region is the Waterberg Plateau National Park. This is a beautiful and lush park with orange cliffs, diverse vegetation and wildlife like rhino, roan, sable, buffalo, leopard, eland, giraffe and many more. The best way to explore the park is on foot and there are various routes up the sides of the mountain - the view from the top is truly spectacular. With over 200 bird species, among them Namibia's only breeding population of Cape vulture, the Waterberg is rich in natural heritage.

Grootfontein is a good place to stock up on supplies if you plan to travel further north towards the Kavango region and the Caprivi Strip. The Hoba Meteorite, which weighs around 50 ton, can be seen at Grootfontein.

The Von Bach Dam near Okahandja supplies most of the capital's water.

Even if you only visited for the views, a trip to the Waterberg Plateau National Park would be worthwhile. (photo: Heiner Dillmann)

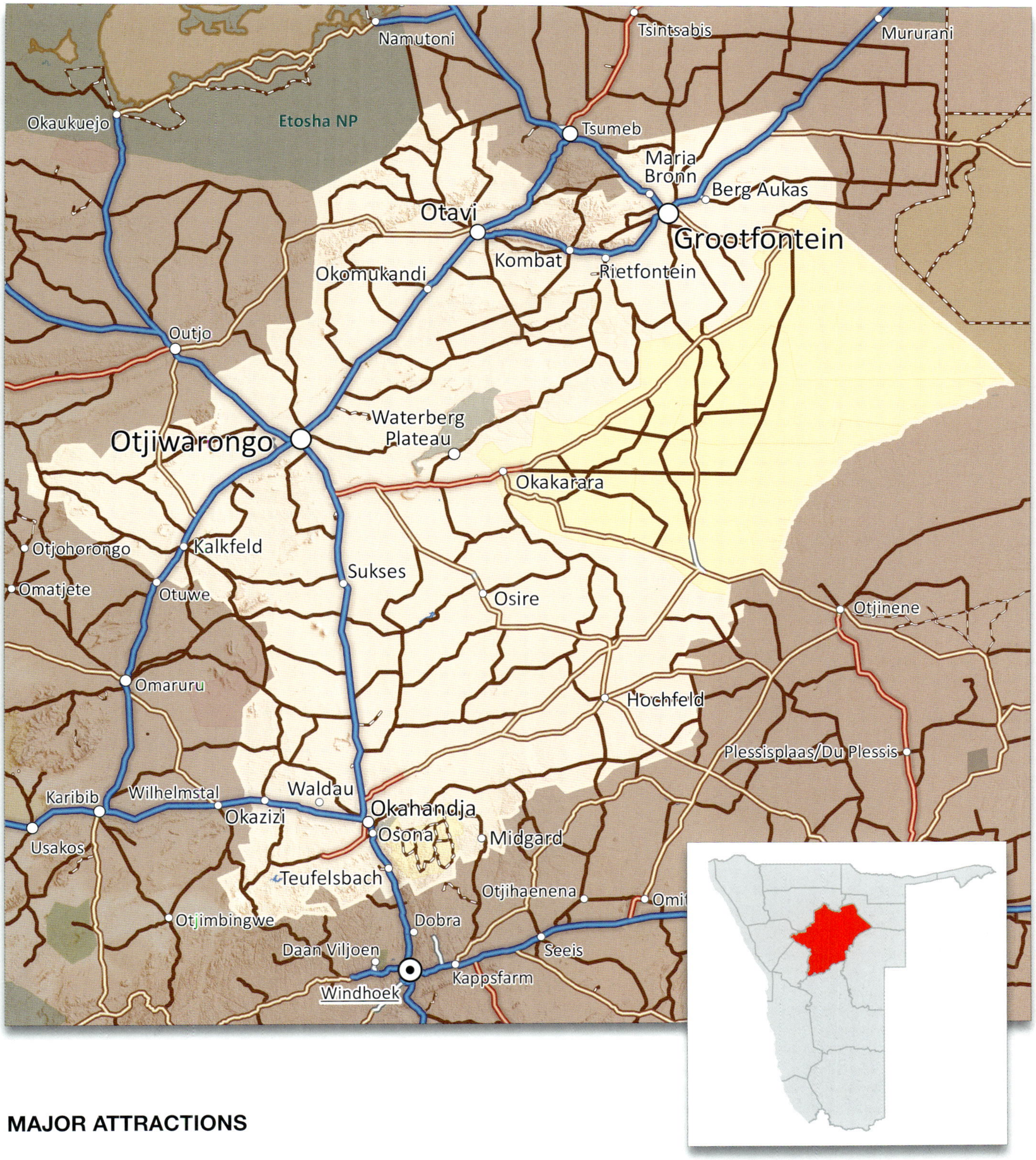

MAJOR ATTRACTIONS

- Waterberg Plateau National Park
- The Von Bach Dam Nature Reserve and holiday resort is popular for water sports and bird watching.
- Three Herero Chiefs were buried in the Herero cemetery in Okahandja and each year in August the Herero people from all over Namibia come to honour their past leaders.
- At the craft market in Okahandja local artists sell their wooden crafts and carvings made from indigenous wood.
- The Gross Barmen Hot Springs Resort has thermal baths and a spa offering luxurious treatments.
- The Grootfontein Museum is housed in the old German Schutztruppe fort.
- Hoba is the world's heaviest metallic meteorite.
- The Cheetah Conservation Fund does research, conservation and education about cheetahs.
- Dinosaur footprints can be viewed at Weavers' Rock Guest Farm.

More details about the attractions are available on our website (www.tracks4africa.co.za) or our Guide App. Our GPS Map can navigate you to each of these attractions.

Grootfontein

(photo: Karin Theron)

HISTORICALLY, GROOTFONTEIN WAS KNOWN to the Herero people as Otjivanda (the place of leopards) and to the Nama as Gei-ous (the big spring). However, in 1885 a group of families from northwest South Africa settled here and referred to it as Grootfontein which means Great Spring. Today this is the centre of a large cattle farming community with mining also prevalent in the area. Grootfontein used to house an important military base in the time when the South African Defence Force was still active in Namibia. The area has a relatively good summer rainfall and turns into a lush paradise of green, purple, blue and red hues as the Jacaranda and Flamboyant trees bloom.

Traveller Description

The section of Namibia around Grootfontein, Otavi and Tsumeb is often referred to as the Otavi Triangle. Grootfontein is a well-developed town which forms the gateway to the north-eastern parts of Namibia. The town offers a variety of good accommodation and is the ideal stop-over for travellers heading for the Kavango and Zambezi regions, it offers both medical services and mechanical repairs.

Grootfontein is best known for being situated 20km from the Hoba Meteorite - the largest known meteorite on Earth. The Ghaub Cave on the guest farm of the same name is well worth a visit, as is a baobab tree with a trunk circumference of 18.5m and branches of up to 12m on the farm Keibeb, 60km north of Grootfontein on the D2855. This tree is romantically known as Tree 1063. In town the old German Schutztruppe fort houses a museum which expounds on local history.

Travel Info

The landline number for the tow-in services is +264(0)67 242 556 (Blitz Panel beaters). The number given on the following page is for the Grootfontein Private Hospital. The Spar has a butchery, bakery and a good selection of fresh produce as well as a coffee shop. Gas refills are offered at the Agri-Mark.

TRAVEL TIP! Because of the vet fence at Mururani you're not allowed to take raw meat or unpasteurised milk from Rundu to Grootfontein; it's allowed if you're travelling north from Grootfontein to Rundu.

Town Info:

Hospital:	+264(0)67 240 064 / +264(0)67 240 066
Police:	+264(0)67 242 111
Doctor:	+264(0)67 243 198
Tow-in:	+264(0)81 242 5430 / +264(0)81 342 4090
Tourism:	+264(0)67 242 456

Turn page to see second map

Bush Baby Safaris — 1

Lodge $

13km or 16min WNW of Grootfontein

w267887

Tel: +264(0)67 243 391, Cell: +264(0)81 829 3711, Fax: +264(0)67 243 393
info@bush-babycamping.com,
www.bush-babycamping.com

Lodge rooms, bush bungalows, tented camp and self-catering flat.

Languages: English

Facilities: VISA FC @

Activities:

Bush Baby Safaris — 2

Camping $

13km or 16min WNW of Grootfontein

w267888

Tel: +264(0)67 243 391, Cell: +264(0)81 829 3711, Fax: +264(0)67 243 393
info@bush-babycamping.com,
www.bush-babycamping.com

Campsites for motorhomes, rooftop tents, caravans or just tents. Campers are allowed to use the lapa area.

Languages: English

Facilities: VISA FC @

Activities:

Dornhügel Guest Farm — 3

Guest Farm $$

39km or 32min ENE of Grootfontein

w137966

Tel: +264(0)67 240 439, Cell: +264(0)81 686 3666, Fax: +264(0)67 240 439
dornhuegel@resdest.com,
www.dornhuegel.com

Three double and two single en-suite rooms. There's a restaurant, pool and library on this 11 000ha farm.

Languages: English, German, Afrikaans

Facilities: @

Activities:

Fiume Lodge — 4

Game/Safari Lodge $$

38km or 33min NE of Grootfontein

w261544

Tel: +264(0)67 240 486, Cell: +264(0)81 595 7855, Fax: +264(0)88 641 161
fiumelodge@iway.na,
www.fiume-lodge.com

Nine stylish chalets with garden views. Venue is ideal stopover for travellers en-route to the north of Namibia.

Languages: English, Afrikaans

Facilities: VISA FC @

Activities:

Fiume Lodge — 5

Farm Camp $

38km or 33min NE of Grootfontein

w262359

Tel: +264(0)67 240 486, Cell: +264(0)81 595 7855, Fax: +264(0)88 641 161
fiumelodge@iway.na,
www.fiume-lodge.com

Single campsite in the middle of the bush. No electricity. Traditional camp environment.

Languages: English, Afrikaans

Facilities: VISA FC @

Activities:

Grootfontein

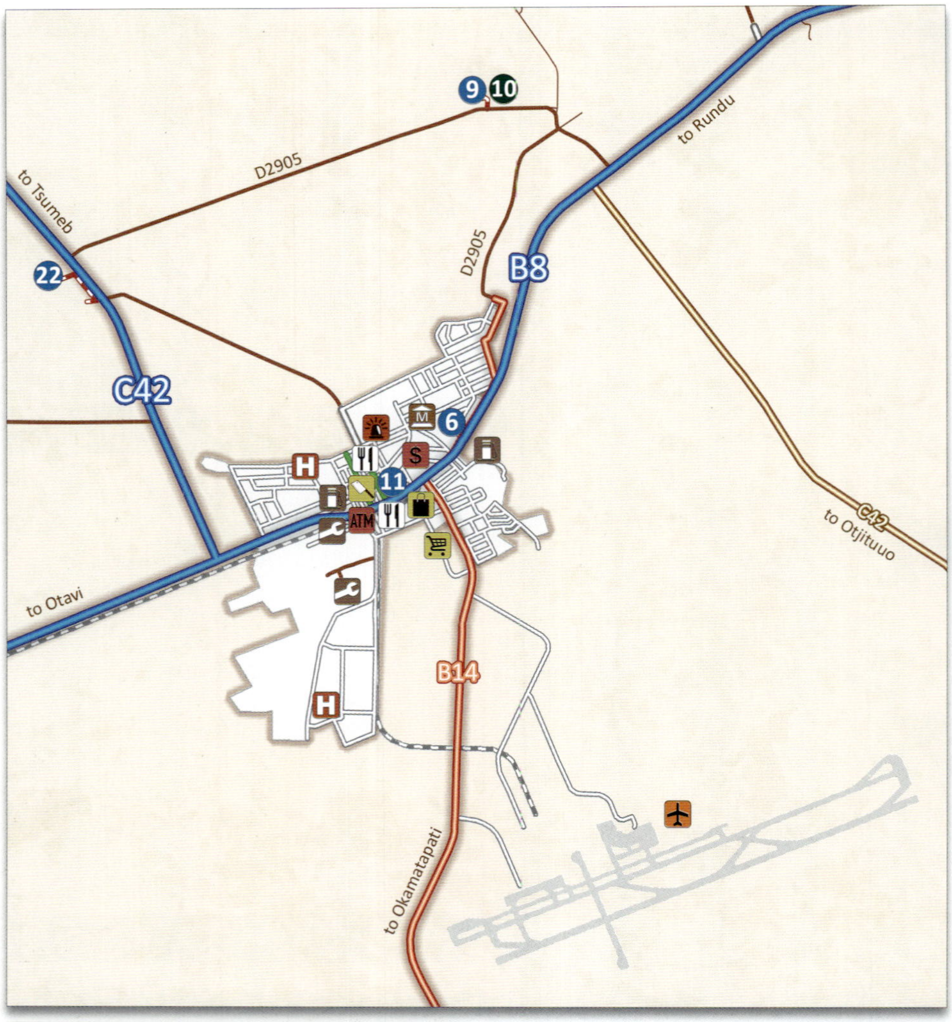

Greenhill Chalets 6

Bed and Breakfast $$
c/o Ericson & Galton St, Grootfontein
w255831

Tel: +264(0)67 243 545, Cell: +264(0)81 382 4138, Fax: +264(0)88 652 1581
greenhillchalets@iway.na

Six double, en-suite chalets of which four are thatched and self-catering. Some chalets have double or twin beds.

Languages: English, Afrikaans

Facilities: FC @

Kalkfontein Guest Farm 7

Guest Farm $$
14km or 12min ENE of Grootfontein
w198416

Tel: +264(0)67 243 731, Cell: +264(0)81 273 3806, Fax: +264(0)67 243 516
kalkfonteinguesthouse@gmail.com

Luxury rooms with and without air-conditioning. There's a pool and an allegedly tame lion...

Languages: English, Afrikaans

Facilities:

Activities:

Kalkfontein Guest Farm 8

Farm Camp $
14km or 12min ENE of Grootfontein
w361589

Tel: +264(0)67 243 731, Cell: +264(0)81 273 3806, Fax: +264(0)67 243 516
kalkfonteinguesthouse@gmail.com

Camp with hot-water ablutions (via 'donkey' system).

Languages: English, Afrikaans

Facilities:

Activities:

Maori Rest Camp 9

Bed and Breakfast $
6km or 8min NNE of Grootfontein
w361605

Fax: +264(0)67 242 351, Cell: +264(0)81 347 1005
katpaul@iway.na
www.maoricamp.wix.com

En-suite rondavels and rooms with shared ablutions.

Languages: English, German, French

Facilities: FC

Maori Rest Camp 10

Camping $
6km or 8min NNE of Grootfontein
w235660

Fax: +264(0)67 242 351, Cell: +264(0)81 347 1005
katpaul@iway.na
www.maoricamp.wix.com

Free firewood for each campsite. Clean ablutions - two toilets and two showers. Facilities include laundry troughs.

Languages: English, German, French

Facilities: FC

Meteor Travel Inn 11

Inn $$
33 Okavango Avenue, Grootfontein
w206897

Tel: +264(0)67 242 078, Cell: +264(0)81 128 3999, Fax: +264(0)67 243 072
methold1@iway.na

Comfortable rooms with en-suite bathrooms, air-conditioning and fans.

Languages: English, Afrikaans

Facilities: VISA

Activities:

Mururani Camp 12

Self-catering $
126km or 1h21min NE of Grootfontein
w361513

Tel: +264(0)67 240 355, Cell: +264(0)81 295 7585, Fax: +264(0)67 240 355
murucamp@mweb.com.na

One room bungalow with own toilet and shower. Plus a self-catering bungalow.

Languages: English, Afrikaans

Facilities:

Activities:

Mururani Camp 13

Camping $
126km or 1h21min NE of Grootfontein
w194686

Tel: +264(0)67 240 355, Cell: +264(0)81 295 7585, Fax: +264(0)67 240 355
murucamp@mweb.com.na

Small, neat, grassed campsite with clean ablutions. Facilities include bar and lapa.

Languages: English, Afrikaans

Facilities:

Activities:

Omega Rest Camp 14

Farm Camp $
82km or 1h2min SSW of Grootfontein
w207998

Tel: +264(0)67 231 560, Fax: +264(0)88 617 392
omega-rc@iway.na

Basic camping facilities on cattle farm that's part of the Ngarangombe or Eland Conservancy.

Languages: English, Afrikaans, German

Facilities:

Activities:

Paradise Rest Camp 15

Self-catering $
85km or 1h5min NE of Grootfontein
w302690

Tel: +264(0)67 232 620, Cell: +264(0)81 617 0998
paradiserestcamp@yahoo.com
www.paradise-rest-camp.webnode.com

Chalets overlooking a lake as well as luxury tents with own beds and bedding.

Languages: English

Facilities:

Activities:

Paradise Rest Camp 16

Camping $
85km or 1h5min NE of Grootfontein
w302688

Tel: +264(0)67 232 620, Cell: +264(0)81 617 0998
paradiserestcamp@yahoo.com
www.paradise-rest-camp.webnode.com

Fully-equipped campsites with ablution blocks.

Languages: English

Facilities:

Activities:

Peace Garden Lodge 17

Guest House $$
7km or 5min WSW of Grootfontein
w138796

Tel: +264(0)67 243 648, Fax: +264(0)67 243 749
reservations@peacegardenlodge.info
www.peacegardenlodge.info

20 Standard chalets (17 twin and three double rooms), each en-suite (shower & toilet), with air-conditioner, DStv, fridge and coffee/tea facilities.

Languages: English, German, Afrikaans

Facilities:

Activities:

Pondoki Rest Camp 18

Guest House $
7km or 7min NE of Grootfontein
w361597

Fax: +264(0)88 613 847, Cell: +264(0)81 310 6795
pondoki1@iway.na

One family room, eight double rooms and one tour guide room. Rooms equipped with air-conditioning, TV, DStv, bar fridge, private bathroom and porch.

Languages: English, Afrikaans

Facilities:

Activities:

Pondoki Rest Camp 19

Camping $
7km or 7min NE of Grootfontein
w241487

Fax: +264(0)88 613 847, Cell: +264(0)81 310 6795
pondoki1@iway.na

Eight campsites, three with power points near the lodge and five in the bush without power points.

Languages: English, Afrikaans

Facilities:

Activities:

Roy's Rest Camp 20

Self-catering $$
59km or 40min NE of Grootfontein
w261556

Tel: +264(0)67 240 302, Fax: +264(0)67 240 264
royscamp@iway.na
www.roys-rest-camp.com

Comfortable, rustic bungalows with en-suite bathrooms, fans and mosquito nets. There's also a bar, restaurant and lounge deck.

Languages: English, Afrikaans

Facilities:

Activities:

Roy's Rest Camp 21

Farm Camp $
59km or 40min NE of Grootfontein
w138422

Tel: +264(0)67 240 302, Fax: +264(0)67 240 264
royscamp@iway.na
www.roys-rest-camp.com

13 Campsites with clean ablutions and washing facilities. Amenities include a bar and curio shop.

Languages: English, Afrikaans

Facilities:

Activities:

Seidarap Guest House 22

Guest House $$
4km or 9min NW of Grootfontein
w207619

Tel: +264(0)67 242 817, Cell: +264(0)81 240 4969,
Fax: +264(0)88 650 7222
seidarap@seidarap.com, www.seidarap.com

Six spacious double rooms with en-suite facilities. Have sundowners on the balcony while enjoying views of the Otavi Mountains.

Languages: English, German, Afrikaans

Facilities:

Activities:

Wildacker Guest Farm 23

Guest Farm $$
141km or 1h43min ENE of Grootfontein
w360756

Tel: +264(0)67 241 004, Fax: +264(0)67 241 005
info@wildacker-namibia.com
www.wildacker-namibia.com

Comfortable bungalows.

Languages: English

Facilities:

Activities:

Roy's Rest Camp, near Grootfontein. See listing above. (photo: Frank Höppener)

Hochfeld

(photo: Johann Groenewald)

HOCHFELD IS A SMALL TOWN located on the C30 main route between Gobabis and Otjiwarongo. The name means High Field in German, due to its higher altitude. It's mainly a farming community as the area has plenty of borehole water and a reasonably good rainfall. There are two manganese mines in the area.

Traveller Description

Hochfeld is situated at the junction of the C30 and C31 and is within reach of Windhoek, Okahandja and Gobabis. It's the ideal stopover for travellers using the Trans-Kalahari (Buitepos/Mamuno) border post, or those heading north for Etosha National Park or Kaokoland, especially if you prefer to avoid the highway and Windhoek.

Travel Info

At the time of writing, a business failure in the town resulted in the closure of the local hotel, fuel pumps, restaurant and general dealer so make advance enquiries if you intend to stop here. This said, good accommodation was still offered in town as well as in the surrounding area.

TRAVEL TIP! Be cautious as there are many wild animals on the C30 between Gobabis and Otjiwarongo, especially around Hochfeld.

Town Info:

Police: +264(0)62 549 132
Tow-in: +264(0)81 129 7490

Farm Wildernis 1

Guest Farm $$
59km or 47min N of Hochfeld
w272018

Tel: +264(0)62 518 044, Cell: +264(0)81 243 2224,
Fax: +264(0)62 518 044
wildernis@iway.na, www.farmwildernis.com

Double rooms with bath or shower. Extra single bed can be added to each room. Wi-Fi in all rcoms. Venue is a 10 000 hectare cattle farm, guest and hunting farm.

Languages: ?English, German, Afrikaans, Herero

Facilities:
Activities:

Hochfeld Guesthouse 2

Guest House $
In Hochfeld
w255872

Tel: +264(0)62 549 073, Cell: +264(0)81 124 5940
rolliheiser@gmail.com
www.hochfeldguesthouse.com

Comfortable single and double rooms. Restaurant on site. Tours offered to nearby olive farm.

Languages: English, German, Afrikaans

Facilities:

Hochfeld Guesthouse 3

Camping $
In Hochfeld
w255873

Tel: +264(0)62 549 073, Cell: +264(0)81 124 5940
rolliheiser@gmail.com
www.hochfeldguesthouse.com

Shaded campsites for up to 20 people. Neat ablutions and braai areas. Campers can also eat at the restaurant.

Languages: English, German, Afrikaans

Facilities:

Ombeameiata Guest Farm 4

Guest Farm $$
20km or 18min ENE of Hochfeld
w139110

Tel: +264(0)62 549 023, Fax: +264(0)62 549 029
zwar-ombe@namibnet.com

Accommodation in single or double rooms.

Languages: English, German

Facilities:
Activities:

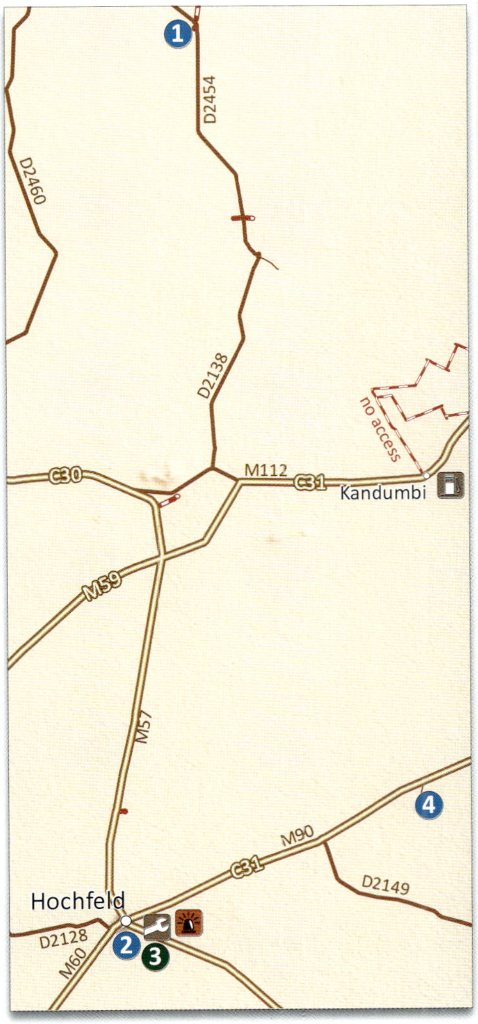

(photo: Neil Harrison)

Okahandja

(photo: Junior Bruwer)

OKAHANDJA IS A HISTORIC TOWN, founded around 1800 by two tribes, the Herero and the Nama. The name means 'The place where two rivers join', the two rivers being the Okakango and the Okumita, both of which only flow after good summer rains.

In 1827 the first European, a German pastor, visited and in 1844 two missionaries were permanently assigned here. After a long period of conflict between the local tribes, a big battle took place between the Herero and Nama groups in 1850 at what is today known as Moordkoppie (translation: murder hill). In 1872 the Rhenish Mission Society founded a mission station and a military post was established in Okahandja in 1894, which is recognized as the town's official founding date.

Okahandja is an important town for the Herero people and the traditional burial place for their chiefs; Maharero day is celebrated annually at the end of August. On this day thousands of Hereros come to Okahandja to pay tribute to their fallen heroes. They make a grand procession, featuring brightly-coloured traditional dresses, military outfits and prancing horses.

Traveller Description

Okahandja is located at the junction of the B1 and B2 - the main route to Swakopmund and the coast. It is the business centre for surrounding cattle and game farms and has a growing industrial area and excellent infrastructure. Many travellers find Okahandja just the place to take a break on their travels, especially if they didn't stop at the capital city, Windhoek.

Just 25km southwest of Okahandja is the Gross Barmen Hot Springs Resort, a popular tourist attraction. The Von Bach Dam southeast of town is a popular resort for water sports, angling and bird-watching. The town is also an important outlet for woodcarvers from the north, who sell their carvings at the craft markets on a co-operative basis, next to the main road at both entrances to Okahandja.

Travel Info

Major shops for travellers include Spar and Woolworths as well as Agra for gas refill.

TRAVEL TIP! The Biltong Padstal, found as you enter on the B2 from Swakopmund, is worth a stop and is open all year round.

Town Info:

Hospital:	+264(0)62 503 030
Police:	+264(0)62 503 013
Doctor:	+264(0)81 144 4911
Tow-in:	+264(0)62 504 250

Elegant Farmstead 1

Lodge $$
30km or 29min ENE of Okahandja
w254427

Tel: +264(0)61 301 934, Cell: +264(0)81 302 8255,
info@the-elegant-collection.com
www.the-elegant-farmstead.com

Eleven rooms with air-conditioning and en-suite bathrooms. Venue is conveniently situated for stopovers.

Languages: English, German, Afrikaans

Facilities:
Activities:

Gross Barmen Resort 2

Resort $$$
27km or 20min SW of Okahandja
w361567

Tel: +264(0)61 285 7200
reservations@nwr.com.na
www.nwr.com.na

Family and bush chalets, on either a B&B or self-catering basis.

Languages: English

Facilities:
Activities:

Gross Barmen Resort 3

Holiday Resort Camp $$
27km or 21min SW of Okahandja
w142539

Tel: +264(0)61 285 7200
reservations@nwr.com.na
www.nwr.com.na

Shaded campsites with ablution facilities and field kitchen.

Languages: English

Facilities:
Activities:

Guestfarm Katjapia 4

Guest Farm $$
52km or 54min ENE of Okahandja
w239943

Tel: +264(0)62 503 713, Cell: +264(0)81 279 8858
tasha@katjapia.com
www.katjapia.com

Five air-conditioned double rooms. Breakfast and dinner served in the main building. Venue is a working cattle farm.

Languages: English, German, Dutch, Afrikaans

Facilities:
Activities:

Guestfarm Katjapia 5

Farm Camp $
52km or 54min ENE of Okahandja
w361730

Tel: +264(0)62 503 713, Cell: +264(0)81 279 8858
tasha@katjapia.com
www.katjapia.com

Cosy camp located near the banks of the Swakop River. Ablution facilities. Breakfast and dinner can be arranged. Venue is a working cattle farm.

Languages: English, German, Dutch, Afrikaans

Facilities:
Activities:

King's Highway Rest Camp 6

Self-catering $
2km or 3min SSE of Okahandja
w140146

Tel: +264(0)62 504 086, Fax: +264(0)62 504 086
okahandja@kingshighway.co.za
www.kingshighway.co.za

Bungalows with communal bathroom. Chalets have their own bathrooms (toilet & shower), and are better equipped.

Languages: English, Afrikaans

Facilities:
Activities:

King's Highway Rest Camp 7

Camping $
2km or 3min SSE of Okahandja
w261548

Tel: +264(0)62 504 086, Fax: +264(0)62 504 086
okahandja@kingshighway.co.za
www.kingshighway.co.za

Seven campsites, each has its own power point, braai, light and water. Communal ablution facilities.

Languages: English, Afrikaans

Facilities:
Activities:

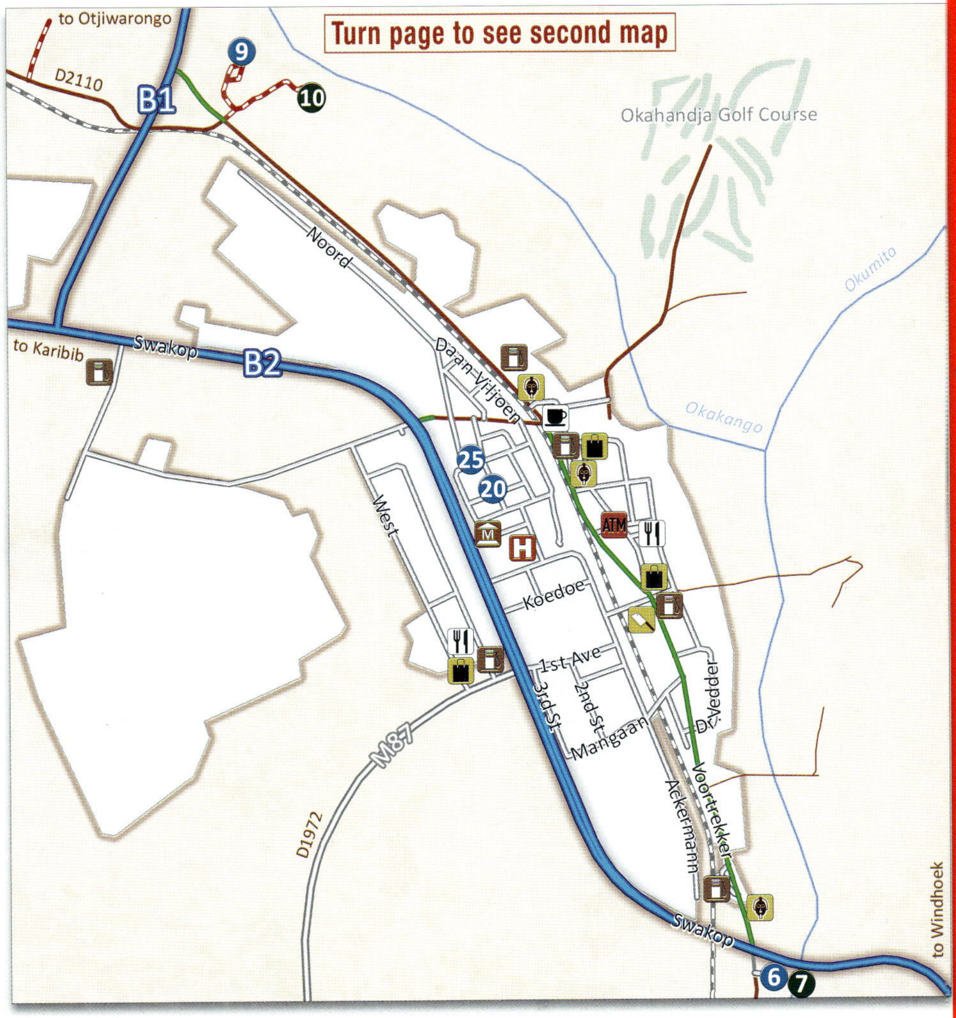

Okahandja

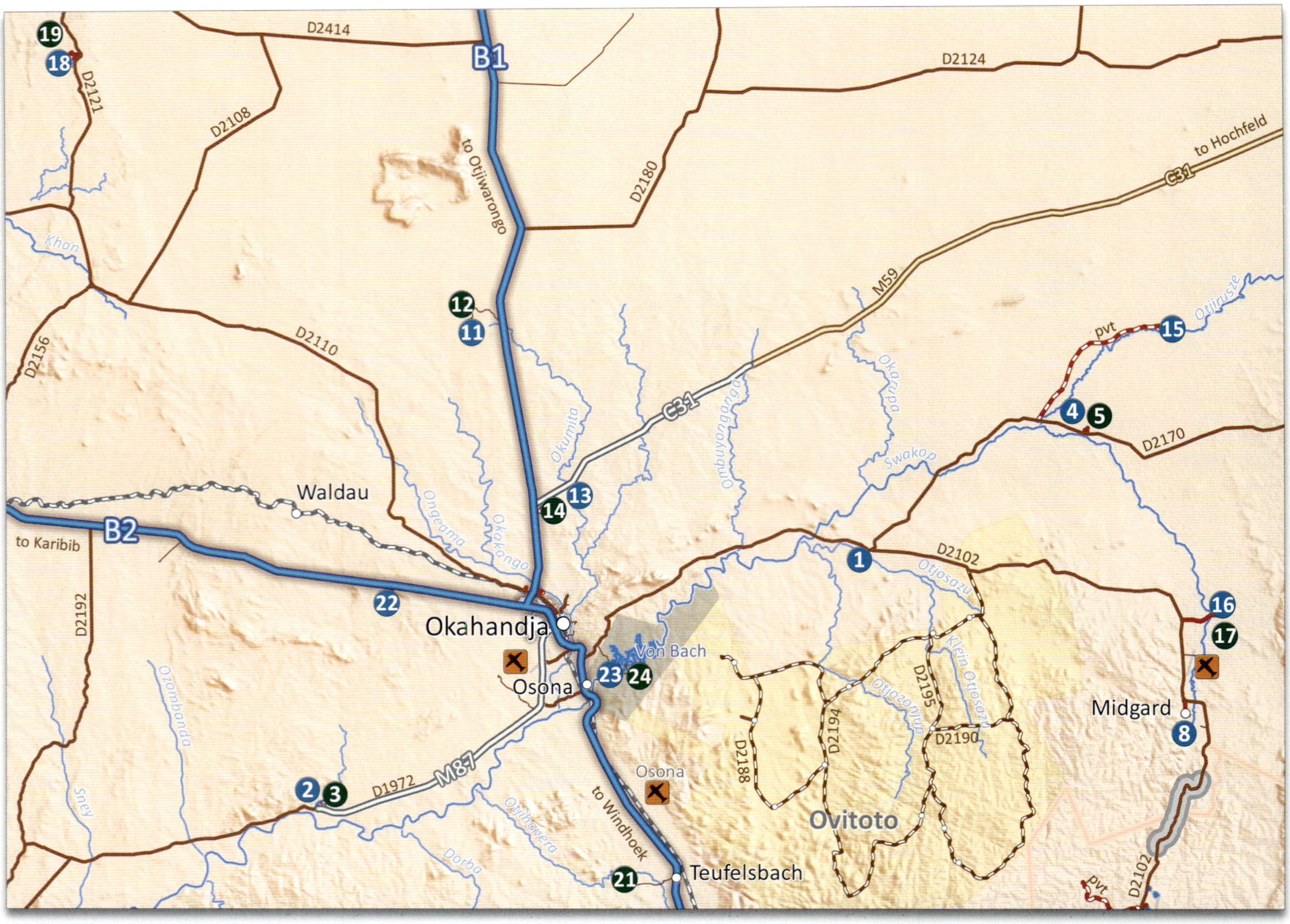

Midgard Country Estate — 8

Lodge $$

63km or 1h8min E of Okahandja

w138484

Tel: +264(0)61 431 8000, Fax: +264(0)62 503 818

midgard.res@ol.na

www.midgardcountryestate.com

Guest rooms and family units, all en-suite with air-conditioning, TV, internet and coffee/tea facilities.

Languages: English

Facilities:

Activities:

Okahandja Country Hotel — 9

Hotel $$

3km or 4min NW of Okahandja

w140270

Tel: +264(0)62 504 299, Cell: +264(0)81 291 6086, Fax: +264(0)62 502 551

okalodge@africaonline.com.na, www.okahandjahotel.com

24 En-suite rooms with air-conditioning and DStv. Venue has a la carte restaurant.

Languages: English

Facilities:

Activities:

Okahandja Country Hotel - Ombonde Campsite — 10

Lodge Camp $

4km or 6min NW of Okahandja

w227984

Tel: +264(0)62 504 299, Fax: +264(0)62 502 551

okalodge@africaonline.com.na

www.okahandjahotel.com

Shaded campsites with powers points, plus hot showers and flush toilet. Some campsites have grass and some have taps.

Languages: English

Facilities:

Activities:

Omatozu Safaris — 11

Tented Camp $$

29km or 28min NNW of Okahandja

w239948

Fax: +264(0)88 634 064, Cell: +264(0)81 643 7100

info@omatozu.com

www.omatozu.com

Three luxury permanent tents, each with en-suite bathroom, air-conditioner and safe.

Languages: English, German, Afrikaans

Facilities:

Activities:

Omatozu Safaris — 12

Farm Camp $

29km or 29min NNW of Okahandja

w239946

Fax: +264(0)88 634 064, Cell: +264(0)81 643 7100

info@omatozu.com

www.omatozu.com

Four campsites, each with own ablution facilities, power point, light and braai. Caravans allowed. Venue is on a game farm.

Languages: English, German, Afrikaans

Facilities:

Activities:

Ombo Rest Camp — 13

Self-catering $$

13km or 12min N of Okahandja

w217079

Tel: +264(0)62 502 003, Cell: +264(0)81 206 2791, Fax: +264(0)62 503 768

omborestcamp@africaonline.com.na, www.ombo-rest-camp.com

Two bed, double bed or luxury, self-catering, family bungalows (air-conditioned).

Languages: English

Facilities:

Activities:

Ombo Rest Camp 14

Transit Camp $
13km or 12min N of Okahandja
w217078

Tel: +264(0)62 502 003, Cell: +264(0)81 206 2791,
Fax: +264(0)62 503 768
omborestcamp@africaonline.com.na,
www.ombo-rest-camp.com

Camping facilities for tents and caravans. Includes warm showers, power points and braai area.

Languages: English

Facilities:

Activities:

Otjiruze Guest Farm 15

Guest Farm $$$
62km or 1h10min ENE of Okahandja
w139500

Tel: +264(0)62 503 106, Cell: +264(0)81 209 5035,
Fax: +264(0)88 632 640
info@otjiruze.com,
www.otjiruze.com

Comfortable rooms with en-suite bathrooms. Furnished in modern style.

Languages: English, German, Afrikaans

Facilities:

Activities:

Otjiterazu Guest Farm 16

Guest Farm $$
59km or 1h5min E of Okahandja
w141661

Tel: +264(0)62 502 441, Cell: +264(0)81 290 0656,
Fax: +264(0)62 501 640
otjiterazu@iway.na,
www.otjiterazu.com

Seven, en-suite double rooms with full housekeeping. Meals and drinks available. Pool and entertainment area.

Languages: English, German, Afrikaans, Herero, Damara

Facilities:

Activities:

Otjiterazu Guest Farm 17

Farm Camp $$
59km or 1h5min E of Okahandja
w261555

Tel: +264(0)62 501 640, Cell: +264(0)81 290 0656,
Fax: +264(0)62 501 640
otjiterazu@iway.na,
www.otjiterazu.com

Two campsites, with ablution facilities. Firewood available.

Languages: English, German, Afrikaans, Herero, Damara

Facilities:

Activities:

Ovita Wildlife Lodge 18

Lodge $
70km or 59min NW of Okahandja
w277771

Cell: +264(0)81 303 6253
info@ovitawildlife.com
www.ovitawildlife.com

Comfortable, lake-facing rooms with desk, outdoor seating area and safety deposit box. There's also braai facilities and a terrace.

Languages: English

Facilities:

Activities:

Ovita Wildlife Lodge 19

Wilderness Camp $
70km or 59min NW of Okahandja
w277772

Cell: +264(0)81 303 6253
info@ovitawildlife.com
www.ovitawildlife.com

Shaded campsites with power points and hot showers. Campers have access to lodge facilities.

Languages: English

Facilities:

Activities:

Sylvanette Guest House 20

Guest House $
311 Hoogenhout St, Okahandja
w138431

Tel: +264(0)62 505 550, Cell: +264(0)81 127 3759,
Fax: +264(0)62 505 560
sylvanette@iway.na,
www.sylvanette.com

Nine en-suite rooms. Meals provided on request. Laundry services available.

Languages: English

Facilities:

Activities:

Teufelsbach River Camp 21

4WD Trail Camp $
29km or 25min SSE of Okahandja
w141477

Tel: +264(0)61 246 225, Cell: +264(0)81 245 2433

The campsite is part of the Okahandja 4WD Trail, which stretches over two farms: Teufelsbach and Bergquell.

Languages: Afrikaans

Facilities:

Activities:

The Rock Lodge 22

Lodge $$
14km or 10min WNW of Okahandja
w139476

Tel: +264(0)62 506 000, Cell: +264(0)81 725 5991,
Fax: +264(0)62 503 170
info@rocklodge.com.na,
www.rocklodge.com.na

Four houses with en-suite rooms, as well as 14 large en-suite rooms with private verandas.

Languages: English

Facilities:

Activities:

Tungeni Von Bach Dam Resort 23

Resort $$
11km or 20min SE of Okahandja
w139612

Tel: +264(0)62 500 162, Cell: +264(0)85 571 2814,
Fax: +264(0)62 500 166
info@tungeni.com,
www.tungeni.com

11 Luxury family chalets and 11 deluxe single room chalets, all fully furnished.

Languages: English

Facilities:

Activities:

Tungeni Von Bach Dam Resort 24

Holiday Resort Camp $
11km or 20min SE of Okahandja
w262941

Tel: +264(0)62 500 162, Cell: +264(0)85 571 2814,
Fax: +264(0)62 500 166
info@tungeni.com,
www.tungeni.com

Basic campsites, each with its own ablution facilities, boat parking bay, braai and small thatched structure.

Languages: English

Facilities:

Activities:

Villa Nina Guest House 25

Guest House $$
327 Conradie St, Okahandja
w141869

Tel: +264(0)62 502 497, Cell: +264(0)81 127 3753,
Fax: +264(0)62 503 350
info@namibiatouristik.de

Comfortable, en-suite, air-conditioned rooms, all well equipped. Self-catering and backpacker accommodation also offered.

Languages: English

Facilities:

Activities:

Otavi

(photo: Johann Groenewald)

OTAVI'S NAME IS DERIVED from the Herero word 'Ondavi' which means 'branch of a tree.' The towns of Otavi, Tsumeb and Grootfontein define an area known as the Otavi, Golden, or Maize Triangle.

The Otavi Mountain is located in the middle of this triangle and it's also referred to as the Otavi Mountain Land.

In the past the area was known for its mineral wealth but most deposits have been exhausted so these days it's largely an agricultural town. Maize is farmed on the fertile plain beneath the Otavi Mountains and it's also a prolific cattle and game farming area.

In 1915 the German Army was defeated at Otavi by South African troops, this led to the signing of the Khorab Peace Treaty. The Khorab Memorial (erected in 1920) is testimony to this event and can be found a few miles outside Otavi.

Traveller Description

Otavi is often used as a refreshment stop when heading towards Etosha National Park. The town itself doesn't hold much attraction for tourists but the surrounding area has beautiful and interesting geological features; for this reason many travellers prefer to stay on guest farms in the surrounding mountains. Since the Total garage complex on the B1 has an ATM, restaurant, kiosk and a shop selling biltong, most travellers don't even drive into town.

Travel Info

Although there's a clinic in town (contact number +264(0)81 161 6544) travellers are advised to consult the private doctor. In town you'll find a Spar with a butchery, a bakery and a coffee shop.

TRAVEL TIP! Tourist attractions in the area include the Khorab Memorial, Ghaub Caves, Hoba meteorite and Mundulea Nature Reserve.

Town Info:

Police: +264(0)67 234 006
Doctor: +264(0)67 234 272
Tow-in: +264(0)81 405 2468
+264(0)81 430 1579

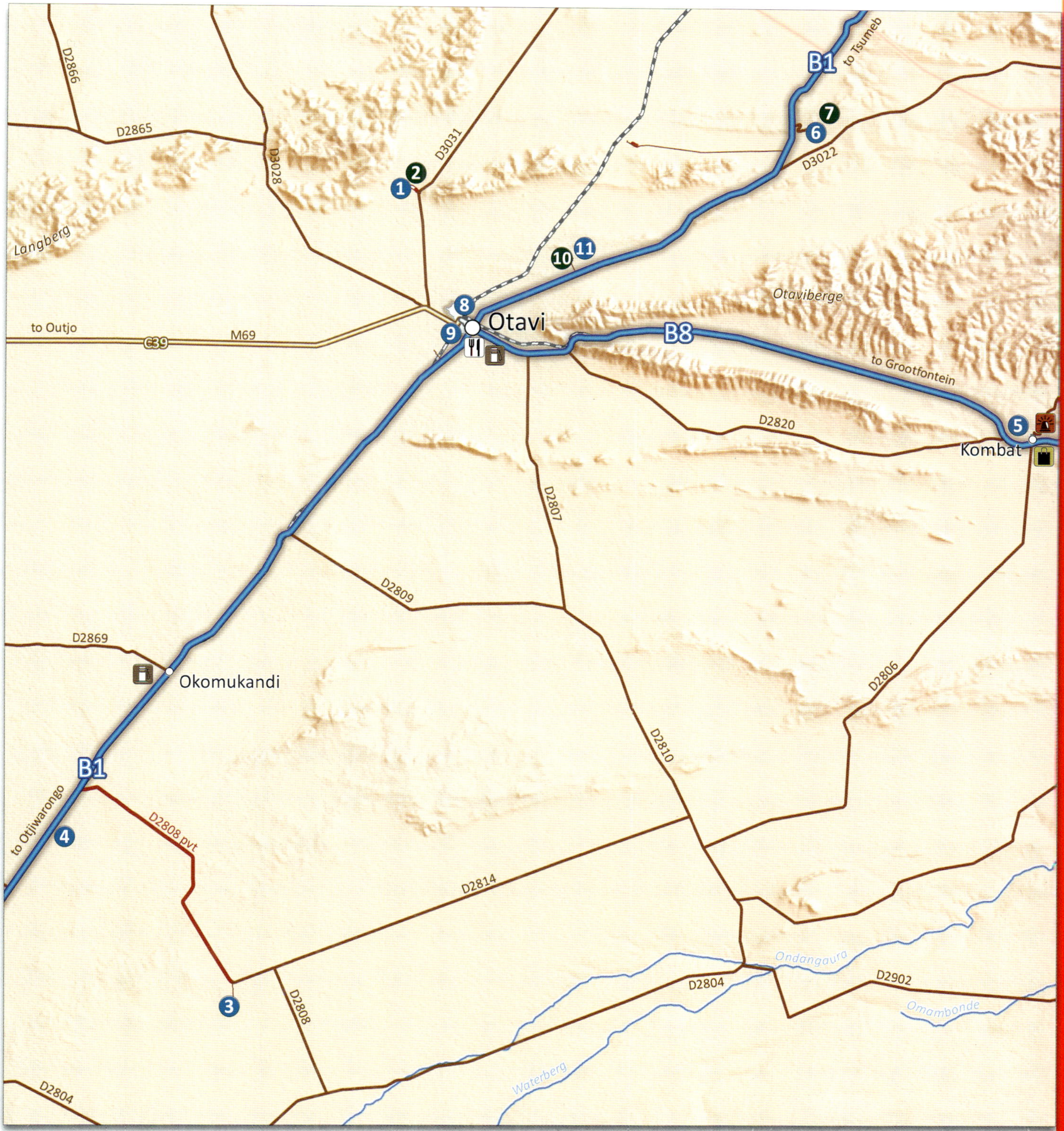

Otavi

Gabus Game Ranch — 1

Lodge — $$
13km or 14min NNW of Otavi
w254410

Tel: +264(0)67 234 291, Cell: +264(0)81 127 9278
kuehl@afol.com.na
www.gabusnamibia.com

Luxurious, en-suite air-conditioned rooms; all overlooking a waterhole ideal for game and bird watching.

Languages: English, German, Afrikaans

Facilities:

Activities:

Gabus Game Ranch — 2

Lodge Camp — $
13km or 14min NNW of Otavi
w361599

Tel: +264(0)67 234 291, Cell: +264(0)81 127 9278
kuehl@afol.com.na
www.gabusnamibia.com

Two campsites with two bathrooms (toilets, showers and big basin), small basin and braai. Campsites have roof for shade

Languages: English, German, Afrikaans

Facilities:

Activities:

Kambaku Safari Lodge — 3

Lodge — $
64km or 44min SSW of Otavi
w142791

Tel: +264(0)67 306 292, Fax: +264(0)67 306 293
reservations@kambaku.com
www.kambaku.com

The lodge is built from natural materials and blends in with surroundings. Guests can relax on the garden terrace or at the pool.

Languages: English

Facilities:

Activities:

Khoi-Khoi Guest House — 4

Guest House — $$
46km or 27min SW of Otavi
w361728

Tel: +264(0)67 309 048, Cell: +264(0)81 280 6318
khoikhoi@iway.na
www.khoikhoiguesthouse.com

16 Comfortable rooms. The venue is situated next to the B1 road, between Otjiwarongo and Otavi.

Languages: English

Facilities:

Activities:

Kombat Lodge Inn — 5

Lodge — $
39km or 35min ESE of Otavi
w192398

Tel: +264(0)67 231 149, Cell: +264(0)81 300 9169,
Fax: +264(0)67 231 151
kombatlodge@gmail.com, kombatlodgeblog.wordpress.com

Private, luxurious, en-suite double rooms. Plus a fully-equipped camp with ablution facilities.

Languages: English, Afrikaans

Facilities:

Activities:

Ohange Safari Lodge — 6

Game/Safari Lodge — $$
137km or 2h5min ENE of Otavi
w279639

Tel: +264(0)61 250 725, Cell: +264(0)81 242 7375,
Fax: +264(0)88 637 655
reservation@resdest.com, www.ohange.com

En-suite bungalows under shady trees. Plus family huts and self-catering rooms.

Languages: English

Facilities:

Activities:

Ohange Safari Lodge — 7

Lodge Camp — $
137km or 2h5min ENE of Otavi
w279638

Tel: +264(0)61 250 725, Cell: +264(0)81 242 7375,
Fax: +264(0)88 637 655
reservation@resdest.com, www.ohange.com

One campsite inside stable block. And another small, shaded campsite next to a game pathway.

Languages: English

Facilities:

Activities:

Otavi Gardens Hotel — 8

Hotel — $
6 Park st, Otavi
w140271

Tel: +264(0)67 234 334, Cell: +264(0)81 285 4388,
Fax: +264(0)67 234 335
sandraotavi@iway.na

10 Luxurious, thatched chalets with en-suite bathrooms. Amenities include a bar, a la carte restaurant and DStv.

Languages: English, Afrikaans

Facilities:

Palmenecke Guesthouse — 9

Lodge — $
96 Hertzog Avenue, Otavi
w252791

Tel: +264(0)67 234 199, Cell: +264(0)81 285 8400,
Fax: +264(0)67 234 199
senotavi@iafrica.com.na, www.palmenecke.co.za

Five affordable, comfortable, en-suite rooms with air-conditioning and TV. Other facilities include a fully-equipped kitchen, secure parking and bar.

Languages: English, Afrikaans

Facilities:

Activities:

Zum Potjie Rest Camp — 10

Farm Camp — $
10km or 9min NE of Otavi
w138221

Tel: +264(0)67 234 300, Cell: +264(0)81 245 6554,
Fax: +264(0)67 234 300
info@zumpotjie.com, www.zumpotjie.com

Twelve grassed campsites, each with tap and lights. Communal ablutions.

Languages: English, German, Afrikaans

Facilities:

Activities:

Zum Potjie Rest Camp Chalets — 11

Self-catering — $$
10km or 9min NE of Otavi
w261568

Tel: +264(0)67 234 300, Cell: +264(0)81 245 6554,
Fax: +264(0)67 234 300
info@zumpotjie.com, www.zumpotjie.com

Bungalows on a full board or B&B basis. Visit the small farm museum or enjoy the walking trails and pool.

Languages: English, German, Afrikaans

Facilities:

Activities:

"There are no foreign lands.
It is the traveler only who is foreign."

Robert Louis Stevenson,
The Silverado Squatters

(photo: Neil Harrison)

Otjiwarongo

(photo: Johann Groenewald)

THE HERERO PEOPLE WERE THE ORIGINAL SETTLERS here and they called this place Otjiwarongo which means 'Place Where Fat Cattle Graze'. The name is still appropriate as Otjiwarongo is home to some of Namibia's largest beef producers.

As with many other Namibian towns, Otjiwarongo developed around a Rhenish missionary station; a treaty was signed in 1891 between German missionaries and the Herero chief. A German military garrison arrived in 1904 when a bloody war broke out between the Hereros and Germans. The town was officially founded in 1906 with the implementation of a narrow-gauge railway from Swakopmund to the mines at Otavi and Tsumeb. Today, Otjiwarongo is the biggest business centre in the province and one of Namibia's fastest-growing settlements. It still has a large population of German speakers and the German influence is evident in its buildings.

Traveller Description

The town has all the amenities usually associated with a large town and is a favourite refreshment stop for travellers en-route to Etosha National Park.

The main point of interest here is Locomotive No 41 which was originally brought from Germany to haul ore between Tsumeb and the port at Swakopmund, it was finally retired from service in 1960. Otjiwarongo is a beautiful town and has a lot to offer; what's more, some of Namibia's best-known private game farms and nature reserves are located nearby.

The town is in close proximity to the popular Waterberg Plateau National Park and other attractions include the Okonjima Cheetah and Leopard Rehabilitation Centre where visitors can get close to cheetahs, as well as Crocodile Ranch, Namibia's first crocodile farm.

Travel Info

Gas refills are offered at Cymot. There's a Wimpy, Spar and Pick 'n Pay in town. The hospital number listed at the top of the facing page, under Town Info, is for the Medi-Clinic private hospital.

Other Useful Numbers:

State Hospital: +264(0)67 300 900
Atex Panelbeaters and Canopies: +264(0)67 303 796

TRAVEL TIP! Otjiwarongo is the ideal place to stock up on your supplies if you are heading for Etosha's Anderson Gate.

Town Info:

Hospital: +264(0)67 303 734, Police: +264(0)67 300 600, Doctor: +264(0)67 308 700, Tow-in: +264(0)81 124 3476, Tourism: +264(0)67 303 830

Turn page to see second map

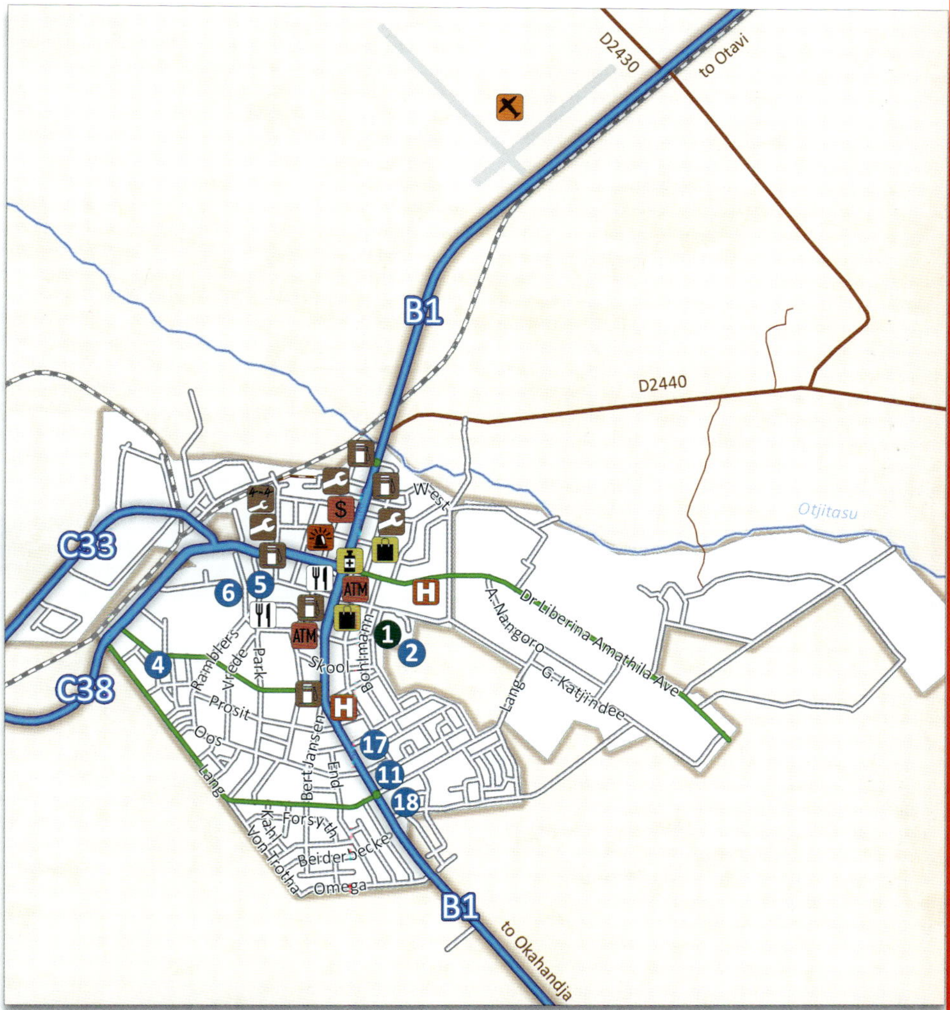

Acacia Park Rest Camp — 1

Caravan Park — $
13/308 Hindenburg St, Otjiwarongo
w141728

Tel: +264(0)67 303 100 Cell: +264(0)81 216 0004,
Fax: +264(0)88 613 766
caciapa@mweb.com.na

Each campsite has an electricity point and braai area. Pets are welcome and children under 5 stay free. Good security.

Languages: English, Afrikaans

Facilities:
Activities:

Acacia Park SC Chalets — 2

Self-catering — $
13/308 Hindenburg St, Otjiwarongo
w222187

Tel: +264(0)67 303 100, Cell: +264(0)81 216 0004,
Fax: +264(0)88 613 766
caciapa@mweb.com.na

One and two bedroom chalets, or a mobile unit. Children under 5 stay for free. Pets welcome.

Languages: English, Afrikaans

Facilities:
Activities:

Aloegrove Safari Lodge — 3

Game/Safari Lodge — $$
39km or 59min ENE of Otjiwarongo
w200952

Fax: +264(0)88 614 602, Cell: +264(0)81 127 4103
aloegrove@mweb.com.na
www.aloegrove.com

Six en-suite rooms, each with own balcony with views of the Waterberg and savannah.

Languages: English, German, Afrikaans

Facilities:
Activities:

Bush Pillow Guest House — 4

Guest House — $$
47 Son Road, Otjiwarongo
w207756

Tel: +264(0)67 303 885, Cell: +264(0)81 128 5323,
Fax: +264(0)88 618 695
artworks@iafrica.com.na,
www.bushpillow.co.za

Rooms with en-suite bathroom (shower, toilet and basin), mini fridge, Wi-Fi and laundry services.

Languages: English

Facilities:
Activities:

Casa Forno Country Hotel — 5

Hotel — $$
21 Ramblers Rd, Otjiwarongo
w360357

Tel: +264(0)67 304 504, Cell: +264(0)81 159 0000,
Fax: +264(0)67 304 916
casaforno@iway.na,
www.casaforno.com

Rooms with private bathroom, TV with satellite channels and kettle.

Languages: English

Facilities:
Activities:

Otjiwarongo

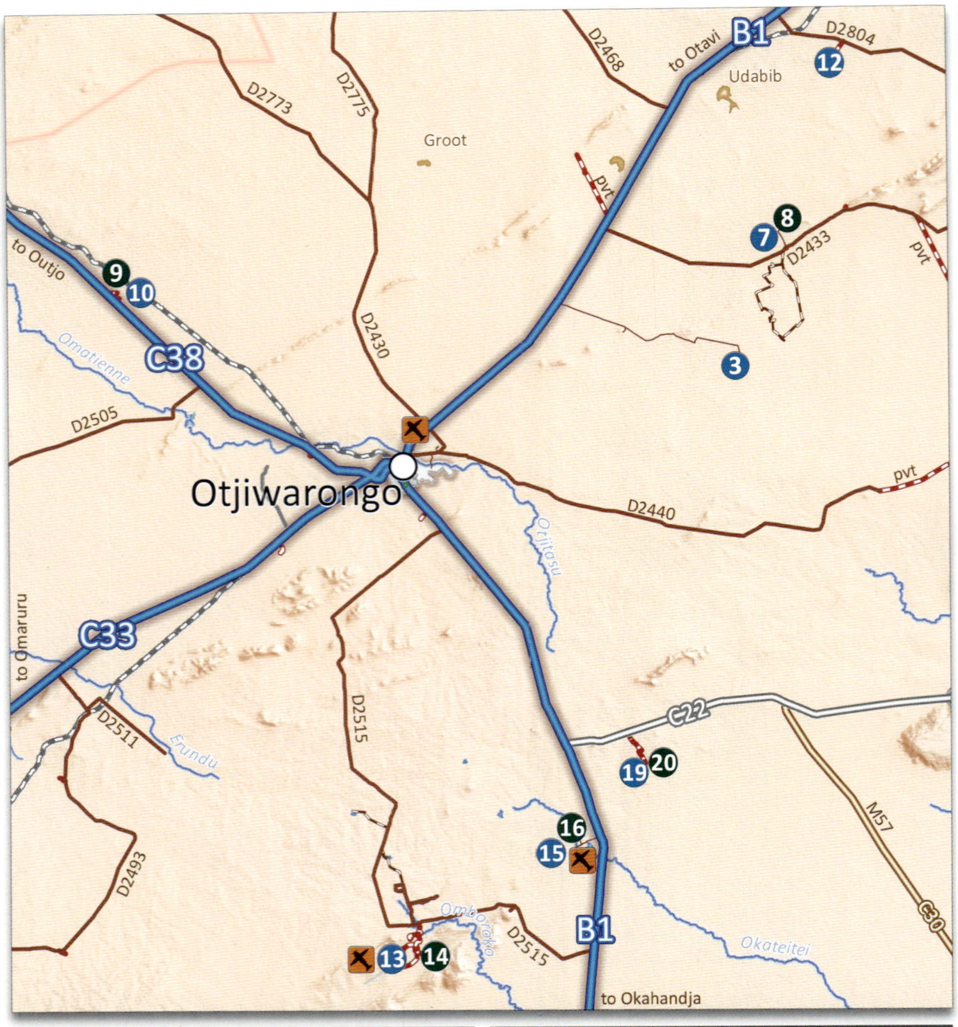

C'est Si Bon Hotel — 6

Hotel — $$

Swembad Road, Otjiwarongo

w207746

Tel: +264(0)67 301 240, Cell: +264(0)81 243 2645,
Fax: +264(0)67 303 208
cestsibon@iway.na,
www.cestsibonhotel.com

Luxury, en-suite twin bed or family rooms. Pool in beautiful garden with aviary. Free Wi-Fi.

Languages: English

Facilities: VISA @

Activities:

Frans Indongo Lodge — 7

Lodge — $$

44km or 31min ENE of Otjiwarongo

w207732

Tel: +264(0)67 307 946, Fax: +264(0)67 307 948
Indongo@mweb.com.na
www.indongolodge.com

Two double rooms, two family units and eight chalets, all beautifully decorated.

Languages: English, German, Afrikaans

Facilities: VISA

Activities:

Frans Indongo Lodge — 8

Lodge Camp — $

44km or 35min NE of Otjiwarongo

w255829

Tel: +264(0)67 307 946, Fax: +264(0)67 307 948
Indongo@mweb.com.na
www.indongolodge.com

Camping facilities offered, a few kilometres from the lodge. Offers great views.

Languages: English, German, Afrikaans

Facilities: VISA

Activities:

Gerus Campsite — 9

Camping — $

33km or 25min WNW of Otjiwarongo

w267389

Tel: +264(0)81 396 4158
danieo@mtcmobile.com.na

Campsites have their own braais, fireplaces, tables and benches. Ablution facilities have hot water.

Languages: English

Facilities:

Gerus Self Catering Accommodation — 10

Self-catering — $

33km or 25min WNW of Otjiwarongo

w361579

Cell: +264(0)81 396 4158
danieo@mtcmobile.com.na

Seven luxury permanent tents. Ablution facilities with hot water.

Languages: English

Facilities:

Hadassa Guest House B&B — 11

Bed and Breakfast — $

36 Long St, Otjiwarongo

w207752

Tel: +264(0)67 307 505, Cell: +264(0)81 774 9382,
Fax: +264(0)67 307 506
hadassa@otjiweb.com,
www.hadassaguesthouse.com

Comfortable, air-conditioned en-suite single, double or family rooms with DStv and fridge. Laundry services and Wi-Fi are available.

Languages: English, Afrikaans, French

Facilities: VISA @

Activities:

Okaputa Guestfarm — 12

Guest Farm — $

59km or 40min NE of Otjiwarongo

w254474

Tel: +264(0)67 307 909, Cell: +264(0)81 250 0131,
Fax: +264(0)67 307 909
reservations@okaputaguestfarm.com,
www.okaputaguestfarm.com

Six double and three family rooms. Venue is a cattle and Arabian stud farm.

Languages: English, German, Afrikaans

Facilities: @

Activities:

Okonjima Lodge — 13

Lodge — $$$

55km or 1h19min S of Otjiwarongo (of which 5km is 4WD)

w137939

Tel: +264(0)67 314 000, Cell: +264(0)81 142 1195,
Fax: +264(0)67 314 005
info@okonjimalodge.com,
www.okonjima.com

Main camp has double rooms and twin tents, all en-suite. The luxury bush camp has chalets, en-suite tents, private suite and villa.

Languages: English

Facilities: VISA FC

Activities:

Okonjima Lodge 14

Lodge Camp $$$
54km or 1h17min S of Otjiwarongo (of which 5km is 4WD)
w139535

Tel: +264(0)67 314 000, Cell: +264(0)81 127 6233 ,
Fax: +264(0)67 314 005
info@okonjima.com,
www.okonjima.com

Camp has open-air showers (hot), flush toilet, washing-up area, electricity points and shared pool.

Languages: English

Facilities:

Activities:

Otjiwa Safari Lodge 15

Game/Safari Lodge $$$
40km or 29min SSE of Otjiwarongo
w137382

Tel: +264(0)67 306 671, Cell: +264(0)81 820 9004,
Fax: +264(0)88 648 765
info@otjiwa.com.na,
www.otjiwa.com.na

Three accommodation facilities: Eagles Rest, Nest and Mountain Lodge. Full board and self-catering. All enjoy great scenery.

Languages: English

Facilities:

Activities:

Otjiwa Safari Lodge 16

Lodge Camp $
40km or 29min SSE of Otjiwarongo
w254367

Tel: +264(0)67 306 671, Cell: +264(0)81 820 9004,
Fax: +264(0)88 648 765
info@otjiwa.com.na,
www.otjiwa.com.na

Otjiwa's campsites are situated underneath big Acacia trees next to a beautiful riverbed. Large and small campsites offered. Ablutions and basic facilities.

Languages: English

Facilities:

Activities:

Out Of Africa B&B Guest House 17

Guest House $$
Long St, Otjiwarongo
w207750

Tel: +264(0)67 303 397, Fax: +264(0)67 302 236
outofafrica@iway.na

Air-conditioned, en-suite rooms with satellite TV and telephone.

Languages: English, Afrikaans

Facilities:

Activities:

Out Of Africa Town Lodge 18

Lodge $$
Long St, Otjiwarongo
w138490

Tel: +264(0)67 302 230, Fax: +264(0)67 302 236
oatlodge@iway.na
www.ooafrica.com

Comfortable, air-conditioned, en-suite rooms, with telephone and satellite TV.

Languages: English, Afrikaans

Facilities:

Activities:

Weaver's Rock Guest Farm 19

Guest Farm $$
37km or 29min SE of Otjiwarongo
w139111

Tel: +264(0)67 304 885, Cell: +264(0)81 128 4098,
Fax: +264(0)67 304 885
srtc@iway.na,
www.weaversrock.com

Comfortable, en-suite rooms. There's also a Wellness Salon and wildlife viewing at the waterholes. Bookings required.

Languages: English, German, Afrikaans, Swiss German

Facilities:

Activities:

Weaver's Rock Guest Farm 20

Farm Camp $
37km or 31min SE of Otjiwarongo
w141514

Tel: +264(0)67 304 885, Cell: +264(0)81 128 4098,
Fax: +264(0)67 304 885
srtc@iway.na,
www.weaversrock.com

Shaded campsites with clean ablutions. Enjoy wildlife and bird watching at the waterholes. Breakfast and dinner can be booked. Massages available at Wellness Salon.

Languages: English, German, Afrikaans, Swiss German

Facilities:

Activities:

"Wherever you go becomes a part of you somehow."

Anita Desai

(photo: Jannie Rykaart www.protea4x4.co.za)

Waterberg Plateau National Park

(photo: Frank Höppener)

THE WATERBERG PLATEAU is a particularly prominent geological feature, it's 50km long and 16km wide and rises from the Kalahari plains to a height of 200 metres. The oldest rock stratum here is over 850 million years old; dinosaur tracks were left some 200 million years ago. The area's first human inhabitants were the San people, who left rock engravings believed to be several thousand years old. A small tribe of the San were still living in the traditional way on the plateau until the late 60s.

The plateau and some 405 km² of surrounding land were declared a Nature Reserve in 1972. The plateau is largely inaccessible so in the early 70s several of Namibia's endangered species were translocated here to protect them from predators and poaching. The programme was very successful and Waterberg now supplies other Namibian parks with rare species like sable and buffalo as well as black and white rhino. The Waterberg is unique, both as a landmark and as an ecosystem. The mountain has perennial springs on its south-eastern slopes, offering a unique habitat to about 500 species of flora and more than 200 bird species.

The Waterberg is also the site of one of the major turning points in Namibian history. It was in the foothills of the Waterberg at the beginning of the 20th century that the Herero people lost their final and greatest battle against German colonial forces. The Hereros were forced to retreat from the Waterberg and flee eastwards to British Bechuanaland (now Botswana). Thousands were killed by the pursuing Germans and many died in the Kalahari Desert due to lack of food and water. The graves of the German soldiers who lost their lives at Waterberg can be seen near the Waterberg Rest Camp in the park.

Traveller Description

There are a few privately-owned lodges around the Waterberg Plateau, and the Waterberg Rest Camp is situated within the national park boundary. From the C22 it will take about 15 minutes on a gravel road to reach the park's main gate. This park is ideal for those who like to explore on foot, although guided game drives can be booked at reception. There are several hiking trails marked, either around the base of the plateau or up to the summit. The hike up to the Waterberg Plateau takes about 30 minutes and will reward you with superb views of the plains below.

Travel Info

History buffs should walk the History Path in the Waterberg Wilderness Private Nature Reserve adjacent to the park. Contact Waterberg Wilderness Lodge on +264(0)67 687 018 or info@waterberg-wilderness.com to obtain permission. This trail has various information points along the route about the 1904 Battle of Waterberg between the Germans and Hereros.

Birders will enjoy the numerous sightings of rosy-faced love birds and Meyer's parrots as well as a number of rare bird species. The only colony of Cape Vultures in Namibia is found in the Waterberg.

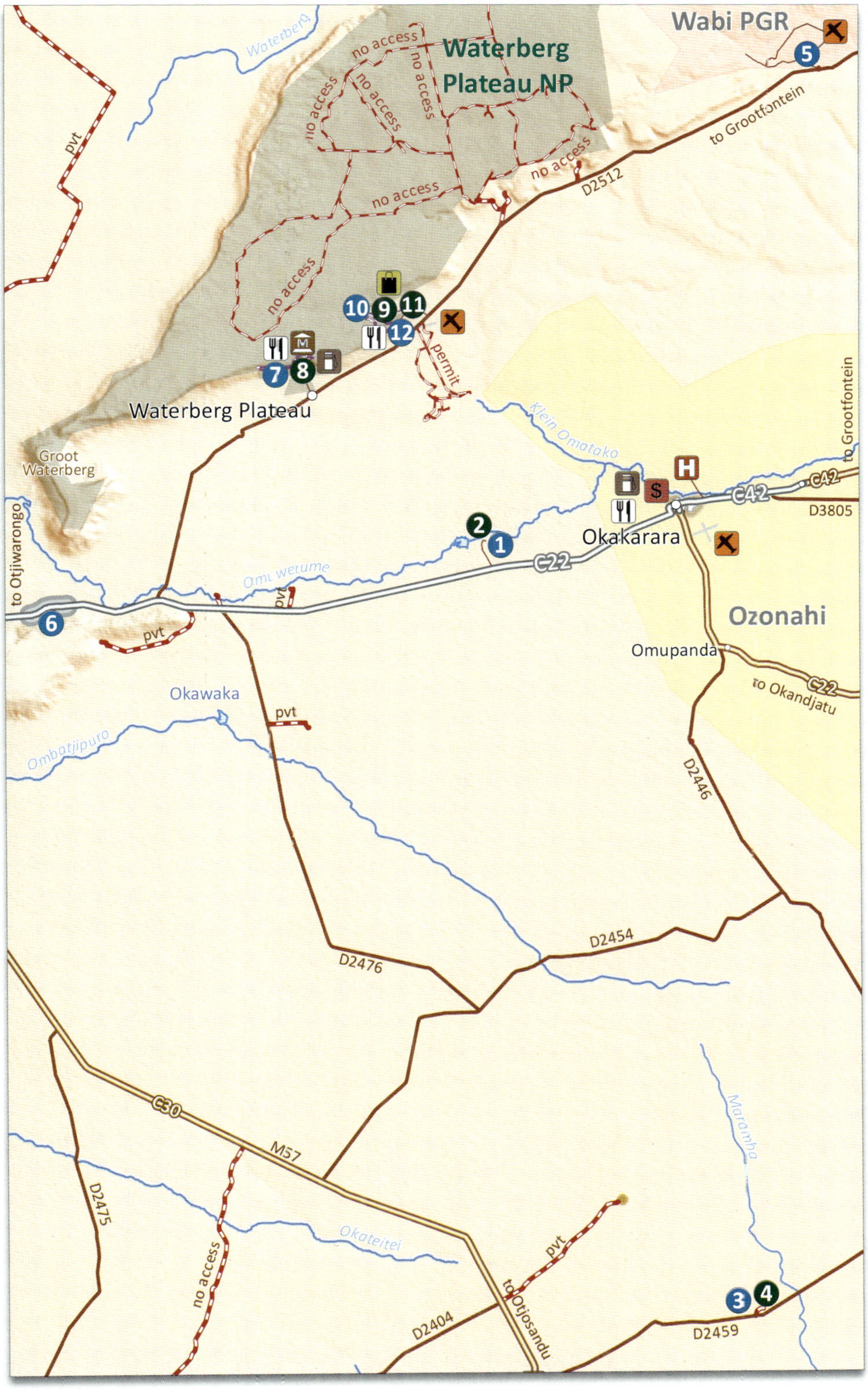

Hamakari Guest Farm 1

Guest Farm $$
92km or 1h4min ESE of Otjiwarongo
w140592

Tel: +264(0)67 306 633, Cell: +264(0)81 249 7927,
Fax: +264(0)67 302 396
hamakari@iway.na, www.hamakari.com

Six comfortable en-suite rooms. Catering and laundry services included.

Languages: English, Afrikaans, German

Facilities:

Activities:

Hamakari Guest Farm 2

Farm Camp $
92km or 1h4min ESE of Otjiwarongo
w175368

Tel: +264(0)67 306 633, Cell: +264(0)81 249 7927,
Fax: +264(0)67 302 396
hamakari@iway.na, www.hamakari.com

Four campsites, each equipped with power point, light, tap and braai. Ablutions have two showers and two toilets.

Languages: English, Afrikaans, German

Facilities:

Activities:

Ouhave Country Home 3

Guest Farm $$
101km or 1h27min SSE of Waterberg Plateau
w207929

Tel: +264(0)67 306 209, Cell: +264(0)81 289 8287,
Fax: +264(0)67 306 209
ouhave@iway.na

Two double, en-suite, air-conditioned rooms with sitt ng room. Breakfast included. Laundry services offered. Rifles can be hired for hunting.

Languages: English, German, Afrikaans

Facilities:

Activities:

Waterberg Plateau National Park

Ouhave Country Home 4

Camping $
101km or 1h27min SSE of Waterberg Plateau
w255838

Tel: +264(0)67 306 209, Cell: +264(0)81 289 8287, Fax: +264(0)67 306 209
ouhave@iway.na

10 Shaded campsites with hot showers.

Languages: English, German, Afrikaans

Facilities:
Activities:

Wabi Game Lodge 5

Lodge $
124km or 1h35min E of Otjiwarongo
w138326

Tel: +264(0)67 687 102, Fax: +264(0)67 687 400
info@wabi.ch
www.wabi.ch

Four standard bungalows with en-suite bathtub, living room and private terrace. Plus, two family suites and garden cottage with two double rooms.

Languages: English, Afrikaans

Facilities:
Activities:

Waterberg Guest Farm 6

Guest Farm $$
63km or 43min ESE of Otjiwarongo
w209672

Tel: +264(0)61 237 294, Cell: +264(0)81 751 4866, Fax: +264(0)67 302 223
reservations@exclusive.com.na,
www.waterbergnamibia.com

Double and twin rooms with en-suite bathrooms (toilet, shower & basin). All rooms have a veranda and private entrance. Thatched bush bungalows also available.

Languages: English, German

Facilities:
Activities:

Waterberg Plateau NP Chalets 7

Bed and Breakfast $
89km or 1h8min E of Otjiwarongo
w207689

Tel: +264(0)61 285 7200, Fax: +264(0)61 224 900
reservations@nwr.com.na
www.nwr.com.na

Luxury and standard units, with DStv and air-conditioning / ceiling fans. Park fees payable on arrival. Reservations advisable.

Languages: English

Facilities:
Activities:

Waterberg Plateau NP Rest Camp 8

Park Camp $$
88km or 1h7min E of Otjiwarongo
w138682

Tel: +264(0)61 285 7200, Fax: +264(0)61 224 900
reservations@nwr.com.na
www.nwr.com.na

Shaded campsites with communal ablutions and field kitchens. Park fees paid on arrival to Ministry of Environment & Tourism. Reservations advisable.

Languages: English

Facilities:
Activities:

Waterberg Wilderness Andersson 9

Park Camp $$
99km or 1h21min E of Otjiwarongo
w216454

Tel: +264(0)67 687 018, Fax: +264(0)67 687 020
info@waterberg-wilderness.com
www.waterberg-wilderness.com

Each campsite has clean water and a braai area. Hot showers are heated via wood-burning stove and there are flush toilets.

Languages: English

Facilities:
Activities:

Waterberg Wilderness Lodge	10
Lodge	$$

99km or 1h22min E of Otjiwarongo
w143023

Tel: +264(0)67 687 018, Fax: +264(0)67 687 020
info@waterberg-wilderness.com
www.waterberg-wilderness.com

Double or family rooms with en-suite bathrooms, and verandas.

Languages: English

Facilities:

Activities:

Waterberg Wilderness Plateau	11
Wilderness Camp	$$

97km or 1h15min E of Otjiwarongo
w143035

Tel: +264(0)67 687 018, Fax: +264(0)67 687 020
info@waterberg-wilderness.com
www.waterberg-wilderness.com

Each shaded campsite has clean water and a braai. Hot showers via a wood-burning stove.

Languages: English

Facilities: FC

Activities:

Waterberg Wilderness Plateau Lodge	12
Lodge	$$$

98km or 1h20min E of Otjiwarongo
w143024

Tel: +264(0)67 687 018, Cell: +27(0)83 626 9409,
Fax: +264(0)67 687 020
info@waterberg-wilderness.com,
www.waterberg-wilderness.com

Seven air-conditioned chalets with en-suite bathrooms.

Languages: English

Facilities:

Activities:

(photo: Heiner Dillmann)

OVAMBOLAND

(above) A typical Ovambo village. (photo: Karin Theron)

(right) The European roller spends its summers in Europe and its winters in Africa. (photo: Karin Theron)

OVAMBOLAND IS SITUATED north of Etosha National Park and is the Ovambo people's homeland. This is one of the most densely populated parts of the country and is the gateway to Angola. Although it doesn't really offer much in terms of tourist attractions, travellers passing through the larger towns of Ovamboland like Oshakati, Ondangwa and Oshikango can find just about all the services they might need for their trip further north.

The landscape is dotted with Makalani palm trees and enormous termite mounds. The Ovambo people weave baskets from the leaves and carve curios out of the palm nuts. The locals supplement their protein intake by fishing in the area's many natural pans. In some places they dry the barbel (catfish) they've caught and sell it next to the road.

Driving the main road you'll pass small villages every few kilometres between the big towns, these settlements give this region a real African feeling. Each village has a shebeen (bar), and each hut has its own kraal with goats and a patch of mealies (maize or corn). Be vigilant, dogs, donkeys, goats and cattle have right of way, even on the main roads through these villages.

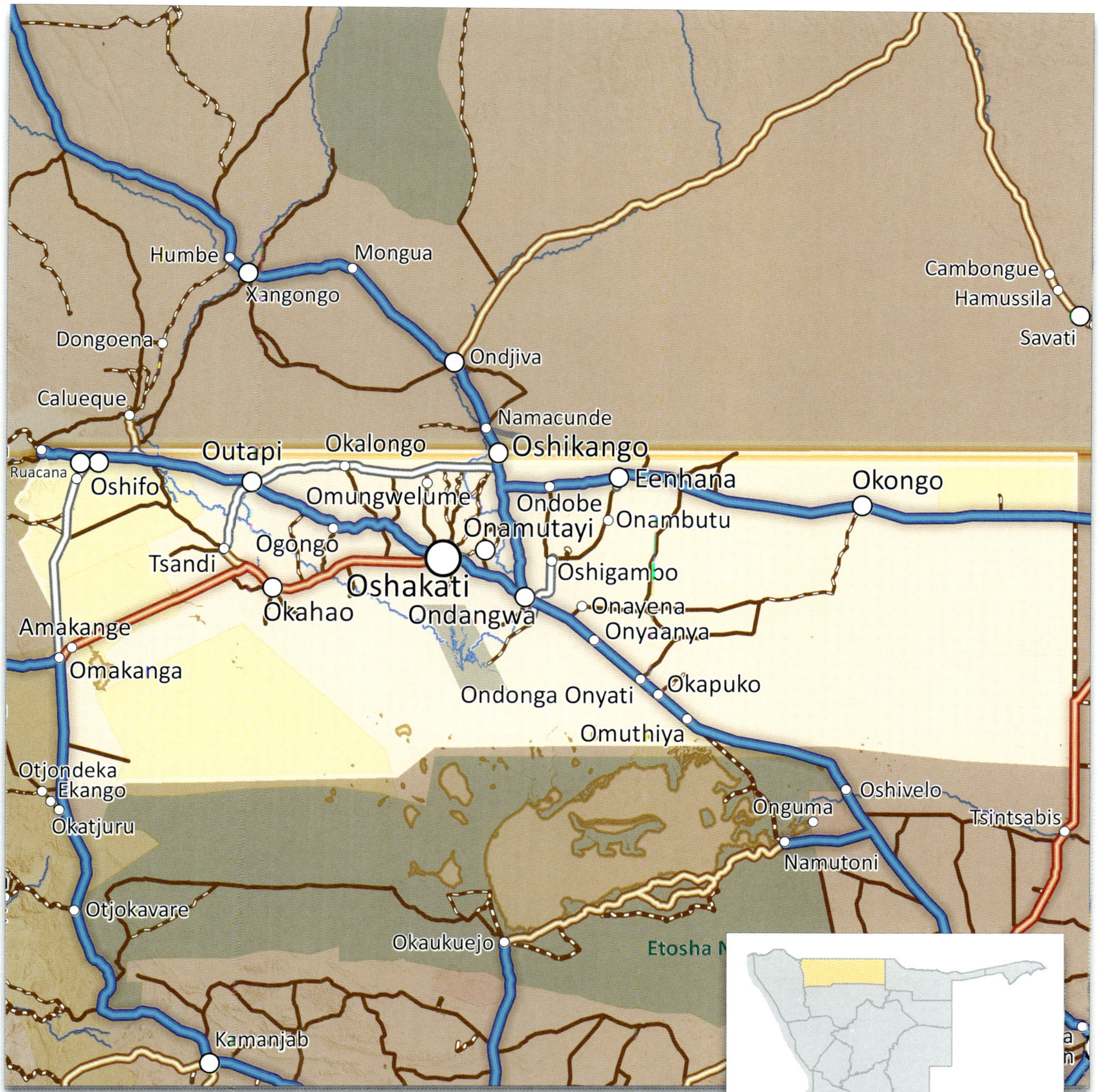

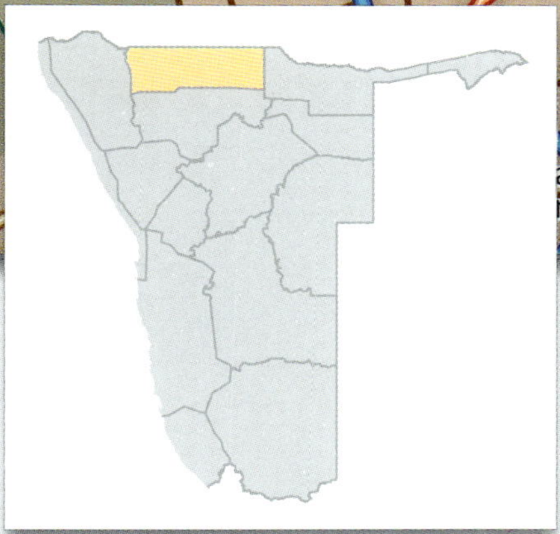

MAJOR ATTRACTIONS

- Ruacana Falls are 120m high and 700m wide when in full flood.
- The Ombalantu baobab in Outapi has a diameter of 26.5m and is estimated to be over 800 years old. It has served as a post office and a chapel in the past and is now preserved as a heritage site.
- The hollow trunk of the Tsandi Baobab once served as the office of the king and is adjacent to the current royal residence.
- The Nakambale Museum near Ondangwa displays the history and culture of the Ovambo tribe.

More details about the attractions are available on our website (www.tracks4africa.co.za) or our Guide App. Our GPS Map can navigate you to each of these attractions.

Ondangwa

(photo: Ian-Ray Nel)

LOCATED SOME 80 KILOMETRES from the Angolan border, Ondangwa is one of the largest towns in the Ovamboland region. After the Finnish Missionary Society was formed in 1859, its first foreign deployment was to Ovamboland, northern Namibia. Here, they opened the first mission station at Onandjokue in 1870, and in 1890, another in Ondangwa. In more recent times, during Namibia's War of Independence the town saw service as a staging base for the South African Defence Force. Though not a destination in its own right, this busy transport hub is a good place to refuel and get provisions.

Traveller Description

Whether you're looking for well-stocked supermarkets, ATMs, or informal traders, you'll find it all here. The town offers a mixture of Africa-style shops and modern shopping centres. Take care when driving around as cattle and goats roam free in the streets. There's a hospital here and the local airport offers flights to Windhoek - worth remembering in the event of an emergency.

Travel Info

Ondangwa has a Shoprite, Spar, Pick 'n Pay and Woermann Hyper and is a convenient overnight stop for those travelling between Etosha and Ovamboland.

TRAVEL TIP! For camping, try Nakambale Community Camp, some 10km out of town. Here you can camp or stay in traditional huts. The camp has a museum where you can learn about Ovambo life, Finnish Mission history and the political history of the area. Traditional food and dance are available on request - as are local guides to Lake Oponono, a large wetland area frequented after heavy rains by a variety of waterbirds such as saddle-billed storks, crowned cranes, flamingos and pelicans.

Town Info:

Hospital: +264(0)65 283 1000
Police: +264(0)65 242 650
Doctor: +264(0)65 248 115
Tow-in: +264(0)81 129 7490

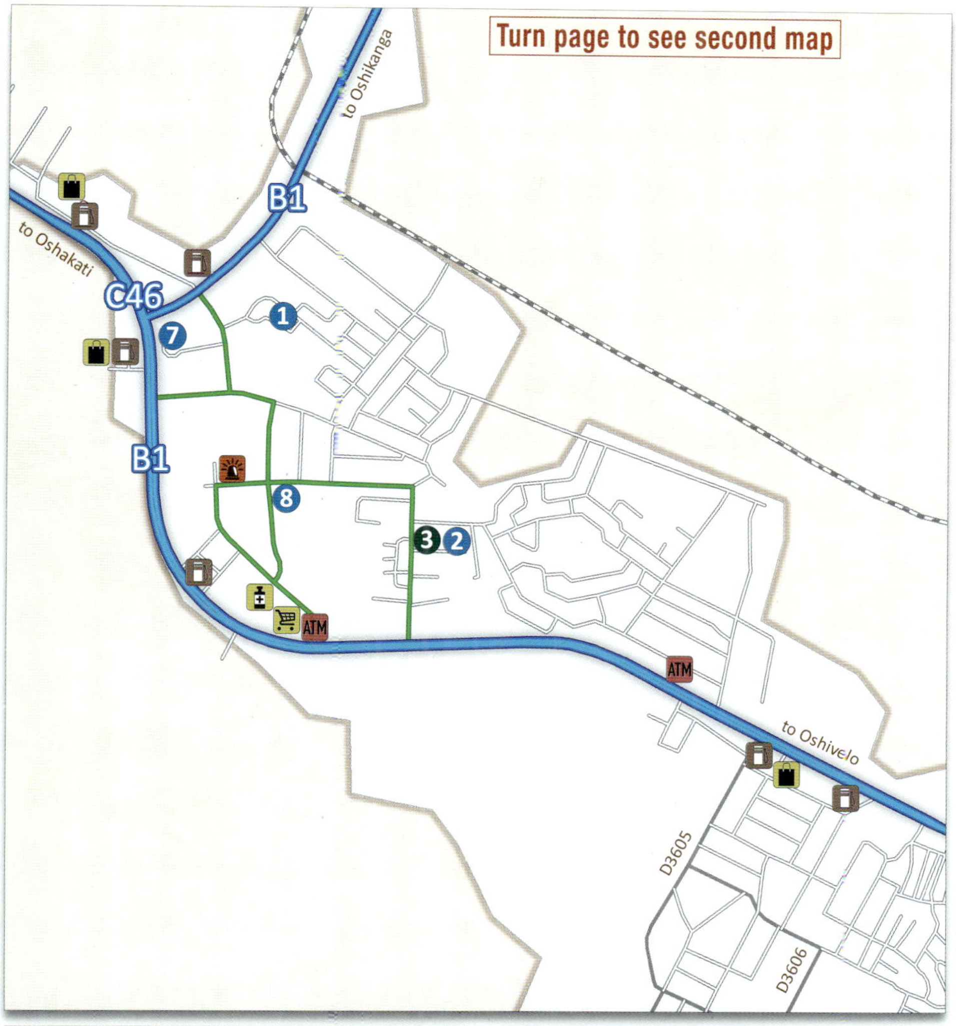

Anot Guest House 1

Guest House $
2133-4 Extension 6, Ondangwa
w359088

Tel: +264(0)65 241 013
anot@iway.na
www.anotguesthouse.com

Luxury rooms with air-conditioning, TV and secure parking. Located in a quiet suburban area of Ondangwa.

Languages: English, Afrikaans, Shona

Facilities:

Fantasia Guest House 2

Guest House $
Ondangwa
w222184

Tel: +264(0)65 240 528, Cell: +264(0)81 648 4871,
cecile@fantasia-guesthouse.co.za
www.fantasia-guesthouse.co.za

17 Air-conditioned, en-suite rooms, each with own entrance, DStv, tea/coffee facilities and mini fridge. They also offer food and drinks.

Languages: English, German, Portuguese, Afrikaans, Ovambo

Facilities:

Fantasia Guest House 3

Camping $
In Ondangwa
w254371

Tel: +264(0)65 240 528, Cell: +264(0)81 648 4871,
cecile@fantasia-guesthouse.co.za
www.fantasia-guesthouse.co.za

Campsites with power points and ablutions (hot showers).

Languages: English, German, Portuguese, Afrikaans, Ovambo

Facilities:

Nakambale Community Camp 4

Community Camp $
10km or 12min SSE of Ondangwa
w140772

Tel: +264(0)65 245 668, Cell: +264(0)81 249 3108,
Fax: +264(0)65 240 472

Three campsites located next to traditional homestead. Venue has ablutions with hot water and flush toilets, a kitchen and wash-up facilities.

Languages: English

Facilities:

Activities:

Ongula Village Homestead Lodge 5

Lodge $$
37km or 32min NE of Ondangwa
w279635

Tel: +264(0)61 250 725, Cell: +264(0)85 625 6551,
Fax: +264(0)88 649 584
ongula@resdest.com, www.ongula.com

Double and family rondawels. All en-suite (shower) with tea/coffee facilities, mosquito nets and enclosed veranda.

Languages: English

Facilities:

Ongula Village Homestead Lodge 6

Lodge Camp $
37km or 32min NE of Ondangwa
w359940

Tel: +264(0)61 250 725, Cell: +264(0)85 625 6551,
Fax: +264(0)88 649 584
ongula@resdest.com,
www.ongula.com

Five campsites with power points, taps and shade. Ablutions with cold showers, flush toilets, hand basins and mirrors.

Languages: English

Facilities:

Protea Hotel Ondangwa 7

Hotel $
Main St, Ondangwa
w177629

Tel: +264(0)65 241 900, Fax: +264(0)65 241 919
gm.ondangwa@proteahotels.com.na
www.marriott.com

88 En-suite rooms with air-conditioning, satellite TV, internet access, coffee/tea facilities and hairdryers.

Languages: English

Facilities:

Activities:

Town Lodge Ondangwa 8

Lodge $
Brian Simaata St, Ondangwa
w222183

Tel: +264(0)65 241 715, Cell: +264(0)81 124 4382,
Fax: +264(0)65 241 717
ondangwatl@iway.na

Air-conditioned rooms with 2 three-quarter beds or one double-bed. Includes DStv, telephone and en-suite shower.

Languages: English

Facilities:

Activities:

Ondangwa

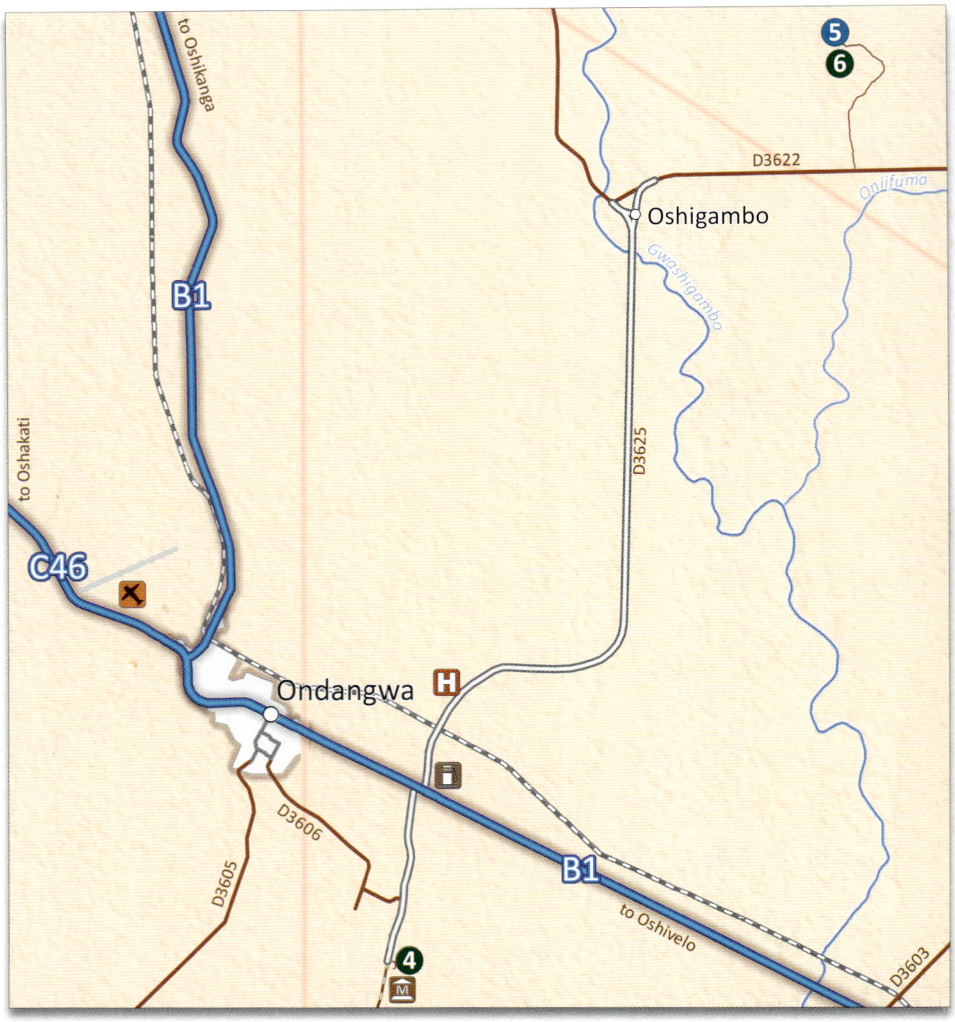

top and above: (photo: Ian-Ray Nel)

(photo: Ian-Ray Nel)

(photo: Ian-Ray Nel)

Oshakati

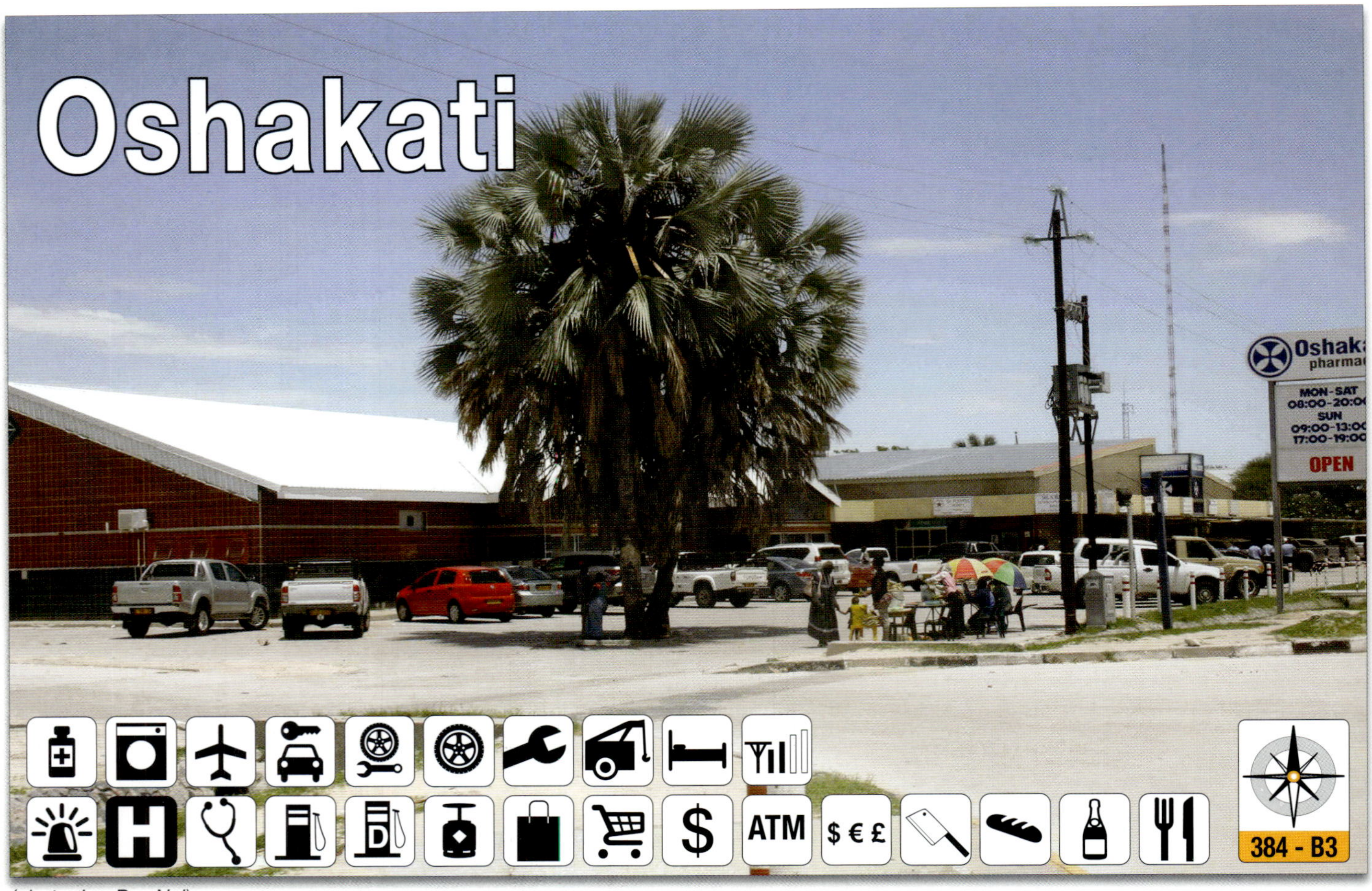

(photo: Ian-Ray Nel)

OSHAKATI IS NAMIBIA'S SECOND LARGEST CITY (though town might be a better description) and is also the capital of the far northern region. The town is focused on transborder trade with Angola; indeed, in the Ovambo language, its name means 'that which is between'. But just to keep things interesting, others believe the name refers to the broadcast tower in downtown which, at 275m, is the tallest freestanding structure in the country.

The town shares an airstrip with nearby Ondangwa and was also a South African Defence Force base during the Namibian War of Independence, also known as the South African Border War or Angolan Bush War. Officially founded in 1966, Oshakati has experienced rapid development since Namibia's independence in 1990. Today, it's a busy place and whether you're looking for open-air markets or modern department stores, you'll find it all here.

The surrounding landscape is crisscrossed by *oshonas* (inland water channels), small farmlands and settlements. In times of heavy rains, the town is prone to flooding.

Traveller Description

Though most accommodation here is geared for business travellers, you will find something to suit those of us journeying at a more relaxed pace. It must be noted that at time of writing there were no camping facilities in or near the town.

Travel Info

There are numerous fast-food establishments as well as more formal restaurants. You'll also find a Pick n Pay, Spar and Shoprite. A number of establishments offer free Wi-Fi.

More useful numbers:

State Hospital tel: +264(0)65 223 3000. Tow-in tel: +264(0)81 129 4154

TRAVEL TIP! Be aware of petty thieves or '*botstotsos*' as the locals call them. Watch out for the distraction technique, while one person engages you in conversation, another steals your gear. Also, be wary of livestock crossing the C46 between Oshakati and Ruacana.

Town Info:

Hospital: +264(0)65 232 911. Police: +264(0)65 223 6000. Doctor: +264(0)65 221 231. Tow-in: +264(0)65 222 014

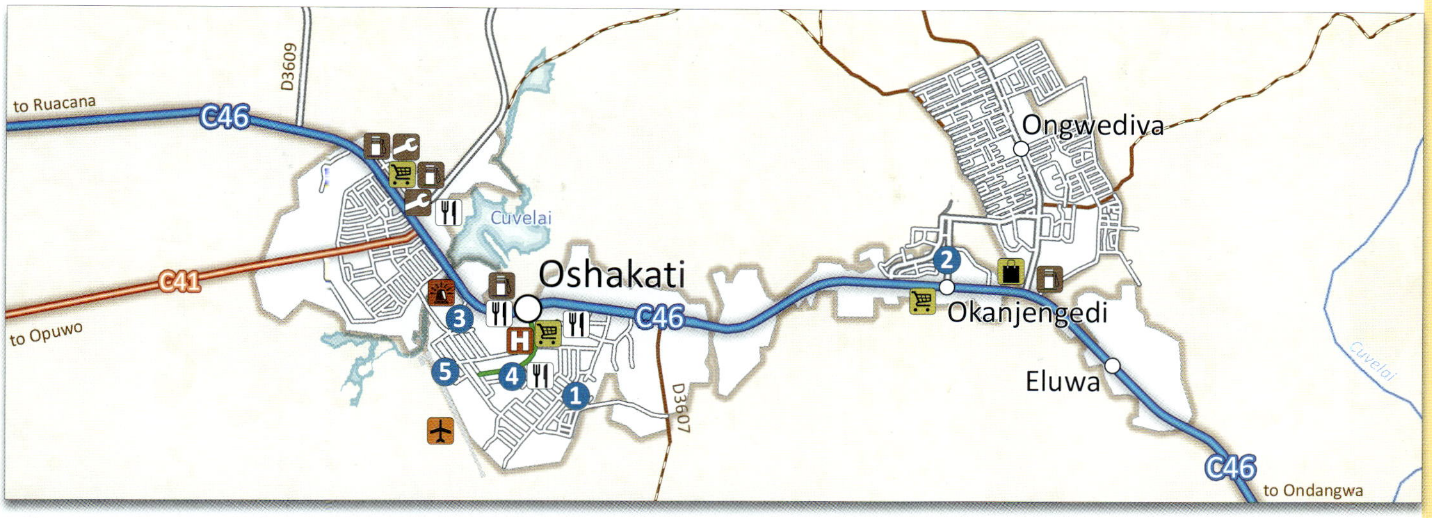

Bahay Susan B&B 1

Bed and Breakfast $
Jakkalsbessie St, Oshakati
w227567

Tel: +264(0)65 221 075, Cell: +264(0)81 256 1445,
Fax: +264(0)65 221 075
bahaysusan@yahoo.com

Rooms with shower, toilet, fridge, DStv and secure parking. Plus pool, garden and your choice of breakfast.

Languages: English

Facilities:

Activities:

Etuna Guest House 2

Guest House $$
5544 Valley of Leopard St, Ongwediva
w208909

Tel: +264(0)65 231 177, Cell: +264(0)81 802 4833,
Fax: +264(0)65 231 178
bookings@etunaguesthouse.com

Air-conditioned single, double and family rooms, and chalets. With en-suite bathrooms, TV, mini bar, laundry and braai facilities.

Languages: English

Facilities:

Activities:

Oshakati Country Lodge 3

Lodge $$
Mandume Avenue, Oshakati
w141630

Tel: +264(0)65 222 380, Fax: +264(0)65 222 384
cro@united.com.na
www.unitedafricagroup.com.na

50 En-suite rooms with modern finishes. Tours as well as white-water rafting can be arranged.

Languages: English

Facilities:

Activities:

Oshakati Guesthouse 4

Guest House $
917 Leo Shoopala St, Oshakati
w255885

Tel: +264(0)65 224 659, Fax: +264(0)65 224 114
bookings@oshakati-guesthouse.com

22 En-suite rooms with air-conditioning. Plus a restaurant that serves breakfast, lunch and dinner.

Languages: English, Afrikaans

Facilities:

Activities:

Oshandira Lodge 5

Lodge $
In Oshakati
w227568

Tel: +264(0)65 220 443, Fax: +264(0)65 221 189
oshandira@iway.na

16 En-suite rooms with satellite TV and air-conditioning.

Languages: English

Facilities:

Activities:

Uukwaluudhi Safari Lodge 6

Lodge $$
163km or 2h19min WSW of Oshakati (of which 12km is 4WD)
w269210

Tel: +264(0)64 418 661, Cell: +264(0)81 319 6585,
reservations@uukwaluudhi-safarilodge.com
www.uukwaluudhi-safarilodge.com

Eight well-appointed, en-suite permanent tents, with views over the Uukwaluudhi plains. Breakfast and dinner served. Lunch optional, can be ordered from a la carte menu.

Languages: English, Afrikaans

Facilities:

Activities:

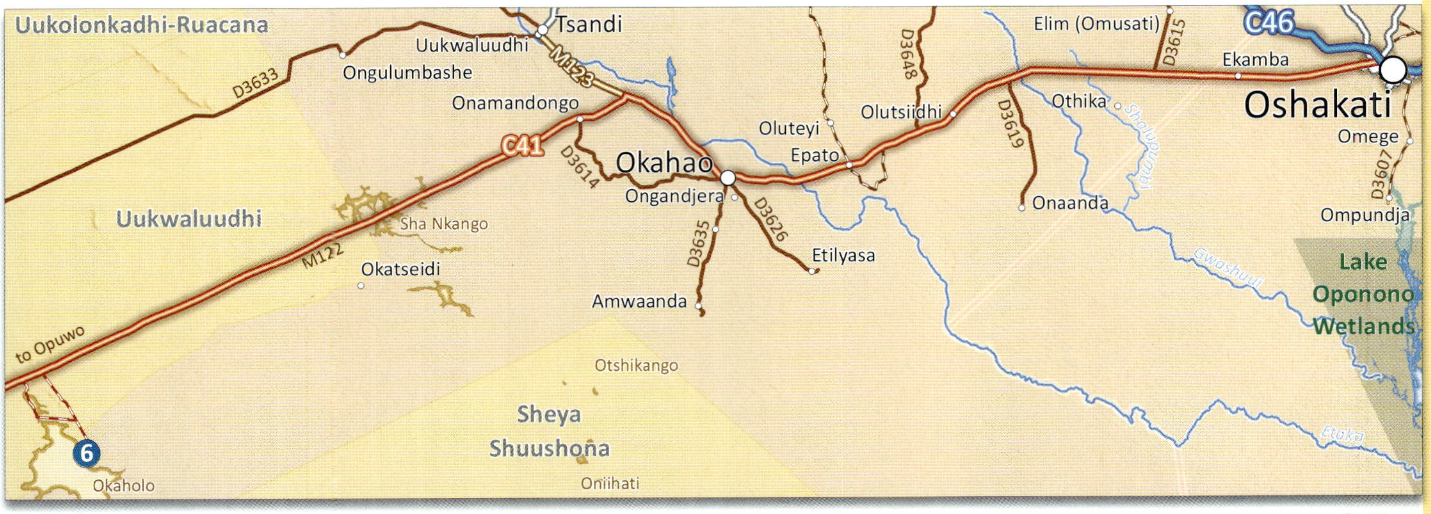

Oshikango

(photo: Ian-Ray Nel)

FORMERLY A SMALL VILLAGE, Oshikango became a border post with Angola after Namibia's independence and experienced tremendous growth. Being a border post town, this is a busy place which sees many big trucks passing through; you'll also observe traders carrying their wares on their heads, on bicycles or even in wheelbarrows.

The town's fortunes are linked to trade with Angola, and with that country's economy heavily reliant on oil exports, the decline in oil prices since 2014 has had a detrimental effect on Oshikango's fortunes. But it's still busy!

Traveller Description

Not a tourist town but the last place for you to replenish stocks and refuel if you're bound for Angola. Some accommodation is available and there's a hospital 8km out of town. Also, this is the last place to access some rudimentary vehicle repairs/maintenance before you tackle Angola's remote areas.

Travel Info

In town you'll find a KFC, Spar, pharmacy, banks, ATMs and medical services. Note that the state hospital is south of town, on the D3608.

TRAVEL TIP! The Oshikango / Santa Clara border post is open 07h00 - 18h00. The contact number is +264(0)65 264 615.

Town Info:

Hospital: +264(0)65 266 604/5
Police: +264(0)65 266 550
Doctor: +264(0)65 265 567

right: (photo: Ian-Ray Nel)
far right: (photo: Karin Theron)

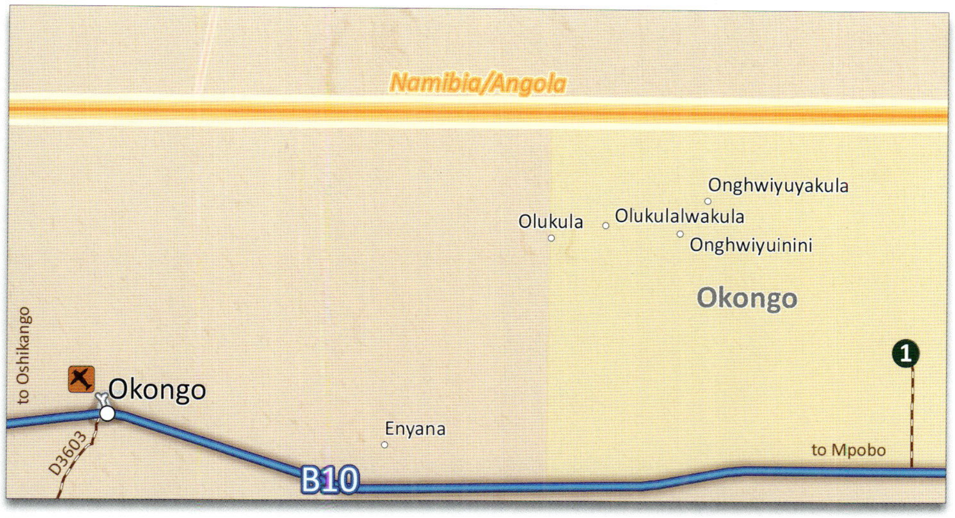

Omauni Community Camp 1

Community Camp $
221km or 2h30min E of Oshikango (of which 9km is 4WD)
w208951

Cell: +264(0)81 318 5133

Not in a very good state but does offer a few taps, shade, flush toilets and cold showers. Approximately 70km from Okongo.

Languages: English

Facilities:

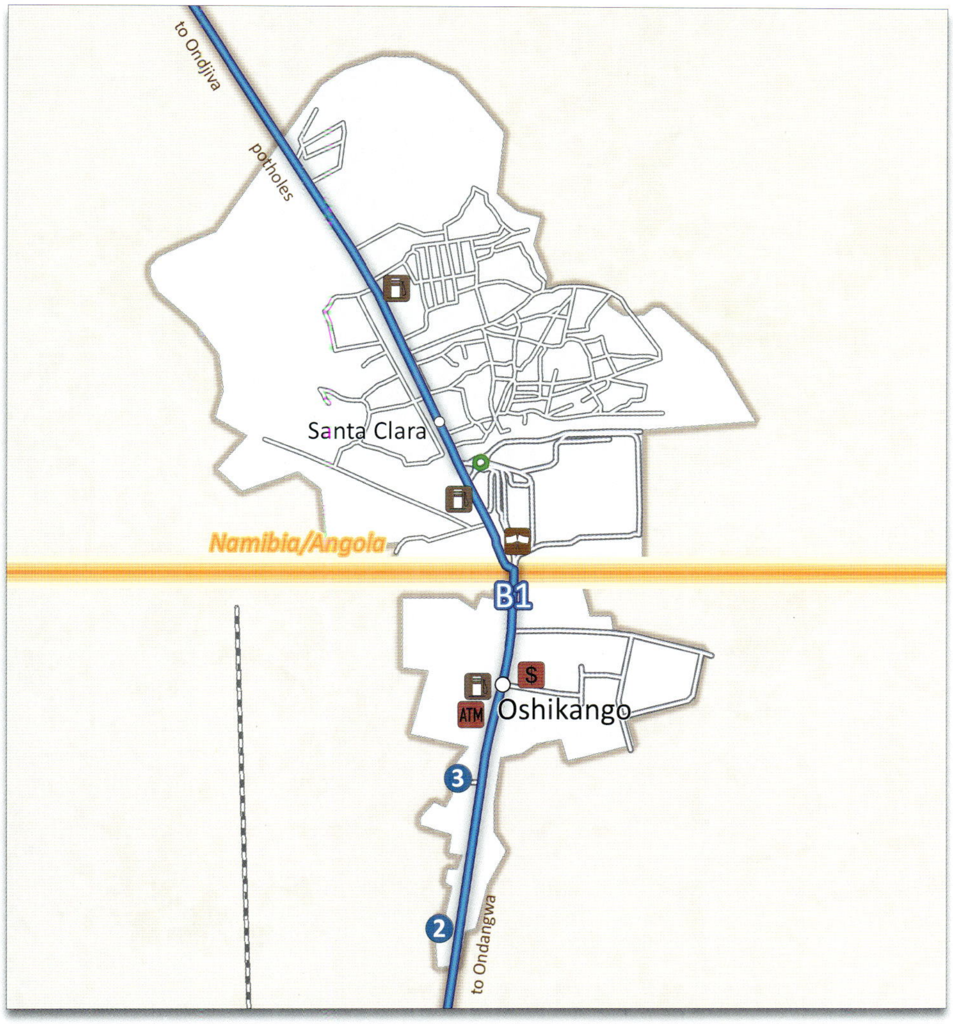

Oshikango Country Lodge 2

Lodge $
Main Road, Oshikango
w219522

Tel: +264(0)65 264 650, Fax: +264(0)65 264 840
maqui@iway.na
www.oshikangocountrylodge.com

Comfortable, luxurious, en-suite rooms with DStv. Restaurant serves Portuguese cuisine. Nightly entertainment on offer.

Languages: English

Facilities:

Activities:

Piscas Accommodation 3

Self-catering $
Main Road, Oshikango
w143420

Tel: +264(0)65 264 761, Fax: +264(0)65 264 763
tomane@iway.na

24 Rooms, restaurant and pool.

Languages: English

Facilities:

Activities:

SKELETON COAST

The inhabitants of the Cape Cross Seal Reserve are not a quiet bunch! (photo: Frank Höppener)

THE SKELETON COAST IS AN EXTREMELY WILD and desolate stretch of land where the Namib Desert and the Atlantic Ocean meet. Its name is most likely derived from the combination of whale and seal skeletons, as well as the numerous shipwrecks along the coastline.

The region consists mainly of the Skeleton Coast and Dorob National Parks, and the main towns of the region are Swakopmund and Walvis Bay. Both towns are tourist friendly and offer many attractions. Henties Bay is another well-known holiday town here, as is Langstrand which is situated about halfway between Swakopmund and Walvis Bay.

This coastline is very popular amongst anglers and keen fishermen make yearly pilgrimages to places like Terrace Bay, Torra Bay, Mile 108, Mile 72 and Jakkalsputz. In past years people used this area as a 4x4 playground causing severe track pollution, strict regulations on off-road driving are now in place. You need a permit to drive on most of the roads, and some areas can only be entered if you're accompanied by an accredited guide.

Although strictly controlled for conservation reasons, the inland parts of the Skeleton Coast also offers a lot of recreational opportunities. On some of the off-road trails, you can view the magnificent Welwitschia plants up close and on the Welwitschia Plains 4WD Trail near Swakopmund you'll drive through an almost surreal moon landscape.

(below right) Some lonely graves at the Cape Cross Seal Reserve. (photo: Frank Höppener)

(below) The wreck of the Zeila is easily viewed from the C34, some 15km south of Henties Bay. (photo: Mietsie Visser)

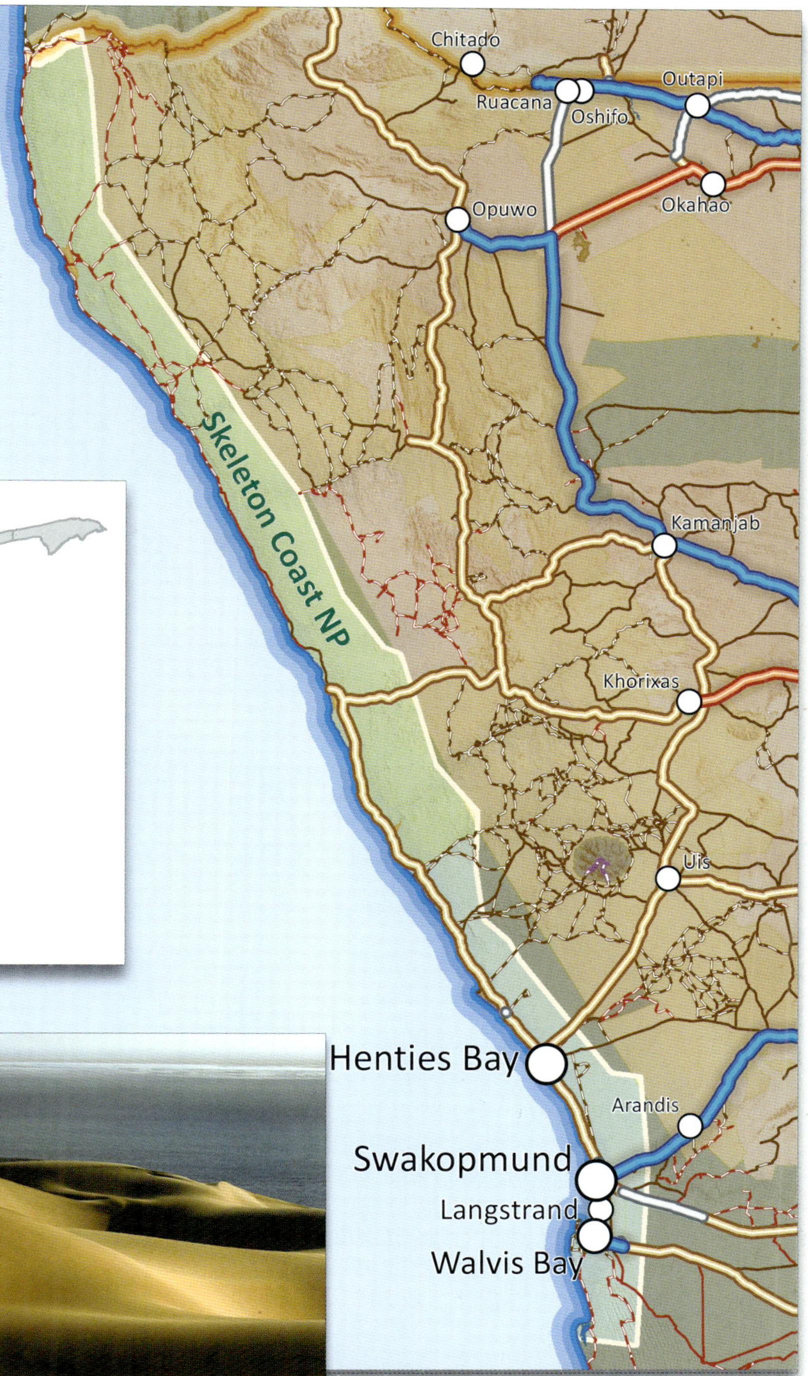

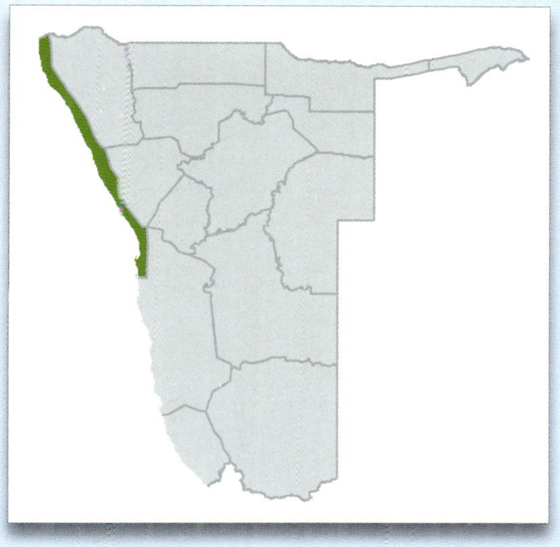

Dune driving near Sandwich Harbour, south of Walvis Bay. (photo: Heiner Dillmann)

MAJOR ATTRACTIONS

- Skeleton Coast National Park
- The Cape Cross Seal Reserve just north of Henties Bay is home to a large colony of Cape fur seals. The area is of historic interest as it marks the spot where the first European, the Portuguese navigator Diogo Cão, set foot on the coast of southwestern Africa in 1486.
- Close to the reserve is a pool which, due to old mining activities, is high in salt and minerals. As one easily floats on these waters, it's referred to as the Dead Sea Swimhole.
- Swakopmund is a charming town offering many attractions like the Aquarium and Snake Park, colonial style architecture, museums, restaurants and a beautiful pier.
- Dune 7 near Walvis Bay is a popular spot for off-road dune and quad bike driving and the bay is ideal for kayaking with dolphins and seals.
- Pelican Point acts as a natural breakwater for Walvis Bay and the lighthouse is worth a visit.
- The Welwitschia Plains 4WD Trail and Moon Landscape are both worthy attractions.

More details about the attractions are available on our website (www.tracks4africa.co.za) or our Guide App. Our GPS Map can navigate you to each of these attractions.

Henties Bay

(photo: Anet Bosman)

HENTIES BAY WAS NAMED AFTER one Major Hendrik 'Hentie' Stefanus van der Merwe. In 1929, during a hunting expedition, he found a natural spring here after running low on water. Recognising it to be a great spot for relaxation, he later returned and built a wooden hut in the riverbed. As friends and family got wind of the place, they began to join him and the place became known as Henties Bay and ultimately developed into a tourist destination. Much of the early attraction was due to the abundance of fish at this spot. In fact, when Portuguese explorer, Bartolomeu Diaz, sailed down this coast back in 1488 he named it Praia das Sardinhas or Coast of Fish for the very same reason. These days fishing is just one of the things that draws people to this small coastal town.

Traveller Description

This is a popular holiday destination for Namibians, especially those who are keen on 4x4ing and/or fishing. Although the municipal area of Henties Bay is excluded from the Dorob National Park, you should take note of restricted roads outside the town. The town is a gateway to adventures like horse riding, 4x4 routes and quad biking in the adjacent Namib Desert, but you need to book these through tour operators. From Henties Bay you can visit the Cape Cross seal colony to the north or Swakopmund to the south. And, don't forget the 9-hole golf course, where the fairways are desert sand!

Travel Info

The town is well populated with small shops, a pharmacy and restaurants. Besides two campsites, guest houses and B&Bs, many holiday houses are available for rent. Every August, the Hentiesfees is celebrated here, featuring a music festival, angling competition, beer tent and various sporting events. Henties Bay is often misty and windy, so remember to take a wind shield if you choose to camp here.

TRAVEL TIP! The abandoned salt mine southeast of Henties Bay is worth a visit. It's situated on the Old Salt Mine 4x4 Trail within the Dorob National Park. The man-made salt pans and old implements are still clearly visible. Take care to drive around the pans as they are porous and your vehicle will get stuck. A heap of whalebones and an old boiler indicate that whales were once processed here. Interesting natural phenomena in the area are quartz crystals, triangular shaped stones and granite boulders. Pay a visit to the new tourism centre for more information on things to do in Henties Bay.

Town Info:

Police:	+264(0)64 500 201
Doctor:	+264(0)64 500 423
Tow-in:	+264(0)81 656 4501
Tourism:	+264(0)64 501 143

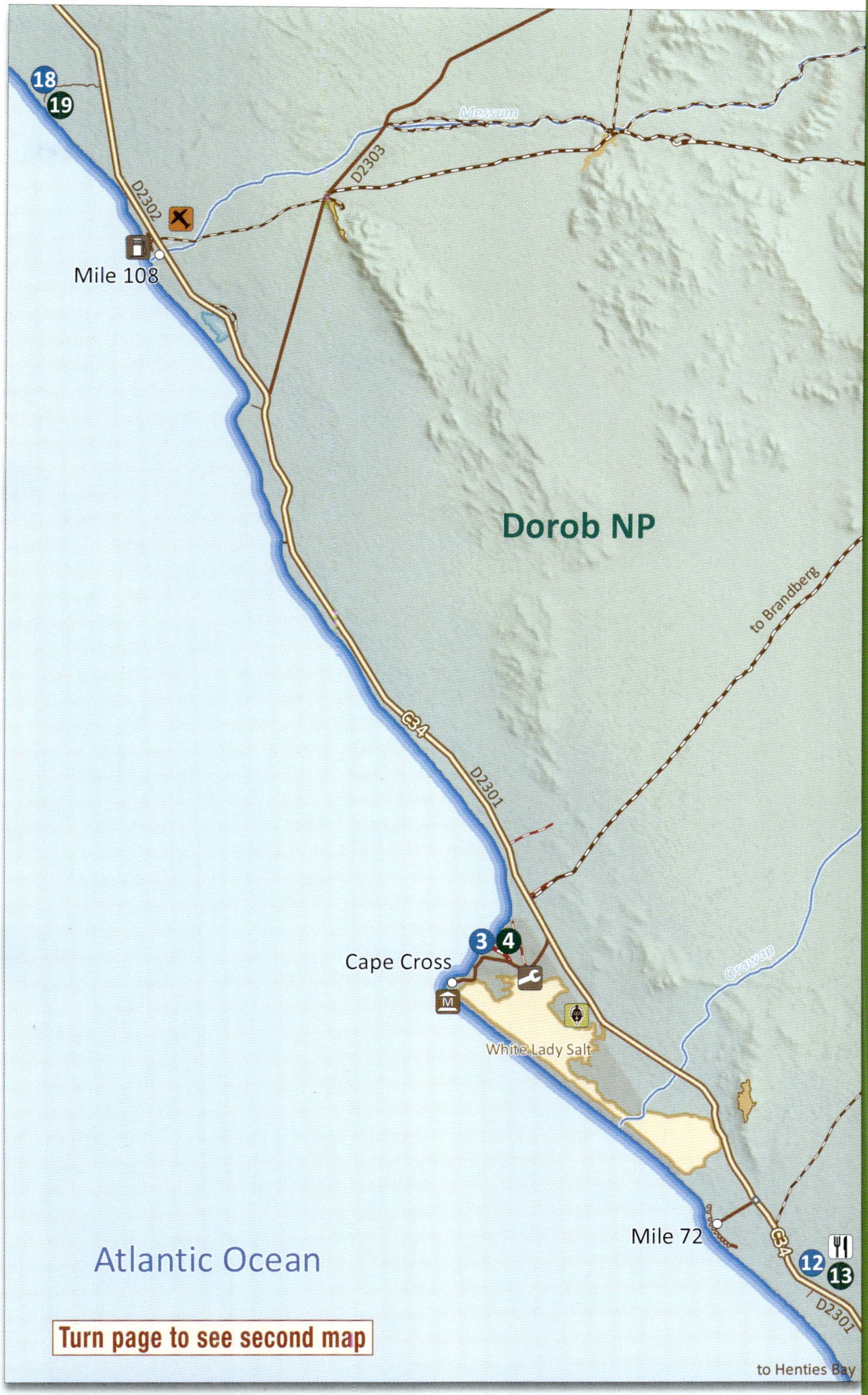

Turn page to see second map

Buck's Camping Lodge — 1

Self-catering — $
Off Nickey Iyambo St, Henties Bay
w139051

Tel: +264(0)64 501 039, Cell: +264(0)81 293 2212,
Fax: +264(0)64 501 039
buckcamp@mweb.com.na

Self-catering chalets.

Languages: English, Afrikaans

Facilities:

Activities:

Buck's Camping Lodge — 2

Caravan Park — $
Off Nickey Iyambo St, Henties Bay
w137639

Tel: +264(0)64 501 039, Cell: +264(0)81 293 2212,
Fax: +264(0)64 501 039
buckcamp@mweb.com.na

45 Campsites, each with its own shower, toilet, wash-up and power point. 24-hour security. Walking distance from shops, pubs, restaurants, golf courses etc.

Languages: English, Afrikaans

Facilities:

Activities:

Cape Cross Lodge — 3

Lodge — $$$
56km or 41min NW of Henties Bay (of which 1km is 4WD)
w137436

Tel: +264(0)64 694 012, Cell: +264(0)81 244 0037,
Fax: +264(0)64 694 013
bookings@capecross.org,
www.capecross.org

Comfortable, double, en-suite rooms with private balcony (wooden chairs and tables). Activities include seal visit, kayaking, surfing, coastal angling etc.

Languages: English, German, Afrikaans

Facilities:

Activities:

Cape Cross Lodge — 4

Lodge Camp — $
56km or 41min NW of Henties Bay (of which 1km is 4WD)
w261539

Tel: +264(0)64 694 012, Cell: +264(0)81 244 0037,
Fax: +264(0)64 694 013
bookings@capecross.org,
www.capecross.org

21 campsites, each with its own light, power point, washbasin, work surface and braai. Central ablution block with flush toilets. Separate bar for campers.

Languages: English, German, Afrikaans

Facilities:

Activities:

De Duine Hotel — 5

Hotel — $$
34 Duine Road, Henties Bay
w138696

Tel: +264(0)64 500 001, Cell: +264(0)81 259 1481,
Fax: +264(0)64 500 724
deduinehotel@iway.na,
www.deduinehotel.com

20 Comfortable, en-suite rooms with air-conditioning and satellite TV.

Languages: English, Afrikaans

Facilities:

Activities:

Henties Bay

Desert Rendezvous	6
Guest House	$$

238 Strandloper St, Henties Bay
w361726

Tel: +264(0)64 500 281, Cell: +264(0)81 255 3751
desertrendezvous@iway.na
www.desertrendezvous.co.za

Guest rooms with seating area, satellite TV and private bathroom (free toiletries and bath). One unit is wheelchair-friendly.

Languages: Polish, English, Afrikaans

Facilities:

Desert Rose Holiday Flats	7
Self-catering	$$

Elf St, Henties Bay
w141529

Tel: +264(0)64 500 181, Cell: +264(0)81 277 3704,
desertrose.firstresorts@gmail.com
www.desertroseresort.co.za

Comfortable, self-catering, 2 and 3-bedroom apartments with en-suite bathrooms. With lounge, braai and secure parking.

Languages: English

Facilities: VISA

Activities:

Die Oord Holiday Accommodation	8
Self-catering	$

Rob St, Henties Bay
w138695

Tel: +264(0)64 500 239, Fax: +264(0)88 633 783
dieoord@iway.na

15 Fully-equipped chalets and bungalows, with bathrooms, separate toilets, kitted kitchens, dining area and braai facilities.

Languages: English, Afrikaans

Facilities: VISA

Eagle Holiday Flats — 9

Self-catering — $
Jakkalsputs St, Henties Bay
w141528

Tel: +264(0)64 500 032, Fax: +264(0)64 500 299
eaglesc@iafrica.com.na

Two bedroom, en-suite chalets which accommodate up to four people. Plus backpackers' hostel. Braai facilities available.

Languages: English, Afrikaans

Facilities:
Activities:

Els Hoekie (Els Corner) Accommodation — 10

Lodge — $
Pylstert st, Henties Bay
w205518

Tel: +264(0)64 500 177, Cell: +264(0)81 271 2111, Fax: +264(0)64 500 177
ltheron@polytechnic.edu.na

Three separate units. One with 12 beds, one with seven beds and one with six beds. Bookings essential during high season.

Languages: English

Facilities:

Fishermans' Guest House — 11

Guest House — $$
2007 Auss St, Henties Bay
w140443

Tel: +264(0)64 501 111, Cell: +264(0)81 303 2694,
reservations@huntandfishnamibia.com
www.huntandfishnamibia.com

Nine, spacious, tastefully-furnished double rooms, all north-facing. This 3-star guest house is 200m from the sea.

Languages: English, Afrikaans

Facilities:
Activities:

Fishermans Inn — 12

Guest House — $$
30km or 22min NW of Henties Bay (of which 1km is 4WD)
w206769

Cell: +264(0)81 129 8162
fishermansinn.henties@gmail.com

This venue has closed.

Facilities:
Activities:

Fishermans Inn — 13

Camping — $
30km or 22min NW of Henties Bay (of which 1km is 4WD)
w261545

Cell: +264(0)81 129 8162
fishermansinn.henties@gmail.com

This venue has closed.

Facilities:
Activities:

Gamsberg Accommodation — 14

Self-catering — $
1847 Brukaros St, Henties Bay
w192913

Tel: +264(0)61 238 800, Fax: +264(0)61 238 167

Two separate units, each accommodating up to 4 people. Units can also be used together as one big house.

Languages: English, German, Afrikaans

Facilities:
Activities:

Haus Estnic B&B — 15

Bed and Breakfast — $
1417 Omatako St, Henties Bay
w141527

Tel: +264(0)64 501 902, Cell: +264(0)81 201 2381,
Fax: +264(0)64 501 902
hausestnic@iway.na,
www.hausestnic.weebly.com

Luxurious, en-suite double rooms (6 people max), equipped with coffee/tea facilities and DStv. Hearty breakfasts available.

Languages: English, Afrikaans, Dutch

Facilities:
Activities:

Huis Klipdrift — 16

Self-catering — $$
142 Kabeljou St, Henties Bay
w192939

Tel: +264(0)64 501 329, Cell: +264(0)81 127 3823,
Fax: +264(0)88 620 856
val@iway.na,
www.huisklipdrift.com

Eight self-catering units. One to four bedrooms, all units equipped with stove, fridge, oven, microwave, cutlery, crockery and bedding. Good security.

Languages: English, Afrikaans

Facilities:
Activities:

Namib Shore Guest House — 17

Guest House — $
303 Dolfyn St, Henties Bay
w142962

Tel: +264(0)64 500 182, Cell: +264(0)81 127 5663,
Fax: +264(0)64 500 182
namshore@iway.na,
www.namshore.iway.na

En-suite rooms with air-conditioning and TV.

Plus, fully-equipped, self-catering unit.

Languages: English, Afrikaans

Facilities:
Activities:

St Nowhere Spa — 18

Lodge — $
103km or 1h14min NW of Henties Bay (of which 1km is 4WD)
w141952

Cell: +264(0)81 252 9422
stnowhere@mtcmobile.com.na

Fishing lodge with five cabins and a main house which sleeps up to 8. Equipped with kitchens, refrigerators, gas stoves, single beds, tables & chairs, cutlery and braai areas.

Languages: English, Afrikaans

Facilities:
Activities:

St Nowhere Spa — 19

Lodge Camp — $$
103km or 1h14min NW of Henties Bay (of which 1km is 4WD)
w141953

Cell: +264(0)81 252 9422
stnowhere@mtcmobile.com.na

Campsites close to the beach, with flush toilets, hot showers and braai area. Wood, ice, braai packs and bait for sale. Meals can be ordered in advance from the restaurant.

Languages: English, Afrikaans

Facilities:
Activities:

"The real voyage of discovery consists not in seeking new landscapes, but in having new eyes."

Marcel Proust

Langstrand

(photo: Karin Theron)

LANGSTRAND IS A BEACH RESORT located between the two coastal towns of Walvis Bay and Swakopmund. The name is Afrikaans for 'Long Beach' and you'll find that some people refer to it by this English translation. This venue achieved some fame for hosting Angelina Jolie and Brad Pitt when Jolie was at the end of her pregnancy with Shiloh.

Traveller Description

Langstrand is not a town, but a holiday resort with a kiosk, bar and restaurant which is only open in high season. It offers a variety of accommodation, from luxury to chalets, and some camping.

Travel Info

While very little happens in Langstrand during the off-season, it's located opposite the Walvisbay dune belt, home to Daredevil Adventures who organise quad bike trips into the dunes.

Damara Tern Self Catering — 1

Self-catering $$
Rand Rifles, Skeleton Coast
w358036

Cell: +264(0)81 124 7246
langford@mweb.com.na

Holiday home with three bedrooms and bathrooms, dining area, kitchen (dishwasher & oven), free Wi-Fi, and private bathroom with a hot tub.

Languages: English

Facilities: VISA @

Activities:

Dolphin Park Accommodation — 2

Self-catering $$
Dolphin Park next to Long Beach
w137626

Tel: +264(0)64 204 343, Fax: +264(0)88 624 909
dolphinpark@iway.na

20 Self-catering chalets with up to four beds. Plus a private VIP chalet with six beds.

Languages: English

Facilities: VISA

Activities:

Long Beach Leisure Park — 3

Caravan Park $
Langstrand
w137707

Tel: +264(0)64 200 163, Cell: +264(0)81 268 9698, Fax: +264(0)88 624 909
longbeachresort@iway.na

Campsites for tents and caravans, with clean ablutions. Open seasonally.

Languages: English

Facilities: VISA

Activities:

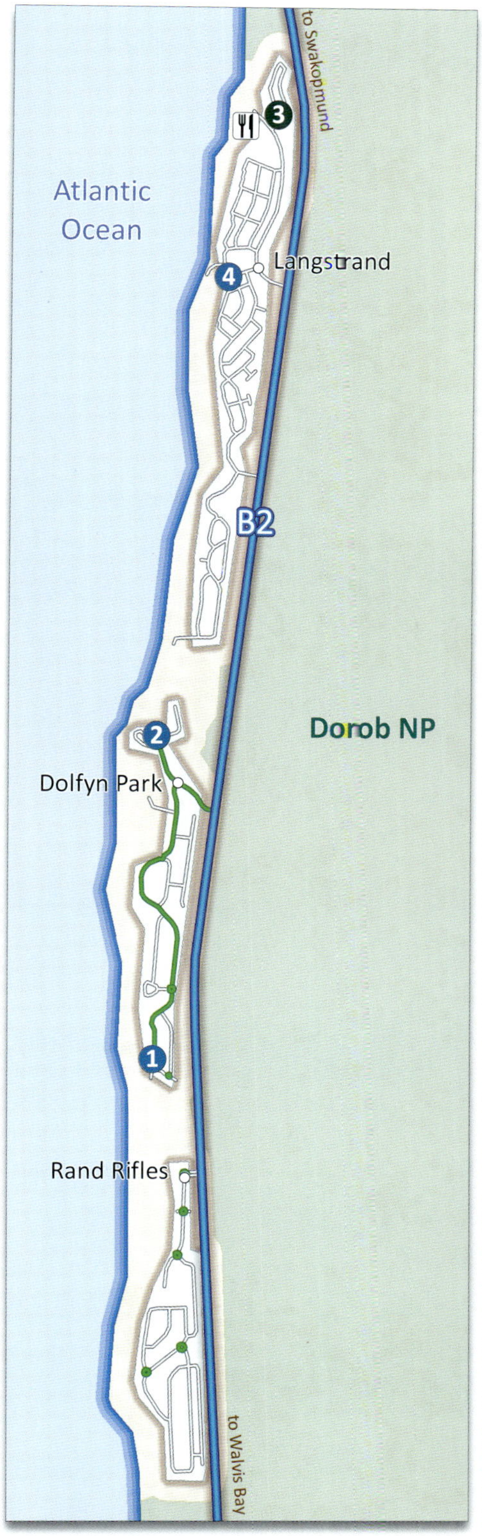

Long Beach Lodge	4
Lodge	$$

Langstrand
w138817

Tel: +264(0)64 218 820, Fax: +264(0)64 218 855
longbeachlodge@iway.na

En-suite rooms with private sea-view patios, DStv, indoor braai area and garden. Breakfast included.

Languages: English

Facilities: VISA FC @

Activities:

"Travel far enough, you meet yourself."

David Mitchell, Cloud Atlas

(photo: Neil Harrison)

(photo: Anet Bosman)

SKELETON COAST • Langstrand

Skeleton Coast National Park

Fishing at Mile 13. (photo: Frank Höppener)

IF YOU REALLY WANT TO ESCAPE the crowds (or if you're a keen angler), be sure to include Skeleton Coast National Park in your itinerary. Within the park, Torra Bay and Terrace Bay are popular resorts and excellent fishing spots. One drives through the park when in transit between Henties and Twyfelfontein. With the necessary fishing permit, you can stop at any of the beaches to fish, or to view the shipwrecks. Access to Torra Bay and Terrace Bay is limited to those with reservations there. To explore the park north of Terrace Bay requires a permit from one of the concession holders - who are generally fly-in safari operators.

Traveller Description

The only places to overnight in the Skeleton Coast National Park are Terrace Bay, Torra Bay and the campsite at Springbokwasser. Torra Bay is only open in December/January and visitors must be self-sufficient as campsites are very basic. The ablution facilities were upgraded in recent years. Terrace Bay Camp is open all year round and offers lodging and other facilities.

If you're lucky you'll find gemstone beaches in this park, places where the sands gleam with wave-polished semi-precious stones like red & maroon garnets, magnetite (magnetic shiny black iron ore), amethysts, agate, ilmenite (containing titanium) quartzes and carnelians. This is a national park so you're not allowed to remove any of this material. Larger items of interest include scattered whale skeletons and shipwrecks.

The park contains rich lichen fields which survive on moisture from the coastal fogs which sweep in nightly. Travellers are requested to not drive off the main tracks as this destroys the lichen fields and other vegetation.

Travel Info

The southern gate is at the Ugab river, some 207km north of Swakopmund. From there it's a further 110km to the camp at Torra Bay and another 50km to Terrace Bay. The northern exit gate is at Springbokwasser, 40km east of Torra Bay. The road through the park is a very good 'salt' road. Fishing from the shore is excellent, but remember that a permit is required. You must also acquaint yourself with bag limits and minimum sizes.

TRAVEL TIP! Terrace Bay and Torra Bay are normally fully booked a year in advance.

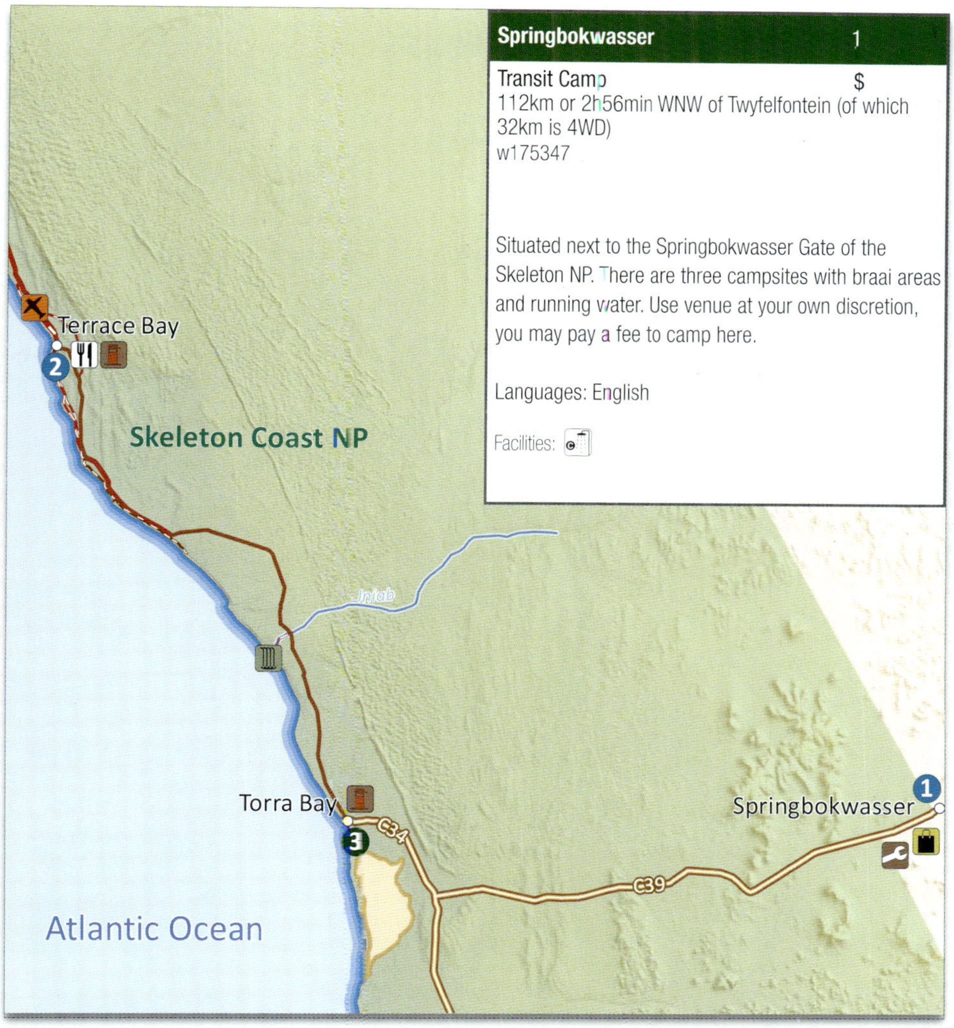

Springbokwasser 1

Transit Camp $
112km or 2h56min WNW of Twyfelfontein (of which 32km is 4WD)
w175347

Situated next to the Springbokwasser Gate of the Skeleton NP. There are three campsites with braai areas and running water. Use venue at your own discretion, you may pay a fee to camp here.

Languages: English

Facilities:

Terrace Bay Camp 2

Lodge $$
Terrace Bay
w138182

Tel: +264(0)61 285 7200, Fax: +264(0)61 224 900
reservations@nwr.com.na
www.nwr.com.na

20 En-suite, double rooms. Plus, two beach chalets for groups or families. Ideal for anglers. No camping. Reservations advisable.

Languages: English

Facilities:
Activities:

Torra Bay Resort 3

Holiday Resort Camp $$$
Torra Bay
w137611

Tel: +264(0)61 285 7200, Cell: +264(0)83 700 0037
reservations@nwr.com.na
www.nwr.com.na

60 Campsites with communal ablutions and basic amenities. Venue open December & January only. Reservations advisable. Angler's paradise.

Languages: English

Facilities:
Activities:

(photo: Ian-Ray Nel)

Swakopmund

(photo: Frank Höppener)

IN 1892 GERMAN SOUTH-WEST AFRICA had a problem. Their rivals, the British, had a natural deep-water harbour just down the coast at Walvis Bay. Not discouraged, they built their own harbour using an artificial breakwater, and so Swakopmund was born – this site was also chosen for its fresh water sources. The town quickly became the main port for imports and exports for the whole German territory but it all came to an abrupt end when German South-West Africa was occupied by the Union of South Africa in 1915.

The change in government saw all harbour activities transferred from Swakopmund to Walvis Bay. In hindsight, it was just as well because the artificial breakwater at Swakopmund, the 'Mole', had already silted up and the port was by now reliant on a somewhat unreliable wooden jetty.

As business, industry and government decamped south to Walvis Bay, the town's growth briefly faltered. But happily, Swakopmund had already started to achieve popularity as a holiday town and the town has continued to grow in this direction to this day. The uranium discovery at Rössing (now the largest opencast mine of its kind worldwide), near Arandis, some 70 km east of Swakopmund, has also had a sizable impact on the town's growth.

Traveller Description

If you're looking for firm evidence of Namibia's German colonial heritage, this is a town to include on your itinerary. In Swakopmund you'll find some fine examples of German architecture which you can admire while sustaining yourself with German pastries and beer in the town's many coffee shops and bars. This is a friendly place and is a firm favourite with Namibians too, especially in the summer months when the coast offers a cool break from the heat of the interior.

Swakopmund is located within the recently-proclaimed Dorob National Park and is a gateway to many adventures in the adjacent Namib Desert, particularly so-called extreme sports like sky diving, quad biking, sand boarding, mountain biking and hot-air ballooning. But whether you're here to chill or scare yourself senseless, this is a town where you can easily spend three days.

Travel Info

Attractions in Swakopmund include the Swakopmund Museum, the National Marine Aquarium and a crystal gallery. Gas refills can be done at Cymot and there is a Spar, Pick n Pay, Shoprite and many other department stores. Alta Brücke is a very well-regarded resort which offers both self-catering chalets and campsites.

Other useful numbers:

State hospital tel: +264(0)64 410 6000

TRAVEL TIP! December is a very busy time here, bookings will definitely be required. Although the municipal area of Swakopmund is excluded from the recently proclaimed Dorob National Park, you should take note of restricted roads outside the town and respect efforts to protect this beautiful coastline.

Town Info:

Hospital: +264(0)64 412 200
Police: +264(0)64 415 000
Doctor: +264(0)64 465 000
Tow-in: +264(0)81 129 0789
Tourism: +264(0)64 404 827

16 @ Plover Studios — 1

Apartment — $$
16 Plover St, Swakopmund
w311191

Cell: +264(0)81 284 6010
christel@16atplover.com
www.ploverfarmhouse.com

Self-catering, air-conditioned apartments with seating area, kitchenette and patio. No children under 12.

Languages: English, Afrikaans

Facilities:
Activities:

Alte Brücke Holiday Resort — 2

Self-catering — $$
Strand St, Swakopmund
w138527

Tel: +264(0)64 404 918, Fax: +264(0)64 400 153
info@altebrucke.com
www.altebrucke.com

Fully-equipped, self-catering chalets. Includes cutlery, bedding and towels. Breakfast included in rate.

Languages: English, Afrikaans

Facilities:
Activities:

Alte Brücke Holiday Resort — 3

Holiday Resort Camp — $$
Swakopmund
w239887

Tel: +264(0)64 404 918, Fax: +264(0)64 400 153
info@altebrucke.com
www.altebrucke.com

Luxury, grassed campsites. Each with their own power point, ablution, braai and wash-up facility.

Languages: English, Afrikaans

Facilities:
Activities:

Alternative Space B&B — 4

Bed and Breakfast — $$
167 Anton Lubowski St, Kramersdorf, Swakopmund
w300098

Fax: +264(0)88 652 8458, Cell: +264(0)81 300 9352
sibylle@thealternativespace.com
www.thealternativespace.com

Four individually designed and decorated, non-smoking, en-suite rooms. Buffet breakfast from 7 till noon.

Languages: English, German

Facilities:
Activities:

Amanpuri Travellers Lodge — 5

Lodge — $
c/o Moses Garoeb & Anton Lubowski St, Swakopmund
w252788

Tel: +264(0)64 405 587, Cell: +264(0)81 250 3668, Fax: +264(0)64 404 597
amanpuri@afol.com.na

Spacious, well-maintained rooms; includes full English breakfast and secure parking. Within walking distance of shops, restaurants, beaches, dunes etc.

Languages: English

Facilities:
Activities:

Swakopmund

to Henties Bay
C34
C34
Beach Lodge
Ernst Konnecke
Dorob NP
Atlantic
Ocean
Tsavorite
Fischreiher
Flamingo
Schwietering
Aldridge
Henties Bay
Vrede Rede
First
Welwitchia
Rakotoka
Nelson Mandela Dr
Noord Strand
Harbour
Moses Garoeb
to Windhoek
B2
Sam Nujoma
Libertina Amathila
Anton Lubowski
Rhode Allee
Swakop
Dorob NP
to Walvis Bay

Anandi Guesthouse Swakopmund 6

Guest House $$
14 Nelken St, Ocean View, Swakopmund
w239931

Tel: +264(0)64 406 553, Cell: +264(0)81 147 7922,
Fax: +264(0)64 406 550
anandiswakop@iway.na,
www.anandiguesthouse.com

En-suite rooms with kettle, fridge and TV. Self-catering units with small kitchenette. There's also a spacious lounge and indoor braai.

Languages: English, Afrikaans

Facilities: VISA @

Activities:

An Der Mole Apartment 7

Self-catering $$
Ludwig Koch St, Swakopmund
w261538

Tel: +264(0)64 462 468, Cell: +264(0)81 129 0026,
Fax: +264(0)64 462 363
info@cornerstoneguesthouse.com

Fully-furnished, luxury apartment with three bedrooms, two bathrooms and a balcony (with braai facilities) overlooking the sea.

Languages: English, German, Afrikaans

Facilities: VISA @

Activities:

Atlantic Villa Boutique Guesthouse 8

Guest House $$
Plover St, Swakopmund
w209714

Tel: +264(0)64 463 511, Cell: +264(0)85 218 4962,
Fax: +264(0)64 463 510
bookings@atlantic-villa.com,
www.atlantic-villa.com

Luxury suites, luxury rooms, deluxe rooms, standard rooms, self-catering units and family units. Each room has an espresso coffee machine, free Wi-Fi and DStv.

Languages: English, Afrikaans

Facilities: VISA FC @

Activities:

Atlantik Sicht Apartment 9

Self-catering $$
Strand St, bt Jetty and Aquarium, Swakopmund
w243164

Tel: +264(0)64 462 468, Cell: +264(0)81 129 0026,
Fax: +264(0)64 462 363
info@cornerstoneguesthouse.com

Three luxurious double rooms with en-suite bedrooms. Two twin rooms share bathroom and private balcony with sea views.

Languages: English, German, Afrikaans

Facilities: VISA

Activities:

Beach Hotel Swakopmund 10

Hotel $$$
1 Strand St, Swakopmund
w279632

Tel: +264(0)64 417 700, Fax: +264(0)88 652 1199
info@beach.na
www.beach-hotel-swakopmund.com

25 Rooms and eight apartments. Each room has a TV, air-conditioner, mini bar, telephone and bathroom. Breakfast included in rates.

Languages: English

Facilities: VISA @

Activities:

Beach Walk House And Cottage 11

Self-catering $$
5 Lumen St, Swakopmund
w313108

Cell: +264(0)81 281 9298
info@jan-jonker.com
www.selfcatering-namibia.com

Self-catering units with satellite TV, seating area, fireplace and fully-equipped kitchen.

Languages: English, Afrikaans, German

Facilities: VISA

Activities:

Beach Lodge 12

Hotel $$
1 Stint St, Vogelstrand, Swakopmund
w140622

Tel: +264(0)64 414 500, Cell: +264(0)81 127 3397,
Fax: +264(0)64 414 501
reservations@beachlodge.com.na,
www.beachlodge.com.na

Standard and luxury twin and family rooms with seafront views. All rooms are en-suite with satellite TV and Wi-Fi access. Portable braais available.

Languages: English, German

Facilities: VISA @ FC Activities:

BON Hotel Swakopmund 13

Hotel $$
5371 Welwitschia, Swakopmund
w313599

Tel: +264(0)64 426 800
skm.reservations@bonhotels.com
www.bonhotels.com

34 rooms, dome- and sea-facing. This 4-star hotel caters for sport groups, leisure, corporates and conferences.

Languages: English, Afrikaans

Facilities: VISA @

Activities:

Brigadoon Guest Cottages 14

Bed and Breakfast $$
16 Ludwig Koch St, Swakopmund
w140336

Tel: +264(0)64 406 064, Fax: +264(0)64 464 195
brigadoon@iway.na
www.brigadoonswakopmund.com

One- or two-bedroom cottages, each with kitchenette and private patio. Twin or double rooms with en-suite bathrooms. Breakfast offered.

Languages: English, Afrikaans

Facilities: VISA @

Activities:

Chala-Kigi Apartments 15

Self-catering $$
16 Riverside Avenue, Kramersdorf, Swakopmund
w224551

Tel: +264(0)64 407 033, Cell: +264(0)81 128 2481,
Fax: +264(0)88 619 395
chala-kigi@gsteu.com

Self-catering unit with views over Namib Desert and Atlantic Ocean. Or palm garden apartment with patio. Secure parking, own entrance and braai facilities.

Languages: English, Afrikaans, Dutch, German

Facilities: FC @

Activities:

Swakopmund

Cornerstone Guesthouse 16

Guest House $$
40 Hendrik Witbooi St, Swakopmund
w219544

Tel: +264(0)64 462 468, Cell: +264(0)81 129 0026,
info@cornerstoneguesthouse.com
www.cornerstoneguesthouse.com

Five en-suite, double rooms, all with separate entrances, TV, Wi-Fi, coffee/tea facilities, bar fridge and safe.

Languages: English, German, Afrikaans

Facilities:
Activities:

Desert Breeze Lodge 17

Lodge $$$
Riverside Ave, Swakopmund
w267636

Tel: +264(0)64 406 236, Cell: +264(0)81 149 4979,
info@desertbreezeswakopmund.com
www.desertbreezeswakopmund.com

12 En-suite bungalows or villas. Venue located just outside Swakopmund next to Swakop River.

Languages: English, German, Afrikaans

Facilities:
Activities:

Desert Sky Backpackers Lodge 18

Backpackers Hostel $$
35 Anton Lubowski St, Swakopmund
w139588

Tel: +264(0)64 402 339, Fax: +264(0)88 650 9638
info@desertskylodging.com
www.desertskylodging.com

Dorms and double rooms. Plus, self-catering kitchen, braai facilities, TV, lounge and lockers.

Languages: English

Facilities:
Activities:

Dunedin Guest Lodge 19

Lodge $
c/o Daniel Tjongarero and Windhoeker Sts, Swakopmund
w139602

Tel: +264(0)64 403 437, Fax: +264(0)64 406 991
info@dunedinstar.com
www.dunedinstar.com

Comfortable single, double or triple rooms with en-suite bathrooms. Assistance offered with booking activities and tours. Venue is close to town centre.

Languages: English

Facilities:
Activities:

Footprints Self-Catering & B&B 20

Bed and Breakfast $$
100 Turmalin St, Hage Heights, Swakopmund
w175373

Tel: +264(0)64 403 042, Cell: +264(0)81 251 3111,
Fax: +264(0)64 403 132
footprin@mweb.com.na,
www.footprints2swakop.com

Self-catering and B&B sections. With TV, business travel luxuries and parking.

Languages: English, Afrikaans

Facilities:
Activities:

Gecko Ridge Guest House 21

Guest House $$
18km or 17min ENE of Swakopmund
w274140

Tel: +264(0)61 250 725, Cell: +264(0)81 214 6567
geckoridge@resdest.com
www.geckoridgeguesthouse.com

10 Campsites, seven self-catering chalets (pet-friendly) and six luxury rooms. Plus fully-equipped gym, pool, TV and Wi-Fi.

Languages: English, German

Facilities:
Activities:

Gut Richthofen 22

Self-catering $
20km or 20min ENE of Swakopmund
w138216

Tel: +264(0)64 404 309, Cell: +264(0)81 129 0758,
Fax: +264(0)64 405 553
richthofen@iway.na

Comfortable, shaded accommodation.

Languages: English, German

Facilities:
Activities:

Hansa Hotel 23

Hotel $$
3 Hendrik Witbooi St, Swakopmund
w142671

Tel: +264(0)64 414 200, Fax: +264(0)64 414 299
reservations@hansahotel.com.na
www.hansahotel.com.na

En-suite rooms with air-conditioning, satellite TV, underfloor heating, safes and coffee/tea facilities. Services include babysitting and laundry.

Languages: English, German, Afrikaans

Facilities: FC
Activities:

Hotel D'Avignon 24

Hotel $
25 Libertine Amathila St, Swakopmund
w139266

Tel: +264(0)64 405 821, Fax: +264(0)64 405 542
davignon@iway.na
www.hoteldavignon.com

Single, double and triple en-suite rooms. Breakfast buffet and secure parking included.

Languages: English

Facilities:
Activities:

Hotel Deutsches Haus 25

Hotel $$
13 Lüderitz St, Swakopmund
w139585

Tel: +264(0)64 404 896, Fax: +264(0)64 404 861
reservations@hotel.na
www.hotel.na

All rooms are modern and have a private shower and toilet. Hotel in traditional German style.

Languages: English, German, Afrikaans

Facilities: FC
Activities:

Hotel Eberwein 26

Hotel $$
c/o Otavi & Sam Nujoma Sts, Swakopmund
w216348

Tel: +264(0)64 414 450, Fax: +264(0)64 414 451
eberwein@iafrica.com.na
www.hotel-eberwein.com

16 Double rooms furnished in Victorian style. All rooms are en-suite and have a TV, mini bar, underfloor heating and hairdryer.

Languages: English, German, Afrikaans

Facilities:
Activities:

Hotel Europa Hof 27

Hotel $$
39 Bismark st, Swakopmund
w140444

Tel: +264(0)64 405 061, Fax: +264(0)64 402 391
info@europahof.com
www.europahof.com

Single, double or family en-suite rooms. All equipped with TV, heater, coffee/tea facilities and free Wi-Fi.

Languages: English, German, Afrikaans

Facilities:
Activities:

Hotel Pension A la Mer 28

Hotel $$
4 Libertina Amathila Ave, Swakopmund
w267594

Tel: +264(0)64 404 130, Fax: +264(0)64 404 170
alamer@iway.na
www.pension-a-la-mer.com

Comfortable single, double and family rooms. All rooms en-suite and decorated in unique African style.

Languages: English, German, Afrikaans

Facilities:

Activities:

Hotel Pension Rapmund 29

Hotel $$
6-8 Bismarck St, Swakopmund
w142695

Tel: +264(0)64 402 035, Cell: +264(0)81 420 6142, Fax: +264(0)64 404 524
rapmund@iafrica.com.na,
www.hotelpensionrapmund.com

20 Standard, two family and two luxury en-suite rooms. Bed and breakfast basis, no other meals supplied.

Languages: English

Facilities:

Activities:

Hotel Prinzessin Rupprecht 30

Hotel $$
15 Anton Lubowski St, Swakopmund
w142667

Tel: +264(0)64 412 540, Fax: +264(0)64 412 541
info@hotel-prinzessin-rupprecht.com
www.en.hotel-prinzessin-rupprecht.com

Single, double and triple rooms, all en-suite. Five small single rooms with communal ablutions. Two family flats. Rooms equipped with telephone, fridge and TV.

Languages: English, German

Facilities:

Activities:

Hotel Zum Kaiser 31

Hotel $$$
4 Sam Nujoma Ave, Swakopmund
w255840

Tel: +264(0)64 417 100, Fax: +264(0)64 417 130
reservations@hotelzumkaiser.com
www.hotelzumkaiser.com

21 Air-conditioned, en-suite rooms, each with TV, coffee/tea facilities, mini fridge, safe and Wi-Fi.

Languages: English

Facilities: @

Activities:

Indulge Guesthouse 32

Guest House $$
12 Moses Garoeb Street, Swakopmund
w142730

Tel: +264(0)64 414 750
stay@indulgenam.com
www.indulgenamibia.com

En-suite rooms with satellite TV, under-floor heating, fridge and coffee/tea facilities. Laundry offered. Secure parking.

Languages: English

Facilities: FC @

Activities:

Jan Jonker Holiday Apartments 33

Self-catering $$
9 Kiebitz St, Vineta, Swakopmund
w301252

Cell: +264(0)81 281 9298
info@jan-jonker.com
www.selfcatering-namibia.com

Comfortable accommodation within walking distance of Swakopmund's beaches.

Languages: English, Afrikaans, German

Facilities:

Activities:

Mile 4 Caravan Park 34

Self-catering $
7km or 12min from Swakopmund central
w261551

Tel: +264(0)64 461 781, Cell: +264(0)81 122 1759, Fax: +264(0)64 462 901
reservation@mile4swkp.com,
www.mile4swkp.com

Three fully-equipped bungalows / flats with 2-3 bedrooms, kitchen / lounge area, braai and garage. Plus fully-equipped, self-catering dorms.

Languages: English, Afrikaans

Facilities: FC

Activities:

Mile 4 Caravan Park 35

Caravan Park $
7km or 13min N of Swakopmund
w137393

Tel: +264(0)64 461 781, Cell: +264(0)81 122 1759, Fax: +264(0)64 462 901
reservation@mile4swkp.com,
www.mile4swkp.com

Numerous campsites with power points. Ablution blocks with cooking facilities. Reportedly, good security here.

Languages: English, Afrikaans

Facilities: FC

Activities:

Prost Hotel 36

Hotel $$
42 Nathaniel Maxuilili St, Swakopmund
w142668

Tel: +264(0)64 429 600, Fax: +264(0)64 429 649
bookings@prosthotel.com
www.prosthotel.com

28 En-suite luxury, family and standard rooms.

Languages: English, Afrikaans

Facilities: FC @

Activities:

Rossmund Lodge 37

Lodge $$
9km or 11min E of Swakopmund
w142669

Tel: +264(0)64 414 600, Cell: +264(0)81 639 1775, Fax: +264(0)64 414 649
lodge@rossmund.com,
www.rossmund.com

21 Luxury, en-suite rooms, eight facing golf course greens, all with fireplace. Plus two VIP chalets.

Languages: English, Afrikaans

Facilities: @

Activities:

Royal Benguela Guesthouse 38

Lodge $$
6km or 9min N of Swakopmund
w254419

Tel: +264(0)64 402 193, Cell: +264(0)81 124 2567, Fax: +264(0)64 402 193
info@royalbenguela.com,
www.royalbenguela.com

Seven rooms in quaint, quiet guesthouse with sea and desert views.

Languages: English

Facilities: FC @

Activities:

Sam's Giardino Hotel-Pension 39

Guest House $$
89 Anton Lubowski St, Kramersdorf, Swakopmund
w139475

Tel: +264(0)64 403 210, Fax: +264(0)64 403 500
request@giardinonamibia.com
www.giardinonamibia.com

En-suite rooms in small, homely guest house offering Swiss hospitality.

Languages: English

Facilities: FC @

Activities:

Swakopmund

Sandcastle Apartments 40

Self-catering $$
4 Woker St, Swakopmund
w208906

Tel: +264(0)64 403 632, Cell: +264(0)81 370 7231,
mail@sandcastle-swakopmund.com
www.sandcastle-swakopmund.com

Fully-equipped, en-suite apartments with satellite TV. Bedding and towels provided.

Languages: English, German

Facilities: VISA FC @

Activities:

Sandfields Guest House 41

Guest House $$
11 Sphinx St, Vineta, Swakopmund
w189422

Tel: +264(0)64 463 136, Cell: +264(0)81 200 4014,
Fax: +264(0)64 463 179
info@sandfieldsguesthouse.com,
www.sandfieldsguesthouse.com

Single, double, twin and triple en-suite rooms with modern amenities in a small, upmarket venue.

Languages: English, German, Italian, Afrikaans

Facilities: VISA FC @

Activities:

Schweizerhaus Hotel 42

Hotel $$
1 Bismarck St, Swakopmund
w142694

Tel: +264(0)64 400 331, Fax: +264(0)64 405 850
reservations@schweizerhaus.net
www.schweizerhaus.net

Standard, luxury and deluxe, en-suite rooms with television and balcony.

Languages: English

Facilities: VISA @

Activities:

Sea Breeze Guest House Swakopmund 43

Guest House $$
48 Turmalin St, Swakopmund
w142696

Tel: +264(0)64 463 348, Cell: +264(0)81 127 0842,
Fax: +264(0)64 463 349
seabreeze@seabreeze.com.na,
www.seabreeze.com.na

Six twin or double rooms with breakfast included. Or four en-suite, self-catering units with kitchenettes. There's a lounge with TV and balcony overlooking the sea. Secure parking.

Languages: English, Afrikaans

Facilities: VISA FC @

Activities:

Sea Side Hotel And Spa 44

Hotel $$
7km or 14min N of Swakopmund
w189055

Tel: +264(0)64 415 900, Cell: +264(0)81 124 7730,
Fax: +264(0)64 415 999
info@ssh.na,
www.seasidehotelandspa.com

30 Rooms and six suites. Venue has a restaurant and spa (sauna, steam room and jacuzzis). Wedding catering offered.

Languages: English, Afrikaans

Facilities: VISA FC @

Activities:

Sophia Dale Base Camp 45

Self-catering $$
13km or 12min ENE of Swakopmund
w255841

Tel: +264(0)64 403 264, Cell: +264(0)81 413 0504
info@sophiadale.org
www.sophiadale.org

Self-catering bungalows and guestrooms. Shop sells basics as well as homemade polonies and other meat specialties. Laundry service.

Languages: English, German

Facilities: @

Activities:

Sophia Dale Base Camp 46

Lodge Camp $
13km or 14min ENE of Swakopmund
w139104

Tel: +264(0)64 403 264, Cell: +264(0)81 413 0504
info@sophiadale.org
www.sophiadale.org

Campsites with braai facilities, lights, power points, table & chairs and rubbish bins. Plus shop selling basic necessities and meat delicacies.

Languages: English, German

Facilities: @

Activities:

Strand Hotel Swakopmund 47

Hotel $$$
An der Mole, Swakopmund
w279637

Tel: +264(0)64 411 4000
strand.res@ol.na
www.strandhotelswakopmund.com

Rooms with air-conditioning, mini bars and TV. Sea or garden views.

Languages: English, German, Afrikaans

Facilities: VISA FC @

Activities:

Strauss Holiday & Overnight Flats 48

Self-catering $$
10 Hidipo Hamutenya St, Swakopmund
w142697

Tel: +264(0)64 412 350, Cell: +264(0)81 124 4937,
Fax: +264(0)64 412 351
straussholidays@iway.na,
www.straussholidays.com

Bed & Breakfast and self-catering units. Conveniently located close to town and beach. Secure parking.

Languages: English

Facilities: VISA

Activities:

Swakopmund Accommodation 49

Self-catering $$
4 Bernstein St, Swakopmund
w141453

Tel: +264(0)64 462 743
info@swakopmundaccommodation.com
www.swakopmundaccommodation.com

Self-catering units about 200m from the beach and within walking distance of shopping mall, restaurants and coffee shops.

Languages: Spanish, Portuguese, Italian

Facilities: VISA @

Activities:

Swakopmund Guesthouse 50

Guest House $$
Hendrik Witbooi St, Swakopmund
w216345

Tel: +264(0)64 462 008, Fax: +264(0)64 461 008
reservations@swakopmundguesthouse.com
www.swakopmundguesthouse.com

Air-conditioned, en-suite rooms with internet access, safe, mini bar and coffee/tea facilities. Five minutes walk from beach. Secure parking.

Languages: English, German, Afrikaans

Facilities: VISA @

Activities:

Swakopmund Hotel & Entertainment Centre 51

Hotel $$$
2 Theo-Ben Gurirab St, Swakopmund
w139262

Tel: +264(0)64 410 5200, Fax: +264(0)64 410 5360
swakopmund@legacyhotels.co.za
www.legacyhotels.co.za

Victorian-style hotel with well-equipped, en-suite, air-conditioned rooms. Plus laundry, cinemas, casino, internet access and a pool.

Languages: English

Facilities: VISA FC @

Activities:

Swakopmund Municipal Rest Camp 52

Self-catering $
c/o Hendrik Witbooi & Swakop Sts, Swakopmund
w138093

Tel: +264(0)64 410 4618, Cell: +264(0)81 128 5893
restcamp@swkmun.com.na
www.swakopmund-restcamp.com

Two-bedroomed fishermen's cabins, luxury four-bed bungalow, A-frame chalets (sleep up to six) and VIP bungalows with private verandas.

Languages: English

Facilities: VISA

Activities:

Swakopmund Plaza Hotel 53

Hotel $$$
42 Libertina Amathila Ave, Swakopmund
w360057

Tel: +264(0)64 426 500, Cell: +264(0)81 129 2799, Fax: +264(0)88 655 7937
info@plaza.na,
www.plaza.na

Air-conditioned rooms with satellite TV and private bathroom (bath or shower).

Languages: English

Facilities: VISA @

Activities:

Swakopmund Sands Hotel 54

Hotel $$
3 Strand St, Swakopmund
w140613

Tel: +264(0)64 405 045, Fax: +264(0)64 404 206
swakopsands@iway.na
www.swakopmundsandshotel.com

14 Luxury en-suite rooms. Beachfront venue has bar, indoor pool, laundry, sauna and gym.

Languages: English, German

Facilities: VISA @

Activities:

The Secret Garden Guest House 55

Guest House $$
36 Bismarck St, Swakopmund
w142698

Tel: +264(0)64 404 037, Fax: +264(0)88 612 196
sgg@iway.na
www.secretgarden.com.na

En-suite rooms with TV, balcony, fully-equipped kitchen, lounge and lock-up garage. Bar on premises. Breakfast included.

Languages: English

Facilities: VISA @

Activities:

The Stiltz B&B 56

Bed and Breakfast $$$
Strand St South, Swakopmund
w142699

Tel: +264(0)64 400 771
info@thestiltz.com
www.thestiltz.com

Luxury villa and nine wooden bungalows on stilts, connected by wooden walkways. Overlooking the sea, riverbed, lagoon and sand dunes.

Languages: English

Facilities: VISA @

Activities:

The Timeless Way 57

Self-catering $
5 Harder St, Vineta, Swakopmund
w139613

Tel: +264(0)61 401 149, Cell: +264(0)81 124 7701, Fax: +264(0)61 401 149
info@thetimelessway.net,
www.thetimelessway.net

Fully-equipped rooms with lounges, kitchens and braai facilities. Bookings essential.

Languages: English, Afrikaans

Facilities:

Activities:

Tiger Reef 58

Camping $$
Sudstrand St, Swakopmund
w239888

Tel: +264(0)64 400 935, Cell: +264(0)81 337 7137, Fax: +264(0)64 400 937
campsite@lighthousegroup.com.na

Basic, shaded campsites with ablution facilities and power points. Located next to Tiger Reef Beach Bar.

Languages: English

Facilities: VISA

Activities:

Veronika B&B 59

Bed and Breakfast $
5 Dolphin St, Swakopmund
w142702

Tel: +264(0)64 404 915, Cell: +264(0)81 208 9359, holiday@veronika-bed-and-breakfast.com
www.veronika-bed-and-breakfast.com

Five spacious single, double and family rooms. Breakfast room and lounge at your disposal.

Languages: English

Facilities: FC @

Activities:

Villa Margherita 60

Bed and Breakfast $$
c/o Daniel Tjongarero and Otavi Sts, Swakopmund
w279633

Tel: +264(0)64 402 991, Cell: +264(0)81 332 4293, Fax: +264(0)64 400 131
info@villamargherita.com.na,
www.villamargherita.com.na

Charming house offering fine accommodation in the heart of historic Swakopmund.

Languages: English, German, Afrikaans, French, Italian

Facilities: VISA FC @

Activities:

Villa Wiese Backpacker's / Guest Lodge 61

Lodge $$
c/o Theo-Ben Gurirab & Windhoeker, Swakopmund
w142664

Tel: +264(0)64 407 105, Cell: ?+264(0)81 715 0226, Fax: +264(0)64 407 106
bookings@villawiese.com,
www.villawiese.com

Single, double and triple rooms as well dorm beds. Free Wi-Fi.

Languages: ?English, German

Facilities: VISA FC @

Activities:

Windpomp14 (Mile 14) Rest Camp 62

Camping $$$
25km or 20min NNW of Swakopmund
w137525

Cell: +264(0)83 700 4414
camp@windpomp14.com

Sea-facing campsites, all with tap, power point and braai facility. Shared ablutions.

Languages: English

Facilities: VISA

Activities:

Walvis Bay

(photo: Anet Bosman)

IN 1487 PORTUGUESE EXPLORER BARTOLOMEU DIAZ put down anchor in a natural harbour he named 'O Golfo de Santa Maria da Conceição' but, for reasons never adequately explained, never laid claim to this land. Almost three centuries later, in 1793, the Cape Colony staked the first colonial title. Just two years on, Walvis Bay was annexed by the British. More recently, in 1910, Walvis Bay was included in the South African Union. It was only in 1994 that this harbour returned to indigenous hands after South Africa and Namibia negotiated its return. Walvis Bay has always been Namibia's main harbour town, with a fishing industry that flourished until its partial collapse in the 70s due to mismanagement. In recent years the harbour has been developed to facilitate more container trade.

Traveller Description

For many years Walvis Bay was the shabby cousin to genteel Swakopmund just up the coast. But these days this harbour town has become a holiday destination in its own right. Harbour activities include dolphin cruises, catamaran trips, fishing expeditions and kayaking; while the adjacent desert offers pursuits like hiking, sand boarding, paragliding, balloon rides, sky diving and quad biking. A lagoon features rich bird life and offers many recreational activities, like kayaking out to Pelican Point to visit the seal colony.

Travel Info

Walvis Bay offers plenty in the way of shops, restaurants and accommodation. And because it's a working harbour you'll also find engineering businesses and the like. So, it's not a bad spot for mechanical repairs and refurbishment.

TRAVEL TIP! Dune 7, the highest dune in the area, lies just outside the town. It's a long trudge to the top but the views are worth the effort. Eco Marine runs kayak tours out to Pelican Point, and if you're looking for a bite to eat, the Raft restaurant offers a memorable dining experience. This wooden building stands on stilts in the lagoon, at the end of its own jetty.

Town Info:

Hospital:	+264(0)64 218 911	Police:	+264(0)64 219 048
Doctor:	+264(0)64 204 356	Tow-in:	+264(0)81 149 8750
Tourism:	+264(0)64 200 606	Embassy:	+264(0)64 206 934

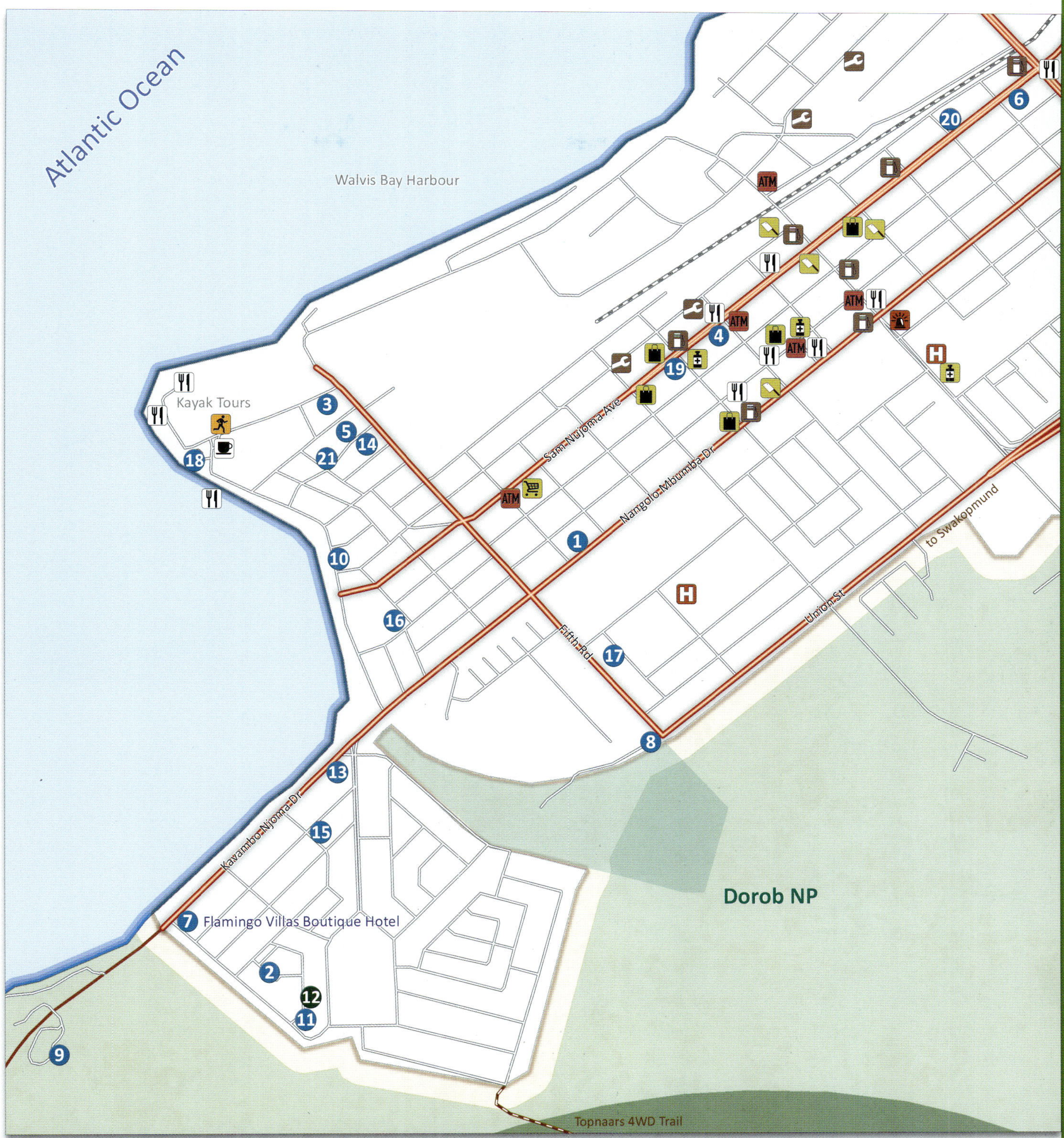

10 de Laan — 1

Self-catering — $

105 Nangolo Mbumba St, Walvis Bay
w311357

Cell: +264(0)81 284 3392

Each unit has a TV, braai facilities and a kitchen with microwave and oven.

Languages: English

Facilities:

Activities:

Amjicaja Guesthouse — 2

Guest House — $$

8 Temple Crescent, Meersig, Walvis Bay
w302659

Tel: +264(0)64 206 225
www.amjicaja.com

Luxury, en-suite rooms, all with DStv, coffee/tea facilities and safe.

Languages: English

Facilities:

Activities:

Ana's Inn Self-catering — 3

Self-catering — $

26 Atlantic St, Walvis Bay
w139935

Tel: +264(0)64 209 164, Cell: +264(0)81 122 0813,
Fax: +264(0)64 209 164
paburger@iway.na,
www.anas-inn.iway.na

Each comfortable, luxurious unit has a fully-equipped kitchen and satellite TV. There's secure parking and braai facilities are available.

Languages: English

Facilities:

Activities:

Walvis Bay

Atlantic Hotel 4

Hotel $
Sam Nujoma Ave, Walvis Bay
w139415

Tel: +264(0)64 213 000, Cell: +264(0)81 128 4501,
Fax: +264(0)64 205 063
reservations@atlantichotel.com.na

Air-conditioned, en-suite rooms with telephone, TV and coffee/tea facilities.

Languages: English

Facilities:

Activities:

Buschtrommel Accommodation & Tours 5

Self-catering $
13 2nd St, Walvis Bay
w206727

Tel: +264(0)64 202 208, Cell: +264(0)81 278 1131,
Fax: +264(0)64 202 208
siggi@buschtrommel-tours.com,
www.buschtrommel-tours.com

One garden flat and four recently-built, en-suite double rooms near the lagoon.

Languages: English, German, Afrikaans

Facilities:

Activities:

Casa Mia Hotel 6

Hotel $$
238 Sam Nujoma Avenue, Walvis Bay
w138719

Tel: +264(0)64 205 975, Cell: +264(0)81 272 5218,
Fax: +264(0)64 206 596
info@casamiahotel.com

Comfortable, elegant rooms with en-suite bathrooms, satellite TV and coffee/tea facilities.

Languages: English

Facilities:

Activities:

Flamingo Villas Boutique Hotel

Flamingo Villas Boutique Hotel **7**

Hotel $$$ 30 Kovambo Nujoma Drive, Walvis Bay w353351

Tel: +264(0)64 205 631, Cell: +264(0)81 162 4917, Fax: +264(0)64 207 869

reservations@flamingovillana.com, www.flamingovillana.com

Comfortable, air-conditioned rooms with private bathroom, DStv, telephone, refrigerator and coffee/tea facilities.

Languages: English

Facilities: Activities:

Dune Chalets Walvis Bay 8

Self-catering $
c/o Union St & Fifth Rd, Walvis Bay
w139938

Cell: +264(0)81 169 6640
bookings@dunechalets.com
www.dunechalets.com

Four self-catering chalets with fully-equipped kitchens. Each chalets sleeps 2 - 3 adults and two children.

Languages: English, German, Afrikaans

Facilities:

Activities:

Esplanade Park 9

Self-catering $
5km or 7min SW of Walvis Bay
w138708

Tel: +264(0)64 206 145, Fax: +264(0)64 209 714
esplandepark@iway.na

27 Fully-equipped cottages, each with braai area and private terrace. Secure parking.

Languages: English

Facilities:

Activities:

Kleines Nest B&B 10

Bed and Breakfast $$
36 Esplanade St, Walvis Bay
w139936

Tel: +264(0)64 203 203, Cell: +264(0)81 278 7050,
Fax: +264(0)64 206 907
kleinnest@iway.na

En-suite rooms with private, lagoon-facing balconies. Equipped with TV, fridge and kettle. Standard rooms have en-suite bathrooms.

Languages: English, German, Afrikaans

Facilities:

Activities:

Lagoon Chalets & Caravan Park 11

Self-catering $
8th Road West, Walvis Bay
w138709

Tel: +264(0)64 217 900, Cell: +264(0)81 128 7151,
Fax: +264(0)64 207 469
info@lagoonchaletswb.com,
www.lagoonchaletswb.com

Fully-equipped chalets accommodate up to six people. Bedding and DStv included. Bookings essential.

Languages: English, Afrikaans

Facilities:

Activities:

Lagoon Chalets & Caravan Park 12

Camping $
8th Road West, Walvis Bay
w255881

Tel: +264(0)64 217 900, Cell: +264(0)81 128 7151,
Fax: +264(0)64 207 469
info@lagoonchaletswb.com,
www.lagoonchaletswb.com

17 Stands with power points. Communal ablutions (warm water).

Languages: English, Afrikaans

Facilities:

Activities:

Lagoon Loge (Lodge) 13

Guest House $$
88 Kowambo Nujoma Drive, Walvis Bay
w138710

Tel: +264(0)64 200 850, Fax: +264(0)64 200 851
french@lagoonloge.com.na
www.lagoonloge.com.na

Eight individually-decorated, en-suite rooms. Lagoon views from balcony / veranda.

Languages: English, French

Facilities:

Activities:

Langholm Hotel 14

Hotel $$
18 - 24 2nd St West, Walvis Bay
w139472

Tel: +264(0)64 209 230, Cell: +264(0)81 127 6987,
Fax: +264(0)64 209 430
desk@langholmhotel.com,
www.langholmhotel.com

12 En-suite double rooms equipped with TV, safe and fridge. There's also a triple room, a luxury room, a family suite and a luxury suite.

Languages: English, Afrikaans

Facilities:

Activities:

Namibia Coast Self Catering & Desert Tours 15

Self-catering $
46 1st North, Meersig, Walvis Bay
w139941

Tel: +264(0)64 205 505, Cell: +264(0)81 129 5505,
Fax: +264(0)64 205 319
grane@mweb.com.na

Three bedroom, self-catering cottage with en-suite bathrooms, kitchen and braai facilities.

Languages: English, Afrikaans

Facilities:

Activities:

Ngandu At Sea / B&B Lodge 16

Bed and Breakfast $
c/o 1st Rd & Theo Ben Guribab, Walvis Bay
w139937

Tel: +264(0)64 207 327, Fax: +264(0)64 207 350
theart@iafrica.com.na

En-suite double rooms, self-catering family unit, and penthouse. Each room has a TV.

Languages: English

Facilities:

Activities:

Omega Bed and Breakfast 17

Bed and Breakfast $$
7 Robert Forbes, Walvis Bay
w272000

Tel: +264(0)64 202 433, Cell: +264(0)81 365 0438
omegabb@iway.na

Comfortable, en-suite rooms with satellite TV and free Wi-Fi. Family rooms also available.

Languages: English

Activities:

Pelican Bay Hotel 18

Hotel $$
Esplanade St, Walvis Bay
w138711

Tel: +264(0)64 214 000, Fax: +264(0)64 200 481
res.pelicanbay@proteahotels.com.na
www.proteahotels.com

50 Comfortable en-suite rooms with air-conditioning. The venue has a restaurant, coffee shop and secure parking.

Languages: English, Afrikaans

Facilities:

Activities:

Protea Hotel Walvis Bay 19

Hotel $$
Cnr Sam Nujoma Ave & 10th Rd, Walvis Bay
w139939

Tel: +264(0)64 213 700, Fax: +264(0)64 213 701
res.walvisbay@proteahotels.com.na
www.proteahotels.com

En-suite single, twin or family rooms. All air-conditioned with TVs and coffee/tea facilities. Some with balconies.

Languages: English

Facilities:

Activities:

Seagull Inn Guest House 20

Self-catering $
215 Sam Nujoma St, Walvis Bay
w138720

Tel: +264(0)64 202 775, Fax: +264(0)64 202 455

Nine self-catering, en-suite rooms, all well equipped, with TV.

Languages: English

Facilities:

Activities:

The Courtyard Pension 21

Hotel $
4 3rd Road, Walvis Bay
w139940

Tel: +264(0)64 213 600, Cell: +264(0)81 258 2060,
Fax: +264(0)64 231 620
courtyrd@iafrica.com.na,
www.thecourtyardhotelwb.com

Single, double or family en-suite rooms with kitchen-ettes.

Languages: English, German, Portuguese, Afrikaans

Facilities:

Activities:

(photo: Anet Bosman)

SOUTH NAMIBIA

One of the great gravel roads in South Namibia, near Ai-Ais. (photo: Karin Theron)

THE SOUTH OF NAMIBIA IS MOSTLY hot and dry but offers the patient traveller a stark but beautiful landscape. In the far south you'll find colourful rock formations and extraordinary plants like the Quiver tree and the Halfmens tree (meaning half human) which are uniquely adapted to the low rainfall.

The Orange River (sometimes called the Gariep in South Africa) is a green belt in this otherwise arid landscape. This mighty river defines the border between South Africa and Namibia and cuts through the Ai-Ais / Richtersveld Transfrontier Park; this consists of the Ai-Ais National Park in Namibia and the Richtersveld National Park in South Africa. The river provides a habitat for hundreds of bird species as well as ideal conditions for canoeing and rafting.

The Ai-Ais National Park is also home to a hot springs resort but its top attraction must be the Fish River Canyon. The Canyon Nature Park and Gondwana Nature Park which border the Ai-Ais National Park to the north and the east add up to quite a large conservation area.

To the east, you'll find an area that's part of the Kalahari, it's characterised by red dunes and tall yellow grass. Through the border post at Mata Mata there's access to the Kgalagadi Transfrontier Park between South Africa and Botswana.

Keetmanshoop is the administrative centre of this region and it's surrounded by karakul sheep and ostrich farms. In the vicinity of Keetmanshoop you'll find quiver trees estimated to be between 200 to 300 years old.

Between Grünau and Seeheim lies the beautiful Klein Karas Mountains with their interesting rock formations. Seeheim is a very small and historic town which will most definitely take you by surprise, it's well worth a visit.

Further north, the landscape softens a bit (especially after good rains) and you'll enjoy rolling grasslands with camel thorn trees and distant blue mountains as you travel towards the central region of Namibia.

(top) Quiver forest at dusk. (photo: Mietsie Visser)

(above) A fun way to cool off! (photo: Frank Höppener)

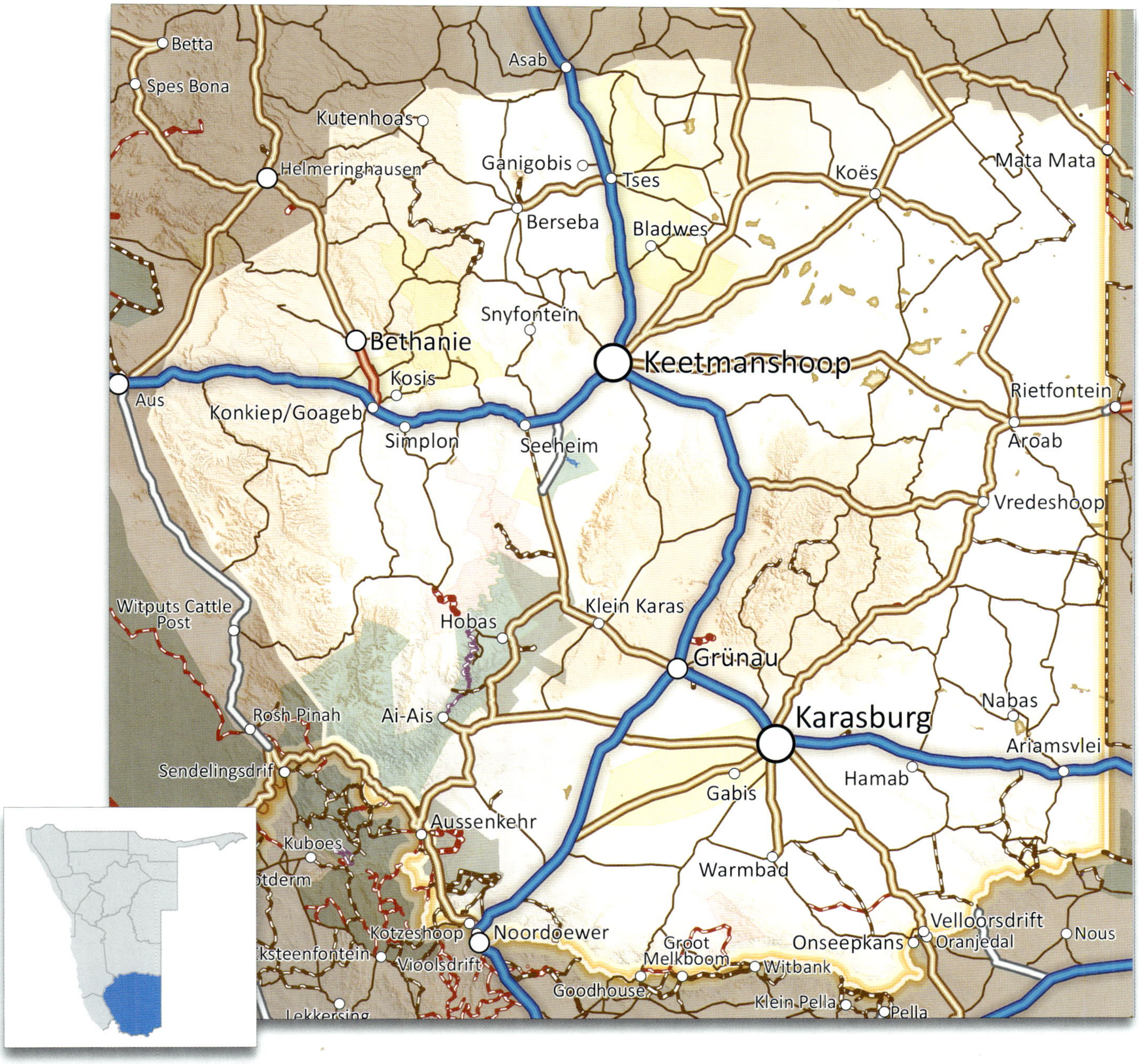

Major attractions

- The majestic Fish River Canyon features a gigantic ravine about 160km long, up to 27km wide and in places almost 550 metres deep. It's the largest canyon in Africa and is also well known for its strenuous hiking trail which traverses 90km over five gruelling days.
- Ai-Ais National Park with the Hot Springs Resort at the southern end of the Fish River Canyon.
- The Aussenkehr Nature Reserve was established to protect the eco-sensitive area around the Orange River. There are two 4WD trails in the reserve, for which permits are required.
- The mule breeding station in the Canyon Nature Park is also the starting point of various mule trails. The mules carry food and equipment for 4 - 5 day guided hiking trails in the Fish River Canyon area.
- The German War Graves in Aussenkehr Nature Reserve are a reminder of the conflict between the Germans and Nama people.
- Rising to 1 588m, the volcanic Brukkaros Crater north of Keetmanshoop towers over the expanse of bare, flat plains that surround it.
- The Mesosaurus Fossils and Quiver Tree Dolerite Park offers visitors a guided tour of fossils of the early *saurian Mesosaurus tenuidens* (a predecessor of the dinosaurs). It also hosts an unspoilt quiver tree forest in the black dolerite hills.
- Captain Josef Fredericks was the leader of the Nama people and the cottage that was built for him in Bethanie by an unknown European in 1883 was declared a national monument in 1951.
- Giants' Playground derives its name from a stack of gigantic 160 - 180 million year old dolerite boulders that resembles a playground. The nearby Quiver Tree Forest is also worth a visit.

More details about the attractions are available on our website (www.tracks4africa.co.za) or our Guide App.
Our GPS Map can navigate you to each of these attractions.

Aroab

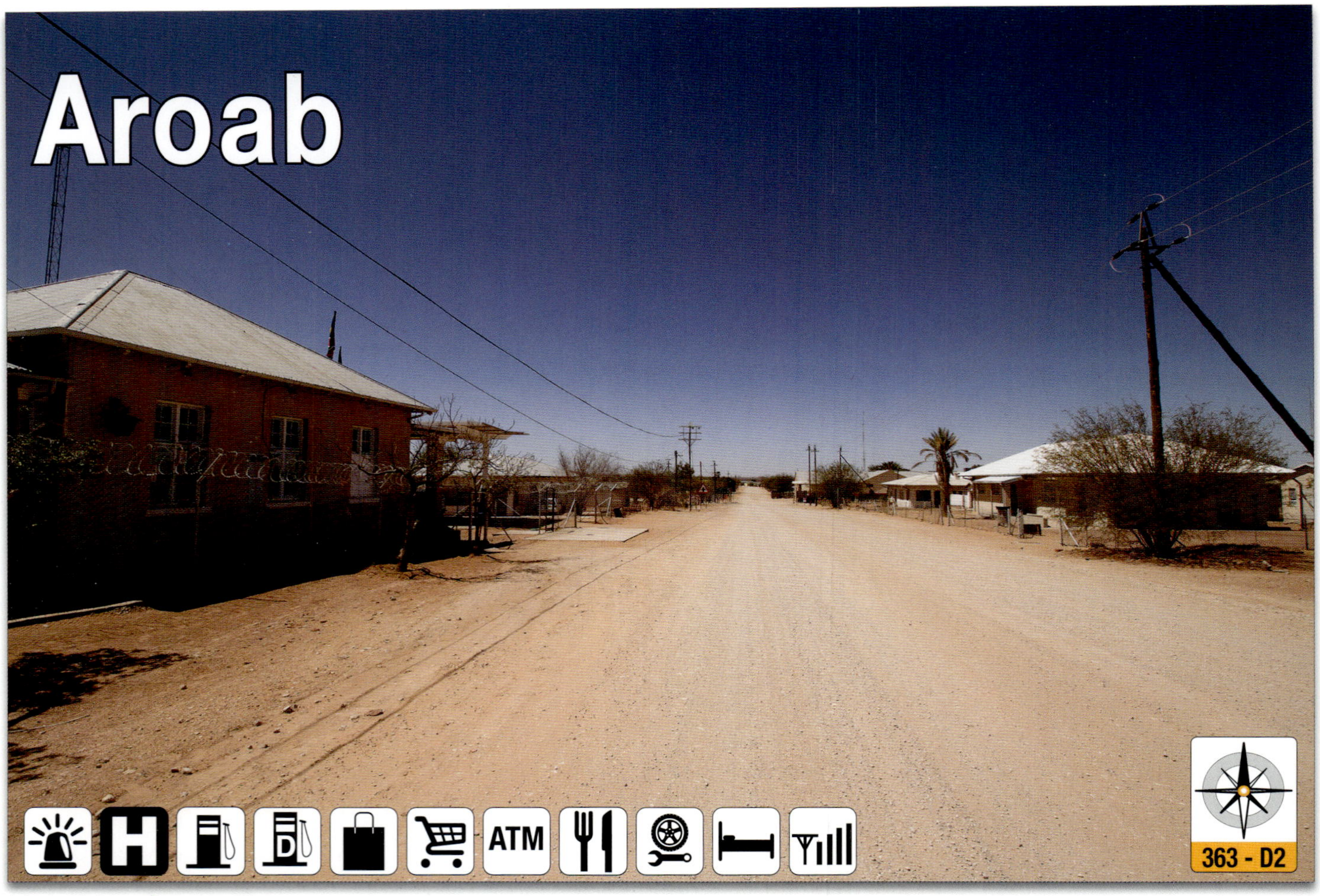

(photo: Johann Groenewald)

AROAB IS A SMALL TOWN some 35km west of the border with South Africa. It's named after the nearby river; the word is an amalgamation of two Nama words: aub meaning dry riverbed and aroe, the type of thorn bushes found in such terrain. Situated on the edge of the Kalahari Desert, this settlement survives on an annual rainfall of just 150 - 200mm. The main industry here is cattle, goat and sheep farming, with game hunting on offer during the winter months.

Traveller Description

Aroab is a small, tidy town with more schools and churches than you'd expect. Even though this is a small village, the general dealer is well-stocked to cater for the farming community.

Travel Info

The ATM occasionally struggles with certain bank cards.

Useful Numbers:

Supermarket tel: +264(0)63 280 581

TRAVEL TIP! The fuel station can help with tyre repairs.

Town Info:

Hospital: +264(0)63 280 511 Police: +264(0)63 280 504

Aroab Village Council 1

Camping $
1km or 2min N of Aroab
w361645

Tel: +264(0)63 280 513
aroabvc@iway.na

Each campsite has a shelter with table & chairs and braai. Ablutions available. Venue is located outside Aroab on the Koës road (C11).

Languages: English

Facilities:

Aroab Village Council — 2

Self-catering — $
43 Rita de Waal Ave, Aroab
w361643

Tel: +264(0)63 280 513
aroabvc@iway.na

Seven self-catering units and two bungalows. All units fully-equipped except bungalows which only have bedding and kettle.

Languages: English

Facilities:

Hunters Inn Guest House — 3

Guest House — $
Aroab
w142602

Tel: +264(0)63 280 581, Fax: +264(0)63 280 581
broncocc@iway.na

Six comfortable, en-suite double rooms, with air-conditioning, fans, coffee/tea facilities and heaters. Communal satellite TV.

Languages: English, Afrikaans

Facilities:
Activities:

(photo: Stephen Cunliffe)

Aussenkehr

(photo: Karin Theron)

AUSSENKEHR IS NOTHING LESS than a miracle in the desert. This agribusiness grew out of the dreams of one farsighted individual, Dusan Vasiljevic, who realised that the climate here was perfect for growing table grapes. Vasiljevic's farm hugs the banks of the Orange River for some 15 kilometres and has spawned its own settlement, a tiny town and some rival agribusinesses. Aussenkehr's success is rooted in the fact that they're able to harvest their grapes three to five weeks earlier than growers elsewhere in the world. During the harvesting season, some 18 000 seasonal workers live here in little reed houses. While this area is famous for its table grapes, other crops like mangoes, citrus, lucerne and dates are also grown here.

Traveller Description

Aussenkehr is on the C13, on Namibia's southern border, some 50 km northwest of the Noordoewer border post with South Africa. It is a well-located stopping point if you're en-route to Ai-Ais Hot Springs, the Fish River Canyon, Lüderitz or Sossusvlei. This said, Noordoewer offers more accommodation and refuelling options. The Aussenkehr riverfront is lush green in the otherwise dry desert surroundings and this stretch of water is very popular for river rafting. There are also various scenic 4WD trails in the nearby Aussenkehr Nature Park - these all require permits which can be purchased from the Spar or at Norotshama River Resort.

Travel Info

You'll find a Spar supermarket and Tops liquor store here. Petrol isn't sold in Aussenkehr but diesel can be purchased at the Aussenkehr Agrimark. The clinic has a nurse on duty and is visited by a doctor once a week.

Useful Numbers:

Spar tel: +264(0)63 297 094
Aussenkehr Agrimark tel: +264(0)63 297 425

TRAVEL TIP! The best place to stay is Norotshama River Resort - here you can buy a permit for the spectacular Canyon Route within the Aussenkehr Nature Park. The agricultural co-op, Aussenkehr Agrimark, is located on the C13 some kilometres south of Aussenkehr, and like many businesses of this type offers a large and interesting selection of well-priced goods (and diesel).

Town Info:
Police: +264(0)63 297 278
Tow-in: +264(0)81 234 3606

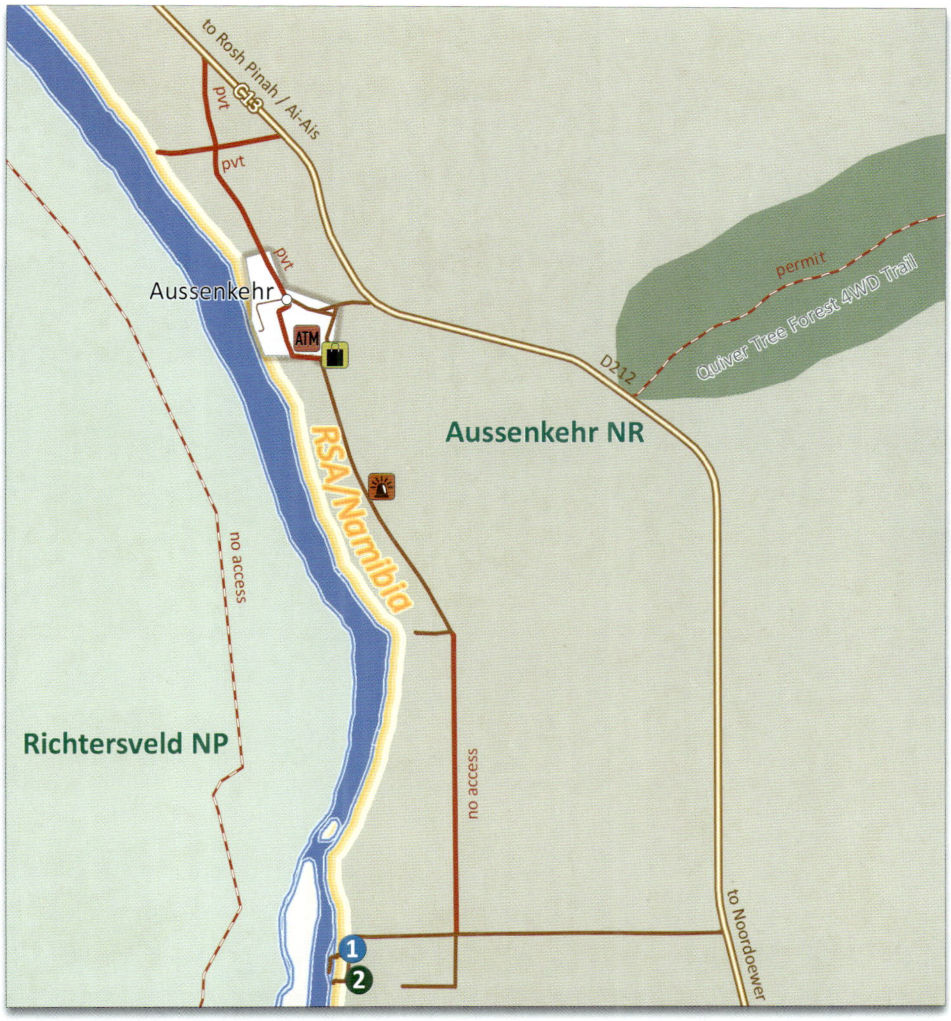

Norotshama River Resort	1
Self-catering	$$

8km or 9min S of Aussenkehr
w255836

Tel: +264(0)63 297 215, Cell: +264(0)81 128 6247,
Fax: +264(0)63 297 217
norotshama@africaonline.com.na,
www.norotshamaresort.com

32 en-suite chalets with air-conditioning on the Orange River.

Languages: English, Afrikaans

Facilities:
Activities:

Norotshama River Resort	2
Holiday Resort Camp	$

8km or 10min S of Aussenkehr
w139518

Tel: +264(0)63 297 215, Cell: +264(0)81 128 6247,
Fax: +264(0)63 297 217
norotshama@africaonline.com.na,
www.norotshamaresort.com

22 Campsites with power points. Ablution block with fresh water and shade.

Languages: English, Afrikaans

Facilities:
Activities:

(photo: Johann Groenewald)

Bethanie

(photo: Johann Groenewald)

THIS SMALL VILLAGE ON THE ROAD between Goageb and Walvis Bay is the site of one Namibia's oldest European settlements. Back in 1814, the London Missionary Society sent a German missionary, one Reverend Heinrich Schmelen, to the area to minister to the Kai/khauan.

His house, the Schmelenhaus, was built on his arrival - it's currently a national monument and a small museum. Unfortunately for Schmelen, his ministries met with few conversions and he departed in despair some eight years on.

With this and other stories to tell, Bethanie is one for the history buffs.

Traveller Description

While it's clear that Bethanie has fair tourist potential, it remains more of a farming town, not that this doesn't allow it a certain charm. Even though this is a small town, you'll find most basic services here.

Travel Info

The clinic number is +264(0)63 283 026. At time of writing there was no private doctor in the town.

TRAVEL TIP! The closest campsite is Konkiep Lapa Rest Camp, 35km from Bethanie.

Town Info:
Police: +264(0)63 283 001
Tow-in: +264(0)81 260 7077

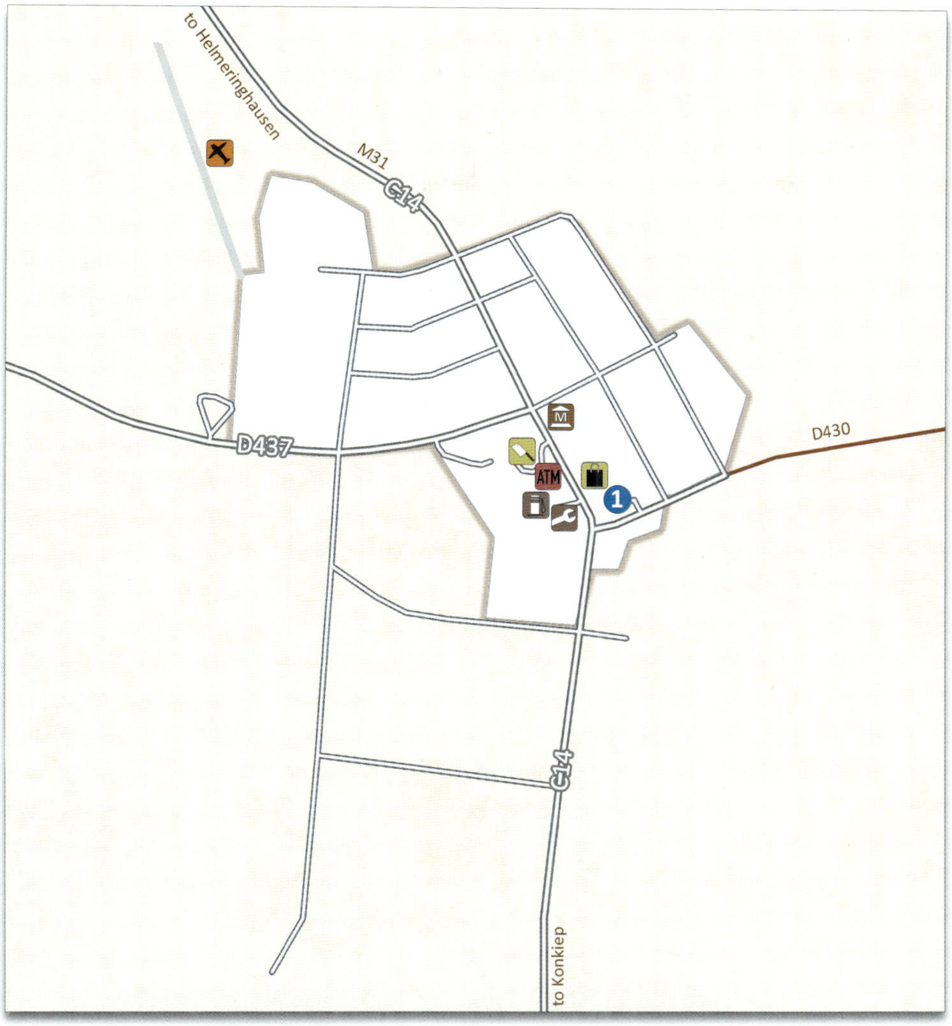

Bethanie Guest House 1

Guest House $
Bethanie
w138153

Tel: +264(0)63 283 013, Cell: +264(0)ɛ1 344 7252
info@bethaniehotel.com
www.bethaniehotel.com

16 Comfortable en-suite rooms. Plus bar, lapa dining area and pool table. Outside rooms share ablutions with campers.

Languages: English, Afrikaans, German, Sign Language

Facilities:
Activities:

As the crow flies, the Brukaros Crater is located some 95km northeast of Bethanie. (photo: Heiner Dillmann)

Fish River Canyon

(photo: Karin Theron)

As well as being the largest canyon in Africa, the Fish River Canyon is one of the largest in the world, ranked just behind the Grand Canyon in North America. This wonder begins south of Seeheim and stretches some 161km south to the point where the Fish river joins the Orange, northwest of Aussenkehr. The Fish river is seasonal, flowing only after heavy rains; most commonly, from January to April.

The 90km Fish River Canyon Hiking Trail, stretches from Hobas down to Ai-Ais, where weary hikers can soothe their aching muscles in the resort's hot springs. The hike is open in the cooler months, from May to September. One of the best places to view the Canyon is from the viewpoint near Hobas Restcamp.

Traveller Description

Ai-Ais is a popular resort and spa located at the southern end of the Fish River Canyon. Its name means 'burning water' and refers to the sulphurous hot springs that were found here in 1850 by a Nama shepherd. Besides the spa complex (which boasts both indoors and open air pools) you'll find chalets, rooms and camping.

This venue has been a very popular holiday destination since the 60s. Its fortunes have waxed and waned, on one occasion almost the entire venue was destroyed by a flood. You can also enjoy a number of walks in the area, from mild to strenuous; there are lots of interesting rock formations to be seen. Plus, this is a great spot for stargazing as there's almost no light pollution in this region. This is also a good spot if you're keen on landscape photography.

Hobas is a recently-renovated rest camp 40km northeast of Ai-Ais, that enjoys some excellent views of the canyon. Both Ai-Ais and Hobas are part of the Ai-Ais / Richtersveld Trans-frontier Park.

Travel Info

The Ais-Ais resort has a restaurant, bar, and small shop selling basic necessities. The last 10km of the access road, the C10, is badly corrugated and features a few sharp bends. Slow down and be on the lookout for oncoming vehicles cutting corners.

While availability isn't guaranteed, diesel and petrol is generally available at Ai-Ais, But be prepared to pay cash should the card machine be offline.

The Hobas Restcamp doesn't have a fuel stop, but features a restaurant, swimming pool, self-catering chalets and a recently-renovated camping terrain.

Canyon Roadhouse Lodge is another popular stop in this region; here, visitors can view a collection of vintage vehicles and enjoy a good meal at the restaurant. Although the lodge accept credit cards, the fuel stop on the premises only accepts cash payments.

TRAVEL TIP! If coming from South Africa, enter Namibia at the Sendelingsdrift border post about 20km from Rosh Pinah. This border crossing features a pontoon across the Orange River, and part of the route from here to Ai-Ais tracks the river along a very scenic gravel road.

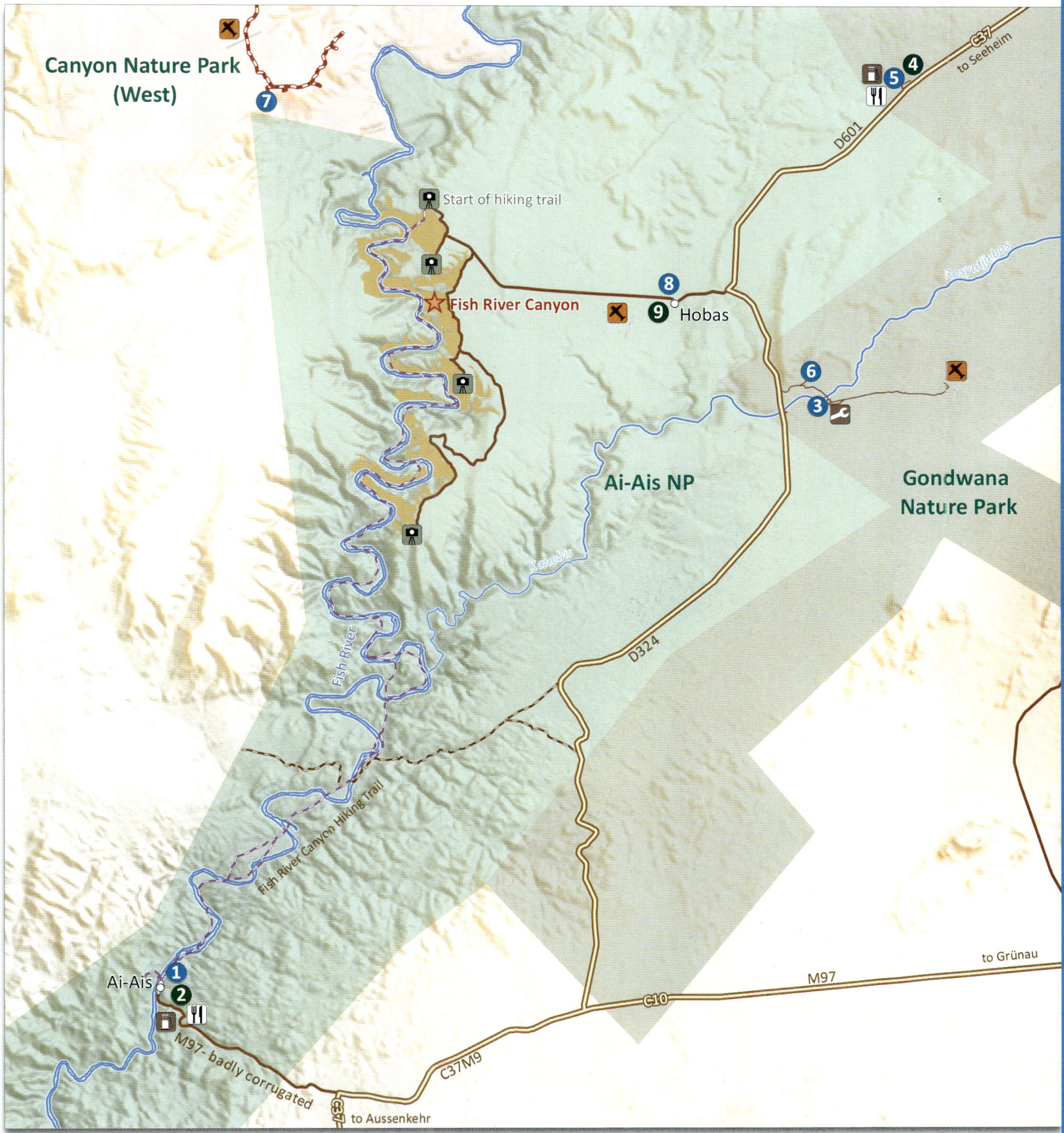

Fish River Canyon

Ai-Ais Hotsprings Resort — 1

Self-catering — $$
Ai-Ais, Ai-Ais National Park
w228675

Tel: +264(0)61 285 7200, Fax: +264(0)61 224 900
reservations@nwr.com.na
www.nwr.com.na

Standard and luxury chalets, each with bathroom and kitchenette. Luxury chalets have balconies. Reservations advisable.

Languages: English

Facilities:
Activities:

Ai-Ais Hotsprings Resort — 2

Holiday Resort Camp — $$$
Ai-Ais, Ai-Ais National Park
w138419

Tel: +264(0)61 285 7200, Fax: +264(0)61 224 900
reservations@nwr.com.na
www.nwr.com.na

Large caravan and camping area with comprehensive facilities at reasonable prices. Clean communal ablutions. Reservations advisable.

Languages: English

Facilities:
Activities:

Canyon Lodge — 3

Lodge — $$$
62km or 54min NE of Ai-Ais
w138347

Tel: +264(0)61 427 200, Fax: +264(0)61 251 863
info@gondwana-collection.com
store.gondwana-collection.com

30 Stone chalets nestled amongst granite boulders. All units equipped with comfortable beds and en-suite bathrooms. Reservations mandatory.

Languages: English

Facilities:
Activities:

Canyon Road Campsite — 4

Lodge Camp — $$
79km or 1h6min NE of Ai-Ais
w139106

Tel: +264(0)61 427 200 , Cell: +264(0)81 129 2424, Fax: +264(0)61 251 863
info@gondwana-collection.com,
store.gondwana-collection.com

Private camp with hot showers and toilets. Reservations advisable.

Languages: English

Facilities:
Activities:

Canyon Roadhouse — 5

Lodge — $$
79km or 1h4min NE of Ai-Ais
w139107

Tel: +264(0)61 427 200 , Cell: +264(0)81 129 2424, Fax: +264(0)61 251 863
info@gondwana-collection.com,
store.gondwana-collection.com

24 en-suite rooms, pool and petrol station. Reservations mandatory.

Languages: English

Facilities:
Activities:

Canyon Village — 6

Lodge — $$
61km or 51min NE of Ai-Ais
w139680

Tel: +264(0)61 427 200, Cell: +264(0)81 129 2424, Fax: +264(0)61 251 863
info@gondwana-collection.com,
store.gondwana-collection.com

Thatched cottages and chalets, with all modern amenities. Restaurant on site. Reservations mandatory.

Languages: English, Afrikaans

Facilities:
Activities:

Fish River Lodge — 7

Lodge — $$$
131km or 2h6min SSW of Seeheim
w139047

Tel: +264(0)61 228 104, Fax: +264(0)88 625 855
reservations@fishriverlodge.com.na
www.fishriverlodge-namibia.com

20 Chalets with views of the canyon. Each chalet has an inside and outside shower. Reservations mandatory.

Languages: English

Facilities:
Activities:

Hobas Rest Camp — 8

Bed and Breakfast — $$
Hobas, Ai-Ais National Park
w361156

Tel: +264(0)61 285 7200, Fax: +264(0)61 224 900
reservations@nwr.com.na
www.nwr.com.na

Six, en-suite chalets on a bed and breakfast basis. The closest camp to the start of the Fish River Canyon hiking trail. Reservations advisable.

Languages: English

Facilities:
Activities:

Hobas Rest Camp — 9

Park Camp — $$
Hobas, Ai-Ais National Park
w137564

Tel: +264(0)61 285 7200, Fax: +264(0)61 224 900
reservations@nwr.com.na
www.nwr.com.na

Campsites with ablutions and shop. No more than eight per site. Only place to camp if you want to photograph the canyon at sunset or sunrise. Reservations advisable.

Languages: English

Facilities:
Activities:

(photo: Jurgen Blignaut)

The camping area at Ai-Ais Hotspring Resort. Note, this venue can become really full over school holidays so if it's peace and quiet you're after, you might want to avoid it at these times. (photo: Janine Reyneke)

(photo: Jurgen Blignaut)

Grünau

(photo: Johann Groenewald)

THIS SMALL TOWN SITS CLOSE to the B1, more or less halfway between the South African border and Keetmanshoop. This location makes it a suitable halfway stop if you're tackling the long road between Windhoek and Cape Town. Some accommodation is available here and you can refuel and buy basic food supplies.

Traveller Description

Many travellers don't visit Grünau at all because it's actually a kilometre or so off the B1. In contrast, the 24-hr Grünau Shell is located right on the B1 just north of the town, and offers food, fuel and accommodation.

Travel Info

The tow-in service is provided by Grünau Motors.

Town Info: Tow-in: +264(0)81 715 2574

Florida B&B — 1

Bed and Breakfast — $
31km or 20min NNE of Grünau
w207724

Cell: +264(0)81 150 0589
floridaguestfarm@gmail.com
www.floridaguestfarm.com

Three fully-equipped, self-catering chalets with braai areas.

Languages: Afrikaans

Facilities:

Goibib Mountain Lodge — 2

Lodge — $
49km or 29min NNE of Grünau
w206788

Tel: +264(0)61 224 712, Cell: +264(0)81 242 7275,
Fax: +264(0)63 683 132
goibib@mweb.com.na,
www.goibibmountainlodge.com

Eight spacious, en-suite rooms. Each with air-conditioning, TV, mini bar, safe, coffee/tea facilities and Wi-Fi.

Languages: English, Afrikaans

Facilities:

Activities:

Goibib Mountain Lodge — 3

Transit Camp — $
49km or 29min NNE of Grünau
w255832

Tel: +264(0)61 224 712, Cell: +264(0)81 242 7275,
Fax: +264(0)63 683 132
goibib@mweb.com.na,
www.goibibmountainlodge.com

Camping area with ablutions and washing-up facilities. Venue is well located for stopovers.

Languages: English, Afrikaans

Facilities:

Activities:

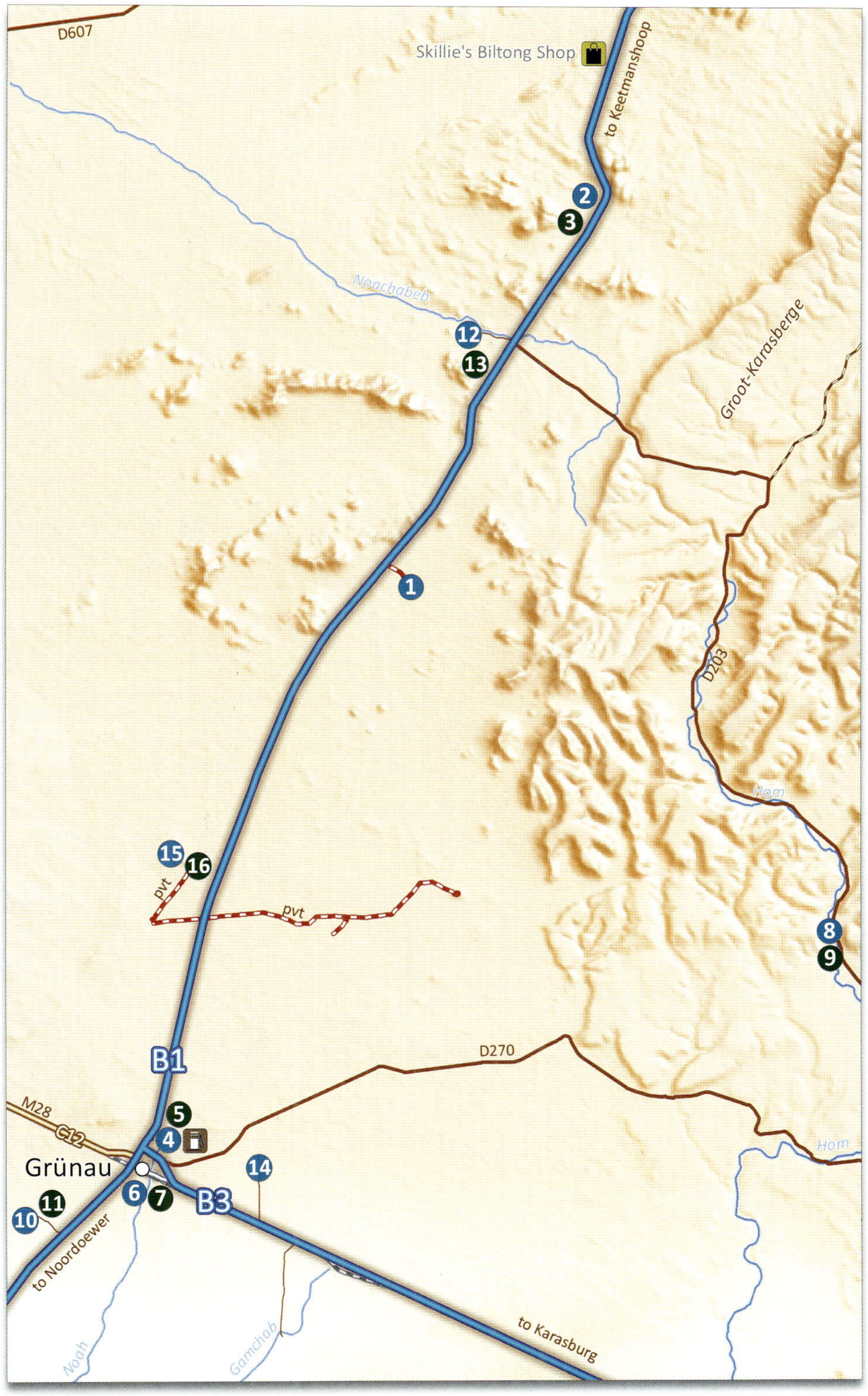

Grünau Chalets 4

Self-catering $
B1, Shell Fuel Stop, 2km or 4min N of Grünau
w140227

Tel: +264(0)63 262 026, Cell: +264(0)81 783 1313,
Fax: +264(0)63 262 017
willa@iafrica.com.na,
www.grunauchalets.com

Six comfortable, air-conditioned chalets with braai areas. Located next to a Shell petrol station with restaurant and shop.

Languages: English, Afrikaans

Facilities:

Activities:

Grünau Chalets 5

Lodge Camp $
B1, Shell Fuel Stop, 2km or 4min N of Grünau
w361637

Tel: +264(0)63 262 026, Cell: +264(0)81 783 1313,
Fax: +264(0)63 262 017
willa@iafrica.com.na,
www.grunauchalets.com

Spacious campsites, each with its own ablution block, braai and wash-up area. Power points and Wi-Fi also available.

Languages: English, Afrikaans

Facilities:

Activities:

Grünau Country Hotel 6

Guest House $
10 Old Main Road, Grünau
w140228

Tel: +264(0)63 262 001, Cell: +264(0)81 808 8909
grunauch@iway.na
www.grunaucountryhotel.com

Single, double or family en-suite rooms. Plus two- or four-bed bungalows with separate communal ablutions.

Languages: English, Afrikaans

Facilities:

Grünau Country Hotel 7

Lodge Camp $
10 Old Main Road, Grünau
w141151

Tel: +264(0)63 262 001, Cell: +264(0)81 808 8909
grunauch@iway.na
www.grunaucountryhotel.com

Four caravan stands / campsites with water and power points.

Languages: English, Afrikaans

Facilities:

Liebenrust 8

Self-catering $
51km or 46min NE of Grünau
w361668

Tel: +264(0)63 262 087
hans@iway.na

Basic accommodation in three-bedroom house. Four single beds and one double. Kitchen with fridge, and one bathroom with corner bath and shower.

Languages: English

Facilities:

Liebenrust 9

Camping $
51km or 46min NE of Grünau
w361686

Tel: +264(0)63 262 087
hans@iway.na

It's not an official campsite but you can camp on the premises and use the house's bathroom. Tranquil farm life.

Languages: English

Facilities:

Grünau

Namgate Guest House — 10

Guest Farm — $$
6km or 5min WSW of Grünau
w140269

Tel: +264(0)63 262 002, Cell: +264(0)81 251 1370,
Fax: +264(0)88 616 689
nammgate@iway.na, www.namgate.co.za

Large, en-suite rooms with air-conditioning. Plus self-catering units.

Languages: English, Afrikaans

Facilities:

Activities:

Namgate Guest House — 11

Lodge Camp — $
6km or 5min WSW of Grünau
w261554

Tel: +264(0)63 262 002, Cell: +264(0)81 251 1370,
Fax: +264(0)88 616 689
nammgate@iway.na, www.namgate.co.za

Camping with power points, water, and braai facilities. Plus ablutions. Wood available on request.

Languages: English, Afrikaans

Facilities:

Activities:

Savanna Guest Farm — 12

Guest Farm — $$
43km or 26min NNE of Grünau
w141513

Tel: +264(0)63 683 127, Cell: +264(0)81 128 0975,
Fax: +264(0)63 683 128
savannagf@gmail.com, www.savanna-guestfarm.com

Self-catering unit, family room or cosy double room. With air-conditioning and private bathrooms.

Languages: English, German, Afrikaans

Facilities:

Activities:

Savanna Guest Farm — 13

Farm Camp — $
43km or 26min NNE of Grünau
w141512

Tel: +264(0)63 683 127, Cell: +264(0)81 128 0975,
Fax: +264(0)63 683 128
savannagf@gmail.com,
www.savanna-guestfarm.com

Camping facilities include kitchen, laundry and ablutions (hot showers). Venue is a 22 000 hectare working farm.

Languages: English, German, Afrikaans

Facilities:

Activities:

Vastrap Guest House — 14

Guest House — $
9km or 18min E of Grünau
w138202

Tel: +264(0)63 262 063, Cell: +264(0)81 127 7142,
Fax: +264(0)63 262 063
vastrap@afol.com.na, www.vastrapguestfarm.com

Nine air-conditioned, en-suite rooms. Plus one flat and four self-catering chalets. Breakfast, lunch and dinner served in dining room. There's a pool too.

Languages: English, German, Afrikaans

Facilities:

Activities:

White House Guest Farm — 15

Guest House — $
17km or 17min N of Grünau
w270493

Tel: +264(0)63 262 061, Cell: +264(0)81 285 6484,
Fax: +264(0)63 262 061
withuis@iway.na, www.withuis.iway.na

En-suite single, double or triple rooms. Choose between self-catering or full board.

Languages: English, Afrikaans

Facilities:

Activities:

White House Guest Farm — 16

Farm Camp — $
17km or 17min N of Grünau
w243044

Tel: +264(0)63 262 061, Cell: +264(0)81 285 6484,
Fax: +264(0)63 262 061
withuis@iway.na, www.withuis.iway.na

Campsites with power points and clean ablutions. Wood and braai grids available.

Languages: English, Afrikaans

Facilities:

Activities:

Opposite page, top: View of the canyon from Fish River Lodge. (photo: Heiner Dillmann)

opposite page,bottom: (photo:Stephen Cunliffe)

right: (photo: Dawid Saayman)

(photo: Johann Groenewald)

IF YOU'RE TRAVELLING to Namibia from Upington, South Africa, the first town of any significant size that you'll encounter in Namibia is Karasburg. It lies in the heart of the southern Namibian sheep farming region and thanks to its position, it's also a major truck stop for such vehicles travelling between Namibia and South Africa.

Traveller Description

This is a good place to replenish stocks, refuel or draw money. This is a great place to stock up on meat - you'll find a number of butchers here offering well-priced cuts. Temperatures here can be extreme, in both winter and summer. While there is accommodation available in town, the nearest campsite is at Kleinbegin, east of Karasburg.

Travel Info

There is a Spar in Karasburg with a butchery and a bakery, as well as a Tops Bottle Store, and fuel station.

TRAVEL TIP! The nearest campsite is at Kleinbegin, 31 km east of Karasburg.

Town Info: Hospital: +264(0)63 270 167
Doctor: +264(0)63 270 030
Police: +264(0)63 270 009
Tow-in: +264(0)81 127 1348

Avondsrus Guesthouse 1

Guest House $
15 25th Avenue, Karasburg
w255816

Tel: +264(0)63 270 023, Cell: +264(0)81 127 3408,
Fax: +264(0)88 621 719
kalkfont@iway.na

Five, air-conditioned, en-suite rooms (with TV) and two self-catering cottages. Restaurant and braai facilities on site.

Languages: Afrikaans

Facilities: VISA @

Kleinbegin Campsites 2

Lodge Camp $
31km or 23min E of Karasburg
w206845

Tel: +264(0)63 269 315, Cell: +264(0)81 124 9186,
Fax: +264(0)88 618 913
kleinbeginlodge@gmail.com

Very private camp with hot showers. Campers may use lodge facilities.

Languages: English, Afrikaans

Facilities: VISA FC @

Activities:

Kleinbegin Game Lodge 3

Guest Farm $$
30km or 23min E of Karasburg
w206846

Tel: +264(0)63 269 315, Cell: +264(0)81 124 9186,
Fax: +264(0)88 618 913
kleinbeginlodge@gmail.com

Seven double, twin and family en-suite rooms with self-catering facilities.

Languages: English, Afrikaans

Facilities: VISA FC @

Activities:

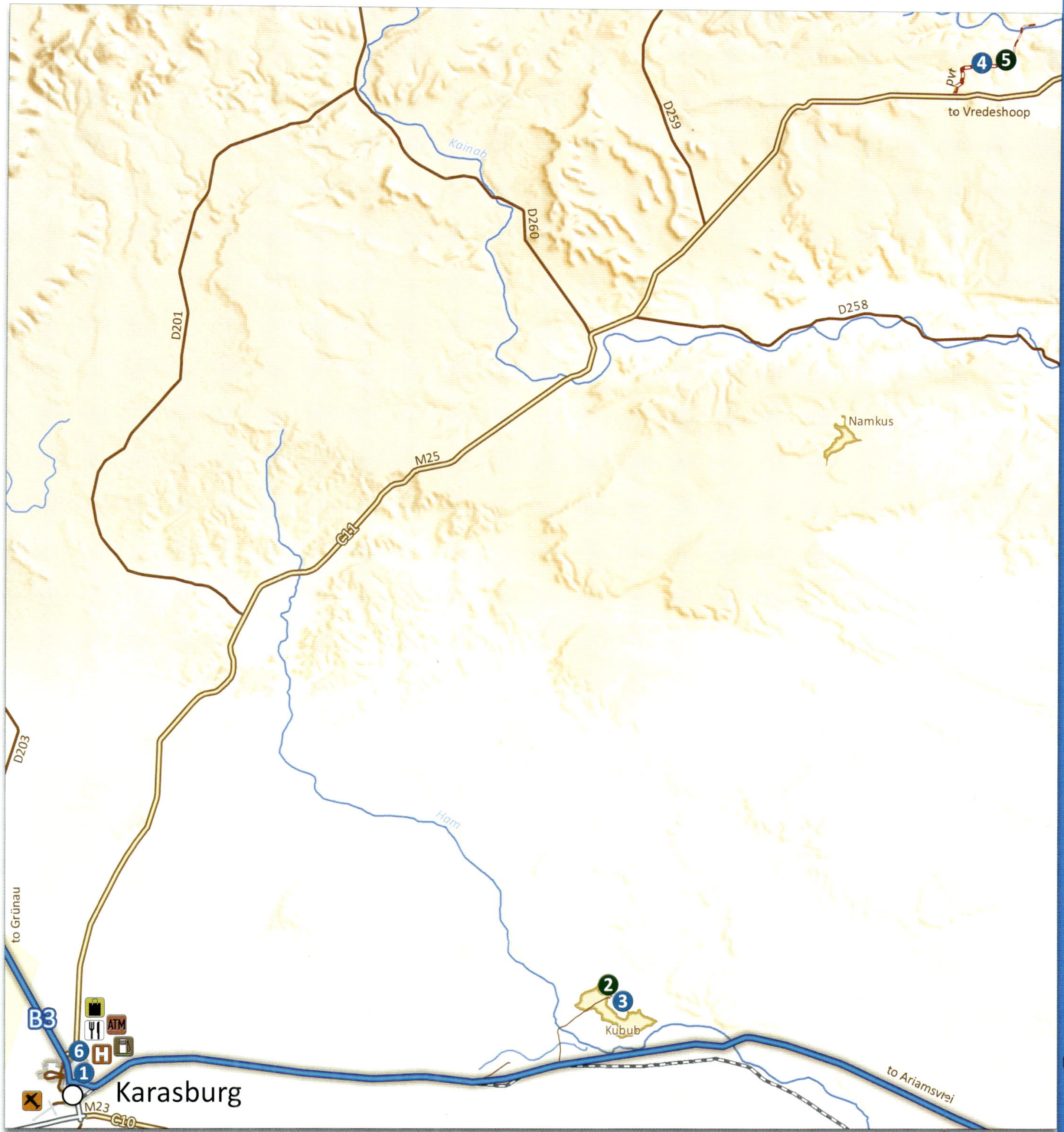

Oas Holiday Farm — 4

Self-catering — $
C11/M25, 83km or 01h09min NE of Karasburg
w138254

Cell: +264(0)81 461 7071
oasstaal@iway.na

Two self-catering, wheelchair-friendly, six-bed chalets. Includes bedding, flush toilets, hot showers, lights, fridge and kitchen utensils.

Languages: English, Afrikaans

Facilities:

Activities:

Oas Holiday Farm — 5

Farm Camp — $
C11/M25, 84km or 01h11min NE of Karasburg
w221348

Cell: +264(0)81 461 7071
oasstaal@iway.na

Campsites for caravans and tents, in solar-powered camp. Male and female ablutions (hot showers). Plus kitchen.

Languages: English, Afrikaans

Facilities:

Activities:

Sunset Chalets — 6

Self-catering — $
Eksteensrus 48, Karasburg
w313060

Cell: +264(0)81 148 7802
sunsetchalets5@gmail.com

Self-catering units facing the Great Karas Mountains. Venue also caters for campers.

Languages: English, Afrikaans

Facilities: VISA FC @

Activities:

Keetmanshoop

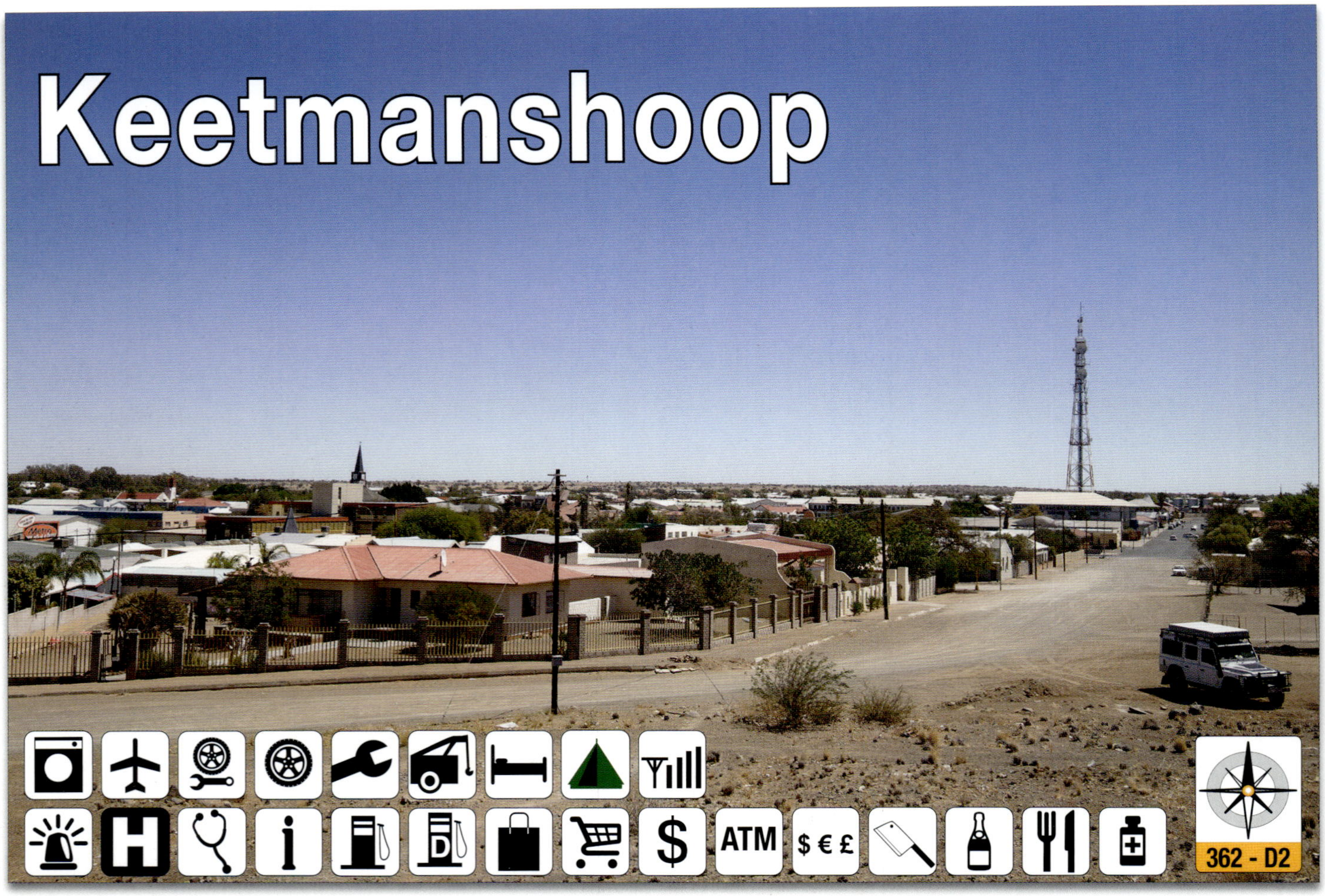

(photo: Johann Groenewald)

BEFORE THE EUROPEAN missionaries arrived, the Nama settlement here was known as Swartmodder ('black mud') which refers to the mud found at a nearby spring. In 1860, some 75 years after the appearance of the first white settler, the Rhenish Missionary Society started a mission here. They named it after a director in the society and someone who provided financial support, one Johann Keetman. These days Keetmanshoop is the economic centre of the Southern Namibia region, it's also an important hub for Karakul sheep farming and houses a number of government offices.

Traveller Description

You'll find Keetmanshoop situated at an important junction, where the B1 (which bisects the country longitudinally) meets the B4, which accesses Lüderitz and the coast to the west. Keetmanshoop can serve as a comfortable base for visiting attractions both further afield, like Ai-Ais National Park and Brukkaros crater, or nearby - the quiver tree forests, Naute Dam and the Mesosaurus fossil site to name but three.

It's also worthwhile spending a few hours in town. You'll find the Keetmanshoop Museum in the Rhenish Mission Church whose unique combination of Gothic architecture cast in African stone makes it one of the architectural masterpieces of the country. Don't forget to look in on the old post office and the old train station too. Thanks to its size, Keetmanshoop offers just about every service that a travel-weary overlander might need.

Travel Info

There's a number of department stores in town as well as a couple of banks.

Town Info:

Hospital: +264(0)63 220 9000
Police: +264(0)63 221 833
Doctor: +264(0)63 226 111
Tow-in: +264(0)63 222 119
Tourism: +264(0)63 221 266

AmBesten Guesthouse 1

Guest House $
116 13th Street, Westdene, Keetmanshoop
w359087

Tel: +264(0)63 222 557, Cell: +264(0)81 040 9999
ambesten@iway.na

Comfortable, air-conditioned, en-suite (shower) rooms. Communal lounge, braai area and garden. Laundry services available.

Languages: English, Afrikaans

Facilities:

Bird's Mansions Hotel 2

Hotel $
6th Avenue, Keetmanshoop
w232243

Tel: +264(0)63 221 711, Fax: +264(0)63 221 730
hotel@birdsaccommodation.com
www.birdsaccommodation.com

Air-conditioned, en-suite rooms with satellite TV, direct-dial telephone and internet access. There's also a beer/ tea garden...

Languages: English, Afrikaans, Nama, Ovambo

Facilities:
Activities:

Birds Nest B&B 3

Bed and Breakfast $
6 Pastorie St, Keetmanshoop
w141283

Tel: +264(0)63 222 906, Fax: +264(0)63 222 261
guesthouse@birdsaccommodation.com
www.birdsaccommodation.com

Comfortable, air-conditioned, en-suite rooms, with direct-dial telephone and satellite TV. There's also a lounge bar, 24-hour room service and secure parking.

Languages: English, Afrikaans, Nama, Ovambo

Facilities:
Activities:

Canyon Hotel 4

Hotel $
5th Avenue, Keetmanshoop
w141627

Tel: +264(0)63 223 361, Fax: +264(0)63 223 714
canyonhotel@iway.na

Basic rooms and facilities, adequate for stopover. Venue is a 3-star hotel used by business people and travelers alike.

Languages: English, Afrikaans

Facilities:
Activities:

Central Lodge 5

Guest House $
5th St, Keetmanshoop
w252804

Tel: +264(0)63 225 850, Fax: +264(0)63 225 850
clodge@iway.na
www.central-lodge.com

Spacious, air-conditioned, en-suite rooms with spa bath, telephone and TV. There's also a coffee shop on site.

Languages: English, Afrikaans

Facilities:
Activities:

Garas Park Rest Camp 6

Camping $
22km or 17min NNE of Keetmanshoop
w139078

Cell: +264(0)81 491 3863
marian.hulme.z@gmail.com

Very basic but clean camp with ablution facilities. Wood, water & snacks available but campers need to be self-sufficient.

Languages: English, German, Afrikaans

Facilities:
Activities:

Keetmanshoop

Home Sweet Home Self Catering — 7

Self-catering — $
Keetmanshoop
w232240

Tel: +264(0)63 225 134, Cell: +264(0)81 127 5397, Fax: +264(0)63 683 390
marica@iway.na

Self-catering accommodation with air-conditioning and braai facilities. Ideal for stopover.

Languages: English, Afrikaans

Facilities:

Keetmanshoop Campsite — 8

Caravan Park — $
Aub St, Keetmanshoop
w139357

Tel: +264(0)63 221 265, Cell: +264(0)81 688 0285

Shaded, electrified campsites, but not grassed. Clean ablution block (hot showers & toilets). Contact manager via cellphone. Central location.

Languages: English, Afrikaans

Facilities:

La Rochelle Guest House — 9

Guest House — $
12 6th Avenue, Keetmanshoop
w360956

Tel: +264(0)63 223 845, Cell: +264(0)81 278 2383, Fax: +264(0)88 631 784
larochelle@iway.na,
www.keetmans.com

Six en-suite rooms with air-conditioning, plus one self-catering room. Breakfast served on request.

Languages: English, Afrikaans

Facilities:
Activities:

Maritz Country Lodge — 10

Lodge — $
6km or 7min SE of Keetmanshoop
w137835

Tel: +264(0)63 224 316, Cell: +264(0)81 619 8740, Fax: +264(0)63 224 309
maritzlodge@iway.na,
www.maritzcountrylodge.com.na

18 Air-conditioned bungalows with TV and braai facilities. Dinner-bed-and-breakfast option available.

Languages: English, Afrikaans

Facilities:
Activities:

Maritz Country Lodge — 11

Lodge Camp — $
5km or 6min SE of Keetmanshoop
w361174

Tel: +264(0)63 224 316, Cell: +264(0)81 619 8740, Fax: +264(0)63 224 309
maritzlodge@iway.na,
www.maritzcountrylodge.com.na

10 Campsites, each with own braai. And ablution facilities.

Languages: English, Afrikaans

Facilities:
Activities:

Mesosaurus Fossil Bush Camp — 12

Farm Camp — $
45km or 50min ENE of Keetmanshoop
w139682

Fax: +264(0)88 650 9622, Cell: +264(0)83 700 0012
mesosaurus.camp@gmail.com
www.mesosaurus.com

Isolated but comfortable bush camp with showers and toilet. Hot water via 'donkey' geyser.

Languages: English, German, Afrikaans

Facilities:
Activities:

Mesosaurus Fossil Camp — 13

Self-catering — $
42km or 32min ENE of Keetmanshoop
w143002

Fax: +264(0)88 650 9622, Cell: +264(0)83 700 0012
mesosaurus.camp@gmail.com
www.mesosaurus.com

Four, self-catering, en-suite chalets (one is a family unit). Catering can be provided by prior arrangement.

Languages: English, German, Afrikaans

Facilities:
Activities:

Pension Gessert Bed & Breakfast — 14

Lodge — $
138 13th St, Keetmanshoop
w259602

Tel: +264(0)63 223 892, Fax: +264(0)63 223 892
gesserts@iafrica.com.na

Seven, en-suite, air-conditioned rooms leading into shady garden. With or without breakfast.

Languages: English, Afrikaans

Facilities:
Activities:

Quivertree Forest Rest Camp — 15

Self-catering — $$
16km or 13min NE of Keetmanshoop
w225373

Tel: +264(0)63 683 421, Cell: +264(0)83 768 3421, Fax: +264(0)63 683 422
quiver@africaonline.com.na,
www.quivertreeforest.com

Guest house, bungalows and family room. Self-catering units or catering package.

Languages: English, German, Afrikaans

Facilities:
Activities:

Quivertree Forest Rest Camp — 16

Farm Camp — $
17km or 15min NE of Keetmanshoop
w137372

Tel: +264(0)63 683 421, Cell: +264(0)83 768 3421, Fax: +264(0)63 683 422
quiver@africaonline.com.na,
www.quivertreeforest.com

Campsites with braais, taps and power points. No meals provided.

Languages: English, German, Afrikaans

Facilities:
Activities:

Schutzenhaus Guest House — 17

Guest House — $
c/o Cathedral Ave & Pastorie St, Keetmanshoop
w142118

Tel: +264(0)63 223 400, Cell: +264(0)81 124 5063, Fax: +264(0)63 225 596
schuetzenhaus@iway.na,
www.schuetzenhaus-namibia.com

Air-conditioned, en-suite rooms with wheelchair access. Self-catering units available on request. Braai facilities, bar and restaurant on site. Camping facilities recently offered.

Languages: English, German

Facilities:
Activities:

right: The Naute Dam, 45km southwest of Keetmanshoop. (photo: Heiner Dillmann)

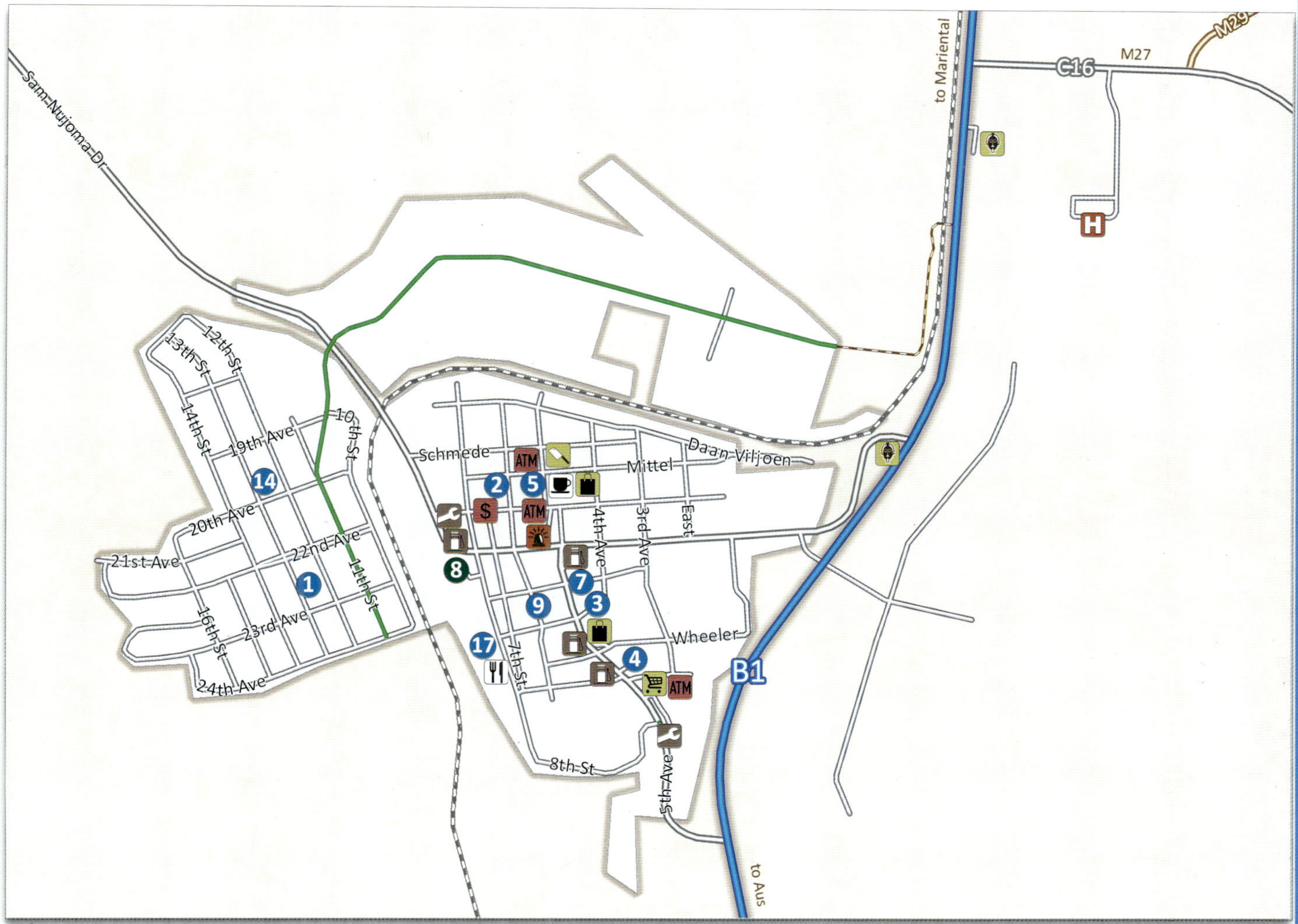
to Mariental
C16
M27
M29
Sam-Nujoma-Dr
12th-St
13th-St
14th-St
10th-St
19th-Ave
20th-Ave
21st-Ave
22nd-Ave
11th-St
23rd-Ave
16th-St
24th-Ave
Schmede
Daan-Viljoen
Mittel
4th-Ave
3rd-Ave
East
Wheeler
7th-St
8th-St
5th-Ave
B1
to Aus
ATM
H
1
2
3
4
5
7
8
9
14
17

Koës

(photo: Johann Groenewald)

KOËS IS A SMALL VILLAGE in the Kalahari; it's located some 130km northeast of Keetmanshoop, en route to the Mata Mata border post. The Koës Pan rally is held here every year and attracts many visitors. Though small, this is an important town for local farmers. During hunting season you can expect this place to get quite busy!

Traveller Description

You'll find fuel pumps, ATM, supermarket, hotel (with quirky bar) and a coffee shop.

Useful Numbers: State clinic: +264(0)63 252 710

TRAVEL TIP! The Koës area is known for hunting in the red Kalahari dunes.

Town Info: Police: +264(0)63 252 702

Koës Pan (photo: Guy Harwood)

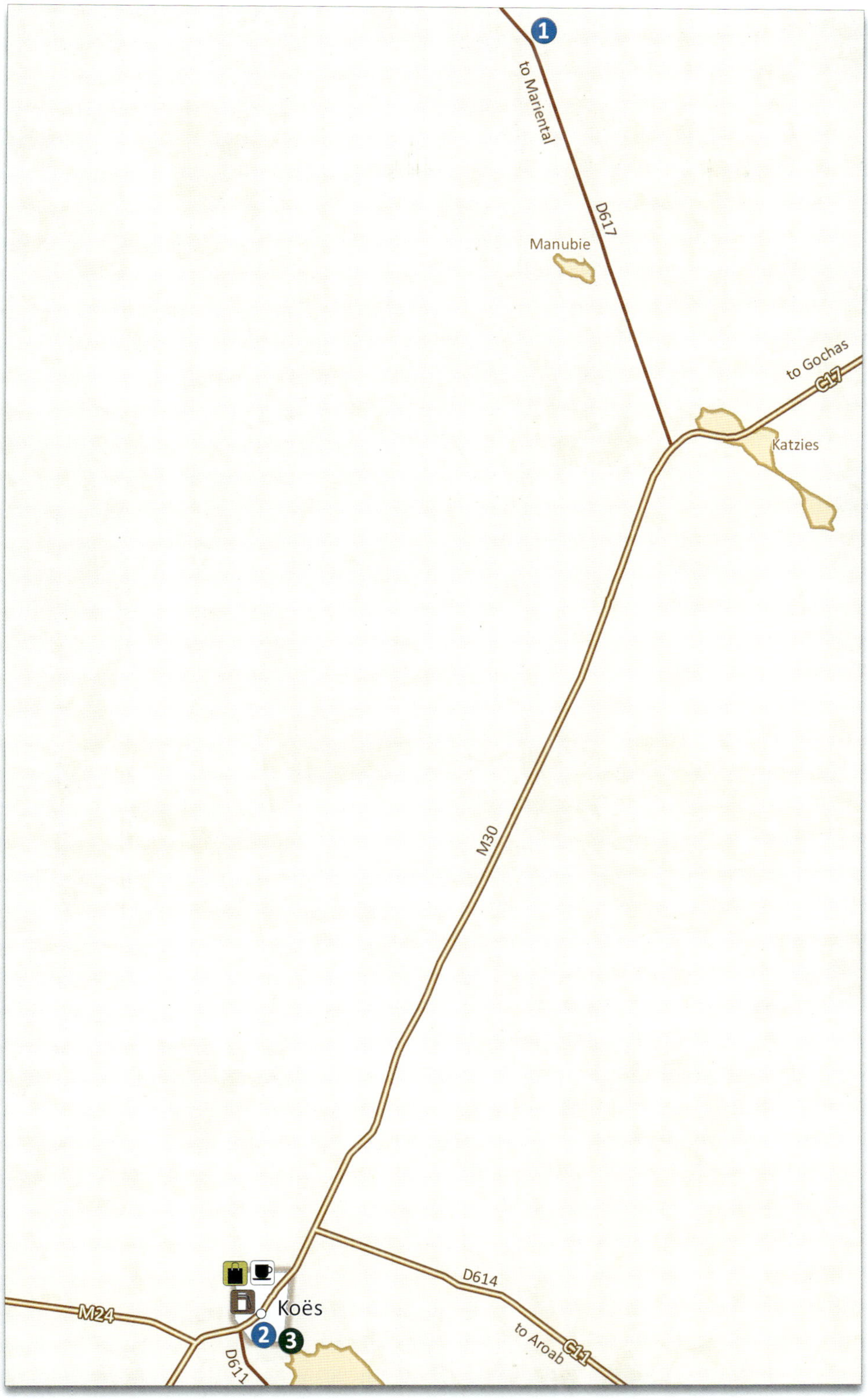

DuneSong Breathers — 1

Self-catering — $
30km or 26min NNE of Koës
w261543

Tel: +264(0)63 252 657, Cell: +264(0)81 122 0175,
Fax: +264(0)88 631 256
dunesong.nell1@gmail.com, www.dunesong.net

Three comfortable chalets, each sleeps four. Built on a red dune on the farm Onze Rust. Plus bush camp.

Languages: English, Afrikaans

Facilities: FC @

Koës Hotel — 2

Hotel — $
2 Fontein St, Koës
w206852

Tel: +264(0)63 252 716, Cell: +264(0)81 206 3686,
Fax: +264(0)63 252 716
koeshotel@gmail.com

Eight en-suite rooms, some share facilities; and one chalet. Breakfast available on request. Plus pool.

Languages: English, Afrikaans

Facilities: VISA

Activities:

Koës Hotel — 3

Lodge Camp — $
2 Fontein St, Koës
w261549

Tel: +264(0)63 252 716, Cell: +264(0)81 206 3686,
Fax: +264(0)63 252 716
koeshotel@gmail.com

Campsites with clean ablution blocks (hot showers & flush toilet). Wood for sale. Breakfast available on request.

Languages: English, Afrikaans

Facilities: VISA

Activities:

(photo: Guy Harwood)

Mata Mata (Namibia)

(photo: Johann Groenewald)

MATA MATA IS A BORDER CROSSING between Namibia and South Africa, located within Kgalagadi Transfrontier Park. On the South African side, there's an adjacent rest camp with the same name, plus fuel pumps and a park shop. Mata Mata rest camp is one of the park's original facilities and is situated on the banks of the Auob riverbed against the Namibian border. On the Namibian side of this border post you won't find any facilities other than the border post and some nearby lodging and camping establishments.

Traveller Description

Mata Mata is a popular rest camp within the Kgalagadi Transfrontier Park and offers campsites and chalets. Traffic through the Mata Mata border post is predominantly comprised of park visitors. The surrounding vegetation is mainly thorny Kalahari Dune Bushveld, a favourite of giraffe. Cheetah are often spotted on the open grasslands south of the camp.

Travel Info

Kgalagadi Transfrontier Park is a popular destination with South Africans so accommodation here is usually booked out well in advance for Easter and the June / July school holidays. Mata Mata accommodation options include campsites and recently-renovated self-catering chalets. Electricity is provided via generator from 05:00 to 21:30 daily. There's a park shop selling curios, alcohol, firewood and basic commodities; and a fuel station supplying petrol and diesel (subject to availability). You'll find a swimming pool to cool down in during the long hot summer days. The Mata Mata interpretation centre focuses on the owl species of the Kgalagadi. There's no restaurant at Mata Mata, only at Twee Rivieren.

Campsite power points at the three main rest camps (Twee Rivieren, Nossob and Mata Mata) have been converted to the caravan-type plug, so a blue converter is required to fit the standard South African three-pronged plug. Wi-Fi is available at Mata Mata but it's not reliable (Wi-Fi vouchers can be purchased at the park shop). While the camp accepts Mastercard and Visa cards, such transactions are dependent on Wi-Fi reception so may not always be accessible.

The park's rough, sandy and corrugated roads aren't suitable for sedan vehicles. The speed limit inside the park is 50 km/h and the recommended tyre pressures are:
Vehicles - 1.6 bar; Trailers - 1.2 bar; and, Caravans - 2 bar.

The border post at Mata Mata is open between 08:00 and 16:30 (no after-hours travel allowed) and operates independently of the Kgalagadi Transfrontier Park rest camp gates and park entry gates which are shown below:
January / February: 06:00-19:30
March: 06:30-19:00
April: 07:00-18:30
May: 07:00-18:00
June / July: 07:30-18:00
August: 07:00-18:30
September: 06:30-18:30
October: 06:00-19:00
November / December: 05:30-19:30

Useful numbers:

Mata Mata Rest Camp: +27(0)54 561 0907
Twee Rivieren Border Post - South Africa: +27(0)54 561 0914
Mata Mata Border - Namibia: +264(0)63 25 2055
Polka 24-hr towing services are based in Okahandja, they service Namibia: +264(0)81 129 7490
Towing services for Kgalagadi Park are available from Upington. Enquire at Mata Rest Camp reception for details: +27(0)54 561 0907

TRAVEL TIP! If you want to use the Mata Mata border post, you have to sleep two nights in the Kgalagadi Transfrontier Park and be able to show proof of such an accommodation booking. Similarly, if you enter at Twee Rivieren you must spend two nights in the park before exiting at Mata Mata. All the South African immigration and custom facilities are located at Twee Rivieren Border Post, there is no South African border post at Mata Mata, just a police station.

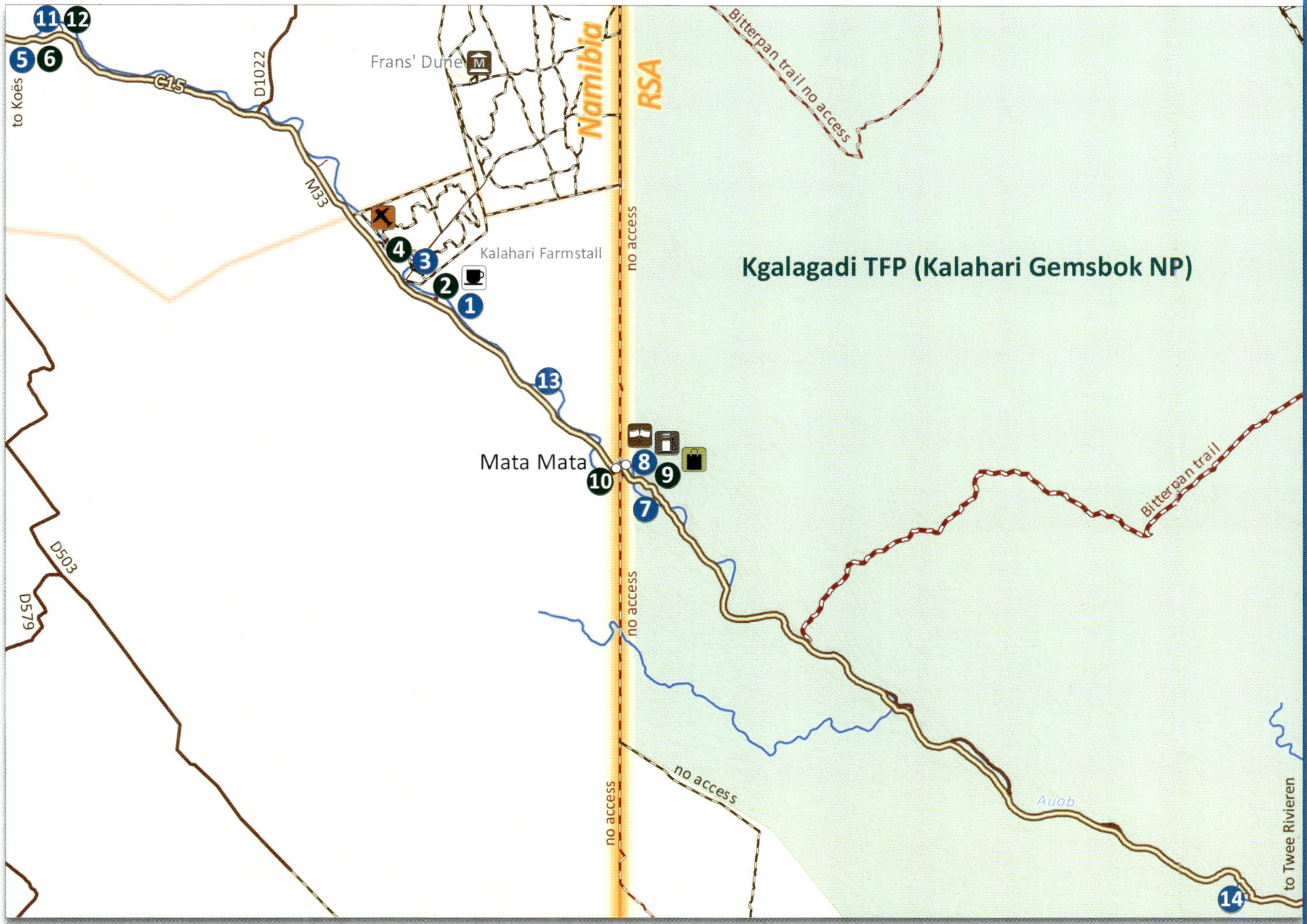

Mata Mata (Namibia)

Kalahari Farmstall and Accommodation 1

Self-catering $
15km or 12min NW of Mata Mata
w239942

Tel: +264(0)63 252 017, Fax: +264(0)63 683 390
info@kalaharifarmstall.com
www.kalaharifarmstall.com

Single, double and family chalets. All en-suite with air-conditioning, kitchen and veranda braai. Breakfast available. Dinner only on request.

Languages: English, Afrikaans

Facilities:
Activities:

Kalahari Farmstall and Accommodation 2

Camping $
15km or 12min NW of Mata Mata
w239940

Tel: +264(0)63 252 017, Fax: +264(0)63 683 390
info@kalaharifarmstall.com
www.kalaharifarmstall.com

Six campsites, each with power point and braai. Four people max per site. Communal ablutions and kitchen facilities.

Languages: English, Afrikaans

Facilities:
Activities:

Kalahari Game Lodge 3

Game/Safari Lodge $$
19km or 17min NW of Mata Mata (of which 2km is 4WD)
w137978

Tel: +264(0)63 252 052, Cell: +27(0)84 443 4241,
reservations@kalaharigamelodge.com.na
www.kalaharigamelodge.com.na

Eight luxurious, en-suite chalets, each equipped with small kitchenette and patio overlooking the Auob riverbed.

Languages: English, Afrikaans

Facilities:
Activities:

Kalahari Game Lodge 4

Lodge Camp $$
19km or 16min NW of Mata Mata (of which 2km is 4WD)
w359847

Tel: +264(0)63 252 052, Cell: +27(0)84 443 4241,
reservations@kalaharigamelodge.com.na
www.kalaharigamelodge.com.na

Six secluded campsites, each with its own covered structure housing shower, toilet, washing-up facility and braai area. No electricity.

Languages: English, Afrikaans

Facilities:
Activities:

Kalahari Sunset Game Farm 5

Guest Farm $
44km or 34min NW of Mata Mata
w361649

Tel: +264(0)63 252 005, Fax: +264(0)88 639 572
oerwoud@africaonline.com.na
www.kalaharisunsetgamefarm.com

Two fully-furnished units on red Kalahari sand dune. Spectacular sunsets views.

Languages: English

Facilities:
Activities:

Kalahari Sunset Game Farm 6

Lodge Camp $
44km or 34min NW of Mata Mata
w361650

Tel: +264(0)63 252 005, Fax: +264(0)88 639 572
oerwoud@africaonline.com.na
www.kalaharisunsetgamefarm.com

Four campsites with power points. Clean ablution facilities. Game drives on request.

Languages: English

Facilities:
Activities:

Kalahari Tented Camp 7

Tented Camp $$
4km or 10min SE of Mata Mata (South Africa)
w151169

Tel: +27(0)12 428 9111, Fax: +27(0)12 343 0905
reservations@sanparks.org
www.sanparks.org

This unfenced camp offers comfortable family tents and honeymoon tents. The tents have bathrooms with hot water. Reservations are advisable.

Languages: English, Afrikaans

Facilities:
Activities:

Mata Mata Rest Camp 8

Self-catering $
In Mata Mata (South Africa)
w179169

Tel: +27(0)12 428 9111, Fax: +27(0)12 343 0905
reservations@sanparks.org
www.sanparks.org

These chalets are located around the dry Auob riverbed overlooking a small waterhole. There is a fuel station, and small shop selling basic necessities. Reservations are advisable.

Languages: English, Afrikaans

Facilities:
Activities:

Mata Mata Rest Camp 9

Park Camp $$
In Mata Mata (South Africa)
w225478

Tel: +27(0)12 428 9111, Fax: +27(0)12 343 0905
reservations@sanparks.org
www.sanparks.org

Situated on the banks of the dry Auob River, the campsites share ablutions and overlook a waterhole. A generator provides electricity. Reservations are advisable.

Languages: English, Afrikaans

Facilities:
Activities:

Sitzas Campsite 10

Transit Camp $
1km or 3min W of Mata Mata Border Control
w200951

Tel: +264(0)61 244 558, Fax: +264(0)86 545 9316
kotzem@mweb.com.na

Three spacious campsites under shady Camel Thorn trees. Shared ablutions (toilet & shower). Suitable for groups who know each other.

Languages: English, Afrikaans

Facilities:
Activities:

Terra-Rouge Guest Farm 11

Guest Farm $$
44km or 34min NW of Mata Mata
w200948

Tel: +264(0)63 252 031, Cell: +264(0)81 129 0280
terrarouge@iway.na
www.terrarougefarm.com

Three self-contained bungalows close to the main house.

Languages: English, Afrikaans

Facilities:
Activities:

Terra-Rouge Guest Farm 12

Farm Camp $
44km or 34min NW of Mata Mata
w359863

Tel: +264(0)63 252 031, Cell: +264(0)81 129 0280
terrarouge@iway.na
www.terrarougefarm.com

Campsites well-positioned for privacy. 10 people maximum per site. Modern ablutions with open-air shower and flush toilet.

Languages: English, Afrikaans

Facilities:

Activities:

Torgos Safari Lodge 13

Lodge $$
10km or 7min NW of Mata Mata
w200950

Tel: +264(0)63 683 168, Fax: +264(0)63 683 169
torgos@iway.na
www.torgoslodgenam.com

Four luxury and four standard tented chalets (includes some self-catering units). Plus two luxury, air-conditioned stone chalets. All en-suite.

Languages: English

Facilities:

Activities:

Urikaruus Wilderness Camp 14

Self-catering $$
50km or 1h16min SE of Mata Mata (South Africa)
w151183

Tel: +27(0)12 428 9111, Fax: +27(0)12 343 0905
reservations@sanparks.org
www.sanparks.org

This camp is unfenced and guests must check in at Twee Rivieren. These self-catering cabins are on stilts with feature fully-equipped kitchens and gas power. Reservations are advisable.

Languages: English, Afrikaans

Facilities:

Activities:

(photo: Johann Groenewald)

Noordoewer

(photo: Karin Theron)

YOU'LL FIND THIS LITTLE TOWN on the eastern flank of the Orange River. Its Afrikaans name means 'North Bank' and points to the fact that the Orange, which forms the border between Namibia and South Africa, runs into the Atlantic due west of this point.

The Namibian border post of the same name lies a short distance outside the town while across the river you'll find Vioolsdrift, its South African counterpart. Besides the industry that a busy border post attracts, this area also boasts grape, date and tomato farms.

Traveller Description

Many South African visitors are drawn to this area by the canoeing and rafting activities offered here. While this dusty brown town doesn't offer much else, there's a reasonable number of accommodation venues in the vicinity located along the lush, green riverfront.

Travel Info

In town you'll find a bank and a supermarket with its own bakery; here you can refill your gas canisters.
Noordoewer Border Post is open 24 hrs. Tel: +264(0)63 297 122. Government clinic tel: +264(0)63 297 109

TRAVEL TIP! You'll find an Engen garage with Wimpy, shop and ATM on the southern side of town.

Town Info:
Police: +264(0)63 297 117

Amanzi River Camp (Abiqua) 1

Self-catering $
13km or 11min WNW of Noordoewer
w274170

Tel: +264(0)63 297 255, Cell: +27(0)72 229 4672,
Fax: +264(0)63 297 255
abiqua@amanzitrails.co.za,
www.amanzitrails.co.za

Furnished (beds & basic kitchen), self-catering chalets. Each with its own outside braai and outdoor ablutions. Wood, ice and meat for sale. Canoeing trips available.

Languages: English, Afrikaans

Facilities:
Activities:

Amanzi River Camp (Abiqua) 2

Holiday Resort Camp $
13km or 11min WNW of Noordoewer
w138869

Tel: +264(0)63 297 255, Cell: +27(0)72 229 4672,
Fax: +264(0)63 297 255
abiqua@amanzitrails.co.za,
www.amanzitrails.co.za

Grassed, shaded campsites. Ablutions with hot water. Meals can be arranged. Located on the banks of the Orange River.

Languages: English, Afrikaans

Facilities:
Activities:

Felix Unite Provenance Camp 3

Lodge $$
10km or 8min NW of Noordoewer
w138668

Tel: +27(0)87 354 0578, Cell: +264(0)81 147 8945,
Fax: +27(0)86 678 8207
cabanas@felix.co.za,
www.accommodationsouthernnamibia.com

En-suite cabanas sleep two. Family Cabanas sleep four. Located a few kilometres from the border post.

Languages: English, Nama, Portuguese, French, Afrikaans

Facilities:

Activities:

Felix Unite Provenance Camp 4

Lodge Camp $$
10km or 8min NW of Noordoewer
w255828

Tel: +27(0)87 354 0578, Cell: +264(0)81 147 8945,
Fax: +27(0)21 702 9493
cabanas@felix.co.za,
www.accommodationsouthernnamibia.com

Campground has access to lodge facilities and overlooks the river. No bookings accepted - availability checked on arrival.

Languages: English, Nama, Portuguese, French, Afrikaans

Facilities:

Activities:

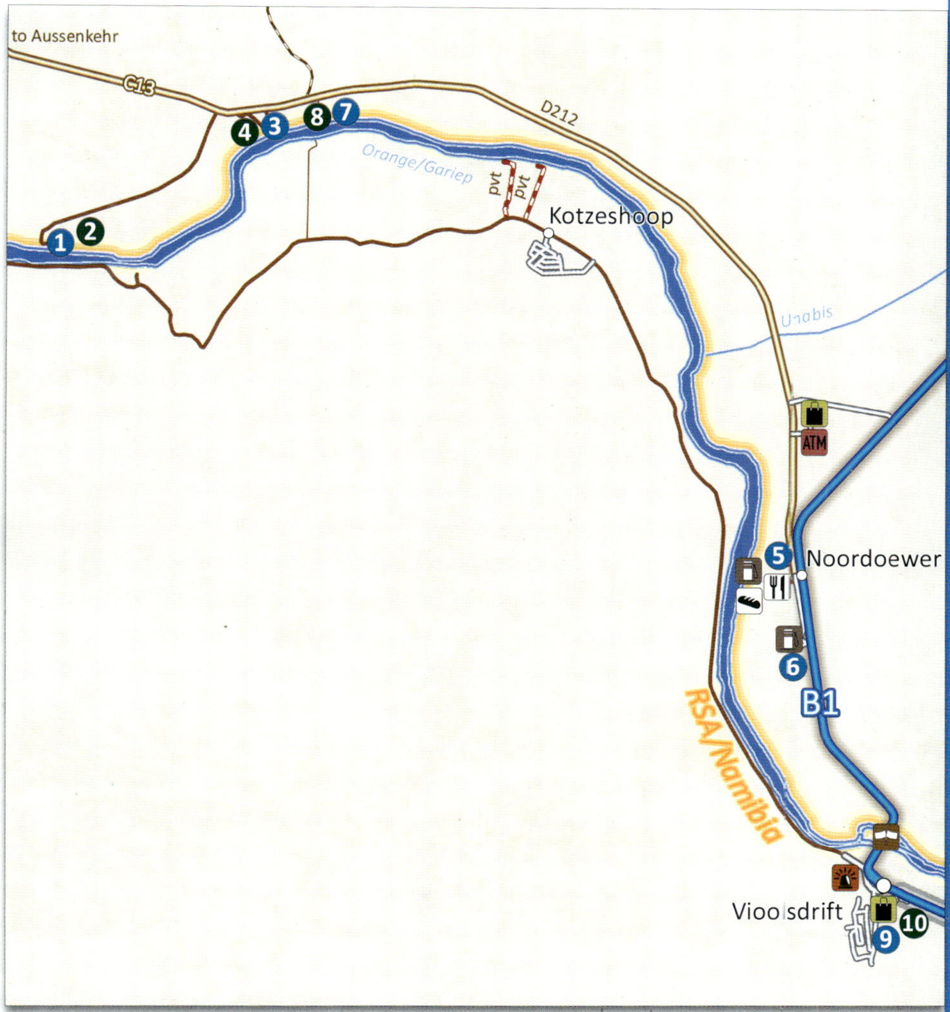

Noordoewer Guesthouse 5

Bed and Breakfast $$
Plot 437, Noordoewer
w140234

Tel: +264(0)63 297 108, Cell: +264(0)81 379 5958,
bookings@noordoewerguesthouse.com
www.noordoewerguesthouse.com

14 Air-conditioned rooms, each with DStv and views of Orange River and Noordoewer farms. Braai packs available.

Languages: Afrikaans

Facilities:

Activities:

Orange River Lodge 6

Lodge $$
Noordoewer
w139322

Tel: +264(0)63 297 012, Cell: +264(0)81 769 2700,
Fax: +264(0)88 621 180
orlodge@iway.na,
www.orlodge.iway.na

Four air-conditioned, en-suite rooms with kitchenettes and coffee/tea facilities. Braai facilities available. No camping.

Languages: English, Afrikaans

Facilities:

Activities:

The River Rafters 7

Self-catering $
10km or 8min NW of Noordoewer
w255839

Tel: +27(0)21 880 2006, Cell: +27(0)83 303 2657,
Fax: +27(0)86 680 5443
info@bundi.co.za,
www.bundi.co.za

En-suite chalets next to Orange River with great views. Includes bar and deck.

Languages: English, Afrikaans

Facilities:

Activities:

The River Rafters 8

Lodge Camp $
10km or 8min NW of Noordoewer
w140235

Tel: +27(0)21 880 2006, Cell: +27(0)83 303 2657,
Fax: +27(0)86 680 5443
info@bundi.co.za, www.bundi.co.za

Five grassed and shaded campsites of various sizes next to the Orange River. Some have power points. Communal ablutions (showers & flush toilets).

Languages: English, Afrikaans

Facilities:

Activities:

Vioolsdrift Lodge 9

Lodge $$
Plot 12, Vioolsdrift
w129662

Tel: +27(0)27 761 8778, Cell: +27(0)82 820 2758,
Fax: +27(0)27 761 8776
info@vioolsdrift.com,
www.vioolsdrift.com

Nine air-conditioned chalets with views over the Orange River. Reservations mandatory.

Languages: English

Facilities:

Activities:

Vioolsdrift Lodge 10

Camping $$
Plot 12, Vioolsdrift
w260517

Tel: +27(0)27 761 8778, Cell: ?+27(0)82 820 2758,
Fax: +27(0)27 761 8776
info@vioolsdrift.com,
www.vioolsdrift.com

Grassed campsites. Ablutions (showers & toilets) and braai facilities but no kitchen area, just a sink. Reservations advisable.

Languages: English

Facilities:

Activities:

Rosh Pinah

(photo: Ian-Ray Nel)

IN 1963, A GERMAN-BORN JEW named Mose Kohan, discovered zinc in the Huns Mountains. This prospector's lucky find turned out be one of the most important sources of lead and zinc in the country. Somewhat appropriately, the name Rosh Pinah is a Hebrew biblical term for cornerstone. Mining continues near to the town to this day, with a heavily-automated plant that produces close to 200 000 tons of zinc concentrate every 24 hours. At the time of writing, primary ownership of the mine had recently passed to the Trevali Mining Corporation, a Canadian company.

Traveller Description

Rosh Pinah lies sandwiched between the Ai-Ais / Richtersveld Transfrontier Park to the east and the Sperrgebiet on the coast to the west. As a mining town, Rosh Pinah offers many facilities and services that an overland traveller will find useful.

Travel Info

The number for the Sidadi Private Clinic is the same as for the doctor: +264(0)63 274 911, a/h +264(0)81 128 0098. There is a supermarket with butchery and bakery and a bottle store.

TRAVEL TIP! The road from Oranjemund to Rosh Pinah was tarred in 2017; a permit is no longer required to travel between these two towns. The public road from Rosh Pinah to Aussenkehr traverses the Ai-Ais National Park. This dirt road hugs the Orange River for the most part, it's a beautiful drive that boasts many spots worthy of a lunch stop or picnic. Note: this road is prone to flooding in the rainy season.

Town Info:

Police: +264(0)63 274 597
Tow-in: +264(0)63 222 119
Doctor: +264(0)63 274 911

Amica Guest House 1

Guest House $$
306 Mukarob Close, Rosh Pinah
w141253

Tel: +264(0)63 274 043, Fax: +264(0)63 274 983
aguesthouse@skorpionzinc.com.na

10 En-suite, air-conditioned rooms with DStv, telephone, internet access, babysitting services, braai area, cocktail lounge, conference centre, restaurant, pool and laundry services.

Languages: English, Afrikaans

Facilities:

Activities:

Four Seasons Lodge 2

Lodge $$
2 Melkbos St, Rosh Pinah
w140954

Tel: +264(0)63 274 416, Cell: +264(0)81 270 6040,
Fax: +264(0)63 274 414
fourseasons@iway.na

Air-conditioned, self-catering, en-suite rooms with TV and refrigerator.

Languages: English, Afrikaans

Facilities: VISA FC @

Activities:

McMillan's Guest House 3

Guest House $
Kokerboom St, Rosh Pinah
w138499

Tel: +264(0)63 274 107, Cell: +264(0)81 274 8849,
Fax: +264(0)63 274 107
rentia.louw@yahoo.com

13 comfortable, air-conditioned rooms with TV. Breakfast served. Restaurant nearby for other meals.

Languages: English, Afrikaans

Facilities: VISA @

Activities:

(photo: Ian-Ray Nel)

Seeheim

(photo: Peter Barber)

THOUGH FOUNDED IN 1896 as a base for the German colonial armed forces, there's evidence to suggest that this spot was a gathering point for the local Nama people who used to cross the river here where the Skaap (sheep) River joins the much larger Fish River. This settlement has seen its fortunes wax and wane over the last century. It enjoyed much prominence during the diamond rush as a junction station where the railway lines from Keetmanshoop diverted to Lüderitz and Karasburg.

In the good times, in the 40s and 50s, the town boasted two hotels, shops and even a legal brothel. In German Seeheim means 'Home by the lake' - during the dry months it's rather difficult to work out why this name was chosen. But should you visit here on the rare occasions when the Fish River floods you'll discover the town as a virtual island, encircled by raging waters.

Traveller Description

In 1974 the B4 main road was rerouted away from Seeheim, leaving the town hidden away at the end of a gravel access road. Small surprise then that today Seeheim is a very quiet little settlement.

Many are drawn to the Seeheim hotel by its castle-like styling and its old world charm; from a historical perspective it's certainly well worth a visit.

Travel Info

Furniture is made and sold here. The hotel also sells petrol and diesel.

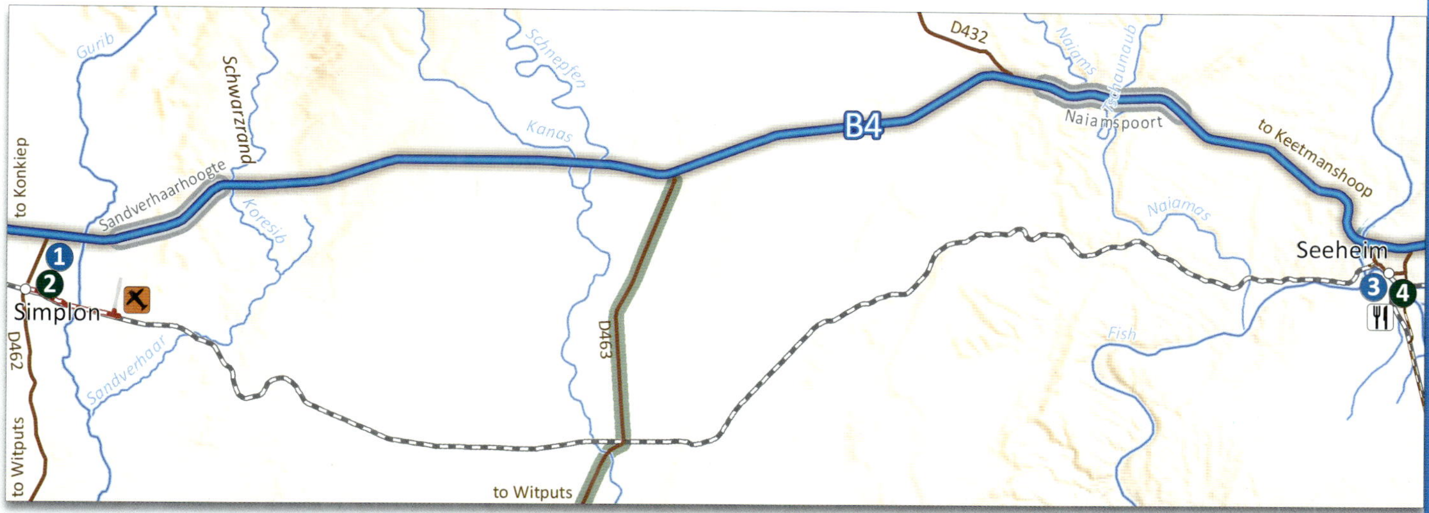

Alte Kalkofen Lodge 1

Lodge $$
52km or 34min W of Seeheim
w267871

Tel: +264(0)63 683 415, Cell: +264(0)81 129 8928, Fax: +264(0)88 633 737
info@altekalkofen.com, www.altekalkofen.com

10 Double/single bungalows and two twin rooms (wheelchair-friendly). Comfortable beds and en-suite bathrooms.

Languages: English, Afrikaans

Facilities:
Activities:

Alte Kalkofen Lodge 2

Lodge Camp $$
52km or 35min W of Seeheim
w359603

Tel: +264(0)63 683 415, Cell: +264(0)81 129 8928, Fax: +264(0)88 633 737
info@altekalkofen.com, www.altekalkofen.com

Three campsites, each with its own bathroom (hot shower, basin & toilet) and washing-up sink.

Languages: English, Afrikaans

Facilities:
Activities:

Seeheim Hotel 3

Hotel $$
Seeheim
w138066

Tel: +264(0)63 683 643, Cell: +264(0)81 128 0349, Fax: +264(0)88 650 9640
seeheim@iway.na, www.seeheimhotel.com

16 En-suite single, double or family rooms. Plus dining and breakfast rooms, bar, curio shop and pool.

Languages: English, Afrikaans

Facilities:
Activities:

Seeheim Hotel 4

Lodge Camp $
Seeheim
w142809

Tel: +264(0)63 683 643, Cell: +264(0)81 128 0349, Fax: +264(0)88 650 9640
seeheim@iway.na, www.seeheimhotel.com

Campsites with own braais on lawn on hotel's lower terrace. Neat ablutions and kitchen area with wash-up facility.

Languages: English, Afrikaans

Facilities:
Activities:

(photo: Karin Theron)

Sendelingsdrif (Namibia)

(photo: Karin Theron)

SENDELINGSDRIF IS A BORDER CROSSING on the Orange River between Namibia and South Africa. The Namibian side has no facilities other than a small border post building but on the South African side of the river you'll find accommodation, fuel and a small shop.

Travel Info

You have to use a pont to cross the river at this border crossing, it's a memorable way to leave or enter Namibia! The pont operates the same hours as the border post, 08:00-16:30, and costs R160 per vehicle and R60 for a trailer (2018 pricing).

Useful Numbers:

Border post: +264(0)63 274 926

TRAVEL TIP! Occasionally, the pont is out of action so call ahead if your travel plans rely on this border post being functional. Particularly during December to April, when the river is prone to flooding.

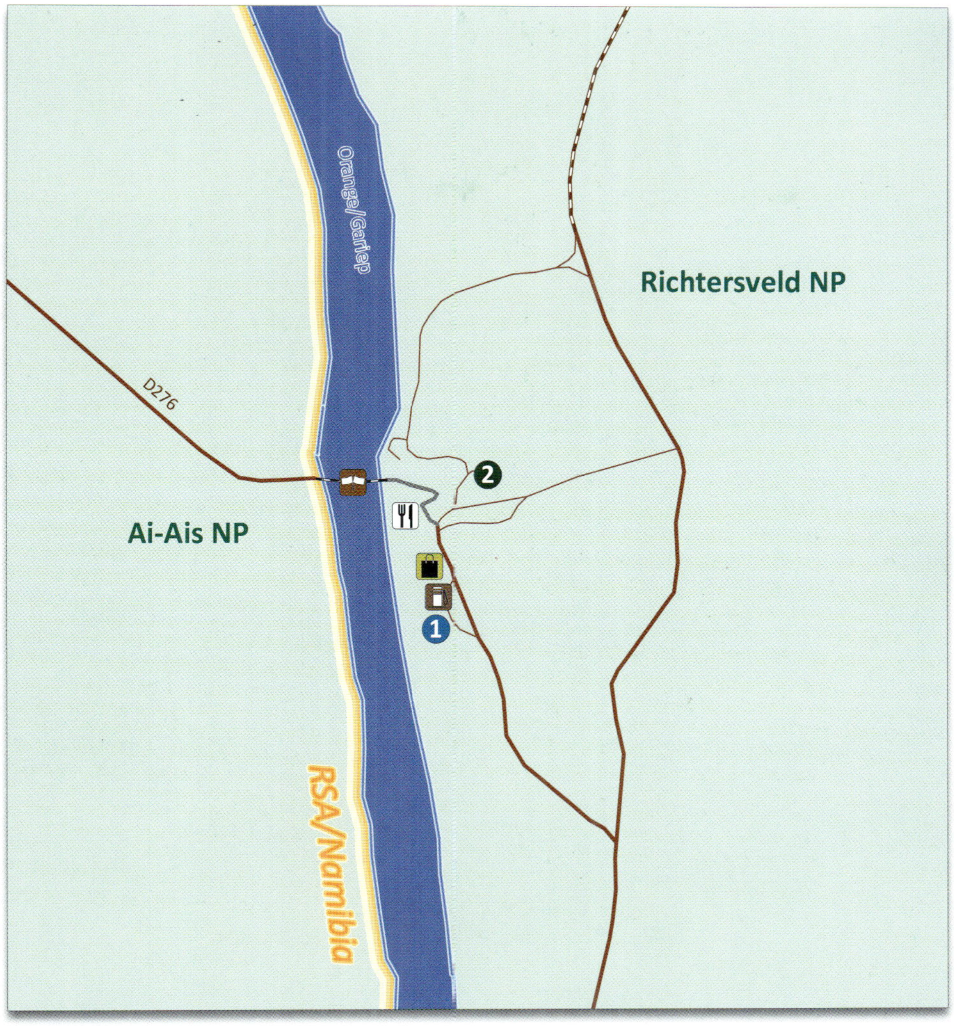

Sendelingsdrif Rest Camp 1

Self-catering $
24km or 32min SE of Rosh Pinah
w260510

Tel: +27(0)27 831 1506, Cell: +27(0)84 742 9797,
Fax: +27(0)27 831 1175
RNPreservations@sanparks.org,
www.sanparks.org

Ten air-conditioned chalets, each with fridge, 2-plate electric stove, shower, and front veranda with views over the Orange River. Plus pool.

Languages: English, Afrikaans

Facilities:

Activities:

Sendelingsdrif Rest Camp 2

Transit Camp $$$
24km or 32min SE of Rosh Pinah
w245953

Tel: +27(0)27 831 1506, Cell: +27(0)84 742 9797,
Fax: +27(0)27 831 1175
RNPreservations@sanparks.org,
www.sanparks.org

Campsites with power point and ablutions (hot showers). There is running water and a pool at this camp. Two vehicles allowed per site.

Languages: English, Afrikaans

Facilities:

Activities:

(photo: Frank Höppener)

SPERRGEBIET

The manager's house at the Pomona ghost town, south of Elizabeth Bay. (photo: Heiner Dillmann)

THE WORD SPERRGEBIET MEANS RESTRICTED AREA - most of this region is closed to the public due to the diamond mining that takes place here. It was declared a restricted area in 1908.

This forbidden territory has a spectacular landscape ranging from rocky outcrops to pure Namib desert. The sand dunes are bordered to the west by the cold, cruel Atlantic Ocean. Like the Skeleton Coast further north, this wild coastline is also a graveyard to many shipwrecks.

Bogenfels, Pomona and Elizabeth Bay are mining ghost towns and day trips are offered from Lüderitz to Bogenfels and Pomona. Various concession holders offer guided 4x4 tours into the desert. Most of them operate from Lüderitz and the adventures are undertaken in the dunes between Oranjemund and Lüderitz.

Oranjemund sits sandwiched between the South African border on the one side (the Orange River) and the Sperrgebiet on the other. Formerly a fully-fledged mining town run by the Namdeb Mining Company, Oranjemund was recently proclaimed a public municipality. With oryx wandering through its neatly-kept streets, this has always been a friendly town for those lucky enough to visit. The end of access restrictions will surely see many travellers passing through here in order to avail themselves of these quaint charms.

The changes discussed in the paragraph above also mean that the Oranjemund border post is open to the public, as is the excellent road between Oranjemund and Rosh Pinah.

The Sperrgebiet was proclaimed a National Park in 2009. It's home to a wealth of endemic succulent plant species and is one of the world's top 25 Biodiversity Hotspots. Because the area has been off limits to the public for so long, the habitat has been left largely untouched, making a visit to the park a truly unique wilderness experience.

Unfortunately, you cannot travel the area at whim; you may only explore it with one of the concessionaires who have permits from the Ministry of Environment and Tourism. These tour operators are based in Lüderitz.

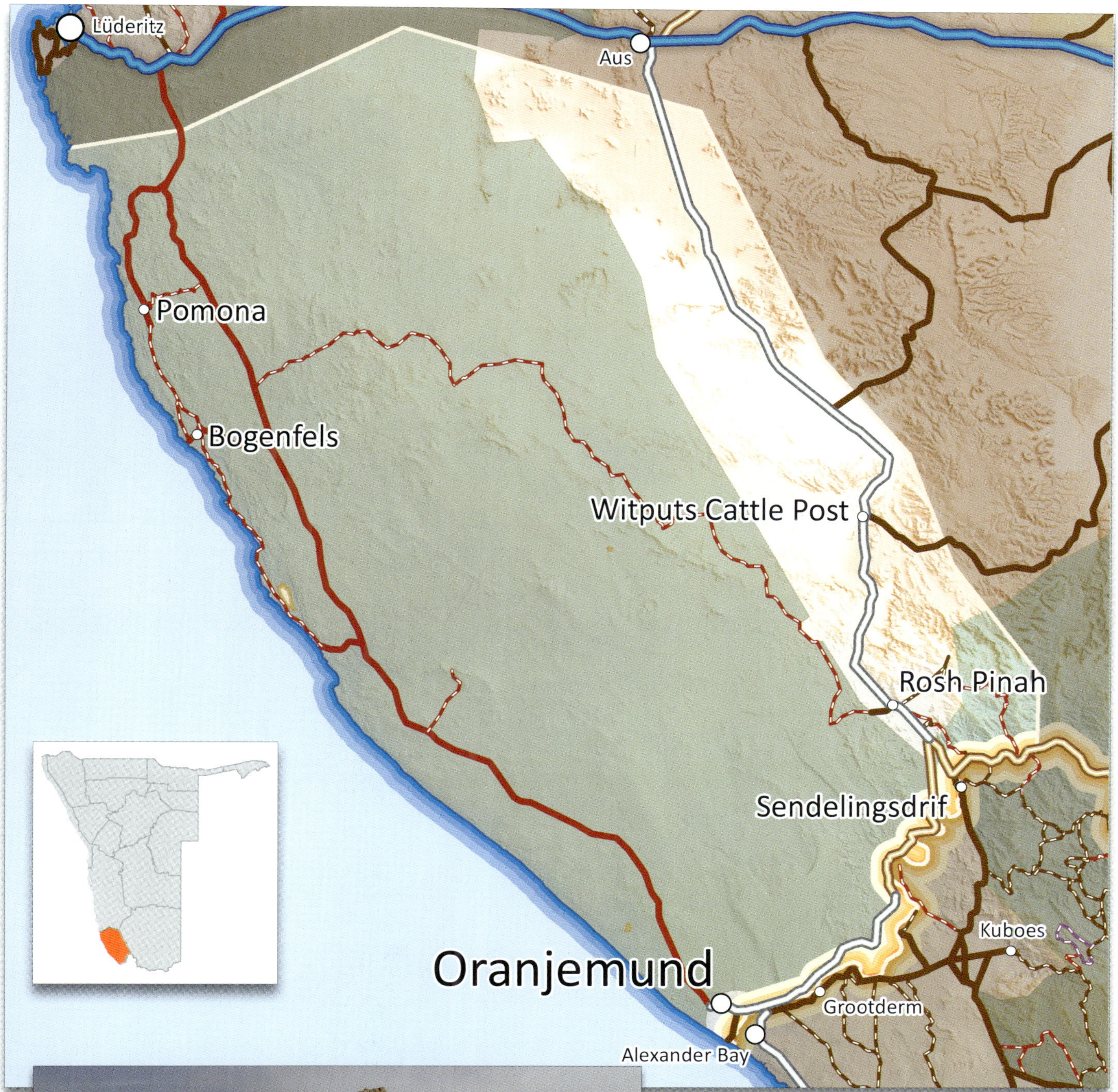

The 55m high Bogenfels rock arch is comprised of lime rock which has been weathered by wind and waves to form a bridge. It's located roughly 100km south of Lüderitz. (photo: Heiner Dillmann)

MAJOR ATTRACTIONS

- Pomona, Bogenfels and Elizabeth Bay are fascinating diamond mining ghost towns.
- The magnificent Bogenfels Arch Rock is a 55 meter high rock arch with one foot of the arch in the Atlantic Ocean and the other in the sand of the Namib Desert.

More details about the attractions are available on our website (www.tracks4africa.co.za) or our Guide App. Our GPS Map can navigate you to each of these attractions.

Oranjemund

(photo: Ian-Ray Nel)

YOU'LL FIND ORANJEMUND JUST NORTH of the Orange river mouth. This mining town was built in 1936 after the discovery of significant diamond deposits on the riverbanks and up the coast to the north. Formerly run by Consolidated Diamond Mines (CDM), the town later fell under the stewardship of Namdeb - a joint venture between the Namibian government and De Beers Centenary AG. These days, as mining in the area begins to wind down, Oranjemund is moving towards independence as a municipal entity. At the time of writing, advanced plans were in place for residents to start paying for services; unrestricted visitor access had already been implemented.

Compared to the surrounding countryside, this neatly-planned town is an oasis with tree-lined streets, parks, and much greenery. A lush 18-hole golf course stands in stark contrast to the four kilometres of wild, unspoilt beachfront adjacent the river mouth. The reed channels at the river mouth (itself part of the RAMSAR proclaimed Gariep River Wetland), are an area of prolific birdlife.

Traveller Description

In the past one needed a permit to visit this town and access was tightly controlled. Oranjemund's future is a little uncertain at the time of writing, but if it manages its transformation cleverly, this town stands every chance of becoming Namibia's southernmost coastal attraction. Many travellers are beginning to use Oranjemund as an entry point to Namibia, taking the newly-tarred road to Rosh Pinah - as this route no longer requires a permit.

Travel Info

You can camp on the beach at the river mouth or along the riverbank, although there are no facilities. Besides the golf course, the town has a bowling club, public swimming pool and putt-putt course. Or you can go explore the river, paddling its reed-lined channels. Fishing is good at the river mouth (especially in December/January) and at the Jasper House Heritage Centre you can see how pioneer miners lived in years gone by. Note: both the sea and the river are rough and dangerous for swimming.

Useful numbers: Oranjemund Border Post: +264(0)63 232 756 (06:00 - 22:00)

Town Info:

Hospital: +264(0)63 238 000, Police: +264(0)63 232 228, Doctor: +264(0)63 238 002/3/6, Tow-in: +264(0)63 232 184

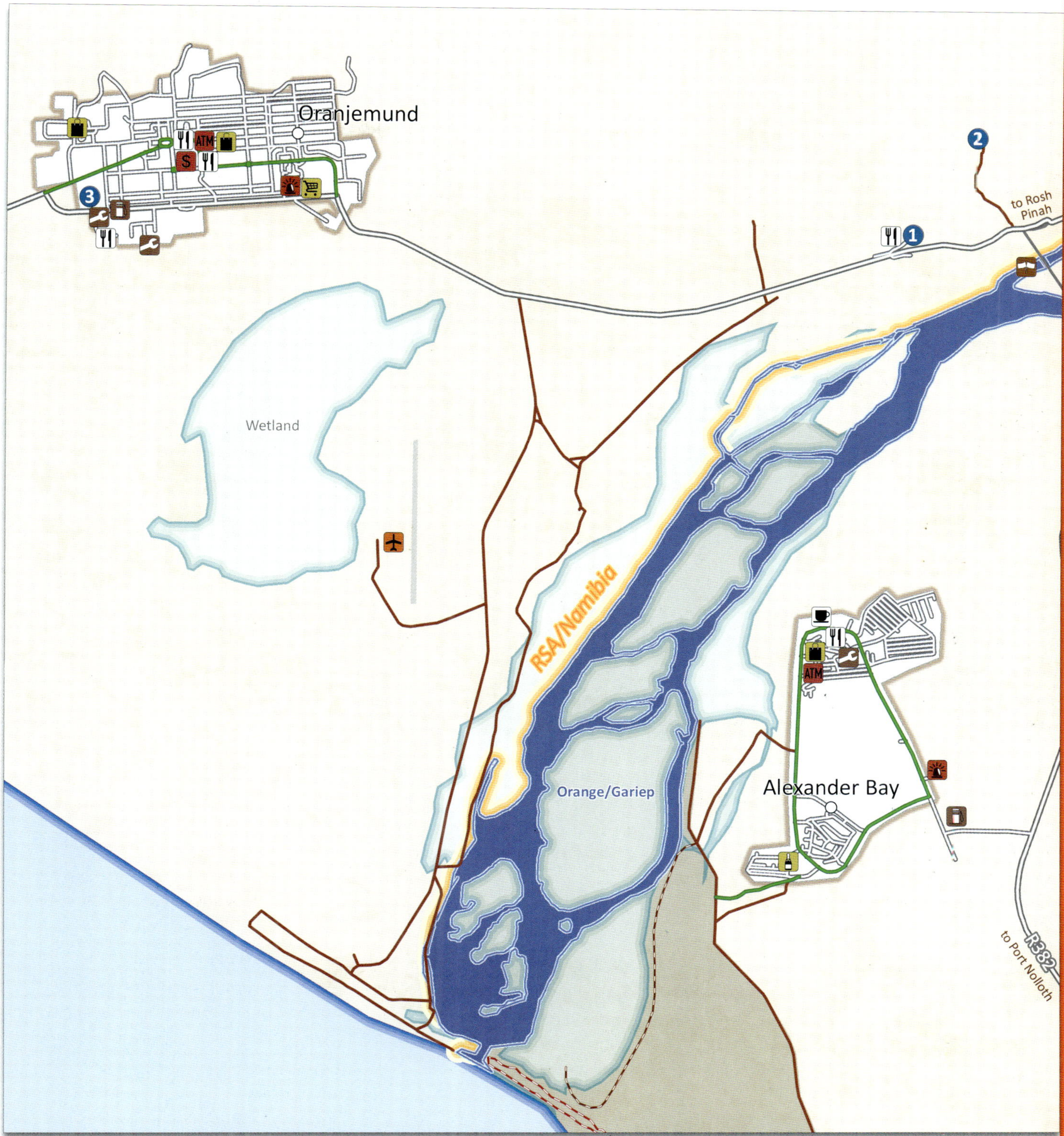

Op My Stoep Lodge 1

Lodge $
7km or 9min E of Oranjemund
w186181

Tel: +264(0)63 23 4223, Cell: +264(0)81 750 1716,
Fax: +264(0)63 232 874
opmystoep@iway.na,
www.opmystoep.com

Luxury rooms and a la carte restaurant.

Languages: English, Afrikaans

Facilities: VISA FC

Activities:

Shepherd's Lodge 2

Lodge $
9km or 13min E of Oranjemund
w138461

Tel: +264(0)63 232 996, Cell: +264(0)81 283 1481,
Fax: +264(0)36 234 996
shepherds@iway.na

Rooms and backpacker dorms, with breakfast included. Situated near Oranjemund in the National Park. Bookings essential.

Languages: English

Facilities: VISA @

Activities:

Tom's Cabin 3

Self-catering $
In Oranjemund
w252805

Tel: +264(0)63 234 207, Cell: +264(C)81 362 1227,
Fax: +264(0)63 234 209
tep@mweb.com.na

Comfortable, self-catering accommodation. Breakfast available at additional charge.

Languages: English, Afrikaans

Facilities: @

Activities:

ZAMBEZI

(above) Bwabwata National Park (all photos: Karin Theron)
(right) A kudu doe in Nkasa Rupala National Park.

IN 2013, A LARGE PART OF THE AREA formerly known as the Caprivi Strip was renamed Zambezi. This region stretches out like an arm between Angola, Zambia and Botswana, touching Zimbabwe at the confluence of the Chobe and Zambezi Rivers. It's a tropical area hosting an array of wildlife and bird species, and offers great fishing.

The area is characterised by an abundance of water, wetlands, large floodplains and thick Mopani woodland. Bwabwata, Nkasa Rupala and Muduma National Parks as well as the Kwando Core Area of the Bwabwata National Park, are the major conservation areas in the Zambezi region. The Bwabwata National Park falls in both the Zambezi and Kavango region, you can read more about this park on page 194 and 342. Be aware that hunting concessions were giving to the local community so this activity takes place, especially in the Buffalo and Kwando Core Areas of Bwabwata. All the parks are well worth a visit and, with over 600 bird species, are a real paradise for bird watchers. Game is plentiful and hippos and crocodiles laze around on the riverbanks.

There are countless fishing camps and lodges along the Zambezi, Kwando and Linyanti Rivers, offering a variety of activities. These rivers define Namibia's borders with Botswana, Zambia, Zimbabwe and Angola.

The Zambezi region is also a gateway to the Okavango Delta and national parks such as Chobe and Moremi in Botswana, and the famous Victoria Falls on the Zambia / Zimbabwe border.

Katima Mulilo is the main town in this region and offers essential services to tourists. Visitors should take malaria precautions when visiting this region.

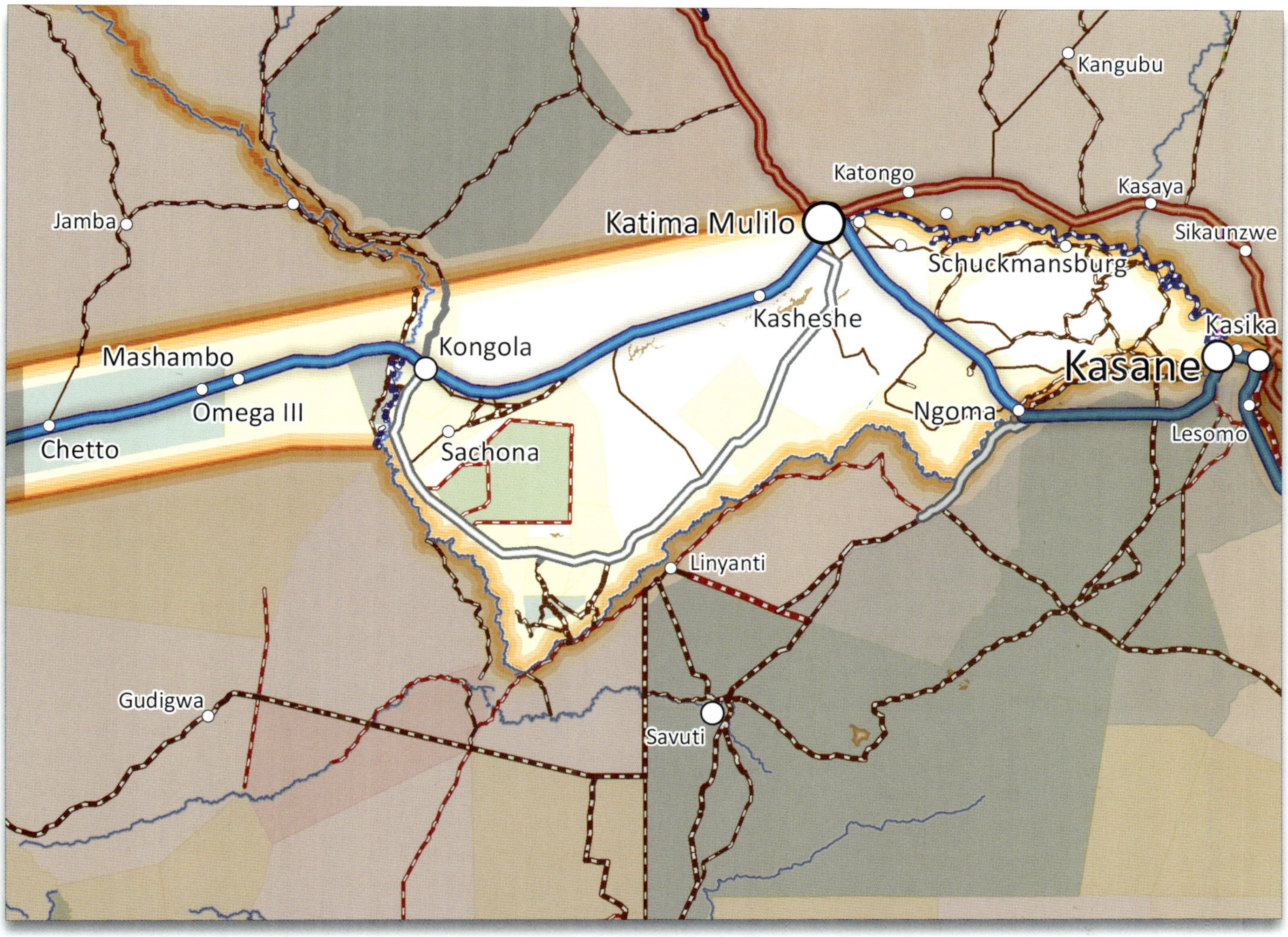

MAJOR ATTRACTIONS

- At Horseshoe Bend in the Bwabwata National Park an oxbow lake was formed in the Kwando River which attracts big herds of elephant and other game.
- Mudumu National Park
- Nkasa Rupala National Park
- Nambwa Community Camp offers a variety of activities like boat trips.
- Visitors can buy lovely baskets and traditional axes at Lipiri Crafts.
- At the craft shop in Kongola you will find baskets, carvings, jewellery and natural remedies.
- The Living Museum of the Mafwe is a village where guests can experience the traditional culture of the Mafwe people.
- Lizauli Traditional Village offers visitors an insight into the Caprivian lifestyle.

More details about the attractions are available on our website (www.tracks4africa.co.za) or our Guide App. Our GPS Map can navigate you to each of these attractions.

Bwabwata National Park
(Kwando Core Area)

(photo: Karin Theron)

BWABWATA NATIONAL PARK, located in the Zambezi and the Kavango Region of northeast Namibia, was formed in 2007 when the Mahango Game Reserve and the Caprivi Game Park were merged. The 6 274km² park is co-managed by the Namibian Government and the local community who benefit from community-based tourism within the park. There are a combination of 'multiple use areas' and 'three core conservation areas', namely the Mahango Core Area, the Buffalo Core Area, and the Kwando Core Area, within Bwabwata National Park.

Traveller Description

The park is home to several large mammals including; lions, leopard, cheetahs, giraffe, zebra, blue wildebeest and buffalo. One of Bwabwata's main attractions, are the elephant herds which still migrate freely through the region, crossing borders into Botswana and Angola. There's also an abundance of birdlife within Bwabwata's borders.

Over 5 000 people still live and farm with livestock and grain in the small villages within the 'multiple use areas' of the park. Tourists can visit the three core areas, but need to be aware that hunting concessions were given to the local community, and that hunting takes place, especially in the Buffalo and Kwando Core Areas.

Travel Info

Accommodation inside the park is limited to the Kwando Core Area, but there are many accommodation options just outside the entry gate into the Mahango Core Area (see Divundu).

TRAVEL TIP! A good time to visit is October. Although it's very hot at this time, game gathers at the remaining waterholes along the Kwando River.

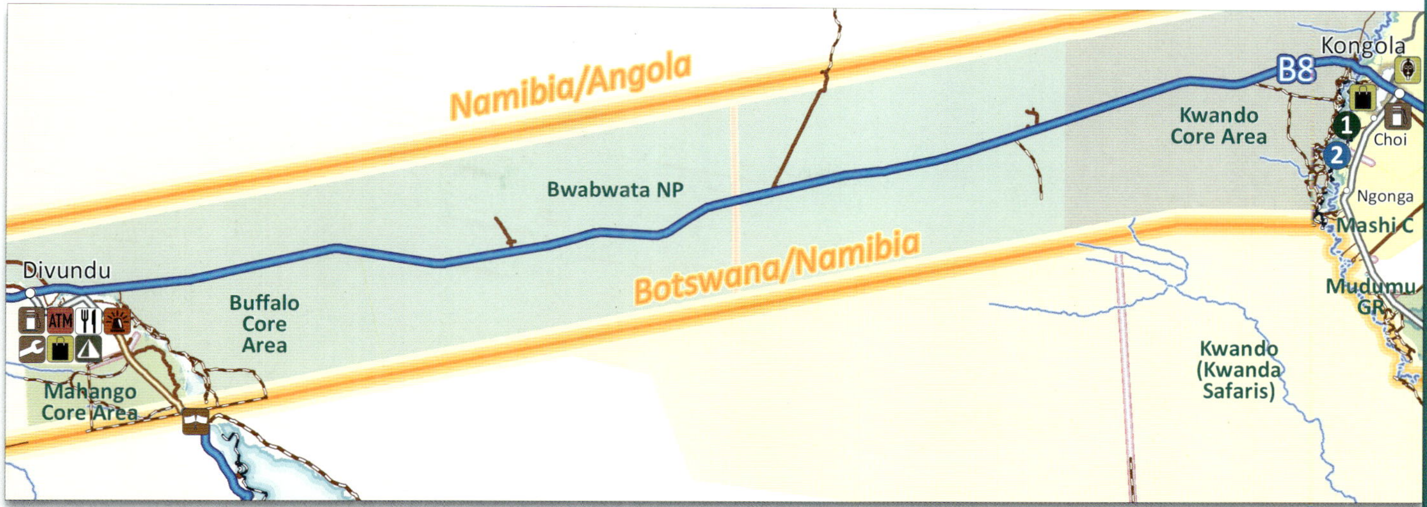

Nambwa Campsite 1

Camping $$$
21km or 46min SW of Kongola (of which 14km is 4WD)
w137401

Tel: +264(0)61 400 510, Cell: +264(0)81 125 2122
reservations@africanmonarch.com.na
www.africanmonarchlodges.com

Four private campsites located on the banks of the Kwando River. Running water, braai areas and ablutions. Hot water via solar. Reservations mandatory.

Languages: English, Afrikaans

Facilities:

Activities:

Nambwa Tented Lodge 2

Lodge $$$
21km or 45min SW of Kongola (of which 13km is 4WD)
w277796

Tel: +264(0)61 400 510, Cell: +264(0)81 125 2122
reservations@africanmonarchlodges.com
www.africanmonarchlodges.com

Luxury tent suites built up in the trees, overlooking the Kwando River and floodplains. Each suite with en-suite bathroom and large inside shower. Reservations mandatory.

Languages: English, Afrikaans

Facilities:

Activities:

(photo: Karin Theron)

Katima Mulilo

(photo: Johann Groenewald)

SOME 1 200KM FROM THE NATION'S CAPITAL and a mere half a kilometre from the Zambian border, you'll find Katima Mulilo, Namibia's most easterly town of any size. Often referred to simply as Katima, this is the capital of the Zambezi region (Caprivi Strip) and it's located on the Zambezi River's banks - the river forms the border with Zambia at this spot. Since the opening of the Katima Mulilo Bridge in 2004, which connects the Zambian Copperbelt with the Namibian deep sea harbour at Walvis Bay, Katima Mulilo has enjoyed much growth.

Traveller Description

Katima Mulilo is home to many cultures and languages. And being an important town on an important trade route (linking the west coast of Africa to the east coast), Katima offers all the facilities and services that an overlander might need.

At the most easterly tip of the Zambezi region you'll find Impalila Island. It's formed by the confluence of the Zambezi and Chobe rivers to the north and south respectively, and the Kasai Channel to the west. Its name means 'the faraway place'. Once a military base for the South African Defence Force, Impalila island now forms part of the Impalila Conservancy and is home to the Lozi tribe. Although part of Namibia, access to the island's lodges is by plane, or boat from Botswana's Kasane Immigration Office. There is no vehicular access to this area.

Travel Info

If you are travelling to Zambia, refuel and buy your provisions in Katima, it's cheaper and the shops are better stocked.

Useful numbers:
Wenela/Sesheke Border Post into Zambia: Open 06:00 - 18:00. Tel: +264(0)66 253 430, +264(0)66 253 153

TRAVEL TIP! If you travel from Katima Mulilo west towards Rundu, there is a vet fence control point just beyond Kongola. You are not allowed to take raw meat from cloven-hoofed animals, cheese and unpasteurised milk beyond this point.

Town Info: Hospital: +264(0)66 251 400 Tow-in: +264(0)81 258 3825 Police: +264(0)66 251 225 Tourism: +264(0)66 252 739 Doctor: +264(0)66 253 321

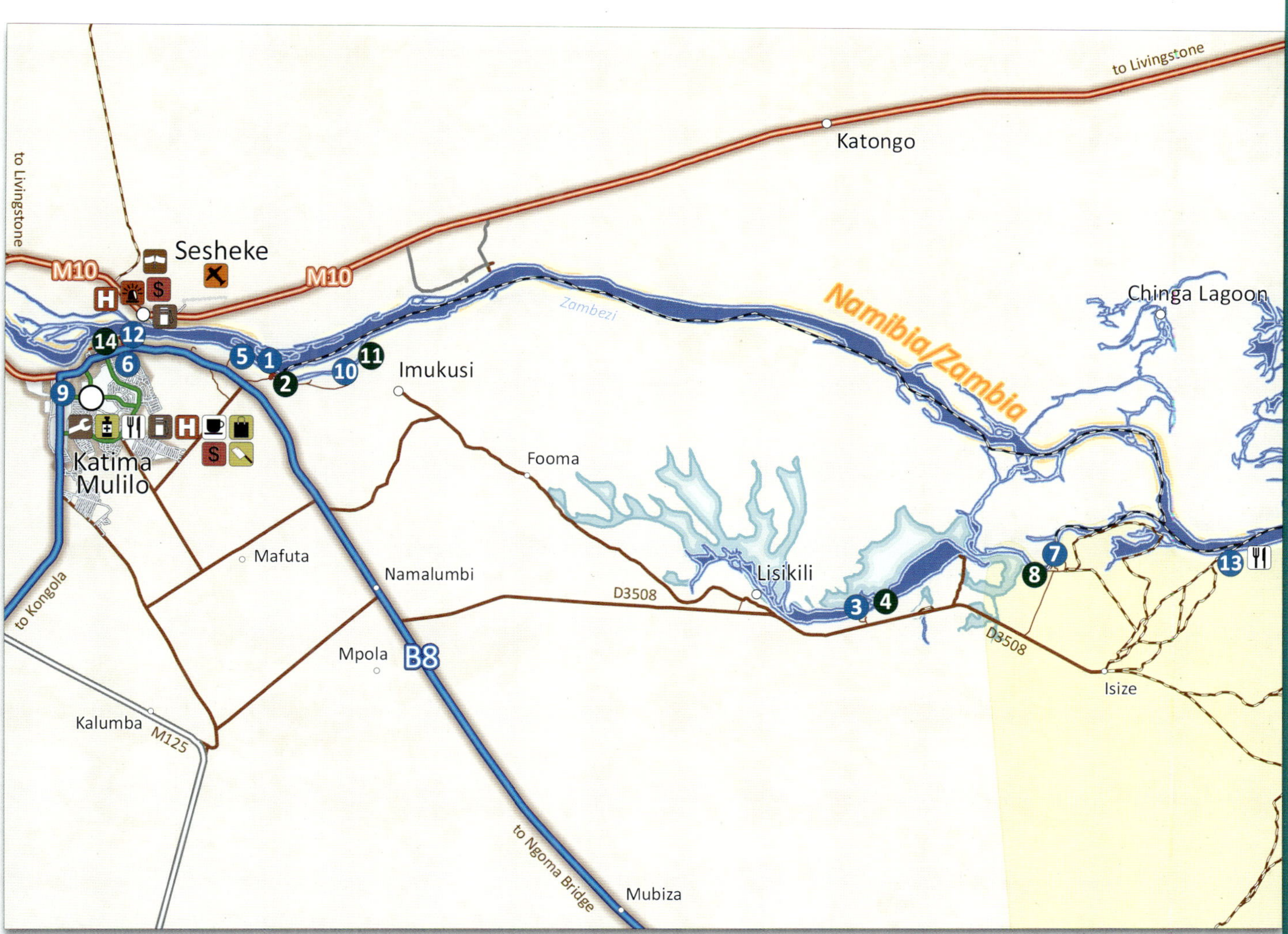

Caprivi Houseboat Safari Lodge	1

Lodge $$
6km or 8min E of Katima Mulilo
w232874

Tel: +264(0)66 252 287, Cell: +264(0)81 129 2811
chs@iway.na
www.zambezisafaris.com

Five rustic, thatched, en-suite chalets with ceiling fans and mosquito nets. Venue located in lush green garden on the banks of the Zambezi River.

Languages: English

Facilities: VISA FC @

Activities:

Caprivi Houseboat Safari Lodge	2

Lodge Camp $
6km or 8min E of Katima Mulilo
w254365

Tel: +264(0)66 252 287, Cell: +264(0)81 129 2811
chs@iway.na
www.zambezisafaris.com

Two large, comfortable campsites, each accommodating up to six people. Communal ablutions.

Languages: English

Facilities: VISA FC @

Activities:

Caprivi Mutoya Lodge	3

Lodge $$
28km or 25min ESE of Katima Mulilo
w357844

Tel: +264(0)66 253 553, Cell: +264(0)81 287 5438
info@caprivimutoyalodge.com
www.caprivimutoyalodge.com

Three safari tents and five spacious, en-suite chalets. Located in a small riverine forest, amongst ancient Jackalberry trees.

Languages: English

Facilities: VISA FC @

Activities:

Caprivi Mutoya Lodge	4

Lodge Camp $$
28km or 25min ESE of Katima Mulilo
w357845

Tel: +264(0)66 253 553, Cell: +264(0)81 287 5438
info@caprivimutoyalodge.com
www.caprivimutoyalodge.com

Landscaped camp with twelve campsites. Includes communal ablutions (hot showers), laundry/kitchen sinks, lights, power points and braai area.

Languages: English

Facilities: VISA FC

Activities:

Caprivi River Lodge	5

Lodge $$
6km or 6min ENE of Katima Mulilo
w139135

Tel: +264(0)66 252 288, Cell: +264(0)81 241 8182,
Fax: +264(0)88 655 1702
hakumata@iway.na

Honeymoon suite, two semi-luxury twin chalets, five standard chalets and comfortable cabins.

Languages: English

Facilities: VISA @

Activities:

Fish Eagle's Nest B&B	6

Bed and Breakfast $
2km or 3min NE of Katima Mulilo
w239884

Tel: +264(0)66 254 287, Cell: +264(0)81 291 7791,
Fax: +264(0)88 625 227
fisheaglesnest@afol.com.na

14 En-suite, air-conditioned rooms equipped with TV, mini bar and coffee/tea facilities. There's a pool and a lapa with braai facilities.

Languages: English

Facilities: VISA FC @

Activities:

Katima Mulilo

Island View Lodge — 7

Lodge — $$
34km or 33min E of Katima Mulilo
w138690

Tel: +264(0)66 252 801, Cell: +264(0)81 306 1445, Fax: +264(0)66 252 573
tiger@islandview-lodge.com, www.islandview-lodge.com

Rustic, fully-equipped, thatched bungalows on self-catering or full board basis.

Languages: English

Facilities: VISA @

Activities:

Island View Lodge — 8

Lodge Camp — $
34km or 33min E of Katima Mulilo
w198323

Tel: +264(0)66 252 801, Cell: +264(0)81 306 1445, Fax: +264(0)66 252 573
tiger@islandview-lodge.com, www.islandview-lodge.com

Five campsites under Mahogany and Acacia trees. Each site with private ablutions. Communal kitchen, braai area and TV lounge.

Languages: English

Facilities: VISA @

Activities:

Mukusi Cabins/Camp — 9

Self-catering — $$
c/o Hage Geingob St and B8, Katima Mulilo
w138242

Tel: +264(0)66 253 255, Cell: +264(0)81 127 4648, Fax: +264(0)66 252 359
mukusi@afol.com.na, www.mukusi.com

Rooms with fan or air-conditioning. Bathrooms for some rooms are communal. Some rooms have TV. Breakfast served at camp.

Languages: English, Afrikaans

Facilities: VISA FC @

Activities:

Namwi Island Lodge — 10

Self-catering — $
9km or 14min E of Katima Mulilo
w193050

Tel: +264(0)66 252 243, Cell: +264(0)81 127 4572, Fax: +264(0)66 252 233
namwiisl@iway.na, www.namwiisland.com

Self-catering cottages and huts of varying sizes. Set in garden with pool.

Languages: English

Facilities:

Activities:

Namwi Island Lodge — 11

Caravan Park — $
9km or 14min E of Katima Mulilo
w193049

Tel: +264(0)66 252 243, Cell: +264(0)81 127 4572, Fax: +264(0)66 252 233
namwiisl@iway.na, www.namwiisland.com

Campsites with own power point, tap and braai. Communal ablutions and wash-up facilities. Located on riverbank, good bird viewing.

Languages: English

Facilities: FC

Activities:

Protea Hotel Zambezi River — 12

Lodge — $$
3km or 4min NNE of Katima Mulilo
w138688

Tel: +264(0)66 251 500, Fax: +264(0)66 253 631
res.zambezi@proteahotels.com.na
www.marriott.com

38 Standard and four luxury, en-suite rooms. With air-conditioning, satellite TV and coffee/tea facilities. River views.

Languages: English

Facilities: VISA FC @

Activities:

Zambezi Mubala Lodge — 13

Lodge — $$
39km or 37min E of Katima Mulilo (of which 5km is 4WD)
w137521

Tel: +264(0)61 427 200, Cell: +264(0)81 129 2424
res6@gondwana-collection.com
store.gondwana-collection.com

Eighteen, spacious double chalets and two family chalets, en-suite and air-conditioned. Contact the lodge prior to arrival during rainy season. Reservations mandatory.

Languages: English, Afrikaans

Facilities: VISA FC @

Activities:

Zambezi River Lodge — 14

Lodge Camp — $
2km or 3min NNE of Katima Mulilo
w206731

Tel: +264(0)66 251 500
gm.zambezi@proteahotels.com.na
www.marriott.com

Small campsites with power points, fire pits and braai facilities. Clean ablution blocks.

Languages: English

Facilities: VISA FC @

Activities:

Salambala Conservancy (photo: Lizette Swart)

Kongola

(photo: Lizette Swart)

KONGOLA IS A SMALL VILLAGE located on the B8 national road between Otavi (750km) and Katima Mulilo (120km). Though the capital of the Kongola Constituency, Kongola offers just basic facilities like a fuel station, wholesaler and curio shop. These days the town has electricity but at the time of writing, safe drinking water still wasn't available here.

Traveller Description

The Mashi Craft Centre is supplied by eleven community craft groups located throughout the Zambezi region (Caprivi). The crafters make a range of products including reed mats, baskets, beaded necklaces, woodcarvings, drums and fish traps. Pottery is a special attraction here, with unique pots sporting interesting patterns and firing techniques on offer.

Travel Info

Take bottled water. You can visit the Namushasha Heritage Centre near Namushasha River Lodge. This is a cultural village and museum where visitors can get an idea of the history, traditions and way of life of the people of the Mashi Conservancy. Entrance fees are N$80 per person (2017) which includes a guided tour with traditional dances. North of Singalamwe you'll find a border crossing into Zambia. This border post is for local vehicles and pedestrians - there are no customs facilities. If you wish to use this crossing, you'll have to visit the nearest conventional border post and complete customs formalities related to bringing foreign vehicles into Zambia.

Useful numbers:

Mashi Craft Centre:
+264(0)81 387 8715

Mashi River Safaris:
Cell: +264(0)81 4619608
mashiriversafaris@gmail.com

TRAVEL TIP! Both, walking safaris in the Mashi Conservancy, and overnight safaris to Njazanga Island, can be arranged via Mashi River safaris, based at Mavunje Camp.

Camp Kwando 1

Lodge $$
28km or 25min SSW of Kongola
w255821

Tel: +264(0)66 686 021, Cell: +264(0)81 206 1514,
Fax: +264(0)66 686 023
reservations@campkwando.com,
www.campkwando.com

13 En-suite, thatched, island tents, each with two beds. Plus larger, en-suite luxury chalets.

Languages: English, Afrikaans

Facilities: VISA FC

Activities:

Camp Kwando 2

Holiday Resort Camp $$
28km or 25min SSW of Kongola
w137653

Tel: +264(0)66 686 021, Cell: +264(0)81 206 1514,
Fax: +264(0)66 686 023
reservations@campkwando.com,
www.campkwando.com

10 Grassed, shaded campsites and four private campsites with power points. Ablutions (hot showers, toilets & basins) and laundry.

Languages: English, Afrikaans

Facilities: VISA FC

Activities:

Living Museum Mafwe 3

Community Camp $
18km or 14min N of Kongola (of which 1km is 4WD)
w360035

Cell: +264(0)81 762 9020
contact@lcfn.info
www.lcfn.info

No facilities other than a dry toilet and no electricity. No bookings accepted. Located at the 'The Living Museum of the Mafwe'.

Languages: English

Facilities:

Malyo Wilderness Camp 4

Tented Camp $
29km or 29min SSW of Kongola
w270489

Cell: +264(0)81 124 1436
deon@karambareservations.com
www.caprivi.biz

Self-catering, permanent tents with hot showers and flushing toilets. Located along the banks of the Kwando River.

Languages: English

Facilities: FC @

Activities:

Malyo Wilderness Camp 5

Camping $
29km or 29min SSW of Kongola
w270490

Cell: +264(0)81 124 1436
deon@karambareservations.com
www.caprivi.biz

Shady campsite on lush lawns. Caravans welcome. Open-air ablutions (hot showers) with some lighting. No refrigeration facilities. Generator use discouraged.

Languages: English

Facilities: FC @

Activities:

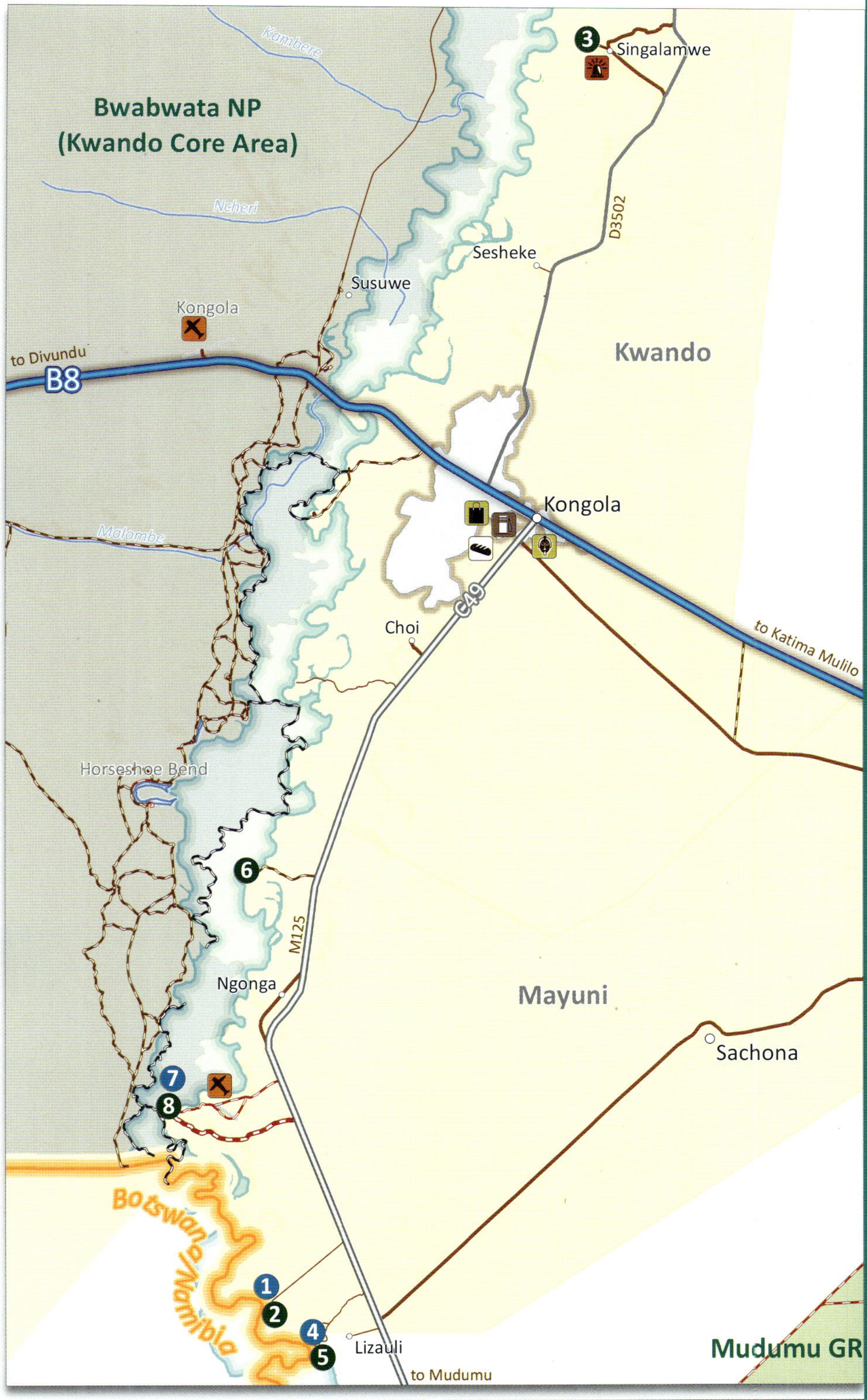

Mavunje 6

Camping $$
15km or 16min SW of Kongola (of which 3km is 4WD)
w274103

Cell: +264(0)81 461 9608
mashiriversafaris@gmail.com
www.mashiriversafaris.com

Private, well-appointed campsites with ablutions (shower & toilet). No electricity or cellphone reception.

Languages: English

Facilities: FC

Activities:

Namushasha River Lodge 7

Lodge $$$
23km or 24min SSW of Kongola (of which 4km is 4WD)
w137716

Tel: +264(0)61 230 066, Fax: +264(0)61 251 863
info@gondwana-collection.com
store.gondwana-collection.com

24 En-suite bungalows. 20 Twin, three triple, one double and one family room. Venue offers small pool, bar, deck, curio shop and buffet restaurant. Reservations mandatory.

Languages: English, German, Afrikaans

Facilities: VISA @

Activities:

Namushasha River Lodge 8

Lodge Camp $$
23km or 24min SSW of Kongola (of which 4km is 4WD)
w239945

Tel: +264(0)61 230 066, Fax: +264(0)61 251 863
info@gondwana-collection.com
store.gondwana-collection.com

16 Grassed campsites under shady trees overlooking the Kwando River. They have private ablution blocks and braai areas. Reservations advised.

Languages: English, German, Afrikaans

Facilities: VISA @

Activities:

Mudumu National Park

(photo: Johann Groenewald)

THIS HAS TO BE ONE OF NAMIBIA'S least-visited parks which is probably just how its fans would like it to stay! On the park's western boundary you'll find the Kwando River and a latticework of lagoons, narrow channels and riverine forest. Botswana lies on the opposite bank, and this reserve forms part of an ancient migration route for large game, connecting Botswana with Angola to the north.

The eastern side of Mudumu, where the bulk of the park is situated, is characterised by dense savannah and Mopane woodlands. Flooding is common during the rainy season. This park boasts a wide variety of wildlife: red lechwe, buffalo, antelope, kudu, impala, zebra and more, not to mention some 430 bird species.

Traveller Description

The tarred C49 runs through the park, linking Kongola and Sangwali villages; no permit is required to travel on this road. But if you want to explore the park's sandy tracks you'll require an off-road vehicle (especially in the rainy season) plus an entry permit (get this from the office just west of the C49, approximately 3km north of the Lianshulu airstrip).

Travel Info

You can camp at Nakatwa Camp on the riverbanks but this is a very basic unfenced camp so you need to be totally self-sufficient. Accommodation is limited here (just three sites, all spaced a few kilometres from each other), most visitors fly in to the luxurious Lianshulu Lodge, situated on the Kwando River. The camp is located in a high-risk malaria area, precautions must be taken.

Lianshulu Lodge 1

Lodge $$$
41km or 42min S of Kongola (of which 4km is 4WD)
w138447

Tel: +264(0)64 403 523, Cell: +264(0)81 622 0498,
reservations@caprivicollection.com
www.caprivicollection.com

10 Luxury, thatched, en-suite chalets with private decks. 4WD recommended during rainy season. Reservations advised.

Languages: English, German, Afrikaans

Facilities: VISA FC @

Activities:

Nakatwa Campsites 2

Community Camp $
46km or 42min S of Kongola (of which 5km is 4WD)
w139063

Cell: +264(0)81 390 0040
mondesimasiku@yahoo.com

Three campsites with no facilities. Water and permit can be obtained at entrance gate. No bookings accepted. Located in Mudumu National Park.

Languages: English

Facilities:

Activities:

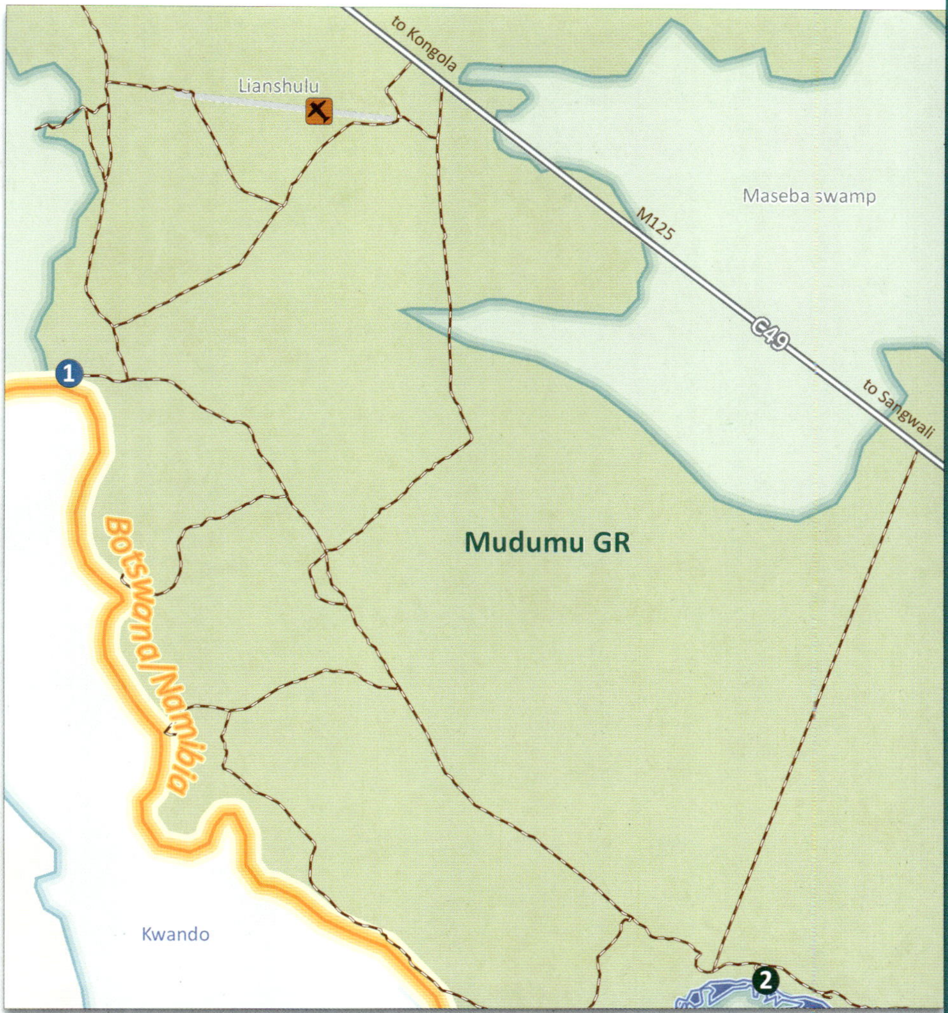

(photo: Johann Groenewald)

Nkasa Rupala National Park

(photo: Karin Theron)

FORMERLY KNOWN AS MAMILI NATIONAL PARK, the park was given its current title in 2013. It's the largest wetland conservation area in Namibia and the name originates from Nkasa and Lupala islands in the Kwando / Linyanti river systems. This park is characterised by large water channels, lagoons, reed islands and pristine wetlands. You'll find elephant, lion, buffalo, giraffe, hippo and over 430 bird species here.

The best time to visit is between April and September. It's transformed by the rainy season (during the hot months of November to March) when most of the area floods and becomes inaccessible. Some call it 'Namibia's own Okavango'.

Traveller Description

Many of the campsites within the park are inaccessible during the rainy season. For this reason the best accommodation options are the ones up north: the Rupara Rest Camp, Nkasa Lupala Tented Lodge and Livingstone's Camp.

Travel Info

The nearest state clinic is in Sangwali Village in the Wuparo Conservancy just north of the park. Here you'll also find the She She Craft Centre.

Livingstone's Camp has large shaded campsites with beautiful ablutions; together with the community, this venue has launched Livingstone's Museum which follows David Livingstone's trail through the region.

TRAVEL TIP! Be extremely cautious of roads that are undriveable during the rainy season. A new bridge was constructed at Sangwali, allowing for easier access when the waters rise.

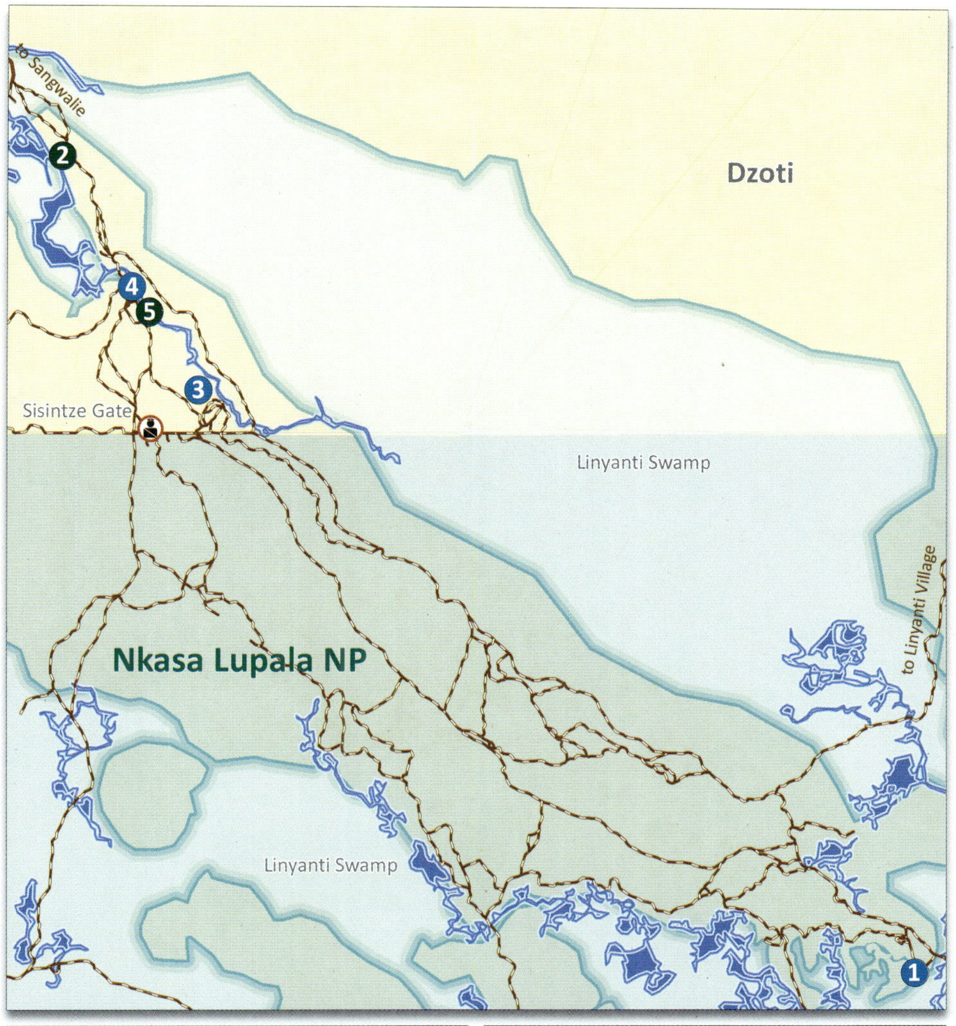

Jackalberry Tented Camp 1

Tented Camp $$$
23km or 1h11min SE of Sangwali (of which 22km is 4WD)
w310849

Tel: +264(0)61 250 725, Fax: +264(0)88 637 655
info@jbcamp.com
www.jbcamp.com

Four double rooms and one double guide room. Plus, restaurant, bar, and lounge area. Reservations advised.

Languages: English

Facilities: VISA

Activities:

Livingstone's Camp 2

Camping $$
5km or 14min SSE of Sangwali (off-road vehicle required)
w139410

Tel: +264(0)66 686 208, Cell: +264(0)81 033 2853
info@livingstonescamp.com
www.livingstonescamp.com

Five exclusive campsites, each with their own private bathrooms (hot showers) and other camping facilities. Reservations advisable.

Languages: English

Facilities:

Activities:

Nkasa Lupala Tented Lodge 3

Tented Camp $$$
82km or 1h33min SSE of Kongola (of which 9km is 4WD)
w189023

Tel: +264(0)61 250 725, Cell: +264(0)81 147 7798, Fax: +264(0)88 643 179
info@nkasalupalalodge.com,
www.nkasalupalalodge.com

10 Luxury, permanent, en-suite tents. Electricity and hot water via solar system. No campsite. Reservations advisable.

Languages: English, Italian

Facilities: VISA FC @

Activities:

Rupara Restcamp 4

Self-catering $$
80km or 1h24min SSE of Kongola (of which 7km is 4WD)
w360969

Cell: +264(0)81 147 7798
info@rupara.com
www.rupara.com

Four self-catering units (one family size), each with tap and fireplace. Hot showers and 12V solar lights available. Reservations advisable.

Languages: English

Facilities: FC

Activities:

Rupara Restcamp 5

Community Camp $$
80km or 1h23min SSE of Kongola (of which 7km is 4WD)
w252844

Cell: +264(0)81 147 7798
info@rupara.com
www.rupara.com

Seven campsites sharing two ablution blocks (hot water via 'donkey' system, and 12V lights). Fireplace and borehole water available. Reservations advisable

Languages: English

Facilities: FC

Activities:

Wuparu Conservancy, near Rupara Restcamp. (photo: Mietsie Visser)

Travel with Track4Africa on your Smartphone

Tracks4Africa content is available in two great apps, both packed with the information and detail that you've come to expect from us. We cover the whole of Africa, and with these apps you can enjoy our maps and content without the need for an internet or data connection.

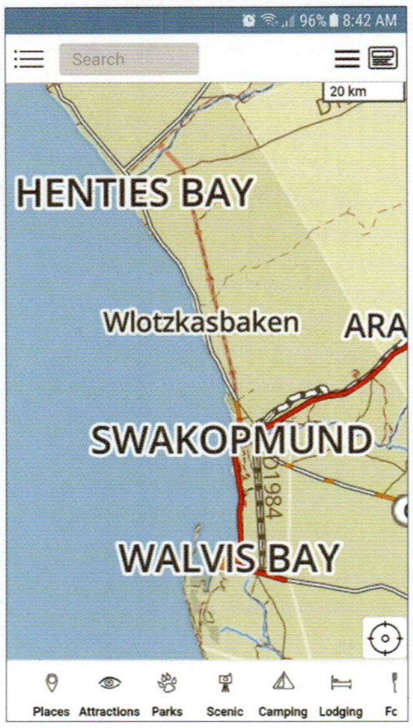

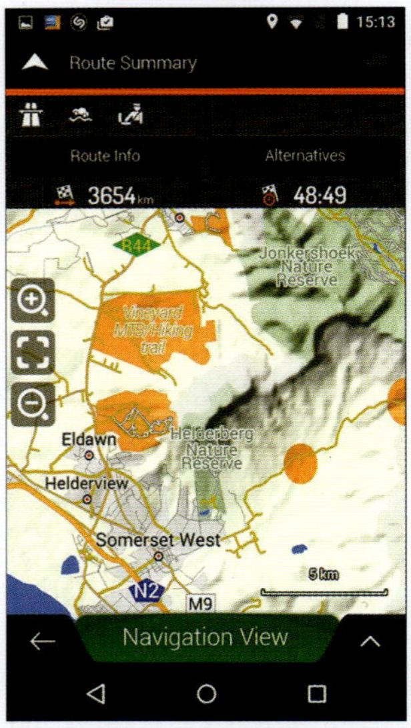

Tracks4Africa Navigator

Don't have a GPS? The Tracks4Africa Navigator app turns your compatible smartphone into a proper overland navigation device. This app is designed to work like a GPS. During installation, maps covering all of Africa are downloaded to your device; this means that once you're on the road you can use this app without an internet or data connection.

Tracks4Africa Guide app

This easy-to-use app will help you discover the places around you. Think of it as an electronic version of a paper map, one which allows you to activate and deactivate different categories of information. The app knows where you are and will show your location on the map. It's packed with rich content on places, very similar to this guide book, but all in your pocket.

	Tracks4Africa Navigator	Tracks4Africa Guide app
Works offline*	✓	✓
Route calculation	✓	✗
Navigation instructions	✓	✗
Shows your location on the map	✓	✓
In-app purchases required	✗	✓
Paper map look & feel	✗	✓
Discovery app	✗	✓
Free updates	✓	✓
Additional information on lodging & camping	✓	✓

**once you've downloaded the app and/or the additional in-app purchase, the maps and content will reside on your device. From here onwards you can use the apps without the need for an internet connection, this makes it ideal for the remoter parts of Africa where you can't access an internet or data connection. No roaming costs!*

GET IT ON Google play

Download on the App Store

TRACKS4AFRICA

Travel Africa Informed

An ATLAS just for the self-drive traveller!

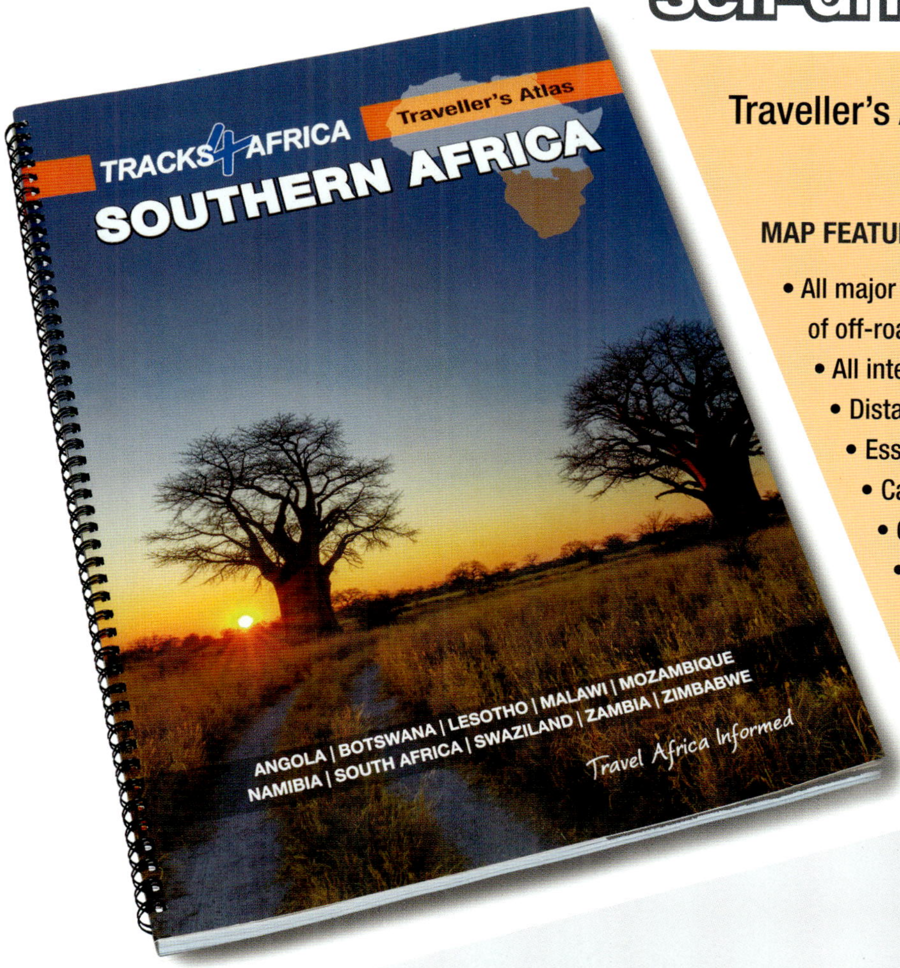

Traveller's Atlas - Southern Africa

MAP FEATURES INCLUDE:

- All major roads as well as more than 100 000km of off-road tracks
- All international airports, with IATA/ICAO codes
- Distance and travel time between towns
- Essential facilities in towns
- Camping and lodging
- 614 Tourist attractions
- 462 Protected areas
- All border crossings, with opening times

AT TRACKS4AFRICA WE KNOW THAT SELF-DRIVE TRAVELLERS have unique requirements. While exploring a foreign country, they need to know what there is to see, where to sleep, get fuel, buy food, and find emergency help. And, of course, they also require up-to-date and accurate maps.

This A3-sized Atlas was conceived and designed to meet all those needs, in one convenient package. It features 108 map pages covering Angola, Botswana, Lesotho, Malawi, Mozambique, Namibia, South Africa, Swaziland, Zambia and Zimbabwe.

South Africa, Lesotho and part of Swaziland are shown on a 1:500 000 scale. Swaziland, Mozambique, Malawi, Zimbabwe, Zambia, Botswana and Namibia are on a 1:1 000 000 scale while most of Angola is on a 1:4 000 000 scale.

You can get a good sense of what the Atlas offers by looking at the maps on the following pages. Bear in mind though, the Atlas is A3 size (twice this page size) and has maps that cover all the countries listed two paragraphs above.

As well as the map pages, you'll also find valuable travel information on each of the ten countries. Things like border crossings requirements, top tourist attractions and driving conditions. This will help you both plan your trip and assist you while you're travelling.

The wiro-bound Atlas weighs 1.3kg (protective canvas bag included), has a laminated cover and the pages are printed on silk matt art paper. Note: the free protective canvas bag is limited to Atlas purchases made from our online store (www.tracks4africa.co.za).
For further information, contact us at sales@tracks4africa.co.za or 021 880 8660.

TRACKS4AFRICA

Travel Africa Informed

Safari Rental
Proudly rented by AVIS

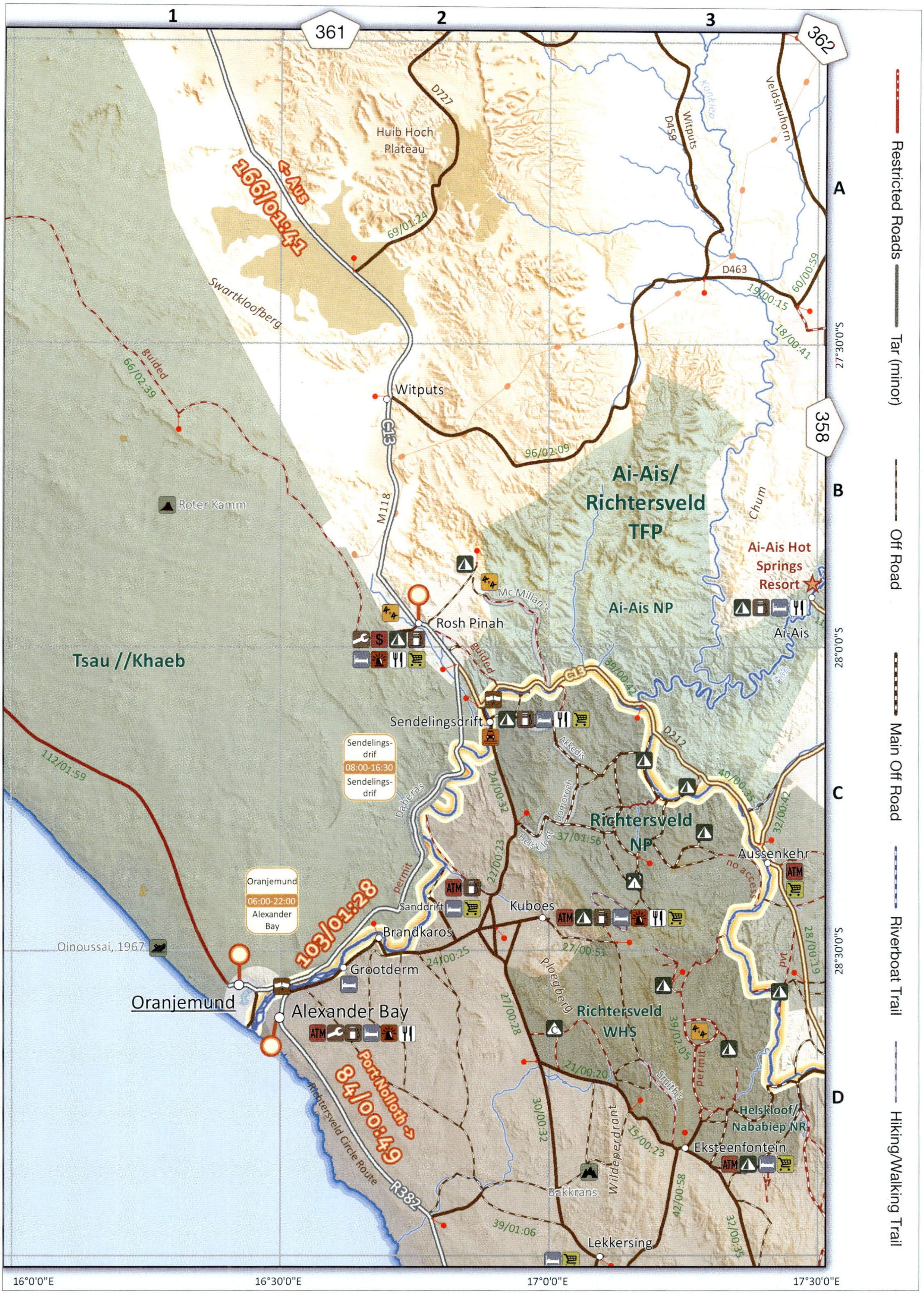
1
2
3
361
362
358
A
B
C
D
Huib Hoch Plateau
D727
D459
Witputs
Konkiep
Veldshuhorn
<- Aus
166/01:47
69/01:24
Swartkloofberg
D463
19/00:15
60/00:59
18/00:41
Guided
66/02:39
Witputs
C13
M118
96/02:09
Ai-Ais/ Richtersveld TFP
Chum
Roter Kamm
Ai-Ais Hot Springs Resort
Ai-Ais NP
Ai-Ais
Mc Millan's
Rosh Pinah
Tsau //Khaeb
Guided
C13
39/00:42
Sendelingsdrift
Sendelings-drif
08:00-16:30
Sendelings-drif
D212
Akkedis
Daberas
24/00:32
Domorogh
Helsk loof
37/01:56
Richtersveld NP
40/00:35
32/00:42
Aussenkehr
no access
112/01:59
permit
22/00:23
Oranjemund
06:00-22:00
Alexander Bay
103/01:28
Sanddrift
Kuboes
Brandkaros
27/00:51
28/00:19
pvt
Oinoussai, 1967
Grootderm
24/00:25
Ploegberg
Oranjemund
Alexander Bay
27/00:28
Richtersveld WHS
39/02:05
permit
Port Nolloth ->
84/00:49
21/00:20
Smith's
Helskloof/ Nababiep NR
Richtersveld Circle Route
30/00:32
Wildeperdrant
15/00:23
Eksteenfontein
42/00:58
R382
Bakkrans
39/01:06
32/00:35
Lekkersing
27°30'0"S
28°0'0"S
28°30'0"S
16°0'0"E
16°30'0"E
17°0'0"E
17°30'0"E
Restricted Roads
Tar (minor)
Off Road
Main Off Road
Riverboat Trail
Hiking/Walking Trail

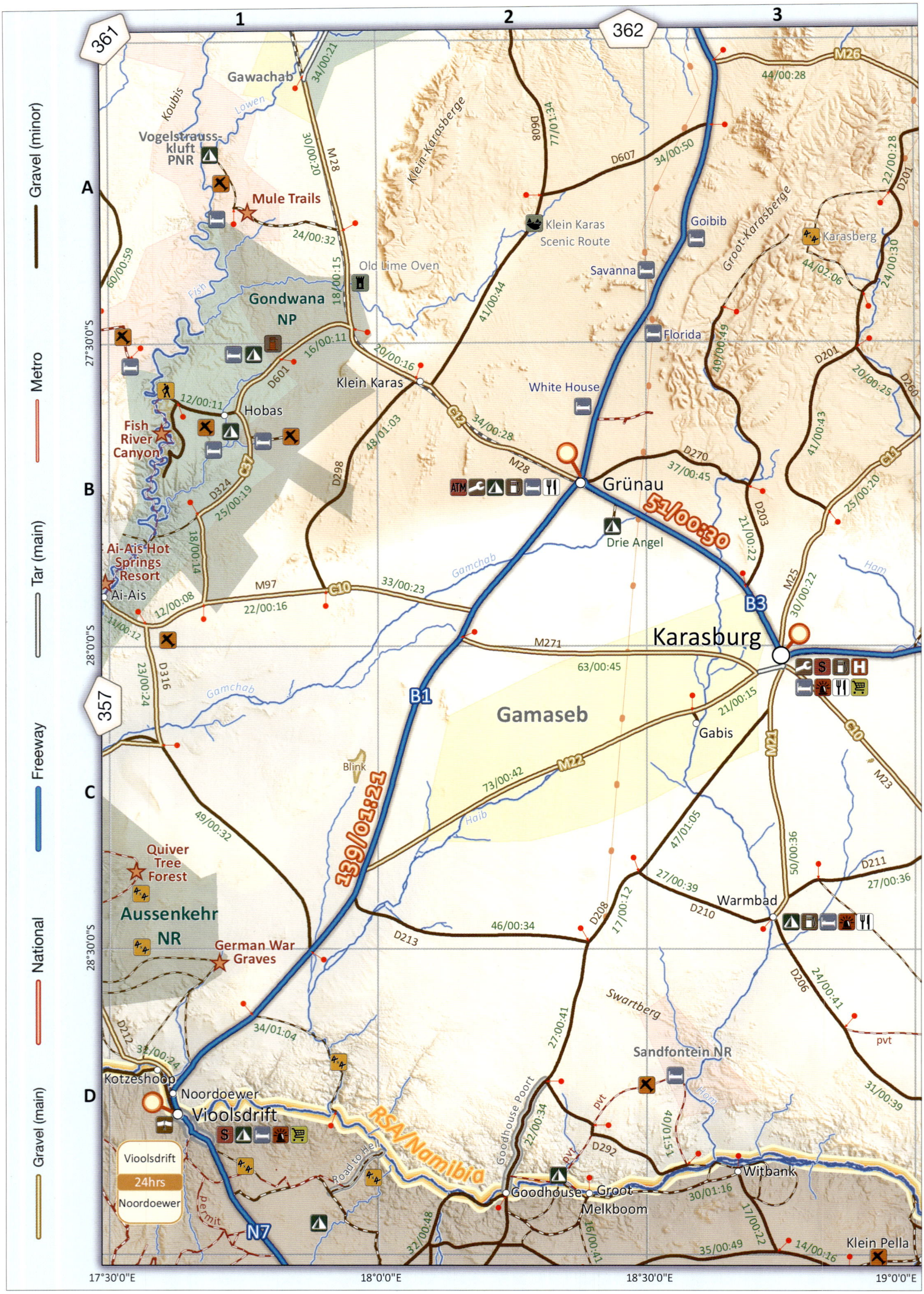

Gravel (minor)
Metro
Tar (main)
Freeway
National
Gravel (main)
1
2
3
A
B
C
D
361
362
357
Gawachab
Koubis
Lowen
Vogelstrauss-
kluft
PNR
Mule Trails
24/00:32
Fish
Gondwana
NP
Old Lime Oven
60/00:59
27°30'0"S
12/00:11
Hobas
Fish
River
Canyon
D601
16/00:11
Klein Karas
20/00:16
48/01:03
D298
D324
25/00:19
C37
18/00:14
Ai-Ais Hot
Springs
Resort
Ai-Ais
12/00:08
M97
22/00:16
C10
33/00:23
11/00:12
28°0'0"S
23/00:24
D316
Gamchab
34/00:21
30/00:20
M28
18/00:15
Klein-Karasberge
D608
77/01:34
D607
34/00:50
Klein Karas
Scenic Route
41/00:44
Goibib
Savanna
Florida
White House
C12
34/00:28
M28
ATM
Grünau
Drie Angel
51/00:30
B3
M26
44/00:28
Groot-Karasberge
Karasberg
44/02:06
22/00:28
D201
24/00:30
40/00:49
D201
20/00:25
D260
41/00:43
C11
25/00:20
D270
37/00:45
D203
21/00:22
M25
30/00:22
Ham
Karasburg
M271
63/00:45
B1
Gamaseb
Gabis
21/00:15
C10
M23
M21
Blink
139/01:21
M22
73/00:42
Haib
47/01:05
50/00:36
49/00:32
Quiver
Tree
Forest
Aussenkehr
NR
German War
Graves
28°30'0"S
D213
46/00:34
D208
17/00:12
27/00:39
D210
Warmbad
D211
27/00:36
D206
24/00:41
Swartberg
34/01:04
D212
31/00:24
Kotzeshoop
Noordoewer
Vioolsdrift
Vioolsdrift
24hrs
Noordoewer
27:00:41
Sandfontein NR
Ham
pvt
31/00:39
RSA/Namibia
Road to Hell
Goodhouse Poort
22/00:34
pvt
pvt
D292
40/01:51
Witbank
30/01:16
Goodhouse
Groot
Melkboom
17/00:22
16/00:41
32/00:48
35/00:49
14/00:16
Klein Pella
permit
N7
17°30'0"E
18°0'0"E
18°30'0"E
19°0'0"E

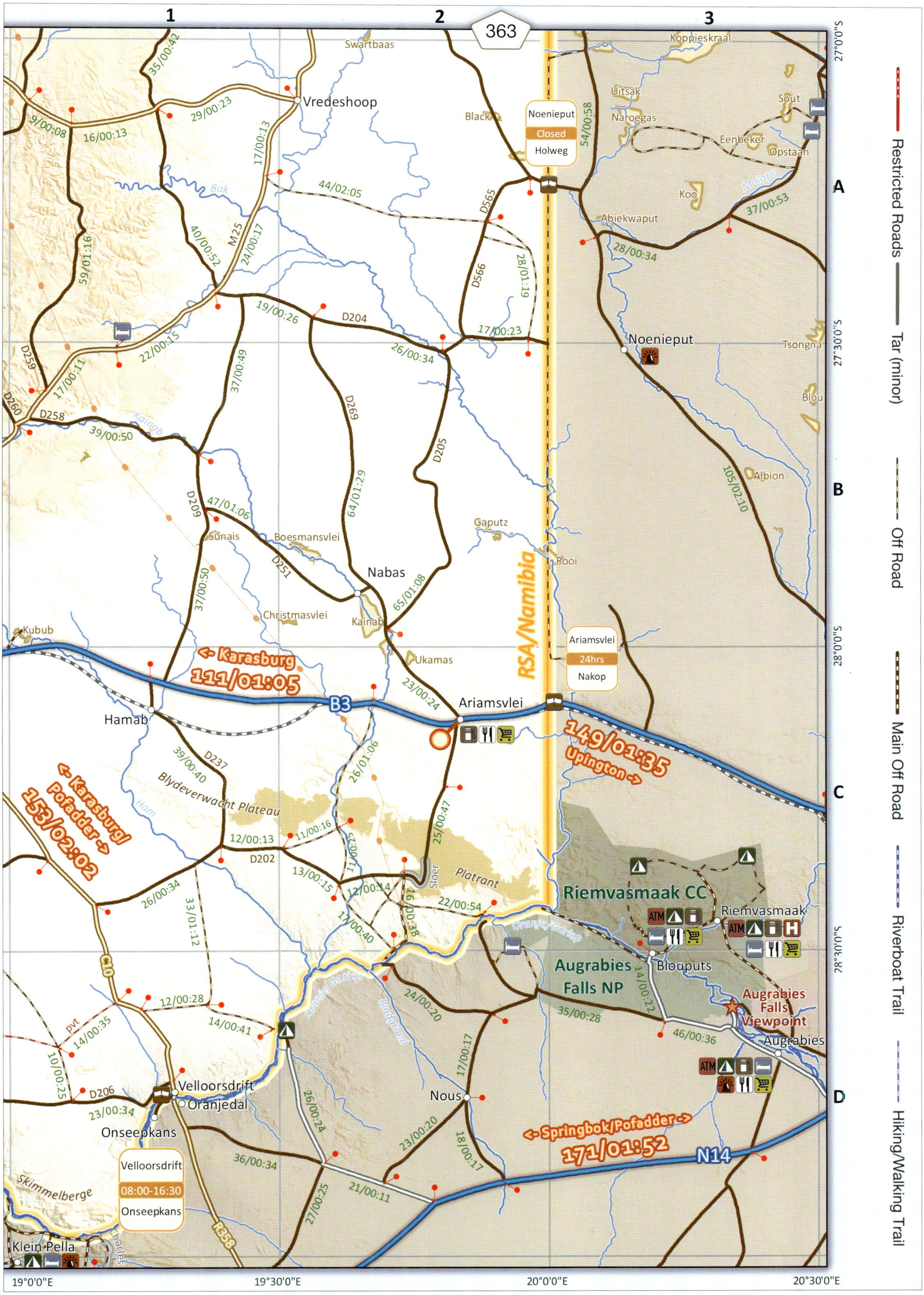
1
2
3
363
A
B
C
D
Swartbaas
Vredeshoop
Black
Noenieput
Closed
Holweg
Koppieskraal
Uitsak
Naroegas
Sout
Eenbeker
Opstaan
Molopo
Koo
Abiekwaput
37/00:53
28/00:34
54/00:58
35/00:42
29/00:23
9/00:08
16/00:13
17/00:13
Bak
44/02:05
D565
D566
28/01:19
40/00:52
M25
24/00:17
59/01:16
19/00:26
D204
17/00:23
26/00:34
22/00:15
D259
17/00:11
D260
D258
Kainab
39/00:50
37/00:49
D269
D205
Noenieput
Tsongna
Blou
105/02:10
Albion
D209
47/01:06
Sunais
Boesmansvlei
D251
64/01:29
Gaputz
Rooi
Nabas
65/01:08
37/00:50
Christmasvlei
Kainab
Kubub
RSA/Namibia
Ariamsvlei
24hrs
Nakop
<- Karasburg
111/01:05
Ukamas
23/00:24
B3
Ariamsvlei
Hamab
149/01:35
Upington ->
39/00:40
D237
26/01:06
<- Karasburg/ Pofadder ->
153/02:02
Blydeverwacht Plateau
Ham
25/00:47
12/00:13
11/00:16
D202
11/00:25
Sloer
Platrant
13/00:15
12/00:14
16/00:38
22/00:54
26/00:34
33/01:12
17/00:40
Riemvasmaak CC
Riemvasmaak
ATM
H
Oranje/Gariep
Augrabies Falls NP
Blouputs
14/00:22
Augrabies Falls Viewpoint
35/00:28
24/00:20
Bladgrond
46/00:36
Augrabies
C10
12/00:28
pvt
14/00:35
14/00:41
17/00:17
10/00:25
D206
Velloorsdrift
Oranjedal
23/00:34
Onseepkans
Nous
26/00:24
23/00:20
18/00:17
<- Springbok/Pofadder ->
171/01:52
N14
Velloorsdrift
08:00-16:30
Onseepkans
36/00:34
21/00:11
27/00:25
Skimmelberge
Klein Pella
Charles
R358
27°0'0"S
27°30'0"S
28°0'0"S
28°30'0"S
19°0'0"E
19°30'0"E
20°0'0"E
20°30'0"E
Restricted Roads
Tar (minor)
Off Road
Main Off Road
Riverboat Trail
Hiking/Walking Trail

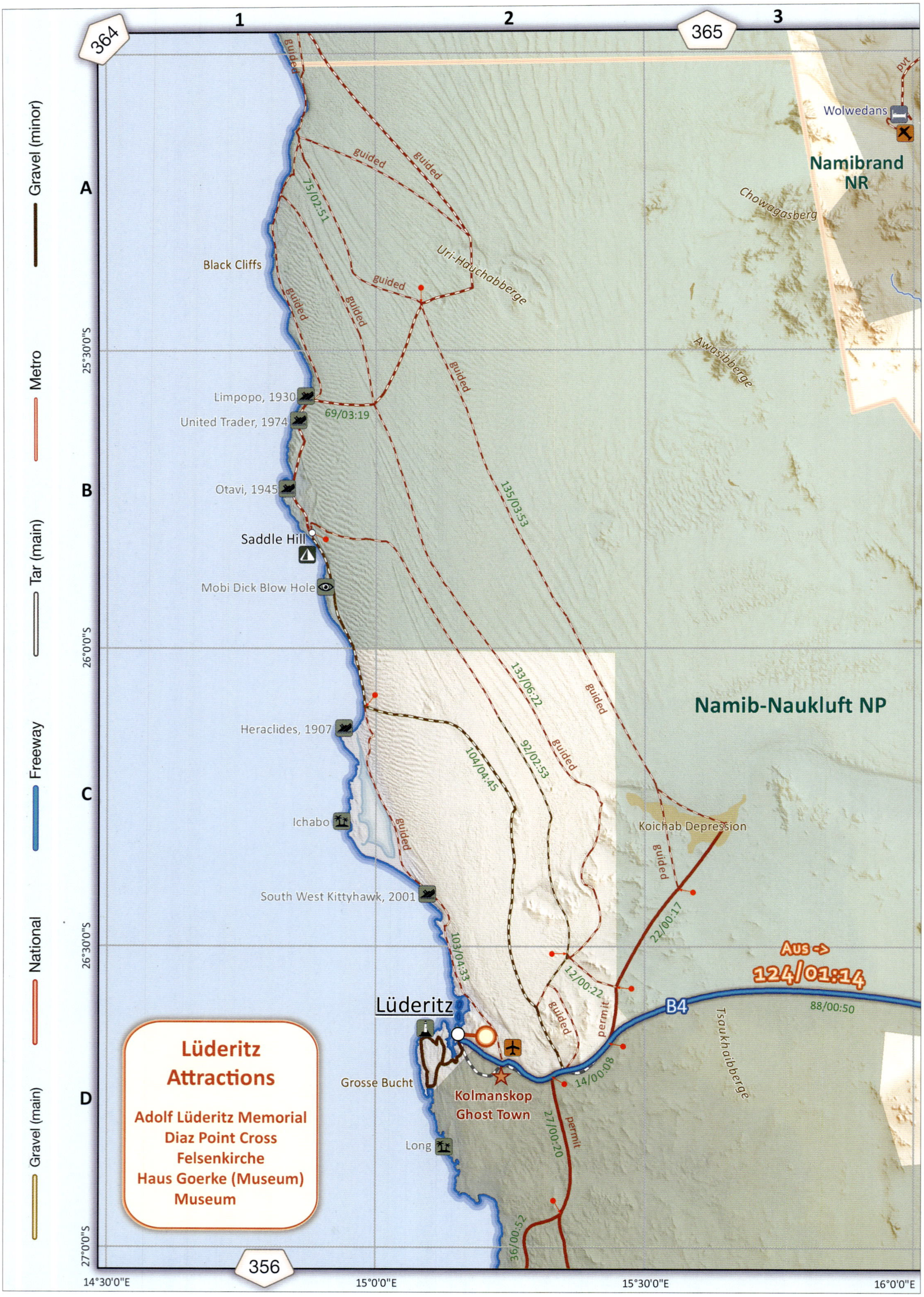

364
365
356
1
2
3
A
B
C
D
Gravel (minor)
Metro
Tar (main)
Freeway
National
Gravel (main)
25°30'0"S
26°0'0"S
26°30'0"S
27°0'0"S
14°30'0"E
15°0'0"E
15°30'0"E
16°0'0"E
Wolwedans
Namibrand NR
Chowagasberg
Uri-Hauchabberge
Awasibberge
Black Cliffs
Limpopo, 1930
United Trader, 1974
69/03:19
75/02:51
Otavi, 1945
Saddle Hill
Mobi Dick Blow Hole
135/03:53
133/06:22
92/02:53
104/04:45
Heraclides, 1907
Namib-Naukluft NP
Ichabo
Koichab Depression
South West Kittyhawk, 2001
103/04:33
22/00:17
Aus ->
124/01:14
12/00:22
B4
88/00:50
Tsaukhaibberge
Lüderitz
14/00:08
Grosse Bucht
Kolmanskop Ghost Town
27/00:20
Long
36/00:52
guided
permit
pvt
Lüderitz Attractions
Adolf Lüderitz Memorial
Diaz Point Cross
Felsenkirche
Haus Goerke (Museum)
Museum

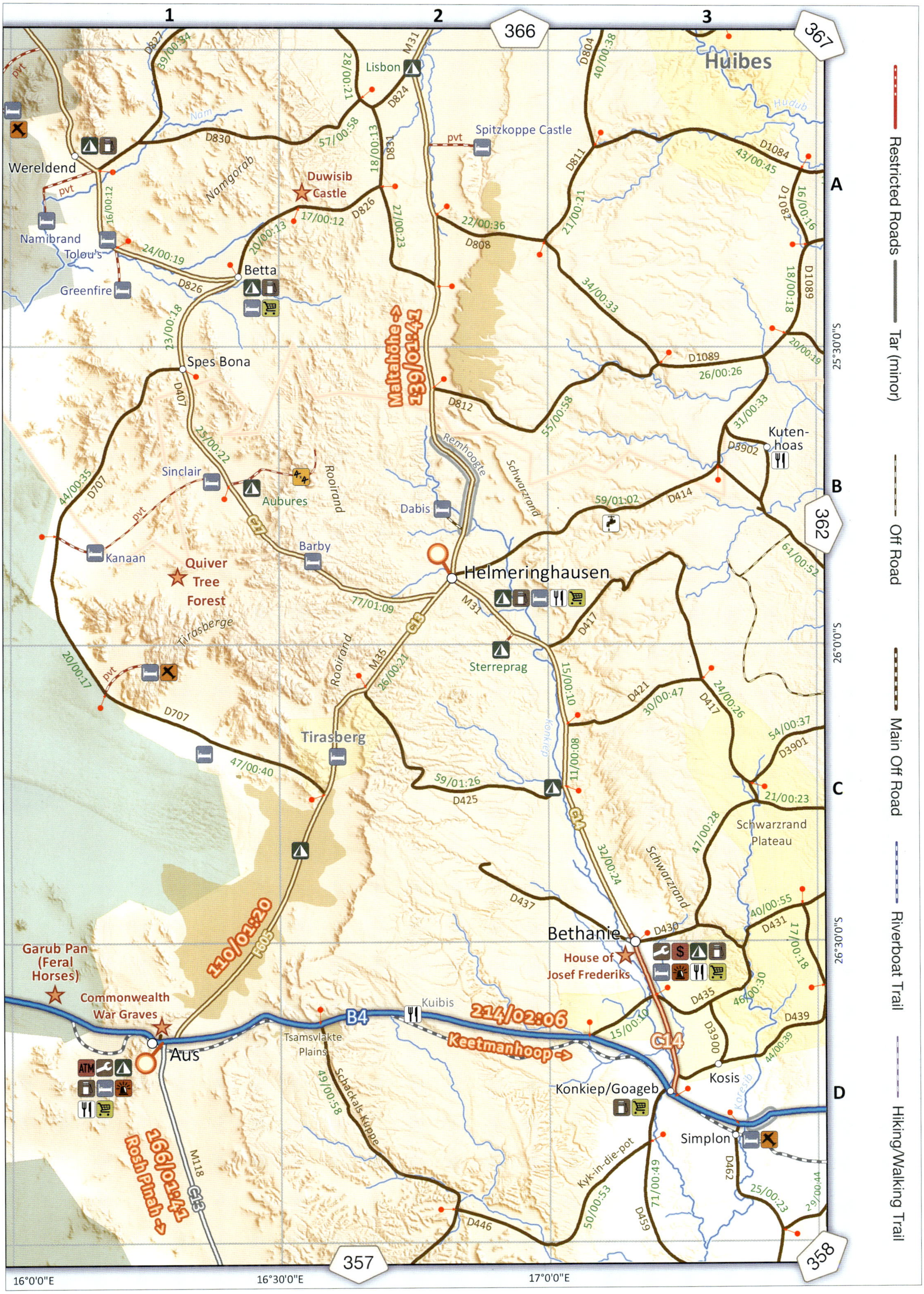

1
2
3
366
367
362
357
358
A
B
C
D
Huibes
Lisbon
Spitzkoppe Castle
Wereldend
Namibrand
Tolou's
Greenfire
Duwisib Castle
Betta
Spes Bona
Sinclair
Aubures
Kanaan
Barby
Quiver Tree Forest
Tirasberge
Rooirand
Namgorab
Maltahöhe -> 139/01:41
Remhoogte
Dabis
Schwarzrand
Helmeringhausen
Sterreprag
Kuten-hoas
Tirasberg
Schwarzrand Plateau
Bethanie
House of Josef Frederiks
Garub Pan (Feral Horses)
Commonwealth War Graves
Aus
Kuibis
Tsamsvlakte Plains
Schackals Kuppe
Keetmanhoop -> 214/02:06
110/01:20
Rosh Pinah -> 166/01:41
Konkiep/Goageb
Kosis
Simplon
Kyk-in-die-pot
Konkiep
Koresib
Nam
Huduub
B4
C13
C14
C12
C27
M31
M35
M118
F605
D707
D407
D826
D830
D824
D831
D808
D811
D804
D827
D1084
D1082
D1089
D812
D414
D3902
D417
D421
D425
D437
D430
D431
D435
D439
D3900
D3901
D446
D459
D462
pvt
16°0'0"E
16°30'0"E
17°0'0"E
25°30'0"S
26°0'0"S
26°30'0"S
Restricted Roads
Tar (minor)
Off Road
Main Off Road
Riverboat Trail
Hiking/Walking Trail

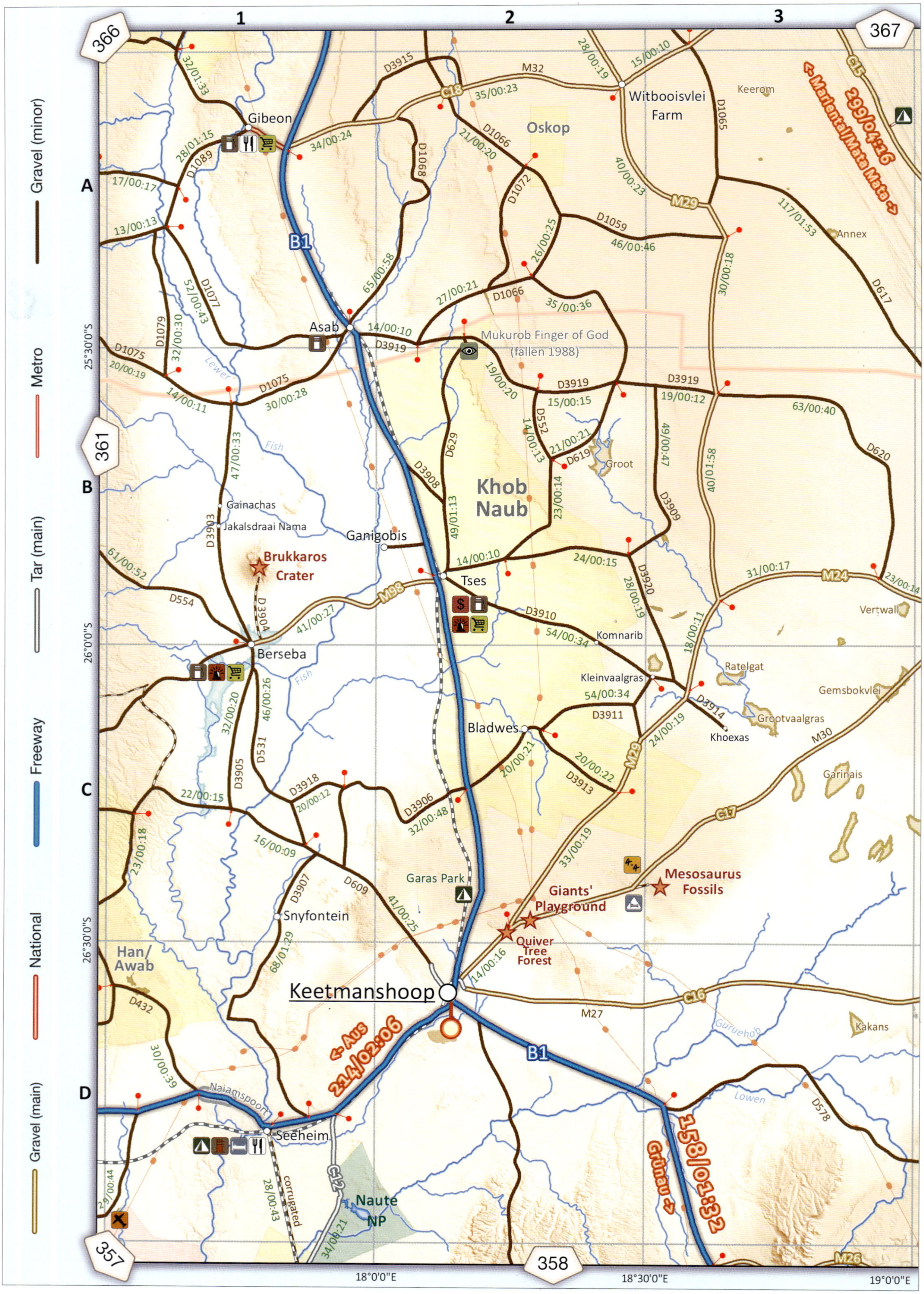

366
367
361
357
358
1
2
3
A
B
C
D
Gravel (minor)
Metro
Tar (main)
Freeway
National
Gravel (main)
Gibeon
Asab
Witbooisvlei Farm
Keerom
Oskop
Annex
Mukurob Finger of God (fallen 1988)
Khob Naub
Groot
Gainachas
Jakalsdraai Nama
Ganigobis
Brukkaros Crater
Tses
Komnarib
Berseba
Kleinvaalgras
Ratelgat
Gemsbokvlei
Grootvaalgras
Khoexas
Vertwall
Bladwes
Garinais
Garas Park
Snyfontein
Giants' Playground
Quiver Tree Forest
Mesosaurus Fossils
Han/ Awab
Keetmanshoop
Kakans
Naiamspoort
Seeheim
corrugated
Naute NP
Lewer
Fish
Guruehab
Lowen
B1
C18
M32
M29
M98
M24
M30
C17
C16
M27
C12
M26
C15
D3915
D1068
D1089
D1066
D1072
D1059
D1065
D617
D1077
D1079
D1075
D3919
D629
D552
D619
D3908
D3909
D3920
D620
D3903
D3904
D554
D3910
D3911
D3914
D3913
D3905
D531
D3918
D3906
D3907
D609
D432
D578
<- Mariental/Mata Mata -> 299/04:16
<- Aus 214/02:06
Grünau -> 158/01:32
25°30'0"S
26°0'0"S
26°30'0"S
18°0'0"E
18°30'0"E
19°0'0"E

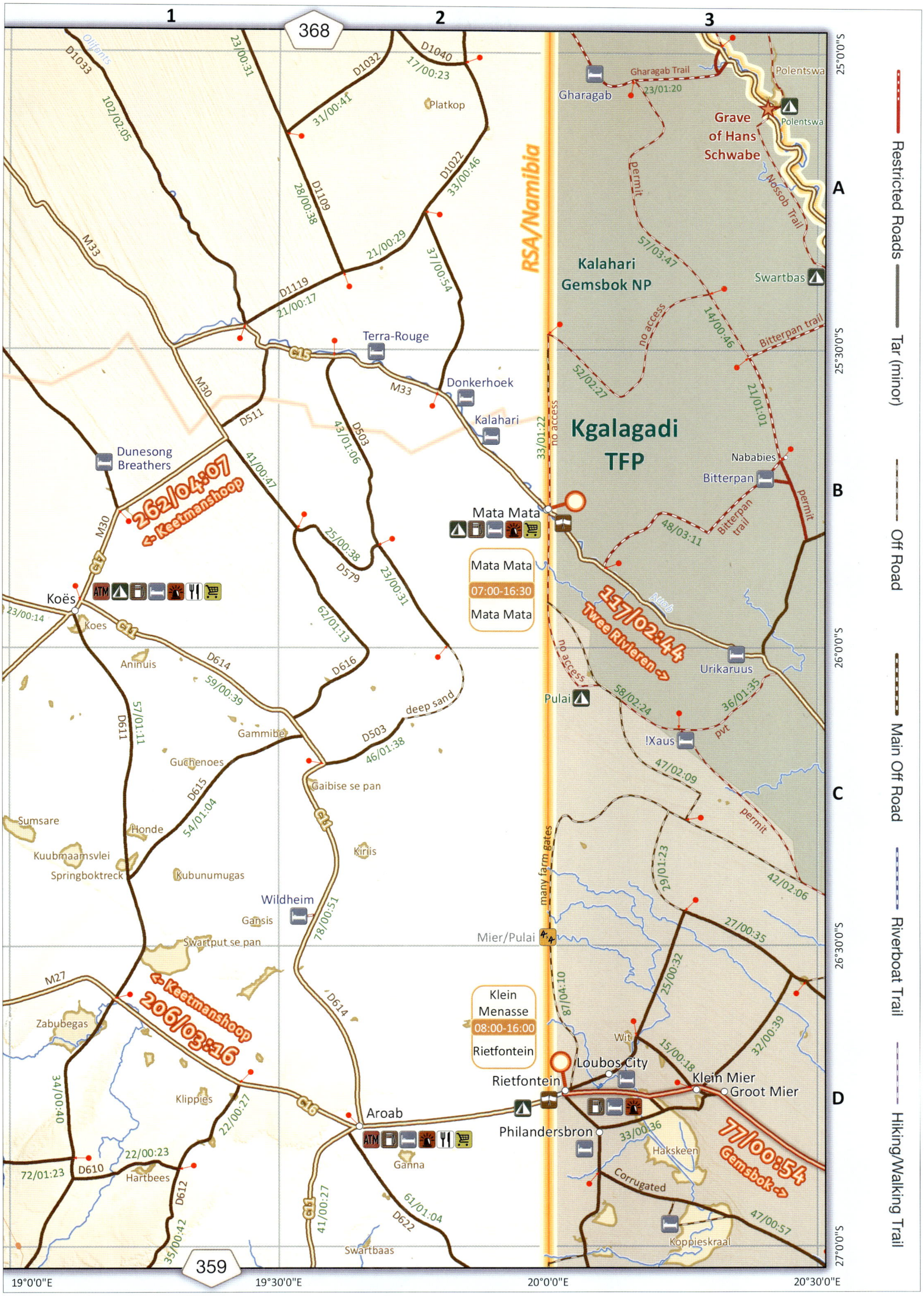

368
359
1
2
3
A
B
C
D
25°0'0"S
25°30'0"S
26°0'0"S
26°30'0"S
27°0'0"S
19°0'0"E
19°30'0"E
20°0'0"E
20°30'0"E
RSA/Namibia
Kalahari Gemsbok NP
Kgalagadi TFP
Grave of Hans Schwabe
Gharagab
Gharagab Trail
23/01:20
Polentswa
Nossob Trail
Swartbas
Bitterpan trail
permit
no access
57/03:47
14/00:46
52/02:27
21/01:01
Nababies
Bitterpan
Bitterpan trail
48/03:11
Mata Mata
07:00-16:30
117/02:44
Twee Rivieren
Auob
Urikaruus
36/01:35
Pulai
58/02:24
!Xaus
pvt
47/02:09
42/02:06
29/01:23
27/00:35
many farm gates
Mier/Pulai
87/04:10
25/00:32
32/00:39
15/00:18
Wit
Loubos City
Klein Mier
Groot Mier
Rietfontein
Klein Menasse
08:00-16:00
Philandersbron
33/00:36
Hakskeen
Corrugated
77/00:54
Gemsbok
47/00:57
Koppieskraal
D1033
Olifants
102/02:05
23/00:31
D1032
D1040
17/00:23
31/00:41
Platkop
28/00:38
D1109
D1022
33/00:46
M33
21/00:29
37/00:54
D1119
21/00:17
C15
Terra-Rouge
Donkerhoek
Kalahari
M30
D511
43/01:06
D503
33/01:22
Dunesong Breathers
262/04:07
Keetmanshoop
41/00:47
25/00:38
D579
23/00:31
Koës
Koes
23/00:14
C17
Aninuis
D614
59/00:39
62/01:13
D616
57/01:11
D611
deep sand
Gammibe
D503
46/01:38
Guchenoes
Gaibise se pan
D615
54/01:04
Sumsare
Honde
Kuubmaamsvlei
Springboktreck
Kubunumugas
Kiriis
Wildheim
Gansis
78/00:51
Swartput se pan
M27
Zabubegas
206/03:16
D614
34/00:40
Klippies
22/00:27
C16
Aroab
22/00:23
72/01:23
D610
Hartbees
D612
35/00:42
41/00:27
C18
Ganna
61/01:04
D622
Swartbaas
Restricted Roads
Tar (minor)
Off Road
Main Off Road
Riverboat Trail
Hiking/Walking Trail

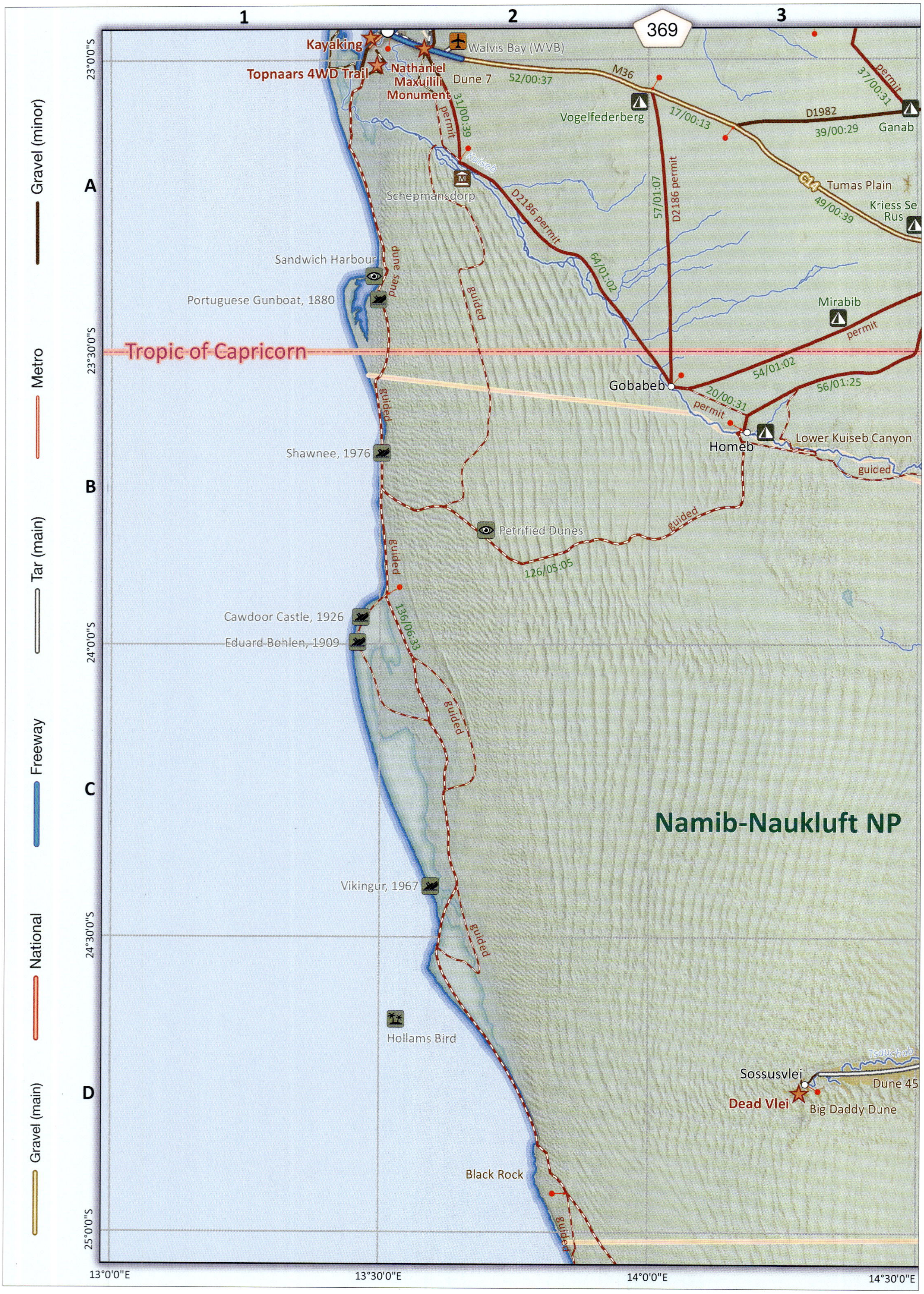

1
2
3
369
A
B
C
D
Gravel (minor)
Metro
Tar (main)
Freeway
National
Gravel (main)
23°0'0"S
23°30'0"S
24°0'0"S
24°30'0"S
25°0'0"S
13°0'0"E
13°30'0"E
14°0'0"E
14°30'0"E
Kayaking
Topnaars 4WD Trail
Nathaniel Maxuilili Monument
Walvis Bay (WVB)
Dune 7
52/00:37
M36
Vogelfederberg
17/00:13
D1982
39/00:29
Ganab
37/00:31
permit
31/00:39
permit
Kuiseb
Schepmansdorp
D2186 permit
64/01:02
57/01:07
D2186 permit
Tumas Plain
49/00:39
Kriess Se Rus
Sandwich Harbour
dune sand
Portuguese Gunboat, 1880
guided
Mirabib
permit
Tropic of Capricorn
54/01:02
Gobabeb
20/00:31
permit
56/01:25
Homeb
Lower Kuiseb Canyon
guided
Shawnee, 1976
guided
Petrified Dunes
126/05:05
guided
guided
Cawdoor Castle, 1926
136/06:33
Eduard Bohlen, 1909
guided
Namib-Naukluft NP
Vikingur, 1967
guided
Hollams Bird
Tsauchab
Sossusvlei
Dune 45
Dead Vlei
Big Daddy Dune
Black Rock
guided

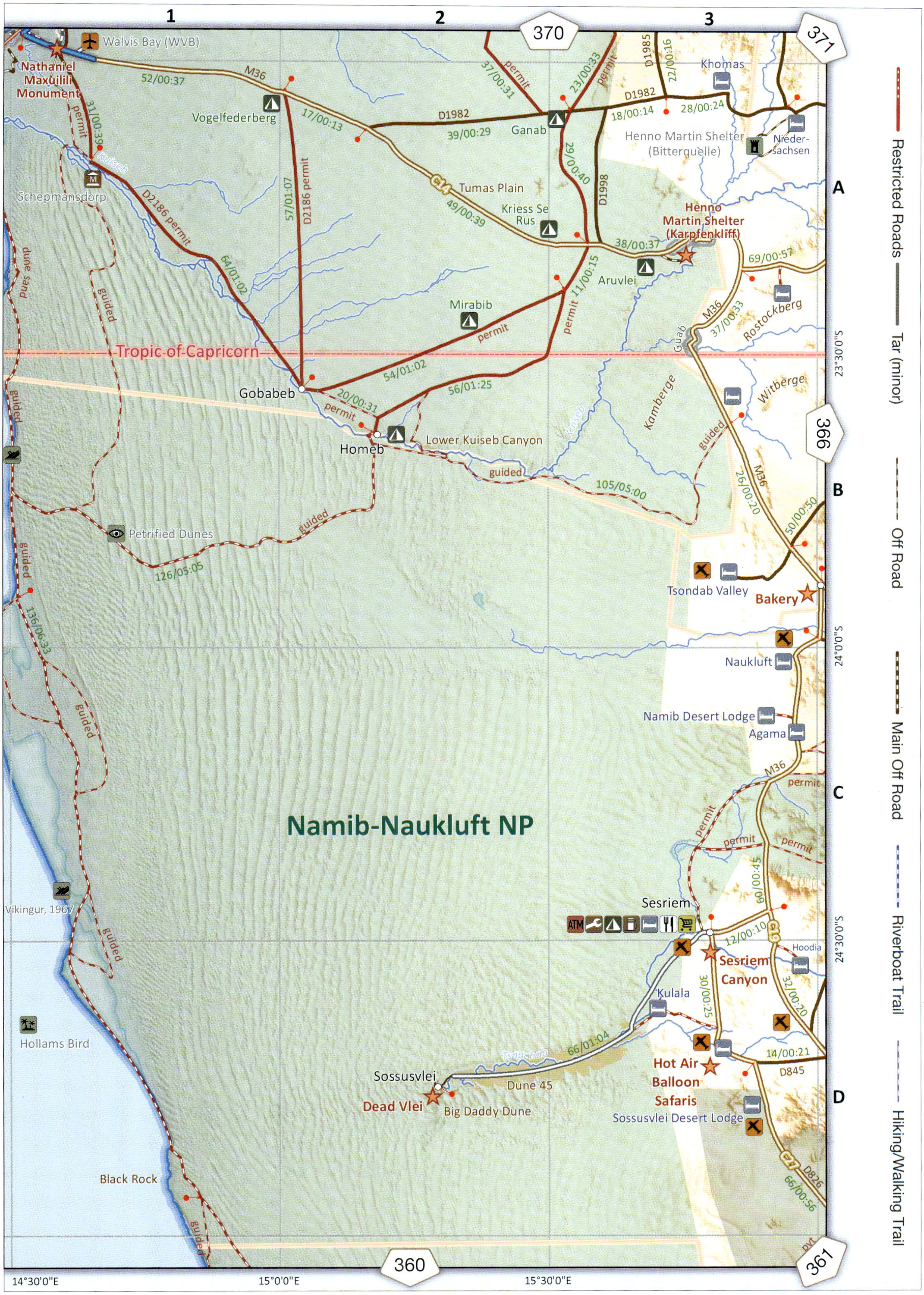
1
2
3
370
371
366
360
361
A
B
C
D
Walvis Bay (WVB)
Nathaniel Maxuilili Monument
52/00:37
M36
Vogelfederberg
17/00:13
D1982
39/00:29
Ganab
37/00:31
permit
23/00:33
D1985
22/00:16
Khomas
18/00:14
28/00:24
Henno Martin Shelter (Bitterquelle)
Nieder-sachsen
31/00:39
Kuiseb
Schepmansdorp
D2186 permit
57/01:07
D2186 permit
C14
Tumas Plain
49/00:39
Kriess Se Rus
29/00:40
D1998
Henno Martin Shelter (Karpfenkliff)
38/00:37
Aruvlei
69/00:57
dune sand
guided
64/01:02
Mirabib
11/00:15
permit
Rostockberg
M36
37/00:33
Gaub
Tropic of Capricorn
Gobabeb
54/01:02
56/01:25
20/00:31
Homeb
Lower Kuiseb Canyon
Kamberge
Witberge
guided
M36
26/00:20
guided
105/05:00
Petrified Dunes
126/05:05
50/00:50
Tsondab Valley
Bakery
136/06:33
Naukluft
Namib Desert Lodge
Agama
Namib-Naukluft NP
M36
permit
Vikingur, 1967
Sesriem
12/00:10
C19
Hoodia
Sesriem Canyon
60/00:45
30/00:25
32/00:20
Kulala
Hollams Bird
Tsauchab
66/01:04
14/00:21
D845
Sossusvlei
Dune 45
Hot Air Balloon Safaris
Dead Vlei
Big Daddy Dune
Sossusvlei Desert Lodge
C27
D826
66/00:56
Black Rock
23°30'0"S
24°0'0"S
24°30'0"S
14°30'0"E
15°0'0"E
15°30'0"E
Restricted Roads
Tar (minor)
Off Road
Main Off Road
Riverboat Trail
Hiking/Walking Trail

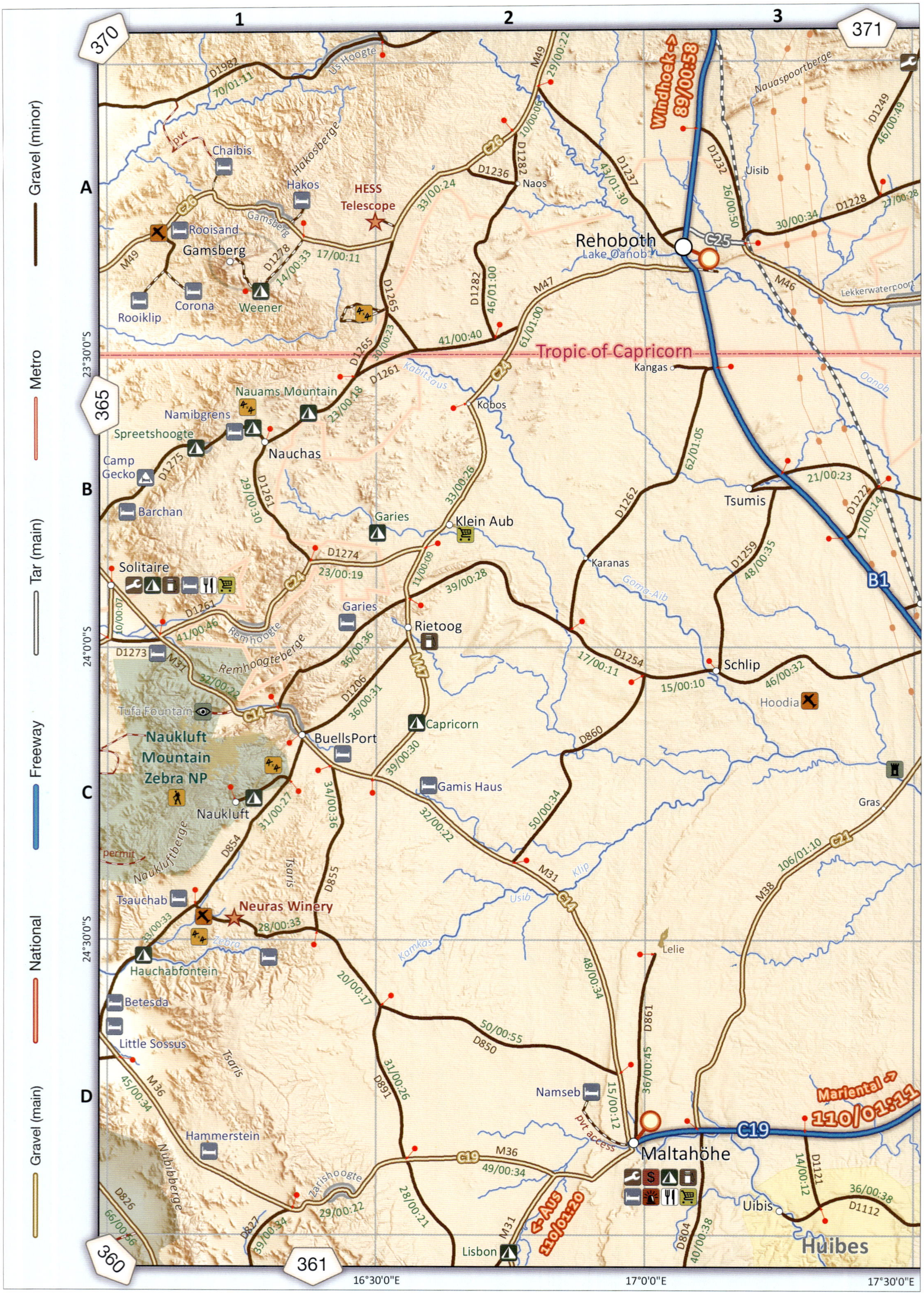
1
2
3
A
B
C
D
370
371
365
360
361
Gravel (minor)
Metro
Tar (main)
Freeway
National
Gravel (main)
23°30'0"S
24°0'0"S
24°30'0"S
16°30'0"E
17°0'0"E
17°30'0"E
D1982
70/01:11
Us Hoogte
M49
29/00:22
Windhoek -> 89/00:58
Nauaspoortberge
D1249
46/00:49
pvt
Chaibis
Hakosberge
C26
10/00:06
D1282
D1236
Naos
D1237
43/01:30
D1232
26/00:50
Uisib
D1228
27/00:28
Hakos
HESS Telescope
33/00:24
Rooisand
Gamsberg
Rehoboth
Lake Oanob
C25
30/00:34
M49
Gamsberg
D1278
17/00:11
14/00:33
D1265
M46
Lekkerwaterpoort
Rooiklip
Corona
Weener
D1282
46/01:00
M47
61/01:00
41/00:40
Tropic of Capricorn
Kangas
D1265
30/00:23
D1261
Kabitsaus
C24
Kobos
Oanob
Nauams Mountain
23/00:18
Namibgrens
Spreetshoogte
Nauchas
62/01:05
Camp Gecko
D1275
D1261
29/00:30
33/00:26
21/00:23
Tsumis
D1222
12/00:14
Barchan
Garies
Klein Aub
D1262
D1274
11/00:09
Karanas
D1259
48/00:35
Solitaire
23/00:19
C24
39/00:28
Goma-Aib
B1
D1261
10/00:07
Garies
Rietoog
41/00:46
Remhoogte
D1273
M31
Remhoogteberge
36/00:36
M47
17/00:11
D1254
Schlip
46/00:32
32/00:22
D1206
36/00:31
15/00:10
Hoodia
Tufa Fountain
C14
Capricorn
BuellsPort
D860
Naukluft Mountain Zebra NP
39/00:30
Gamis Haus
Gras
Naukluft
34/00:36
31/00:27
32/00:22
50/00:34
C21
106/01:10
permit
Naukluftberge
D854
Tsaris
D855
M31
Klip
M38
Tsauchab
Usib
C14
Neuras Winery
28/00:33
33/00:33
Zebra
Kamkas
Lelie
Hauchabfontein
48/00:34
20/00:17
Betesda
D861
50/00:55
D850
Little Sossus
Tsaris
M36
31/00:26
D891
36/00:45
45/00:34
Namseb
15/00:12
Mariental -> 110/01:11
pvt access
C19
Maltahöhe
Hammerstein
Nubibberge
C19
M36
49/00:34
D1121
14/00:12
36/00:38
Zarishoogte
D1112
D826
<- Aus 110/01:20
Uibis
66/00:46
D827
29/00:22
28/00:21
39/00:34
M31
D804
40/00:38
Huibes
Lisbon

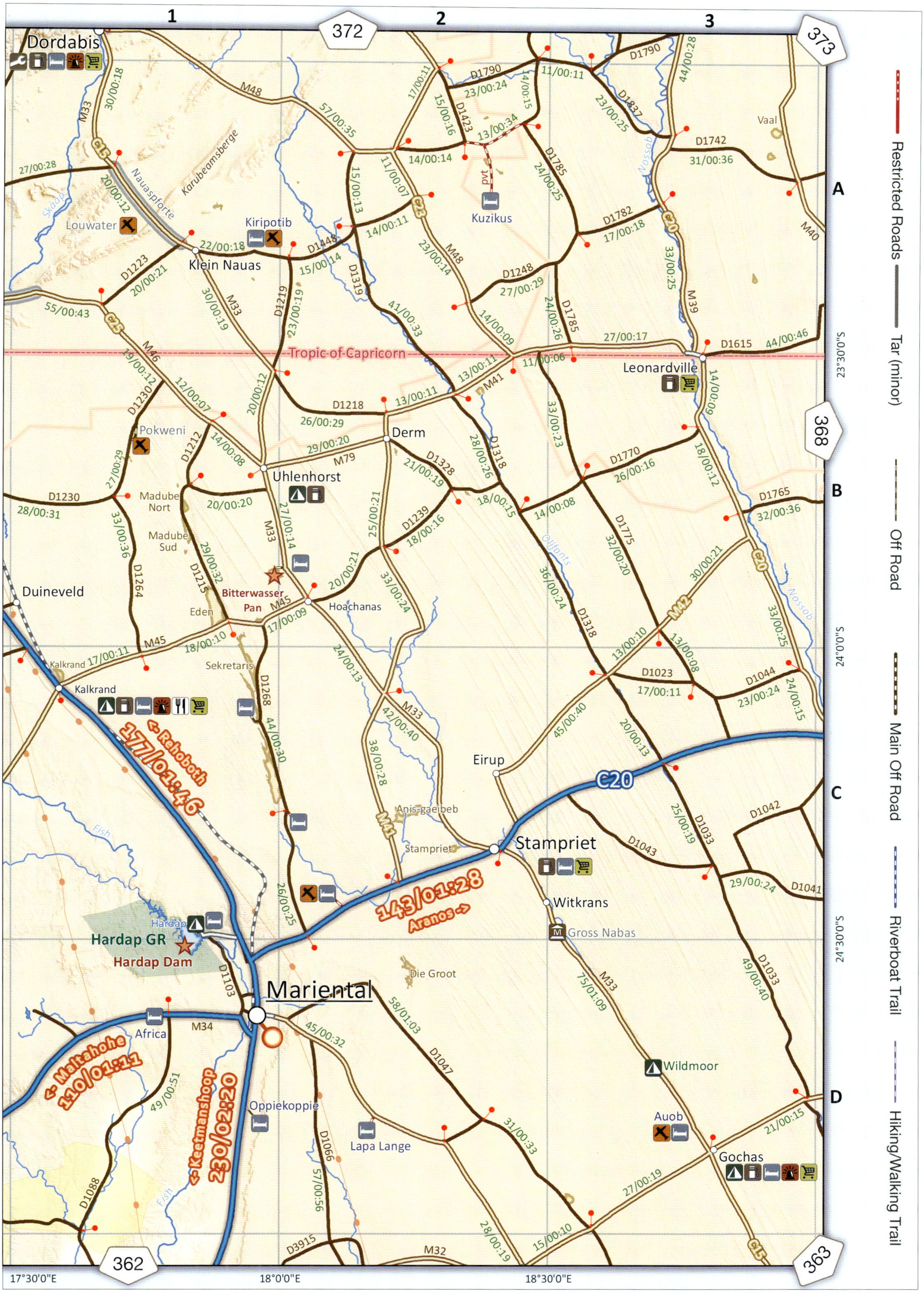

372
373
368
362
363
1
2
3
A
B
C
D
Dordabis
Louwater
Kiripotib
Klein Nauas
Kuzikus
Karubeamsberge
Nauaspforte
Tropic of Capricorn
Leonardville
Vaal
Nossob
Pokweni
Derm
Uhlenhorst
Madube Nort
Madube Sud
Duineveld
Bitterwasser Pan
Eden
Hoachanas
Sekretaris
Kalkrand
Oljfonts
Eirup
Anis-gaeibeb
Stampriet
Witkrans
Gross Nabas
Hardap
Hardap GR
Hardap Dam
Mariental
Die Groot
Africa
Oppiekoppie
Lapa Lange
Wildmoor
Auob
Gochas
Fish
C20
<- Rehoboth 177/01:46
143/01:28 Aranos ->
<- Maltahohe 110/01:11
<- Keetmanshoop 230/02:20
17°30'0"E
18°0'0"E
18°30'0"E
23°30'0"S
24°0'0"S
24°30'0"S
Restricted Roads
Tar (minor)
Off Road
Main Off Road
Riverboat Trail
Hiking/Walking Trail

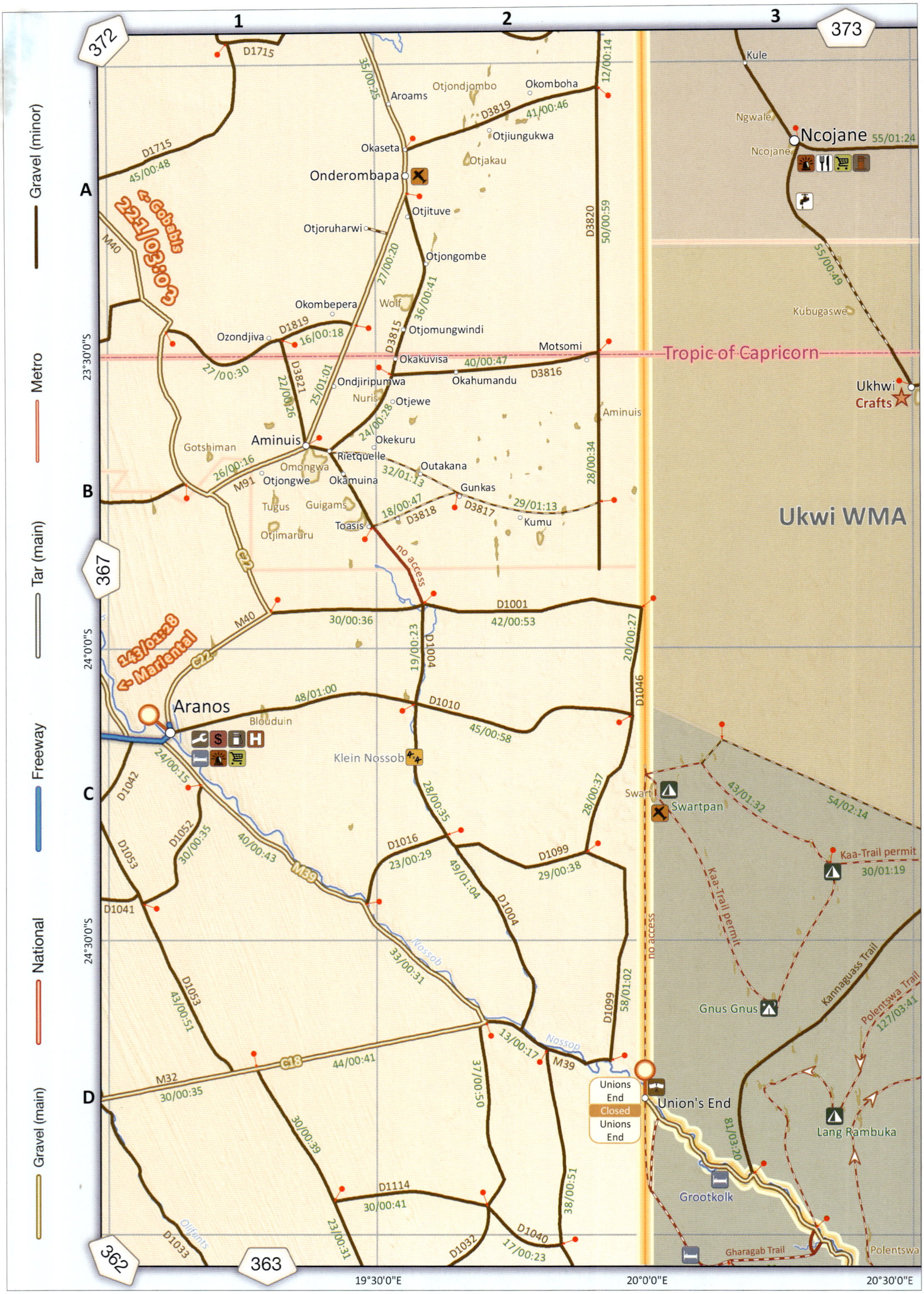
Gravel (minor)
Metro
Tar (main)
Freeway
National
Gravel (main)
1
2
3
372
373
367
362
363
A
B
C
D
Ncojane
Aranos
Aminuis
Onderombapa
Tropic of Capricorn
Ukwi WMA
Ukhwi Crafts
Kule
Ngwale
Kubugaswe
Motsomi
Okakuvisa
Okahumandu
Aroams
Otjondjombo
Okomboha
Otjiungukwa
Otjakau
Okaseta
Otjituve
Otjoruharwi
Otjongombe
Okombepera
Wolf
Otjomungwindi
Ozondjiva
Ondjiripumwa
Nuris
Otjewe
Okekuru
Rietquelle
Outakana
Gunkas
Kumu
Gotshiman
Omongwa
Otjongwe
Okamuina
Tugus
Guigams
Toasis
Otjimaruru
no access
Klein Nossob
Blouduin
Swartpan
Kaa-Trail permit
Gnus Gnus
Kannaguass Trail
Polentswa Trail
Lang Rambuka
Union's End
Unions End Closed Unions End
Grootkolk
Gharagab Trail
Polentswa
Nossob
Olifants
221/03:05 ← Gobabis
143/01:28 ← Mariental
D1715
45/00:48
D3819
41/00:46
12/00:14
35/00:25
D3820
50/00:59
27/00:20
36/00:41
D1819
16/00:18
27/00:30
D3815
D3821
22/00:26
25/01:01
40/00:47
D3816
24/00:28
26/00:16
M91
32/01:13
18/00:47
D3818
D3817
29/01:13
28/00:34
M40
C22
D1001
30/00:36
42/00:53
19/00:23
D1004
20/00:27
D1046
48/01:00
D1010
45/00:58
24/00:15
D1042
D1052
30/00:35
D1053
40/00:43
M39
28/00:35
D1016
23/00:29
49/01:04
D1099
29/00:38
28/00:37
43/01:32
54/02:14
30/01:19
55/00:49
55/01:24
D1041
33/00:31
D1053
43/00:51
58/01:02
13/00:17
37/00:50
M32
30/00:35
C18
44/00:41
30/00:39
D1114
30/00:41
23/00:31
D1032
D1040
17/00:23
38/00:51
D1033
81/03:20
127/03:41
23°30'0"S
24°0'0"S
24°30'0"S
19°30'0"E
20°0'0"E
20°30'0"E

376
377
370
364
365
1
2
3
A
B
C
D
Salt
Benguela Eagle, 1975
Menhir Rocks
52/02:17
52/00:52
17/00:23
15/00:44
21/00:50
Ancient Damara Settlement
Brandberg West
flash floods
45/02:30
11/00:21
19/00:16
26/00:28
24/00:56
21/00:52
White Lady Rock Painting
Mt Brandberg NR
Umoab
Ugab
Stormkus, 1977
Winston, 1970
35/00:35
Dorob NP
D2303
14/00:10
Gobobosebberge
16/00:15
36/01:06
15/00:15
13/00:25
16/00:17
10/00:20
Messum
St Nowhere
Bakkrans
Messum Crater
19/00:21
33/01:00
Mile 108
15/00:10
14/00:17
24/00:38
16/00:46
24/00:26
26/00:44
35/00:33
Drawuo
Heideveld, 1968
28/00:18
D2301
20/00:14
Dead Sea Swimhole
Cape Cross
Cape Cross Seal Colony
Dorob NP
C35
30/00:40
11/00:10
riverbed
Mile 72
27/00:17
Uis
124/01:32
Omaruru
M76
riverbed
15/00:24
C34
Henties Bay
Old Salt Mine 4WD Trail
Jakkalsputz
Zeila of Hangana, 2008
71/01:06
Wlotzkasbaken
Vipava, 1968
Mile 14
Natal Coast, 1955
Gertrud Woermann, 1903
Swakopmund Attractions
Aquarium
Kristall Galerie
Living Desert Snake Park
Martin Luther Steam Locomotive
Museum
Old Jetty
Omeg Haus
Town Hall
Swakopmund
34/00:25
D1984
Quad biking
Langstrand
Pelican Point
Walvis Bay
Kayaking
Topnaars 4WD Trail
Nathaniel Maxuilili Monument
21°30'0"S
22°0'0"S
22°30'0"S
13°0'0"E
13°30'0"E
14°0'0"E
Restricted Roads
Tar (minor)
Off Road
Main Off Road
Riverboat Trail
Hiking/Walking Trail

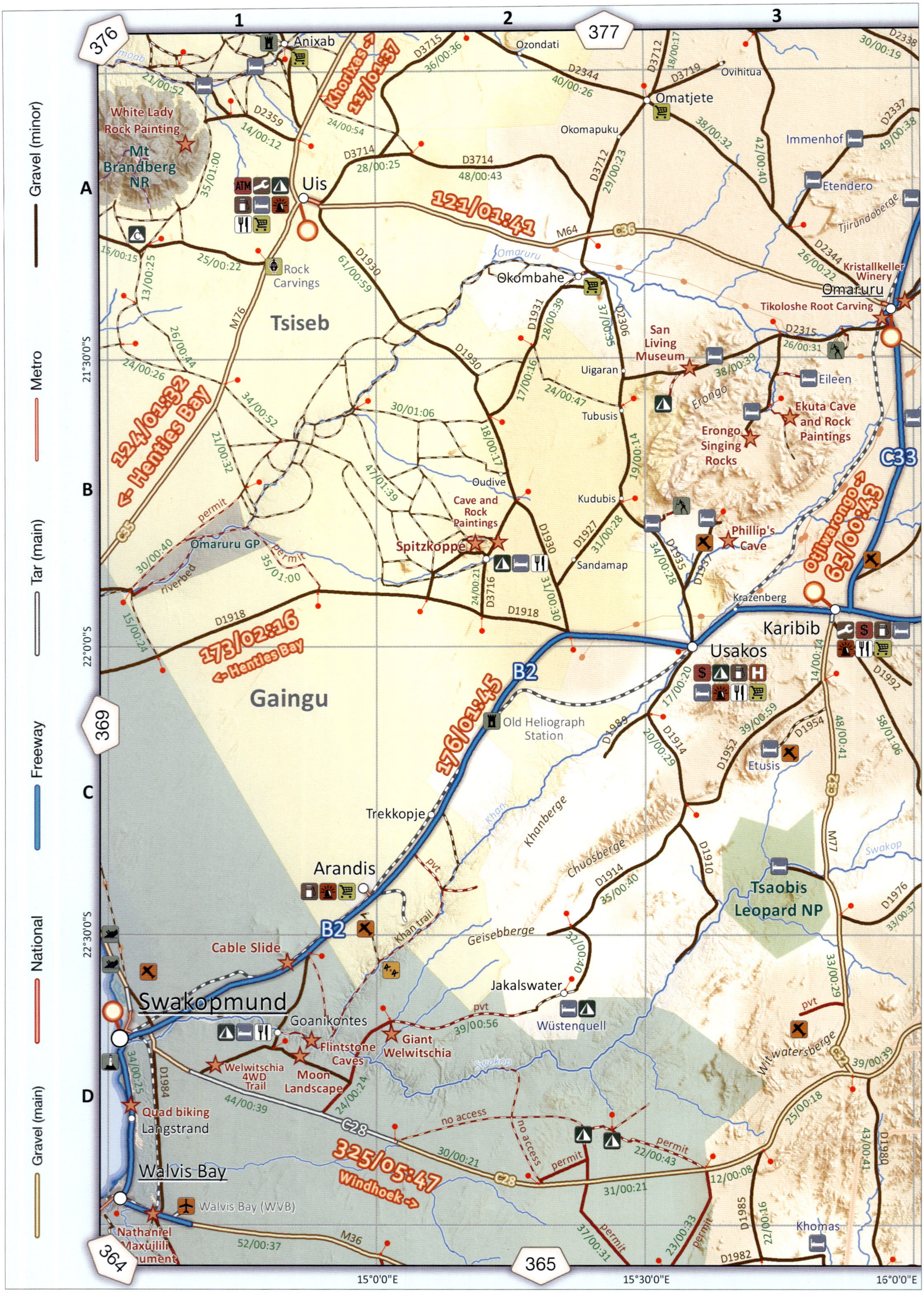

Gravel (minor)
Metro
Tar (main)
Freeway
National
Gravel (main)
1
2
3
A
B
C
D
376
377
369
364
365
Anixab
Khorixas -> 147/01:37
Ozondati
D3715
36/00:36
D3712
18/00:17
D3719
Ovihitua
D2338
30/00:19
D2344
40/00:26
Omatjete
White Lady
Rock Painting
Mt Brandberg NR
21/00:52
D2359
14/00:12
24/00:54
35/01:00
Okomapuku
38/00:32
42/00:40
Immenhof
D2337
49/00:38
D3714
28/00:25
D3714
48/00:43
29/00:23
Etendero
Uis
121/01:41
M64
C36
Tjirundoberge
D1930
61/00:59
Omaruru
D2344
26/00:22
Kristallkeller Winery
Omaruru
Tikoloshe Root Carving
15/00:15
25/00:22
13/00:25
Rock Carvings
Okombahe
D1931
28/00:39
37/00:35
D2306
San Living Museum
D2315
26/00:31
Tsiseb
M76
26/00:44
D1930
17/00:16
Uigaran
38/00:39
Eileen
24/00:26
124/01:32
<- Henties Bay
34/00:52
30/01:06
24/00:47
Tubusis
Erongo
Ekuta Cave
and Rock
Paintings
18/00:17
Erongo
Singing
Rocks
21/00:32
47/01:39
19/00:14
C33
Oudive
Cave and Rock Paintings
Kudubis
permit
C35
Omaruru GP
permit
35/01:00
30/00:40
Spitzkoppe
D1930
D1927
31/00:28
D1935
Phillip's Cave
Otjiwarongo -> 65/00:43
riverbed
24/00:21
D3716
Sandamap
34/00:28
15/00:24
31/00:30
D1918
D1918
Krazenberg
Karibib
173/02:16
<- Henties Bay
Usakos
B2
Gaingu
176/01:45
17/00:20
14/00:14
D1992
Old Heliograph Station
D1989
D1914
20/00:29
D1952
39/00:59
D1954
48/00:41
58/01:06
Etusis
C32
Khan
Khanberge
Trekkopje
Chuosberge
D1910
M77
Swakop
Arandis
pvt
D1914
35/00:40
Tsaobis Leopard NP
D1976
33/00:37
B2
Khan trail
Geisebberge
32/00:40
Cable Slide
33/00:29
Jakalswater
pvt
Swakopmund
Goanikontes
pvt
39/00:56
Wüstenquell
Flintstone Caves
Giant Welwitschia
Witwatersberge
C32
39/00:39
Welwitschia 4WD Trail
Moon Landscape
Swakop
34/00:25
D1984
24/00:24
25/00:18
Quad biking
Langstrand
44/00:39
C28
no access
no access
D1980
325/05:47
Windhoek ->
30/00:21
permit
permit
22/00:43
43/00:41
Walvis Bay
C28
12/00:08
31/00:21
Walvis Bay (WVB)
37/00:31
permit
23/00:33
permit
D1985
22/00:16
Khomas
Nathaniel Maxuilili ...ument
52/00:37
M36
D1982
21°30'0"S
22°0'0"S
22°30'0"S
15°0'0"E
15°30'0"E
16°0'0"E

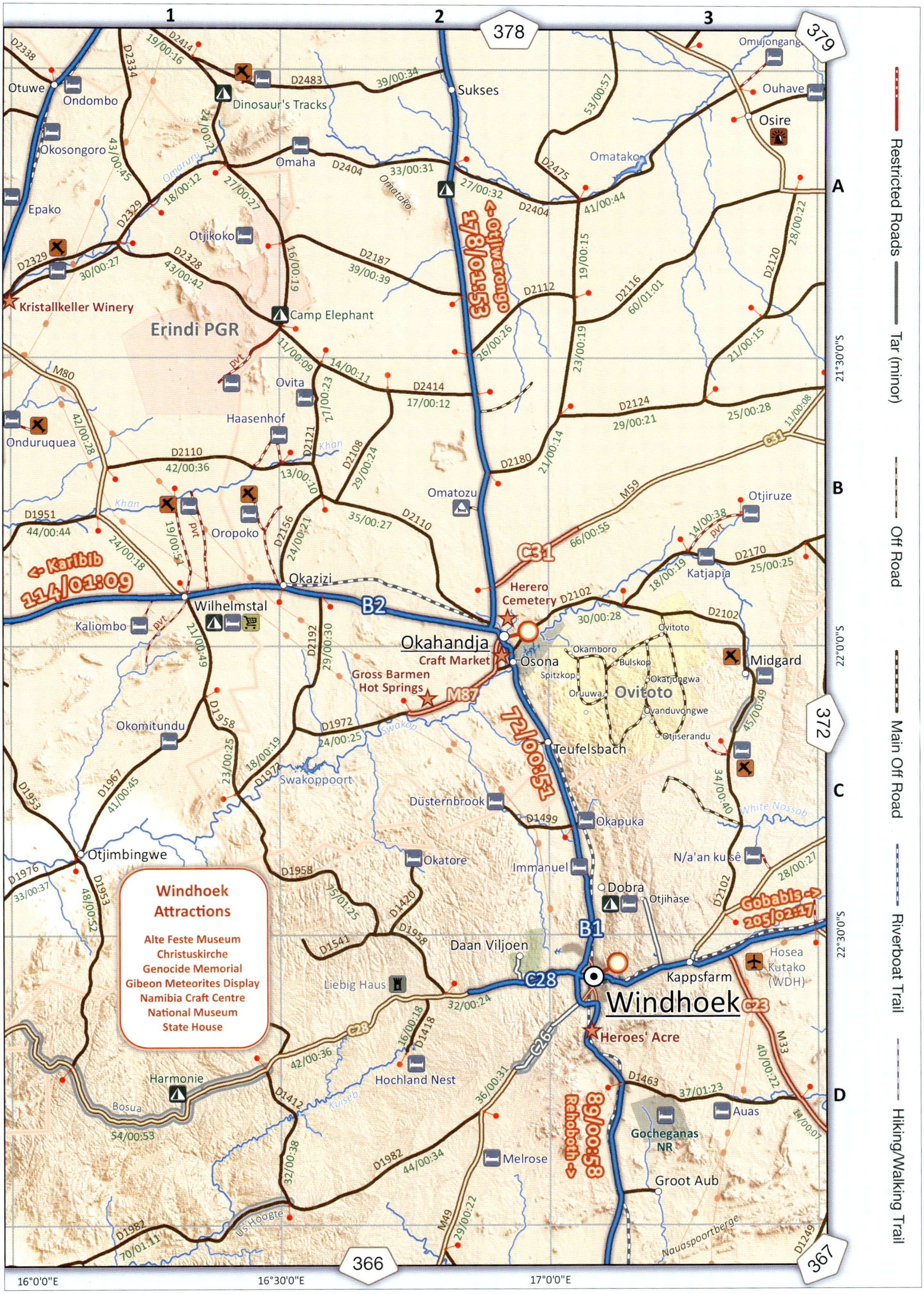
1
2
3
378
379
372
366
367
A
B
C
D
Restricted Roads
Tar (minor)
Off Road
Main Off Road
Riverboat Trail
Hiking/Walking Trail
21°30'0"S
22°0'0"S
22°30'0"S
16°0'0"E
16°30'0"E
17°0'0"E
Otuwe
Ondombo
Okosongoro
Epako
Dinosaur's Tracks
Omaha
Sukses
Omujongang
Ouhave
Osire
Omatako
Otjikoko
Kristallkeller Winery
Erindi PGR
Camp Elephant
Ovita
Haasenhof
Onduruquea
Omatozu
Otjiruze
Katjapia
Oropoko
Okazizi
Wilhelmstal
Kaliombo
Herero Cemetery
Okahandja
Craft Market
Osona
Gross Barmen Hot Springs
Midgard
Okamboro
Bulskop
Spitzkop
Okatjongwa
Oruuwa
Ovitoto
Ovanduvongwe
Otjiserandu
Okomitundu
Swakoppoort
Teufelsbach
Düsternbrook
Okapuka
Otjimbingwe
Okatore
Immanuel
N/a'an ku sê
Dobra
Otjihase
Daan Viljoen
Kappsfarm
Hosea Kutako (WDH)
Liebig Haus
Windhoek
Heroes' Acre
Harmonie
Bosua
Hochland Nest
Melrose
Gocheganas NR
Auas
Groot Aub
Us Hoogte
Nauaspoortberge
Khan
Swakop
White Nossob
Kuiseb
Omaruru
<- Otjiwarongo 178/01:53
<- Karibib 114/01:09
72/00:51
Gobabis -> 205/02:17
89/00:58 Rehoboth ->
B1
B2
C28
C26
C23
C31
M87
M59
M33
M49
M80
Windhoek Attractions
Alte Feste Museum
Christuskirche
Genocide Memorial
Gibeon Meteorites Display
Namibia Craft Centre
National Museum
State House

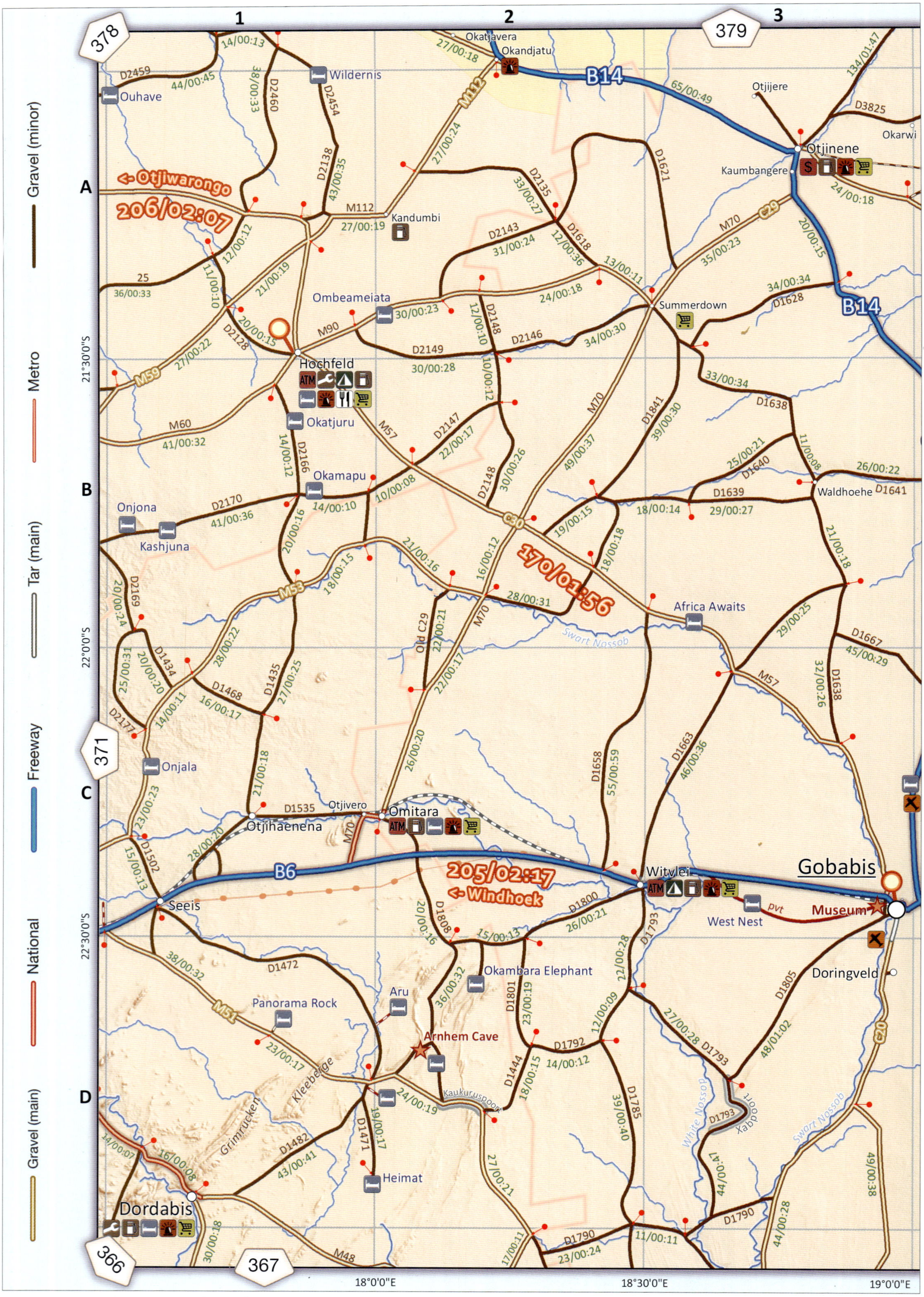

Safari Rental
Proudly rented by AVIS

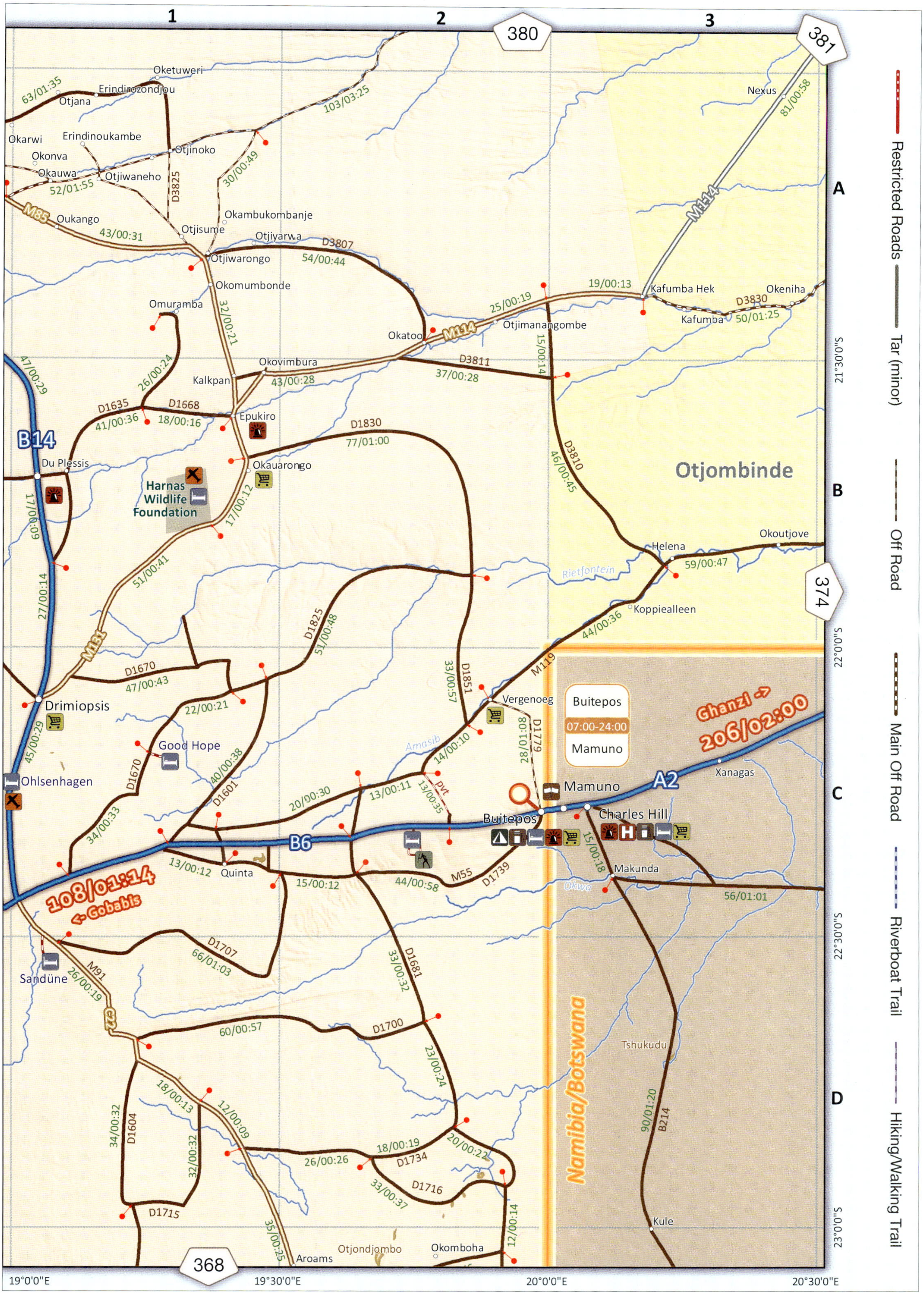

1
2
3
380
381
374
368
A
B
C
D
Oketuweri
Erindirozondjou
Otjana
63/01:35
103/03:25
Okarwi
Erindinoukambe
Okonva
Otjinoko
Okauwa
Otjiwaneho
52/01:55
D3825
30/00:49
M85
Oukango
43/00:31
Okambukombanje
Otjisume
Otjiyarwa
D3807
Otjiwarongo
54/00:44
Okomumbonde
Omuramba
32/00:21
Okatoo
M114
Otjimanangombe
25/00:19
19/00:13
Kafumba Hek
Okeniha
D3830
Kafumba
50/01:25
Nexus
81/00:58
47/00:29
26/00:24
Okovimbura
Kalkpan
43/00:28
D3811
37/00:28
15/00:14
D1635
D1668
41/00:36
18/00:16
Epukiro
B14
D1830
77/01:00
D3810
46/00:45
Du Plessis
Okauarongo
Harnas Wildlife Foundation
Otjombinde
17/00:09
17/00:12
Helena
Okoutjove
59/00:47
Rietfontein
27/00:14
51/00:41
Koppiealleen
44/00:36
D1825
51/00:48
M81
M119
D1670
47/00:43
33/00:57
D1851
Drimiopsis
22/00:21
Vergenoeg
D1779
28/01:08
Buitepos
07:00-24:00
Mamuno
Ghanzi ->
206/02:00
Good Hope
45/00:29
Amasib
14/00:10
Ohlsenhagen
D1670
40/00:38
D1601
20/00:30
13/00:11
13/00:35
pvt
Mamuno
A2
Xanagas
Charles Hill
34/00:33
Buitepos
B6
15/00:18
13/00:12
Quinta
15/00:12
44/00:58
M55
D1739
Makunda
108/01:14
<-Gobabis
Okwa
56/01:01
D1707
66/01:03
D1681
33/00:32
Sandüne
M91
26/00:19
C22
60/00:57
D1700
23/00:24
Tshukudu
Namibia/Botswana
18/00:13
12/00:09
34/00:32
D1604
32/00:32
18/00:19
D1734
20/00:22
26/00:26
90/01:20
B214
33/00:37
D1716
D1715
12/00:14
Kule
35/00:25
Aroams
Otjondjombo
Okomboha
19°0'0"E
19°30'0"E
20°0'0"E
20°30'0"E
21°30'0"S
22°0'0"S
22°30'0"S
23°0'0"S
Restricted Roads
Tar (minor)
Off Road
Main Off Road
Riverboat Trail
Hiking/Walking Trail

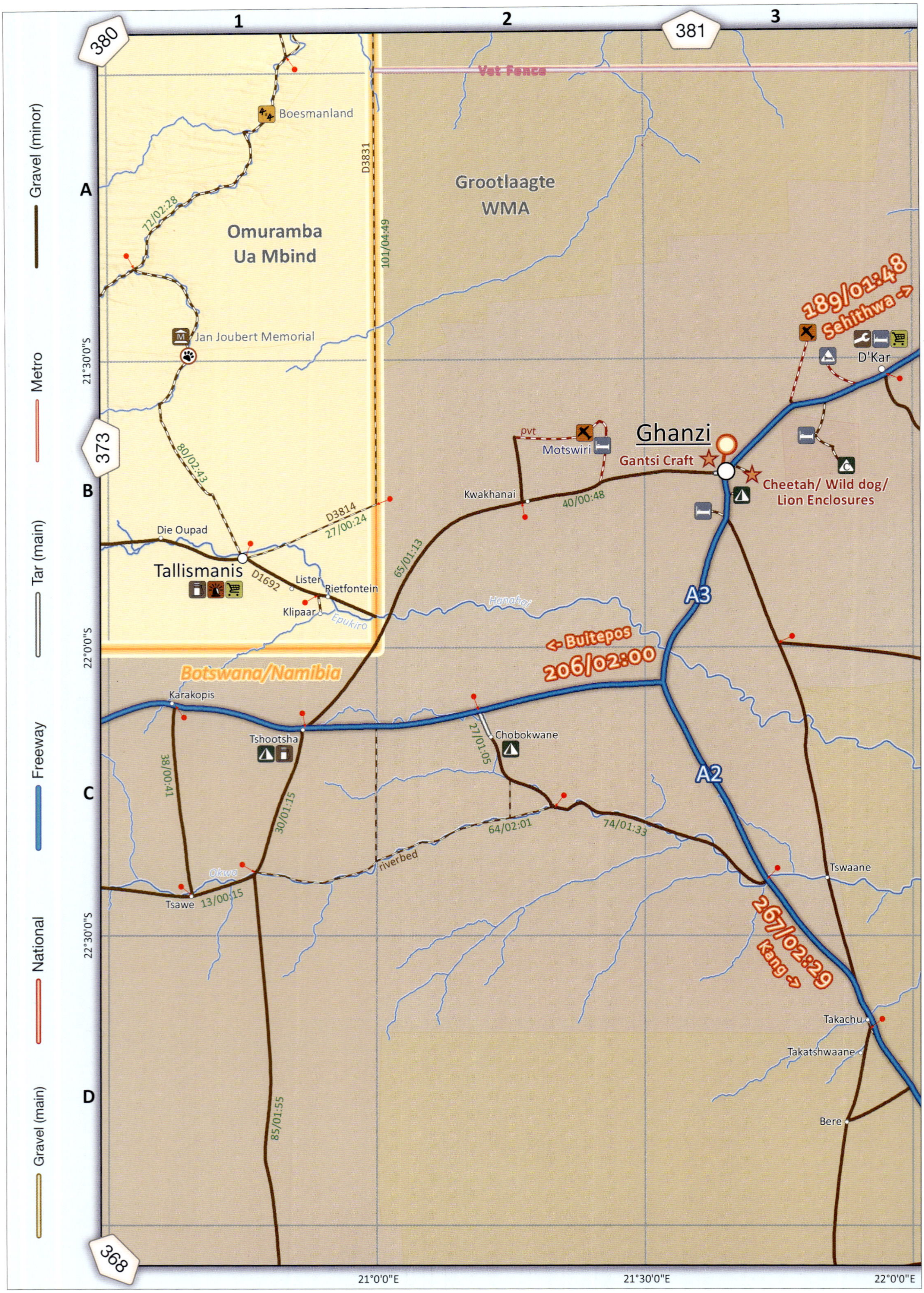

Gravel (minor)
Metro
Tar (main)
Freeway
National
Gravel (main)
1
2
3
A
B
C
D
380
381
373
368
21°30'0"S
22°0'0"S
22°30'0"S
21°0'0"E
21°30'0"E
22°0'0"E
Vet Fence
Boesmanland
D3831
Grootlaagte
WMA
Omuramba
Ua Mbind
72/02:28
101/04:49
Jan Joubert Memorial
189/01:48
Sehithwa ->
D'Kar
80/02:43
pvt
Motswiri
Ghanzi
Gantsi Craft
Cheetah/ Wild dog/
Lion Enclosures
Kwakhanai
40/00:48
D3814
27/00:24
Die Oupad
Tallismanis
D1692
Lister
Rietfontein
Klipaar
Epukiro
65/01:13
Hanahai
A3
<- Buitepos
206/02:00
Botswana/Namibia
Karakopis
Tshootsha
27/01:05
Chobokwane
A2
38/00:41
30/01:15
64/02:01
74/01:33
riverbed
Okwa
Tsawe
13/00:15
Tswaane
267/02:29
Kang ->
Takachu
Takatshwaane
85/01:55
Bere

1
2
3
382
383
376
369
A
B
C
D
Sir Charles Elliot,1942
Westies
Karimona, 1971
Suiderkus, 1977
Mowe Bay
Ganias Plains
Amspoort Gorge
Gui-Uiri Swamp
Hoarusib
55/01:35
30/01:04
guided
D2302
guided & permit
ATLANTIC OCEAN
19°30'0"S
20°0'0"S
20°30'0"S
11°30'0"E
12°0'0"E
12°30'0"E
Restricted Roads
Tar (minor)
Off Road
Main Off Road
Riverboat Trail
Hiking/Walking Trail

Gravel (minor)
Metro
Tar (main)
Freeway
National
Gravel (main)
382
383
375
369
1
2
3
A
B
C
D
19°30'0"S
20°0'0"S
20°30'0"S
21°0'0"S
13°0'0"E
13°30'0"E
14°0'0"E
14°30'0"E
C35
Oromauwa
Dolomite
no access
Otjokavare
Omuramba
<- Omakange 204/02:54
M76
Ehirovipuka CC
Hobatere
permit
Fort Sesfontein
Ongongo Hot Spring
Sesfontein
Anabeb
Warmquelle
De Wet
Khowarib
D3710
D3706
D3707
Anabeb
Hoanib Skeleton Coast
Fearless
flash floods
Hoanib
Mbakodja
Okememuno
Kharokhaob Plains
Blackridge
Palmwag Crowther's
Theun's Camp
Crowther's
Xai Ais Fountain
Aub-Barab
Etendeka
Palmwag
Grootberg
Humor
Khoadi//Heas
Condor
Atlanta
Erwee
Rodeon
Estorff
D2650
D2646
Otjitheka
pvt
Skeleton Coast NP
Terrace Bay
Atlantic, 1978
Uniab Delta Pools
Uniab
Desert Rhino
Spaarwater
Bergsig
Ruspoort
Huab
D2633
Torra Bay
Salt
Springbokwasser
C39
Springbok
Koigab
Torra
Vrede
Fonteine
Xaragu
Rendezvous
De Riet
Slangpos
D2612
Living Museum of the Damara
Desolation Valley
Jan Snel
Twyfelfontein
World Heritage Site
Organ Pipes
Kuidas
Doro!nawas
Doros Crater
Montrose, 1973
D2302
C34
Vinte e Oite de Maio, 1966
Toscanini
Divorce
flash floods
Ugab

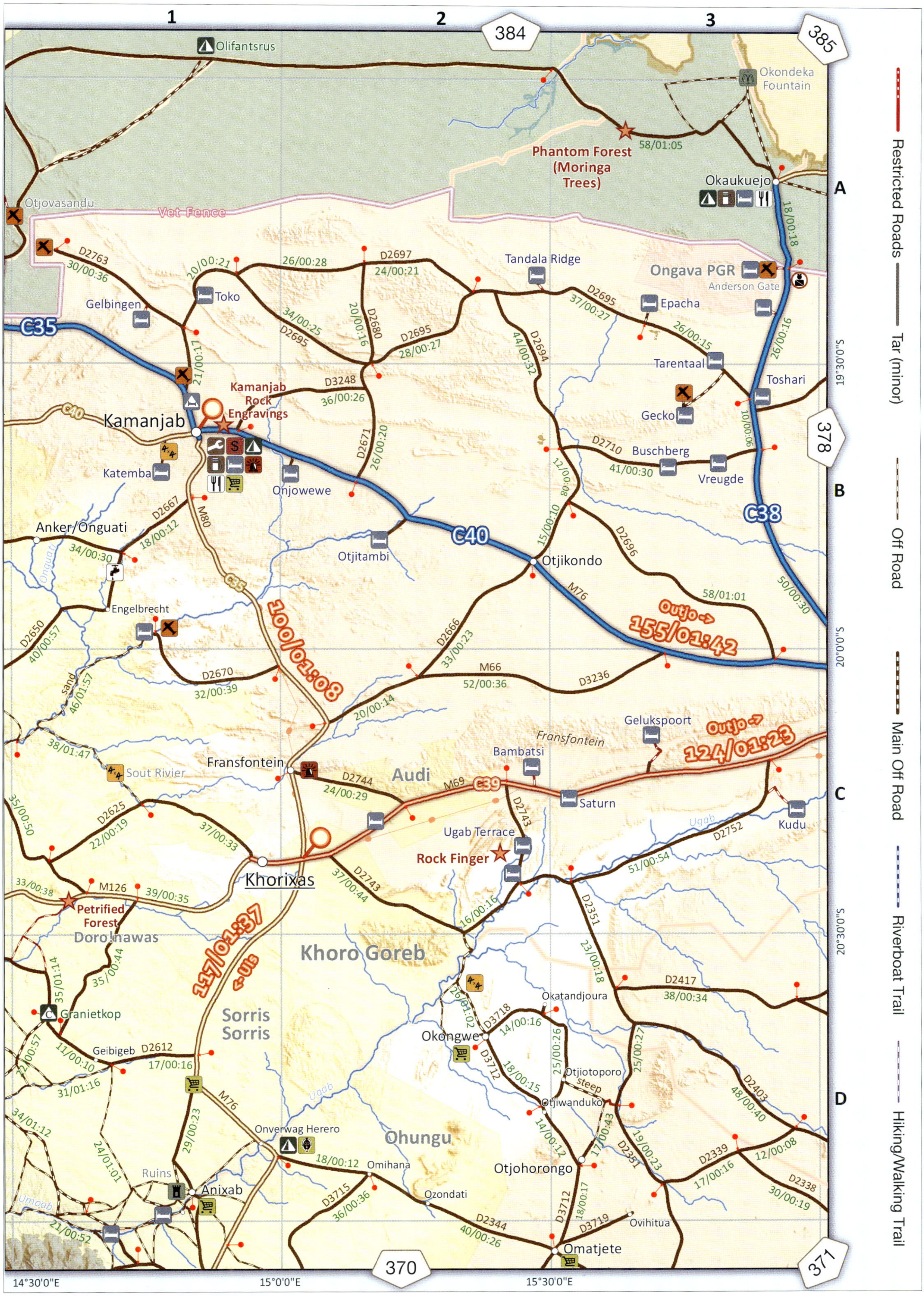
1
2
3
384
385
378
370
371
A
B
C
D
Olifantsrus
Okondeka Fountain
Phantom Forest (Moringa Trees)
58/01:05
Okaukuejo
18/00:18
Otjovasandu
Vet Fence
D2763
30/00:36
20/00:21
26/00:28
D2697
24/00:21
Tandala Ridge
Ongava PGR
Anderson Gate
Toko
Gelbingen
C35
34/00:25
D2695
20/00:16
D2680
D2695
28/00:27
37/00:27
Epacha
26/00:15
44/00:32
D2694
Tarentaal
26/00:16
Toshari
21/00:17
Kamanjab Rock Engravings
D3248
36/00:26
Gecko
10/00:06
C40
Kamanjab
Katemba
Onjowewe
D2671
26/00:20
D2710
41/00:30
Buschberg
Vreugde
12/00:08
C38
D2667
18/00:12
M80
Anker/Onguati
34/00:30
C40
15/00:10
Otjitambi
Otjikondo
D2696
Onguati
C35
100/01:08
M76
58/01:01
50/00:30
Engelbrecht
Outjo
155/01:42
D2650
40/00:57
D2666
33/00:23
D2670
32/00:39
M66
52/00:36
D3236
sand
46/01:57
20/00:14
Geluksspoort
Fransfontein
Bambatsi
Outjo
124/01:23
38/01:47
Sout Rivier
Fransfontein
D2744
24/00:29
Audi
M69
C39
D2743
Saturn
Kudu
35/00:50
D2625
22/00:19
37/00:33
Ugab Terrace
Ugab
D2752
Rock Finger
Khorixas
51/00:54
37/00:44
D2743
33/00:38
M126
39/00:35
Petrified Forest
Doro !nawas
16/00:16
D2351
117/01:37
Uis
Khoro Goreb
23/00:18
35/01:14
35/00:44
D2417
38/00:34
Okatandjoura
Granietkop
Sorris Sorris
D3718
14/00:16
Okongwe
25/00:26
25/00:27
22/00:57
Geibigeb
D2612
17/00:16
D3712
18/00:15
Otjiotoporo
steep
11/00:10
31/01:16
Otjiwanduko
D2403
48/00:40
M76
Ugab
34/01:12
29/00:23
Onverwag Herero
Ohungu
17/00:43
14/00:12
19/00:23
D2351
24/01:01
18/00:12
Omihana
Otjohorongo
D2339
17/00:16
12/00:08
D2338
30/00:19
Ruins
Anixab
Umoab
D3715
36/00:36
Ozondati
D3712
18/00:17
D3719
Ovihitua
21/00:52
D2344
40/00:26
Omatjete
14°30'0"E
15°0'0"E
15°30'0"E
19°30'0"S
20°0'0"S
20°30'0"S
Restricted Roads
Tar (minor)
Off Road
Main Off Road
Riverboat Trail
Hiking/Walking Trail

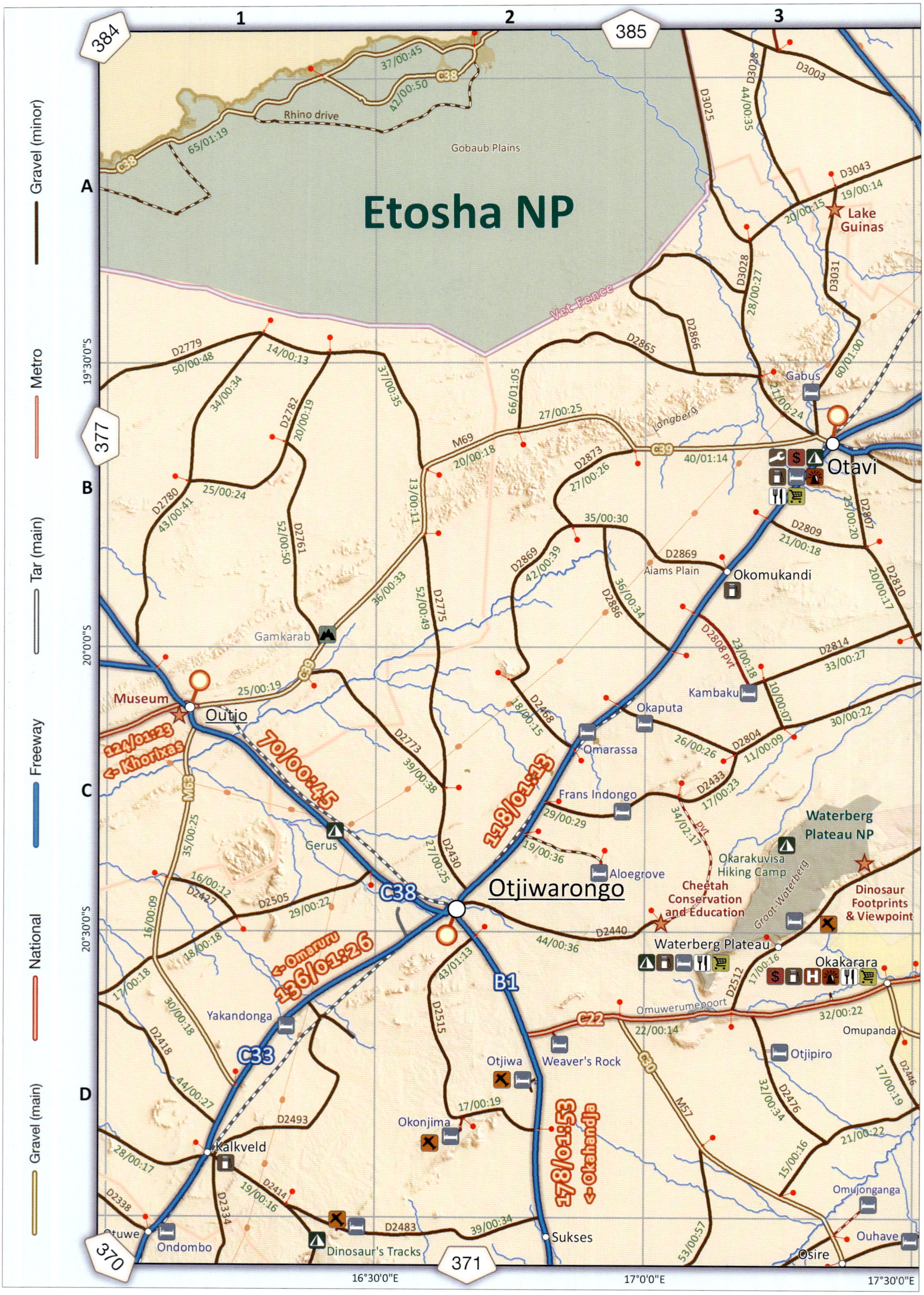

Etosha NP
Gobaub Plains
Rhino drive
Vet Fence
Lake Guinas
Gabus
Otavi
Okomukandi
Aiams Plain
Longberg
Gamkarab
Museum
Outjo
124/01:23 <- Khorixas
70/00:45
118/01:13
Kambaku
Okaputa
Omarassa
Frans Indongo
Aloegrove
Gerus
Otjiwarongo
Cheetah Conservation and Education
Waterberg Plateau NP
Okarakuvisa Hiking Camp
Groot-Waterberg
Dinosaur Footprints & Viewpoint
Waterberg Plateau
Okakarara
Omuwerumepoort
Omupanda
Otjipiro
<- Omaruru 136/01:26
Yakandonga
Otjiwa
Weaver's Rock
Okonjima
178/01:53 <- Okahandja
Kalkveld
Omujonganga
Ouhave
Osire
Sukses
Otuwe
Ondombo
Dinosaur's Tracks
C38
C39
C33
C22
C30
B1
M63
M69
M57
D3025
D3028
D3003
D3043
D3031
D2865
D2866
D2779
D2782
D2780
D2761
D2773
D2775
D2873
D2869
D2886
D2808 pvt
D2809
D2807
D2810
D2814
D2804
D2433
D2468
D2430
D2427
D2505
D2440
D2512
D2515
D2418
D2493
D2414
D2483
D2334
D2338
D2476
D2446
pvt
1
2
3
A
B
C
D
384
385
377
370
371
19°30'0"S
20°0'0"S
20°30'0"S
16°30'0"E
17°0'0"E
17°30'0"E
Gravel (minor)
Metro
Tar (main)
Freeway
National
Gravel (main)

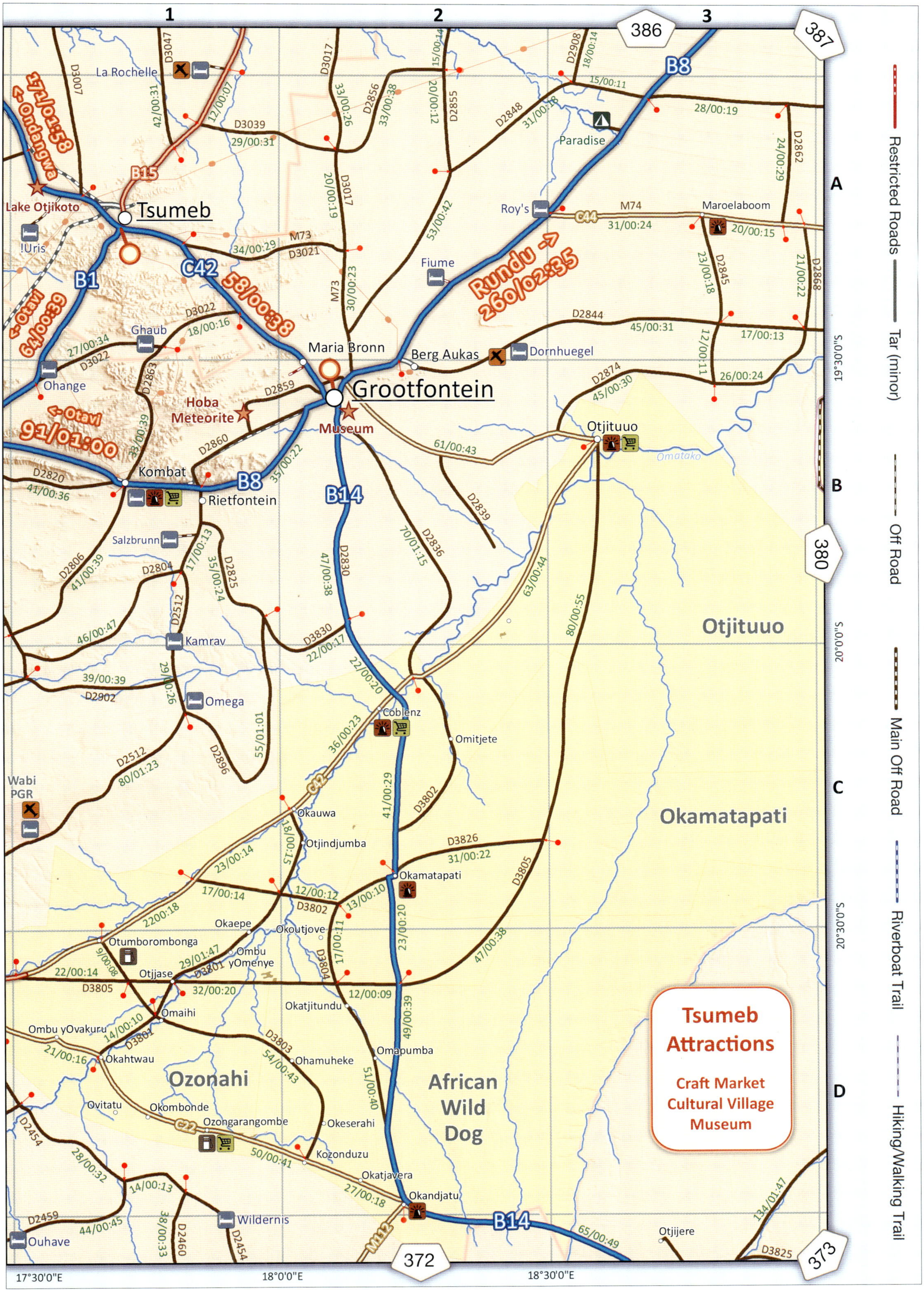

1
2
3
386
387
380
372
373
A
B
C
D
Tsumeb
Grootfontein
Lake Otjikoto
!Uris
La Rochelle
Ghaub
Ohange
Hoba Meteorite
Museum
Maria Bronn
Berg Aukas
Dornhuegel
Kombat
Rietfontein
Salzbrunn
Kamrav
Omega
Wabi PGR
Paradise
Roy's
Fiume
Maroelaboom
Otjituuo
Omatako
Coblenz
Omitjete
Okauwa
Otjindjumba
Okamatapati
Okaepe
Okoutjove
Otumborombonga
Ombu yOmenye
Otjjase
Omaihi
Ombu yOvakuru
Okahtwau
Okatjitundu
Omapumba
Ohamuheke
Ovitatu
Okombonde
Ozongarangombe
Okeserahi
Kozonduzu
Okatjavera
Okandjatu
Otjijere
Wildernis
Ouhave
Otjituuo
Okamatapati
Ozonahi
African Wild Dog
Tsumeb Attractions
Craft Market
Cultural Village
Museum
17/01:58 <-Ondangwa
<-Otavi 64/00:39
<-Otavi 91/01:00
58/00:38
Rundu -> 260/02:35
B1
B8
B14
B15
C42
C44
C22
M112
M73
M74
D3007
D3047
D3039
D3017
D2856
D2855
D2848
D2908
D2862
D2845
D2868
D2844
D2874
D3021
D3022
D2863
D2859
D2860
D2820
D2806
D2804
D2825
D2512
D2902
D2896
D2830
D2836
D2839
D3830
D3802
D3826
D3805
D3804
D3801
D3803
D2454
D2459
D2460
D3825
17°30'0"E
18°0'0"E
18°30'0"E
19°30'0"S
20°0'0"S
20°30'0"S
Restricted Roads
Tar (minor)
Off Road
Main Off Road
Riverboat Trail
Hiking/Walking Trail

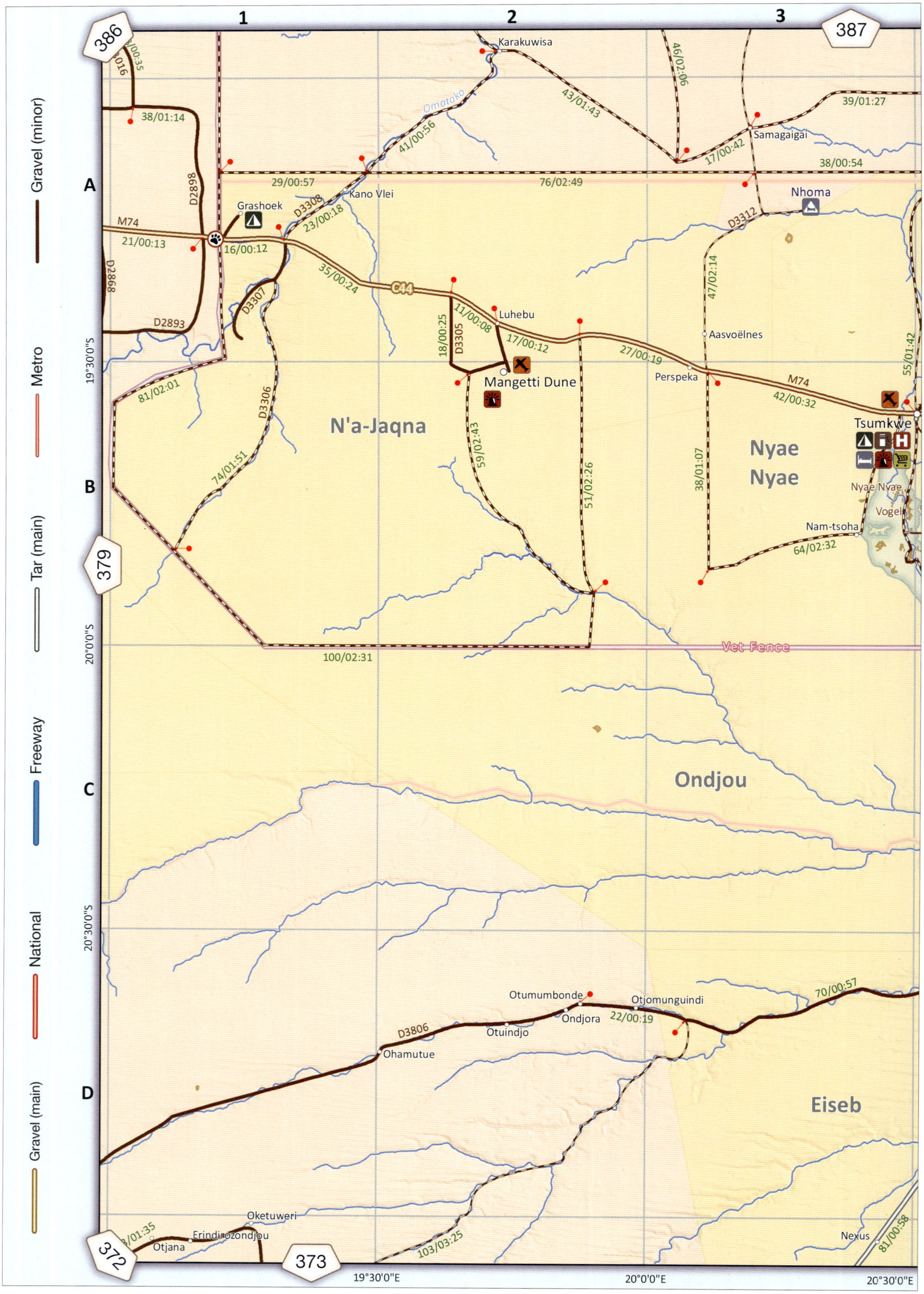

Safari Rental
Proudly rented by AVIS

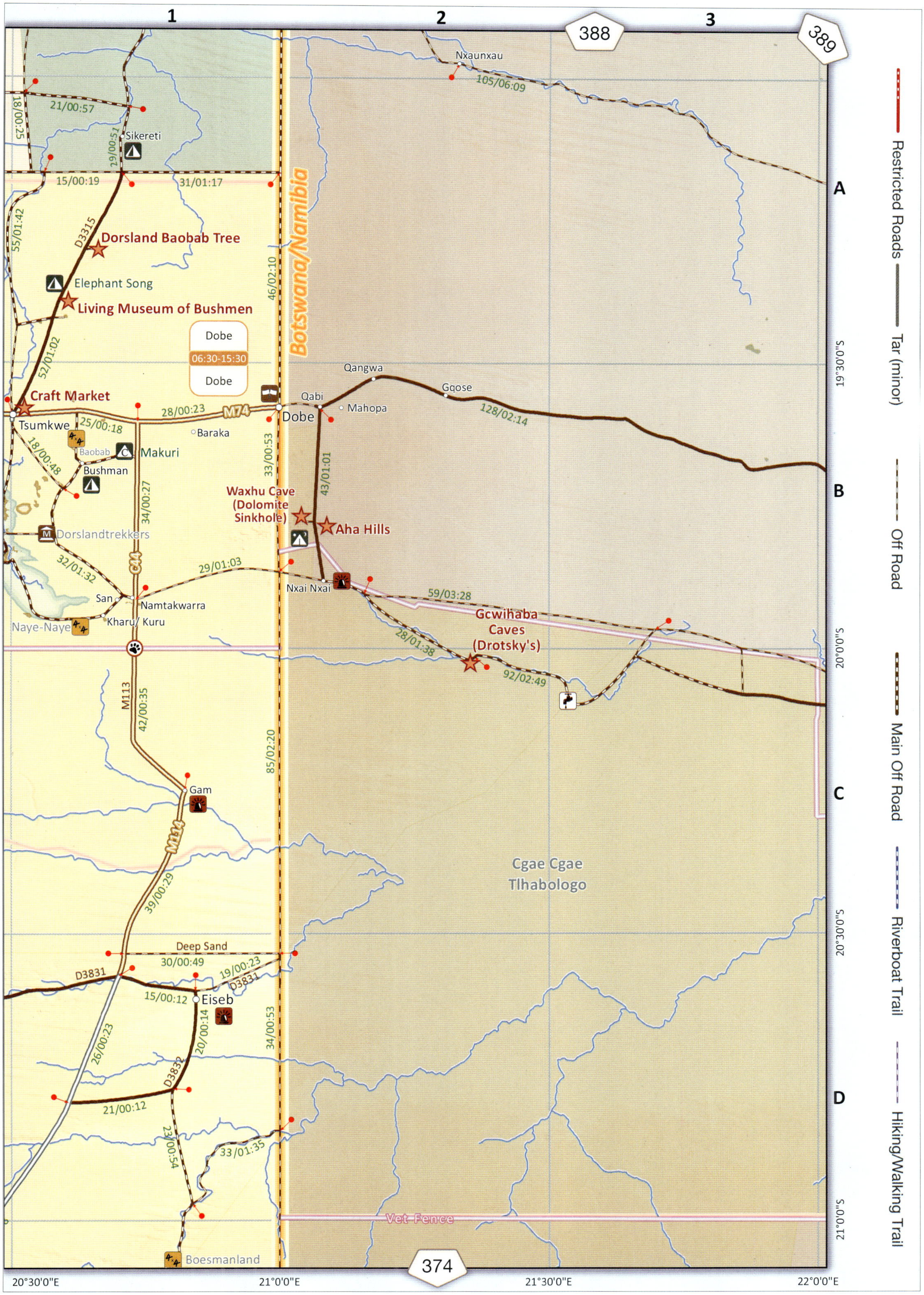
1
2
3
388
389
A
B
C
D
Nxaunxau
105/06:09
18/00:25
21/00:57
Sikereti
19/00:51
15/00:19
31/01:17
55/01:42
D3315
Dorsland Baobab Tree
Elephant Song
Living Museum of Bushmen
46/02:10
Botswana/Namibia
Dobe
06:30-15:30
Dobe
52/01:02
Craft Market
Tsumkwe
25/00:18
28/00:23
M74
Dobe
Qabi
Qangwa
Gqose
Mahopa
128/02:14
Baraka
18/00:48
Baobab
Makuri
Bushman
33/00:53
43/01:01
34/00:27
Waxhu Cave
(Dolomite
Sinkhole)
Aha Hills
Dorslandtrekkers
C44
32/01:32
29/01:03
Nxai Nxai
59/03:28
San
Namtakwarra
Kharu/ Kuru
Naye-Naye
Gcwihaba
Caves
(Drotsky's)
28/01:38
92/02:49
M113
42/00:35
85/02:20
Gam
M113
39/00:29
Cgae Cgae
Tlhabologo
Deep Sand
30/00:49
19/00:23
D3831
D3831
15/00:12
Eiseb
26/00:23
20/00:14
34/00:53
D3832
21/00:12
23/00:54
33/01:35
Vet Fence
Boesmanland
374
19°30'0"S
20°0'0"S
20°30'0"S
21°0'0"S
20°30'0"E
21°0'0"E
21°30'0"E
22°0'0"E
Restricted Roads
Tar (minor)
Off Road
Main Off Road
Riverboat Trail
Hiking/Walking Trail

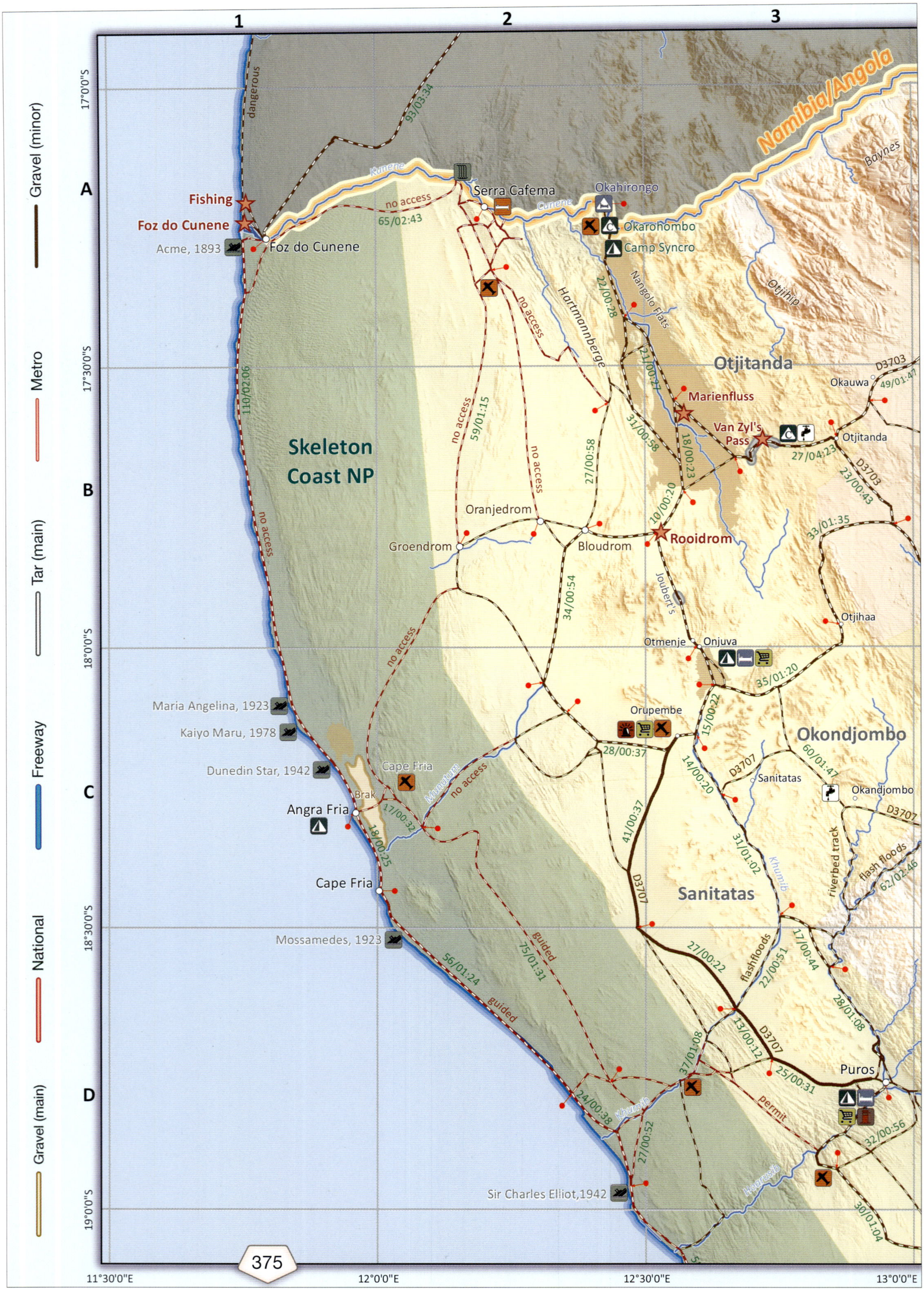

1
2
3
A
B
C
D
17°0'0"S
17°30'0"S
18°0'0"S
18°30'0"S
19°0'0"S
11°30'0"E
12°0'0"E
12°30'0"E
13°0'0"E
Gravel (minor)
Metro
Tar (main)
Freeway
National
Gravel (main)
Namibia/Angola
Kunene
Cunene
dangerous
93/03:34
Fishing
Foz do Cunene
Acme, 1893
Foz do Cunene
no access
65/02:43
Serra Cafema
Okahirongo
Okarohombo
Camp Syncro
Baynes
Otjihip
Nangolo Flats
22/00:28
Hartmannberge
no access
Otjitanda
D3703
Okauwa
49/01:47
Marienfluss
21/00:17
Van Zyl's Pass
Otjitanda
27/04:23
D3703
23/00:43
31/00:58
18/00:23
110/02:06
Skeleton Coast NP
no access
59/01:15
27/00:58
no access
Oranjedrom
Groendrom
Bloudrom
10/00:20
Rooidrom
33/01:35
no access
34/00:54
Joubert's
Otjihaa
Otmenje
Onjuva
no access
35/01:20
Maria Angelina, 1923
Kaiyo Maru, 1978
Dunedin Star, 1942
Orupembe
15/00:22
Okondjombo
28/00:37
Cape Fria
Brak
Angra Fria
Munutum
no access
17/00:32
18/00:25
D3707
Sanitatas
60/01:47
14/00:20
Okandjombo
D3707
41/00:37
riverbed track
flash floods
62/02:46
31/01:02
Khumib
Cape Fria
D3707
Sanitatas
Mossamedes, 1923
guided
75/01:31
56/01:24
guided
flashfloods
22/00:51
17/00:44
27/00:22
28/01:08
13/00:12
D3707
37/01:08
25/00:31
Puros
permit
24/00:38
Khumib
27/00:52
32/00:56
Hoarusib
Sir Charles Elliot, 1942
30/01:04
375

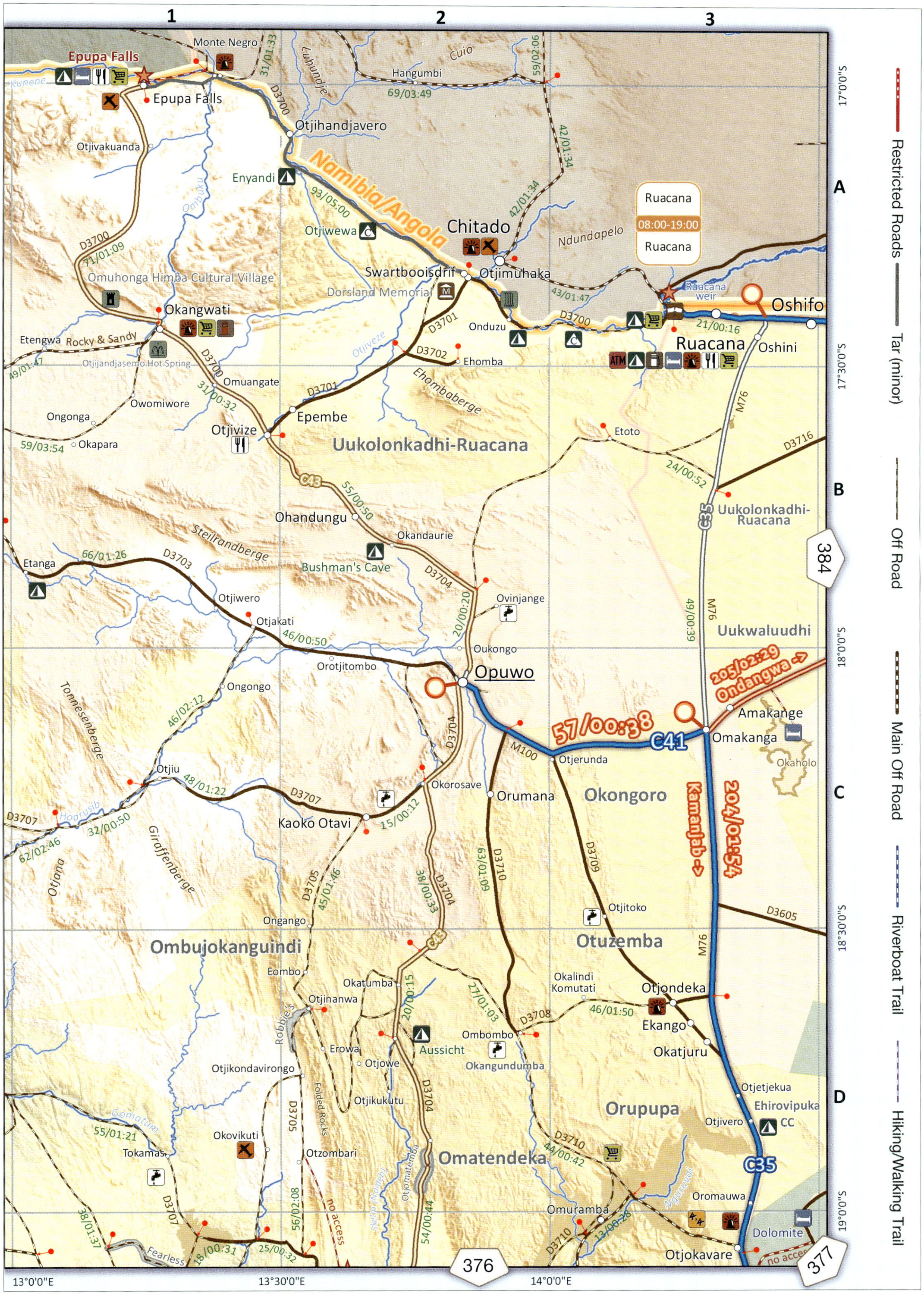
1
2
3
A
B
C
D
Epupa Falls
Monte Negro
Kunene
Epupa Falls
31/01:33
Luhundje
Cuio
Hangumbi
69/03:49
59/02:06
D3700
Otjihandjavero
Otjivakuanda
42/01:34
Enyandi
Omboku
Namibia/Angola
93/05:00
Ruacana
08:00-19:00
Ruacana
Otjiwewa
Chitado
42/01:34
Ndundapelo
D3700
71/01:09
Omuhonga Himba Cultural Village
Swartbooisdrif
Otjimuhaka
Dorsland Memorial
43/01:47
Ruacana weir
Oshifo
Okangwati
D3701
Onduzu
D3700
21/00:16
Etengwa
Rocky & Sandy
Ruacana
Oshini
49/01:47
Otjijandjasemo Hot Spring
Otjiveze
D3702
Ehomba
Omuangate
Ehombaberge
M76
Ongonga
Owomiwore
31/00:32
D3701
Epembe
Otjivize
Etoto
59/03:54
Okapara
Uukolonkadhi-Ruacana
D3716
C43
24/00:52
55/00:50
Uukolonkadhi-Ruacana
Ohandungu
C35
Steilrandberge
Okandaurie
Etanga
66/01:26
D3703
Bushman's Cave
384
D3704
Otjiwero
Ovinjange
49/00:39
M76
Otjakati
20/00:20
Uukwaluudhi
46/00:50
Oukongo
Orotjitombo
205/02:29
Ondangwa ->
Opuwo
Ongongo
Tonnesenberge
Amakange
57/00:38
46/02:12
Omakanga
C41
D3704
Okaholo
M100
Otjerunda
Otjiu
48/01:22
Kamanjab ->
204/01:54
Okorosave
D3707
D3707
Orumana
Okongoro
Hoarusib
Kaoko Otavi
32/00:50
15/00:12
62/02:46
Giraffenberge
D3709
Otjana
63/01:09
D3710
38/00:33
D3705
45/01:46
D3704
Otjitoko
D3605
Ongango
Otuzemba
M76
C43
Ombujokanguindi
Okalindi
Komutati
Eombo
Okatumba
Otjondeka
20/00:15
27/01:03
Otjinanwa
46/01:50
D3708
Ekango
Robbie's
Ombombo
Aussicht
Okatjuru
Erowa
Okangundumba
Otjowe
Otjikondavirongo
Otjetjekua
Ehirovipuka
Folded Rocks
D3705
Otjikukutu
D3704
Orupupa
CC
Otjivero
55/01:21
D3710
Okovikuti
44/00:42
Tokamas
Otzombari
Omatendeka
C35
D3707
Oromauwa
38/01:37
56/02:08
no access
54/00:44
Omuramba
Fearless
18/00:31
25/00:32
13/00:28
D3710
Dolomite
Otjokavare
no access
376
377
17°0'0"S
17°30'0"S
18°0'0"S
18°30'0"S
19°0'0"S
13°0'0"E
13°30'0"E
14°0'0"E
Restricted Roads
Tar (minor)
Off Road
Main Off Road
Riverboat Trail
Hiking/Walking Trail

Gravel (minor)
Metro
Tar (main)
Freeway
National
Gravel (main)
1
2
3
A
B
C
D
17°0'0"S
17°30'0"S
18°0'0"S
18°30'0"S
15°0'0"E
15°30'0"E
16°0'0"E
Dongoena
Tchipeke
Cunene
Cuamato
45/01:28
71/03:17
Ondjiva
35/00:51
Oshikango
08:00-19:00
Santa Clara
30/01:20
potholes
Namacunde
Naulila
Calueque
32/00:57
Calueque
08:00-19:00
Omahenene
17/00:30
20/00:28
15/00:21
Omahenene
Namibia/Angola
Ruacana
168/03:23
Santa Clara
Oshikango
Oshifo
Mahenene
Epalele
Okalongo
D3608
Okambembe
Ongenga
Ohaingu
Omafo
Epoko
Outapi
Ombalantu Baobab Tree
Olushandja
D3616
Omungwelume
Onuno
Onesi
30/00:48
191/02:27
Okando
D3611
44/00:54
D3609
39/00:26
Cuvelai
D3716
29/00:36
Lilyateko
M123
Ketu-Kuyela
Omagalanga
Endola
Onekwaya
Epalala
Oshikuku
Omulamba
D3638
Ogongo
Onamutayi
B
Ongulumbashe
D3633
Tsandi
M123
D3648
25/00:30
D3615
19/00:11
C46
Ekamba
63/00:46
383
Onamandongo
Oluteyi
Oshakati
C41
Okahao
D3619
Omege
D3614
D3607
M122
Sha Nkango
D3635
D3626
Etilyasa
Onaanda
Ompundja
Ondangwa
Amwaanda
D3605
205/02:29
Omakanga
Uukwiyuushona
Oponono
33/00:59
Lake Oponono
Lake Oponono Wetlands
Sheya Shuushona
Otjivalunda Salt #1
Natukanaoka
Otjivalunda Salt #2
Etosha NP
Olifantsrus
Okondeka Fountain
376
377

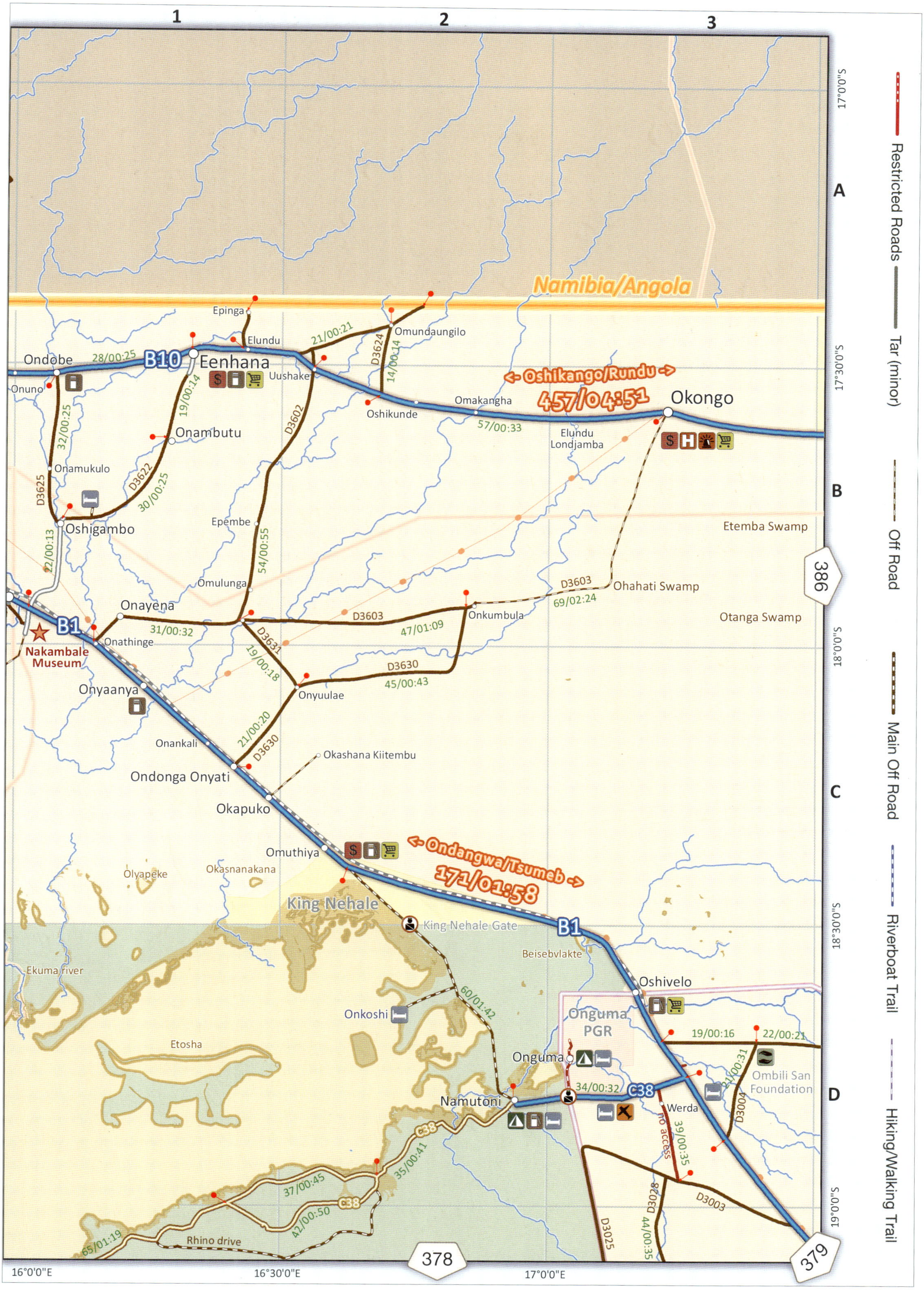

1
2
3
A
B
C
D
17°0.0"S
17°30'0.0"S
18°0.0"S
18°30'0.0"S
19°0.0"S
16°0'0"E
16°30'0"E
17°0'0"E
Namibia/Angola
Epinga
Elundu
Omundaungilo
21/00:21
Ondobe
28/00:25
B10
Eenhana
Uushake
Onuno
D3624
14/00:14
Oshikunde
Omakangha
<- Oshikango/Rundu ->
457/04:51
Okongo
57/00:33
Elundu
Londjamba
19/00:14
Onambutu
D3602
32/00:25
Onamukulo
D3622
30/00:25
D3625
Oshigambo
Epembe
Etemba Swamp
386
22/00:13
54/00:55
Omulunga
D3603
Ohahati Swamp
69/02:24
Onayena
D3603
Onkumbula
Otanga Swamp
B1
31/00:32
47/01:09
Nakambale Museum
Onathinge
D3631
19/00:18
D3630
45/00:43
Onyaanya
Onyuulae
21/00:20
D3630
Onankali
Okashana Kiitembu
Ondonga Onyati
Okapuko
Omuthiya
<- Ondangwa/Tsumeb ->
171/01:58
Olyapeke
Okasnanakana
King Nehale
King Nehale Gate
B1
Beisebvlakte
Ekuma river
Oshivelo
Onkoshi
60/01:42
Onguma PGR
19/00:16
22/00:21
Etosha
Onguma
21/00:31
Ombili San Foundation
34/00:32
C38
Namutoni
Werda
no access
39/00:35
D3004
C38
35/00:41
37/00:45
C38
42/00:50
D3028
D3003
65/01:19
Rhino drive
D3025
44/00:35
378
379
Restricted Roads
Tar (minor)
Off Road
Main Off Road
Riverboat Trail
Hiking/Walking Trail

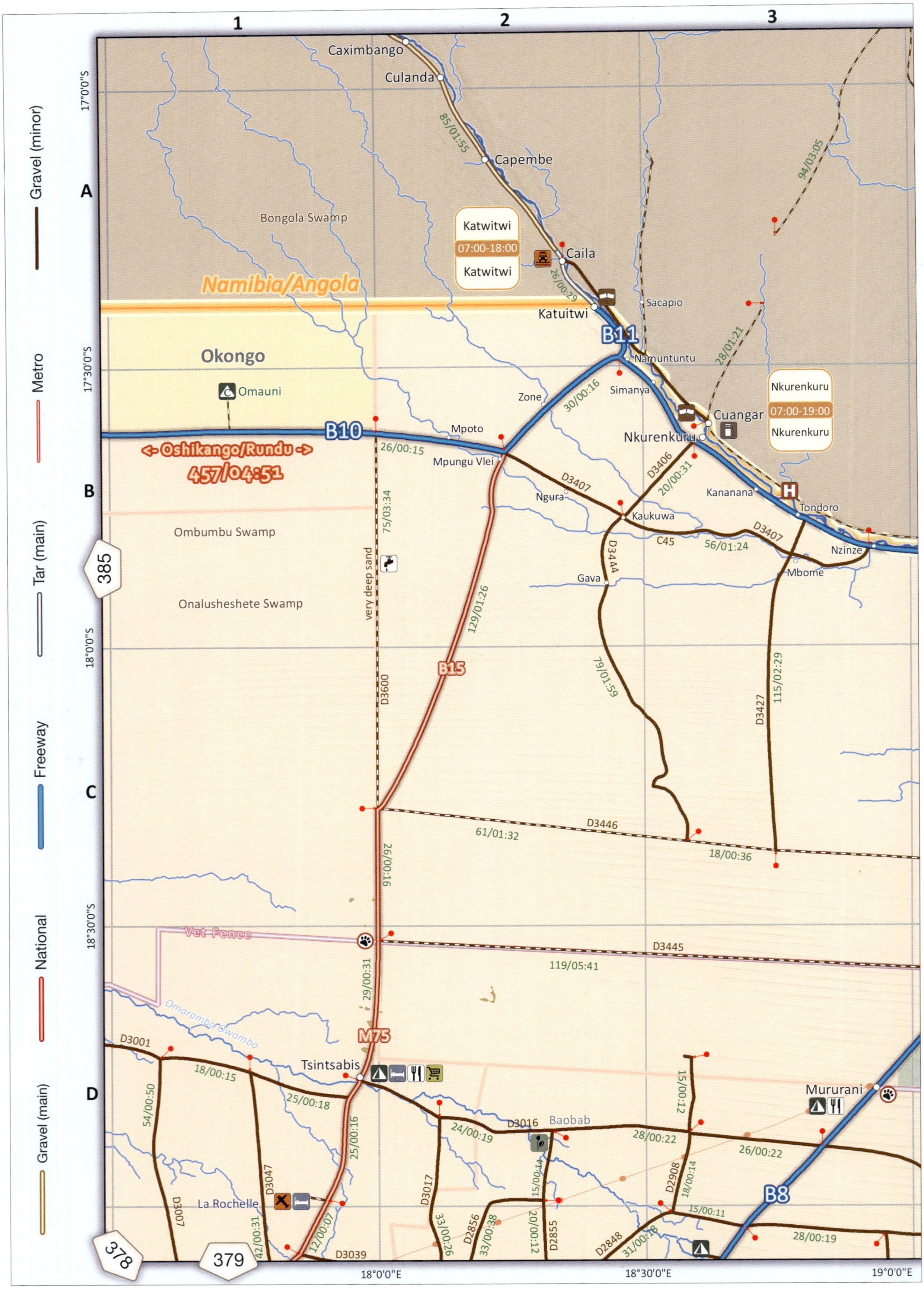

1
2
3
A
B
C
D
Gravel (minor)
Metro
Tar (main)
Freeway
National
Gravel (main)
17°0'0"S
17°30'0"S
18°0'0"S
18°30'0"S
18°0'0"E
18°30'0"E
19°0'0"E
Caximbango
Culanda
85/01:55
Capembe
Bongola Swamp
Katwitwi
07:00-18:00
Katwitwi
Caila
26/00:29
Namibia/Angola
Katuitwi
Sacapio
94/03:05
B11
Namuntuntu
28/01:21
Okongo
Omauni
Zone
30/00:16
Simanya
Nkurenkuru
07:00-19:00
Nkurenkuru
Cuangar
Nkurenkuru
B10
Mpoto
26/00:15
Mpungu Vlei
<- Oshikango/Rundu ->
457/04:51
D3407
D3406
20/00:31
Kananana
Ngura
Tondoro
Kaukuwa
D3407
C45
56/01:24
Nzinze
Ombumbu Swamp
75/03:34
385
D3444
Mbome
Gava
very deep sand
129/01:26
Onalusheshete Swamp
79/01:59
B15
D3600
D3427
115/02:29
D3446
61/01:32
18/00:36
26/00:16
Vet Fence
D3445
119/05:41
29/00:31
Omarambo Owambo
M75
D3001
18/00:15
Tsintsabis
15/00:12
Mururani
54/00:50
25/00:18
D3016
Baobab
24/00:19
28/00:22
26/00:22
25/00:16
D3047
D3017
D2908
18/00:14
15/00:14
B8
La Rochelle
D3007
15/00:11
12/00:07
33/00:26
D2856
33/00:38
20/00:12
D2855
D2848
31/00:18
28/00:19
42/00:31
378
379
D3039

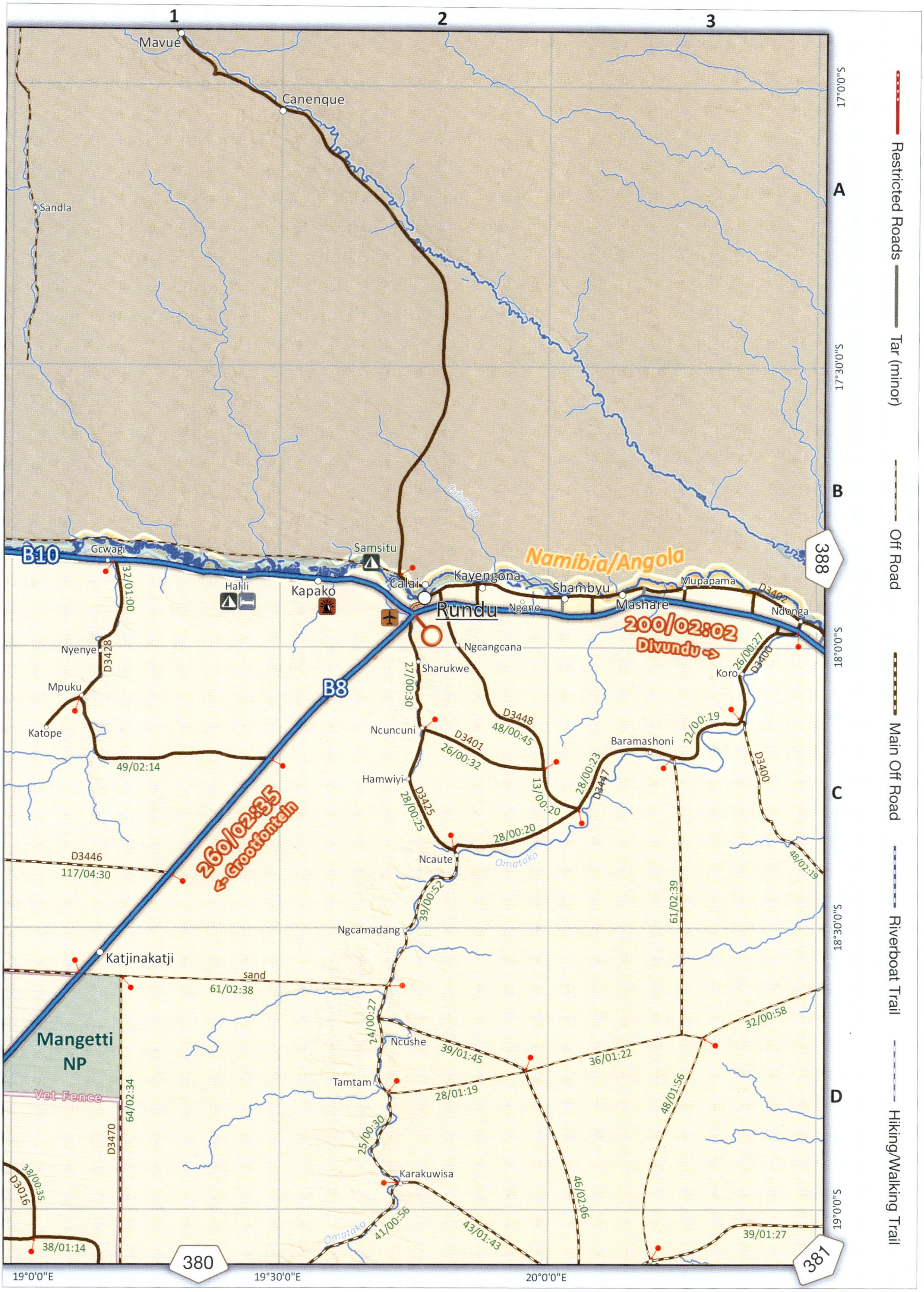

1
2
3
A
B
C
D
17°0'0"S
17°30'0"S
18°0'0"S
18°30'0"S
19°0'0"S
19°0'0"E
19°30'0"E
20°0'0"E
Mavué
Canenque
Sandla
Cubango
Namibia/Angola
B10
Gcwagi
Samsitu
Halili
Kapako
Calai
Kayengona
Rundu
Ngone
Shambyu
Mashare
Mupapama
D3402
Ndonga
200/02:02
Divundu ->
32/01:00
Nyenye
D3428
Mpuku
Katope
49/02:14
B8
Ngcangcana
Sharukwe
27/00:30
Koro
26/00:27
D3400
D3448
48/00:45
Ncuncuni
D3401
26/00:32
Baramashoni
22/00:19
Hamwiyi
D3425
28/00:25
13/00:20
28/00:23
D3447
28/00:20
Ncaute
Omatako
48/02:19
D3446
117/04:30
260/02:35
<- Grootfontein
39/00:52
61/02:39
Ngcamadang
Katjinakatji
sand
61/02:38
24/00:27
Ncushe
39/01:45
36/01:22
32/00:58
Mangetti NP
Vet Fence
Tamtam
28/01:19
48/01:56
64/02:34
D3470
25/00:30
38/00:35
D3016
Karakuwisa
46/02:06
41/00:56
43/01:43
39/01:27
38/01:14
388
380
381
Restricted Roads
Tar (minor)
Off Road
Main Off Road
Riverboat Trail
Hiking/Walking Trail

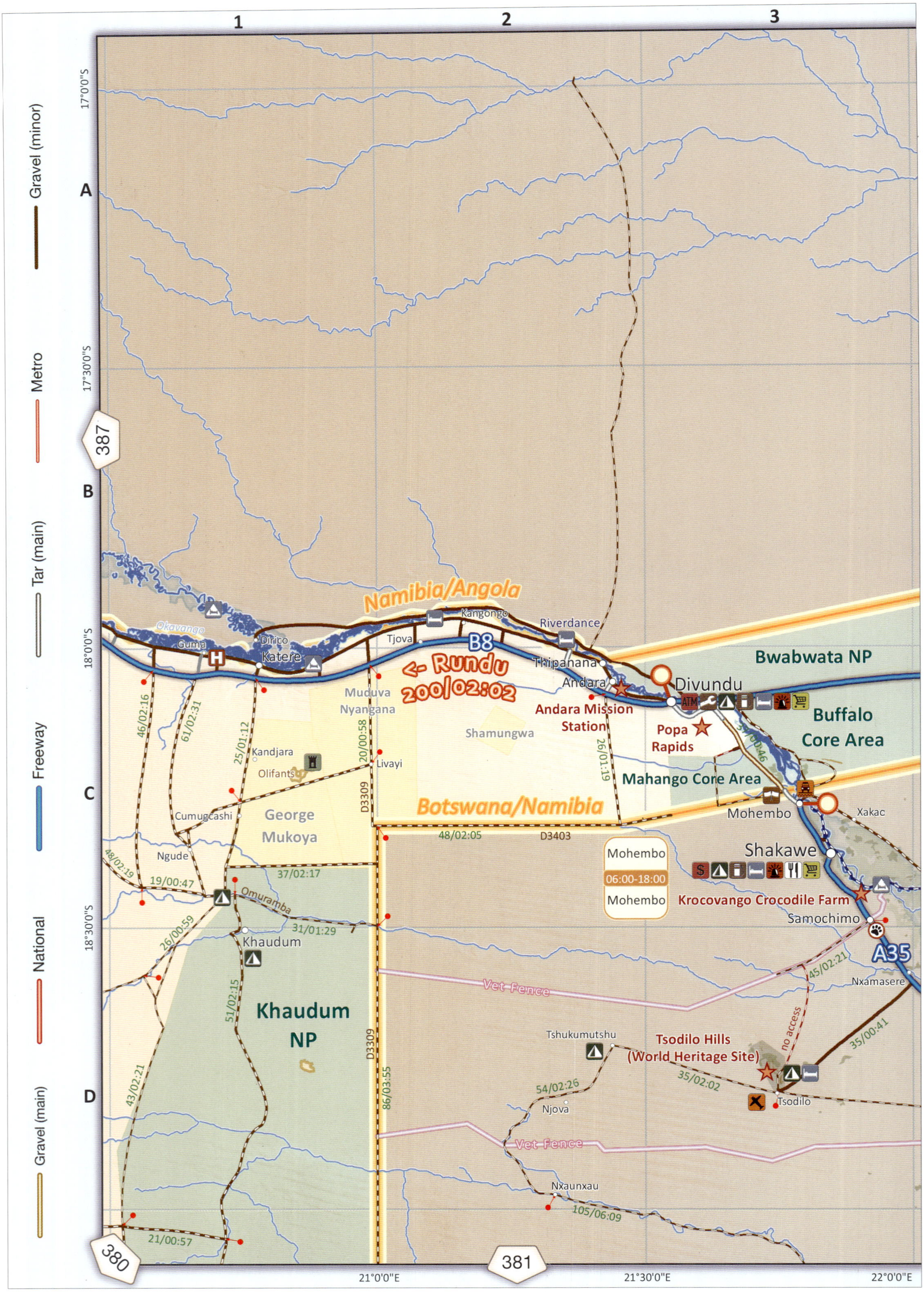
Gravel (minor)
Metro
Tar (main)
Freeway
National
Gravel (main)
1
2
3
A
B
C
D
17°0'0"S
17°30'0"S
18°0'0"S
18°30'0"S
21°0'0"E
21°30'0"E
22°0'0"E
387
380
381
Namibia/Angola
Botswana/Namibia
Okavango
Guma
Dirico
Katere
Tjova
Kangongo
Riverdance
Thipanana
Andara
Divundu
B8
<- Rundu 200/02:02
Bwabwata NP
Buffalo Core Area
Andara Mission Station
Popa Rapids
Mahango Core Area
Muduva Nyangana
Shamungwa
Kandjara
Olifants
Livayi
Cumugcashi
George Mukoya
Ngude
Mohembo
Xakac
Shakawe
Mohembo
06:00-18:00
Mohembo
Krocovango Crocodile Farm
Samochimo
A35
Nxamasere
Omuramba
Khaudum
Khaudum NP
Vet Fence
Tshukumutshu
Tsodilo Hills (World Heritage Site)
no access
Tsodilo
Njova
Nxaunxau
D3309
D3403
46/02:16
61/02:31
25/01:12
20/00:58
26/01:19
48/02:05
37/02:17
48/02:19
19/00:47
31/01:29
26/00:59
51/02:15
43/02:21
86/03:55
21/00:57
45/02:21
35/00:41
54/02:26
35/02:02
105/06:09

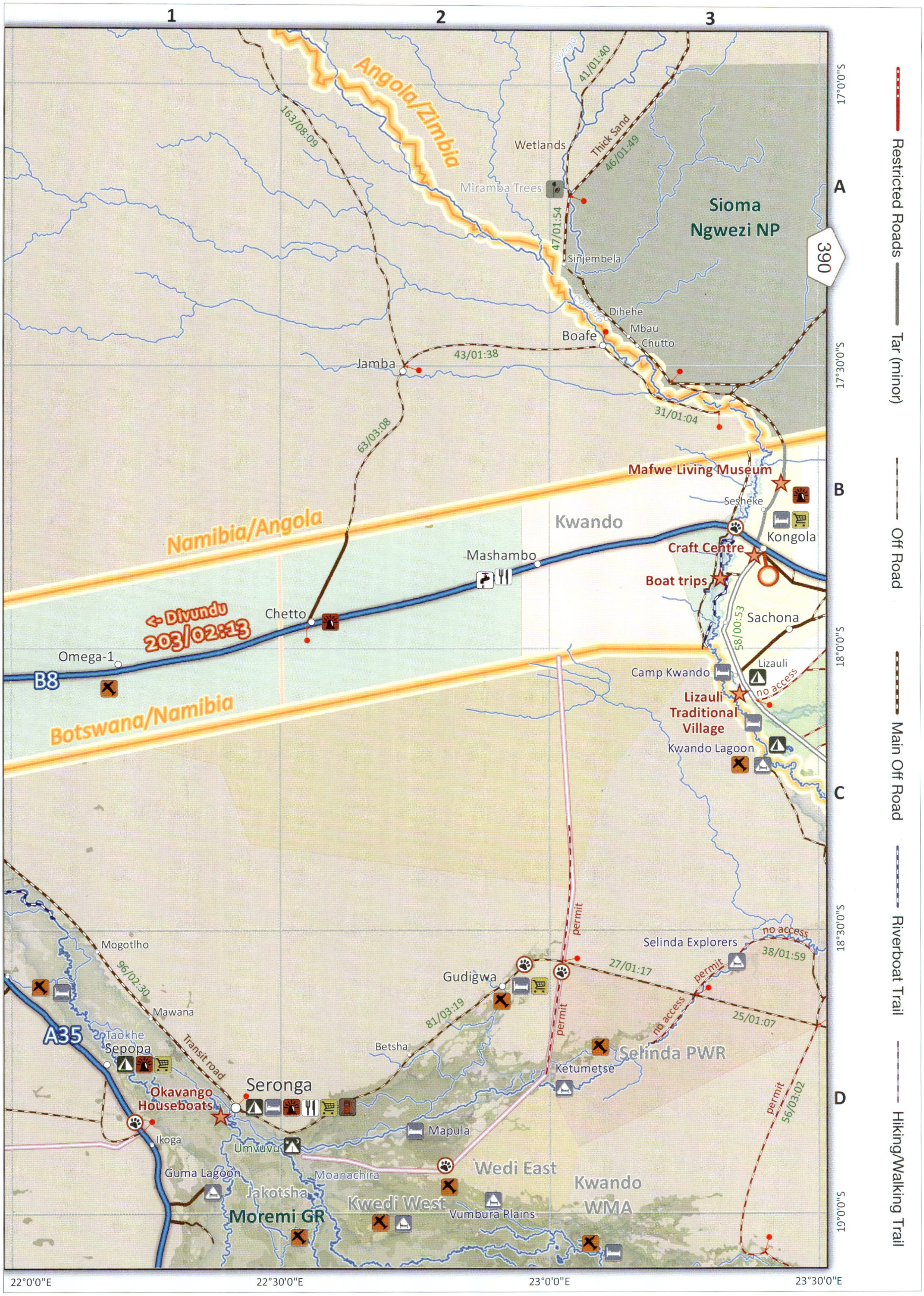
1
2
3
A
B
C
D
390
Angola/Zimbia
163/08:09
Wetlands
Thick Sand
46/01:49
41/01:40
Miramba Trees
47/01:54
Sinjembela
Sioma Ngwezi NP
Dihehe
Mbau
Chutto
Boafe
43/01:38
Jamba
63/03:08
31/01:04
Mafwe Living Museum
Sesheke
Kongola
Kwando
Mashambo
Craft Centre
Boat trips
Namibia/Angola
Chetto
<- Divundu
203/02:13
Sachona
58/00:53
Omega-1
B8
Camp Kwando
Lizauli
no access
Lizauli Traditional Village
Kwando Lagoon
Botswana/Namibia
permit
Mogotlho
96/02:30
Mawana
Transit road
A35
Taokhe
Sepopa
Okavango Houseboats
Ikoga
Seronga
Gudigwa
81/03:19
Betsha
Selinda Explorers
no access
38/01:59
27/01:17
25/01:07
Selinda PWR
Ketumetse
permit
56/03:02
Mapula
Umvuvu
Moanachira
Guma Lagoon
Jakotsha
Moremi GR
Wedi East
Kwedi West
Vumbura Plains
Kwando WMA
17°0'0"S
17°30'0"S
18°0'0"S
18°30'0"S
19°0'0"S
22°0'0"E
22°30'0"E
23°0'0"E
23°30'0"E
Restricted Roads
Tar (minor)
Off Road
Main Off Road
Riverboat Trail
Hiking/Walking Trail

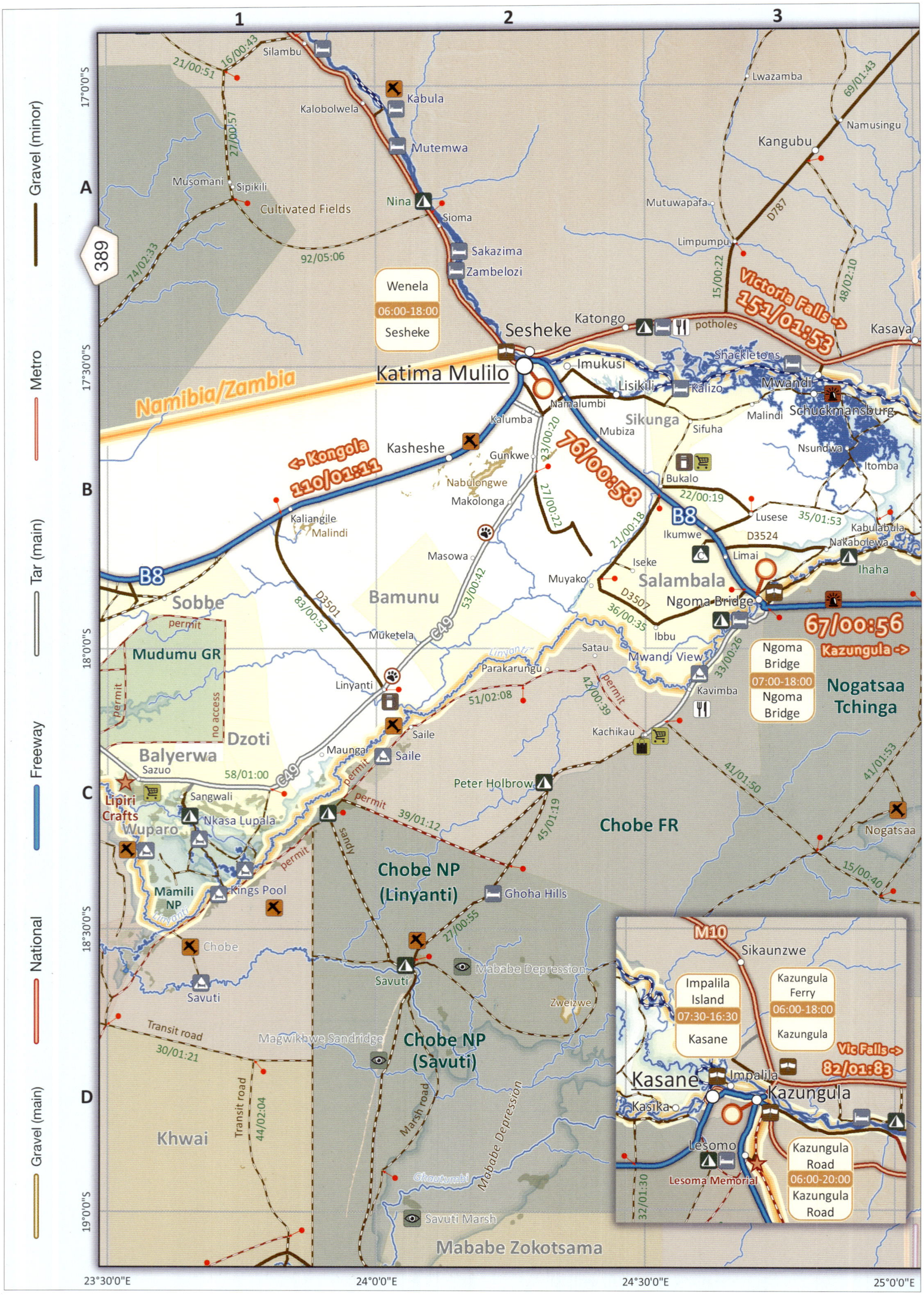
Gravel (minor)
Metro
Tar (main)
Freeway
National
Gravel (main)
1
2
3
A
B
C
D
389
17°0'0"S
17°30'0"S
18°0'0"S
18°30'0"S
19°0'0"S
23°30'0"E
24°0'0"E
24°30'0"E
25°0'0"E
Silambu
21/00:51
16/00:43
Kabula
Kalobolwela
Mutemwa
27/00:57
Musomani
Sipikili
Cultivated Fields
Nina
Sioma
92/05:06
74/02:33
Sakazima
Zambelozi
Wenela
06:00-18:00
Sesheke
Katongo
potholes
Lwazamba
69/01:43
Namusingu
Kangubu
Mutuwapafa
D787
Limpumpu
15/00:22
48/02:10
Victoria Falls ->
151/01:53
Kasaya
Namibia/Zambia
Katima Mulilo
Imukusi
Shackletons
Lisikili
Kalizo
Mwandi
Namalumbi
Schuckmansburg
Kalumba
Sikunga
Malindi
Mubiza
Sifuha
Nsundwa
Kasheshe
Gunkwe
23/00:20
76/00:58
Itomba
<- Kongola
110/01:11
Nabulongwe
Makolonga
27/00:22
Bukalo
22/00:19
B8
Lusese
35/01:53
Kabulabula
Kaliangile
Malindi
21/00:18
Ikumwe
D3524
Nakabolelwa
Masowa
Limai
Ihaha
Iseke
B8
Sobbe
Bamunu
Muyako
Salambala
D3501
53/00:42
D3507
Ngoma Bridge
permit
83/00:52
36/00:35
67/00:56
Kazungula ->
Mudumu GR
Muketela
C49
Ibbu
Satau
Mwandi View
Linyanti
Parakarungu
33/00:26
Ngoma Bridge
07:00-18:00
Ngoma Bridge
Nogatsaa Tchinga
permit
Linyanti
51/02:08
42/00:39
permit
Kavimba
no access
Dzoti
Saile
Kachikau
Balyerwa
Maunga
Saile
Sazuo
58/01:00
C49
permit
41/01:50
41/01:53
Lipiri Crafts
Sangwali
Peter Holbrow
permit
Nkasa Lupala
39/01:12
Chobe FR
Wuparo
sandy
45/01:19
Nogatsaa
permit
Chobe NP (Linyanti)
15/00:40
Mamili NP
Kings Pool
Ghoha Hills
Linyanti
M10
Sikaunzwe
Chobe
27/00:55
Impalila Island
07:30-16:30
Kasane
Kazungula Ferry
06:00-18:00
Kazungula
Savuti
Mababe Depression
Savuti
Zweizwe
Vic Falls ->
82/01:83
Transit road
30/01:21
Magwikhwe Sandridge
Chobe NP (Savuti)
Kasane
Impalila
Kazungula
Kasika
Transit road
44/02:04
Marsh road
Mababe Depression
Khwai
Lesomo
Kazungula Road
06:00-20:00
Kazungula Road
Ghoutumbi
Lesoma Memorial
32/01:30
Savuti Marsh
Mababe Zokotsama

(photo: Chris Davies)

INDEX

INDEX continued

INDEX continued

NAMIBIA TRAVEL-TIME & DISTANCE TABLE

Distance in km; Travel time in hr:min	Aranos	Aus	Betta	Buitepos	Epupa Falls	Gobabis	Grootfontein	Grünau	Helmeringhausen	Henties Bay	Karasburg	Karibib	Katima Mulilo	Keetmanshoop	Khorixas	Koës	Leonardville	Lüderitz	Maltahohe	Mariental	Okaukuejo	Omaruru	Opuwo	Oranjemund	Oshakati	Oshikango	Otavi	Otjiwarongo	Outjo	Palmwag	Puros	Rehoboth	Ruacana	Rundu	Seeheim	Sesriem	Solitaire	Stampriet	Swakopmund	Torra bay	Tsumeb	Uis	Vioolsdrift	Windhoek
Aranos		500	352	329	1231	220	614	531	391	679	582	506	1381	372	733	309	90	623	253	143	754	530	1053	766	955	981	687	570	638	845	1058	299	1081	872	417	419	418	80	683	916	674	651	673	322
Aus	05:28		204	776	1470	667	1017	298	109	738	350	744	1785	214	971	339	540	124	248	363	993	769	1292	270	1270	1297	926	808	876	1083	1296	468	1319	1276	168	376	410	420	672	975	989	890	325	556
Betta	03:44	02:49		628	1322	519	869	428	124	555	480	597	1637	344	823	443	392	328	100	215	845	621	1144	471	1122	1149	778	660	728	936	1149	320	1171	1128	298	137	226	272	489	792	841	742	570	408
Buitepos	03:34	08:43	06:59		1145	109	493	825	667	671	875	498	1260	665	686	602	240	899	529	437	668	522	967	1042	833	860	559	484	552	828	1041	401	995	751	711	616	533	374	674	908	552	643	967	314
Epupa Falls	14:18	17:05	15:20	13:39		1036	743	1567	1360	767	1617	819	1411	1407	545	1407	1150	1593	1222	1179	616	753	178	1736	402	466	780	663	592	409	431	1001	227	902	1453	1211	1129	1220	836	555	687	646	1709	910
Gobabis	02:27	07:37	05:53	01:06	12:34		394	716	558	561	766	388	1161	556	576	493	132	791	420	328	559	413	858	933	735	761	461	375	443	719	932	292	885	652	602	506	424	265	565	798	454	534	858	205
Grootfontein	07:19	11:01	09:16	05:45	09:47	04:51		1115	908	583	1165	410	768	955	412	954	526	1140	770	726	394	345	565	1283	340	367	91	209	278	554	767	549	505	259	1000	759	676	767	587	630	60	466	1257	457
Grünau	05:15	03:19	05:03	08:41	17:30	07:35	11:26		304	1015	52	842	1883	161	1069	287	584	421	496	389	1090	866	1389	328	1368	1394	1024	906	974	1181	1394	566	1417	1374	129	571	659	451	1019	1252	1087	988	142	654
Helmeringhausen	04:04	01:24	01:28	07:19	15:40	06:13	09:36	03:34		629	356	635	1676	220	862	286	431	233	139	253	883	659	1182	376	1161	1187	817	699	767	974	1187	359	1210	1167	175	267	301	310	563	866	880	781	446	447
Henties Bay	07:24	09:03	07:08	07:22	09:51	06:17	06:16	10:36	07:38		1065	173	1351	855	238	855	597	861	491	627	436	238	589	1004	700	765	492	374	354	366	579	449	616	842	901	411	329	667	71	240	555	123	1157	358
Karasburg	05:46	03:50	05:34	09:12	18:01	08:06	11:57	00:31	04:05	11:07		892	1933	212	1119	337	635	473	546	439	1141	917	1440	367	1418	1445	1074	956	1024	1231	1444	616	1467	1424	181	622	709	501	1069	1302	1137	1038	147	704
Karibib	05:22	08:09	06:24	05:19	09:51	04:15	04:13	08:34	06:44	02:02	09:05		1178	682	268	682	425	868	497	454	342	65	641	1011	663	690	319	201	225	380	593	276	668	669	728	372	289	495	177	410	382	187	984	185
Katima Mulilo	15:33	19:18	17:33	14:00	16:20	13:05	08:16	19:43	17:53	14:32	20:14	12:30		1723	1180	1722	1293	1908	1538	1494	1162	1113	1233	2051	1000	956	859	977	1046	1322	1486	1317	1123	513	1768	1527	1444	1426	1355	1398	824	1234	2025	1225
Keetmanshoop	03:43	02:12	03:56	07:09	15:58	06:02	09:54	01:36	02:27	09:04	02:07	07:02	18:11		909	127	425	337	336	229	930	707	1230	480	1208	1235	864	746	814	1021	1234	406	1257	1214	47	486	499	291	859	1092	927	828	303	494
Khorixas	08:15	11:02	09:17	07:39	06:59	06:35	04:24	11:28	09:38	03:03	11:58	03:18	12:41	09:55		909	651	1095	724	681	215	203	367	1237	479	543	321	203	132	162	375	503	395	671	955	647	564	721	307	218	384	118	1211	412
Koës	03:31	03:36	04:51	06:57	16:06	05:51	10:02	03:00	03:38	09:12	03:31	07:10	18:19	01:28	10:03		362	463	343	228	930	706	1229	606	1208	1234	863	746	814	1021	1234	405	1257	1214	172	510	506	231	859	1092	927	827	429	494
Leonardville	01:02	06:06	04:22	02:41	13:25	01:35	06:26	05:59	04:42	06:31	06:30	04:29	14:41	04:27	07:22	04:15		663	293	196	673	449	972	806	866	893	606	488	556	764	977	210	999	784	470	459	394	134	601	834	585	570	726	241
Lüderitz	06:45	01:19	04:06	10:00	18:22	08:54	12:18	04:35	02:41	10:19	05:07	09:25	20:34	03:29	12:19	04:53	07:23		371	486	1116	892	1415	273	1394	1420	1049	932	1000	1207	1420	591	1443	1400	292	500	533	543	796	1098	1113	1013	450	680
Maltahohe	02:35	02:54	01:09	05:51	14:12	04:44	08:08	05:02	01:29	06:11	05:33	05:16	16:25	03:29	08:09	03:43	03:14	04:10		115	745	521	1044	514	1023	1049	679	561	629	836	1049	221	1072	1029	313	167	163	172	426	728	742	643	638	309
Mariental	01:23	04:07	02:23	04:49	13:38	03:42	07:34	03:53	02:43	06:44	04:24	04:42	15:51	02:21	07:35	02:28	02:07	05:24	01:15		702	478	1001	629	980	1006	635	518	586	793	1006	177	1029	986	274	282	278	63	631	864	699	599	531	266
Okaukuejo	08:10	10:57	09:12	07:30	08:02	06:26	04:15	11:22	09:32	05:27	11:53	03:43	12:32	09:50	02:35	09:58	07:17	12:13	08:04	07:30		276	439	1259	314	341	303	186	115	299	512	524	466	654	976	734	652	743	518	432	245	316	1232	433
Omaruru	05:40	08:27	06:42	05:38	09:08	04:33	03:30	08:53	07:03	02:45	09:23	00:43	11:47	07:20	02:34	07:28	04:47	09:44	05:34	05:00	03:00		576	1035	598	625	254	136	160	315	528	301	603	604	752	438	355	519	242	370	317	121	1008	209
Opuwo	11:26	14:13	12:29	10:47	02:51	09:43	06:56	14:39	12:49	07:00	15:09	06:59	13:28	13:06	04:08	13:15	10:33	15:30	11:20	10:46	05:10	06:17		1558	225	289	603	485	414	231	253	824	139	724	1275	1034	951	1042	658	377	509	469	1531	732
Oranjemund	08:28	03:04	05:49	11:43	20:05	10:37	14:01	04:24	04:24	12:03	04:43	11:09	22:18	05:12	14:02	06:36	09:06	03:15	05:54	07:07	13:57	11:27	17:13		1536	1563	1192	1074	1143	1350	1563	734	1585	1542	435	642	676	686	938	1241	1255	1156	239	822
Oshakati	11:29	14:17	12:33	09:56	05:37	09:02	04:10	14:43	12:53	08:30	15:13	07:30	10:52	13:10	05:38	13:19	10:37	15:34	11:24	10:50	05:23	06:47	02:45	17:17		75	344	462	525	456	477	802	165	492	1253	1012	929	1020	769	625	285	580	1510	711
Oshikango	11:53	14:41	12:56	10:19	06:12	09:25	04:34	15:06	13:16	09:05	15:37	07:53	10:23	13:34	06:13	13:42	11:00	15:58	11:48	11:14	05:46	07:10	03:20	17:41	00:54		371	489	558	520	542	829	179	447	1280	1039	956	1047	867	689	311	644	1536	737
Otavi	07:19	10:05	08:21	06:22	09:28	05:27	00:55	10:31	08:41	05:20	11:02	03:18	09:12	08:58	03:29	09:07	06:26	11:22	07:12	06:38	03:20	02:35	06:36	13:05	04:11	04:35		118	187	463	676	458	509	350	909	668	585	676	496	539	63	375	1166	366
Otjiwarongo	06:06	08:52	07:08	05:26	08:15	04:22	02:09	09:18	07:28	04:07	09:49	02:05	10:26	07:45	02:16	07:54	05:13	10:09	05:59	05:25	02:07	01:22	05:23	11:52	05:25	05:49	01:13		70	346	559	340	512	468	792	550	467	558	378	421	181	257	1048	249
Outjo	06:50	09:37	07:52	06:11	07:28	05:06	02:56	10:02	08:12	04:20	10:33	02:23	11:12	08:30	01:29	08:38	05:57	10:54	06:44	06:10	01:20	01:40	04:36	12:37	06:07	06:35	02:00	00:47		274	487	408	441	537	860	618	535	626	402	350	250	234	1116	317
Palmwag	10:03	12:49	11:05	09:37	06:03	08:32	06:21	13:15	11:25	04:30	13:46	05:05	14:38	11:42	02:23	11:51	09:10	14:06	09:57	09:22	04:00	04:22	03:11	15:49	05:57	06:32	05:26	04:13	03:26		213	615	371	813	1067	775	692	834	435	146	526	230	1323	524
Puros	13:53	16:39	14:55	13:27	07:19	12:22	10:11	17:05	15:15	08:20	17:36	08:55	17:56	15:32	06:13	15:41	13:00	17:56	13:47	13:12	07:50	08:12	04:27	19:39	07:13	07:48	09:16	08:03	07:16	03:49		828	392	977	1280	988	905	1047	648	359	739	443	1536	737
Rehoboth	02:54	05:14	03:29	04:16	11:50	03:12	05:46	05:39	03:50	04:56	06:10	02:54	14:03	04:07	05:48	04:15	02:35	06:31	02:21	01:47	05:42	03:13	08:59	08:14	09:03	09:26	04:51	03:38	04:22	07:35	11:25		851	808	451	242	159	218	453	686	521	422	708	88
Ruacana	11:53	14:39	12:55	11:13	04:06	10:09	06:07	15:05	13:15	07:26	15:36	07:26	12:27	13:33	04:34	13:41	11:00	15:56	11:47	11:13	05:37	06:43	01:40	17:39	01:57	02:19	06:09	05:50	05:02	04:52	06:08	09:25		615	1302	1061	978	1069	685	541	450	496	1559	760
Rundu	10:06	13:50	12:06	08:33	10:53	07:38	02:49	14:16	12:26	09:05	14:47	07:03	05:35	12:44	07:14	12:52	09:13	15:07	10:58	10:24	07:05	06:20	08:01	16:50	05:25	04:56	03:45	04:58	05:45	09:11	12:29	08:36	07:00		1259	1018	935	918	846	889	315	725	1516	717
Seeheim	04:10	01:44	03:28	07:36	16:25	06:30	10:21	01:36	01:59	09:31	02:07	07:29	18:38	00:31	10:22	01:55	04:54	03:01	03:29	02:48	10:17	07:47	13:33	04:44	13:38	14:01	09:26	08:13	08:57	12:10	16:00	04:34	14:00	13:11		441	475	337	737	1138	973	873	271	540
Sesriem	04:36	04:27	01:54	07:28	14:57	06:23	08:53	06:37	03:02	05:18	07:08	05:09	17:09	05:30	08:18	05:43	05:14	05:44	02:01	03:15	08:49	05:52	12:05	07:27	12:09	12:33	07:57	06:44	07:29	09:46	13:36	03:28	12:31	11:42	05:02		83	339	346	648	731	532	713	303
Solitaire	04:30	04:48	02:53	06:24	13:53	05:19	07:49	06:58	03:24	04:15	07:29	04:06	16:06	05:26	07:15	05:39	04:29	06:05	01:57	03:11	07:45	04:49	11:01	07:48	11:05	11:29	06:54	05:41	06:25	08:42	12:32	02:24	11:28	10:39	05:24	01:03		338	263	566	648	449	801	220
Stampriet	00:45	04:43	02:58	04:11	14:00	03:05	07:56	04:30	03:18	07:06	05:00	05:03	16:10	02:57	07:57	02:49	01:29	05:59	01:50	00:37	07:51	05:22	11:08	07:43	11:12	11:36	07:00	05:47	06:32	09:44	13:34	02:09	11:34	10:43	03:25	03:50	03:44		671	904	739	640	593	299
Swakopmund	07:15	08:21	06:27	07:13	10:40	06:08	06:06	10:27	06:57	00:51	10:58	01:53	14:23	08:55	03:51	09:03	06:22	09:38	05:30	06:35	05:36	02:36	07:48	11:21	09:18	09:46	05:11	03:58	04:16	05:18	09:08	04:47	08:14	08:56	08:57	04:37	03:33	06:57		309	559	192	1161	362
Torra bay	10:09	11:47	09:53	10:06	08:03	09:02	07:32	13:21	10:23	02:48	13:52	04:46	15:49	11:49	03:07	11:57	09:16	13:04	08:56	09:29	05:43	05:05	05:11	14:47	07:54	08:29	06:36	05:23	04:36	01:59	05:49	07:41	06:50	10:21	12:16	08:03	06:59	09:50	03:36		602	285	1394	595
Tsumeb	07:59	10:47	09:02	06:25	09:12	05:31	00:40	11:12	09:22	06:01	11:43	03:59	08:53	09:40	04:10	09:48	07:06	12:03	07:54	07:20	03:56	03:16	06:20	13:47	03:35	03:58	00:41	01:55	02:41	06:07	09:57	05:32	05:32	03:26	10:07	08:39	07:35	07:41	05:52	07:18		438	1229	430
Uis	07:11	09:58	08:13	07:09	08:22	06:04	05:01	10:23	08:33	01:33	10:54	02:13	13:18	08:51	01:33	08:59	06:18	11:15	07:05	06:31	03:57	01:30	05:30	12:58	07:01	07:35	04:06	02:53	02:51	03:21	07:11	04:43	05:56	07:51	09:18	06:48	05:45	06:53	02:21	04:04	04:47		1130	330
Vioolsdrift	06:43	04:02	06:31	10:09	18:59	09:03	12:55	01:28	05:02	12:05	01:34	10:02	21:11	03:04	12:56	04:29	07:28	05:19	06:30	05:22	12:50	10:21	16:07	03:26	16:11	16:35	11:59	10:46	11:31	14:43	18:33	07:08	16:33	15:44	03:04	08:05	08:26	05:58	11:56	14:49	12:41	11:52		796
Windhoek	03:24	06:12	04:27	03:21	10:56	02:17	04:52	06:38	04:48	04:02	07:08	02:00	13:09	05:05	04:53	05:13	02:31	07:29	03:19	02:45	04:48	02:18	08:04	09:12	08:08	08:32	03:56	02:43	03:28	06:40	10:30	00:58	08:30	07:42	05:32	04:07	03:03	03:05	03:53	06:47	04:38	03:49	08:06	

The above values are based on a 'fastest travel time' route calculation as opposed to a 'shortest distance' calculation. Distance/time values in the above table should be used for estimate purposes only as they're dependent on many factors, some of which may change from time to time.

ATLAS KEYPLAN

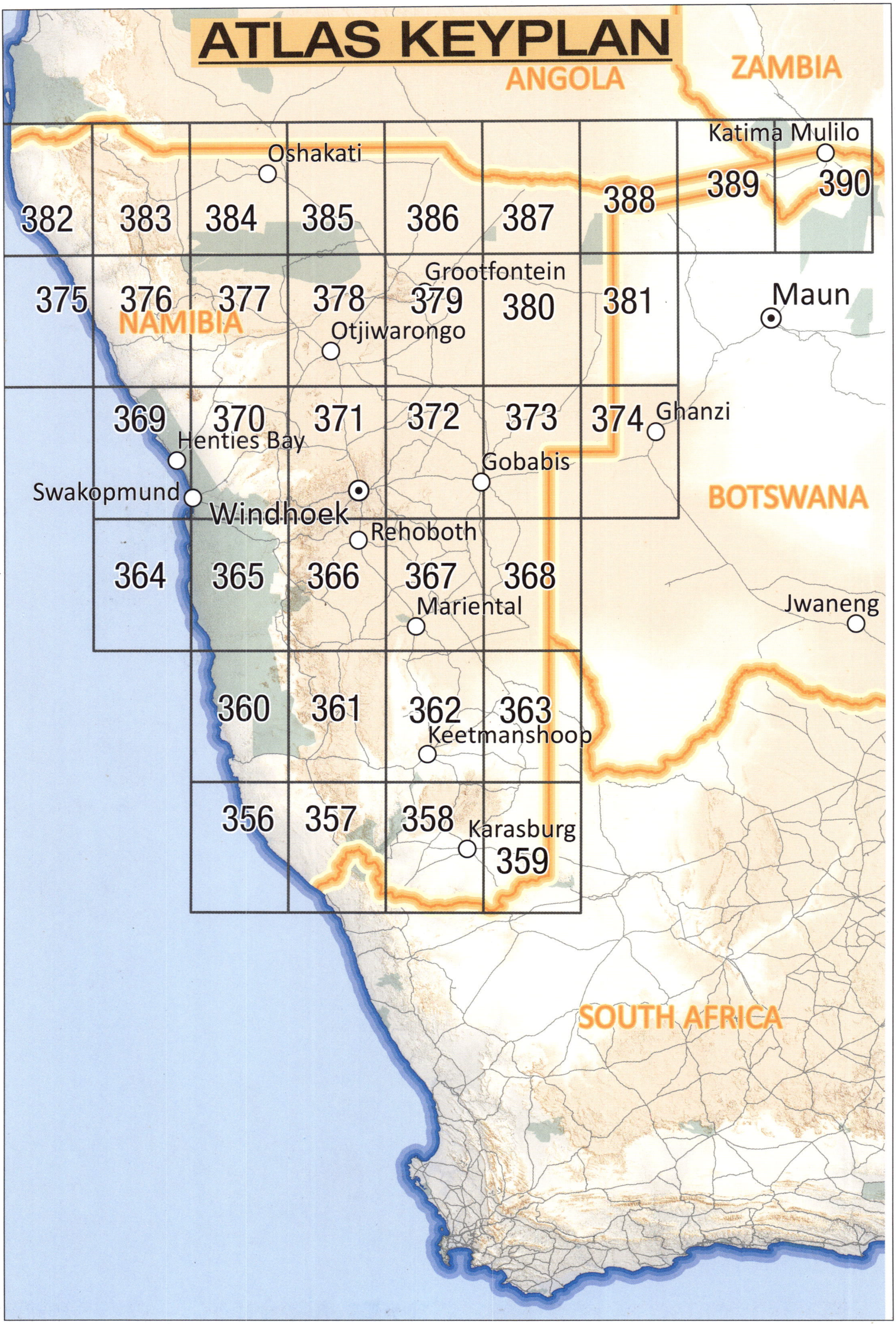